The United States,
Revolutionary Russia,
and the Rise of
Czechoslovakia

The United States, Revolutionary Russia, and the Rise of Czechoslovakia

by
Betty Miller Unterberger

THE UNIVERSITY OF
NORTH CAROLINA PRESS

Chapel Hill | London

Library of Congress Cataloging-in-Publication Data

Unterberger, Betty Miller.
The United States, revolutionary Russia, and the
rise of Czechoslovakia / by Betty Miller Unterberger.
p.   cm. — (Supplementary volumes to
The papers of Woodrow Wilson)
Bibliography: p.
Includes index.
ISBN 0-8078-1853-4 (alk. paper)
1. World War, 1914–1918—Diplomatic history.
2. United States—Foreign relations—Czechoslovakia.
3. Czechoslovakia—Foreign relations—United States.
4. Soviet Union—History—Allied intervention, 1918–1920.
I. Title.   II. Series.

D619.U63   1989   88-38687
940.3'22—dc19   CIP

68722
Manufactured in the United States of America

93 92 91 90 89 5 4 3 2 1

To my beloved family
Robert R.
Gregg Russell
Gail Lynn
Glen Alan

Contents

Maps

Illustrations

Preface

When Soviet troops moved into Czechoslovakia in August 1968 to end the "liberalization" policies of the incumbent Czech government, few persons in either Czechoslovakia or the United States expected the American government to do more than exercise moral pressure to aid the Czechs. Fifty years earlier, however, in the midst of the First World War, when the Czech and Slovak peoples opposed the autocracy of the Austro-Hungarian regime at home and the Czecho-Slovak Legion in Russia became involved in a military struggle against the Bolsheviks and Austro-German prisoners of war, the American government responded quite differently. The situation in 1918 was even more complex than fifty years later because the United States had to deal not only with the issue of self-determination for the Czechs while seeking a separate peace with Austria-Hungary, but also the complicated interrelationships and struggles for power released by the Bolshevik revolution, which, in turn, had opened the way for Japanese imperialism in Russia and Manchuria. The United States thus found itself in the anomalous position of seeking to preserve the territorial integrity and right to self-determination of both Russia and China against not only the Central Powers but also its own allies. This work explores how and why President Woodrow Wilson and the United States came to support the Czecho-Slovak movement for self-determination and to aid in the "rescue" of the Czecho-Slovak army in Russia. The result of this support and aid directly affected the breakup of the Austro-Hungarian Empire, the establishment of Czechoslovakia as an independent state, the role of the United States in the Allied intervention in Russia, and the initiation of the United States's most aggressive effort to stop Japanese imperialism in Northeast Asia.

Within the context of Wilsonian diplomacy, this study explores the interrelationships of policy decisions and "on the scene" actions during the Allied struggle for victory in the First World War, the international rivalries stimulated by that war, the desperate policies of the disintegrating Austro-Hungarian Empire, the revolutionary turmoil of the Bolshevik government, the appalled response of the Allies to the first Communist revolution, the imperialistic urge to expansion of the military clique in Japan, the weak and fumbling efforts of a revolutionary China to preserve its territorial and administrative integrity while itself in the throes of continuing civil strife, and, finally, Woodrow Wilson's efforts to implement the principles for which the United States had entered the war and which he sought to apply universally.

The winning of independence for Czechoslovakia is part of an epic of grand proportions. An historic struggle for freedom, it includes the flight from Austria-Hungary of Thomas G. Masaryk, the distinguished Czechoslovak scholar-statesman and his brilliant diplomatic campaign of propaganda in the Allied capitals; the revolts of the Czech and Slovak troops in the Austrian army and their desertion to the Russians and Italians; the formation of Czech legions in France, Italy, and Russia; the heroic anabasis of the Czech Legion across Siberia and its campaign against the Bolsheviks; the courageous deeds of heroism of thousands of exiled Czechs and Slovaks for the cause of independence; and the silent endurance of persecution by those at home.

The Czecho-Slovak army, composed of some 70,000 soldiers trapped in the interior of Russia when the Bolsheviks initiated an armistice with the Central Powers, found itself in grave difficulty in its efforts to reach the Western Front. Once in France, the Czechs hoped to fight for their independence with the aid of the United States and the Allies. Instead, they found themselves fighting against Austro-German prisoners of war and Bolsheviks.

Upon Bolshevik withdrawal from the war, President Wilson, who for six months had withstood intense Allied pressure for intervention in Russia in order to reestablish an Eastern Front, finally decided reluctantly in the mid-summer of 1918 to send American troops to the Russian Far East to "rescue" the Czechs. American and Allied relations with the Czechs in Russia and the impact of that relationship on eventual Allied and American recognition of Czech independence is a crucial aspect of this study.

The early story of American-Czechoslovak relations has its setting in Washington, London, Paris, Vienna, Rome, Prague, Geneva, Moscow, Peking, and Tokyo where, throughout the war years, Woodrow Wilson sought to interpret and gain acceptance for his historic view of self-determination and to decide on the appropriate areas for its application. Here Wilson's struggle to order his principles of peace, self-determination, nonintervention, antiimperialism, the Open Door, and international organization; the role of Czech and Slovak minorities in the United States; the relationship between Wilson and Masaryk, who later became the first president of Czechoslovakia; and finally the pressures of public opinion and of Wilson's European and Asian associates—all contributed to the formation of America's attitude and policy toward the Czechoslovak struggle for independence.

Strangely, in the years ending in eight—1918, 1938, 1948, and again in 1968—the Czechoslovak peoples strove either to gain, maintain, or regain their independence. However, only in 1918 did the United States play a crucial role in those efforts. This study, then, will endeavor to present a history of the role of the United States in the dissolution of the Austro-Hungarian Empire and the rise of the Czechoslovak nation within the context of two of the most cataclysmic events of the twentieth century—the First World War and the Bolshevik revolution. It will delineate Wilson's persistent efforts to implement his "new diplomacy," not only toward Austria-Hungary, the Bolsheviks, and the Czechs, but also toward his own allies.

Today, the United States struggles almost desperately to formulate rational and effective policies toward the rising nationalism and aspirations for self-determination of many of the peoples of Eastern Europe, Asia, Africa, the Middle East, and Latin America. It seeks guidelines to determine when and where American intervention to aid peoples struggling against Communism, colonialism, and domination is appropriate and can be effective. It confronts regularly the problem of when to grant recognition to revolutionary new peoples and states. It faces the pressures of minority ethnic and religious groups at home who seek to influence policy toward their home countries. Finally, it strives to gain support for its own policies from the major powers of the world. In 1918, the United States faced each one of these problems in attempting to formulate a policy toward the rebellious peoples of Czechoslovakia. Moreover, it was forced to determine its policy while simultaneously attempting to cope for the first time with involvement in a world war, with the ensuing Communist revolution and civil war in Russia, and with the growth of Japanese imperialism in Northeast Asia. A careful analysis of American foreign policy toward Czechoslovakia—one of the several areas in Eastern Europe seeking self-determination in the First World War—can bring us greater understanding in dealing with the strikingly similar problems that confront the United States throughout the world today.

I want to express my deep appreciation to George F. Kennan, who first suggested the possibility of this work, and to Arthur S. Link, who quickly supported it. Each has read the manuscript and has provided valuable commentary. I owe a special debt of gratitude to Arthur S. Link for providing access to the invaluable Woodrow Wilson Collection at Princeton at a time of deep, personal tragedy. The collection contains a wealth of important documents not heretofore available, both from foreign as well as American archives. My warm thanks go to George J. Kovtun, of the European Division of the Library of Congress, who provided assistance with Czech documentation, and to Mary A. Giunta, of the National Historical Publications and Records Commission, for her invaluable assistance. I am also grateful to the staffs of the following repositories: Manuscript Division, Library of Congress; Diplomatic and Military Branches of the National Archives; Public Record Office, London; Columbia University Library; Georgetown University Library; Harvard University Library; Hoover Institution on War, Revolution and Peace; Missouri Historical Society; New York Public Library; Princeton University Library; U.S. Military Academy Library; Library of University of California at Berkeley; University of Chicago Library; University of Pittsburgh Library; Wisconsin Historical Society; Yale University Library; and YMCA Archives, University of Minnesota. I would also like to acknowledge the grant support of the American Philosophical Society, the Woodrow Wilson Foundation, and Texas A&M University.

At different stages of the typing and preparation of this manuscript, various individuals provided assistance. These include Laurie Caldwell, Terry Hammond, Jacob Sulzbach, Carole Knapp (now deceased), Gail Lynn Unterberger, Vicki Reinke, and Rosa Richardson. Jude K. Swank prepared the final draft. However, the author alone assumes full responsibility for the accuracy of the manuscript.

I wish also to express my deep appreciation to my husband, Robert R., and to my children, Gail Lynn and Gregg Russell, for their patience, understanding, and loving support during the many years of the research for and writing of this book.

The United States,
Revolutionary Russia,
and the Rise of
Czechoslovakia

1

The Bohemian Liberation
Movement Abroad

In the nineteenth century, the Habsburg Empire was the oldest ruling dynasty in Europe. Its location in Central Europe signified not only its strategic geographical position, but also its political dominance. Its capital city, Vienna, was situated in the heart of Central Europe. After the Habsburgs became the rulers of Austria in the thirteenth century, they extended their dominion over various historical political entities, which they held together by dynastic ties. Some of these various peoples, such as the Magyars, Czechs, and Poles, could recall a glorious past, when they had been important states in their own right, specifically the Kingdom of Hungary (the lands of the Crowns of St. Stephen) and the Kingdom of Bohemia (the lands of the Crowns of St. Wenceslaus). Other peoples, like the Slovaks, Slovenes, and Rumanians, had no historical "right" to revive and defend. From the historical and geographical standpoint, the disposition of the Czech and Slovak lands became the pivot on which the survival of Austria-Hungary turned. By the close of the First World War, even the loss of Galicia, Bukovina, Transylvania, the South Slavic lands, and the Italian Irredenta would have left Austria-Hungary still the most powerful state between Russia and Germany and Italy. However, without Bohemia, Austria-Hungary could hardly survive. Thus every Entente war aim that favored the establishment of a separate Czech state, with or without the Slovaks, necessarily doomed the existence of a Danubian empire.[1]

From the outset of the war, the Austro-Hungarian government used dictatorial and terroristic means to keep its subject peoples in line.[2] Nevertheless, most Slavs remained loyal to the monarchy.[3] Certainly this was true of the two largest Czech political parties: the Agrarians and the Social Democrats. The clerical parties also supported the Habsburg monarchy. Two of the leaders of the dissenting parties had acquired real stature several decades before the war. Karel Kramář, young, educated, moderately wealthy, and married to a Russian, was the leader of the Young Czechs. He had gradually accepted and spread

among the party members the idea of an eventual Slavic domination of
Austria-Hungary, including the eventual dissolution of the Austro-
German alliance and its replacement by alliances with Russia and
France, so as to escape the threat of pan-Germanism. The pan-Slavic
views of many of Kramář's followers were encouraged by the early
successes of Russian armies in the autumn of 1914.[4]

Thomas G. Masaryk (1850–1937), the only deputy whom the Realist
party sent to Vienna, did not share the pro-Russian views of Kramář
and his followers. He believed that the future of Bohemia lay with the
Western democracies. Masaryk, an intellectual and ethical giant, had
made the long step from his father's serfdom to a professorship at
Charles University in Prague, where before the war he educated two
generations of scholars in all walks of life. A Renaissance man steeped
in history, philosophy, sociology, political science, and literature, he
derived his philosophy from Hume, Mill, Spencer, and Comte. His
views were reinforced by his marriage to an American, Charlotte
Garrigue. His study of Czech history had made him an admirer of John
Hus; Comenius, the renowned pedagogical writer and a moral leader
in the struggle against foreign domination; and František Palacký,
Bohemia's greatest historian. Masaryk's rejection of pan-Slavism and
the Russophilism of Kramář was the result of his own profound
researches into the social and political structure of tsarist Russia. He
had frequently visited Russia, and his well-known study, *The Spirit of
Russia*, published in 1913, had made him the most eminent student of
Russia outside of that country. His program had been to create a just
and federalized state composed of politically independent nations of
the old Empire. He regarded himself as a man with a mission. The
history of nations was not the result of chance, but the plan of Provi-
dence. It was the task of historians and philosophers, indeed of all
people, to recognize this plan in the world, to discern and define their
own place in it, and to engage in every effort to implement its realization. This historical profession of faith revealed his deep interest in and
sympathy with this aspect of Leo Tolstoy's historical outlook. It was a
position that Woodrow Wilson would later find congenial to his own
spiritual philosophy.[5]

Masaryk, Dr. Edvard Beneš (1884–1948), then a young lecturer in
sociology at Charles University, and a small group of like-minded men
formed the nucleus of what later became a revolutionary movement
known as the Maffia. As Masaryk considered the meaning and objectives of the war and the political maneuvering behind the scenes in
both the East and the West, he concluded that the future of the Czech

Dr. Thomas G. Masaryk (National Archives)

people depended on the defeat of the Central Powers. For Masaryk's group, German domination of the Danube basin was synonymous with Slavic slavery. Thus, the only possible hope for the peoples of the Habsburg Empire lay in an Entente victory. When, in late 1914, Masaryk learned from his English friend, Henry Wickham Steed, the foreign editor of *The Times*, that many in England predicted a long war, he realized the importance of publicizing the Slavic cause to the Entente leaders.[6]

Led off to war against their Slavic brothers, the Russians and Serbs, Czech regiments in the First, Third, and Fourth Armies fought so bravely on the Eastern Front that even the Russians paid tribute to them. On the other hand, many Czech soldiers mutinied.[7] They threw themselves in front of the military trains, preferring to die rather than to bear arms against their brothers for a government they despised. They wrote inscriptions on the cars, such as "Hurray for Russia and Serbia," and "Fresh meat for the Russian bear."[8] Early in the war, Masaryk had drawn Steed's attention to the discontent among the Czech troops through the good offices of Emanuel Voska, a wealthy Czech-American caught in Prague by the war, who agreed to act as a courier for Masaryk. Masaryk sought Steed's assistance in suggesting to the Russian Supreme Command a way to facilitate the desertion of the Czech troops. He arranged with St. Petersburg that the singing of the pan-Slav hymn, *Hej Slované*, would be a signal to the Russians to hold their fire so that the Czech or Slovak soldiers could cross the Russian lines.[9]

In the autumn of 1914, Masaryk made three trips abroad to discover the real aims and prospects for victory of the Entente. While abroad he initiated contact with two British scholars on Austro-Hungarian affairs, Robert Seton-Watson and Steed, and the renowned French scholar, Ernest Denis. Seton-Watson's first memorandum of his conversations with Masaryk was later transmitted to Steed, the British Foreign Office, the French Foreign Minister, Théophile Delcassé, and, later, Professor Paul Vinogradoff of Oxford, who personally handed it to the Russian Foreign Minister, Sergei Sazonov.[10]

Although Masaryk recognized the need to educate Western opinion about Bohemian aims and aspirations, he was surprised that people in England expected Bohemian claims for independence to rest on the principle of nationality rather than on historic state rights.[11] Masaryk was now aware of the great educational and propagandist work required to support Bohemian nationalistic aspirations. As he explained to Seton-Watson, the future of the Czechs depended on the breakup of the Austro-Hungarian Empire and the transformation of Central Europe. While ready to demand an independent state, he realized at this early stage that it could "only be a kingdom, not a republic."[12]

Masaryk left Prague for his third trip abroad in December 1914. Warned while in Switzerland that his return would result in his arrest, Masaryk determined to stay abroad and develop an organization that would work openly for Czecho-Slovak national liberation.[13] On July 6, 1915, the five hundredth anniversary of the martyrdom of John Hus, Masaryk officially inaugurated the revolutionary movement abroad with a lecture on Hus in Zurich. He then traveled on to Paris and London.

Beneš, who was about half Masaryk's age, joined him in Paris and became his lifetime collaborator. A man of progressive social thought, he had followed Masaryk's teaching in Prague. He identified wholly with Masaryk's political philosophy. Ironically, he wrote his doctoral dissertation on the necessity of preserving the Austro-Hungarian Empire. After joining his mentor, he began explaining the intricacies of the Czech problem to Allied leaders in the French capital. Beneš had a unique talent for analysis and a discernment for historical parallel. These qualities, plus a retentive memory and an enormous capacity for work, made him a tremendous help to Masaryk in the ensuing years.[14]

Masaryk and Beneš were engaged in no easy task. For years they had studied seriously the forces that had shaped Europe since the Renaissance and Reformation. They saw the First World War as something more than merely a conflict between Germans and Slavs; it was more universal, more fundamental—a great struggle between two parts of Europe that had developed historically to different stages. It was a struggle between two ideas. Western Europe, in spite of many contradictory manifestations, had evolved into democratic states that emphasized the freedom of the individual and the concept that the state existed for the people. In contrast, Germany, Austria, and Russia had not outgrown the feudal and aristocratic conceptions of the Middle Ages. To Masaryk and Beneš, the historical experience of the Czech nation fitted into the scheme of events in Western Europe. They were convinced that the Czechs and Slovaks had to integrate their policies into the general framework of European development to win freedom. After careful study of the political scene, these two pioneers concluded that their philosophy of European and Czech history was substantially correct and that the time was ripe for action.[15]

In Paris, Masaryk also met Milan R. Štefánik (1880–1919), another

Dr. Edvard Beneš (National Archives)

former student whom he had befriended in earlier days. A colorful young Slovak, who had received his doctorate in 1904, Štefánik was a mathematician who had decided to become an astronomer. He soon excelled in this field as well as in social relationships. Although he accepted French citizenship, when the war broke out he gave himself unsparingly to the Czech cause. Štefánik combined the attributes of the scholar and the bon vivant, both of which opened the doors of political and intellectual salons to Beneš and Masaryk. Pierre T. C. Maurice Janin, the French general later to become commander of the Czech Legion in Russia and who knew Štefánik intimately during the war, described him as a "real bundle of nerves . . . with a precious gift of brilliance, supersensitive with a unique power of persuasion." Although Štefánik's views were basically antidemocratic, he had a profound respect and admiration for Masaryk, whose leadership he accepted easily and naturally.[16]

At the outbreak of the war, Czechs and Slovaks abroad had been quick to show where their sympathies lay. Some 70,000 of them were living in Russia and Siberia, concentrated mostly in Petrograd, Moscow, Kiev, Warsaw, and Odessa. In France, the Paris colony, which had an active Sokol (patriotic athletic club), numbered approximately 2,000 Czechs and Slovaks; several thousand more lived elsewhere in France. The numbers were considerably smaller in England and Italy, where they were scattered and disorganized. In the United States, the approximately one and a half million Czechs and Slovaks were soon effectively utilized in the struggle for Czecho-Slovak independence.[17] The move for independence soon developed along three major lines: propaganda and political-diplomatic work, organization of Czech and Slovak prisoners of war, and recruitment of troops.[18]

Masaryk journeyed to London in the early autumn of 1915 to seek political support. Since he was technically an enemy alien, he was immediately arrested and was set free only through the good offices of Sir William Wiseman, a friend of Seton-Watson, who had told him that Masaryk was "a great Czech patriot, and that the enemy would give an army corps to have him dead or alive." On Masaryk's release, he and Wiseman had a long discussion, thereby establishing a relationship that was to be mutually beneficial.[19] Masaryk initially chose to concentrate his political activity in London because it was the political center of the war effort, as Paris was the military center. Moreover, England was well placed for courier service to Prague.[20]

The Czech colony in England was small, poor, and insignificant, but Masaryk endeavored to use it to help shape public opinion. Seton-

Watson believed that the most effective way to introduce Masaryk to the British public would be to find him a post at a British university, where his special qualities as scholar and teacher would impress academic circles. This would also implement Seton-Watson's plan for the foundation of a school for Slavonic studies, a Slavonic library, and a chair at London University. After the principal of King's College was persuaded to accept the idea, Seton-Watson invited Masaryk to accept the post of lecturer on Slavonic history and literature.

On October 19, 1915, Masaryk delivered the inaugural lecture of the new School of Slavonic Studies. Although illness prevented Prime Minister Herbert Asquith from presiding over the meeting, he sent a message which emphasized that the Allies were waging war for the protection of small nations. The occasion brought together Masaryk and Lord Robert Cecil, then the Under Secretary of State for Foreign Affairs.[21] Masaryk made other contacts with officials of the British Foreign Office, particularly with Sir George Clerk, a senior official. While in England Masaryk made himself available as a speaker for various clubs, as well as a lecturer at London University, Cambridge, and Oxford.[22] He also wrote articles for various newspapers and magazines and persuaded Seton-Watson to start a weekly review because he regarded the London papers as being so "wretchedly bad."[23] The first number of the weekly, *New Europe*, appeared on October 19, 1916. Masaryk became a regular contributor; he had an article in the first issue about German war objectives. With access to secret information from Masaryk, the Maffia, and other sources, *New Europe* rapidly established itself as an authority on Eastern European affairs.[24] The destruction of the Austro-Hungarian monarchy became its most important objective.

The question of military service played an important part in the activities of the Czech exile movement in all of the Allied countries. Masaryk and the Czech leaders sought to persuade the various Allied governments not to intern the Czechs but to allow them to serve in the army. In addition, in those countries where there were a sufficient number of Czechs or Czech prisoners of war, they sought permission to form separate military units. Masaryk convinced the Czechs in England that they could serve the cause best by volunteering for the British army and distinguishing themselves by their ability, discipline, and courage. By July 1917, approximately 90 percent of the Czechs who were physically fit had volunteered for service with the British army.[25]

The British Foreign Office tended to view the activities of Masaryk and his group with a certain ambivalence. Although it desired to encourage activities that might weaken the Central Powers, it was unwilling to accept the ultimate aim of the complete dismemberment of Austria-Hungary and actually feared the consequences of its disappearance. While Asquith regarded the Austrians as "quite the stupidest people in Europe," he and other British statesmen feared that dismemberment would simply produce a group of Russian satellite states.[26] Although British intellectuals concerned with the fate of Austria-Hungary engaged in a vital and searching debate, their spirited controversy was not duplicated within the British Cabinet, except for Winston S. Churchill, who believed that ultimately Austria would be "resolved into its component parts."[27] Indeed, the idea of encouraging national minorities to rebel as a weapon of victory received little consideration in British official quarters at this time.[28]

Nevertheless, the British did give some consideration to the dissolution of the Austro-Hungarian Empire, as was indicated by a British Cabinet paper written on August 7, 1916, by Sir Ralph Paget and Sir William Tyrrell, private secretary and confidant of Sir Edward Grey, the British Foreign Secretary. The paper supported the view that nationality should be a governing factor in arranging territory after the war. While admitting that the future of Austria-Hungary would depend upon the military situation at the end of the war, the authors posed the strong probability that the Dual Monarchy would be broken up as the result of the secession of all of its non-German parts. However, while agreeing that dissolution would be in accordance with the principle of nationality, the authors rejected the notion of either an independent Czech state or a joint Czech and southern Slavic state. They believed that the most desirable solution would be to link Bohemia to an independent Poland, a proposal they felt would receive the approval of both Czechs and Poles.[29]

France, too, at the outset of the war regarded the maintenance of Austria-Hungary as essential to the balance of power in Europe. In 1913, President Raymond Poincaré observed that Austria-Hungary's continued existence was in the best interest of France. Georges Clemenceau himself had said, "Alas, we must have the courage to say that our programme, when we entered the War, was not one of liberation."[30] Even André Chéradame, a leading French scholar on Austro-Hungarian affairs and one of Masaryk's most devoted supporters, agreed with these views.[31] Another of Masaryk's supporters, Ernest Denis, was a renowned Slavic scholar, professor at the Sorbonne, and author of a classic history of Bohemia. He established the journal, *La Nation tchèque*, on May 1, 1915, to publicize the Czech cause. Denis arranged for both Masaryk and Beneš to lecture at the Sorbonne and also helped to promote a journalistic campaign in the Paris newspapers.[32]

Despite the lack of official support, on September 8, 1915, the Czechs presented a memorandum to Poincaré announcing their intention to work wholeheartedly for Czech independence. Two months later, they took bolder action. On November 14, 1915, the Czecho-Slovak Foreign Committee in Paris issued an official declaration of war upon the Habsburg Empire and demanded the establishment of an independent Czecho-Slovak state within the historical boundaries of the two peoples. Masaryk had insisted earlier on the acceptance of this manifesto by the leaders at home and in America, England, and France.[33] Its publication marked the initial phase of Czech and Slovak organized activity abroad.[34]

Soon thereafter, the Czecho-Slovak National Council was formed with representation in the major Allied capitals. Upon authority from the leaders of the political parties of Bohemia and Slovakia and the leaders of the Czecho-Slovak Foreign Committee in Paris, the Czecho-Slovak National Council proclaimed its intention to gain the independence of all countries that once had formed the independent Czech (and Slovak) state and those countries that were then inhabited by the Czechs and Slovaks: Bohemia, Moravia, Austrian Silesia, Slovakia, and neighboring regions. With headquarters in Paris, the council organized a general secretariat to conduct its activities and to direct the liberation movement. It planned to organize offices in London, Rome, Petrograd, Moscow, Kiev, New York, Chicago, and Pittsburgh. In addition, it established centers of political and journalistic activity in Switzerland and Holland. The general secretariat of the council functioned as a government institution with Masaryk as President, Josef Dürich and Štefánik as Vice Presidents, and Beneš as Secretary General.[35]

In late January 1916, Masaryk joined Beneš and Štefánik in Paris to aid their political and diplomatic efforts. They conducted an extensive journalistic campaign in *Le Matin* and presented a series of lectures on Slavonic affairs at the Sorbonne. Beneš was able to secure the support of Socialist Albert Thomas, Minister of Munitions. Štefánik arranged a meeting for Masaryk with Premier Aristide Briand.[36] This was a prime opportunity for Masaryk to explain his diagnosis of the general situation—the pan-German plans of Berlin, the vassalage of Austria-Hungary, and the Czecho-Slovak aim to break up the Habsburg monarchy and return Germany to her own territorial limits. He outlined a reorganization of central Europe based on the liberation of the small nations and explained the relevance of this plan to the interests of France and the Entente. Masaryk emphasized that "to weaken Austria was to weaken Germany." To destroy Austria "was to strike Germany in a vital place by ruining her scheme of a European central state."[37] Briand, in an official communiqué, immediately expressed the sympathy of France for the Czecho-Slovak movement. Masaryk was elated. He never forgot that Briand was "the first statesman who publicly promised to our nation the help of France."[38] Briand's official reception of Masaryk, the establishment of the Czecho-Slovak National Council in Paris, and the precise formulation of a party program marked the end of the initial stage of Czecho-Slovak political activity.

From this point onward, Masaryk and Beneš became military organizers and later diplomats. Even before the November manifesto, Masaryk had emphasized the importance of establishing a large army: "Neither the Allies nor Vienna will be able to pass us by in silence if we have soldiers. . . . Without a decisive military struggle we shall obtain nothing from anybody." By its military activity, the Czecho-Slovak National Council became associated with France, then desperately defending itself against enormous pressure from Germany.[39]

The country where the successful establishment of an independent Czecho-Slovak army seemed most likely was Russia. Driven by the oppressive rule of the Habsburgs, Czechs and Slovaks had migrated to Russia in relatively large numbers near the end of the nineteenth century. Slavic by race, some looked at the World War as a means to fight the oppressors of their fathers—Austria-Hungary and Germany. Others, politically apathetic, were encouraged to take a loyal position by the Tsar's policy, which interned all enemy aliens and confiscated their property.[40] In the earliest phase of the war, the Russian Czechs and Slovaks had enlisted in the crusade against the Central Powers by forming the John Hus Battalion at the Mikhailov Monastery in Kiev on August 14, 1914. This battalion was an independent unit of the Russian army and became known as the *Česká Družina* ("Czech Comrades").[41]

The attitude of the tsarist government toward the formation of an independent Czech unit was somewhat ambivalent. On the one hand, it welcomed the aid offered and admired the bravery of the Czechs on the battlefield. Russian leaders were naturally interested in weakening the Austrian Empire, their most dangerous and immediate competitor in the Balkans. Therefore, although the Russian government took remarkably little interest in war aims toward Austria-Hungary, it adopted a friendly attitude toward the efforts of the Czechs to organize their movement. The Tsar on August 20 and September 16, 1914, and

Foreign Minister Sergei D. Sazonov on September 15, received Czech delegations and heard their desires and requests. However, neither made a firm commitment in favor of an independent Bohemia. Yet in certain comments each suggested sympathy with the Czech cause and perhaps a willingness to consider the creation of a smaller Austria-Hungary consisting of three autonomous units: the Czech land, the Austrian land, and Hungary.[42] Despite the vacillating attitude of the Tsar, a strongly organized federation of Czecho-Slovak societies in Russia was constituted by the spring of 1915.[43] Masaryk referred to this organization as the Czech League.

Actually, there were many reasons for the Tsar's government to fear and suspect the Czech liberation movement.[44] As one Czech historian explained, Russia could hardly support the principle of nationality and the "right of the peoples to determine their own fate—principles in the name of which dissolution of the Dual Monarchy was called for— because this constituted a precedent which could detach from Russia all of her heterogeneous ethnic population."[45] Such a policy might boomerang upon the Romanov dynasty itself and might also unduly embarrass certain territorial ambitions of Russian imperialism.[46] According to Papoušek, Masaryk's one-time secretary, Russia was willing to support the plan for organized Czecho-Slovak military detachments only to the extent "required for the breaking of military power of Austria-Hungary by the instigation of a revolt in the Czech lands."[47]

However, considering the Slavic kinship of the Czechs and Russians, the Russian government could not neglect entirely the Czech residents on Russian soil and those who later came into the Russian lines as prisoners or deserters. In fact, the Slavic deserters were separated from the German, Austrian, and Hungarian prisoners, given preferred treatment, and also subjected to a systematic pan-Slav campaign.[48] In January 1916, the original Česká Družina grew into the first Czecho-Slovak regiment of John Hus, followed by a second regiment named for John Žižka and a third named for George Podiebrad, the last Bohemian King of Czech blood. The way had been paved by the propaganda of Czecho-Slovak prewar organizations in Russia.

Volunteers from Czech prisoners of war were eager to join these regiments, but the tsarist government placed many obstacles in their way. Some were permitted to join the Russian army as volunteers or to work in ammunition factories. Others undertook a campaign of education among the Russians; they issued six newspapers, three of them dailies, in which they explained the aims of the war and spread their ideas from the Ukraine to Siberia.[49] In the meantime, entire battalions of Czecho-Slovaks were deserting from Austrian regiments.[50] However, they were not permitted to join the original Czecho-Slovak organization. Instead, along with other Austrian and Magyar war prisoners, they were sent to prison camps. Some of them later escaped and joined the Czecho-Slovak army.[51]

Initially, the *družina*, and subsequently, the First Regiment, were used by different Russian divisions as small detachments for reconnaissance. Their knowledge of the German language and their acquaintance with the Austro-Hungarian organizations rendered their services particularly valuable. At the end of October 1914, 700 volunteers with Russian officers left Kiev for the Southwestern Front, where they first met General Mikhail K. Dietrichs, former quartermaster general at the Stavka, the Russian general staff headquarters at Mogilev, who became one of their most influential Russian friends. They were employed chiefly as spies and agitators among Czech regiments in the Austrian army. The *družina* gradually won favor, but internal disputes and suspicion of the Russian military authorities prevented any great increase until October 1915, when the Czechs and Slovaks of Volhynia, who owed military service to Russia, were added. This concession was in part due to the fine conduct of Czech military units during the disastrous retreat from the Carpathians in 1915.[52]

The first public manifesto of the Czecho-Slovak Foreign Committee, signed by Bohumír Čermák and Bohdan Pavlů as representatives of the Czechs living in Russia, had not settled the question of relations between Czecho-Slovak organizations in Russia and the Paris headquarters. As in Bohemia, the Czechs and Slovaks were divided concerning the nation to which they should look for leadership and support of their movement. Many thought that the Czecho-Slovak question should be solved by the Russians themselves in accordance with their interests. Others were convinced that the future of a new Czech state lay in a close alliance with the Western Allies under the leadership of Masaryk.[53] The Russian government had not taken Masaryk seriously as leader of the tiny Realist party in Austria-Hungary. However, once the Czecho-Slovak National Council had been organized and Masaryk had had an official audience with Briand, the Tsar's government, which feared British and French influence in Central Europe, began to adopt a vigorous policy of transforming the Russian Czech organizations into tools of tsarist policy. The Russians naturally feared any independent Czech state in Central Europe with a Western orientation, particularly under the leadership of Britain. During the summer of 1916, therefore, the Tsar actually approved for a brief time the release of Slavic prisoners and the establishment of the various Czecho-Slovak military units.[54]

It was events in Paris that led to an independent Czech army in Russia. In the spring of 1916, Russia had agreed to send about 400,000 soldiers to the French front, but only about 10,000 arrived. When obstacles to the dispatch of Russian troops were discussed by Czech and French representatives in Paris, they suggested the possibility of sending to France, together with the Russian troops, detachments of Czecho-Slovak prisoners of war then in Russia to form the national Czecho-Slovak army in France. Masaryk and the Czecho-Slovak National Council agreed to concentrate on recruiting prisoners of war among the Allies as a whole, but particularly in Russia and in Italy. The French government agreed to pay the costs of recruitment, and Dürich was sent to initiate it in Russia.[55]

By the spring of 1916, Russian diplomats had begun to view Masaryk's activities in France with considerable distrust. Thus, when Dürich, a former ardent exponent of pan-Slavism, arrived in Russia, he was easily subverted to support a competing Czecho-Slovak movement in Russia. In fact, before Dürich had left Prague in May 1915, Kramář had instructed him to "work for a great Slav empire."[56] Suspecting the loyalty of Dürich, Štefánik had persuaded Masaryk and Beneš to send him also to Russia in order to insure the successful organization of Czech prisoners of war under the leadership of the National Council. His fears about Dürich were shared by Briand and others in the French Ministry of Foreign Affairs. Štefánik succeeded in gaining the support of both General Janin and General Mikhail Vasilevich Alexeev, the Tsar's Chief of Staff. He also persuaded the Petrograd Czechs to accept the Kiev memorandum of August 29, 1916, in which for the first time all of the Czecho-Slovak groups in Russia recognized the authority of the Czecho-Slovak National Council, with Masaryk at its head. The Russian Foreign Ministry, however, refused to acknowledge the Kiev memorandum, induced Dürich to repudiate it, and drew up competing plans for the establishment of a Czecho-Slovak army under Russian leadership.

The result was violent internal warfare. The Petrograd opposition was led by Bohdan Pavlů, former Slovak editor of the *Národní Listy* and then editor of *Czechoslovak* of Petrograd. He had recently been to France to see both Masaryk and Beneš and to sign the political manifesto of the Czecho-Slovak Foreign Committee of November 14 in the name of the Czechs and Slovaks of Russia. Despite extensive agitation and Štefánik's personal intervention with Foreign Minister Sazonov, the Russian government sanctioned Dürich's proposal for a separatist national council and granted him financial support. The Paris National Council expelled Dürich, but the Russian movement was now divided into two groups. Although the Provisional Government established by the Russian Revolution repudiated both Dürich and his organization, the movement was not fully unified until Masaryk himself arrived in Russia in the spring of 1917.[57]

During the first few years of the war, the Czech liberation movement faced perhaps even greater difficulties in Italy than it did in Russia. Up to and even after the war had begun, Italy had been an ally of Austria-Hungary. However, on April 26, 1915, the Foreign Minister, Sidney Sonnino, repudiated the Triple Alliance and concluded with the Allies the Treaty of London, which recognized Italian claims, not merely to the Trentino, Trieste, and other Italian districts of Austria, but also to Istria and a large part of Dalmatia that encompassed a population of close to a million Slovenes and Croats. Italy entered the war the following month. Whereas the Italians could accept the possibility of Czecho-Slovak independence, they were primarily concerned with the maintenance of a balance of power in the Adriatic and therefore viewed the ambitions of the South Slavs with great distrust and fear. Thus, they saw Slavic nationalism as applied to the Habsburg monarchy as detrimental to their interests.[58] In accordance with his interpretation of the Treaty of London, Sonnino consistently supported the preservation of an Austro-Hungarian Empire even though reduced in territory by Italian claims.

In January 1917, Beneš went to Rome for conferences with some of the officials in the Italian Foreign Ministry. Although Sonnino declined to receive him personally, Beneš was able to make friends in diverse circles. He established an office of the National Council and laid the foundation for an Italian committee for Czecho-Slovak independence. The only satisfaction that he received concerning the question closest to his heart—that of recruiting a legion among the Czech and Slovak prisoners of war in Italy—was a promise that they would be separated from the Austrians and the Hungarians.[59]

2

Wilson's Early Wartime Policy
toward Austria-Hungary

While a sophomore at Princeton, Woodrow Wilson demonstrated his knowledge of the multinational Habsburg Empire with his first published work, an essay on Bismarck.[1] Later in 1889, Wilson analyzed the character and problems of Austria-Hungary in a book on comparative government entitled *The State*. He described precisely both the complexities and frailties of the Dual Monarchy. He revealed profound knowledge of the competing and potentially disruptive nationalisms, including the desperate quest of the Czech leaders for a larger measure of home rule. Aware of Bohemia's individuality and her strenuous and persistent devotion to independence, he wrote: "No lapse of time, no defeat of hopes, seem sufficient to reconcile the Czechs of Bohemia to incorporation with Austria. . . . They desire at least the same degree of autonomy that has been granted to Hungary." The phrase "no lapse of time" later became the battle cry of Czech propaganda in the United States during the First World War. First quoted by a Czech spokesman at a hearing before the Committee on Foreign Affairs of the House of Representatives on February 25, 1916, it was printed on the title page of the first issue of *The Bohemian Review* (later the *Czechoslovak Review*).[2]

When Wilson wrote his chapter on the Dual Monarchy in the 1880s, he was probably in a far more contemplative mood than he was some thirty years later when burdened with the responsibility of making decisions involving the Habsburg Empire and the people who lived in it. Nevertheless, the Czechs and Slovaks interpreted his various benevolent statements as support for their cause. They based their electoral support for him in 1916 on the grounds that he had "always stood for all those sacred principles so dear to all Slavs." They regarded Wilson as the great exponent of liberation for minority peoples.[3]

Wilson's espousal of the principle of self-determination as a central element of the peace was not simply a reaction to Bolshevik initiatives and wartime exigencies, as some scholars have claimed.[4] He had early embraced this concept under his own favored expression of self-government and had referred to it in relation to the war as early as November 4, 1915.[5] Although he does not appear to have used the term "self-determination" publicly until February 11, 1918, his addresses of May 27, 1916, and January 22, 1917, as well as his early wartime addresses are permeated with the ideas later incorporated in the catchall phrase "self-determination." For example, in his address to the League to Enforce the Peace in Washington on May 27, 1916, he emphasized the fundamental right of every people "to choose the sovereignty under which they shall live."[6]

Prior to the war, relations between Austria-Hungary and the United States had consisted largely of diplomatic formalities. Wilson had appointed Frederick Courtland Penfield, a former newspaperman, as Ambassador. An egotist, ill-equipped for his post, Penfield was unable to command the respect of his subordinates.[7] His counterpart in Washington was the experienced diplomat, Count Constantin Theodor Dumba, who had arrived from Stockholm in 1913. Dumba, an accomplished practitioner of the "old diplomacy," impulsive, congenial, and polished, soon gained a reputation as one of the most astute members of the diplomatic corps in Washington.[8]

Wilson sent an appropriate message of sympathy to Emperor Franz Joseph when he learned that the heir to the Austrian and Hungarian thrones had been assassinated.[9] Immediately after war was declared, Wilson offered the good services of the United States to end the war through mediation. The aged Habsburg Emperor's reply was scarcely conciliatory.[10] He could accept the President's offer only "at such time as the honor of the flag will permit and when the objectives of war shall be obtained." The replies of the other powers were equally discouraging.[11] Wilson's response was to issue numerous proclamations of neutrality, which established the position of the United States in unequivocal terms.[12]

From the beginning of hostilities, the American public and the press were strongly sympathetic toward Britain and France. These sympathies had been reinforced by the abrupt Austrian ultimatum to Serbia, the German violation of Belgian neutrality, and the ensuing devastations in that little country. While striving to remain neutral, Wilson suspected that Austria-Hungary shared responsibility with Germany for the war. He read "with genuine interest" an article in the *New York Times* by Albert Bushnell Hart of Harvard University, which had been sent by his friend and admirer, Charles R. Crane. Hart bitterly criticized the Vienna government for the "arrogant and contemptuous language" of its ultimatum to Serbia and emphasized the conciliatory and dignified response of the Belgrade ministry.[13] Commenting on the Hart piece, Wilson wrote that the more he read about the conflict, the more deserving it was of "utter condemnation." By December 1914, Wilson had adopted a peace-without-victory outlook and rejected the theory of exclusive German responsibility for the war.[14] The possible disintegration of the Habsburg Empire apparently caused him no great regret, since he thought that it "ought to go to pieces for the welfare of Europe."[15]

After the war had begun, Dumba requested the President's intervention in relieving the abysmal conditions of Austro-Hungarian prisoners in Siberia.[16] In response, Wilson wrote personally to the Tsar on behalf of the war prisoners. As a result of these exchanges, the American Ambassador in St. Petersburg and all American Consuls throughout Russia became by international law intermediaries between the Austro-Hungarian prisoners of war and the Russian government.[17] Dumba was expelled in September 1915 on account of a foolish indiscretion and was succeeded by the Austrian Chargé d'Affaires, Baron Erich von Zwiedinek.[18]

The most threatening controversy in Austro-American relations was the sinking in the Mediterranean of the *Ancona*, an Italian passenger ship, presumably by an Austrian submarine in November 1915.[19] Since Secretary of State Robert Lansing thought that there was sufficient evidence from the Austro-Hungarian side alone to justify a stern reaction, he drafted an unusually severe note.[20] Although Wilson regarded the note as "peremptory," he agreed to send it to Vienna on the following day.[21] Vienna's reply did not ease the situation. Because Lansing was irritated by its "technicalities and quibbles," Wilson found it necessary to soften his draft response and to add courteous references before sending it to Vienna on December 19.[22] During the tedious discussions that followed, it appeared that Count Stefan Burián von Rajecz, Austro-Hungarian Foreign Minister, would suggest arbitration as a way out, a possibility that Wilson believed the United States could scarcely "refuse to consider," since refusal would be "contrary to all our traditions and would place us in a very difficult pos[i]tion to justify in the opinion of the rest of the world."[23] Wilson had begun to believe that Lansing was moving too fast, especially after he wrote on December 28 that the United States might soon have to break relations with the Habsburg government, and that perhaps Wilson ought to consider laying the facts before Congress to obtain its approval.[24]

Wilson found it difficult to believe that sufficient new elements had entered the picture to justify a breach of diplomatic relations. He considered it unwise to lay the matter before Congress. Believing that the Austrians should be given every opportunity to clarify the *Ancona* case, he could not refuse to discuss the matter until all the world was convinced that "rock bottom" had been reached.[25]

Foreign Minister Burián sent a full and responsive reply on the *Ancona* affair to Washington on December 29 and thereby made a presidential showdown with Lansing unnecessary. The note was a complete vindication of the American position on submarine warfare.[26] Thereafter, the Austrian government avoided serious complications by promising to curb the action of its few submarines. Wilson emerged from the encounter with "a most favorable impression of the friendly and reasonable attitude" of the Vienna authorities.[27]

As 1916 opened, Wilson was optimistic both about continued American neutrality and the prospects for a negotiated peace. The Austrian attitude afforded him "something more than a ray of hope for a satisfactory settlement."[28] However, this outlook was not officially shared in Vienna, where Franz Joseph told Kaiser Wilhelm: "There will be no peace concluded unless our enemies sue for it."[29] Yet Penfield reported that there was not one person in the Dual Monarchy who was not heartily sick of the war and wished for an early peace. The coffers of the Dual Monarchy were practically empty, and skeptics believed that the resources of the Empire could not last another six months.[30]

The British government publicly shared the official view of its enemies. In September 1916, David Lloyd George, an important figure in the Asquith government and leader of the Radicals, publicly supported a "crushing military victory" over Germany that would be "complete and final."[31] Asquith himself had declared that the "sword of the United Kingdom would never be sheathed" until "the rights and independence of small nations had been placed in unassailable foundation; and until Prussian military domination had been finally destroyed."[32]

Despite these militant views, Colonel Edward M. House, negotiator of the well-known House-Grey memorandum, repeatedly assured Wilson that both British and French leaders wanted peace and that American mediation was possible. House "not only misinformed and mislead" Wilson but also encouraged him to believe that American efforts might well be effective.[33] It soon appeared that Wilson's hopes for negotiating a separate peace with Austria-Hungary were not shared by Penfield. He feared that Wilson's frequent statements supporting the right of every race to govern itself had made the Austrians suspicious. This position was hardly pleasing to the Austro-Hungarian monarch who ruled Austrians, Hungarians, Bohemians, Slavs, Croats, and other races.[34]

While the war continued in the trenches of France, German Chancellor Theobald von Bethmann Hollweg met Burián at Imperial headquarters in Pless, Germany, to clarify the position of Austria after the war, as well as to discuss their latest war aims. A memorandum outlining the final conclusions placed the integrity of the Austrian monarchy at the head of the seven main terms.[35] It clearly reflected the Austrian fear that the Entente wished to divide the Central Powers.

With Wilson's reelection in November 1916, the Central Powers began to send peace feelers throughout Europe. Wilson received the first inkling of the Austrian peace terms through the British embassy at Washington on November 19; however, the dispatch specified that the Austrian offer was "good until November 20, after which date the Austrian minister was to request further instructions."[36] The instructions referred to the German intention to use unrestricted submarine warfare, a policy that began under pressure from the military leaders in the winter of 1916.[37]

In view of the nebulous nature of the Austrian peace proposal and the public opposition of Lloyd George and Briand to a negotiated peace, the time seemed most inauspicious for an American peace proposal. Nevertheless, as early as November 14, Wilson had told House that he desired to send a note to the belligerents demanding that the war cease. He feared that unless this was done immediately, war with Germany over the submarine issue would be "inevitable."[38] Franz Joseph died in the midst of the prenegotiations, on November 21.

Throughout Vienna, considerable speculation now arose concerning a possible change in Austrian foreign policy. In Viennese circles, the new monarch, young Charles, the grandnephew of the old Emperor, was considered more liberal than his predecessor. His accession to the throne reinforced the peace party. However, Charles faced an exceedingly difficult situation. The war had been going on for more than two years, and the military and economic forces of the nation were beginning to fail.[39] To combat antidynastic feeling, Charles needed to renew the splendor of the dynasty, give his people the long desired peace, and bring about a settlement among the different nations composing the Habsburg monarchy. At the outset, Charles emphasized his firm intention to end the terrible conflict, an objective strongly supported by his wife, Zita, by her mother, the influential Maria Antonia of Parma, and by his brothers-in-law, Sixtus and Xavier, who as early as November 1916 tried to get in touch with the Entente powers.[40]

Charles I of Austria (Charles Francis Joseph) (Bildarchiv der Österreichischen
Nationalbibliotek, Vienna)

Penfield reported that Charles not only spoke English well but also appeared to understand the United States. Rumors circulated that he was anxious to end hostilities and might be receptive to proposals for a separate peace, particularly if they sought to preserve the Empire. Vienna press reports revealed a tendency to look to the United States to inaugurate peace proposals.[41] Masaryk immediately disagreed. He believed that the new Emperor had no real authority and could not act as a unifying factor in the same way as Franz Joseph had. He predicted that Charles would be unable to resist German influence and that the Germans would secure even greater control of Austria-Hungary.[42]

Masaryk's view was not borne out in the first message Charles issued to his Empire: "I have to do all in my power to end, as soon as may be, the horrors and sacrifices of the war, and to restore to my peoples the vanished blessings of peace."[43] This statement contrasted markedly with his predecessor's belief in total victory. Charles reinforced his policy with the appointment of Ottokar Czernin as the Minister of Foreign Affairs to replace Burián. An intelligent and resourceful diplomat, Czernin pursued a strong nationalist policy while in office. Nevertheless, he showed greater inclination than most of his class to meet the wishes of aspiring democracy. This major change of ministers was the "sensation of the day and wholly unlooked for."[44] The scene was now set for the peace moves of the Central Powers and Woodrow Wilson in December. However, if Wilson's effort to negotiate a peace with Austria-Hungary was to succeed, he would have to support the integrity of the Empire—a policy that would surely displease both Masaryk and the Bohemian liberation movement in general. But their attitude and response can be better understood after a review of their early efforts to secure American support for their cause.

Count Ottokar Czernin von und zu Chudenitz (Bildarchiv der Österreichischen Nationalbibliotek, Vienna)

3

American Supporters of Bohemian Liberation

In 1914, approximately a million and a half Czechs and Slovaks lived in the United States. After Prague, Chicago was the second largest Czech city in the world. Czechs were also particularly numerous in the areas surrounding Cleveland, Pittsburgh, and New York, and in the midwestern states and Texas. They had organized extensive patriotic organizations, newspapers, churches, and Sokols.[1] Before 1910 periodical literature on the Czechs and Slovaks was practically nonexistent, and Bohemian history was virtually unknown among the general American public. If Americans thought of Bohemia at all, it was apt to be as the land of the gypsies.[2] At the outbreak of the war, many Czechs and Slovaks in the United States, deeply sympathetic to the Serbs, grieved that Czech and other Slavic regiments were being sent to fight against them. Aware of Austro-Hungarian censorship, some believed that it was their responsibility to protest against this "barbarous and fratricidal war" and seek greater freedom and independence for the Czechs.[3] Meetings held across the country resulted in the formation of the Bohemian National Alliance on August 18, 1914. Dr. Ludvik J. Fisher became the head of the national organization, located in Chicago, while Emanuel Voska became the leader of the movement in New York. It spread throughout the country and by the end of the war numbered some 250 branches.[4]

When Voska returned from Bohemia in late 1914 with the news of Masaryk's preparations for the liberation of the Czechs and Slovaks, the initial task of the Bohemian National Alliance was clear. It had to convince the American Czechs that political action was now necessary and opportune. By the end of 1915 the majority of Czechs had been persuaded to join the Bohemian National Alliance.[5] The Slovak League, headed by Albert Mamatey of Pittsburgh, cooperated with the movement and sent members to a joint conference. The Sokols, the National Mutual Aid Organization, and, later, the Slovak Catholics also joined the Bohemian National Alliance.[6] In April 1915, 3,000 Bohemians

Dr. Ludvik J. Fisher (*Bohemian Review*)

met in New York City and adopted a resolution endorsing President Wilson's neutral course.[7] When the Czecho-Slovak Foreign Committee in Paris issued its declaration of war against Austria-Hungary and its manifesto for Czecho-Slovak independence on November 14, 1915, Czech and Slovak organizations in the United States immediately announced their support. In the early years of the war, the Bohemian National Alliance sought to publicize its program by lectures, articles, memoranda to Wilson, and the conversion of prominent Americans to the Czech cause.[8]

The movement slowly won adherents among Americans. The first was Charles R. Crane, who became the most important friend the Czechs had in the United States. Head of the Crane Plumbing and Manufacturing Company and a wealthy philanthropist, Crane had endowed the School of Slavonic Studies at the University of Chicago. He became a Czechophile gradually, but at a time when this was so unusual as to make him an eccentric. In 1896, when Crane was planning a trip to Russia and East Central Europe, his intimate friend, William R. Harper, President of the University of Chicago, urged him to get in touch with Masaryk.

During the visit, the two men spoke at length of their mutual interest in Slavic affairs. So rare was it for an American to be sympathetic to the welfare of the Slavic peoples that both Masaryk and his wife believed that Crane, whom they thought was a mild-mannered idealist, must be a missionary out on a fund-raising tour. Crane became one of Masaryk's closest friends. He invited Masaryk to lecture at the School of Slavonic Studies at the University of Chicago. This brought Masaryk to the United States and acquainted him with Slavic people throughout the nation. Thus, it was not surprising that Crane was the first American whose help Masaryk sought for the Czech cause at the outbreak of the war.[9]

Their friendship was propitious. As Crane became increasingly close to Wilson, various Cabinet members, and House, he was able to influence Wilson's attitude toward Masaryk and Czech nationalistic aspirations.[10] Crane, who greatly admired Wilson, had a feeling of genuine responsibility toward him—the responsibility of understanding and interpreting him to the world. He played an active role in Wilson's first presidential campaign and was the largest single financial contributor to it. Like many of Wilson's admirers, Crane saw him as the prophet for whom the world had been waiting.[11]

Wilson had "the warmest admiration and affection" for Crane. In 1914, he invited him to become Ambassador to Russia, but Crane declined because of his father's recent death.[12] During early 1915, Crane moved from Chicago to Woods Hole, Massachusetts. From there he was better able to visit Colonel House and to entertain members of Wilson's Cabinet and other persons of note in Washington. Later during the summer, his son Richard was appointed secretary to Lansing. The elder Crane was deeply gratified by his son's appointment.[13]

The elder Crane was also instrumental in winning support for

Masaryk from Samuel N. Harper. In 1900, Crane had taken William R. Harper along as a guest on one of his visits to Russia. Harper became so impressed with Russia and Russian affairs that he and Crane persuaded Harper's son, Samuel N., to make Russian studies his life's work. Samuel N. Harper was another person to whom the Czechs could turn for support and whose help Masaryk sought in 1918 in his final effort to gain American recognition of Czech independence. Young Harper also saw Masaryk frequently when the Czech leader was in Moscow attempting to organize the Czech Legion.[14]

Masaryk's charisma also transformed the early purely academic interest of Herbert A. Miller in the Czechs to dynamic personal and professional support. In 1912, after a week's visit with Masaryk, Miller regarded him as "one of the noblest men who ever lived, a man fearless in standing for the highest principles." Miller's paper on Bohemian nationalism, printed in *The North American Review* in December 1914, was the first magazine article on that subject published in the United States.[15] Charles Pergler, Czech-American journalist, speaker, lawyer, and signer of the Czecho-Slovak demand for independence, was another dedicated worker. Successively he was a Vice President of the Bohemian National Alliance, Director of the Slav Press Bureau in New York, Director of the American office of the Czecho-Slovak National Council in Washington, and secretary to Masaryk while he was in the United States. For two years Pergler lobbied for a nation that did not exist and a cause that was demanding no legislation.[16]

Emanuel Voska was an outstanding Czech-American supporter in another arena of the Czech struggle—that of intelligence. Voska had offered his support to Masaryk as a courier to London and America in 1914. An ardent Bohemian nationalist who had been exiled as a youth by the Austro-Hungarian government for socialist activity, he had come to the United States in 1894 and made a comfortable fortune. He became prominent in the Bohemian colonies and President of the American Sokols. When Masaryk had visited the United States in 1902 and 1907, Voska had arranged a series of lectures for him before branches of the Sokol.[17]

Voska's dedication to the Czech cause was tireless. As head of the propaganda section of the Bohemian National Alliance in the eastern United States, he was in constant contact with Masaryk. Upon meeting Captain Sir Guy Gaunt, British Naval Attaché in Washington and the head of British naval intelligence in the United States, Voska offered him the services of his organization in the hope that Czechs could make themselves "so useful that when Britain and France dictated peace they

Charles Pergler (*Bohemian Review*)

could not deny our claim to an independent republic."[18] Although initially Voska's organization worked without British financial support, in 1916 arrangements were made to provide operating expenses from British intelligence sources.[19] Voska's agents were active in espionage, counterintelligence, and propaganda aimed at thwarting Austrian and German plots against the Entente in the United States and played important roles in a number of well-known Allied espionage coups by infiltrating the Austrian embassy and several German organizations.[20]

When Sir William Wiseman became the head of the British counterintelligence operations in the United States in December 1916, Voska began to work for his organization. He soon had eight agents working for him, and Wiseman came to regard Voska's services as "the luckiest thing" that had happened to him in his intelligence activities. Voska was later hailed as one of the most outstanding "secret agents of the first war."[21] The work of the Czech agents in the United States was the most valuable assistance given to the Entente by any organization before 1917.

Masaryk and the Czechs had other dedicated American supporters. Mary McDowell, head of the University of Chicago Settlement House and an old friend of both Masaryk and his daughter, Alice, had befriended many Czechs and Slovaks whom she had seen grow up in Chicago. She had not only arranged Professor Miller's introduction to Masaryk, but she had also encouraged Professor Emily Greene Balch of Wellesley—at one time with the Chicago Settlement House—to continue her sensitive writings about Czech immigrants and inspired other academicians to do deeper research about the Czechs.[22] McDowell's services on behalf of the Czechs were later to win for her the Order of the White Lion of the Czechoslovak Republic.

Masaryk desperately needed funds, not only to relieve the men and families "who had become victims of military absolutism, reigning all over Austria and particularly in Bohemia," but also to help to organize the political movement abroad. Naturally he approached both the Bohemian communities in the United States, a comparatively wealthy group, and Crane, his friend and benefactor. Fearful of police interference if he wrote to Crane directly from Bohemia, Masaryk had been forced to communicate through an intermediary. Once he left Prague, he wrote Crane directly about his plan to organize Czech journalistic activities abroad and communicate with the "politicians of the Triple Entente." He was convinced that once the Russians advanced to the Bohemian provinces, the time would be ripe to secure freedom and independence at home. He reported on his initial efforts to organize

Bohemian legions in Russia and in France and urged Crane not only to contribute personally but to elicit the support of his friends for the Bohemian cause. "Please help us," Masaryk wrote, "in obtaining a high and noble end."[23] Crane not only sent money, but also assured the Czech leaders in the United States that if they kept within reasonable limits, he saw no reason for the administration to put obstacles in the way of their agitation for "racial" independence.[24]

One event, particularly, engendered great sympathy for the Bohemian liberation movement—the arrest and threatened execution of Dr. Alice Masaryk, Professor Masaryk's daughter, on the charge of high treason.[25] The widespread publicity given the Alice Masaryk case was the consequence of the determined efforts of Charles R. Crane; selected leaders of the women's movement in Chicago, New York, Boston, and Washington; and the Bohemian National Alliance.

News of Dr. Masaryk's imprisonment was confirmed in November 1915. She had been arrested on October 28 in Prague and then, on November 7, confined in the Landesgerichtliches Gefangenhaus in Vienna. Penfield in Vienna had difficulty in obtaining further information because she was being prosecuted by the military authorities.[26] Masaryk, then in England, immediately wrote to Crane for help. He surmised that his daughter had been imprisoned for "putting aside" certain of his books and manuscripts, although he had asked her to do this soon after he left Prague, at a time when such communication was not a political crime. As the days wore on, Masaryk became even more deeply concerned, and, on November 29, he again cabled Crane asking him to "intervene as asked last letter."[27]

The elder Crane immediately set aside personal plans and vowed to "do anything in the world" to publicize the "Alice Masaryk Affair," to the point where it would create as much public disapproval as the "Edith Cavell Case."[28] He alerted American and Bohemian newspapers and news agencies and also induced the *New York Times* and the *Christian Science Monitor* to publicize the case. He enlisted the support of both Mary McDowell in Chicago and Lillian D. Wald, head of the Henry Street Settlement in New York. Crane also solicited the help of his son Richard through the State Department. Finally, he sent a personal cable to the Austrian Chancellor himself, whom he knew, warning him in a friendly way of the "dynamite" in the matter.[29]

The newspapers speculated that the arrest of Alice Masaryk was a move by the Austrians to silence her father. Members of the various Bohemian organizations brought the case to the attention of Congressman Adolph J. Sabath, Democrat of Illinois, in an effort to secure the government's intervention. Sabath, a Bohemian-born Chicago lawyer, was a devoted friend of the Bohemian cause.[30] Upon learning of Alice's imprisonment, he wired immediately to Vienna to withhold any action until it had heard from the United States.[31] He also brought the case forcefully to the attention of the State Department "in the name of the Bohemian people in Chicago."[32] Dr. Julia Lathrop, chief of the Children's Bureau of the Department of Labor, requested that the State Department cable for information about the well-being of Miss Masaryk.[33] Penfield responded that she had been imprisoned presumably on the charge of high treason, and that her trial would be delayed because, "owing to the mass of evidence, the preliminary investigation [would] take some time." He was unable to obtain any further news.[34]

On April 27, the *Chicago Daily Tribune* headlined the caption, "Alice Masaryk Already Executed, New York Hears."[35] Chicago members of the Bohemian National Alliance, aided by Jane Addams and other Hull House workers, urged a State Department inquiry into the reported execution, but the State Department had no confirmation of the report.[36] However, in May, news from Professor Hugo Münsterberg of Harvard University, who supposedly had a good deal of influence at the Austrian embassy, revealed that Miss Masaryk was safe and was being held only for preliminary trial by the Austrians.[37] Several weeks later this report was confirmed.[38] On August 20, Alexander von Nuber, the Austrian Consul General in the United States, announced Miss Masaryk's release.[39] According to the reports in *Denní Hlasatel*, Austrian officials could find no proof of any subversive activities on her part. The account suggested that the great interest of the American public in Alice Masaryk's fate, combined with the stream of protests sent to Vienna, may well have influenced the Austrian authorities.[40] According to one eminent authority, the life of Alice Masaryk was saved only by the agitation in the United States that induced the American government to intervene on her behalf.[41]

Both Charles R. Crane and the Bohemian National Alliance, while deeply sympathetic to the plight of Miss Masaryk, had used every opportunity in publicizing her case to present the cause of the Bohemian liberation movement as eloquently and persuasively as possible. Virtually all news articles covering the affair presented it against the historic background of Bohemian aspirations for freedom and independence. Thus, the quest for Alice Masaryk's freedom had provided an effective opportunity to arouse popular antagonism to the Austro-Hungarian regime and promote interest in the Czecho-Slovak independence movement in the United States.

4

Search for Friendly Relations
with Austria-Hungary

In November 1916, Wilson was reelected President as the man "who kept us out of war." Both the November referendum and his own personal inclination now moved him to initiate a peace move. The time seemed propitious, for not only had the new Austrian Emperor shown a genuine interest in peace, but also reports from Germany revealed a marked increase of peace sentiments among the general public and high official circles. At the same time, Wilson feared that the German leaders had already violated the *Sussex* pledge of May 1916, by which they had agreed to cease their attacks against merchant ships without warning. This might necessitate a break in diplomatic relations, a step which Wilson deeply deplored. Before doing this, he wished to make another serious effort at peace through negotiation.[1]

Before Wilson could bring his own plan to fruition, both the Austrian Emperor and the German Chancellor initiated their own peace moves. On November 21, 1916, Charles began secret negotiations through his brothers-in-law, Princes Sixtus and Xavier of Bourbon-Parma, then serving in the Belgian army. Through influential contacts in France, they began a long series of secret negotiations with President Poincaré and his government, which continued until May 1917.[2] On December 12, after discussing Wilson's mediation efforts with both Joseph C. Grew, the American Chargé in Berlin, and Johann Heinrich von Bernstorff, the German Ambassador to the United States, the German Chancellor announced his decision to send a preliminary peace note to the enemy powers.[3]

Deeply interested in the outcome of "these unexpected overtures," Wilson announced his own intention to present a peace proposal.[4] On December 18, Wilson invited all the belligerent governments to state their aims in the war and their conditions for peace. Neither proposing peace nor offering mediation, he noted that both sides proclaimed the same objectives. Moreover, each professed a willingness to consider the formation of a league of nations, but only after the war had terminated with peace terms that each believed would safeguard its independence, territorial integrity, and political and commercial freedom. Wilson put forth the suggestion, if not the threat, that the United States might become a belligerent if the war was not ended soon.[5]

On December 26, the Central Powers officially expressed their unwillingness to state their war aims publicly; at the same time, they proposed a "direct exchange of views" with the Entente.[6] The German Chancellor had written the note knowing that if the peace move did not bear fruit by February 1, 1917, the German High Command would almost certainly begin unrestricted submarine warfare.[7] Vienna, while welcoming peace, cast its unofficial comments in "a guarded form," obviously fearing to prejudice its chances of obtaining the best possible terms by appearing too receptive. Wilson's recent statement indicating that every people had the "inherent right to self-government" had clearly given umbrage to the ruling groups. Thus the official Austrian response, while friendly, was essentially the same as that of the Germans.[8]

When Wilson's note arrived in the Allied capitals on December 20, the Allies were formulating their reply to the note of the Central Powers. Skeptical of the sincerity of the German peace offer, they refused to accept an invitation to discuss peace when the Central Powers had not indicated their terms in the note.[9] The new British Prime Minister, David Lloyd George, summed up Allied terms as "complete restitution, full reparation, and effectual guarantees for the future."[10]

Such an atmosphere was not congenial to an enthusiastic consideration of Wilson's note. Most Allied officials considered Wilson's interference an "outrage." They felt that his failure to distinguish the ethical differences that separated the two groups of belligerents showed an utter lack of moral discernment.[11] As official spokesman for the Allies, Ambassador Jean Jules Jusserand in Washington voiced his anger directly to Lansing.[12] Nevertheless, because the Entente, and the British in particular, still sought to draw the United States into the war on their side, they agreed to state their war aims in the hope of impressing upon the President the similarity of those aims with his principles.[13]

Masaryk agreed with the Allies in part. Although he rejected Wilson's statement that the announced objectives of the war were virtually the same on both sides, he agreed that the "concrete objects" of the war had never been definitely stated. Masaryk naturally considered "very dangerous" and "absolutely unacceptable" Wilson's view of settling the issues of the war upon terms that would safeguard the independence, territorial integrity, and commercial freedom of the nations involved. This implied the status quo ante, or a German peace. He also doubted Wilson's commitment to the protection of smaller and weaker peoples. "How," said Masaryk, "could the liberty of smaller nations be secured without *territorial* changes?" Nevertheless, he re-garded the opportunity to issue an Allied reply to Wilson as "psycho-logically favorable" for presenting a proper account of the Austro-Hungarian problem and of Czech and Slovak national demands.[14]

Despite Masaryk's hopes and earlier evidence of official British sympathy, neither of the first British drafts responding to Wilson's peace proposal contained a specific reference to the Czechs and Slo-vaks. Yet in December 1915, the then Foreign Secretary, Edward Grey, had advocated giving free play to the aspirations of the national minor-ities in the Dual Monarchy to insure an Entente victory, because he believed that the non-German parts of Austria-Hungary would cer-tainly secede.[15] Moreover, in November 1916, Arthur James Balfour, the new British Foreign Secretary, had written a memorandum supporting the "principle of nationality." Although he advocated the maintenance of the Dual Monarchy, he believed that it should be "shorn" of various of its territories, including "Bohemia," where "Germanic civilization [was] profoundly distasteful."[16] Even more sympathetic to the Bohe-mians was Wiseman, who on December 13 cabled to London: "If British reply to German peace proposal contains no mention of Bohemian aspirations, it is probable that the work done for us here by Czechs will suffer, and possible that if too much discouraged they might listen to bids from Central Empires. This might cause us considerable harm."[17]

Neither Wiseman's telegram nor the earlier efforts of Masaryk and Seton-Watson at the Foreign Office produced any specific reference to the Czechs in the final British draft. The reply, however, did include references to national self-determination, primarily to appeal to Wilson and the popular American interest in the nationalities, particularly the Poles.[18] Beneš immediately initiated a series of conversations with key officials at the French Foreign Ministry to secure specific Allied sup-port for the liberation of the Czechs and Slovaks. While the French were sympathetic, they were opposed to making any public promise that would oblige the French to fight until the Empire had been com-pletely broken up.[19]

In the meantime, the British and French had drafted a joint response to Wilson's peace proposal at a conference in London between December 26 and 28. Lord Robert Cecil later admitted that he had never thought about the Czechs and Slovaks until a French delegate to the conference, probably Foreign Minister Stéphen Pichon, suggested that their liberation be included in the document. Yet no mention of the Czechs and Slovaks appeared in the original joint draft. On January 4, during a final interview at the Quai d'Orsay, the French informed Beneš that they were resolved to do something for the Czechs but would probably not determine on the appropriate form until an inter-Allied conference met in Rome. The last business taken up by the conference at Rome was the answer to Wilson's peace appeal.[20] Although the Allies had agreed to express in general terms the necessity to liberate the Austro-Hungarian Slavs, Italians, and Rumanians, the Italian delegates opposed the specific mention of the Czechs and Slovaks because they felt that it would necessitate a similar reference to the Yugoslavs, a policy to which they were fundamentally opposed.[21] At the last minute, Briand finally succeeded in inserting in the already completed draft of the note to Wilson the explicit demand for Czech and Slovak liberation.[22] Russia did no more than assent to the collective replies of the Allies.[23] It was not until January 7 that Beneš learned that the Allies had accepted the French proposal for "the liberation of Italians, of Slavs, of Roumanians and of Czecho-Slovaks from foreign domination."[24]

Although some might interpret the term "liberation" as autonomy rather than independence, Beneš argued that it more logically implied the destruction of the Habsburg Empire, particularly in light of his earlier discussions at the French Foreign Ministry.[25] Briand, concerned over events on the Eastern Front, welcomed the declaration in the hope that it would encourage the people of Bohemia and Moravia to detach themselves from the Austro-Hungarian Empire. And yet, according to his biographer, Briand's attitude did not represent "the expression of a firm will."[26] In any case, the British believed that they had in no way committed themselves to the "practical break up and partition of the Austro-Hungarian Empire."[27]

The Allied reply to Wilson's peace note of January 10, 1917, was the first official and public declaration of war aims by either coalition. Significantly, the reference to the Czechs and Slovaks represented the first major diplomatic achievement of the Czechs in exile. Despite its vagueness and ambiguity, the Czechs interpreted the Allied statement optimistically—as the announcement of a policy of dismemberment of Austria-Hungary. Masaryk now believed that "the victory of the Allies would bring them freedom from Austrian domination."[28] Joy reigned throughout the various Czech and Slovak headquarters abroad. Telegrams and letters of congratulations poured into Paris from emigrés in Russia, the United States, Italy, Switzerland, and elsewhere.[29]

The Czech politicians in Prague did not share the enthusiasm of the exiles abroad. Comment in the press was virtually unanimous in rejecting the idea of dismemberment. There appeared to be little surface doubt of Czech loyalty to the Empire.[30] When statesmen in Vienna learned that the Entente war aims included the liberation of the Czechs and Slovaks, they were terrified. Czernin immediately denounced the Entente for seeking "the annihilation and spoliation of the Austro-Hungarian Monarchy."[31] Equally disturbed, the Hungarian Premier, Stephen Tisza, informed Penfield that the Allied conditions of peace involving "the dismemberment of Austria-Hungary" were equivalent to a war of destruction.[32]

In general, the American press was silent about the Allied "peace terms" relating to the liberation of the Czechs and Slovaks. An occasional foreign correspondent such as Norman Hapgood emphasized the European importance of the Bohemian question. He cabled the *Chicago Tribune* that next to the problem of Constantinople, only Bohemia had a "pressing and unavoidable bearing" upon the geography in Europe.[33] It was Hapgood also who wrote to Wilson about Masaryk, the scholarly leader of the "Independent Bohemia party," then "under sentence of death" by the Austro-Hungarian government. At Masaryk's request, Hapgood enclosed a published memorandum written by Masaryk entitled *At the Eleventh Hour*. An analysis of the military situation, it included strong arguments to demonstrate that Austria and Hungary were the "tools and puppets" of pan-Germanism and that an independent Bohemia, Poland, and Greater Serbia were vital to stop "Prussian" aggression.[34]

Despite the minimal response in the American press to the cause of Bohemian independence, Czech and Slovak exiles took heart on reading Wilson's "Peace without Victory" address to the Senate of January 22, 1917. In laying down the general principles for a lasting peace, Wilson emphasized: "No peace can last, or ought to last, which does not recognize and accept the principle that governments derive all their just powers from the consent of the governed, and that no right anywhere exists to hand peoples about from sovereignty to sovereignty as if they were property."[35] Aspiring national minorities immediately identified this as the program of national self-determination.[36] Yet some weeks later Wilson explained to Jusserand that he had intended to suggest, not the break-up of the Habsburg Empire, but broad autonomy for its subject nationalities.[37]

Wilson's address was followed by preparations for a confidential peace move. Wilson informed the German government that he intended to negotiate on the basis of his "Peace without Victory" address and that he was quite willing to abstain from participation in the settlement of territorial questions. However, by this time, Wilson's fears of a violation of the *Sussex* pledge had materialized. German submarines had been sent out with appropriate instructions on January 25, 1917. Nevertheless, the German High Command was willing to permit Bethmann Hollweg and Bernstorff to make one more attempt at negotiation, provided it did not interfere with the submarine campaign. Consequently, on January 29, Bethmann sent Wilson the terms upon which Germany's peace note of December 12 was based. They arrived on the same day as the announcement that unrestricted submarine warfare would commence on February 1. The Chancellor tried to counteract the bad effects of this news by expressing Germany's willingness to modify its plans if Wilson's efforts would insure a peace acceptable to Germany.[38] Wilson was so deeply distressed by the Berlin U-boat decision that on February 3 he announced to a joint session of Congress the severance of diplomatic relations with Germany. At the same time, he expressed his continued hope for peace by announcing that he would not go to war because of the German violation of the *Sussex* pledge, provided the Germans did not sink *American* ships without warning.[39]

In the Habsburg monarchy, Czernin, Tisza, and Charles received with deep gloom the news that Washington had severed diplomatic relations with Berlin. They were convinced that the almost certain intervention of the United States would bring forth catastrophic consequences.[40] In the United States, however, President Fisher of the Bohemian National Alliance reported the joy of 500,000 loyal Bohemian-Americans in a telegram of congratulations to Wilson.[41]

As fate would have it, on February 3, the same day that Bernstorff and his staff were handed their passports, Count Adam Tarnowski, the new Austrian Ambassador-designate to the United States, arrived at the State Department to present his credentials. Austria-Hungary had been without an ambassador in the United States since the expulsion of Dumba over eighteen months earlier. Tarnowski, a Pole, had been in the diplomatic service for twenty years. Penfield had praised him highly as a person "friendly to the United States." In urging Tarnowski's acceptance, Penfield emphasized that Austria was "not a partner in the submarine menace."[42]

William Phillips received Tarnowski. Phillips had acquired strong anti-German feelings as a result of his first appointment as private unpaid secretary to the Ambassador to Britain in 1903. Although a

Republican and the chief of the Division of Far Eastern Affairs, he had accepted Wilson's appointment as Third Assistant Secretary of State in 1914, becoming Assistant Secretary three years later.[43] Phillips, who had been informed only that morning of the severance of relations with Germany, described the turn of events to Tarnowski.

Tarnowski appeared much overcome by the news and immediately offered to urge his government not to associate itself with Germany. While Phillips agreed to send the message, he doubted whether Wilson would accept Tarnowski's credentials in view of the current crisis.[44] Apparently Phillips was unaware that, on February 1, Lansing had agreed with Wilson and House on the advisability of retaining the Austrian Ambassador with the hope of making "peace proposals through the Austrians."[45]

Lansing's ensuing conversation with Tarnowski was quite cordial. Deeply disturbed over the attitude of the German government, Tarnowski hoped that his government would not follow its example.[46] His hopes were not realized. He had scarcely departed when Lansing received a telegram announcing, albeit reluctantly, Vienna's decision to identify itself with Berlin on the submarine question. However, the Austrian note approved Wilson's speech of January 22 and threw the blame for the failure of the peace efforts on the Entente, which would be content with nothing less than Austrian dismemberment.[47] Tarnowski, visibly perplexed, presented two messages for transmission to Vienna. The State Department in the meantime withheld publication of the Austrian note aligning Vienna with the German submarine policy.

The desire of the Austrian government to maintain friendly relations with the United States was dramatically illustrated on February 4. Although it was a Sunday morning, Phillips decided that he must prepare instructions in the event that a decision was made to sever relations with Vienna. Zwiedinek called at the State Department and left a cablegram for his government urging once again that it not join Germany in its present course. Tarnowski also was doing "everything in his power to hold the situation as it was."[48] In Vienna on the same day, Czernin took the unusual step of calling personally at the American embassy to transmit a personal message to the American government explaining the motives behind Austria's decision to renew unrestricted submarine warfare. The responsibility for that decision, he emphasized, rested solely upon the Entente, which had declined to enter peace negotiations on Wilson's formula of no "victors and no vanquished." Austria-Hungary, however, would always be ready to commence peace negotiations on the basis of Wilson's formula if appropriate guarantees would be given.[49]

During the next few days, Austrian representatives in Washington continued their efforts to persuade their government to take a moderate stand. Lansing, however, was reluctant to send any further messages for Tarnowski until he knew the official attitude of the Austrian government.[50] Two days later, Lansing learned of Czernin's wish both to maintain diplomatic relations with the United States and to "negotiate honorable conditions of peace, a peace without victory." However, Czernin insisted that so long as the Entente would not give up its program of dismemberment, it was impossible to talk about peace. He also said that a technical modification of the submarine war was impossible, not only because it would necessitate an exchange of views with Germany, but, more importantly, because many submarines had already left their ports and could not be reached by radio. He concluded with the plea that Wilson continue to use his moral influence to persuade the Entente to accept his proposal for a peace without victory. If Wilson should succeed, "not only the terror of the submarine war, but the war in general would come to a sudden end and Mr. Wilson's name will shine with everlasting letters in the history of mankind."[51] On the next day, Czernin directed Tarnowski to do all in his power to prevent a breach. He added: "Am sending $100,000 for influencing the press."[52]

Actually, the Austrian government had accepted the policy of unrestricted submarine warfare under duress rather than as retaliation against the Entente's threat of dismemberment. As early as January 12, Czernin had protested vigorously against the U-boat decision, and these protests had been reiterated at a meeting on January 20 by Czernin, Tisza, and the Emperor. Their protests were in vain, for Germany had sent the note to Washington announcing the resumption of unrestricted submarine action on January 20, the day before the Vienna conference. Czernin, incensed not only by the German decision but also by such cavalier treatment of an ally, toyed with the notion of breaking with Berlin. Yet "with a heavy heart," he felt himself compelled to acquiesce in the German verdict. Charles, too, protested bitterly but ultimately gave in.[53]

During the next six weeks, American and Austrian diplomats in Washington and Vienna made a determined effort to prevent a severance of relations. The United States initiated dual negotiations: to dissuade the Austrian government from submarine warfare and to persuade it to negotiate for a separate peace. These latter efforts were carried on in Vienna and also in London through Ambassador Walter Hines Page. Phillips, conducting almost daily conversations in the State Department with either Tarnowski or Zwiedinek, tried to hammer out an acceptable Austrian submarine policy.[54] However, Wilson himself initiated the negotiations for a separate peace. Czernin's message, which Wilson had personally picked up at Lansing's office on February 7, was the "first really unequivocal response from Europe" to his appeal for a negotiated peace. With mounting hope and excitement, Wilson worked throughout that evening on a note that would break the deadlock. He typed the final copy on his own typewriter and carried it personally to Lansing on the following afternoon. At midnight on February 8, Lansing sent the message in a top-secret code to Page.[55]

Wilson directed Page to convey his views in strictest confidence and with the utmost sincerity to the leading members of the British government and to ascertain informally and unofficially their response. Wilson sought first of all to avoid breaking with Austria-Hungary, "in order to keep the channels of official intercourse" open for the pursuit of peace. He saw the threat of "radical dismemberment" stated in the Entente peace terms as the major obstacle to such a peace. If, therefore, he could persuade the Allies to renounce this threat and approve official American negotiations with Vienna, he believed that he could force the acceptance of peace in accordance with the terms laid down in his recent address to the Senate.[56]

When Page discussed Wilson's note with Lloyd George, the latter seemed evasive at first. He argued that Austria was an economic and military burden for Germany and that releasing her from the war would only strengthen Germany rather than embarrass her. Moreover, he believed that the "just demands" of the Rumanians, the Slavs, the Serbians, and the Italians "must be met by the principle of nationality." However, he had no objection to the Emperor's retaining Hungary and Bohemia, as Britain had "no policy of sheer dismemberment." Lloyd George added that if Wilson desired to receive specific proposals from Austria, he would be perfectly willing to receive them confidentially and respond to them when the time was propitious. In a dramatic conclusion, he urged Wilson to enter the war, "not so much for help with the war as for help with the peace." "If he sits in the conference that makes peace," Lloyd George added, "he will exert the greatest influence that any man has ever exerted in expressing the moral value of free government."[57]

Lloyd George's conversation seemed to indicate that although Britain felt bound by contractual obligations to her allies through the treaties of London and Bucharest, it was not equally bound by the broader promises made in the Entente note of January 10, which had included the liberation of the Czechs and Slovaks largely at the insistence of the French. British policy itself was ambivalent. It revolved upon the question of military expediency. Just as the Central Powers had decided upon unrestricted submarine warfare in order to break the military deadlock, the Entente had decided to attack Germany through her weakest link—Austria.[58] On the other hand, less than a month earlier the British War Cabinet had discussed certain tentative approaches recently made in Christiania, Norway, by alleged Austrian agents who sought a possible separate peace between Austria-Hungary and the Allies. General Sir Henry H. Wilson, chief of the Imperial General Staff, had declared that a separate peace with Austria would be a decided advantage from a military point of view. It would eliminate 47 Austro-Hungarian divisions then located on the Eastern Front, set free 149 Russian divisions to deal with 78 German divisions located on the Eastern Front, and also remove the submarine menace in the Adriatic. He believed that these advantages would more than counterbalance the possibility of Italy withdrawing from the war. The War Cabinet had then agreed that any Austrian approaches to the British should be probed to determine their reality.[59]

On February 20 and 21, Page reported that Lloyd George had modified his first views after discussing the subject with some of his associates, apparently in the War Office and the Admiralty. Page, earlier irritated by Lloyd George's inconsistency, reported that now the Prime Minister was ready to receive a formal offer of peace from Austria "to consider it on its merits." He also expressed "his willingness not to disrupt the Austro-Hungarian Empire by the loss of its older units of Hungary and Bohemia."[60]

Armed with this support, Wilson immediately instructed Penfield to assure Czernin confidentially and in absolute secrecy that the "Allied Governments have no desire or purpose to disrupt the Austro-Hungarian Empire by the separation of Hungary and Bohemia from Austria unless a continuance of the war causes a change of conditions." Moreover, Wilson might be able to obtain "a definite assurance of this" if the "Austrian Government, indicating a desire for an early peace," wished him to "act secretly to that end." No mention was made of a peace commission proposal as Wilson wanted first "to try out the temper of the Austrian Government."[61] In a series of four highly confidential meetings, all held at Penfield's residence, Czernin expressed keen interest in Wilson's proposal. However, he affirmed that Austria could only enter into negotiations for peace simultaneously with her allies, and that "she must receive the guaranty that the Monarchy would remain intact." Czernin agreed that peace had to come eventually through Wilson.[62] In the meantime, in a personal interview on March 6, Wilson made clear to Jusserand his belief that Austria-Hungary should not be dismembered and that its diverse races would have to be satisfied with autonomy.[63] Nevertheless, even after conversations with the Emperor, Czernin reported that a separate peace was out of the question. If the Allies were willing to discuss a general peace, Czernin agreed to send his representative to meet with an Entente representative on neutral territory "to discuss secretly and freely the basis and the conditions of negotiations for peace."[64] Wilson urged Czernin to reconsider his attitude while he might still "obtain for his country certain advantages which this Government feels *might* be obtained under existing conditions which may not continue long and may not come again."[65] However, neither Czernin nor the Emperor was moved "to debate any arrangement meaning a breaking away from Austria's allies."[66]

Lansing was not discouraged by Czernin's response. He believed that Penfield's reported rumors of Austria-Hungary's tiring of the overlordship of Berlin had a substantial foundation. Obviously, Czernin had to maintain an appearance of perfect loyalty to Austria's allies, not only to satisfy the Austrian sense of honor, but also to avoid possible danger from an enraged Germany should the matter be made public. Thus Lansing saw Czernin's willingness to engage in *secret* conferences for a general peace as very significant and worth encouraging.[67]

Meanwhile, Phillips and Lansing, in discussions with Tarnowski, sought to secure a modification of Austria's submarine policy so as to make continued peace negotiations possible. When Wilson had announced the severance of relations with Germany because of its violation of the *Sussex* pledge, he had not mentioned Austria-Hungary, although it had accepted the German U-boat decision. The State Department had received this information early on the morning of February 3, the very day that Wilson gave his speech.[68] Yet this information would not have influenced Wilson to announce a break with Austria-Hungary, since he had already decided to initiate a diplomatic effort to secure a separate peace.[69]

With this objective in mind, the State Department had agreed to hold back publication of the Austrian U-boat note until Tarnowski or the State Department received further information. During the next week, notes from Austria-Hungary appeared encouraging. They indicated not only that its submarine decision had been made largely at the urging of its powerful ally, but also that it was "ready to commence negotiations for peace" in accordance with Wilson's earlier proposal.[70] The State Department continued to transmit confidential messages from the Austrian government to the Austrian embassy in Washington in the hope that something would work out.[71]

Phillips personally had "very little hope." Nevertheless, in the next few days he was able to devise a possible way for Austria to modify her submarine policy. Tarnowski emphasized his government's desire to maintain friendly relations with the United States and promised to do everything in his power to make this possible. Tarnowski was anxious to begin conversations at once. Lansing and Wilson, eager to initiate negotiations for a separate peace with Austria-Hungary, approved the suggestions offered by Phillips as a basis for resolving the submarine issue. At this point Lansing informed Wilson that if the Entente governments could be persuaded to modify their peace terms to allay Austrian fears of dismemberment, he thought that Austrian dependence on Germany could be lessened. Lansing believed that any weakening of the German-Austrian alliance would be a decided step toward peace.[72]

In the meantime, the German government was pushing Austria to break off diplomatic relations with the United States. It urged that Tarnowski withhold his credentials until the situation between Germany and America was clear, that he protest against Wilson's effort to make the neutrals turn against Germany, and that he be recalled on the outbreak of war with Germany.[73] Czernin refused the first two items but accepted the last. While admitting that the Austrians were unable to prevent Germany from beginning their U-boat warfare, he believed that his government should use all possible means to maintain relations with the United States and thus enable it later to play the part of mediator. For Czernin, this period was absolutely crucial.[74]

On February 26, in a further effort to avoid war, Wilson went before Congress for extraordinary powers to maintain "armed neutrality." Even as he did so, news of the notorious Zimmermann note was creating a great stir in the State Department. This note proposed that Mexico and perhaps Japan enter an offensive alliance with the Central Powers should war occur between Germany and the United States. On February 27, the Austro-Hungarian response to the American proposal for a separate peace arrived. Though disheartened, Lansing was not totally discouraged by the response. Nevertheless he was virtually convinced that the Zimmermann note was the straw that had "broken the camel's back."[75]

As the newspapers exploded over the Zimmermann note, the Austrian submarine reply arrived on March 4. A twenty-seven-page discourse, it upheld the principle of promiscuous submarine warfare but reiterated that American trade would not be affected, because Austrian submarines were not operating in the Atlantic. Although Vienna, for some unknown reason, had given out the text of its reply publicly, Lansing felt that the United States should not follow its example.[76] At this crucial point in early March, Wilson was confined to his bed with a cold. As a result, the Austro-Hungarian decision was held in abeyance. In Vienna, both Penfield and Joseph C. Grew, Counselor of the embassy, continued to be optimistic. At this stage, a new difficulty arose between Vienna and Washington.[77]

Czernin began to press daily for news as to why Tarnowski had not been fully received. Since Charles had requested the information, Penfield foresaw difficulty if the matter was not settled. Penfield, without instruction, had continually assured Czernin that Wilson would receive Tarnowski. The situation was an especially delicate one, because Dumba had been dismissed and the Emperor himself had appointed Tarnowski. Although Phillips believed that it would probably be wise if Tarnowski were to retire,[78] Lansing, unwilling to give up, wrote Penfield a long explanation and expressed his hope of finding a way to eliminate "existing difficulties." He professed his willingness to receive any suggestions on the matter from Czernin.[79] Only the day before, Lansing and Wilson had discussed Czernin's response opposing separate peace talks but agreeing to *secret* general peace talks. Lansing had urged a follow-up. Clearly, this would be a most inappropriate time to dismiss Tarnowski.

Meanwhile, the newspapers were hailing enthusiastically the fall of the Russian Tsar and the formation of the new Russian Provisional Government. Wilson immediately authorized recognition of the new government.[80] It now looked as though Wilson's hope for a "league to enforce peace" was coming into being "quite naturally by the rapid extension of democratic governments." The Allied side appeared greatly strengthened, not only by the events in Russia, but also by the willingness of China to join the democratic powers in severing relations with Germany as a result of Wilson's plea to the neutral powers to do so.

The first Russian revolution, which dethroned Nicholas II, had a profound effect upon American willingness to fight on the Allied side and also upon the attitude of many Czechs who favored democracy. Wilson was much more willing to fight alongside a young Russian republic rather than one of the most absolute despotisms in Christendom. Similarly, many Czechs and sons of Czechs who had been born under the Tsar had seen no point in fighting for tsarism against kaiserism.[81]

On March 26, as the newspapers urged recognition of the new Russian Provisional Government and dismissal of the Austrians, Tarnowski once again called at Lansing's home and discussed his embarrassment and his government's position as a result of the long delay in his official reception by Wilson. Lansing immediately sought advice from Wilson, who was forced to agree reluctantly that he had no choice but to say that the "explicit acceptance and avowal" by Tarnowski's government of the policy that led to America's breach of diplomatic relations with Germany made it impossible to receive Tarnowski. Wilson instructed Lansing to convey this response regretfully and "in the most friendly spirit."[82]

Lansing received Tarnowski at his home in the evening of March 29 and informed him of Wilson's decision. At the same time, Lansing indicated that the American people felt little or no animosity against Austria, in contrast to their strong indignation against Germany. Moreover, despite Wilson's inability to receive an Ambassador at this critical time, he was sincerely concerned that Austria-Hungary should have diplomatic representation in Washington. Accordingly, Wilson had instructed Penfield to return to Washington for consultation so as to entrust both embassies to Chargés. Grew was to remain in Vienna. Tarnowski departed genuinely distressed and personally regretful over the embarrassment of the situation.[83]

On the evening of April 2, Wilson appeared before a joint special session of Congress to request a declaration of war against Germany. He described the submarine controversy with Germany as warfare against all mankind. Wilson asked that the United States formally accept the status of belligerent that had been thrust upon it. Germany's submarine warfare and violation of the freedom of the seas were declared as the casus belli. Wilson declared that the United States had no quarrel with the German people, but only with the autocratic government responsible for the present crisis. The world, he said, must be made safe for democracy against autocratic governments.[84]

In declaring the war to be a crusade for the safety of democracy, it would have been quite consistent for Wilson also to recommend a declaration of war against Germany's allies. However, Wilson did not do so. He fell back upon his original premise of making war only to defend American rights. The operations of German submarines had forced him to adhere to his commitments under the *Sussex* pledge. This was not true in the case of Austria-Hungary.[85] Wilson believed that because its unrestricted submarine warfare was the result of "Prussian influence," it was not necessary to sever "diplomatic relations with Vienna." He pointed out: "We enter this war only where we are clearly forced into it because there are no other means of defending our rights."[86] Obviously, Wilson still hoped and desired to separate Austria from Germany.[87]

On April 6, in the midst of Tarnowski's last-minute confidential efforts to initiate new peace negotiations, Congress voted to declare war on Germany. On April 9, Austria severed diplomatic relations with the United States. Orders were immediately given to seize all Austrian ships in the United States, and Zwiedinek and Tarnowski received their passports.[88]

Shortly thereafter, a British war mission headed by Balfour arrived in Washington to exchange views on the Allied and American war efforts. Wilson emphasized his intention to throw himself wholeheartedly into the conflict and to see it through to a finish. Yet Balfour interpreted Wilson's most important pronouncement to be his refusal to "bind himself by any treaty obligations such as those into which the other Allies had already entered with each other." Wilson's rationale was the unpopularity of such treaties in the United States. "Aware of the general tenor of the mutual engagements by which the European Allies" had "bound themselves," Wilson believed the United States "being themselves unfettered might exercise a powerful and valuable influence," in the event that Allied adherence to the letter of the treaties might make them inflexible over "some question of detail."[89]

After visiting with Wilson, Balfour lunched privately with Jusserand and expressed his general satisfaction with Wilson's support and intentions. However, he regarded "the fate of Austria" as one of the "most difficult points to settle" and one about which there was "most to fear from differences of opinion." Jusserand, who had already shared with the French Foreign Ministry Wilson's view of the question, believed that Balfour's view did not differ greatly from Wilson's. Balfour, too, thought it better to let Austria survive, "even though enfeebled by the quasi-independence of several of its provinces," rather than risk a dismemberment that might result in the ultimate absorption of its strongly pro-German parts by Germany.[90] Nevertheless, although not committed to Bohemian unity and independence, Balfour favored giving Bohemia a status within the Habsburg Empire equal to that of Hungary.[91] Later, after a long discussion over boundaries in Europe, Balfour and House agreed that Austria should be composed of three states—Bohemia, Hungary, and Austria proper with an independent Poland. They also thought well of negotiating with Austria for a separate peace. Two days later at dinner, Wilson, Balfour, and House went over much of the same ground and, according to House, arrived at exactly the same conclusions.[92]

Most Czechs and Slovaks in the United States greeted America's break with Germany with joy because it lifted the moral and legal restrictions that American neutrality had imposed on their activities during the first period of the war. Although the Bohemian National Alliance had pledged its neutrality in letter and in spirit in a manifesto to Wilson in 1916, it had indicated that, within the limits of neutrality, it would seek to present the merits of the Bohemian cause to the American people. Albert Mamatey, President of the Slovak League of America, presented a handsomely engraved testimonial of loyalty to Wilson, who received it with deep appreciation.[93] Similar testimonials were presented to Congress.[94] From every city with a considerable Bohemian population came a deluge of telegrams commending Wilson's vigorous stand and pledging the absolute loyalty of citizens of Bohemian birth. Officers of the Bohemian Alliance urged their young members to prove their patriotism by enlisting in the army. They emphasized that "now the cause of the United States and the cause of Bohemia are one and the same and that fighting for America is fighting for the liberation of Bohemia."[95] Enormous parades and mass meetings of Americanized Slovaks and Bohemians supported patriotic causes, notably the American Red Cross. Frequently, a Cabinet member or Wilson himself would be invited to speak or to send a few words of support.[96] Even more often, Czech and Slovak Americans held huge bazaars or festivals in cities and towns throughout the nation.[97] Through these means and the private support of philanthropists like Crane, "the whole Czecho-Slovak movement was originally financed by the subscriptions from America," which continued to be the main source of its funds.[98] One of the most important steps in publicizing the Czecho-Slovak cause was the establishment of the Slav Press Bureau in New York City. Determined to keep senators and congressmen fully informed, the bureau sent them copies of all appropriate publications.

By May 1917 these efforts had begun to show results.[99] Sabath, who had earlier supported a resolution favoring the Bohemians, and Senator William S. Kenyon, Republican of Iowa, agreed to introduce resolutions in Congress supporting the establishment of an independent "Bohemian-Slovak State."[100] Although the congressional resolution never came to a vote, it bolstered the morale of the Czecho-Slovaks, called the attention of Congress to the Czech cause, and stimulated comment from the press.

In presenting the case for an independent Bohemian-Slovak state, spokesmen emphasized the concept of nationality in an ethnic sense, a relatively new idea at that time. They rejected federalization as impracticable, if not wholly impossible, because the will to cooperate—a fundamental attribute for nationality—was unknown in Austria. Not only would federalization simply lead to the continued domination of the Bohemians, but the preservation of the Austro-Hungarian state, even in a mutilated condition, would simply provide a resurgent Germany once again with an opportunity to realize its pan-German plans for Middle Europe and "the consequent conquest of the world." Spokesmen also emphasized that the Czech question was one of restoration. The Habsburgs had been called to the Bohemian throne by the free will of the representatives of the Bohemian state, and they had taken solemn oaths and pledges to protect and safeguard the independence of that state. The violation of these pledges and the deprivation of Czech independence by force had not done away with these legal rights. The fact that the Czechs at one time had been a strong, powerful, and well-organized state was presented as sufficient proof of inherent political capacity. Furthermore, the Czechs had proved the viability of independence by their economic and cultural development. The Czech lands were described as the richest of the Austrian "provinces." This economic strength would be reinforced by the undeveloped resources of Slovakia, whose people formed a part of the same ethnic group as the Bohemians and desired to be joined with the Bohemians in one state. Thus, the case for Czecho-Slovak independence rested upon two major arguments: the right of any nation to independence once its viability was demonstrated, and the necessity of dissolving Austria in the interests of permanent peace.[101]

On June 23, 1917, the Slav Press diary recorded that "a particularly friendly" letter from John Sharp Williams, senior senator from Mississippi, had arrived for Pergler. Williams's letter was not a mere courtesy. He had long been interested in the Austro-Hungarian problem and had very quickly become sympathetic to the Czech cause. Scholar, planter, lawyer, and aristocrat, Williams had been trained at the Universities of Virginia, Heidelberg, and Dijon. An experienced legislator, he had served as United States Congressman from 1893 to 1909 and as

United States Senator since 1910. Moreover, he was on excellent terms with Wilson. Williams early became particularly interested in the question of self-determination. Along with Pergler, he, too, had addressed the meeting of the American Academy of Political and Social Science in April 1917. Here he had made it clear that, if he could dictate the terms of a durable peace immediately, he would "free Bohemia from the Habsburg rule." This meant, of course, the ultimate crushing of the House of Habsburg.[102]

Toward the end of April, Williams wrote Wilson that "the country is full of Slovaks and Slovenes and Bohemians . . . and Poles who are anxious to fight Austria and Germany both." He urged the recruitment of these various subjects into foreign legions, as France had done. He proposed raising an army of 250,000 or 300,000 men.[103] Wilson immediately took up the legality of creating such a corps with Secretary of War Newton D. Baker.[104] However, Baker believed that creating such foreign units at that time might have a bad effect by setting a precedent for other volunteers. He was concerned that the public might get the idea that the government was trying to use "the foreigners instead of our own people." He advised waiting until the next Congress, when trained officers would be available to carry out Williams's suggestions. While Williams agreed with Baker's reasoning, and particularly with his concern about the timing of such an organization, he urged that "every effort ought to be made to keep from chilling the initiative and enthusiasm of these Slovak, Italian and Bohemian and other groups."[105]

Williams's scheme for the creation of a Bohemian legion would surely have met with the approval of the Czecho-Slovak National Council in Paris. Since the beginning of 1917, Beneš had been directing the major effort of the National Council in organizing an army in France and Italy. The Russian Revolution and America's entry into the war had provided the council with an even greater incentive to carry out these plans, as well as to create new opportunities to recruit additional legions in the United States and in Russia. Štefánik had gone to Russia in the hope of making final plans for the creation of a Czecho-Slovak army in Russia to be transferred as soon as possible to the Western Front. While in Russia in late 1916, he had evolved a plan of going to the United States to assist in recruiting a volunteer national army of 20,000 men from the 1,500,000 Czechs and Slovaks living there. It was precisely at this time that the Poles with French support were also seeking to form a legion from among their American emigrés.[106] The Polish effort had the powerful backing of House and the sympathetic support of Lansing and Phillips.[107]

Workers for Czecho-Slovak independence; *left to right:* A. Hrdlička, F. Bielek,
A. Mamatey, C. Pergler, General Štefánik, E. V. Voska, L. J. Fisher, I. Daxner,
F. Písecký (*Bohemian Review*)

Štefánik desired not only to recruit volunteers for the autonomous
Czech army in France but also to win the sympathy of the United States
government for the Czecho-Slovak cause. With the help of Beneš, he
was able to secure the support of the French government for the
project. The French government sought to expedite the enterprise by
sending a special political mission to the United States headed by Henri
Franklin-Bouillon, Vice President of the French Chamber of Deputies,
to secure American consent to the recruitment of volunteers from the
emigrants in America for the Polish and Czecho-Slovak armies in
France. Franklin-Bouillon sailed for America on August 10.[108]

By mid-June, the belief in Austrian dependence upon Germany was
widespread and well publicized in the United States.[109] Wilson himself
expressed this judgment publicly in his Flag Day speech of June 14
when he declared that the military masters of Germany were also "the
masters of Austria-Hungary."[110] Wilson struck a deeply sympathetic
chord among the Czech peoples when he elaborated on the pan-
German program of "binding together racial and political units which

could be kept together only by force," among them "the proud states of Bohemia and Hungary."[111] The Bohemians were so delighted with Wilson's address that they immediately sought House's help to send a delegation to express their appreciation to Wilson personally.[112]

Wilson's address was important for still another reason. The Czechs believed that for the first time Wilson had begun to look upon the Austro-Hungarian problem in the light of the interpretation presented by the French publicist, André Chéradame. In *Pan-Germany, The Disease and Cure* and *The Pan-German Plot Unmasked*, Chéradame had held that the Bohemian problem was preeminent because none of the subject nationalities could be really freed unless Bohemia was liberated. He also favored the creation of an independent state out of the non-Germanic elements of Austria-Hungary, which would be like "a confederacy of the United States of Central Europe."[113] Pergler saw evidence of Wilson's virtual adoption of Chéradame's view even more clearly in his speech to the American Federation of Labor Convention at Buffalo on November 12. There Wilson traced historically Germany's efforts to dominate Middle Europe and emphasized that "Germany has absolute control of Austria-Hungary."[114] Nevertheless, despite this view, Wilson refused even in the face of bitter criticism to declare war on Austria-Hungary.[115] He refused to be drawn into a greater conflict as long as there was the possibility of separating Austria from Germany.

5

Decision for War with
Austria-Hungary

The severance of diplomatic relations between the United States and
Austria-Hungary did not affect their friendly relationship nor their
continued efforts to negotiate a peace. However, the American diplomats differed about the likelihood of successful peace efforts.[1] While
Penfield regarded Austria as a mere vassal of Germany, Grew
remained optimistic about the possibilities of negotiations. He continued to believe that the Austrian people and government were
deeply desirous of peace.[2] Allen W. Dulles, who had just been transferred from Vienna to Bern, had written both Lansing, his "Uncle
Bert," and John W. Foster, former Secretary of State and his grand-
father, that there was a "growing party in Austria" that would "welcome a severance from Germany."[3] Abram I. Elkus, American Ambassador in Turkey, agreed and reported "an ardent desire for peace"
among Austrians.[4]

Washington's desire to maintain friendly relations with Vienna was
clearly dramatized at Lansing's last interview with Tarnowski. Lansing
tried to convince him that Americans had little or no animosity toward
Austria and that nothing would alter this public feeling except the
active connivance of Austrians in subversion, sabotage, or treason.
Supremely self-confident of the inevitable victory of the Allies over the
Central Powers, Lansing assured Tarnowski that, when the entire
"miserable business" was over, "unless something happens to change
American sentiment Austria will not have a merciless enemy in America." Tarnowski immediately responded passionately: "But the Allies
desire to partition the Austrian Empire according to their own terms.
How can we make peace? How can we?"[5] Lansing replied, "I do not
believe that it will come to actual partition. . . . Austria will never be
absorbed unless it is by one power. . . . Germany alone threatens
Austrian independence." As the men parted each professed the hope
that when the war ended, both nations would be "very good friends."[6]

Austrian statesmen were clearly reluctant to see Tarnowski leave the United States. Two days after their last interview, Lansing received a personal note from Tarnowski, then in New York, offering to remain in the United States "alone and as a private man" in order to continue unofficial conversations. Vienna had received the report of his last conversations with Lansing with "much interest" and had expressed "full appreciation" for Lansing's "friendly assurances."[7] Tarnowski also telephoned Phillips with a similar personal message from Vienna. Both Phillips and Lansing strongly opposed the idea. Nevertheless, Tarnowski reiterated that in the future he would gladly return to the United States at a moment's notice.[8] In Austria, Czernin was "very defeatist." Having no faith in the German submarine campaign and convinced that Austria would soon collapse, he advocated peace moves "immediately even at the expense of great sacrifices."[9] Both Czernin and Charles had been badly shaken by the Entente's statement of war aims the previous January. As they witnessed the Russian Revolution in March, the activities of the various ethnic groups within the Empire, and the mounting dissatisfaction with the war among all groups, they naturally feared a similar catastrophe at home.

The Emperor had already attempted to preserve his regime by initiating a peace move through his brother-in-law, Prince Sixtus de Bourbon-Parma, who had taken several messages to President Poincaré of France. This bizarre affair, which later involved Lloyd George and Sonnino, was soon to demonstrate the pitfalls of personal diplomacy.[10] When Lloyd George was informed secretly of the Emperor's overture, he enthusiastically agreed to plan an early meeting with the Italian Premier and Foreign Minister. By April 17, Lloyd George had made the necessary arrangements to travel with the French Prime Minister to the small town of St. Jean de Maurienne in the Swiss Alps for "a conference about possible peace with Austria."[11]

At this point Sonnino, an old foe of Austria, flatly declined to negotiate with Austria-Hungary. He regarded the Emperor's letter as simply another trick to separate the Allies. Since Sonnino had been mainly responsible for bringing Italy into the war on the side of the Allies, Lloyd George and Clemenceau attached great importance to his views.[12] Sonnino assured his Allied colleagues that a peace that did not bring Italy the Trentino, Trieste, Dalmatia, and all of the islands in the Adriatic would result in a revolution in Italy. Facing such inflexibility, the Allied leaders concluded that they could do nothing more with the Emperor's letter.[13] Although Lloyd George admitted that the British would willingly have "shaken hands" with Austria "if she would leave Germany," Italy's "bitter feelings" made this impossible.[14]

Later, the British discovered that a week before the Allied meeting, Italian General Headquarters had sent an agent to offer the German and Austrian Ministers in Switzerland a peace with Italy on the sole condition of the cession of the Trentino—with no demand made for Dalmatia, Trieste, or even Gorizia. Apparently Sonnino knew nothing about the offer. General Luigi Cadorna, then chief of the Italian General Staff, had initiated this attempt to make a secret peace with Austria because of his fear that the war-weary Italians were on the brink of revolution. His apprehensions were justified just a few months later by the Italian collapse at Caporetto. But at St. Jean de Maurienne neither the British nor the French knew that the highest military leaders in Italy had doubts about the morale of their troops.

By early May, the British War Cabinet had become even more deeply convinced of the need for a separate peace with Austria. It feared Russia's possible defection from the war and the signing of a separate peace. This would give the Central Powers a tremendous stock of wheat, oil, and other available materials and permit the release of large German forces for service on the Southern and Western Fronts.[15] As the French military situation became more desperate and the possibilities of a Russian defection more real, Lloyd George became even more insistent on exploring Austrian peace possibilities. The British radicals were then condemning the Allies for not following up enthusiastically the Austrian peace offer, which they presumed had been made in April 1917.[16] Moreover, Lloyd George was becoming increasingly irritated with the intransigence of the Italians.[17]

Before Charles learned of the disappointing results of the Allied meeting at St. Jean de Maurienne, Czernin had attempted to warn the German Kaiser of Austria's economic and military exhaustion and of the folly of exaggerating the potency of the submarine weapon. Convinced that "another winter campaign would be absolutely out of the question," he advocated an end to the war at all costs by the late summer or autumn in order to avert revolution and the resulting collapse of the Empire.[18] Both Charles and Czernin were greatly disturbed when this information fell into the hands of the Entente, apparently through the efforts of the secret Czech Maffia.[19] The German response to the Austrian plea was glowingly optimistic. Pointing to the success of German arms in the West and the internal difficulties of Russia in the East, German leaders exuded confidence in the success of the unrestricted U-boat campaign. In these favorable circumstances, there could be no consideration of peace.[20]

Wilson's desire to continue to seek a separate peace with Austria-

Hungary was in part responsible for his decision not to participate in the first inter-Allied military war conferences held in London, Paris, and Rome after America's entrance into the war. Prior to his departure from the United States, Balfour had sent Wilson texts of some of the secret treaties between Great Britain and her Allies, as well as his statements to the Imperial War Council containing the main terms.[21] Although the State Department did not receive copies of these secret treaties, Balfour did send Lansing a document, known later as the Balfour Memorandum, which outlined Britain's commitments to her allies in considerable detail.[22] While certainly not favorably impressed with Allied war aims, Wilson appeared not to be unduly disturbed by them.[23] Apparently he believed that at the conclusion of the war, he would be able to force the Allies to his way of thinking because of their financial dependence upon the United States.[24] He wanted to "be able to enter the peace conference free from the ambitions of the various allies." To this end, he preferred not to join in war councils that might well deal with military strategy involving Austria-Hungary, Bulgaria, and Turkey, with whom the United States was not at war.[25]

As the summer of 1917 drew to an end, a strong current for peace existed not only in Austria-Hungary but in Germany as well.[26] At this point, Pope Benedict XV offered himself as "the disinterested servant of the Prince of Peace."[27] The Pope's peace proposal, announced to the world on August 15, provoked considerable interest. Wishing to halt these "useless massacres," he called for the restoration of Belgium and evacuation of French territory in exchange for the restitution of German colonies. He made no reference to the principle of self-determination. The proposed settlement clearly favored the Dual Monarchy, since it called for a status quo ante bellum peace.[28] The Vienna Cabinet welcomed the papal initiative more cordially than did any other belligerent government.[29] It was not surprising then that both Beneš and Masaryk vehemently denounced the Pope as Czernin's agent.[30] Wilson's immediate reaction was to make no reply at all to the Pope's offer, since he believed that the Vatican favored the Central Powers, yet he sympathized with the "humane purpose of the Pope" in his desire to end the war on "terms honorable to all concerned."[31]

Wilson's advisers differed sharply on the appropriate American response to the Pope's proposals. On grounds of policy, House wished to be conciliatory. Told by a trustworthy source, in "the deepest confidence," that the Pope might be able to get Austria to consent to a separate peace, he intended to "watch this lead and try to follow it closely."[32] Lansing advocated a firm rejection of the Pope's appeal, which he believed emanated from Austria-Hungary and was probably sanctioned by the German government. He believed that the Pope was probably acting unwittingly "out of compassion for Austria-Hungary."[33]

Except for House, Lansing and the British and French governments had counseled Wilson either to ignore the Pope's appeal or to respond in a very informal fashion.[34] The latter was Wilson's initial inclination. He informed Balfour privately that if he were to make a response, it would be to sympathize with the Pope's desire to end the war, but that he would also make it clear that the terms suggested constituted no real settlement and would leave affairs in Europe in the same condition that had originally led to the war. Wilson believed that no peace could be assured that rested upon the promises of the "morally bankrupt" autocratic German regime. Moreover, Lincoln Steffens, the former muckraking journalist, had recently arrived with a message for Wilson from the Russian Premier, Alexandr Feodorovich Kerenskii, which stressed the importance of the "secret treaties" and the necessity for revision of Allied war aims. Without such revisions, Kerenskii believed that the Russians would be unable to continue the fight.[35]

Wilson, in answering the Pope's note, found it difficult to present a full statement of American war aims for fear that "it might provoke dissenting voices from France or Italy," even though their territorial claims did not "interest" the United States.[36] His response began with an eloquent expression of appreciation for the humane motives that had inspired the Pontiff's note. But Wilson made it clear that a return to the status quo ante bellum could in no way provide the basis for a lasting peace. He declared that "peace should rest upon the rights of peoples, not the rights of governments—the rights of peoples great or small, weak or powerful—their equal right to freedom and security and self-government and to a participation upon fair terms in the economic opportunities of the world." "Punitive damages, the dismemberment of empires, the establishment of selfish and exclusive economic leagues," Wilson deemed "inexpedient and in the end worse than futile, no proper basis for a peace of any kind, least of all for an enduring peace."[37]

Wilson's response, published on August 29, evoked general commendation and praise. Describing its "spontaneous and enthusiastic reception" by the American people, House called it "the most remarkable document ever written." Phillips labeled it "a magnificent document." John R. Mott, close friend and admirer of Wilson and general secretary of the YMCA, agreed. Both Lord Grey[38] and Lord Robert

Cecil conveyed their deep satisfaction and the general approval of the British press. The British attached "great importance" to the endorsement of "President Wilson's attitude . . . as far as possible by all the Allies unitedly."[39] Senator Williams commended the note as "one of the best state papers ever offered to the world."[40] For many Czechs and Slovaks in America, Wilson's response confirmed opinions and policies they had previously both criticized and hailed. They were delighted to hear Wilson say once again that the intolerable wrongs done by the German government ought not to be repaired "at the expense of the sovereignty of any people." But they were infuriated at his statement opposing the dismemberment of empires.[41] Nevertheless, Wilson's response had tactfully and courteously dealt the coup de grace to the papal peace initiative.

At this same time, British troops were locked in fierce combat with the Germans on the Western Front, where the great British offensive of 1917 was just getting under way. By late August, despite murderous British losses, the German defenses showed no signs of cracking. Meanwhile Russia was hanging by a slender thread; mutinies made the French army virtually unfit for any serious offensive; unrest with the war continued to mount in Italy; and the United States had not yet been able to place a significant number of men in Europe. As the British War Cabinet considered the threat of Russia's withdrawal from the war and received intelligence that the Austrians were clamoring for peace, they argued the pros and cons of reconsidering or revising their war aims in order "to reduce the number of our adversaries."[42]

Discouraged by British failures on the Western Front, Lloyd George longed to attack the enemy in more vulnerable areas—Austria or Turkey—where an Allied victory might force the weakening Austro-Hungarians into serious discussions of a separate peace. In an effort to secure American backing for this eastern strategy, Lloyd George in early September entrusted Lord Reading, already scheduled to go to Washington as a special envoy, with the responsibility of explaining the idea to Wilson.[43] He dispatched Wiseman to convince House. Lloyd George hoped that this strategy would result in Wilson's acceptance of an invitation to attend an Allied military conference and lend American support, if not outright sponsorship, to the plan for attacking Austria or Turkey. That the United States was at war with neither of the latter powers seemed not to disturb Lloyd George unduly.[44]

Wilson appeared noncommittal about both the scheme to attack Austria and participation in the Allied military council. When Reading officially presented Lloyd George's proposals on September 20, Wilson's response was courteous but reserved. However, he did order the War Department to evaluate Lloyd George's eastern strategy. It was not until three weeks later that he made his decision.[45] Although the War Department finally vetoed Lloyd George's proposal, Wilson decided to send House to London if the Allied conference scheduled for October 15 could be postponed to November.[46] House was far more interested in planning the pursuit of peace than in participating in decisions for waging the war. However, the British were ambivalent. While they considered a visit from House "naturally very useful," since he was one of their "best and strongest friends," they preferred that he remain close to Wilson, as they were coming to rely on his "well-known pro-British sympathies" in the presentation of their views to Wilson.[47] Apparently, House showed Wiseman "everything he got" and discussed "practically everything" with him, even internal American affairs.[48]

Wilson realized that if he wished to formulate American war aims precisely and educate his associates to his position, he had to consider their possible objections to America's war objectives. These concerns led him to establish "The Inquiry." Organized in New York in September 1917 under House's nominal leadership, this semiofficial committee was to gather full information about the objectives his associates would be likely to insist upon as part of the final arrangement for peace. Wilson wished The Inquiry to "formulate our own position whether for or against them . . . in brief, prepare our case with the full knowledge of the position of all the litigants."[49] The bulk of the work of The Inquiry was to deal with *Mittel Europa*—all those Central European and Near Eastern areas stretching from the North Sea and the Baltic to the Persian Gulf and the Indian Ocean.[50]

House was enthusiastic about his new job. He appointed Sidney E. Mezes, his brother-in-law and President of the College of the City of New York, as director. He selected Walter Lippmann from the staff of the *New Republic*, then currently on special assignment to Baker in the War Department, as secretary. House justified his choices to Wilson on the grounds that "the small group around me must be in thorough sympathy with your purposes."[51]

As a result of discussions with Sidney E. Mezes and David Hunter Miller of The Inquiry, Lansing began to consider the policy of weaning Austria away from Germany through separate peace negotiations.[52] He drew upon an earlier memorandum prepared in May by Albert H. Putney, chief of the State Department's Near Eastern Division. Putney, former Dean of the Illinois College of Law, author, and intimate of various Slavic spokesmen in Washington, had been the first high State Department official to become seriously involved with the problem of the Slavs in Eastern Europe. Stimulated to explore the possibility of exploiting nationalist unrest in Austria as a result of conversations with Balfour and Sir Eric Drummond, Balfour's private secretary, during their visit to the United States, Lansing had instructed Putney to submit a memorandum on "nationalistic aspirations in the Near East."

Putney's memorandum and follow-up report paid particular attention to the Czechs, among whom he included the Bohemians, the Moravians, and the Slovaks. He reported that "the members of this race, both at home and in this country, are practically unanimous in their demand for an independent Bohemia" and that "no autonomous quasi-sovereign Bohemia would be acceptable to the majority" of them. He assured Lansing that there was "no nationalistic aspiration more entitled to the sympathy, and . . . the support of the American people, than that of the Bohemian people."[53] Putney recommended the creation not only of independent Yugoslav and Polish states, but also the "complete independence" of Bohemia. He stressed that independence would be a "death blow" to Germany's "dream of Drang nach Osten."[54]

The latter argument was the one that appealed most strongly to Lansing. He was now clearly beginning to see the principle of nationality as the solution to the perplexing problems of East Central Europe. Yet, he did not submit the Putney report to Wilson, for he was keenly aware that Wilson's views were quite different.

Putney's memoranda appeared to be clearly on Lansing's mind in late October when he was beginning to question the possibility of a stable peace without "rendering the German military power impotent for the future." As he reconsidered his conversations with Mezes and Miller on October 23, Lansing found that he was losing the little faith he had concerning the possibility of discrediting Prussianism with the German people. Instead, he favored depriving the German Empire completely of the means to wage successful war. To check the extension of German power, Lansing proposed serious consideration of "the establishment along the Danube and the Adriatic and also along the eastern boundaries of the German Empire of strong, populous and independent states, even though this would deprive Russia and Austria of large areas of territory." Up to this point, Lansing had clung to the hope of peace through possible negotiations with Austria. Now he thought that the "fear of German revenge" would "keep the Dual Monarchy intact faithful to an alliance which makes it a vassal of her powerful neighbor."[55]

Lansing's memorandum marked a turning point in his thinking. Although willing to continue efforts for peace negotiations with the Austrians, he regarded the possibility as almost hopeless. Yet his consideration of the creation of independent states in Eastern Europe was motivated primarily by his growing conviction that such a policy would best limit Germany's ambitions in Eastern Europe and thereby provide the basis for a durable peace.[56] In contrast to Lansing's thinking, the earliest tentative Inquiry documents did not mention independence for the minorities within Austria-Hungary, but rather discussed a reorganized empire in which the Czechs and others would have "the political power to which their numbers entitled them."[57]

As The Inquiry struggled to establish a repository of source material on the problems relating to Austria-Hungary, Štefánik, still in the United States, continued his efforts to win official support to recruit for a Czecho-Slovak legion. When the Fisher-Mamatey interview with Lansing in early June failed to produce an invitation for Štefánik to negotiate arrangements for such recruiting, he determined to pursue the effort as a French officer, and, with Jusserand's aid, he met with Acting Secretary of State Frank L. Polk while Lansing was on leave. In a second interview on July 28, Polk granted him permission to recruit Czech and Slovak residents in the United States not subject to the draft, so long as he did it in a "discreet manner." Secretary Baker approved the project, as long as the French would bear the financial burden. Subordinates in the War Department dropped their objections at the end of September, when they were forced into action by the Poles, backed by House, who sought approval of a similar project.[58] Štefánik's efforts were no doubt also helped by the news that the French government had granted the Czecho-Slovak National Council official permission to constitute a Czecho-Slovak army of liberation.[59] Štefánik's instructions for all persons involved in the recruitment program were detailed and carefully organized. He had admonished his aides about the seriousness of the program: "We are dealing with the formation of a real army, not with an amateurish play."[60] His efforts ultimately led to the recruitment of the first Czecho-Slovak contingent of approximately 2,000 men. When he returned to France in November 1917, he led the first eighty Czecho-Slovak volunteers from America.[61]

During his stay, Štefánik also worked on American public opinion. He established the American branch of the Czecho-Slovak National Council in Washington and appointed Charles Pergler as director. The Bohemian National Alliance and the Slovak League recognized the council as their common executive agency.[62] Štefánik also secured their cooperation in the organization of a public mass meeting at Carnegie Hall in New York, where Franklin-Bouillon urged Czechs and Slovaks who could not join the United States forces to go to France and join the new Czecho-Slovak army being formed there. He then "electrified" his audience with the declaration that the Allies intended the formation of a separate Czecho-Slovak state at the end of the war.[63]

Before Štefánik left for France, Roland Thomas interviewed him for a long feature article in the New York *World*—one of the first serious discussions of the Czecho-Slovak problem in the American press. Štefánik emphasized that the only way to insure that the present war would be the last one was "to establish the right of men of every nationality, great or small in numbers, to choose their rulers and their form of government," as Wilson had said. Štefánik's own anti-German scheme envisaged nationalized states in Central Europe composed of the non-Teutonic parts of the continent, including an independent Czecho-Slovakia.[64]

Mezes found the interview "delightful reading as an antidote to Central Europe" but thought it leaned "appreciably backwards." He was then hardly ready to consider the dissolution of the Habsburg monarchy as the answer to the problems of Eastern Europe.[65] Such a position explains why Štefánik returned to France disillusioned with both American democracy and Wilson. He had expected to receive tremendous support for his efforts to liberate Bohemia but instead found the Czech cause almost unknown. Moreover, it was impossible for him to understand why the United States could not become involved in Czech matters while still at peace with Austria-Hungary. If the United States was fighting to make the world safe for democracy, why was it not yet at war with Austria-Hungary?[66]

As winter approached, the Allied cause was overwhelmed by a double disaster: the Austrian-German victory over the Italians at Caporetto and the Bolshevik takeover in Russia. Italy seemed in imminent danger of complete collapse.[67] Rumania's fate was inextricably tied to that of Russia, whose expected withdrawal from the war would leave Rumania completely isolated. A few days after the Allies learned of the full magnitude of the Italian disaster, news arrived from Petrograd that Lenin and the Bolsheviks had overthrown the Provisional Government and seized control on November 8. The Bolshevik program demanded an immediate, general, and democratic peace with the Central Powers. By the end of November, military operations on the Russian front had ceased. Preliminary peace negotiations between Russia and Germany were scheduled to begin on December 2.[68] These events set the capstone on the fears of the Allied leaders, who had watched with increasing panic the collapse of Russia's military power.[69] The Italian situation now made it more necessary than ever to retain Russia as an effective ally. Desperate to avert ultimate tragedy, the Allies had considered various schemes to raise the morale of the Russian army through the creation of a Polish legion or the dispatch of an American or Japanese contingent. Reading had discussed each of these possibilities with Wilson.[70] The hope of saving the Russian situation also led the British to put pressure on Wilson to undertake American supervision and reorganization of the Russian railways and to grant financial aid to "the Polish Cossacks and others who were willing to fight Germany."[71] The British were painfully aware that a separate peace between Russia and Germany would free Germany to transfer at least forty divisions from the Eastern to the Western Front.

The French, desperate for manpower in the West, began to negotiate with the Czecho-Slovak National Council in the spring of 1917 to expand the *družina*, the Czecho-Slovak force in Russia. The National Council had drawn up the main principles of the new military organization in Russia with the French government. The agreement of June 1917 between Albert Thomas and Masaryk stipulated that the soldiers of this new Czech army would take an oath of allegiance to the Czecho-Slovak nation. Recruiting was to be carried out only in the name of the National Council, and the French authorities were to act merely as executive bodies. Only the National Council, in agreement with the French government, would appoint and promote officers, and Czecho-Slovaks were to have the preference. The language of command was to be Czech, although all important documents were to be bilingual. The commander of the army was to be a French general, appointed after agreement with the National Council. In financial matters, Czech troops would receive the same pay as the French, and all expenditures were to be recorded in special accounts to be settled after the war.[72]

The Thomas-Masaryk agreement gave the National Council a much stronger tactical position. Beneš negotiated additional arrangements for the organization and recognition of an autonomous Czecho-Slovak army in Russia under the general direction of the French Supreme Command on August 4, and these were finally signed officially, although kept provisionally secret, on December 6, 1917, by President Poincaré, Premier Clemenceau, and Foreign Minister Stéphen Pichon. The army was to be evacuated to France as rapidly as possible. By recognizing the Czechs' right to form their own army, the French, in effect, gave de facto recognition to Czecho-Slovakia as a sovereign and independent nation and granted political direction of the army to the Czecho-Slovak National Council—a right usually granted only to an independent state. The French agreement had far-reaching political importance. It ended France's vacillation about Austro-Hungarian affairs and proved that France had ceased to rely on the possibility of a separate peace with the Habsburg Empire; to the Czechs, it demonstrated that France had decided definitely to support "to the end the struggle of the Austro-Hungarian peoples for freedom and independence."[73]

While Beneš in Paris and Masaryk in Russia were making arrangements concerning the Czecho-Slovak army in Russia, the Czech and Slovak prisoners in Italy were also active. In September, Sonnino, impressed by the French recognition of the Czecho-Slovak army and the implication contained in the Thomas-Masaryk agreement, recognized the right of the council to represent the Czechs and Slovaks in Italy. He agreed to the formation of labor battalions of Czecho-Slovak prisoners, but initially he rejected Beneš's request for the formation of military units under the council's control. However, the disaster at Caporetto in late October shook Italian political leadership and eventually resulted in Štefánik's concluding a treaty with Premier Vittorio Orlando and General Vittorio Zupelli, Minister of War. The treaty, signed on April 21, 1918, permitted the formation of an independent Czecho-Slovak army in Italy controlled by the National Council in Paris but commanded by General Andrea Graziani, with Italian, Czech, and Slovak officers. This treaty with the Italians was the first one that clearly recognized the National Council as a sovereign political body and a de facto government. It was a particular triumph because of the earlier prejudice of Italians against the Czecho-Slovaks. The number of Czecho-Slovak troops in Italy soon reached 22,000.[74]

From the Allied standpoint, nothing could be strategically more successful than a serious blow at the morale of the Central Powers, particularly in their most vulnerable spot—the manpower of Austria-Hungary. The prospect of a Czecho-Slovak unit of respectable size fighting on the French and Italian fronts alongside the troops of the Entente constituted not only a grave danger for the Central Powers but also a great propaganda coup for the Allies. The French had now begun to count upon a substantial number of Czech troops from Russia, America, and Italy, especially after the disaster at Caporetto and the imminent Russian withdrawal from the war. This was the gravest crisis faced by the Allies since 1914, and it ultimately convinced Wilson that the United States had to send a representative to the new Supreme War

Council, established at the inter-Allied conference at Rapallo, Italy, on November 7, 1917, and to send House to Paris.[75]

Formed on October 30, 1917, the new Italian government headed by Orlando immediately appealed to the Allies for help, particularly an American declaration of war against Austria-Hungary.[76] Foreign Minister Sonnino had observed privately and unofficially to Ambassador Thomas Nelson Page that, "if America declared war on Austria, it would have great effect morally."[77] The French government agreed. But Ambassador William G. Sharp in Paris opposed the measure until there was concrete proof that Austrian troops were actually being employed on the Western Front. Having recently discussed Austrian proposals for peace with George D. Herron, an expatriate American publicist in Switzerland, Sharp was reluctant to advocate a course that "might place beyond our reach an influence which events may make of great service to us."[78]

Increasingly alarmed by the depressing messages pouring into the State Department after Caporetto, Wilson finally authorized Lansing to cable a message of sympathy to the Italian people on November 13. He also cabled his full approval to the establishment of the Supreme War Council and appointed General Tasker H. Bliss as the American representative.[79] Shortly thereafter, Wilson also pledged the fullest possible support to the King of Rumania.[80]

In this crucial period, Clemenceau, *le tigre de France*, came to power as both Premier and Minister of War, "determined to eradicate all forms of defeatism in France." On November 29, he met with Lloyd George, Sonnino, and House to discuss the latest Austrian peace proposals. Rumors of such proposals had been drifting into the State Department since the beginning of the month.[81] The first major Austrian victory since 1915 had not succeeded in raising the spirit of the Austrians, who appeared as "anxious as ever for peace."[82] They had immediately initiated another round of secret peace proposals throughout Europe, even assuring the British government that, despite their recent victory, they would be willing to guarantee the territorial integrity of Italy as it existed before the war.[83]

Prior to the inter-Allied meeting, Lloyd George had told House of the various advances that Austria had made to the British. House "cheerfully agreed" to support Britain in insisting that Austria's latest offer be probed. Apparently Sonnino and Clemenceau also agreed.[84] Thereupon the Foreign Office instructed its representatives in Switzerland to ascertain what terms Austria would offer for a separate peace. Lloyd George was clearly enthusiastic. His interest in peace negotiations with Austria had grown in direct proportion to his increasing awareness of the probability of Russian withdrawal from the war.[85]

Lloyd George selected General Jan C. Smuts of South Africa to conduct the peace explorations. Smuts immediately departed for Switzerland to confer with Count Albert Mensdorff of Vienna, a former Austrian Ambassador to Britain. The meetings, attended also by Philip Kerr, Lloyd George's private secretary, took place on December 18 and 19, 1917.[86] Negotiations continued into the following spring but revealed little possibility of a successful outcome. Nevertheless, when Smuts returned to London, he told Lloyd George that Austria was "now in a mood to talk, apparently behind the back of her Ally." Both Lloyd George and Smuts were clearly excited by the results of the conversations and now thought that a separate peace with Austria was possible.[87]

While the inter-Allied conference was meeting in Paris, Charles realized that he should have been negotiating with Wilson rather than the Entente. To this end, he discussed with a former intermediary how Austria might break away from Germany. The Emperor stated "that he stood ready to reorganize his government in such a way as to approach as near as feasible the principles governing the federation of Switzerland," and that, among other things, he would give Bohemia home rule. He viewed this action as a possible forerunner of a united states of Europe.[88]

By the time that Sharp conveyed this new information to Washington, Wilson had already decided on war with Austria-Hungary.[89] A variety of factors had contributed to that decision, including the Bolshevik revolution and the Italian disaster at Caporetto. Actually, once the United States joined the Supreme War Council, its position had become increasingly more embarrassing. It was cooperating in the efforts of a group jointly devising war plans against the combined armies of Germany and Austria-Hungary, thereby aiding in the prosecution of the war against a country with which the United States was at peace.[90]

Presenting a "convincing case" to justify a declaration of war against Austria-Hungary was not easy.[91] The Austrian government had committed no aggressive acts of war against the United States since the sinking of the *Ancona* in November 1915. It had specifically refrained from submarine operations in the Atlantic and the Mediterranean where American ships were traveling. Sabotage and espionage activities had ceased with the ousting of Dumba in September 1915.

Wilson himself had refrained from asking for a declaration of war on Germany's allies in his war address on April 2, because they had committed no acts of war against the United States. Lester H. Woolsey, Solicitor-General of the Department of State, was forced to "burn the midnight oil" in the effort to prepare an effective case.[92] Lansing believed that Wilson had actually decided on war because of his failure to separate Austria from Germany.[93] While this was partially true, Wilson also believed that war against Austria was necessary to bring hostilities to a speedier conclusion. For over a year, he had sought a separate peace and had been rebuffed, while Germany had won victory after victory at the expense of his associates. Now he was seeking not so much a declaration of war as a declaration of principle. Germany represented everything that he had sworn to eradicate, and Austria was its official ally. Wilson was slowly arriving at the conviction that the only way to end the war was to defeat Germany.[94]

On December 4 Wilson appeared before Congress to request a declaration of war on Austria. He began by excoriating Germany with a fervor befitting the occasion. He emphasized his belief that Austria-Hungary was "not acting upon its own initiative or in response to the wishes and feelings of its own people," but was simply the "vassal of the German government." Therefore, it was necessary to treat the Central Powers as one. War must be declared against Austria-Hungary. And yet, said Wilson, war "shall not end in vindictive action of any kind; . . . no nation or people shall be robbed or punished because the irresponsible rulers of a single country have themselves done deep and abominable wrong." Pointing specifically to the Bolshevik formula of "no annexations, no contributions, no punitive indemnities," Wilson agreed that "this crude formula expresses the instinctive judgment as to the right of plain men everywhere," even though it was being utilized by the "masters of German intrigue to lead the people of Russia astray." But, said Wilson, "that a wrong use has been made of a just idea is no reason why a right use should not be made of it." He then announced his continued opposition to the dismemberment of Austria-Hungary: "We do not wish in any way to impair or rearrange the Austro-Hungarian Empire. It is no affair of ours what they do with their own life, either industrially or politically. We do not purpose or desire to dictate to them in any way. We only desire to see their affairs are left in their own hands, in all matters, great or small."[95]

The address was one of Wilson's most eloquent messages. Lansing regarded it as his greatest address, while Phillips called it magnificent, "the most remarkable of his many messages." It was obviously intended for people in the enemy countries. Wilson's request, however, came "like a thunder cloud." Apparently, no one expected it—not even his Cabinet. Most of those close to Wilson had expected him to author-ize immediate help to Italy and then allow Austria to declare war on the United States. Nonetheless, when he made his war request, the entire Congress rose to its feet and cheered.[96] Although Wilson had "a very serious doubt about its effects upon the international situation," he "seemed relieved" and "plainly pleased at its reception."[97] The armi-stice between Russia and the Central Powers was signed the same day that Wilson addressed Congress. On December 7, the day that Austria declared war on the United States, Wilson signed the joint resolution declaring a state of war between the two countries.[98]

Although Wilson's war message was greeted enthusiastically by the Allies, many noted Americans questioned his opposition to the dis-memberment of Austria-Hungary.[99] The response from Austria-Hun-gary was somewhat mixed. Although he vehemently rejected Wilson's description of Austrian subservience to Germany, Czernin noted with satisfaction his assurances of disinterest in the Empire's internal affairs. This was far superior to the Entente's policy, which was based on the so-called "right of nations to govern themselves."[100] While most mem-bers of the Reichsrat approved Czernin's stand, František Staněk, the Czech, pleaded for the creation of a representative committee to carry on negotiations for peace, while Kramář preached the gospel of self-determination. There was a mixed response from fellow Czechs and South Slavs.[101]

Masaryk, then in Russia, where he had been since May 1917 to expedite the formation of an independent Czecho-Slovak army to join the Allies on the Western Front, cabled his enthusiasm over the war declaration and his disappointment over Wilson's failure to support Austrian dismemberment. Describing Austria as an "organization of violence," he reminded Wilson of the Allied note of January 10, 1917, which demanded the liberation of Italians, Armenians, Slavs, and Czecho-Slovaks. Speaking in the name of the Czecho-Slovak National Council, he insisted that there could be "no liberation of Europe from German militarism and imperialism without the dismemberment of Austria-Hungary and the creation of a zone of free and independent states in Eastern Europe to prevent a Prussianized Europe."[102]

Masaryk's views were shared by many Czechs and other represen-tatives of Austro-Hungarian nationalities in the United States. They had hoped that if they could not get a declaration favoring Austro-Hungarian dissolution, that at least the reverse would have been left unsaid.[103] Wilson's address of December 4 was a clear check to the revolutionizing of Austria-Hungary. The official Austro-Hungarian press immediately used Wilson's war message to discourage the nationalities who sought their independence. To American Czechs who had vigorously backed the declaration of war against the Habsburgs, Wilson's speech revealed that much still remained to be done if Czech liberation was to be made an official objective of American foreign policy.[104] Both Pergler and Voska feared that the high morale of the Czechs in support of the war would be dampened by Wilson's statements regarding the integrity of the Empire, while the Austro-Hungarian government would "tear the sentences in question from their context in order to discourage Czecho-Slovak opposition within the Austro-Hungarian Empire."[105]

Yet the cause of Czecho-Slovak independence was generating increased support in the United States. This was indicated by the almost simultaneous appearance of several sympathetic articles in large American magazines in the autumn of 1917. By the end of the year, a substantial, well-organized, and broadly supported effort by the Bohemian and Slovak national associations was well under way and had begun to make a small impact on the news media as well as on various public figures.[106] Yet, at no point in 1917 did this publicity or Bohemian efforts of any kind have any serious influence on the formation of America's official policy. Wilson's positive statements opposing Austro-Hungarian dismemberment had placed him well behind the Western Allies in support of Czecho-Slovak independence.

Wilson put peace first. This meant placing primary importance on separating Austria-Hungary from the Central Powers. Although the Entente powers had announced their verbal support of the national aspirations of the peoples of Eastern Europe, Wilson refused to follow their example. He had become convinced that raising the specter of Austro-Hungarian dismemberment would inhibit his efforts in peace negotiations with the monarchy. Despite the failure of his peace efforts thus far, Wilson did not reconsider his opposition to the policy of dismemberment. Instead, he moved in the direction of supporting a federation within the monarchy.[107]

6

Wilson, Masaryk, and the Russian Revolution

The two Russian revolutions of 1917 affected the Russian and Far Eastern policies of both Wilson and Masaryk in dramatic ways that neither could have foreseen when the United States entered the war. Masaryk saw in the first Russian revolution a unique opportunity for the Czecho-Slovak liberation movement. Whereas the tsarist authorities had displayed a reactionary outlook toward the Czechs, several leading members of the new government, especially Foreign Minister Paul N. Miliukov, were Masaryk's close friends and sympathized with the aspirations of the lesser Slavic nations.[1] Miliukov was willing to cooperate with Masaryk in the formation of both an independent Czech army and a Czecho-Slovak state.[2]

On arriving in Russia in mid-May 1917, Masaryk planned to work with the leaders of the new Russian government and the newly selected leaders of the Russian branch of the Czecho-Slovak National Council—Professor Prokop Maxa, Dr. Bohdan Pavlů, and the poet, Rudolf Medek. Like the National Council in France, the Czecho-Slovaks in Russia had welcomed the March revolution as a victory of Russian democracy. Two months later, the second Czecho-Slovak Congress at Kiev adopted unanimously a resolution recognizing the Czecho-Slovak National Council headed by Masaryk as the supreme body in charge of the "national struggle." It now appeared that all obstructions to the formation of a strong and independent Czech army had been eliminated.[3] Although some of the Russian leaders had begun to fear that the Czecho-Slovak military detachments might be used by the counterrevolutionaries, their concerns were allayed after the battle of Zborov on July 2, when the Czechs won a decisive victory as a part of Minister of War Kerenskii's attempt to start a great Russian offensive. The Russian leaders then permitted the expansion of the *družina* into an entire army corps.[4]

Once the Provisional Government had been established, desertions of individual Czechs and Czech regiments from the Austro-Hungarian army to the Russian side to join the new Czecho-Slovak army increased. The Bohemian National Alliance used these mass desertions as valid evidence of Czech hostility against the Austrian government and of sympathy for the Allies. Bohemian-Americans were enthusiastic about the organization of an independent Bohemian army in Russia.[5] Surely a nation with its own army "must be reckoned with in the councils of the diplomats."[6]

Masaryk, uneasy over the feebleness of the Provisional Government and the strength of the Petrograd Soviet, with its cries for immediate peace, now increased his efforts to gain official consent for the organization of an independent Czecho-Slovak army to take to France. General Nikolai N. Dukhonin, chief of staff of the Russian army in the Kerenskii government, finally agreed to an independent unit under French command, but under the political control of the National Council in Paris. Albert Thomas, the French Minister of Munitions, who had just arrived in Petrograd, renewed the request for the transfer of at least 30,000 Czecho-Slovak prisoners of war, which was approved by the Russian Government on June 13, 1917. Beneš arranged for the dispatch of a special French mission to Russia to expedite the transport of the Czech prisoners and soldiers. Headed by Major Arsen Vergé, the mission organized the transfer of the first Czecho-Slovak contingents, which arrived in France in October 1917 and February 1918.[7] Prior to Vergé's arrival in August, the Russian Ministry of Foreign Affairs and the staff of the Supreme High Command had issued orders to the Kiev Military District in late July to prepare the Czech troops' movement toward Archangel.[8]

On October 9, Masaryk finally secured the consent of the Russian Provisional Government to expand the Czecho-Slovak army. Thereafter, he appointed Vladimir Shokorov, a Russian general, as commander of the Czech corps and Mikhail K. Dietrichs, a former Russian general, as chief of staff. Masaryk was also forced to choose Russians for the other superior commands, since the Czechs had only subalterns among their prisoners, most of whom were young and inexperienced. On November 7, the day of the Bolshevik coup d'état, Masaryk cabled specific instructions to Jiří Klecanda, the authorized representative of the Czecho-Slovak National Council on the Russian General Staff, and through him to Prokop Maxa, the commissary of the Czecho-Slovak army, to maintain a strict and absolute neutrality toward internal Russian politics.[9] In the autumn of 1917, the Czech Legion in Russia grew larger and more disciplined and cohesive. But the situation in the East was deteriorating. As the Bolsheviks seized power, they urged the soldiers to throw down their rifles and induce the Germans to do the same. The entire Russian military system was disintegrating.[10]

The two Russian revolutions of 1917 also had a profound effect on Wilson and his war policy. The first Russian revolution had eased his task of declaring war against Germany. Eager to aid Russia, the United States immediately began negotiations to establish Russian credits in the United States. Wilson also sent two missions to Russia. The first was to aid in the rehabilitation of the Russian railway system. The second mission, headed by Elihu Root, was to extend American friendship and goodwill to Russia and to find the best means of cooperating in a successful prosecution of the war.

The arrival of the Root mission in Russia gave Masaryk the opportunity to visit at length with his devoted friend, Charles R. Crane, as well as John R. Mott and Samuel N. Harper, also attached to the mission. Up to this point, Crane had known Masaryk largely as a scholar and counselor; now he saw a new side of Masaryk's personality—a man of action, intent and active in making definite and practical arrangements for the exodus of Czech troops from Russia. Crane was clearly impressed.[11] He informed Wilson that no one understood "the international situation quite so well as Professor Masaryk."[12]

The Root mission provided the stimulus for still another Russian project, one involving propaganda and the Czechs. Root cabled Wilson about the project, which coincided with one then being carried on by the British.[13] The British Foreign Office was already spending large sums of money on propaganda in Russia. It now sought to involve the United States in a cooperative propaganda effort to expose German intrigue and spur the Russians to a renewed military effort. The scheme itself sprang from the fertile brain of Wiseman, who hoped to counteract German propaganda and intrigue by sending a mixed group of pro-Allied refugees, including leaders from the Czecho-Slovak and Polish societies in the United States, to Russia as "lecturers and propagandists." House, Polk, and Lansing approved of the enterprise and were the only ones informed of the proposal.[14] Lansing assured Wilson that Washington's role would be invisible, since it would be possible to work through British connections in the United States. One of the most important aspects of the plan was to send a trusted Czech-American leader to Russia to organize the "Czechs and Bohemians" there. An estimated 220,000 Bohemian prisoners of war had surrendered to Russia early in the war; about 20 percent of them were skilled mechanics, and almost all of them were entirely reliable from the Allied point of view. If released, these prisoners, along with the other Czechs in Russia, could form the nucleus of an important and bitterly anti-German organization.[15] The British government agreed to underwrite the venture with $75,000, while Wilson allocated a similar amount. Although the British wanted Washington to undertake the venture alone, Wilson was unwilling to proceed without British participation. Wiseman agreed to make reports to House.[16]

W. Somerset Maugham, the British novelist, was Wiseman's top agent in Petrograd.[17] He was joined in September by Voska and three of Voska's colleagues—Reverend Alois Koukol, a Presbyterian minister from New York; Joseph Martínek, editor of a Czech-language newspaper; and Dr. Vac Švarc, attorney for the Slovak League in the United States. Masaryk helped Voska to establish a Slavic press bureau in Petrograd, which was to use a Czech organization consisting of 1,200 branches and 70,000 men to disseminate anti-German propaganda and to help keep Russia in the war. However, Masaryk warned Voska to keep his hands off the Czech Legion since it was in a delicate position— "a guest in the country." Although Wiseman's propaganda scheme ultimately came to naught, both Maugham's and Voska's reports in part provided the basis for urging Allied and American support for General Aleksei Maksimovich Kaledin's Cossacks, allegedly bolstered by a Polish and Czech corps (estimated at 80,000 each) already in Russia for a renewed effort to reestablish an Eastern Front.[18]

Toward the end of November, the British War Cabinet, deeply concerned over the cataclysm occurring on the Eastern Front, considered proposals for getting Russia back into the war. There was some sentiment in the War Office to act quickly and decisively with an expeditionary force. Initially, its role was to be twofold: the destruction of the antiwar Bolshevik regime and the stiffening of the backbone of Russian soldiers. Brigadier General Alfred Knox, senior adviser to the War Office on Russia, argued: "There . . . will never be a Russian army till some outside force with machine guns makes an example of a few undisciplined units."[19]

The desire to revitalize the Eastern Front with the introduction of foreign armies became the mainspring of British intervention in Russia until the Central Powers were defeated. In late 1917, the problem was to find "loyal" Russians who desired both the destruction of Bolshevism and the continuation of the war. Major General Sir George Mark Watson Macdonogh, director of British military intelligence, believed that Kaledin represented the best hope of keeping Russia in the war and might "well become dictator of Russia," since he controlled the "coal supplies of the Empire." If an Allied force of "say two American divisions" could support Kaledin, Macdonogh wrote, it would be possible to create an army of pro-Allied elements in Eastern Europe consisting of "500,000 Poles, 400,000 Cossacks, 80,000 Czechs and Slovaks, 300,000 Rumanians, 15,000 Serbians, 105,000 Armenians and 25,000 Georgians, etc." With the addition of other elements, Macdonogh was confident that an army of 2,000,000 men could be organized.[20]

On November 21, the War Cabinet instructed the chief of the Imperial General Staff to "get into touch with General Kaledin."[21] The French also sought to encourage anti-Bolshevik and anti-German resistance in the Ukraine and the Don region. They hoped to maintain Rumania in the war, foster the formation of a southern coalition of Ukrainian and Russian anti-Bolshevik forces around the Rumanian army, and "facilitate the reestablishment of order and a legal government." The French supreme commander, Marshal Ferdinand Foch, like Maugham, also urged the formation of Polish and Czecho-Slovak, as well as Ukrainian, divisions to cooperate with the counterrevolutionary centers in southern Russia to support the Rumanian front.[22]

In response to the requests of British and French representatives in Paris, who wished to send Czech soldiers to the Rumanian front, Masaryk went to Jassy, then seat of the Rumanian government, to confer with representatives on the scene. He soon discovered that Rumania was thinking of peace and would find it exceedingly difficult to supply 50,000 additional Czech troops. Masaryk thus opposed the plan of the Allied representatives both on the scene and in Paris.[23] Bolshevik historians have claimed that the Czechs at Jassy planned an attack against the Bolshevik government at the end of 1917. Presumably they were aware that Allied, White Russian, Rumanian, and Czecho-Slovak delegates had met and discussed the ability of the Czecho-Slovak Legion to march against the Soviet government. A Czech officer presumably present at this meeting recalled a specific discussion of the question.[24] One Bolshevik historian later claimed in an official history that General Alexeev had planned to bring the Czecho-Slovak regiments nearer to the Don to cooperate in a joint offensive against the Bolsheviks.[25] However, when, in late January 1918, Alexeev appealed to the head of the French military mission in Rumania to direct the Czecho-Slovak Legion to march to the Don and join up with the volunteer army, he was unsuccessful.[26] On December 3, 1917, the British War Cabinet had decided to "support any responsible body in Russia that would actively oppose the Bolsheviks" and "give money freely, within reason, to such bodies as were prepared to help the

Allied cause." Sir George Buchanan, the British Ambassador in Russia, was given discretion to make the necessary arrangements with appropriate national groups.[27]

As a result of the Maugham and other reports[28] and Wiseman's intercession with House, Wilson agreed to give "whatever aid . . . possible to the Polish, Cossacks, and others" who were "willing to fight Germany." And, while he had "no power to lend money direct to such un-organized movements," he was "willing to let France and England have funds to transmit to them if they consider it advisable."[29]

The Bolshevik seizure of power plunged the Czechs in Russia into heavy seas. Armies of the Central Powers, who were deadly enemies of the Czechs and considered them traitors to Austria, were advancing speedily into the heart of the Ukraine. All of Russia seemed on the point of breaking up into autonomous states of dubious political color and of highly uncertain orientation with regard to their former enemy, Germany. The Ukrainian Rada (parliament) announced its intention to sue for a separate peace with Germany and Austria.[30] Masaryk began negotiations in Petrograd with the Soviet authorities to evacuate the Czech corps in Russia to France as rapidly as possible. However, no definite arrangements could be made until after the ratification of the Brest-Litovsk Treaty on March 15, 1918. During this period, the Czech corps stationed around Kiev maintained its unity and military discipline.

From December 1917 through early February 1918, the Ukrainian Rada controlled somewhat tenuously the territory in which the Czech corps was stationed, but when it proclaimed its independence on January 24, 1918, and began to negotiate with the Germans, the position of the Czech Legion became hazardous. Before the negotiations could be concluded, the Red Army under Commander Mikhail Artemovich Muravev reached Kiev and took the city. Now the position of the Czech corps became even more complicated, for it found itself occupying the territory of a government in the process of concluding peace with its enemy. Moreover, with the conquest of the region by the Red Army, intensive Communist propaganda was promoted within the ranks of the Czech army.[31]

To oppose Communist propaganda and restore confidence in the West among both leaders and the Allies, the Czech League convened its third congress in Kiev on January 30. It made a solemn promise of fidelity to Masaryk and reaffirmed its determination to fight against Austria-Hungary until it was destroyed and Czecho-Slovakia was independent. On January 31, Masaryk and Maxa began to negotiate with the Bolsheviks, and on February 16, Masaryk received word that the Bolshevik Commander in Chief would present no objections to the departure of the Czecho-Slovak contingents for France.[32] On February 20, Masaryk and the French military mission in Russia ordered the legion to evacuate the Ukraine and depart for France to "fight against the ancient enemy." From March 8 to March 13, the Czech Legion, in cooperation with the Bolsheviks, fought violently and successfully against the Germans at Bakhmach. These engagements had a strong psychological effect on the Czechs and contributed greatly to the improvement of their morale.[33] Even as the Germans were marching into the Ukraine, Emperor Charles sent a special envoy to the Czech Legion with the promise that if they would disarm they would be "amnestied" and their land would receive "autonomy." The Czechs refused to negotiate.[34]

The Czecho-Slovak victory at Bakhmach had checkmated the clever German move to cut the railroad leading to the east, and troop trains now began to move regularly toward western Siberia. The way now seemed open for a Czecho-Slovak exit from the Ukraine. The Commander in Chief of the Ukrainian Bolshevik troops publicized a testimonial to their Czech "comrades . . . who fought honorably and bravely near Zhitomir defended Kiev and won a victory at Bachmach." The Bolsheviks vowed that "the Revolutionary Armies" would "not forget this brotherly help."[35]

Masaryk, after completing his discussions with the Bolshevik leaders, believed that they now had no objections to the evacuation of the Czech corps via Vladivostok. He decided in late February to leave Moscow for Vladivostok to secure in America and Europe the shipping to transport the corps from Vladivostok to Europe.[36] Before leaving Moscow, Masaryk gave Klecanda full power to conduct any further political negotiations. Klecanda was determined to adhere strictly to Masaryk's policy of noninterference. On March 15, Klecanda negotiated with members of the staff of the Moscow Military District about the departure of the Czecho-Slovak army from Russia. Semen Ivanovich Aralov and Iosif V. Stalin were among the members present. They appeared grateful for Czecho-Slovak assistance and telegraphed Lenin, who agreed to a speedy transport of the Czecho-Slovak army to Vladivostok. Shokorov then issued orders to prepare for the long trip across Asia and to leave the Bolsheviks such equipment as might prove a hindrance to travel.[37]

It was at this point that the Bolsheviks and the French Ministry of War—now committed to a limited rapprochement with the Bolsheviks—discussed the possibility of employing the "Czech contingent as nucleus" of a new Russian army. General Jean Guillaume Lavergne, newly appointed chief of the French military mission in Russia, even telegraphed the French General Staff that the Bolsheviks had accepted such a proposal. The French General Staff replied on March 21 that the transfer of Czech troops via the Trans-Siberian Railway did not "appear so urgent," that these "good troops could be employed where they are," and that their transport to Siberia should be resumed only if they could not be so employed. On March 23, Lavergne once again talked with Leon Trotskii, Bolshevik War Minister, about the use of the Czech troops, and Trotskii appeared most agreeable. However, when Lavergne approached the members of the Czecho-Slovak National Council, they were opposed to the suggestion and eager to go to the French front.[38]

On March 26, the Bolsheviks sent a telegram confirming an agreement at Penza between the legion, the Bolsheviks, and Vergé that guaranteed the Czechs unmolested passage to Vladivostok. Stalin, the Moscow commissar, telegraphed to the local soviets that the Czecho-Slovaks were traveling through Siberia as free citizens, not as an armed unit, and that they carried a certain number of weapons as protection against counterrevolutionaries. He added: "The Soviet of the People's Commissars wishes every assistance to be given them on Russian soil" in recognition of their "honorable and distinguished loyalty." The way now seemed clear for the Czecho-Slovak exodus.[39]

It was at this juncture that the YMCA began its service to the Czecho-Slovak troops. In 1917 the General Secretary of the YMCA was John R. Mott, an old friend of Wilson. As a member of the Root mission, Mott had secured official approval of the Provisional Government to begin a vast YMCA service program to Russian troops and civilians. It eventually brought some 400 American YMCA workers to Russia.[40] The organizer of the work with the Czechs was a YMCA secretary, Kenneth D. Miller, who had earlier spent eighteen months in Bohemia, principally at Prague, studying the Bohemian language and people. Upon his return, he had served several years as resident worker at John Hus Memorial Church House in New York City. Leaving for Russia in September 1917, he had gone from Petrograd to Kiev, from whence he started his pilgrimage with the Czech troops.[41] Miller and the YMCA workers received a royal reception. The Czechs and the American YMCA "uncles" soon developed deep and lasting bonds of friendship and loyalty.[42] As Miller put it, "One thing is sure, our work among the Czechs is going to be a great thing, and if Bohemia is made free at the end of the war it will pave the way for a great work in Bohemia."[43] The YMCA men were to provide the most effective and reliable information regarding the Czechs and their movement to the various American diplomatic representatives throughout Russia. Moreover, six of the best men who served the YMCA in Russia accepted positions as American Vice Consuls. The reports of many of these men, whether as YMCA secretaries or as Vice Consuls, were of inestimable help in piecing together the story of the Czech movement across Siberia.[44]

After the signing of the Treaty of Brest-Litovsk, Ethan T. Colton, head of the YMCA in Russia, summoned the seventy-three restless and distraught YMCA secretaries then located in European and Asiatic Russia to headquarters, which had been moved from Moscow to Samara, far from the German lines.[45] Colton had just come from the United States with cablegrams from New York, including Mott's assurances that Wilson had urged the YMCA to continue its work to demonstrate American interest in the Russian people. While he cautioned the YMCA men not to participate in Russian politics, Wilson hoped that they would stay.[46]

Another American group—the Stevens railway mission—also found its efforts to aid in the rehabilitation of the Russian railways complicated by the Bolshevik revolution. The organization of the railway mission had come about in an extraordinary way. On March 30, 1917, Stanley Washburn, correspondent of the London *Times* in Russia since September 1914, met in Washington with the Council of National Defense, which had been appointed by the President to advise the administration on problems of economic mobilization if war should come. Fearful that the Germans would take Petrograd and cut off Russia's supplies from the West, Washburn emphasized the strategic importance of the Trans-Siberian Railway, then in pitiable condition and poorly managed, as the only Allied access to Russia. Washburn suggested sending some expert American railway operators to aid that country's transportation system. He estimated that they could triple the road's capacity.[47] Wilson consulted with Secretary Baker about the best way to handle the matter and approved a draft dispatch to Ambassador David R. Francis. It asked if the Russian government would "welcome" an American railway mission prepared to inspect and recommend improvements in the operation and equipment of the Trans-Siberian Railway. The Russians were delighted to accept. Thus, on May 3, Stevens and five other railway experts sailed for Vladivostok.[48]

John F. Stevens, a great railway and engineering genius, was regarded by experts as "the best qualified man for the [Russian] job in the United States."[49] Wilson had explained his conception of the railway commission's purpose with care: "It is not going to ask What can [the] United States do for Russia? but only to say We have been sent here to put ourselves at your disposal to do anything we can to assist in the working out of your transportation problem. They are to report nothing back to us. They are delegated to serve Russia on the ground, if she wishes to use them, as I understand she does."[50] The mission arrived at Vladivostok early in June 1917 and proceeded across Siberia in a special train provided by the Russian Railway Administration. Once it had finished its survey and made its recommendations, the mission returned to the United States. Stevens, however, remained in Russia as a special adviser in the Ministry of Ways and Communications to assist in executing the measures that the railway and the Russian officials had agreed were vital. In fact he was given absolute control of the terminals at Vladivostok.[51]

Throughout 1917, the Allies had watched the gradual weakening of the Eastern Front with a concern that approached panic as military operations came to a complete halt in December. To bolster the weakening front initially, and later to reconstitute it against the German invasion of Russia, the Allies seriously considered the possibility of sending a Japanese military expedition to Russia as early as January and February 1917.[52] When the French began to urge the use of Japanese troops to restore the Russian front in June 1917, Wilson rejected the proposal as both unwise and impractical.[53] Later in the autumn, when Russian soldiers were abandoning the Eastern Front, Joseph Noulens, the French Ambassador in Petrograd, approached the Provisional Government with a proposal to use Japanese troops. Both Kerenskii and Foreign Minister Mikhail Ivanovich Tereshchenko refused. They were completely opposed to having Russian territory traversed by their "old enemy of 1905."[54] In late 1917, after the Bolsheviks had seized power, the French, desperately struggling to hold the Germans on the Western Front, became quite vigorous in their demands for military intervention in Siberia. The British backed their efforts and sought American support for a proposal either to send troops to Russia or to support a Japanese intervention via the Trans-Siberian Railroad. Various American officials, particularly Ambassador Francis, emphasized the moral effect of American troops on the Russian front.[55] Others, however, like House, were completely opposed to the French suggestion and to any proposals for a Japanese expeditionary force.[56] Senator Williams had advised Wilson earlier of the "demoral" effect of sending American troops to Russia. Wilson was impressed with his

Colonel George H. Emerson, *left,* and John F. Stevens (National Archives)

argument.[57] By late December, the British were informed of American opposition to either lone Japanese intervention in eastern Siberia or a joint Japanese-American intervention.[58]

In the meantime, Stevens, following the Russian adoption of his railway plan, awaited the arrival of 300 American engineers requested by the Provisional Government at his suggestion. The representatives of the British, French, and Italian governments had also agreed to lend all possible aid in the administrative reorganization of Russia and had appealed to Washington to aid in reorganizing the Russian railways.[59] According to Stevens's plan, American engineers would serve as advisers along the different sections of the Trans-Siberian and Chinese Eastern Railways. The Provisional Government agreed to meet all expenses involved. The American engineers were specially commissioned by the Secretary of War as officers of the Russian Railway Service Corps and placed under the command of Colonel George H. Emerson. On December 14, the U.S.S. *Thomas*, an army transport ship, reached Vladivostok with the railway engineers aboard but could not land because of chaotic conditions. The corps had no choice but to return to Japan to await developments.[60]

Stevens, though disappointed, went to Harbin in Manchuria and opened negotiations with officials of the Chinese Eastern Railway. On February 16, he notified the State Department that he had arranged for the American railway engineers to begin work on that railway, and that he would move them to Harbin on February 27. He also reported: "Japanese inquisitive. No sympathy for the assistance of the United States. They desire intervention to seize the railway [themselves]."[61] Stevens's message was a clear portent. It is now apparent that, while the Czech Legion had embarked upon its great odyssey across Siberia via the Trans-Siberian Railway, its success in large measure would depend upon the effectiveness of Stevens and the Russian Railway Service Corps in keeping the Trans-Siberian Railway open and in expediting traffic along its tortuous length. Indeed, Czech success might ultimately depend upon the ability of the Allies to keep Siberia free from either German or Japanese control. Thus, while the efficient management and operation of the Trans-Siberian Railway was crucial to the Allies for strategic purposes, it was a matter of survival to the Czech Legion.

By the end of 1917, agitation for intervention in Siberia had begun in earnest. The chaotic conditions in Vladivostok gave rise to constant rumors of Japanese intervention. Even American representatives were advising the landing of an Allied force to preserve order in the city. The

State Department vehemently opposed these suggestions. Meanwhile, on December 14, Sir W. Conyngham Greene, the British Ambassador to Japan, discussed informally with Japanese officials the problem of protecting the Amur and Trans-Siberian railways and the stores and munitions at Vladivostok. These discussions, unknown to the United States, resulted in the dispatch of warships to Vladivostok.

The Far Eastern Division of the State Department was well aware of Japan's interest in keeping the Chinese Eastern Railway, the key segment of the Trans-Siberian Railway crossing Manchuria, out of the hands of the Bolsheviks. The secret documents published by the Bolsheviks in Petrograd in December 1917 revealed agreements concerning relations between Russia and Japan. One was an alleged convention of July 3, 1916, including certain secret clauses not previously disclosed, whereby Russia agreed to transfer that portion of the Chinese Eastern Railway between Changchun and the Sungari River to Japan in payment for military supplies. Moreover, Article 1 of that convention was a positive pledge by each to assist the other and to adopt measures to prevent any third power hostile to either one from acquiring political influence in China. According to Edward T. Williams, Chief of the Division of Far Eastern Affairs, this convention was "undoubtedly aimed at the United States which country is continually represented as seeking political control in China and as constantly aiming to thwart Japan's legitimate ambitions in that country."[62] Article 2 recognized that the measures upon which Russia and Japan might agree would be likely to create ill feeling upon the part of the third power to which reference was made (i.e., the United States) and that this feeling might conceivably lead to war, in which case the party not attacked would at the first summons come to the assistance of the other.[63] V. K. Wellington Koo, the Chinese Minister in Washington, who was deeply concerned over Japanese actions at Vladivostok, had informed Polk that the "Japanese wish to land in Russian Siberia. . . . that they were not so much afraid of Russians as they were glad of opportunity to land."[64] It was information of this kind that led the Far Eastern Division of the State Department to be exceedingly wary of any proposal involving lone Japanese intervention in Siberia. Wilson clearly shared its concern.[65]

The Allies confronted still another problem stemming from the chaotic situation in Russia. The Chinese Eastern Railway formed a part of the great Trans-Siberian line linking Asia with Europe. The Russian imperial government had gradually assumed complete authority within the railway zone, which had by 1917 become in effect a Russian crown colony in China, despite the fact that Chinese authority had never been renounced within the railway area.[66] By the end of 1917, General Dmitri L. Horvath was established as Russian governor and general manager of the railway and maintained the pretense of representing the defunct Provisional Government. Within the next few months, the railway zone became the center of counterrevolutionary activities against the Bolsheviks. England, France, and Japan soon extended financial aid to these anti-Bolshevik groups.[67]

One of the most notorious of the anti-Bolshevik leaders was Captain, later Ataman, Gregorii M. Semenov, who appeared on the Siberian scene in December 1917 as the "savior of Russia." He was said to be the son of an old Cossack Ataman by a Mongol Buriat woman. Later, as his fame spread, the Buriat woman became a descendant of Genghis Khan. Promoting himself to colonel, Semenov raised and armed a volunteer force of a few hundred men, which he took west to Manchuria Station, where he engaged the Bolsheviks. The sole effect of this move was to cut the Trans-Siberian Railway at the Manchurian border and to separate the Chinese Eastern on the west from the Trans-Siberian Railway. This of course immensely complicated Stevens's job.

The British representatives rather casually invited their American counterparts to join them in paying Semenov $50,000 per month, claiming that, with three to five thousand men, he could easily push on to Irkutsk and thus stop the movement of both prisoners of war and supplies from Vladivostok west to Germany. Although the French and Japanese joined the British in openly paying and supplying Semenov, the United States, even after repeated requests, refused to do so. Manifestly, had the United States at any time supported Semenov against the Bolsheviks, Stevens and his railway men would have been barred thereafter from the Siberian railways, and at that time they were being employed on the Chinese Eastern only because they hoped eventually to extend their operations to the Siberian lines. For this reason alone, the United States was absolutely opposed to the support of Semenov.[68] Wilson fully agreed with Stevens "that it would be a fatal mistake for the Allied powers to attempt to support or countenance any counterrevolution . . . to obtain control in favor of less radical elements." Wilson emphasized the futility and danger of antagonizing the Bolsheviks "by attempting any sort of armed intervention even in eastern Siberia."[69]

7

Self-Determination without Dismemberment of Nations

On January 8, 1918, Wilson made his Fourteen Points Address, his most memorable statement of American war aims. Wilson hoped that such a statement would unite the world against Germany as well as answer the Bolshevik invitation to negotiate a general peace.[1] Wilson's expectations did not reflect a realistic appreciation of the serious gap between America's position and that of the Entente nations. The French and Italians adamantly opposed any statement of war aims that might conflict with the Treaty of London of April 26, 1915, whereby each nation had agreed to remain in the war to its conclusion. They agreed that a statement of war aims in accordance with Wilson's request would mean, in effect, an abrogation of the London Treaty and three years of war fought in vain.[2]

In Paris, at Wilson's request, House had presented for approval to the inter-Allied conference in November a general declaration that the Allies were not "waging war for the purpose of aggression or indemnity," but rather to eliminate militarism and provide nations with the right to "lead their lives in the way that seems to them best for the development of their general welfare." Although the British had agreed to support House's proposal, it was clearly not acceptable to the French and the Italians.[3] Thus the inter-Allied conference agreed that each government should be free to instruct its Ambassador in Petrograd in accordance with its own special interests, but only until Russia "had a stable government with whom they could act."[4] However, the combination of Russian withdrawal from the war and the possibility once again of securing a separate peace with Austria-Hungary prompted British reconsideration of war aims.

Once Lenin and Trotskii seized power, they demanded an immediate, general, and democratic peace with the Central Powers "without annexations and contributions with the right of all nations to self-determination." The German Supreme Command announced its agreement. On November 29, both sides ceased military operations and prepared for preliminary peace negotiations on December 2. They invited all of the Allies to participate in attaining a speedy armistice on all fronts and securing a universal democratic peace.[5] The Bolsheviks also annulled unconditionally all the secret treaties that the tsarist government had negotiated, thereby renouncing Russia's claims to any territory promised by an Entente victory.[6] Furthermore, on November 15, they had implemented their promise of self-determination by publishing "The Rights of Peoples of Russia to Self-Determination," a decree that sanctioned even the separation and formation of independent states in portions of the former Russian Empire.[7]

When the Entente governments and the United States refused to accept the Bolshevik invitation to the peace negotiations, the Russians on December 3 suspended hostilities with Germany and its allies for two weeks. They persuaded the Central Powers to allow the Allies more time to define their war aims and decide whether to participate in the negotiations. On December 6, Trotskii asked Francis whether the Allies were prepared to indicate "their readiness or their refusal to take part . . . and, in case they refuse, to openly, before the face of the whole of humanity, declare, clearly, precisely, and definitely in the name of what aims must the nations of Europe shed their blood during the fourth year of war."[8]

After several attempts to entice or intimidate the Allies into joining the negotiations, the Bolsheviks published the six points for world peace that they had laid down for the guidance of the peace conference. Five of the six dealt with self-determination. Although the Allies failed to perceive it until Trotskii pointed it out two days later, this time the points were directed at them as much as the Central Powers. The points were (1) no forced annexation of any territories conquered during the war; (2) political independence of nationalities enjoying the same before the war; (3) the right of national groups within all national states to choose by referendum under which suzerainty they should be placed; (4) the right of national minorities to cultural autonomy; (5) no indemnities of any kind; and (6) points one through four to govern the solution of colonial problems.[9]

The delegations of the Quadruple Alliance, headed by the German Foreign Secretary Richard von Kühlmann and Czernin, agreed to accept the Russian thesis "if the Entente would also agree to negotiate a Peace on similar terms."[10] On Christmas Day 1917, Czernin gave his assent to the principle of self-determination of national groups in the reply of the Central Powers to the conference. However, Czernin said, it could not be applied in the East so long as Russia's allies did not apply

Trotskii (National Archives)

it in the West. Moreover, the right of self-determination of nationalities within existing states had to be "solved by each State independently together with the nationalities concerned, and in accordance with the constitution of that State."[11] The Bolsheviks accepted the response of the Central Powers as a great triumph. The Allied statesmen were embarrassed even more when the Central Powers agreed to still another postponement of negotiations to permit the Bolsheviks to send their third invitation to the Entente.[12]

On December 29, with six days still remaining for the Entente powers to exercise their option to participate in the negotiations, Trotskii sent them his longest and most impassioned appeal. Once again his central argument concerned self-determination. Trotskii demanded that the United States and the Allies state their peace program "clearly and precisely." Trotskii continued:

If the Governments of the Allied Countries were to manifest the readiness—along with the Russian Revolution—to construct peace on the basis of an entire and complete recognition of the principle of self-determination for all peoples and in all states; if they were to begin with the actual giving of this right to the oppressed peoples of their own states: this would create international conditions under which the compromise program internally contradictory of Germany and in particular of Austria-Hungary would manifest all its inconsistencies and would be overcome by the pressure of the peoples concerned.[13]

Trotskii's address was clearly an ideological challenge. Not only did he call for violent proletarian revolution against the Allied governments, but he had also shrewdly based his appeal on Wilson's own principle of self-determination. His interpretation was a direct challenge to Wilson's view of that principle. Yet Trotskii's address was an even greater challenge to the Entente in terms of practice.

The Allies could not publicly refute Trotskii's charge that they had not even "advanced that one step towards peace" made by the Central Powers. Nevertheless, at the inter-Allied conference in December, Lloyd George had secured the Allies' support to investigate Austria-Hungary's latest peace offers. These investigations had resulted in the Smuts-Mensdorff discussions on December 18 and 19.[14] Smuts had reported to Lloyd George that Austria was "now in a mood to talk, apparently behind the back of her Allies." Both Lloyd George and Smuts believed that a separate peace with Austria-Hungary was now possible.[15] The timing of these events, then, became important. Smuts had informed Lloyd George of his views on the day after Czernin had accepted the Soviet peace principles as a basis for peace discussions. Czernin's response to the Bolshevik overtures for peace on December 25 seemed to concede, at least as far as phraseology was concerned, all that the British were fighting for. It now became essential to ascertain what Czernin's utterances actually meant.[16]

On January 3, 1918, the War Cabinet discussed war aims. It declared its readiness to "go to the extreme limit of concession" to emphasize to the British people, their Allies, and the peoples of the Central Powers that Britain's object "was not to destroy the enemy nations." As for the

Austro-Hungarian problem, it agreed to indicate general support of Italian claims for union with the peoples of Italian nationality then under Austrian rule, without specific reference to the whole of the Italian war aims. It decided that some reference ought to be made to "the Italians, Croats, Slovaks, Czechs, etc., who are under Austrian rule, and who seek some form of Autonomy." The War Cabinet also once again discussed whether to consult the Allies before publishing a statement. It decided to act independently in order to give a prompt answer.[17]

The War Cabinet then discussed three drafts of the proposed statement submitted by Cecil, Smuts, and Philip Kerr. Lloyd George urged his colleagues to evaluate the drafts primarily as counteroffensives to the German peace move, because he believed that, in its hour of triumph, Germany would never accept the terms set out in the draft documents. Therefore, it was essential to consider the British statement as a war move rather than a peace move. "Its real importance would be its effect on Austria." Lloyd George emphasized that there would be a great difference between an Austria that desired to fight and one that was lukewarm.[18] On the following morning, January 4, Lloyd George showed a rough draft of the statement to Albert Thomas, who indicated that "it would suit France."[19] He also secured the approval of both Asquith and Grey so that he could later say that the draft represented the views of the entire nation.

In its final form, the statement regarding Austria-Hungary read: "Though we agree with President Wilson that the break-up of Austria-Hungary is no part of our war aims, we feel that, unless genuine self-government on true democratic principles is granted to those Austro-Hungarian nationalities who have long desired it, it is impossible to hope for the removal of those causes of unrest in that part of Europe which have so long threatened its general peace." The final statement was as clear and precise an enunciation of Wilson's position as had yet been made.[20]

Meanwhile, Wilson, too, was pondering the entire issue of war aims. He hoped that by stating a concrete and morally strong program of common Allied war aims he might persuade the Entente nations to liberalize their own program. He wanted to persuade the Germans, particularly the German Socialists, to negotiate or perhaps convince the German people of the purity and justice of Allied war aims and thus lead them to repudiate their autocratic masters. A refusal would lay the responsibility for continuing the war squarely upon the Germans. A liberal program would also answer Bolshevik demands for a statement of American war aims and might even cause Russia to remain loyal to the Allies. By this time, Wilson had received two invitations from the Bolsheviks to join in general peace negotiations, or at least to state the Allies' reasons for continuing the war.[21] Wilson himself believed that "something would have to be done to counteract the Bolshevik propaganda, and he might have to do it soon."[22] Moreover, Czernin's statement of possible peace terms in response to Bolshevik overtures was so similar in its essentials to the principles that Wilson had laid down that he felt he had to respond.[23] Finally, Wilson still cherished the hope that such a program, if carefully worded, might persuade Austria-Hungary to separate from its allies.

Although it appears that he never fully realized it, Wilson was in an ideological corner: either he must accept the Bolshevik argument that all peoples, in all states, including all colonies, had the right to immediate self-determination, or he must reject it. If he rejected it, he would have to offer some reasonable alternative. Although sympathetic to the principle of self-determination as enunciated by Lenin, Wilson had no illusions concerning the German attitude toward self-determination. By the end of December, it was clear that self-determination, as understood by the Germans, justified the severance from Russia of Russian Poland, most of the Baltic provinces, and parts of Belorussia (White Russia). Moreover, by mid-December the Russian response to Lenin's program of self-determination seemed to forebode similar disaster, with the Ukraine, Finland, and the Transcaucasus in the process of declaring themselves independent. It seemed clear that if Petrograd was to have peace according to both the German interpretation of self-determination and the Russian implementation of Lenin's program, it was to be purchased at the price of the dismemberment of the Empire.[24] Wilson was sternly opposed to such an interpretation of self-determination.

If Wilson's concept of self-determination did not anticipate the dismemberment of nations, what then did it really mean? This question of meaning had been raised incisively on December 29, when Trotskii had issued what Lansing called his "insidious" address to the peoples and governments of the Allied nations. Trotskii had made it clear that to demand self-determination for the peoples of enemy states and to refuse self-determination to the peoples within the various Allied states or their own colonies would "mean the defense of the most naked, the most cynical imperialism."[25]

To Wilson, it seemed clear that a response was necessary. William Phillips, Polk, and Basil Miles, head of the Russian Division, agreed.[26]

On January 1, Wilson questioned Lansing on "the most feasible and least objectionable way" to establish "unofficial relations with the Bolsheviki."[27] Lansing's response was one of total opposition. His position was based on his social conservatism, his personal animosity to Bolshevik ideology, and, most importantly, his insight into the logical and political requirements for a meaningful application of the principle of self-determination in foreign policy, despite his own personal commitment to Austro-Hungarian dismemberment. His advice to Wilson betrayed the contradictions that still existed in his thinking. Lansing wrote:

> I believe it would be unwise to make a reply to this insidious address; but if it seems advisable not to ignore it, I think the only course should be to state frankly the false premises upon which it is based and the vagueness of the unit of the independent communal power which they propose to set up. In view of the threat against existing governments and the promised aid to revolutionists I would personally prefer to see the communication unanswered whatever the consequences might be. Lenine, Trotskii, and their colleagues are so bitterly hostile to the present social order in all countries that I am convinced that nothing could be said which would gain their favor or render them amenable to reason. I feel that to make any sort of reply would be contrary to the dignity of the United States and offer opportunity for further insults and threats, although I do not mean that it may not be expedient at some time in the near future to state our peace terms in more detail than has yet been done.[28]

In his analysis of Bolshevik reasoning, Lansing also sought to persuade Wilson that self-determination was an undesirable means of settling territorial problems. The current concept of the sovereignty of states in international relations would be destroyed if the "mere expression of popular will" became the governing principle in territorial settlements. He reminded the President of the decision of the United States in regard to popular sovereignty in its own civil war. Wrote Lansing: "We, as a nation, are . . . committed to the principle that a national state may by force if necessary prevent a portion of its territory from seceding without its consent especially if it has long exercised sovereignty over it or if its national safety or vital interests would be endangered." The Bolshevik proposal, Lansing warned, would be "utterly destructive of the political fabric of society and would result in constant turmoil and change."[29]

One of the strongest points in Lansing's analysis was his discovery that the whole discussion of self-determination up to that point had a major ideological flaw. There was no definition of the "distinguishing characteristic" of the unit to which the principle was to be applied. Trotskii had discussed the right of nationalities without defining what a nationality was. Was it based on blood, habitation of a particular territory, language, or political affinity? Clearly, accurate definition of the word was necessary if the terms proposed were to be properly interpreted; otherwise, they were far too vague to be intelligently considered. He added that if the Bolsheviks intended to suggest that every community could determine its own allegiance to a particular state or to become independent, then the political organization of the current world would be shattered. The result, he said, would be international anarchy. Wilson now had before him two totally divergent views on self-determination. Whereas Trotskii had pushed the political logic of the principle to its limits, Lansing had negated the usefulness of self-determination in settling world issues.

Wilson was clearly at odds with the logic of both points of view. At the core of his thought, self-determination meant government by consent of the governed—a moral necessity. This logic did not conceive of the implementation of the concept in its broader sense apart from the parallel existence of a league of nations. Unlike Trotskii, Wilson did not call for a worldwide series of plebiscites as the first requirement for universal peace. Throughout 1917, and over the opposition of many persons, including Lansing, Wilson's policy set forth the dual principles of government by the consent of the governed and world security through an international organization of states as the only principles for the constitution of a permanent peace. He never conceived of these principles as being divided or as being applied separately. He had concluded that the primary cause of aggression by one state against another was a desire for territorial and economic security in the absence of international political security. The hallmark of this lack of international security was the bipolar alliance system that operated in an atmosphere of struggle for the elusive balance of power. This being the case, Wilson reasoned that if security could be restored to the various states, the motive for political and economic aggression would be removed. Wilson believed that an international organization of states through the common resources of a community of power would provide the required security. Once states had become adjusted to working for the common welfare and without resorting to exploitation, then the existing inequities regarding points of sovereignty could be resolved by that international organization based on the principle of government with the consent of the governed. This was Wilson's long-range view of the application of this principle. Even before the United States entered the war, Wilson had come to regard a league of nations as central to his thought—the key to the whole future peace of the world.[30]

On January 2, the day that Wilson received Lansing's letter opposing the Bolsheviks and their concept of self-determination, Balfour cabled him a report on the Smuts-Mensdorff conversations. Although the Austrians had held out little hope of a separate peace, Balfour reported that Austria was anxious for peace. Mensdorff had evinced great satisfaction with Smuts's statement that the destruction of Austria "was no part of the British war aims." He also seemed very sympathetic to the British desire "to see the various nationalities of which the empire is composed given an opportunity for autonomous development." To Balfour, this sympathy reflected opinions in the "highest quarters."[31]

On the following day, January 3, Wilson revealed in a highly confidential conversation with Sir Cecil Spring Rice, retiring British Ambassador, his own concern over war aims. He had been pondering both the impact of the Bolshevik peace appeal and Lansing's criticisms of it.[32] He realized now that the problem was "in the main a psychological one." He wanted to determine a course of action "which commended itself to the great majority of the American people whose interpreter he was."[33] Yet, he could scarcely be unsympathetic to the Bolshevik appeal to the peoples of the belligerent nations over the heads of their governments, since he had made a similar appeal to the German people "with the full consent of the American people." Recognizing the tremendous power of the Bolshevik statement and its potentially devastating effect on the morale of the peoples of Italy, England, and France, he believed that if it was not counteracted, "the effect would be great and would increase." While Wilson sympathized with the Bolsheviks' desire to settle the war on the basis of self-determination, "in point of logic, of pure logic, this principle which was good in itself would lead to the complete independence of various small nationalities now forming part of various empires." Pushed to its extreme, the principle would mean the disruption of existing governments, to an indefinable extent. This was already occurring in response to Lenin's decrees on self-determination. Moreover, if Petrograd accepted peace according to the German interpretation of self-determination, the price would be the dismemberment of Russia.[34]

Allied policy itself complicated Wilson's position. He believed that the Allies would find it extremely difficult to agree on any definite program that "did not look as if its main objective was aggression and conquest." Therefore, to evoke the enthusiastic approval of the American people, his own program had to represent the highest principles for which the United States was fighting. He had to oppose the aggressive war aims for which the Germans were fighting, distinguish between American and Allied war aims, make clear to the Russian people continued American sympathy and support, and pledge noninterference in their affairs.[35] Lansing's advice and Balfour's report on peace discussions with Austria all tended to move him to clarify his concept of self-determination and to emphasize his opposition to the German dismemberment of Russia as a part of the peace settlement. He also wished to indicate his opposition to any Allied effort to intervene in Russia's affairs in any way that might deny to the Russian people the right of self-determination or result in the detachment of Russian territory. By this time, Wilson was deeply concerned over the Allied desire to sanction Japanese intervention in Siberia as their mandatory—a policy which he regarded as tantamount to giving Japan the right to do in the East what Germany was already doing in the West.[36]

Once Wilson had decided upon an independent statement of war aims, he had asked House in collaboration with The Inquiry to draw together the materials necessary for such a declaration. The Inquiry's approach to specific territorial problems, general peace principles, and war aims was quite different from Wilson's. Concentrating on the psychopolitical landscape of Europe, it placed primary emphasis on economic and strategic factors. Less concerned with the justice of a particular settlement than with its economic viability, it gave little attention to Wilson's concept of self-determination.[37]

On January 4, House dined with Wilson and spent the evening discussing the general terms of his proposed message to Congress. Poring over the many maps and documents provided by The Inquiry, they worked until 11:30 that evening and met once again on the following morning to complete the final outline of the speech. It was at this time that they went through The Inquiry's report of December 22, 1917. Wilson's shorthand marginal notes constitute the first version of the Fourteen Points. Interestingly enough, the full account of that historically momentous conference revealed no direct reference to the independence of Bohemia as opposed to autonomy.[38] And yet the genesis of the point concerning Austria-Hungary cannot be understood without reference to events occurring almost simultaneously with the Wilson-House discussions just described.

Toward the end of 1917, Julius Meinl, an able, cultivated Vienna businessman and industrialist reputed to be a friend of Emperor Charles, initiated a peace feeler that was conveyed to the State Department by Hugh R. Wilson, the American Chargé in Switzerland, who believed that Meinl was acting on official instructions. Meinl's peace memorandum included the following: "Submission of all outstanding questions of European peoples and nationalities to the peace congress on the basis of consideration of the wishes of the people." In conversation, Meinl stipulated that "Austria has no desire to dominate the Balkans" and that the Austrian Reichsrat had declared "for no annexations." Moreover, Poland would be a separate kingdom.[39] Meinl also suggested that the President should ask pointedly in a public speech whether the German government spoke for the German people or the German militarists and whether or not it unreservedly accepted the "peace resolution of July 19th of the German *Reichstag*."[40]

Wilson enthusiastically endorsed Meinl's views, which, as he said, advanced "a long stride in fact nearly all the way, towards our position." He was anxious to learn more about Meinl and "what importance may be attached to his statements."[41] On the following evening, Lansing cabled Bern for immediate information. While no reply was received from this inquiry until January 8, within twenty-four hours Phillips's office sent a memorandum to Lansing, which in all probability he immediately forwarded to Wilson.[42] This memorandum said that Meinl was an important Viennese capitalist; more significantly, he was a political conservative and one of the first men in Austria-Hungary to take an advanced stand for peace. He was said to have the complete confidence of Czernin and Julius Andrássy, a prominent Hungarian statesman, and probably also Charles. The memorandum added that Meinl was probably the direct agent of the government. While some of the facts concerning Meinl's affiliations with Czernin and the presumed official character of his inquiries were later questioned, that information was not sent to the President until January 8, and could therefore have had no bearing on the Fourteen Points Address, which was completed on January 6.[43] It appears, then, that Hugh Wilson's belief in the official character of Meinl's peace feelers, combined with Balfour's report on the Smuts-Mensdorff conversations, strengthened Wilson's belief in the reliability and sincerity of Austrian peace offers at the very moment when he was in the midst of drafting his address. Both offers emphasized an appreciation of the ideas expressed by Lloyd George and Wilson that dismemberment of Austria-Hungary was no part of British or American war aims and that there was support in high official centers in Austria-Hungary for the view that the various nationalities of the Empire should be given *"an opportunity for autonomous development."*[44]

So it was that Wilson's marginal note on The Inquiry's report of December 22, 1917, stated: "The peoples of Austria-Hungary, whose place among the nations of the world we wish to see safeguarded and assured must be accorded the freest opportunity of autonomous development."[45] Wilson sought no outside criticism concerning the points he had drafted except the one relating to the Balkan settlement. In drafting this point he had confined himself to vague generalities, rather than presenting specific recommendations. Obviously, Italian war claims added another strong argument to Wilson's unwillingness to accept dismemberment of the Austro-Hungarian Empire. As he later explained, he could not "pledge" the American "people to fight for the eastern shore of the Adriatic."[46] As drafted, Point Nine asked only for a "readjustment of the frontiers of Italy along clearly recognizable lines of nationality," while Point Eleven called for the evacuation of Rumania, Serbia, and Montenegro, restoration of occupied territories, free and secure access to the sea for Serbia, relationships of Balkan states to one another based on historical lines of allegiance and nationality, and international economic and political guarantees for the Balkan states.[47]

Wilson delivered his Fourteen Points Address to a joint session of Congress on January 8. Replying specifically to the Bolsheviks, Wilson made clear that self-determination for Russia included opposition to the detachment of her territory by any of the belligerents, Allied or enemy, and preservation of the right of the Russian people to determine their own government without any outside interference. He praised the Russian representatives for insisting "very justly, very wisely, and in the spirit of democracy" on full publicity for the Brest-Litovsk proceedings and also expressed his desire to assist "the people of Russia to attain their utmost hope of liberty and ordered peace."[48] Point Six represented the official attitude of the American government toward Russia:

> The evacuation of all Russian territory and any such settlement of all questions affecting Russia as will secure the best and freest cooperation of the other nations of the world in obtaining for her an unhampered and unembarrassed opportunity for the independent determination of her own political development and national policy and assure her of

a sincere welcome into the society of free nations under institutions of her own choosing; and, more than a welcome, assistance also of every kind that she may need and may herself desire. *The treatment accorded to Russia by her sister nations in the months to come will be the acid test of their good will, of their comprehension of her needs as distinguished from their own interests, and of their intelligent and unselfish sympathy.*[49]

Wilson's position on self-determination was also reflected in his desire to draft a statement regarding Austria-Hungary that would both preserve the integrity of the Empire and also provide for government by the consent of the governed through an autonomous federation of states, a position that now appeared to have the sanction of Austria-Hungary as revealed in the Smuts-Mensdorff conversations.[50]

Although the meaning and purpose of Wilson's Point Ten can best be understood in the light of The Inquiry memorandum, Balfour's report on the Smuts-Mensdorff conversations, the Meinl note, and Lansing's diatribe of January 2 against the Bolshevik definition of self-determination, it has nevertheless been interpreted variously from "vague" to "ambiguous." Mamatey questions "whose place among the nations did the President wish to see safeguarded and insured? Austria-Hungary's, or her peoples?"[51] Actually, Lippmann's advice had determined Wilson's use of the term *peoples*. In the original memoranda on Austria-Hungary and Czecho-Slovakia written by Professor Robert J. Kerner, The Inquiry's Czech expert, Lippmann had questioned his use of the terms *nations* and *races* and indicated his preference for the term *peoples*. It was so used in the final Inquiry memorandum.[52] Wilson himself did not intend any ambiguity. When Jusserand questioned the meaning of Point Ten, Wilson made clear that it was the place of the *peoples* of Austria-Hungary whom he wished to see made secure. He had told Jusserand earlier that he had not meant to suggest the destruction of the Habsburg Empire, which would not be desirable in any event. What he desired was a grant of "broad autonomy to the subject nationalities of the empire."[53]

That Wilson intended a federation of autonomous states within a strong and democratic Austria-Hungary is clearly indicated by his discussions with Jusserand, by Lansing's comments regarding Point Ten, and The Inquiry's interpretation of it, combined with its subsequent search for the appropriate formula to implement it. Although Wilson had not consulted the State Department in formulating his war-aims address, nevertheless, he had in his possession Lansing's memo-

Self-Determination

randum of January 2. Moreover, on January 7, Wilson had read his address to Lansing.[54] That Lansing understood Wilson's meaning in Point Ten is clear in a memorandum he wrote just two days after Wilson's speech. In it, he discussed various subjects open to debate in Wilson's address, noting that he hesitated to "include the question of independence for the nationalities within Austria-Hungary, such as the Czechs, Rumanians, and Southern Slavs, because the President, except in the case of Poland which is mostly outside of the empire, had indicated a purpose to preserve the dual monarchy intact."[55] Thus Lansing not only knew and understood the meaning of Point Ten, but had determined to alter Wilson's interpretation of it. The position of The Inquiry was somewhat different. While it, too, advocated a federation of states within the Austro-Hungarian Empire, it had also advised the use of psychological warfare to encourage the subject peoples to revolt, thereby weakening the Empire and encouraging it to negotiate for a separate peace. However, there is no evidence that in January 1918 Wilson had agreed to such an opportunistic policy.[56]

The Entente's reaction to Wilson's speech was generally favorable, except in Italy. Wilson himself was deeply gratified to learn that his own program of peace was "so entirely consistent" with that of Lloyd George, and also of Balfour, who spoke in Edinburgh on January 10.[57] However, both Wilson's and Lloyd George's addresses, insofar as they concerned Italy, fell far short of what Italy desired and what her government and press had led the Italian people to expect.[58] Some Italian newspapers noted that Wilson apparently had ignored the London Treaty, and even though he had not been a party to it, the treaty was critical, since it defined "the conditions and obligations of the European Allies one to another, when they entered the war."[59] When Wilson learned that Orlando had gone to London and Paris to protest against his and Lloyd George's speeches and to demand that the Allies live up to the full term of their secret treaties, he was eager to know Lloyd George's response. He was clearly not sympathetic with either Italian war aims or the part that the Italians had played in the war.[60]

The Czechs and Slovaks both abroad and at home were deeply disappointed by Point Ten. They assumed that the Allied desire for victory had induced Wilson to accept mere autonomy of the nationalities rather than complete independence. They regarded the pronouncements of both Lloyd George and Wilson as not only moral failures, but also as diplomatic and military mistakes.[61] Within Prague itself, the radicals who had believed that the Entente powers were committed to the dissolution of the Habsburg state were deeply agitated. In the United States, the Bohemian National Alliance was also deeply concerned over Wilson's further retreat from the position of declaring himself in favor of the aspirations of the Czechs and Slovaks.[62] Yet it was confronted by a rather delicate situation. How could it indicate its opposition and at the same time not antagonize the White House?

Wilson was particularly anxious about the response of the Central Powers to his speech. An elated House, who had analyzed the official and public responses from German and Austrian papers, reassured him. It "looked" to House as "if the chasm which they were trying to create by this speech was more successful than they had dared to hope."[63] Austrian workers had gone on strike and had used the war-aims addresses of Wilson and Lloyd George as a basis for demanding a discussion of peace. The reaction in Vienna was generally favorable.[64] There were of course many reasons for this. The most important were the bare realities of war, which by January 1918 had had a cataclysmic impact on Austro-Hungarian life. The nation had suffered nearly two million casualties on the Eastern Front. The army was exhausted, the internal situation confused, and Germany's firm grip over the monarchy's policy unshaken. With the Hungarian refusal to send food to German Austria and elsewhere, the people were starving and clamoring for peace. Furthermore, the Soviet publication of the various secret treaties was now known throughout Europe.[65] If the Austrian government accepted Wilson's tenth point, it might well force Wilson to persuade his Allies to abandon the Treaty of London.

Given these considerations, Czernin had returned hurriedly from the peace negotiations at Brest-Litovsk on January 22 to answer Wilson's speech in the friendliest terms.[66] He declared that he could accept Wilson's proposals "with great pleasure." He reiterated that he had demanded from Russia "not a spare meter, not a penny," that his negotiations had been based strictly on the principle of no annexations and no indemnities.[67] To Czernin, Wilson's program contrasted strongly with the terms now self-evident in the Treaty of London. He was convinced that Wilson had spoken honestly and sincerely. As he later wrote eloquently: "A new star had risen on the other side of the ocean, and all eyes were turned in that direction. A mighty man had come forward and with one powerful act had upset the London Resolution and in so doing, had reopened the gates for the peace of understanding."[68] Not surprisingly, it was Meinl who conveyed the news of Czernin's willingness to enter into conversations to the American legation at Bern.[69]

In the meantime, Count Ladislaw de Skrzynski, Counselor of the Austrian legation at Bern, had informed the British War Cabinet that Vienna approved many of the points in the speeches of both Lloyd George and Wilson, and that some of these might well provide the basis for a successful discussion. Skrzynski indicated that Czernin was ready to come to Switzerland to meet Lloyd George, if he would agree to a meeting. The British government interpreted this information as a bona fide, serious approach for negotiations. Although Lloyd George felt personally unable to meet Czernin—since such an interview would be regarded as tantamount to the initiation of negotiations for peace— he suggested a Smuts-Czernin meeting.[70]

Lloyd George thought that the whole situation had undergone a considerable change since the war-aims speeches of Wilson and himself. He believed that Czernin and Kühlmann were acting in concert and were meeting with opposition from the German military commanders, Marshal Paul von Hindenburg and General Erich Ludendorff. Given this split between the civil and military authorities, he believed that Smuts might be able to drive a wedge into the gap separating them. Moreover, "the verdict of the future and probably even of contemporary history would strongly condemn a government which had failed to take any notice of so important an overture."[71] Yet for over a week the War Cabinet continued to temporize. It was unwilling to appear too eager, and Balfour had asked that the matter be postponed until after Orlando's visit. In the meantime, once Czernin had delivered his speech, it became clear that he had suggested a conversation with Wilson's representative rather than London's. Obviously there was now some question as to whether the moment was favorable for a British approach to Vienna through Smuts. Notwithstanding, the War Cabinet decided to telegraph Wilson of its desire to resume the conversations, if he agreed.[72]

So it was that by the end of January the stage was set for a new round of peace negotiations. To Colonel House the situation looked "as if things were at last beginning to crack." To his diary, he confided: "I hope the Entente will keep still and not do anything, for past experience makes one fearful lest they do the wrong thing. . . . The situation is so delicate and so critical that it would be a tragedy to make a false step now."[73]

8

Building a Bridge between
Vienna and Washington

Almost inevitably, Switzerland became the "psychic center" of the war. Because of its geographical location and neutrality, Switzerland literally swarmed with the agents, emissaries, and spies of all tribes and nations. Frequently, each of the foreign offices and war departments of the various countries had its own set of intelligence officers—often unknown to each other—spying on the enemy and sometimes on another department of its own government. This was sometimes carried on by the representatives of the heads of governments themselves. For instance, Smuts came to Switzerland to negotiate with Mensdorff as the personal representative of Lloyd George and without the knowledge of many of the British War Cabinet. Mensdorff's position was similar to that of Smuts. Given these conditions, the American legation in Switzerland, regarded by Lansing as "the most important post in Europe," carried an almost insuperable burden. It was the only post from which to observe Austria-Hungary, Bulgaria, Poland, and occupied Rumania; the nearest point for observation of the distant lands of Turkey; and well placed for observing Germany and German affairs, particularly southern Germany. Gathering information included following the press of various countries and interviewing travelers, emigrés, and neutral diplomats. It meant establishing secret services and intercourse with deserters and with those ready to betray their countries for gain or through conviction. Thrust into the flank of Eastern and Central Europe, the American legation thus had the responsibility of keeping the President informed of events throughout this wide area.[1]

During the winter and spring of 1918, while Minister Pleasant A. Stovall was absent from Bern, Hugh R. Wilson, the American Chargé, headed the legation. Stovall, the owner and editor of the *Savannah Press*, had revealed little insight or ingenuity during his tenure in Switzerland.[2] Hugh Wilson, however, had an excellent reputation in the State Department. In early 1918, the Bern legation was flooded with telegrams from Washington clamoring for information. Wilson's solution to this avalanche was to propose the establishment of a historical data committee to take up the questions of European nationalities and to synthesize and systematize international information for the State Department and especially for the President and his Cabinet. Hugh Wilson was satisfied that this information was absolutely necessary to insure a Wilsonian peace and the "existence and development of the society of nations."[3] Both the President, who had expressed the keenest satisfaction with both the Swiss legation and Hugh Wilson's personal work, and Lansing agreed.[4]

It was not long before Hugh Wilson made the acquaintance of Dr. Stefan Osuský, who headed the permanent Czecho-Slovak center in Geneva. Wilson was impressed with Osuský's burning patriotism and, most important, his value as a source of information on the politics and policies of the Dual Monarchy. Gradually, Wilson became aware of the magnitude of Czech efforts. Osuský introduced Wilson to Beneš, whom Wilson found to be deeply sincere, a "man of tireless energy" and "great penetration."[5] Osuský also introduced Wilson to Captain Voska, then in the Military Intelligence Division of the American army, who provided useful information on Central Europe.[6]

When Hugh Wilson met George Davis Herron in the spring of 1917, he immediately saw his value as an American negotiator, not only because he was the most suitable man on the spot at the crucial moment, but also because he had a wide group of acquaintances in intellectual and political circles within the enemy empires who consulted him whenever they came to Switzerland. A pacifist preacher and a socialist internationalist, Herron had spent the major portion of his life in radical criticism of the public order and had given his life to the advocacy of peace. Born of devoutly religious parents, he received the Doctor of Divinity degree and became convinced of his destiny to devote his life to religious pursuits and to play a messianic role in the regeneration of the world.[7]

Herron had written a variety of books in the field of applied Christianity, which tended toward a progressive interest in politics. About 1914 he was living very quietly near Geneva, writing articles for various journals on political and ethical subjects and maintaining an extensive correspondence with persons of like mind.[8] By the summer of 1917, Herron was recognized in Europe as the spokesman for both President Wilson and America. Wilson himself, upon reading Herron's book entitled *Woodrow Wilson and World Peace*, had been amazed at Herron's "singular insight into all the elements of a complicated situation and into my own motives and purpose."[9]

Although Herron had never met President Wilson, he had fallen under the spell of his personality and took him at his word "as implicitly as an early Christian Apostle took Jesus at his word."[10] To Hugh Wilson, Herron's fervor, whether enthusiasm or invective, seemed to carry "the conviction of sincerity of an Old Testament prophet." Not only was he able to convince enemy subjects of the crusading spirit, of the purity of purpose, and of the lofty ambition that animated the American spirit in the war, but the President himself evinced a genuine trust and "entire confidence in Herron's integrity."[11] Once Hugh Wilson recognized the value of Herron's information, he invited him to receive the various missions that came to Switzerland from Germany, Austria, Bulgaria, and elsewhere and carry on conversations or negotiations with them on behalf of the State Department and the legation. Because Herron shared President Wilson's belief in the possibility and hope of a negotiated peace, he was eager to comply.[12]

Herron's deep interest in a separate peace, particularly with Austria-Hungary, did not prevent his consideration of movements toward the complete independence of subject nationalities. Yet Herron recognized that the only hope of detaching Austria from Germany lay in assuring it of the integrity of the Empire. This, however, did not rule out the possibility of federalizing it. While he gave full and unqualified assent to the Wilsonian idea of self-determination, he believed that it was not the greatest war aim. The most important goal was the defeat of Germany, which he regarded as the epitome of evil.[13] However, as early as January 1918 Herron eloquently expressed his confidence in the Czech nationalist movement. He regarded the Czechs as "the one people who seemed . . . to pursue a straight and honorable and consistent course, throughout the whole period of the war and the peace conference." Osuský had played the major role in convincing him of the stability of the Czech organization and goals.[14]

Herron participated in the most colorful, important, and tragic of the Austro-Hungarian negotiations for peace with Heinrich Lammasch of Vienna. A venerable figure of unquestioned integrity, well known to students of international law throughout the world, Lammasch had been a tutor to Emperor Charles and continued to exercise considerable influence over him intellectually. Lammasch was a devoted advocate of a democratized Austro-Hungarian confederation of autonomous units. When, late in January 1918, Lammasch told Herron that he wished to see him to deliver a most important message, Hugh Wilson was deeply interested because he knew of Lammasch's reputation. Moreover, Meinl had arranged the initial overture for the conversation.[15]

Meinl served as emissary between the Emperor and Lammasch, who was then sick in Zurich. Lammasch, in turn, had charged Dr. Benjamin de Jong van Beek en Donk, former Director of the Ministry of Justice in Holland and General Secretary of the Association for a Durable Peace, to make the immediate arrangements for the meeting with Herron. The State Department knew Lammasch as a "devoted adherent of the idea of a democratized" and federalized Austria.[16] Actually, in August 1917, the Emperor had offered the chancellorship to Lammasch, who had refused because he believed the time was "not ripe to put his ideas into execution." Apparently Charles was again urging Lammasch to accept the task of forming a Cabinet. Lammasch would only accept under the explicit condition that Austria "should not negotiate for peace through Prussia but should make a separate peace." Although the Emperor had accepted these conditions "unreservedly," Lammasch's health prevented his immediate acceptance. In these circumstances, plans had to be made with great secrecy because of the omnipresence of the spies of all belligerent governments and of Czernin's personal spies. Herron believed that Czernin's response to Wilson's Fourteen Points Address had been insincere and that the Emperor had given him no choice but to speak as he did or to resign.[17]

Meinl's telegram to Lammasch stated the general conditions necessary for Austria-Hungary to negotiate a separate peace with the Allies through American mediation. Lammasch confided that Meinl's telegram revealed only one-tenth of the real truth, which would never have passed the censor. When questioned on details, Jong reported that there were two parties in Vienna: one represented by Lammasch, the other the reactionary court party. The Emperor was now apparently prepared to break with all his former associates and cast his lot with "a nation founded on consent of the governed."[18]

During the next few days Herron had a series of conversations with Jong, who presented a rough draft and clarified the principles supported by the Emperor. Lammasch then requested a meeting to assure President Wilson of the authenticity and accuracy of the message and to give a full statement of the Emperor's views. Meeting at Château Hofgut, the home of Dr. Wilhelm von Muehlon, a German friend, in the town of Gümligen near Bern, Herron was delivered there in Hugh Wilson's automobile, with the blinds drawn and accompanied by an armed guard.[19] Within the next few hours behind locked doors, Lam-

Heinrich Lammasch (Bildarchiv der Österreichischen Nationalbibliotek,
Vienna)

masch outlined to Herron the confidential message from Emperor
Charles for President Wilson alone. Lammasch corroborated Herron's
view that Czernin was not to be trusted and that the Emperor had
forced him to make the speech of January 24. Charles now desired to
lay his plans confidentially before the President. He wanted Wilson to
recognize publicly that Czernin's recent speech demonstrated Vienna's
desire for peace in accordance with Wilsonian principles. The Emperor
would then reply by letter to the Pope, expressing his desire to implement the Wilsonian concept of self-determination within the framework of the Dual Monarchy, as suggested in the Fourteen Points. The
Emperor also promised to assure the Pope of his enthusiastic support
of both disarmament and a league of nations established on the principles expounded by President Wilson. Were Wilson to propose all these
things to him as a condition of peace, the Emperor gave his word that
he would accept it. Austria would then present these terms to Germany and demand their acceptance; if the latter refused, Austria was
ready to make a separate peace. This was his plan for "building a
bridge between Vienna and Washington." Thus concluded the first
conversation.[20]

Herron was unimpressed. He saw the Emperor's proposal as an
effort to use the United States and the Pope as a means of restoring the
Holy Roman Empire in modernized form. Although Lammasch
emphasized that "never before in history had the world so looked to a
nation as it now looks to America," or to a man as it "now looks to
President Wilson and has never trusted a man as it trusts President
Wilson," Herron reluctantly came away with the feeling that "we must
let Austria wait."[21]

On the next day, Herron urged Lammasch to persuade Charles to
act alone upon his own initiative and assume the moral leadership of
Europe. He would then put himself beside President Wilson upon the
same platform and "compel the issue of the war in a spiritual victory"
that would prove redemptive to all nations. Herron assured Lammasch
that both the Austrian people and the "whole America as with one
great voice would join him." Herron's appeal touched Lammasch
deeply, both as an academician and as an eminent Christian in the
Catholic church. His conscience was aroused; he promised that he
would try to convince the Emperor of the need for this great initiative.
All that he asked was that Wilson should publicly take notice of Czernin's speech, which the Emperor himself had dictated. Herron promised to submit this request to the President with his endorsement.[22]

The State Department's decision not to inform the French and

British of the Herron-Lammasch discussions revealed its concern over the lack of unity of policy between the United States and the various Allied governments regarding peace. The President confessed to House that he was disturbed by the letters from Europe emphasizing the reluctance of Allied leaders to follow him and insisting that peace was none of his business. To Wilson, these criticisms simply furnished additional arguments for showing how "each item of a general peace was everybody's business."[23] As for Italy, Wilson thought that its response might be "merely the resentment brought about by the prospect that, without our support, Italy cannot get what she went into the war, on cold-blooded calculation, to get."[24] Wilson also disagreed with Lloyd George and Balfour who had been unimpressed with Czernin's response to his war-aims speech.[25] Wilson became more deeply disturbed when he learned that the Supreme War Council on February 4 had issued a statement from Versailles that completely rejected whatever specific peace overtures appeared in the speeches of both Czernin and the German Chancellor, Count Georg von Hertling, who had replied to Wilson on January 24.[26] Clemenceau and Lloyd George had, in fact, drafted the statement. Wilson saw "infinite stupidity" in this action, while House called it a "monumental blunder."[27] When Wilson had given his active support to the creation of the Supreme War Council, he had never intended it to express any opinion on political subjects. Unburdening his anger to Lansing, Wilson stated: "These people have a genius for making blunders of the most serious kind and neutralizing each thing that we do."[28] In these circumstances, Wilson felt it "more necessary than ever" to offset the declaration of the Supreme War Council by addressing Congress again on war aims in answer to Hertling and Czernin.[29]

On February 7, the cables from Bern filled with the Herron-Lammasch conversations began coming into the State Department. All seemed to indicate the desire of Austria for a separate peace with the United States and the Allies. Hugh Wilson, who saw the Emperor's proposal as a "vast step in advance for all oppressed racial units of Austria-Hungary," did not see how the United States could lose by a declaration such as the Emperor desired.[30] Lansing, who had met Lammasch personally at The Hague in 1910, spoke highly of his sincerity and integrity and told the President that his overture represented authentic evidence of Austria's desire for a separate peace and the Emperor's wish to "reestablish the Empire on democratic principles."[31] On the same day, Balfour sent a secret message to the President, which in part seemed to allay the substance of what had been given out by the Supreme War Council. Balfour pointed out that the Austrian public was becoming impatient with the prolongation of negotiations with Russia without results; that Czernin was understood to favor a separate peace but wished a pretext for breaking with Germany; and that the Austrian Emperor, fearing the "Red Wave," also desired a speedy peace. Moreover, tension between Austria and Germany was greater than ever before. The Germans were furious with Czernin for having responded in such a conciliatory way to Wilson's address. Balfour thought that if Austria could be assured of financial help from the United States in case of a separate peace, public opinion would force the issue. He especially emphasized the importance of the United States as a desirable intermediary. However, he warned Wilson to remember that any rumor of negotiations in Vienna on the basis of an undivided Austria not only caused great alarm in Italy but was also used by the Austrian diplomats as proof that the Entente had abandoned the cause of all the subject nationalities under the Habsburg rule, a view "which greatly reduced our friendships and heartens our enemies."[32]

The American Congress was greatly surprised when, on February 11, fifteen minutes before the session opened, the President sent a message that he wished to address a joint session. Lansing had been aware of Wilson's intention for less than an hour.[33] In the first half of his speech, Wilson drew incisive contrasts between the stands of Vienna and of Berlin on war aims. He applauded the "very friendly tone" of Czernin's speech and the hints of further discussion. Aware of the substance of the Herron-Lammasch conversations, he assumed that the Cabinet in Vienna agreed with him in the matter of constitutional reorganization for the satisfaction of minority aspirations. He acknowledged that the Fourteen Points were only a "provisional sketch of principles" and might not represent the best or the only foundation for a durable settlement of the war. Nevertheless, he emphasized that self-determination was not "a mere phrase" but an "imperative principle of action, which statesmen will henceforth ignore at their peril." Yet the context of his address made clear that his interpretation of self-determination was "consent of the governed," or self-government, and not necessarily independence. Wilson also observed that Czernin would probably have walked farther along the road to peace if he had not been embarrassed by dependence upon Germany. Clearly this was a none too subtle effort to accelerate the rising antipathy to Germany then prevalent in the Empire. Wilson concluded by indicating that the test for any further comparison of views for either government rested upon its willingness to apply four principles: first, the final settlement of each particular case had to rest upon essential justice and the adjustments that most promised permanent peace; second, "Peoples and provinces are not to be bartered about from sovereignty to sovereignty, as if they were mere chattels and pawns in a game"; third, territorial settlements had to be made in the interest and for the benefit of the populations concerned, notwithstanding the claims among the rival states; and fourth, all well-defined national aspirations should be accorded the utmost satisfaction without introducing elements that might ultimately break up the peace of Europe and the world.[34]

Within the next few days, House heard the response of the minority nationalities, and particularly the Czechs, to both Wilson's recent speech and his Fourteen Points Address. André Chéradame wrote at length indicating the dangers. Seton-Watson, who had already impressed upon House the risks of negotiating with Austria, sent him a memorandum clearly supportive of the aspirations of the Empire's minorities.[35] On February 13, Charles R. Crane came to call. Voska, too, visited both House and the State Department, where he was informed of the Emperor's unofficial proffer of peace and Lammasch's peace proposal. Voska, who had never heard of Lammasch, offered to investigate the attitudes of Masaryk and the Czecho-Slovaks and to write a report for Wilson within a few days. Thereupon he consulted with Chéradame for three days and nights on a report designed not only to express Masaryk's possible criticisms, but also "to blow the Lammasch plan out of the water." For about two weeks, Voska dropped nearly everything else and talked to people influential within the administration. He then turned in his report.[36] Apparently he was greatly heartened by his interviews and felt more certain than ever that the Allies intended to break up the Habsburg Empire. Spring Rice had told him that he considered the Lammasch plan of little importance. Richard Crane and his colleagues in the State Department felt that the more Wilson studied the plan, the less it would impress him. When George Creel finally dismissed it with a shrug, Voska considered the incident closed.[37]

However, both Wilson and Lansing were very interested. That interest was confirmed by a message sent to Hugh Wilson at Bern on February 15. Apparently in response to Balfour's suggestion, Lansing asked Hugh Wilson to convey "secretly, unofficially and orally" to Lammasch or his agent that if Germany deprived Austria of financial support for trying to arrange a cessation of hostilities and negotiations for peace at the present time, Washington would help Austria obtain comparable financial aid in the United States.[38]

Hugh Wilson thereupon arranged for Heinrich York-Steiner, an Austrian who was a close friend, warm admirer, and political disciple of Lammasch, and a person known personally to Grew, to deliver the message to Lammasch in Vienna.[39] During the next few days, there continued to be encouraging signs that the Emperor would respond positively to Wilson's speech.[40] On February 15, Lammasch invited Herron to visit Vienna for a personal discussion with the Emperor. Every preparation had been made to enable him to journey incognito. Although authorized by the President to accept the invitation, Herron first waited to receive a reply to the suggestions he had laid before Lammasch. Four days later, Lammasch informed him that the Emperor had approved their discussion and would soon take appropriate action. Lammasch now considered "peace through America highly probable."[41] The imperial response sent on the same day, however, was not the one Herron had suggested. It was sent secretly from Vienna to King Alfonso of Spain for delivery to President Wilson through the Spanish Ambassador in Washington. As had happened so frequently in the past, British intelligence intercepted the secret message on February 20 and sent it on to Washington on the same day. Thus, Wilson had an additional period of grace in which to consider a reply.[42] On the following day, the sincerity of the Emperor's proposal was indicated by a note from Czernin to the Austrian Ambassador at Madrid: "If Mr. Wilson assents to the King's proposal and sends a representative to discuss matters with me, he should send someone who speaks either French or German as I do not know English well enough to discuss such weighty matters."[43]

At first reading, the Emperor's reply appeared to be a direct peace offer based upon a friendly acceptance of the four principles of peace that Wilson had laid down in his recent speech. However, it mentioned neither the Fourteen Points nor any consideration of self-government for the peoples of Austria-Hungary. Little mention was made of territorial problems, and nothing was said of German claims. There appeared to be no willingness to concede any of the Italian claims. In effect, the proposal was for a general peace based on the status quo ante rather than a separate peace.[44]

Prior to the arrival of the Emperor's secret message, Lansing had advised Wilson to give the text of the expected message to "our principal cobelligerents" so as not to "arouse any suspicion or cause any offense among the Allies."[45] After attending church on Sunday morning, February 24, Wilson and House decided to seek Balfour's opinion concerning a reply to Charles. Wilson then typed the cablegram on his own typewriter. At the same time, he asked Balfour how far it was "necessary to go in apprising the Entente Governments of the character of the message from Austria."[46]

The next few days were filled with deep concern and excitement. As House confided to his diary, "No one can know the amount of discussion the President, Lord Reading, Sir William Wiseman, Lansing, Gordon Auchincloss and I have had concerning what action the President should take regarding this note from the Emperor of Austria and what attitude he should assume toward the Entente in regard to it." It was "one of the most delicate and difficult situations" House had confronted.[47] He therefore remained with Wilson, who wished to make a decision promptly. They were both inclined to encourage further discussion. Wiseman, however, begged them to await Balfour's views.[48] Yet Lansing, after conferring at length with House and later with Wilson, saw "no peace in sight."[49]

On February 26, the Spanish Ambassador delivered the note from Emperor Charles. According to House, Wilson had "difficulty in composing his face and trying to look surprised," especially since he had already written a reply the night before. House described Wilson's reply as noncommittal.[50] Two days later, Wilson asked House to show the note to Lansing while he discussed the Austrian communication with Jusserand.[51] Both Lansing and House were greatly surprised over Wilson's speedy action. Although not too happy with Wilson's proposed reply, Lansing was pleased that he had agreed to leave out any intimation in the note that he would accept a substitute for any of his fourteen war aims. Deeply concerned about the effect of apparent secrecy upon the Allied representatives, Lansing begged Wilson to give them copies of the Austrian communication.[52] As Lansing fretted, Balfour's response arrived. Balfour found little in the Emperor's proposal that could be reconciled with Wilson's public declarations on peace terms. He feared it was a "German scheme concocted at Berlin."[53] On the other hand, he was "profoundly impressed" with the Herron-Lammasch conversations, which had been sent to him by the British Minister in Bern. He believed they represented the opinions of the Emperor himself, unaffected by German influence. Yet he found two objections even to these: first, they ignored Italy; and second, the proposition might well alienate the subject races of Austria "whom PRESIDENT desires to benefit." He saw the future of the war as depending largely on supporting both Italian enthusiasm and the anti-German zeal of the Slavic populations of Austria. He perceived both the Italians and Slavs as very easily discouraged and quick to find evidence that their interests were being forgotten or betrayed. More-over, Balfour feared that Austrian statesmanship would not be above using any sympathetic response from Wilson as a means of convincing the Slavs that they had nothing to hope for from the Allies and had best make terms with the Central Powers.

Nevertheless, since some risks must be run, Balfour advised that if Wilson wished to keep open the door to further discussion, then he should investigate the Lammasch conversations to see if the Emperor was prepared to treat them as a basis of discussion. While Balfour saw no reason to conceal the Emperor's letter from the "great belligerents," he advised that if Wilson should decide to follow up the Lammasch-Herron line, he should simply tell the Allies very confidentially that he was carrying on informal conversations with Austria and would com-municate with them further if the occasion arose.[54] In a private and wholly unofficial conversation with Page, Balfour reiterated his concern over the Italian response to separate peace discussions between the United States and Austria. If this information "leaked out" and was made known by Germany, Italy might abandon the war. Again Balfour admitted that while the Treaty of London was "regrettable," nev-ertheless Great Britain and France were "honor bound" to it, and he saw no way in which it could be "overcome to square with the Presi-dent's just conditions of peace."[55]

Despite Balfour's less than enthusiastic response, Wilson replied that if the Emperor's message indicated "a genuine desire to meet the just demands of the Allies, it ought not to be rejected."[56] He then forwarded to the Emperor his reply, which he had typed himself to insure secrecy. Expressing his pleasure over the Emperor's acceptance of his four principles as a basis for formulating the conditions of peace, Wilson asked the Emperor for as equally explicit a program implement-ing the four principles for peace as the one that he had laid out in his Fourteen Points Address. Assuring Charles of his willingness to con-sider any solution offered, Wilson then asked him to define his attitude toward the Balkans, the national aspirations of the Slavic peoples, the Adriatic question, just concessions to Italy, and the protection of the non-Turkish peoples subject to Turkish rule. Wilson reiterated that he sought "no strategic advantage nor any advantage of a personal nature but a just settlement which will confer on the world a just and lasting peace."[57] On March 1, Wilson instructed Lansing to inform the other major Allies about the communication from the Austrian Emperor, the general nature of his own reply, and his agreement with the Emperor's wishes that the exchange of messages "be personal and private."[58]

Although his associates feared that he might be playing into German hands by his conversations, Wilson was not "in the least afraid of walking into a German trap" or "playing into the hands of the pacifists and pro-Germans." He thought it would be "a pity to discountenance . . . all processes of diplomacy even in the midst of arms."[59]

While Wilson awaited the Emperor's response, the devastating news arrived on March 3 that Russia had signed the Treaty of Brest-Litovsk. As a result, eastern Poland, the Ukraine, Lithuania, Estonia, and Latvia were separated from Russia and taken over by Germany. The disastrous terms of the treaty contrasted sharply with the peace program that Wilson had outlined. According to Clemenceau, it was at this point that the war aims of the Entente changed from national defense alone to the liberation of the peoples of Eastern Europe.[60] Actually, on February 7, Clemenceau and Beneš had signed an agreement authorizing the organization of an independent Czecho-Slovak army in France. This action virtually bound France to the support of an independent Czecho-Slovakia and thereby to the dissolution of the Austro-Hungarian Empire.[61]

At the same time, the British War Cabinet was having serious second thoughts about the matter. The British had learned through Skrzynski that Czernin was ready to declare formally that Austria would discuss only her own affairs in any conversation she might have with England, America, and the Allies. Skrzynski had intimated that now was the moment to act against Germany, particularly in view of Kühlmann's recent public insults to Austria. He stressed Austria's need of financial help from America after the war, and he offered to furnish a written declaration regarding his earlier observations. He made it fairly obvious that Austria desired a separate peace. Lloyd George now became very apprehensive that Wilson's four conditions of peace could easily be interpreted as hostile to the Allies. His inclination was to tell Wilson that "we consider any such conversations dangerous" and follow up the messages from Skrzynski to "ascertain what was the real position."[62] The War Cabinet was obviously concerned about the wisdom of letting Wilson assume the role of negotiator, particularly since the British had had a mandate from their Allies. Their discussions resulted in a decision to investigate the earlier peace feelers to the British government.[63]

Lansing's deep anxiety over negotiating secretly with Austria was obviously not shared by either the British or the French, who were busy investigating their own secret peace feelers from Vienna. Czernin had clearly not put all his eggs in one basket. Toward the end of February, the French concluded fruitless discussions between Count Abel Armand, an intelligence officer of the French General Staff, and Count Nicholas Revertera, an Austrian diplomat.[64] The British War Cabinet also received still another message from Bern indicating Czernin's willingness to enter into conversations with an appropriate British agent. The War Cabinet recommended immediate investigation of the proposal. The question immediately arose as to whether Wilson should be notified of the impending action. After hearing divergent opinions on the matter, Balfour urged that Wilson be told everything with complete candor, thereby inviting reciprocity from him.[65]

On the following day, March 6, the War Cabinet received highly secret information through unofficial channels concerning Wilson's reply to Charles. Once again there was vacillation about policy.[66] Since Wilson's reply was satisfactory from the British point of view, some thought it might now be better to leave the matter in his hands and not investigate Austrian peace feelers. Yet upon further consideration, the War Cabinet concluded that the interest of the British Empire in this vital matter ought not to be entrusted to any other nation. Thus it agreed to adhere to the decision of the previous day.[67] Thereupon Balfour informed Wilson of the British decision to resume conversations with Austria. He assured the President that British action would not be "inconsistent with" or "harmful to interchange of messages" that Wilson was conducting with the Emperor of Austria.[68]

In the meantime, Italy had apparently got wind of the secret negotiations, and Orlando had left for London immediately.[69] Nevertheless, Balfour was not intimidated. He hoped that Czernin was prepared to discuss terms apart from Germany with an English Cabinet Minister. In that event, he intended to broach the matter with Orlando and, with his approval, to send Smuts to meet Czernin.[70]

On March 9, Smuts returned once again to Bern, accompanied by Kerr. The first discussion with Skrzynski appeared promising. Convinced that the Germans were prolonging the war because of annexationist ambitions, the Austrians now seemed prepared to negotiate a separate peace, withdraw from Prussian influence, and remodel their institutions on federal lines. However, within a week, British hopes foundered because of the Russian collapse before the German advance and the improved military situation for Germany in the West. Czernin may well have decided to abandon separate negotiations in order to see what terms military necessity or a new peace offensive against the civilian populations of the Allies might effect. Moreover, since the President's telegram had arrived in Vienna on March 8, Czernin may also have decided that it would be easier to do business via America, particularly as Wilson's general peace conditions required no sacrifices on Austria's part, and the United States was not bound by the secret treaties as was Great Britain. Whatever the reason, the Austrian mood appeared to have changed from peace to victory.[71]

While the War Cabinet was bemoaning the passage of diplomatic leadership to Wilson in the Austrian negotiations, Lammasch recognized the effect of the Treaty of Brest-Litovsk on the impending negotiations and decided to speak to the Austrian Parliament in order to bolster the spirit of the secret exchanges. He told the members that Austria had never been so close to an honorable peace as at that moment. The only danger threatening the country was "anarchy from East." This danger, however, could not be met in Russia or the Ukraine, but only by "fighting it in our own country—by fulfilling peoples' just desires, by giving nationalities [the] right to self-government, and by giving peoples bread, peace, and an opportunity for quiet work." He pointed out that if Wilson's program was now refused, the war would last for years. In defending a peace of compromise, Lammasch was by implication also defending the Emperor. He denounced the games of the Central Powers and the logic of Austria fighting to protect German control of Alsace-Lorraine. As his colleagues jeered, he implored them to work for peace and federation within the Empire before it was too late.[72] His passionate pleas were rejected. At the conclusion of his speech, the majority of the delegates rose and demanded victory instead of peace.

The German government was furious. Insisting that Lammasch was engaged in pernicious agitation against Germany, it demanded that Charles disavow him or face the prospect of German occupation of Vienna. The Austrian government was thus forced to announce a public tentative disapproval of Lammasch's negotiations. Lammasch, however, had announced that he would "fight to death to complete Austrian federation with autonomous states, complete separation from German policy, and a reorientation in accord with the Western Powers."[73] Lammasch and Charles appeared to be caught between the subject nationalities, who desired Austria's defeat, and the ruling nationalities, encouraged by the Treaty of Brest-Litovsk, who now dreamed of victory and annexation. Thus, there seemed to be little support for the Emperor's position.[74]

Actually, a struggle of tragic historical significance was taking place in Vienna. Herron learned the details in a visit with Count Ludwig Windisch-Graetz, a disciple and associate of Lammasch, who remained until the end an honest and self-sacrificing apostle of Austrian federalism. It seemed for a few days after Lammasch's return from the January talks with Herron at Gümligen that the very radical program to federalize Austria was about to be accomplished—a deed whereby Austria would become the microcosm of the United States of Europe. The program was substantially an adaptation of the Swiss cantonal system to the six or seven nationalities of the Austrian Empire, with a plebiscite reserved for the Italian Irredenta, and Trieste transformed into a free Hanseatic town and port. Under the first impulse of the report that Lammasch had so fervently presented, the Emperor asked Windisch-Graetz to prepare a constitution for the new confederation. The Count had previously prepared the way before Lammasch arrived at Gümligen by presenting to the Emperor, "with all the moral force he possessed," the necessity of breaking with Germany and creating the United States of Austria. He told the Emperor candidly and insistently that he must choose between reconstruction or dissolution. In cooperation then with Lammasch, Windisch-Graetz wrote a constitution for the expected federation.

But when this constitution was ready for the Emperor's signature and promulgation, he first asked to reflect for two days; six weeks later there was still no answer. Then began a lengthy drama of indecision and vacillation by the Emperor, and "treachery and stupidity on the part of all of those about him." One day Charles was ready to sign and promulgate the constitution—and to do the great deed; the next day he would defer action. For six months, this Hamlet-like debate with himself and his ministers proceeded. The opportunity was apparently infinitely greater than the man. It was an action that required great mental capacity as well as moral heroism; and, according to Windisch-Graetz, his Emperor was only "a poor weak thing," without either mental capacity or adequate force of character. It was the opportunity that comes once in a thousand years—an opportunity to change the course of history—and the man to whom the opportunity came was no match for it.[75]

President Wilson had received the complete report of the Herron-Lammasch conversations on March 8. He had found it a "very pregnant" document and had been deeply affected by Charles's reiterated desire for the reorganization of the Empire and his declaration that only Wilson could bring things to a head in Vienna.[76] He now waited in vain for a reply from Vienna. Although it was sent from Vienna to Madrid on March 23, Alfonso XIII of Spain, perhaps fearing to compromise Spain's neutrality, decided that he could no longer transmit Austrian messages. At this point Czernin intervened and had the imperial message recalled from the Austrian embassy in Madrid.[77] Just as Wilson was becoming tired of the procrastination of both the Spanish and the Austrian monarchs, the Emperor's message, intercepted by British intelligence, finally arrived in Washington unofficially in early April. The note was equivocal and did not differ greatly from the previous message. Again the Emperor suggested direct oral discussions between representatives of the two powers. Again he repeated that the only obstacle to peace that could not be solved by open discussion was the French and Italian "lust for conquest." If the President could induce both these states to renounce their plans of annexation, the Emperor believed he would render "the cause of universal peace the greatest service."[78]

By the time this message reached Washington, Germany had massed for the second Battle of the Marne, and Wilson was forced to "suspend the public debate over war aims and the secret parleys over peace conditions." It seemed to Wilson that "every man with any vision must see that the real test of justice and right action is presently to come as it never came before."[79] During the first week of the German general offensive, the British were wheeled back forty miles, and panic struck in Paris and London. As Czernin witnessed the initial German successes at the end of March, he apparently concluded that Austria's only hope for the future was to exist as a satellite of a powerful Germany. Stovall in Switzerland had arrived at this same conclusion many months before.[80] Balfour concurred in a note that reported recent British conversations with an Austrian agent and laid to rest any possibility of an immediate settlement. The manner in which Czernin had shifted his ground clearly "betrayed the weakness of [the] Austrian government."[81] Actually, once the German government had learned of the Herron-Lammasch conversations, it had treated the Austro-Hungarian Empire as a conquered and vassal province. It had ordered Vienna instantly to discontinue all further peace conversations and to disown Lammasch. No negotiations were held concerning the matter; Vienna was simply told what to do at once, without argument or equivocation. The German campaign against Lammasch had been "furious and murderous." It was clear that the Germans had determined upon his political extinction.[82] Czernin's position seemed to be for the moment secure. Backed by Germany, he refused to be dismissed. He was now in a stronger position than the Emperor himself. He was in effect acting as German viceroy. The troops of Austria-Hungary were now wholly commanded by German officers. Berlin virtually ruled Vienna entirely, as well as the much more willing Budapest.[83]

On April 2, after the initial German victories in the second Marne offensive in late March, Czernin felt that the time was ripe for a renewed effort to bolster Austrian morale and perhaps also to attempt a general peace along the lines of the Emperor's secret letters and the President's address of February 11, which he now proceeded belatedly to acknowledge. He also accepted the four principles as a basis upon which a general peace could be discussed. However, he questioned whether Wilson would be able to "rally his allies on this basis." He then revealed that before the western offensive, Clemenceau had actually attempted to initiate peace talks and had asked the basis upon which Austria was ready to negotiate.[84]

Czernin also intimated that on a previous occasion the Allies were willing to negotiate but had then changed their mind. He laid the blame for this change on various elements within the monarchy and singled out Masaryk and the Czechs for particularly scathing attack: "The wretched and miserable Masaryk is not the only one of his kind. There are also Masaryks within the borders of the Monarchy." Nevertheless, Czernin concluded his remarks optimistically: "Alas, the decisive struggle is at hand. All hands on deck. Then we will win."[85]

So ended Czernin's last speech as Foreign Minister. The Czechs responded to Czernin's insults by organizing a defiant demonstration of solidarity with Masaryk in Prague and proclaimed a solemn oath to resist until "our nation's freedom is in our grasp."[86] While the participants at home enthusiastically cheered Masaryk and Wilson, Czech propagandists abroad used Czernin's inadvertent tribute to Masaryk as propaganda to convince those who still were in doubt that Czech resistance to Habsburg rule was strong enough to call forth denouncement from the highest authorities.

However, Czernin's removal as Foreign Minister was not long in coming. His indiscreet revelations concerning the Armand-Revertera negotiations pitted him against Clemenceau. Having taken power with the promise to lead France to victory, Clemenceau was humiliated by the revelation that he had in fact begged Austria for peace. He immediately denied the story and, to support his denial, published a letter written by the Austrian Emperor to the French President, suggesting a peace on terms advantageous to France at the expense of Germany. The document, popularly called the Sixtus Letter since Prince Sixtus de Bourbon was the intermediary in its delivery, was authentic; but to pacify his German allies, the Emperor immediately denied the incident.[87] Czernin was apparently unaware of the Emperor's letter, which had promised his support of France's "just claims in Alsace Lorraine." So also were the Germans. Czernin insisted that Clemenceau had lied.[88] Emperor Charles denied his correspondence with President Poincaré and insisted that the French documents were forgeries.[89] However, when he finally admitted that he had indeed written some of the letters, a tragic story ended. A showdown occurred between the Minister and his Sovereign, with Czernin forced to assume blame for "his Majesty's blunder." He resigned on April 15, and the embarrassed Foreign Ministry declared the incident closed.[90]

The Sixtus affair had far-reaching repercussions on Austro-German relations. Charles, ordered to attend a conference with the Kaiser at Supreme Headquarters in Spa, Belgium, on April 15, was forced to apologize for his "wicked" letters and to promise not to conduct any further negotiations concerning peace. He also agreed to the German demand for the resignations of Czernin and Lammasch.[91] As proof of his good faith, the Emperor surrendered Austrian army control to the German High Command for twenty-five years.

Clemenceau's impetuous action in publishing the Sixtus correspondence ignited varied and intense reactions throughout the Allied capitals. Clemenceau himself felt that his own position was actually at stake because of Czernin's intimation that he had been secretly dickering with the enemy. It could only provide fuel for his political opponents, perhaps even force a Cabinet crisis, which he could scarcely permit, with the Germans only miles from Paris. Moreover, Clemenceau felt little responsibility for the negotiations, since they started long before he came to power and had been continued under his ministry with some reluctance. He was also concerned over Italian reaction, since Italy was always suspicious of any secret negotiations with Vienna. His action, therefore, brought forth applause from Rome and stimulated a strong nationalistic fervor in his people to win the war.[92]

The Czecho-Slovak National Council also regarded the Clemenceau-Czernin controversy of profound importance for its cause. Beneš interpreted the events as a "sentence on the Hapsburg Empire." Shortly thereafter, Clemenceau declared his willingness in principle to agree to the recognition of Czecho-Slovak independence and of the National Council as a de facto government. On April 11, 1918, the French government issued an official communiqué announcing that all the documents relating to the Clemenceau-Czernin incident were to be submitted to the Parliamentary Committee on Foreign Affairs. This was done a month later and led to declarations by Clemenceau that proved decisive insofar as French policy toward Vienna and the Czechs was concerned.[93]

The British War Cabinet was deeply concerned about Clemenceau's revelations, particularly since it had regarded the discussions via the Emperor as authentic. It feared severe political repercussions once the British public knew that the Allies had passed up an opportunity to consider serious peace negotiations. Actually, the British had pursued the negotiations up to the point of Italian refusal to cooperate. The War Cabinet discussed the advisability of publishing in Britain and in France a facsimile of the original document with the hope of sowing seeds of discord between Austria and Germany. However, it rejected such a course because "revealing the Emperor Karl as a traitor to his Allies and a liar to us . . . would finally close any avenue to a separate understanding between the Allies and Austria." It decided simply to announce to the House of Commons that "His Majesty's Government, after giving careful thought to the matter, considered that it was not in the public interest to have any public discussion on this subject."[94]

American reaction to the Clemenceau-Czernin affair was deep disappointment. On April 6, the first anniversary of the American declaration of war, Wilson had delivered a speech partly in response to Czernin's speech of April 4. Designed to bolster Allied morale, Wilson emphasized the brutality of the war and the autocracy of the Central Powers. He declared that, after the harsh terms imposed on Russia at Brest-Litovsk, the only American response possible was "force, force to the utmost."[95] Yet, despite the bellicosity of his speech, he had once again carefully refrained from attacking Austria specifically. He held the Germans alone responsible for the misfortunes of Russia and Rumania, despite the fact that Austria had seized Rumanian territory in contradiction to her own professions of a peace without annexations. Wilson also made no comment on the arrival of Austrian troops on the Western Front. There was still hope of resuming negotiations with Vienna.

That hope, however, was almost completely shattered by news of Clemenceau's "unpardonable blunder," which had "thrown Austria boldly into the arms of Germany." To Lansing, now "only a military victory on the western front" could "again open the door which Clemenceau has slammed shut."[96] Herron wrote graphically that Clemenceau had "delivered Charles and his Empire, bound and helpless, into the arms of the beast we are all fighting. Germany has not been served so well since the war began, diplomatically speaking, as M. Clemenceau has served her." He reported "a widespread conviction that the action was aimed as a secret blow at American diplomacy—at the President's hope of detaching Austria whose dismemberment England and France are now determined for."[97] Herron continued to interpret Clemenceau's action as symbolic of the great gulf that separated Wilsonian ideals from the ideals of France and her Allies. He urged the President to "combat their Scheme."[98]

Herron's informants also agreed on the "now inevitable dissolution of the Austro-Hungarian empire" and held the Czernin-Clemenceau controversy responsible. They saw the breakup as occurring either through a complete collapse of the whole political-social system, as in the case of Russia, with perhaps the impetus coming from Austrian Bolsheviki—or a "revolution of each of the several states," particularly the Czechs and the Yugoslavs. Herron was very much aware of the strength of the second possibility. The Czechs, he pointed out, were already in a state of active revolution, at least politically speaking. They now only awaited the opportune hour for action.

But, incurable optimist that he was, Herron was unwilling to give up hope completely, despite Clemenceau's "apparently fatal blow" to the President's policy. To him, any effectual program for preventing another world war rested upon Middle Europe and the existing Austro-Hungarian Empire. Even Charles had once said to a confidant that the reform of Austria-Hungary and its separation from Germany "would be a permanent political and moral defeat of Germany, and a defeat of the autocratic principles throughout Europe." Herron believed "we must hold fast even to the shadow of this hope, even looking and working for it where and when we have no hope."[99]

9

Growth of Support for Czecho-Slovak Liberation

In April 1918, the Congress of Oppressed Nationalities convened in Rome. It met at approximately the same time that the Clemenceau-Czernin feud was erupting over the Sixtus affair, while the Allies were frantically seeking some means of reestablishing an Eastern Front, and while the Czechs in Russia began to encounter serious difficulties in making their way to the Western Front. The purpose of the congress was to galvanize all secessionist forces in a common campaign against the House of Habsburg and to attempt a more precise definition of Italo-Yugoslav relations. The leaders of the oppressed nationalities had been profoundly disappointed in the solutions proposed for their peoples by the respective war-aims addresses of Lloyd George and Wilson in January. Herron had written that the proposal of "autonomy" had produced not merely a feeling of deep resentment among the exiles of the nationalities in Switzerland, but even "hatred" of Wilson.[1]

The plans and arrangements for the Congress of Oppressed Nationalities had been made at the Inter-Allied Conference on Propaganda in London in March 1918. In February 1918, Lloyd George had agreed to the establishment of the Department of Propaganda in Enemy Countries, with headquarters in Crewe House, under the directorship of Lord Northcliffe, who was responsible only to him. Northcliffe, along with Steed and Seton-Watson, the two codirectors of propaganda against Austria-Hungary, had arranged the London meeting.[2] The Allied representatives to the London meeting were all close friends of the Czechs and advocates of the policy primarily aimed at destroying the Habsburg Empire. They drew up an inter-Allied agreement on joint propaganda, which was officially approved by the three Allied governments.[3]

Steed, selected by Northcliffe to conduct propaganda on the Italian front, had successfully negotiated the agreement between the South Slavs and the Italian government for a conference of the subject races of Austria, to be held on April 8 in Rome, to plan the best means of inciting these peoples to revolt. He had adopted the ideas of Henri Moysett, a student of Central European affairs and the private secretary of the French Minister of Marine, who had argued in London that "the Allies must launch a 'war of ideas' on Germany." Steed, in turn, had urged a policy of breaking the power of Austria-Hungary by supporting and encouraging all anti-German and pro-Allied tendencies. Balfour had instructed the Ministry of Information to base its policy on the support and encouragement of all anti-German and pro-Allied peoples in Austria-Hungary—without promising them independence. The Allied propaganda offensive, conceived on quite a grand scale, went into action in early April under the supervision of a central inter-Allied commission set up at the Italian headquarters. The commission included representatives of the South Slav, Czecho-Slovak, and Polish exiles committees. Shortly after the launching of the first leaflet campaign on the Italian front, the first meeting of the Rome Congress convened.[4]

Crewe House alone was involved in the congress; the Foreign Office was hardly interested. While it was considered an aspect of Allied propaganda, the congress was not otherwise related to foreign policy, and the Foreign Office did not consider its resolutions to be official.[5] Similarly, while the chairman of the Rome Congress was the Italian senator, Francesco Ruffino, Sonnino refused to participate in the meeting out of fear that his presence would compromise the government and especially the Treaty of London. Italy refused to appoint official representatives to the congress or to recognize its resolutions.[6] The British were clearly following a policy of playing both ends against the middle, because they had still not determined upon a definite policy toward Austria-Hungary. Propaganda, with the objective of liberating the oppressed nationalities and dismembering the Habsburg Empire, might force the Empire to pursue a separate peace more quickly. If, however, this result was not achieved, the dissolution and collapse of the Empire would accelerate the liberation of its peoples. In any case, "no promise should be made to the subject races in Austria which we could not redeem: for example, we must not promise complete independence if the best we could get was autonomy." Thus, Balfour refused to shut the door to any possibility of peace with Charles by any definite promise about the independence of the oppressed peoples.[7] Clemenceau, with far deeper commitment, had also approved the plan and had lent a French officer to Steed for propaganda work. Steed, who had left on March 23 for Italy, had also been accompanied by aides presumably supplied by the Italian government. En route to Italy, he had visited members of the American embassy in Paris. His parting words to Sharp had been, "We have thirty-one million friends in Austria-Hungary and twenty million enemies, why not help our friends."[8]

The British delegates were Steed and Seton-Watson. The French representatives were Franklin-Bouillon and Albert Thomas. The Czechs and Slovaks were led by Beneš and Štefánik. There were representatives also for the Russian and Austrian Poles, the South Slavs, and the Rumanians. Other Italian politicians and public figures were there in addition to Senator Ruffino; one of them was Benito Mussolini, a passionate defender of national liberty for the Czecho-Slovaks and Yugoslavs. Nelson Gay, a wealthy well-known American who then resided in Rome, was the only American member of the conference. However, he made it plain that he had no official instructions.[9]

During the two days of deliberations in Rome, committees of the congress, meeting privately, devised plans to coordinate psychological warfare against the monarchy; to encourage the formation of autonomous armies composed of members of the subject peoples under the jurisdiction of the various national committees abroad; to recognize such armies as Allied cobelligerent forces; to grant these soldiers the same status as their own soldiers; to use these armies preferably on the Italian front against Austria; and to accord civilian members of the oppressed peoples residing in Allied countries the status of Allied citizens. The formal resolutions of the gathering denounced Vienna as the submissive tool of Berlin and demanded that the Allied governments include in their war aims the liberation of subject peoples of Austria-Hungary.[10] This Pact of Rome, as the public resolutions of the congress were called, could not be regarded as an official treaty, but rather a program, since the delegates to the congress were actually private persons.

Page in Rome kept the State Department fully informed about the progress of the meetings. Colonel Mervyn C. Buckey, the American Military Attaché in Rome, reported that the Allied purpose in supporting the aims of the Czechs and Yugoslavs was "to cause internal trouble in Austria, to cause disaffections among Austrian troops, and to obtain troops to fight in the Allied ranks against Austria."[11] Page also reported "a general feeling of disapproval" among Czechs in Bohemia because the United States had not openly approved the proceedings of the Rome Congress of Oppressed Nationalities. He added that the British mission there strongly recommended American recognition of the Czecho-Slovak movement within the next few weeks. However, his conversations with Sonnino were less positive. While Sonnino believed that anything tending to create disaster in Austria-Hungary and weaken her military power was advantageous, he thought that it was unwise to support a new declaration in favor of a "Jugoslav state with the dismemberment of Austria-Hungary which would make the latter fight desperately and would bring about possible amalgamation of Austria with Germany greatly strengthening latter."[12] Nevertheless, in view of the imminent Austrian offensive, Page urged Washington to take immediate steps to approve the liberation movement, since it would have a pronounced effect on the Slavic troops in the Austrian army.[13] In effect, Page's report forced the State Department to reconsider its policy toward the subject races.

In fact, the State Department had not been wholly satisfied with the soundness of its Austrian policy since the autumn of 1917. Certainly, from the very outset Albert Putney had urged the importance of supporting the aspirations of the subject races. He had influenced Lansing, who by October 1917 had begun to reconsider his Austrian policy. By the time of Wilson's Fourteen Points speech, Lansing believed that the dismemberment of the Austro-Hungarian Empire was necessary. Wilson, on the other hand, had continued to think in terms of autonomy for the subject peoples within an enlarged Austro-Hungarian federation. Inspired by Wilson's views, Mezes, head of The Inquiry, had sought information on the best possible means of establishing such a confederation. Yet, within The Inquiry at least one of the main experts on the nationalities problem, Robert J. Kerner, had already strongly endorsed the independence of the Czecho-Slovaks. He had been encouraged by a continuing flood of memoranda from Britain by Steed, Seton-Watson, and the historians, H. W. Temperly and Arnold J. Toynbee, as well as from Albert Thomas.[14]

House, who had strongly advocated the policy of seeking a separate peace with Austria-Hungary, had begun to have second thoughts and had become supportive of plans by the Committee on Public Information (CPI), headed by George Creel, to use American propaganda in Austria-Hungary as the "most effective weapon that the United States could wield in the war."[15] By the early spring of 1918, the CPI had drafted a complete memorandum on "awakening the deep enthusiasm and support for the Allied cause among the immigrants of the Austro-Hungarian peoples in the United States." Such a program envisaged removing the classification of enemy aliens from all the subject peoples, enabling them to volunteer or be drafted, and then keeping them together to ensure the "greatest possible increase of enthusiasm and determination for independence for their brethren abroad." Baiting of those who spoke languages other than English was to be stopped and attempts to compel citizenship authoritatively discouraged. Immigrant support was to be secured by propaganda in the public press and speeches before American patriotic meetings. Governmental cooperation was also to be provided in raising and financing such forces as the Polish National Army, the Yugoslav Volunteers at Salonika, and the Bohemian legions.[16] House approved the plan, and it was presented to Wilson.

The CPI program to distribute propaganda to Austria-Hungary had the special support of the Bohemian National Alliance and Emanuel Voska, who had visited the State Department throughout early 1918 and urged acceptance of his plans. About May 1918, Voska was assigned temporarily to the CPI and sent to Europe to do the things the Czechs and Slovaks had done in the United States: obtain military information, keep the channels open between the revolutionists in Austria and their associates in the Allied world, and help to break down the morale of the Austrian army. Among other things, he was to act as a liaison between the revolutionists in Bohemian territory and the Czecho-Slovak National Council in Paris. Appointed director of the Central European Division of the CPI, Voska had approximately two hundred men and women in the eastern sector of his territory and the same number working from the Netherlands. Voska was regarded as a man who "could be trusted absolutely." Indeed, Creel considered him to be "the greatest secret agent in the war, that's all!"[17]

As Masaryk was traveling across Siberia via Japan to the United States to aid in the propaganda effort there, Wilson was being deluged by his associates to support an intervention in Russia to reestablish an Eastern Front. Although he had rejected all Allied arguments, by late May he was beginning to weaken. His major advisers, except for the military, appeared to favor such intervention. Masaryk wrote in disagreement. Indeed, he advocated the de facto recognition of the Bolshevik government. Although aware of the weak points of the Bolsheviks, he was equally aware of the weakness of the counterrevolutionary groups and had no faith in the monarchical movement, the Cadets, or the Social Revolutionaries; he felt the same way about Semenov. Convinced that the Bolsheviks would maintain their power longer than their adversaries supposed, he was nevertheless hopeful that ultimately a coalition government acceptable to the Allies might be established in Russia. He urged the United States to weaken Germany by abandoning any thought of a separate peace with Austria and to aid in transporting the Czech corps in Russia to the Western Front.[18] He advocated extensive propaganda under American supervision throughout eastern Siberia. Finally, he specifically opposed lone Japanese intervention, which he feared would estrange Russia from all the Allies.[19]

Masaryk offered similar observations to Eugène Louis Georges Regnault, the French Ambassador in Tokyo, on April 15. Officials in Washington, Paris, and even his friends in London received his comments with considerable dismay.[20] Certainly, for various members of the State Department and even Wilson himself, the depiction of Lenin as "an honorable man" was decidedly at variance with the image portrayed by their official diplomatic representatives in Russia. When Long informed the Secretary of the Treasury of Masaryk's impending arrival, he described him as traveling in the interests of the Bolshevik government of Russia.[21]

By the spring of 1918, virtually all American diplomats in Europe had begun to urge support for the aspirations of the oppressed peoples. They were particularly sympathetic to the cause of the Czecho-Slovaks. Herron, too, began to change his attitude. He informed Hugh Wilson on April 19 that the Czechs were politically "already in a state of active revolution" and were "only biding their time, awaiting the opportune hour for action."[22] Hugh Wilson and Stovall now sought instructions in the event of an anticipated Austrian peace drive. How were they to respond? Stovall concluded: "Before long our representatives should have a clear understanding whether, as the Allies appear to wish, all negotiations and hope of detaching Austria shall be abandoned or whether as the President has previously indicated, a more favorable tone should be adopted to protect Austria."[23]

In the meantime, Steed's propaganda on the Italian front had been so successful that Slavic regiments had been replaced by non-Slavic troops that the Austrian generals had been holding in reserve in anticipation of an offensive. Moreover, Orlando had informed Steed that the reason for the German push on the British front was an Austrian ultimatum to Germany stating that unless she could have peace by the first of May, she could no longer hold the various elements of the Empire together. Steed believed that if propaganda among the subject races of Austria could be successfully continued, the Austrian commanders would not dare to risk an offensive.[24]

The British were urging as much Allied moral and material support as possible to the Czecho-Slovak National Council in its struggle against the Central Powers. They asked Washington to sign a general convention recognizing the existence of a single Czecho-Slovak army placed for political purposes under the authority of the Czecho-Slovak National Council.[25] Page in Italy also strongly recommended American public support for Allied activities in the movement of liberation for the oppressed nationalities. He sent a memorandum of the secret convention negotiated between Italy and the Czecho-Slovak National Council in Rome on April 21, signed by Orlando and Štefánik. Now that Czecho-Slovak units were taking part in the fighting on the Italian front, the Italian government had recognized the Czecho-Slovak army as an autonomous Allied army with supreme judicial, political, and military authority vested in the Czecho-Slovak National Council. Štefánik had informed Buckey that within the preceding two weeks 80 percent of the Slavic prisoners of war had voluntarily enlisted in the autonomous army and now formed in Italy the strength of about 12,000 men commanded by General Andrea Graziani. General Janin was the Commander in Chief of all the Czech armies, and Štefánik had been nominated second in command by order of Marshal Foch. Page reported that London was considering a similar and stronger convention, and that a second congress of "oppressed races in Austria" was to be held within the next three weeks in Paris, where it was probable that a provisional government with all appropriate functions would be organized.[26]

At this point, Masaryk arrived in the United States accompanied by Pergler, his American secretary. On his arrival in Chicago on May 5, he was greeted with a "spectacular reception."[27] He reached Washington on May 9, just as the Congress of Oppressed Nationalities issued its declaration in Rome. The failure of the peace negotiations with Austria-Hungary had now become apparent as a result of Clemenceau's indiscreet disclosures. The British were now seeking to inaugurate an intervention policy in Russia that rested upon the military and political cooperation of the Czech Legion. Hence they were pressing Washington to support a policy of sympathy and aid to the Czech liberation movement, and both Britain and Italy were in the process of negotiating formal arrangements for the recognition of a Czecho-Slovak national army under the authority of the Czecho-Slovak National Council.

While Lansing was seeking the formulation of a new Austro-Hungarian policy, the British and French were besieging him with appeals for intervention in Siberia and northern Russia, and the French were urging American support in the evacuation of the Czechs from Vladivostok to the Western Front. Moreover, Masaryk's arrival in Washington occurred when powerful friends in high places were exerting their influence to gain support for the Czecho-Slovak cause, and major newspapers in the country had come out in support of the Czech liberation movement.[28] Influential congressional leaders were also exerting pressure in support of Czecho-Slovak independence. Senator Williams, who was now publicly insisting on Bohemian independence, urged Wilson to tell an expected delegation of Bohemians that he would "look with the utmost favor on the efforts of the Bohemians to 'regain their old independence and liberty.' "[29] Wilson, who shared "the same sympathy with the Bohemians" that Williams felt, assured him that he would "speak sympathetically to them" when he had "the opportunity."[30] Other members of Congress were equally supportive. Both Representatives George H. Tinkham, Republican of Massachusetts, and Thomas C. Gallagher, Democrat of Illinois, called on Lansing to urge that recognition be granted to the "nationalities in Austria."[31]

Upon his arrival in Washington, Masaryk had reason to be exceedingly grateful both to the elder Crane, and to his son Richard, through whom he made the personal acquaintance of Phillips, Polk, Long, Baker, Lane, and, finally, both House and Wilson.[32] Charles R. Crane saw Lansing on May 6 and sought to arrange a Lansing-Masaryk meeting.[33] He also wrote to Wilson praising Masaryk as the "wisest and most influential Slav of our day" and asking him to "set aside a little time for a talk." Crane believed that Masaryk could "materially aid" the President "in a technical way" with "his world program."[34] Having already read Masaryk's memorandum of April 10 "with the closest attention," Wilson responded that he would not "attempt an interview unless something material" could be added to what that memorandum contained.[35]

At this opportune moment, Putney sent to Lansing his long memorandum on "the Slavs of Austria-Hungary," a comprehensive, legal, historical 236-page document, which placed greatest emphasis on the Czecho-Slovaks and the Yugoslavs. It stressed that not only would German control of Austria-Hungary be destroyed forever if the Slavs— a majority within the Empire—were given full political rights, but also that the creation of new national states on the ruins of the Dual Monarchy would provide an insurmountable "barrier" to German expansion and provide stability in postwar Europe, a view that Lansing had been tentatively considering since October 1917. Drawing heavily upon the views of Masaryk and the Polish and Serbian national leaders, Putney urged all possible support to the national minorities for moral reasons as well as reasons of expediency. He concluded with a summary of the arguments favoring American support of the aspirations of the Slavs of Austria-Hungary.[36]

On the day that Masaryk arrived in Washington, Lansing was in the throes of reconsidering American policy toward the subject nationalities. As he read Putney's report and reexamined recent developments in Europe, he became convinced that a change in policy toward the Habsburg monarchy was mandatory. The famous Clemenceau-Czernin imbroglio had created a new political situation that tied Austria-Hungary to Germany even more closely. Coincidentally, the Congress of the Oppressed Nationalities in Rome showed both the unity of the nationalities in their struggle for independence and the "clear desire" of all the Allies to support the aspirations of the Slavic peoples. Moreover, by May 1918, France had virtually recognized the Czecho-Slovak National Council as a de facto government, Russia had recognized the autonomy of an independent Czecho-Slovak army in Russia, and Italy had followed the French example in recognizing an independent Czecho-Slovak army on the Italian front. The London government was about to follow the example of its Allies. In addition, the Allies had independently assumed responsibility for promoting a program of propaganda within Austria-Hungary without Washington's cooperation. Moreover, by May 7, Rumania had signed the Treaty of Bucharest with the Central Powers. Thus, the situation in Central Europe was completely changed.

On the day after receiving the Putney memorandum, Lansing informed Wilson of the changed conditions in Europe resulting from the Sixtus letter and from the presumed Austrian overtures toward Italy. Germany, he wrote, was firmly entrenched in Austria. Given Emperor Charles's lack of power and courage to work for a confederative state, the whole structure of the Empire might give way as it had in Russia, with the possible Bolshevization of Austria. Lansing was convinced "unquestionably" that a "revolution or its possibility in the Empire would be advantageous." He believed that the German government's success in the disorganization of Russia by appealing to the national jealousies and aspirations of the different peoples under the Tsar's sovereignty was a strong inducement to employ the same methods in relation to Austria's various nationalities, regardless of whether the United States liked the method. Should we, he asked Wilson, "continue to favor the integrity of Austria" or "declare that we will give support to the self-determination of the nationalities concerned."[37] The policy he favored was obvious.

Wilson's position is more difficult to determine. He had just written the wife of Ignace Jan Paderewski that to declare a Polish Day was not "wise" at a time when there was "a movement among Americans of Bohemian origin . . . to take some active part against the Central

Powers, and questions are arising . . . similar to the . . . admirable and commendable purposes of the Polish peoples."[38] Wilson was reluctant to commit himself further to the Poles and thereby give the Czecho-Slovaks a reason for pressing their claims. While his letters to Madame Paderewski, to Senator Williams, and to Dr. Fisher all indicate sympathy for the national aspirations of the Czechs, they also reveal an unwillingness to commit the United States to anything more.

On May 10, Wilson summoned Lansing to the White House for a conference to discuss the whole range of problems concerning Central and Eastern Europe. With regard to the Austrian nationalities, Lansing's views apparently prevailed, for Lansing noted in his diary "Pres't . . . favors Slavic movement in Austria."[39] Wilson also agreed to a public declaration supporting the Austrian nationalities, but he continued to refuse an appointment with Masaryk.[40] The younger Crane was not even able to persuade Wilson to see his father, who wanted to explain the importance of a presidential interview with Masaryk.[41]

Although Lansing had urged a reconsideration of the nationalities question on the basis of the failure of peace negotiations with Austria-Hungary, Wilson had not yet authorized more than a public declaration of sympathy for the cause of the nationalities.[42] On May 11, Lansing cabled Page in Rome about the deep interest of the United States in the proceedings of the Congress of Oppressed Nationalities of Austria-Hungary. He instructed him to make known to the proper authorities that the aims of the Czech and South Slav peoples of Austria for "free and independent development" had "the earnest support of this government."[43] Lansing also sent Wilson the draft of a similar public statement in the United States, which he thought would have a "very great influence among a large body of our population."[44]

Lansing's cable to Page did not constitute a public announcement. Italy's response revealed that however favorable the United States was to the oppressed peoples, Sonnino regarded it as unwise to make any new declarations. He was willing to weaken Austria by exciting the Czecho-Slovaks with the hope of independence, or at least self-determination, but he was unwilling to encourage the Yugoslavs because of their relations with the Serbs, whose ambitions and claims overlapped those of Italy along the Adriatic.[45] After receiving Italy's "selfish" response, Lansing asked Wilson whether the department should "listen to Italy, knowing her motive and give no encouragement to the Slavs of the south?" He believed that a speedy decision must be reached, because if the suppressed nationalities of Austria-Hungary were to be aroused, the appropriate time seemed to have arrived.[46]

Meanwhile, the political storm in Vienna and Budapest continued. The Dual Monarchy was rocked by political disagreements and food shortages. Unity between the Czechs, Poles, and Germans appeared to be impossible. The Vienna *Arbeiter Zeitung* reported ninety-nine separate demonstrations in Vienna and lower Austria on May Day alone. Given this crisis, Stovall asked Lansing and House whether the psychological moment had not come for the United States to decide whether to "support the individual nationalities which want political freedom or whether . . . to continue to trust the intentions of the emperor?" Hugh Wilson was all for throwing American strength on the side of the oppressed nations. Stovall and Carl Ackerman, whose reports on Austria-Hungary for the *New York Times* had been received favorably by the State Department, supported these views.[47]

Within the next week, Lansing prepared the draft of a public announcement and sent it to Wilson for approval.[48] He had composed the memorandum with special care and had conferred with Phillips about it at least seven times. There were clear differences of opinion within the department. Although Long regarded the scheme of "fomenting" the Czecho-Slovaks "to revolt against Austria" as "utterly impractical," Phillips sought to strengthen the memorandum by changing the term "sympathy" to "support."[49] Phillips also discussed the issues involved with both Count Macchi di Cellere, the Italian Ambassador, and Lioubomir Michailovitch, the Serbian Minister, without indicating the department's intent to make a public statement. While di Cellere intimated that the use of the words "national aspirations" might be misunderstood in Italy as indicating territorial ambitions, the Serbian Minister urged the retention and even the strengthening of the term as necessary for Austrian consumption.[50] Lansing did not consult Masaryk, who was then out of town.

At this same time, the State Department was besieged with requests for intervention in Siberia by the British and the French. Long was increasingly concerned over the possibility of lone Japanese intervention not only in Siberia, but also in Manchuria. On May 18, two days after a luncheon with Masaryk, Long received word of a Japanese-Chinese exchange of notes on the German menace in Siberia signed on March 25. The Japanese Ambassador had handed Lansing a strictly confidential memorandum containing this information. In effect, these notes gave the Japanese a free hand to send troops into both Siberia and Manchuria to combat the alleged German menace and prevent the spread of Bolshevik anarchy. To Long, the notes permitted a Japanese "hegemony of the Far East—same as twenty-one demands—now for

Siberia." Deeply concerned, Long dashed off a memorandum to Lansing that apparently had been the product of some discussion among various underlings in the State Department. Noting the advance of Semenov in Siberia, Long suggested "that the Czecho-Slovak troops organized by Professor Masaryk would be most useful." He reported that 6,000 of them had arrived at Vladivostok, 50,000 were preparing to go to Archangel, and an additional 50,000 were in the process of organization. "Might not some of these be taken over by the United States Government and assisted by American officers in support of Semenoff?" asked Long.[51] Here was the germ of an idea that was to be modified, debated, and elaborated by various members of the State Department during the next weeks.

Although Masaryk's friends brought increasing pressure to bear, Wilson refused to see the Czech leader. Yet Masaryk seemed to have little difficulty in getting the ear of the lower echelon members of the State Department and even of Lansing himself.[52] Moreover, Charles R. Crane was actively involved in promoting Masaryk's appearance throughout the country to make his views known to the larger American public.[53] Thus Masaryk's opposition to current American policy in regard to Austria-Hungary received widespread coverage both in New York and in Washington.[54]

Given all the pressures for support of the subject peoples coming in from both abroad and at home, Wilson decided to go ahead with a public announcement of policy. On May 29, Lansing declared publicly that Washington had followed the proceedings of the Congress of Oppressed Races of Austria-Hungary and that the nationalistic aspirations of the Czecho-Slovaks and Yugoslavs for freedom had "the earnest sympathy of this Government."[55]

The State Department was flooded immediately with hundreds of telegrams from Czech, Bohemian, and Slavic groups throughout the United States, all thanking the government for "its expression of earnest sympathy with the aspirations of the Czechs for freedom."[56] Abroad, the declaration also met with widespread enthusiasm. The Allies quickly announced their association with Wilson's declaration.[57] At the same time, they pronounced themselves for "the creation of a united and independent Polish state." These simultaneous announcements made clear the Allied distinction between the independence of Poland and that of the other nationalities, since they extended only sympathy to the Czecho-Slovak and Yugoslav movements. Masaryk and others brought this distinction to Lansing's attention and asked him to reconcile the differences between the two statements. Lansing agreed.[58]

The Allied military propaganda committee in Italy gained as much mileage as possible from the declaration of May 29. On June 15, the long-awaited Austrian offensive was launched on the Piave. It failed, according to a communiqué from the Austrian High Command, because of revelations of Slavic deserters, who had apparently alerted the Italian command "in the nick of time."[59] The policy favoring the nationalities had begun to bring tangible results. Yet Wilson had adopted the policy without enthusiasm. His feelings were best explained in a conversation with Wiseman. Referring to the Austrian peace overtures, he said that it was "a thousand pities" that Clemenceau had acted as he did. While Wilson had no great sympathy for Emperor Charles, he did think that the Emperor had been seeking a means of breaking away from Germany, but Clemenceau's action had forced him into an even more permanent alliance with Germany. Deeply disappointed, Wilson told Wiseman that the United States now had "no chance of making a separate peace with Austria, and must look to the other way—the way which he disliked most intensely—of setting the Austrian people against their own government by plots and intrigues." He believed Americans "were not good at that work, and generally made a failure of it," but the "saw no other way." He intended to support the Czechs, Poles, and Yugoslavs.[60]

10

Early Complications for the Czech Legion

While the Americans and Allies conducted secret talks with Austro-Hungarian agents in Switzerland, events in Russia involving the Czecho-Slovak Legion played a crucial role in the evolution of Allied and American policy toward Austria-Hungary and the Bolsheviks. The British sought to secure the use of the Czech Legion for the reestablishment of an Eastern Front in Russia, while the Allies encouraged Japanese intervention in Siberia, in both cases with little regard for the approval of the Bolsheviks or indeed the United States. But these developments can be better understood against the background of the Czech Legion's efforts to leave Russia for the Western Front.

After the Czecho-Slovaks repelled the Germans at Bakhmach in mid-March, their troop trains began to move regularly toward Penza, some 300 miles southeast of Moscow, to begin the long journey across the Trans-Siberian Railway. Various Czech accounts indicate that the relations between the Czecho-Slovaks and the Russians had not only been correct but even cordial.[1] Lenin and Trotskii seemed eager to get the corps out of Russia as fast as possible, and Masaryk's negotiations with the Soviet government had convinced him that it was perfectly possible to do business with the Bolsheviks.[2] Nevertheless, no sooner had the corps actually begun its movement than serious obstructions appeared.[3]

According to Czecho-Slovak testimony, the Bolsheviks attempted to hire or to bribe the Czechs to enter Soviet service with the prospects of a later Soviet declaration of war against Germany. The Czecho-Slovaks rejected these efforts because they distrusted the Soviets and suspected German influence. Moreover, Masaryk had warned them strictly against interfering in Russian affairs. On March 21, the Omsk Soviet suddenly halted the Czecho-Slovak trains as they were proceeding eastward to Vladivostok. Fearful that "the Czecho-Slovaks might be used as counter-revolutionists and imperialists," the Omsk authorities wired a request to Moscow asking that the soldiers be sent to

France via Archangel. They then wired the Kazan Soviet that sixty trains of Czecho-Slovaks "armed to the teeth" were proceeding from Kursk to eastern Siberia. "To let them through is treason to the Soviet." Tsentrosibir, the Soviet government in Siberia at Omsk, insisted that the "echelons be disarmed and sent out by the way of Archangel." The telegram concluded, "You are hereby ordered to stop these trains at any cost."[4] In view of the chaos and confusion then existing in Siberia, Tsentrosibir was naturally alarmed at the prospect of an armed legion passing through the area. Moreover, "Comrade Stalin had informed them that only Soviet armed detachments could be permitted in the territories of the Soviet Republic and thus the Czecho-Slovaks must be disarmed."[5]

The Czecho-Slovak advance was also stopped at Penza. Four trains carrying 3,000 men had arrived; the other trains were scattered westward along the railroad at intervals of fifty to one hundred miles. Some 2,000 Bolshevik troops were stationed at Penza with considerable artillery commanding the town and the railroad. Vasilii Vladimirovich Kurajov, the President of the local soviet, informed Captain Vladimír Hurban of the first Czecho-Slovak train that he had orders from Moscow to hold the Czecho-Slovak movement, and he produced four telegrams sent by different officials at Moscow. One read: "Let the Czecho-Slovaks pass to Siberia, the sooner the better, their trains are filling the railroad station and paralyzing the traffic." The second said: "Order the Czecho-Slovak armies to encamp on this side of the Ural mountains, where there is plenty of bread, to await the organization of the Soviet armies. War will be declared against Germany in two or three months and the Czecho-Slovaks will be an essential help against the Germans." The third telegram stated: "Stop the Czecho-Slovaks at Penza. Do not let them pass further." The fourth one read: "Disarm the Czecho-Slovaks at once."[6] Actually, each one of these conflicting telegrams was the result of both the negotiations then being carried out by the Bolsheviks with the Germans and the British simultaneously and the fear of the Bolshevik authorities that the Czech corps would join either Semenov in the Trans-Baikal or the Japanese then threatening intervention in the east.[7]

The question of disarming the Czecho-Slovaks now became a serious one and contributed in large measure to the hostilities between them and the Soviet government. It is quite possible that German and Austrian influence was exerted to secure disarmament. DeWitt C. Poole, Jr., American Consul in Moscow, later reported that Foreign Minister George V. Chicherin had informed him personally that the

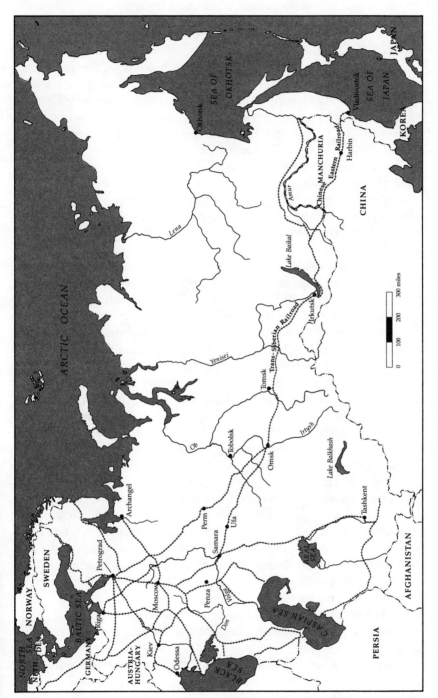

Map 1. The Russian Empire

135

Czech order had been the result of German pressure.[8] On the other hand, the Soviets may well have been apprehensive about the conduct of a well-armed and experienced force in the midst of so many political and military uncertainties. It is also possible that Trotskii's arrival in Moscow as Commissar for War on March 17 might have initiated a review of the arrangements made for the Czech forces to pass through Soviet territory.[9] Then, too, the general disorganization gave reasonable grounds for distrust among the unprotected and suspicious localities along the line of movement.

On March 26, a telegram from Stalin, Commissar of Nationalities, confirmed an agreement negotiated at Penza between the Czecho-Slovak corps, the Bolsheviks, and Vergé, the French liaison officer with the Second Czech Division. According to Captain Hurban's account, ten rifles and one machine gun were to be retained for each one thousand Czecho-Slovaks as a means of protection against lawless forces and counterrevolutionists.[10] All other arms were to be surrendered. Hurban explicitly confirmed this arrangement in later testimony, affirming that at the end of March Czech "relations with the Bolsheviks were still good and . . . to prove indisputably our loyalty, we turned over to the Bolshevikii everything, all our arms with the exception of a few rifles which we kept for . . . our personal safety."[11] In early April, an Associated Press dispatch reported that, on orders from Trotskii and the French Ambassador in Petrograd, the Czech corps in Penza had been disarmed, giving up its arms to the local Soviet authorities.[12] Other reports state no less definitely that the number retained was 30 rifles per 100 men. The Penza order was anything but popular with the Czechs who, to a large extent, evaded it successfully. They hid their rifles, cartridges, and hand grenades where they could under the cars and in partitions they had made inside the cars. Moreover, two whole regiments that had not yet reached Penza remained fully armed and refused to surrender a gun or rifle. Indeed, it was this retention of arms, including hand grenades, which made it possible for the Czechs to defend themselves later. Beneš himself admitted that after the Penza agreement, the troops with the Czecho-Slovak National Council's consent did not fully commit themselves to the terms, and Major Homer H. Slaughter, United States Assistant Military Attaché in Russia, later confirmed the legion's possession and use of these weapons.[13]

The telegram to the Omsk Soviet had instructed the Czecho-Slovaks to "proceed not as fighting units, but as a group of free citizens, taking with them a certain quantity of arms for self-defense against the attacks of counter-revolutionists." The Soviet authorities agreed to "help" them in every way possible as long as they remained on Russian territory, "provided they maintained an honest and sincere loyalty." However, they were ordered to expel "counter-revolutionary commanders immediately." New commissaries were to be designated to accompany the legion and protect them on their journey to Vladivostok, with instructions to inform the soviets en route "of everything connected" with their movement. Similar telegrams were to be sent by the Soviet of National Commissaries to all interested soviets. On April 9, after the Japanese landing at Vladivostok, the Soviet attitude hardened even more. Stalin ordered the complete disarmament of the Czech trains and their transportation in small groups at spaced intervals and "in no case all at once." Clearly aware that the Czechs considered themselves a part of the French army, he wanted them to understand that his instructions must be implemented "without hesitation." There was, he said, "no other way to do it."[14]

While on paper it appeared that everything had been straightened out, the reality was quite different. Neither the Bolshevik government nor the Czecho-Slovaks observed the specific promises of Penza. The local soviets were still ignorant of the purpose of the Czech movement to the Pacific; thus, as the Czech Legion traveled to Vladivostok, the trains were constantly halted by the local soviets of Samara, Ufa, Zlatoust, Omsk, and Chita, each soviet making new demands for further disarmament. Captain Jacques Sadoul of the French military mission in Russia reported the further aggravation of the situation by Communist agitators sent by the Bolshevik government to induce the Czechs to enter the Red Army.[15] The Siberian Bolsheviks also feared that the Czecho-Slovaks might join the counterrevolutionary bands of Semenov on the Manchurian frontier. Concurrently, while the Czechs were seeking to move as rapidly as possible to the east, Germany was clamoring insistently for the return of its prisoners from Siberia, who were needed badly on the Western Front. As early as April 21, the Krasnoyarsk Soviet received a telegram from Chicherin announcing that since Germany was expecting an attack upon Siberia by Japan, it wished a speedy evacuation of German prisoners from eastern to western Siberia or Russia immediately. He advised the Krasnoyarsk Soviet to give priority to the German movement and not feel compelled "to keep the Czecho-Slovak trains moving toward the east."[16]

Unquestionably, the circumstances under which the Czecho-Slovak army moved were difficult and trying in the extreme. From the Czech point of view, it seemed clearly to the Bolsheviks' advantage to have the

Czechs leave Russia as quickly as possible. Yet, the legion's boxcars and trains barely crawled along the vast railroad line. Moreover, the Bolsheviks were angered that there were still many former tsarist officers in the Czecho-Slovak military ranks. They believed that these officers were inciting the legion to oppose the Bolsheviks actively and propagating the view that Lenin and Trotskii were German agents who planned to return the legionnaires to Austria as deserters and traitors. In his memoirs, Trotskii later wrote that since the Czecho-Slovaks were under the command of counterrevolutionary officers and had Russian arms in their hands, he "put forward the condition that all arms be returned to the Soviets."[17] However, it must be noted that after the Penza act was signed, most of the imperial officers had disappeared.[18] Nevertheless, the few Russian commanders who remained after the March 26 order were strongly anti-Communist and very likely had considerable influence on their men, thus contributing to a stiffening of the Czechs' attitude against the Bolsheviks.

The Czechs blamed German propaganda and German influence at Moscow primarily for the development of friction but ascribed the immediate responsibility to the local soviets. The evidence is often conflicting. On the one hand, the Czechs cited the orders of the central authorities as favorable to the Czech movement, but described the central authorities as entirely dominated by the Germans. Similarly, while the official Czech account accused the local authorities of being hostile to the Czechs in disobedience to the instructions from Moscow, it also accused them of obstructing the Czech movement on orders from German-controlled central authorities. Yet Admiral Austin M. Knight, commander of the United States Asiatic Fleet, reported that the Vladivostok Soviet received the Czecho-Slovak echelons very well, and friendly relations prevailed until mid-June when tension developed, apparently due to news about Czech clashes with the soviets elsewhere in Siberia.[19]

Another grievance emphasized by the Czecho-Slovaks in blaming the Bolsheviks for initiating hostilities was their use of Czech deserters as Soviet liaisons with the Czech Legion. The Penza Soviet appointed some of these deserters to the commission charged to receive the arms from the Czecho-Slovaks. Other deserters, holding documents from the Soviet political and military authorities, joined the Czecho-Slovak echelons to carry on agitation for the Red Army and to seek hidden arms. They called themselves social revolutionists, internationalists, and Communists and claimed that stalling the Czech transport and creating other obstacles caused dissension within the Czech ranks and gained many recruits for the Red Army. Indeed, they declared that the Soviet government encouraged the Czechs to go to Archangel so that, in a region where no food was to be had, they could halt the Czech corps and compel them from very hunger to join their ranks.[20] These were the explanations, often inconsistent, given by the Czechs for the friction and hostility which forced them into open, bitter warfare with the soviets and Bolsheviks. Often the Czech statement of the case bears a suspicious resemblance to the reactionary propaganda against the Bolsheviks then current.

Clearly, the Penza agreement had not solved the Czech difficulties. Fearful that the Japanese landing at Vladivostok on April 5[21] was the precursor of full-fledged intervention, Moscow had become suspicious of the eastward movement of the Czechs and, on April 7, ordered them to halt. A few days later, after the excitement over the Japanese landing had subsided, the order was rescinded. From this time on, the movement of the corps was hindered by increasing tension and confusion.[22] On April 13, the commanders of the First Division of the Czech Legion held a conference at Kirsanov, not far from Penza, and arrived at a secret agreement. Believing that it was impossible to rely on any Bolshevik promise, they agreed not to surrender any more arms in accordance with the Penza agreement, but rather to recover the arms and munitions already surrendered and to force their own passage to Vladivostok if necessary. It is quite likely that the White Russian officers played an important role in this decision, which was later to become the position of the Czecho-Slovak corps as a whole.[23]

Throughout early April, American representatives described the difficulties of the Czecho-Slovak troops as they moved across Siberia. The first units arrived at Samara on March 30. Orsen M. Nielsen, Vice Consul temporarily stationed at Samara, reported that they hoped to leave for the east, despite their slow progress and the suspicious Bolsheviks, who were inclined to hamper their movements as much as possible. He added: "Numbers were arrested by Tambov government and some arms taken from them. If plans work out, the entire force will pass through Samara in the course of the next ten days. Their ultimate destination is France."[24] On April 3, David B. Macgowan, American Consul at Irkutsk, reported that Trotskii had sent orders all along the Siberian line to allow the Czecho-Slovaks to proceed eastwards but with long intervals between the trains. However, the legionnaires were to be disarmed to the point requisite for the protection of property, and if the slightest opposition was shown, they were to be arrested.[25]

Through the efforts of Kenneth D. Miller, the YMCA man traveling with the Czech Legion, Nielsen was able to get yet another viewpoint. At a meeting with Miller and a representative of the Czecho-Slovak National Council, Nielsen learned that both the national Soviet and Lenin favored the departure of the Czechs from Russia, but that Trotskii, who had visions of a new Russian army, was opposed to letting them go. The representative of the Czecho-Slovak National Council stated that Czecho-Slovaks "would surrender all their arms if necessary; that they were desperately trying to avoid friction and wished to remain neutral in any of Russia's internal troubles." Although he anticipated future difficulties with the local soviets along the route, he felt certain that the national Soviet was friendly. Nielsen, however, had been "reliably informed" that Trotskii had sent a telegram to every station master along the Trans-Siberian route stating that if one Czecho-Slovak soldier or officer was guilty of any misconduct along the way, that act would be sufficient cause to hold up the entire force. Nielsen also reported the uneasiness among the leaders of the Czech Legion caused by unfriendly newspaper articles written by Czecho-Slovak war prisoners who had adopted Bolshevism. These articles denounced the legion for recruiting among the prisoners to obtain men for a bourgeois army officered by bourgeoisie in an imperialistic war. On the other hand, Nielsen observed that some of the White Russian officers in the Czecho-Slovak forces had been indiscreet in their bearing toward various Soviet officials.[26] The Czecho-Slovak Bolsheviks, clearly receiving support from the government, endeavored in mid-April to prove that the majority of the soldiers were unwilling to go to France to fight again and that they were opposed to the legion command. By early April, the Soviet government had apparently decided to increase its support of these Bolsheviks and to establish a special commissariat for Czecho-Slovak affairs in Moscow. These developments merely served to increase the tension between the Czechs and the Soviets.[27]

At least three other factors had a decided bearing on the Czech position in Siberia by May 1918. One was the rumored danger from German and Austrian war prisoners, the second was the Japanese landing at Vladivostok in early April, and the third was the determined effort by at least one of the Allies, the British, to retain the Czechs in Russia to fight the Germans and ultimately reestablish the Eastern Front, either with or without the Bolsheviks. Throughout 1918, the threatened activities of Austro-German war prisoners played an important role, not only in the Siberian situation itself, but in Allied pleas for intervention. Some 30,000 Austrian and German prisoners were reported in the Baikal region and eastern Siberia as early as December 15, 1917, but according to Major Walter S. Drysdale, the American Military Attaché at Peking, they constituted no serious menace to Allied interests. However, a week later, John K. Caldwell, Consul at Vladivostok, warned that many of these prisoners were escaping. He feared that in the event of a separate peace between Russia and Germany, their presence would necessitate Allied control of Vladivostok and the surrounding area. Throughout February and early March 1918, Stevens, Emerson, Ernest L. Harris, and Willing Spencer, the Chargé at Peking, reported increasing activity among the German war prisoners. Yet Spencer observed that much of the news emanating from Irkutsk came from the French Consul General, whose views were "slightly colored by his desire for immediate intervention on the part of Japan." Paul S. Reinsch, American Minister in Peking, agreed.[28]

Rumors of the danger of armed prisoners of war increased after the signing of the treaty of Brest-Litovsk, particularly after Count Wilhelm von Mirbach, German Ambassador to the Soviet government, arrived in Moscow on April 26. Some observers disagreed with these reports. Admiral Knight wrote to Secretary of the Navy Josephus Daniels that there was "no danger of German influences at work in Siberia and that there was no real need for intervention."[29] When Major Drysdale was sent on a special mission to investigate the rumors, he reported that prisoners of war were armed only in certain localities. Both Trotskii and Raymond Robins, head of the American Red Cross Mission to Russia, also denied the rumors. A special investigatory team from Moscow led by Captain William B. Webster, a member of the American Red Cross mission, and Captain W. L. Hicks, a member of the British mission in Moscow, reported that the activities of war prisoners did not endanger Allied interests. Clearly the views of the Webster-Hicks mission differed materially from those of the Allied Consuls and other sources of information in Siberia. Webster accounted for those differences by the anti-Bolshevik attitudes of the Allied Consuls at Irkutsk, their failure to examine Soviet sources concerning the danger, their reliance on information from anti-Bolshevik sources, and the ineffectiveness of Allied investigations because of limited staff.[30] General William S. Graves, head of the American expeditionary forces in Siberia, agreed.[31] Reinsch also saw "no evidence of a concerted plan on the part of the Germans to control Siberia through the prisoners." Nor did he believe such an attempt could succeed.[32] Masaryk, too, who traveled through Siberia in early April en route to the United States, was convinced that there was "no organized German influence in Eastern Siberia."[33] These views were shared by Russell M. Story, YMCA director at Vladivostok, who also crossed Siberia in the early spring of 1918 and was "persuaded that there was much exaggeration in the official and semi-official reports submitted."[34]

The potential and alleged threat represented by the rumored release of German and Austro-Hungarian prisoners in Siberia caused concern, not only to the Czechs and the American consular staff in Siberia, but to Lansing as well.[35] But his position can be better understood in the context of events in Europe and the Far East bearing upon the response of the American government to Allied pleas for intervention in Russia. While the German-Bolshevik peace negotiations were taking place, the Allies had continued to besiege Wilson with appeals for lone Japanese military intervention in Siberia as the mandatory of the Allies. Although Wilson regarded the Allied proposals as dangerous from a political standpoint and could see no military advantage to justify the political risks involved, he was persuaded by Wiseman and House to cable Bliss, American military representative on the Supreme War Council, for his advice before expressing a definite opinion.[36]

Bliss found the British military section of the Supreme War Council unanimous in urging the military necessity of intervention. These officers advocated Japanese occupation of the entire length of the Siberian Railway, which meant practically all of Siberia. They believed that Siberian sentiment, although extremely socialistic, was also anti-Bolshevik, and that Japanese intervention would aid in the consolidation of this sentiment both in Siberia and in western Russia. They regarded intervention as the last hope for preventing Russia from falling under German domination.[37] Despite Bliss's disapproval, the British, French, and Italians unanimously favored an immediate occupation of the entire length of the Siberian railway. Bliss then wrote General Peyton C. March, American Chief of Staff, that "the intervention of a large Japanese army over a large portion of Siberia raises the question of how and when they can be made to get out" and "suggests a possible way in which another war may be brought about."[38] March immediately urged the Secretary of War to "keep out of Siberia."[39]

Meanwhile, events in eastern Siberia and northern Manchuria were becoming increasingly serious. Early in February, Stevens had warned the State Department of the gravity of the situation along the Chinese Eastern and Trans-Siberian railways and urged the Allies to "act vigorously or they may later on be at war to hold north [route] across the Pacific." Roland S. Morris, Ambassador to Japan, reported that the

Japanese were seriously discussing some plan of immediate action in Siberia, but desired approval by the United States and the Allies. Japanese Foreign Minister Ichiro Motono had hinted broadly that the Japanese were planning to take control of the area along the lines of the Trans-Siberian and Chinese Eastern railways between Vladivostok and Chita.[40]

Wilson was clearly suspicious about Japanese intentions. By mid-February, he was aware that the British and French had acceded to the Japanese request for a "free hand" in the event of intervention in Siberia. The British embassy had presented confidential memoranda to the State Department suggesting that Japan, acting as the mandatory of the Allies, be asked to occupy the Chinese Eastern and Amur railways, and that Washington consider the practicability of having Japan occupy the entire Trans-Siberian Railway. France had agreed to the Japanese request. Wilson was clearly displeased with these requests and declined to take any part in their execution, because he saw "nothing wise or practicable" in them.[41] He saw no reason to antagonize unnecessarily the "various elements of the people" now in control of "the power in Russia." Moreover, should the necessity for intervention arise, Wilson believed it should be handled through international cooperation rather than unilateral action and that Chinese military forces should guard and protect the Chinese Eastern Railway.[42]

By the end of February, Japan appeared ready to act alone. It proposed to China a joint military occupation of Siberia and of the Trans-Siberian Railway to restore order in Siberia. Further intelligence revealed that Japan was preparing a military expedition to assist the Russians for the same purpose. When a Japanese agent had approached General Dmitri L. Horvath, Director of the Chinese Eastern Railway, with an offer of assistance, Horvath had agreed to accept the leadership of conservative Russians in Siberia against the Bolsheviks, if assured of Allied support.[43] Horvath had already agreed to support Semenov and Ataman Ivan Kalmikov of the Ussuri Cossacks, even though he knew they would "operate independently as Napoleons."[44] On February 26, 1918, Koo in Washington sought American advice regarding Japan's request. He feared that while the Japanese might retire eventually from Siberian territory, they would not retire from Chinese territory.[45]

Breckinridge Long, Third Assistant Secretary of State, was deeply concerned over these proposals. It was he who had made the deepest study of the secret treaties regarding both the Russo-Japanese plans to control and dominate Manchuria and Japanese insistence on retaining

General Dmitri L. Horvath (National Archives)

all territories wrested from the Germans during the course of the war. He had urged Lansing to read the secret diplomacy and correspondence as soon as possible. He confided to his diary his innermost thoughts on the effects of the Bolshevik peace: "In the Far East it means—I feel and believe—the increased aggression of Japan and the probable annexation of Siberia—or eastern Siberia—by her, and unless we can keep China in control of that part of the Trans-Siberian which crosses Chinese territory, the annexation of northern China—eventual not immediate."[46] Long's suspicions ran even deeper: "The real danger lies with the possible coalition of Japan with Germany—under an agreement for well-defined spheres and a sharp line of difference between the territories of each. The poor people of Siberia! They hate Germany and Japan equally but cannot even choose between them."[47]

Long's suspicions over Japanese intentions in the Far East had led him to watch with particular interest the progress of Bolshevik negotiations with the Germans. If Lenin would take a stand once again against the Germans, Long was determined to "recommend to the sec'y that we immediately recognize the Lenine-Gov't and offer them all material military and moral support in their fight against Germany." This possibility was at least briefly considered by both House and Wilson, not only because of their concerns over Japanese intentions in Siberia and Manchuria, but also as a part of their policy to induce Austria to desert Germany. "It was in line with what Wiseman described as hope of 'talking' the Austrians into peace." Apparently Wilson and House saw two benefits from Bolshevik recognition: first, it would encourage the liberals in Germany and Austria, and, second, it would rob the Germans, who had a de facto relationship with the Bolsheviks, of an opportunity to link in propaganda the Western powers with Russian reactionaries.[48]

Long's fears over lone Japanese intervention were shared by Reinsch and the Department's Far East expert, Edward T. Williams, who agreed with Reinsch on the feasibility of using the Chinese as a military force in Russia to oppose the Germans and deny Japanese intervention. He wrote: "Japan ought not to be allowed to dominate China or to intervene alone in Siberia. To permit this it seems to me is to allow the building up of another great military autocracy and to sacrifice to it the only democratic people in the Far East."[49] Charles R. Crane agreed. Thomas F. Millard, Far East expert then in China, who had been keeping Crane well informed about Japan's "proposed action in Siberia," had urged Crane to bring Japan's aggressive tendencies to the attention of the proper authorities.[50] Wilson shared the views of both Crane and the Far Eastern Division because he, too, feared the consequences for both the Chinese and Siberian peoples of a Japanese intervention in Siberia and Manchuria.[51] When informed of Japan's proposal to China for a joint military intervention against the Bolsheviks, he suggested that the "wisest course [was] for the Chinese government to take over and guard that part of the Trans-Siberian railroad system which passed through China."[52]

Reports from Siberia throughout February and March indicated a growing unanimity among American officials in the Far East supporting international intervention in Siberia rather than unilateral Japanese intervention. These reports came from General William V. Judson, Military Attaché recently returned from Russia; DeWitt C. Poole, Jr.; Maddin Summers, Consul and Consul General in Moscow; and Ambassador Francis, who advocated immediate occupation of Vladivostok, Murmansk, and Archangel. While Reinsch opposed lone Japanese troops, he noted that a majority of Russians would welcome Allied intervention to prevent German control. Even John F. Stevens, who had been solidly opposed to any kind of intervention in Russia, advised that German influence was growing and would have to be met by force soon. Indeed, now that German prisoners were being released and armed, he believed that even Japanese action was necessary if Siberia was to be saved from German control. On February 26, Marshal Ferdinand Foch, generalissimo of the Allied armies, added his plea for active intervention in Siberia by Japan and the United States.[53]

The British War Cabinet considered the problem on February 20. Japanese intervention was no longer necessary to aid the Cossacks because they no longer existed as an efficient fighting force. Nevertheless, the problem of countering German influence in Russia remained. Here the members of the War Cabinet were confronted by two principal views concerning Japanese action: one was the French, which saw in Japan the only means of opposing German power and influence in Russia; the other was the American, "which apart from jealousy and suspicion of Japanese enterprises, considered the Japs as the worst possible agents of the Allies in Russia."[54]

The War Cabinet met five days later to discuss Balfour's recent interview with the Japanese Ambassador regarding intervention in Siberia. The Ambassador had declared that his government was eager to proceed at once, even as a mandatory of the Allies, but not accompanied by Allied detachments, because of the opposition of Japanese public opinion. Although the War Cabinet realized how difficult it would be to persuade Wilson to agree to this policy, the French government openly favored it, with the distinct understanding that Japan would agree to occupy the entire Siberian railway. The War Cabinet agreed, therefore, to advocate Japanese intervention in Siberia up to Cheliabinsk and to obtain concurrence from the United States.[55]

On February 27, Reading presented Wilson with two secret messages from Balfour. The first urged that the United States, Great Britain, France, and Italy invite Japan to occupy the Siberian railway in order to protect Allied military stores in Vladivostok and prevent the enemy from obtaining access to the vast stores of agricultural resources west of Lake Baikal. Reading admitted reluctantly that Japan would not tolerate cooperation, although it was willing to accept an Allied mandate. The final decision rested with the United States. Furthermore, Reading added, common action would be impossible if the United States disapproved. In that event, Great Britain feared that Japan would act alone and would not then be subjected to the Allied safeguards.[56] The second message concerned the activities of German prisoners in Siberia.[57] Wilson agreed to consider the matter and discussed the question freely with Reading. He was anxious that Balfour understand that his reservations about the proposal stemmed largely from his "conviction that the Russian people would regard any manifesto of disinterestedness on the part of the Allies on a par with similar manifestos issued by the Central Powers in European Russia, and that the Allies would consequently lose the moral force of their position."[58]

Balfour's appeal was followed by a cablegram from Pichon reporting that Foreign Minister Motono was willing to announce publicly Japan's pledge of disinterest, to carry on military activities as far as the Ural Mountains, and to comply with all Allied demands. Jusserand later met with Lansing and developed these arguments very persuasively.[59] Yet Wilson seemed to be "against any intervention by the Japanese in Siberia, with the Allies or for the Allies and would prefer if Japan would intervene at Vladivostok, that she should do it on her own initiative, thus leaving it open for America and the Allies to make any representations that they may hereafter think fit to Japan."[60] But recent messages from the British and French governments had made a deep impression upon Lansing. He feared that Japan intended to "go into Siberia anyway" and that a public declaration of disinterest such as Motono proposed might be a "restraint upon her." He thought that Washington's role should be to assure that the United States would not object to Japan's action. Given the urgency of the matter, Lansing requested Wilson's "guidance at the earliest possible moment."[61] As Lansing waited, he received further disquieting news of serious conditions at

Irkutsk, where German prisoners were allegedly being armed by the Bolsheviks and that Japan was prepared to act at once and might at any moment inquire about the attitude of the American government.[62]

Lansing's change of heart, apparently approved by House, combined with the increasing pressure for intervention from the Allies, and Wilson's own diplomatic staff abroad, particularly Stevens, now caused Wilson to waver in his position. Even Bliss had agreed to the military efficacy of a limited occupation of the Trans-Siberian Railway from Vladivostok to Harbin by a Japanese force, after obtaining suitable guarantees from Japan.[63] The War Department, too, although concerned over possible Japanese complications, had agreed that "every possible effort should be made to obtain possession" of the supplies stored in and near Vladivostok.[64] Because Wilson had so frequently been at odds with his Allies, he was now "particularly anxious not to appear as obstructing any of [Balfour's] schemes."[65] Finally, Japan's declaration of disinterest prompted his serious reconsideration of the matter.[66] On March 1, 1918, Wilson decided that if England, France, and Italy invited Japan to be their mandatory, he would not oppose such action, but would indicate the American position separately.[67]

Wilson thereupon drafted a new declaration of policy stating that although he had "not thought it wise to join the governments of the Entente in asking the Japanese Government to act in Siberia," he would not object to such a request being made by the other Allies.[68] On the same day, at Wilson's suggestion, Lansing sent an elaboration of Reinsch's plan for more extensive "military participation of China in the War."[69] The plan made it clear that China's desire to assist was "thwarted by Japan" but that the "situation in Siberia makes urgent the need of preparing China for participation in the war."[70] Eager to lessen the chance "of China's falling entirely under Japanese domination," E. T. Williams recommended the use of Chinese troops in Siberia to lessen factional strife within China, unite the country, and win "a standing before the world that would deserve a place in the Peace Conference."[71] Not surprisingly, then, Wilson's new declaration emphasized especially his understanding that in putting an armed force into Siberia, Japan was acting as Russia's ally solely "to save Siberia from the invasion of the armies and intrigues of Germany" and would "leave the determination of . . . the permanent fortunes of Siberia to the Council of Peace."[72] Wilson sent his statement to the State Department on March 1, and Polk showed it to Jusserand and Colville A. Barclay, the British Chargé, on the same day and to the Italian Ambassador, Count Macchi di Cellere, on the following day. The Japanese Chargé, however, was not informed.[73]

Meanwhile, House had begun to have serious second thoughts.[74] After discussing the matter with Ambassador Boris Bakhmetev and Elihu Root, he wrote Wilson an urgent note saying that Root and Bakhmetev shared the President's concerns about the "danger of the proposed Japanese intervention."[75] On the same morning, Auchincloss, at House's request, had sent Wilson a message from William C. Bullitt, then serving in the State Department as adviser both to the White House and to Lansing on developments in enemy countries. Bullitt's memorandum, "Our Policy in Regard to Japan's Proposed Invasion of Siberia," played a crucial role in Wilson's decision to withdraw the original statement.[76] It said that America's moral position in the war would be "irretrievably compromised unless we protest publicly against Japan's invasion of Siberia." Bullitt insisted that the United States was about to assent tacitly to Japan's invasion of Siberia because it feared that, if opposed, Japan would switch to the side of Germany. "Japan will take this step because of her desire to annex eastern Siberia, which she covets so intensely." To assent to an invasion of Siberia "by this autocracy" was to "compromise on all the principles for which we are asking our soldiers to die."[77]

Bullitt also pointed to the anomaly of Wilson's position: "If the United States assents to the imperial Japanese army invading territory controlled by the Bolsheviki, for the ostensible purpose of restoring order, the United States cannot object to the Imperial German army invading territory controlled by the Bolsheviki for the ostensible purpose of restoring order." He concluded: "In Russia today there are the rudiments of a government of the people, by the people, and for the people. . . . Unless the Soviet government is overthrown by enemy imperialists it will continue to control Russia. Are we going to make the world safe for this Russian democracy by allowing the Allies to place Terauchi in Irkutsk, while Ludendorff establishes himself in Petrograd?"

Wilson was clearly moved by these appeals, which, after all, merely repeated his own opinions concerning lone Japanese intervention.[78] Wilson's change of mind was also strongly reinforced by three memoranda he received on March 5 in response to his request for information from the War Department. The two memoranda from General Judson, one of which he had discussed earlier with Secretary Baker, and the third from Lieutenant Colonel Sherman Miles all strongly supported the rationale presented by Bullitt and vehemently opposed lone Japanese intervention.[79]

Wilson now called Auchincloss and told him "that in view of this [Bullitt's] memorandum and of a letter . . . from Colonel House," he wished to withdraw his original telegram. He asked Auchincloss to get House's reaction to his proposed new telegram over the telephone and call him back.[80] He also instructed Polk to delay transmission of the original message to Tokyo. Polk now found himself in an embarrassing position, since he had already given the contents of the earlier note to all of the Allies except Japan. Moreover, as a result of the note of March 1, the British government had agreed that Japan should take independent action in Siberia as the mandatory of the Allies.[81]

Wilson now opposed Japanese intervention even if Japan gave explicit assurances that she would not impair the political or territorial integrity of Siberia. Gone from the context of the new note was the crucial statement that the United States had no objection to the request being made by the other Allies.[82] Wilson was clearly concerned over the moral issues involved in intervention. His case rested on two assumptions: first, the policy would alienate Russian opinion from faith in the Allies and America; secondly, the course proposed was contrary to America's democratic war aims and would fatally compromise the American moral position.[83] Convinced that Russian self-determination itself was at stake, Wilson told Reading that if the United States agreed to Japanese intervention, she would deal Russian democracy another blow "by invading Russian territory in opposition to the wishes of the Bolshevic authorities."[84]

The response to Wilson's new note was mixed. Balfour appreciated the frank exposition of Wilson's views. He assured Wilson that until the Treaty of Brest-Litovsk he too had been opposed to Japanese intervention. However, when the Bolsheviks surrendered unconditionally, it became crucial to prevent the rich supplies in Siberia from falling into German hands, and Japanese intervention was the only method to secure this. Moreover, despite reports of enemy prisoners being armed by the Bolsheviks in Siberia, other intelligence revealed that the Bolshevik government still intended to organize resistance to German aggression.[85] Balfour wrote that the British decision to ask Japan to take independent action in Siberia as the mandatory of the Allies was a result of Wilson's first note. The British feared that "considerable resentment would be aroused in Japan if, the Japanese Government being willing to act on behalf of the Allies, a mandate were refused. A formidable pro-German party in Japan would have asserted that such a refusal was due to mistrust, and . . . however, erroneous in fact, this sentiment would have predominated in Japanese opinion."[86] Nevertheless, in their note, they had advised Japan to give the "utmost publicity to her aims and methods" so as to insure there was not the "least resemblance" between operations which Germany was carrying on in European Russia and those which Japan might undertake in Siberia acting as the mandatory of the Allies.[87]

The War Cabinet, on March 4, 1918, received news from Russia that prompted still another response. British Rear Admiral Thomas W. Kemp at Murmansk wired that Trotskii had broken off peace negotiations with the Germans and was preparing to defend Petrograd to the last drop of blood. The local soviets had been ordered to do "everything they could to defend the Murmansk line" and to "cooperate with the Allied missions in everything." The War Cabinet immediately authorized Kemp to land troops if in his judgment "any useful assistance could be given by them to any Russian forces operating against the Germans."[88] The French were in agreement. On the same day, R. H. Bruce Lockhart, British Special Representative in Russia, urged a suspension of the proposed intervention of Japan in Siberia, since the Bolshevik government swore to organize resistance to German aggression despite having signed a peace treaty. It was this intelligence that impelled Balfour to advise the Bolsheviks to seek Japanese and Rumanian cooperation against the Germans.[89]

Meanwhile House was "perplexed and rather worried" about lone Japanese intervention in Siberia, particularly in view of the impending Fourth All-Russian Congress of Soviets in Moscow on March 12 to ratify the Treaty of Brest-Litovsk. He questioned Wilson about sending a reassuring message to Russia. His thought was "not so much about Russia" as to "seize this opportunity to clear up the Far Eastern situation but without mentioning it or Japan in any way." House concluded: "What you would say about Russia and against Germany, could be made to apply to Japan or any other power seeking to do what we know Germany is attempting."[90] Wilson fully agreed and drafted a strong and impressive statement that was sent to Russia on March 11. The message expressed "sincere sympathy" for the Russian people and assured them that the United States would "avail itself of every opportunity" to secure for Russia complete sovereignty and independence in her own affairs.[91]

The concern of both Wilson and House over lone Japanese intervention gave Reading hope for an American change of policy closer to Balfour's position. However, Balfour preferred not to press for such a change until after the Japanese response.[92] To the surprise of both Wilson and House, Tokyo refused to intervene without American support unless developments in Siberia should "jeopardize the national security or vital interest of Japan" and compel it "to resort to prompt and efficient measures of self-protection." In any event, Japan professed that whatever action it might take in Russian territory would be "wholly uninfluenced by any aggressive motives or tendencies."[93]

Because the British proposals for Japanese intervention had been rejected by both the United States and Japan, Balfour believed that a new plan or approach was absolutely essential.[94] On April 1, the British War Office approached the Czecho-Slovak National Council with a proposal to use the Czech Legion in Russia or Siberia. Doubtful that the legion could actually get to France via Vladivostok, the War Office suggested that a part of the Czech Legion be transported to the Western Front by way of Archangel. Although Trotskii had demanded earlier that the Czech Legion remain in Russia to form the nucleus of a reorganized Russian army, the Czechs had refused. However, the British military authorities believed that it would be possible either to occupy Siberia in the region of Omsk or else establish a military base at Archangel and maintain communication with Siberia through Perm. They also suggested the possibility of having the Czech Legion pass beyond Lake Baikal and provide support for Semenov.

In Paris, Beneš discussed the matter with General Henri Edouard Alby, Chief of the General Staff in the French Ministry of War, and with Janin, the Commander in Chief of the Czech troops; Beneš then sent a reply to Clemenceau on April 2. He opposed the use of the Czech troops in western Siberia, but he agreed to permit them to be sent via Archangel for the sake of a more rapid transport to France. Moreover, it was Beneš's wish that if the Czechs remained in eastern Siberia, it would be only until vessels for their transport were made available. The French government agreed.[95] Although the British War Cabinet obviously desired to utilize the Czecho-Slovaks in Russia and Siberia, France's official policy was to bring the legionnaires to the Western Front, a plan Balfour considered absurd. Yet, as late as April 20, Clemenceau, who regarded the Czecho-Slovak legionnaires as "admirable soldiers," told Beneš that he wanted them on the French front at all costs to guarantee victory.[96]

By early April, Lockhart had had a very satisfactory discussion with Trotskii, who seemed willing to discuss the possibility of Allied troops being sent via Siberia to Russia. He even seemed to pose no objection to the use of Japanese troops. The Allied ambassadors had met with their military attachés and had agreed to permit their officers to continue assisting technically in formulating plans for a new Red Army in the hope of inducing the Soviets to request Japanese and other Allied intervention.[97] These discussions of collaboration with the Soviets were going on even as the British and French were supporting the anti-Bolshevik efforts of the Cossack forces in southern Russia and of Semenov along the line of the Chinese Eastern Railway. Sadoul, Lockhart, Raymond Robins, and even Francis for a time continued to entertain the notion that they could still secure Bolshevik cooperation in the war against Germany. Lockhart was convinced that the Bolsheviks were still the most likely party to oppose German interests in Russia. Trotskii in turn encouraged the consideration of such cooperation. Early in March, he had welcomed the landing at Murmansk of a small British force sent to oppose the Germans and Finns, who were threatening the Murmansk Railway. Moreover, he had also suggested to Sadoul and Lockhart the possibility of using the Czecho-Slovak Legion, at that time stationed in the Ukraine, for the same purpose.[98] British representatives on the scene were enthusiastic about the possible use of the Czechs, having already arrived at this view independently. Various American representatives, including Summers, Francis, Robins, and Major Thomas D. Thacher of the American Red Cross, shared their views.[99]

By April 8, the British had succeeded in getting the approval of the permanent military representatives of the Supreme War Council to Joint Note No. 20, which pushed the concept of a Siberian expedition grouped around the Japanese, despite Wilson's clear opposition to such a proposal. It projected the advance of an Allied expeditionary force from Vladivostok to the Ural areas and possibly the Volga. Although the Japanese were to form the nucleus of the force, the plan envisaged "the eventual assistance *of Czech and other elements which can be organized on the spot.*"[100] Bliss had abstained from signing the note.

Although Wilson's note of March 5 had clearly opposed intervention, his support of Stevens and the Russian Railway Service Corps in Siberia was bringing the United States at least one step closer to eventual armed intervention in that area. The Bolshevik revolution had necessitated Stevens's return to Japan, but after the major disturbances along the Chinese Eastern Railway had subsided, he returned to Harbin in February 1918 to confer with General Horvath on the best means of utilizing the services of the Russian Railway Service Corps. The Japanese government had watched these conversations closely. Charles K. Moser, American Consul at Harbin, had warned earlier that unless America took over direction of the railroads, Japan would do so. As a result of negotiations with Horvath, Stevens had been authorized to return to Harbin with Colonel Emerson and part of the Russian Railway Service Corps and to begin work in cooperation with the railway authorities of the Chinese Eastern Railway.[101] Before the corps could begin its work, Stevens received word that German prisoners were now armed at Irkutsk and Chita and that, without the aid of armed forces, he would be able to place only four railway units, not seven as planned. He was, therefore, compelled to hold at Nagasaki one-half of the contingent. Stevens feared that if the Germans actually controlled Petrograd, they would at once send orders to destroy the bridges and tracks of the Trans-Siberian Railway, which would seriously cripple any future movements in Siberia.[102] Balfour immediately advised Wilson to instruct Stevens "to do anything" he could to protect the lines "with or without the assistance of General Semenoff." Balfour was now convinced of the "extreme urgency" of action by the Japanese.[103]

On March 11, the eve of the signing of the Brest-Litovsk Treaty, Wilson had once again declared to the Russian people through the Congress of the Soviet that "the whole heart of the American people" was with the Russian people in their attempt to "free themselves forever from autocratic government and become the masters of their own life."[104] When the Japanese Foreign Office inquired as to how Russia should be regarded in the future, Wilson replied that the United States would continue to regard Russia "as an ally." He argued that since the United States had not recognized the Soviet government on whom Germany had "just forced, or tried to force a peace" even as a de facto government, none of its acts needed to be officially recognized by the United States. He asked all his allies to "continue to treat the Russians as in all respects our friends and allies against the common enemy."[105]

At this point, Lansing decided to approach Wilson concerning a possible change in policy toward the Russians, in light of the alleged menace of the German prisoners of war.[106] Wilson, however, refused to change his position because he found nothing in the various memoranda presented to him to justify altering his viewpoint. Responding specifically to Lansing's plea that the German menace in Siberia constituted a sufficient reason for Japanese intervention, Wilson replied that he did not believe the situation "yet warranted change of policy."[107] Although House was inclined to agree, he was coming to believe that regardless of the intrinsic value of the Siberian scheme, it might be advisable and even necessary to put it into effect for the sake of Allied morale. Reading agreed. House, however, showed a "disposition always to revert to making assent of Russia [an] indispensable feature of American policy."[108]

The British, rebuffed by Wilson's opposition to the recent Allied joint appeal, now devised a new plan of action. They proposed that an expedition of American, British, and Japanese troops be substituted for a lone Japanese force. By this scheme, they hoped to overcome not only Bolshevik objections to military action in Siberia, but also Wilson's opposition.[109] Even though the Japanese Foreign Minister "disagreed with President of U. States' belief that it would be possible to consolidate Bolsheviks to resist Germans," and Balfour had earlier expressed strong doubt on the matter, Balfour had agreed with House that the "ideal arrangement would be for Bolshevikii to request Japanese, American, Allied assistance against German aggression." He had informed House that Lockhart had been instructed to do everything he could to bring about Bolshevik assent. Balfour had suggested that such an invitation might be hastened if Robins could be asked to second Lockhart's endeavors, since he was on "such excellent terms with the Bolshevik leaders."[110]

By early April, Lockhart's efforts seemed to be bearing fruit. On March 27, he had had a very satisfactory discussion with Trotskii, who indicated that Russia would welcome help from the Allied countries, even if to obtain this help "it should become necessary for the socialist forces to fight in cooperation with the imperialist army." Although Trotskii demanded Allied guarantees on certain points, he agreed that if "other Allied forces were present he thought there was no objection to the use of Japanese troops." Lockhart was optimistic although cautious about negotiating an arrangement on this question. He now believed the Bolsheviks' attitude toward the Allies had completely changed and that it was important that this attitude not be jeopardized by a counterrevolution.[111]

On April 5, a Japanese armed force landed at Vladivostok and began to patrol the city. The announced reason was the murder of three Japanese nationals in the business district the day before.[112] The British also landed fifty armed sailors on the afternoon of April 5, ostensibly to protect the British consulate, but in reality "to ensure that any move made would be an Allied one, not an independent Japanese venture." On the next day, the Japanese landed 250 additional sailors. The French Consul asked the Japanese to guard the French consulate, but the American Consul felt it unnecessary to ask for protection.[113]

In Bolshevik circles, the Japanese-British landing was regarded as

Depot and terminal of Trans-Siberian Railroad in Vladivostok, Siberia
(National Archives)

the beginning of intervention against the Soviet regime. The Council of People's Commissars called upon the "toiling masses" to resist the "imperialist blow from the east."[114] Chicherin addressed a note of protest to the French Consul General in Moscow, to Lockhart, and to Robins, demanding immediate withdrawal. Reading feared that Trotskii's orders "to resist the invasion" would only serve to harden the American view. He found Wilson more opposed than ever to Japanese intervention without Russian consent. Even members of the administration previously inclined to favor American cooperation with the Japanese intervention now leaned in the opposite direction.[115] Wilson made clear to Reading that no sailors would be landed from American vessels unless American life and property were attacked.[116] Keenly aware that "Russian trust of America was held by a very slender thread," he was unwilling to jeopardize that trust by any support of Japanese actions, which he believed would only "drive Russia toward Germany."[117]

In the week following April 5, both Lenin and the central Siberian soviets were deeply apprehensive and concerned over the passage of the Czech troops through their territory. Nielsen reported that this hesitancy accounted for orders being issued to halt all Czecho-Slovak trains. Bolshevik posters about the Czecho-Slovaks appeared in the railway depots. One announced: "In view of the hostile attitude of international imperialism and threats of foreign landing at Vladivostok, the Central Executive Committee of Soviets in Siberia considers the concentration there of these forces dangerous and inadmissible." The Siberian Central Executive Committee asked for instructions, adding that its position was to mobilize all available forces, declare Siberia in a state of military emergency, offer resistance if the Japanese attempted to seize territory, and say to the Allies that the Vladivostok Soviet was strong enough to assure the protection of foreign nationals. The note ended with the query: "What do you now think about arming the socialists made prisoners of war?" Lenin agreed and indicated his intention to begin negotiations with the German Ambassador. It was "clear" to Lenin "that no faith can now be put in any assurances and that solid military preparations on our part constitute the sole reliable guarantee."[118]

By April 10, the Vladivostok Soviet, which up to that point had been able to handle the Czechs arriving at that city without mishap, telegraphed Moscow that "the situation is not hopeless as there appears to be great disagreement among the Allies." As a result of this more optimistic message, the Sovnarkom (the Soviet of People's Commissars) issued a new order on April 12, which permitted the Czechs to continue their movement.[119] Although the Bolsheviks regarded the Japanese landing as a hostile act against the Soviet government, they still appeared willing to negotiate an intervention in Siberia, provided it was an Allied rather than an exclusively Japanese affair.[120] The Soviet protest was not without effect among the Allies. The British government instructed Lockhart to assure Trotskii that the landing was made "solely with the object of affording security for the life and property of foreign residents in Vladivostok" and had no relation to the larger question of Allied intervention in the Far East. The Japanese government professed agreement with this position.[121] The British regarded the official silence maintained by the United States as a sign of disapproval.[122]

By April 17, Moscow had once again changed its mind. Martial law was proclaimed in Siberia and, on April 21, Chicherin wired all the Siberian soviets that "the fear of a Japanese advance into Siberia" and "German determined demands" necessitated "a quick evacuation of

German prisoners from eastern Siberia into western Siberia or to European Russia. . . . The Czecho-Slovak detachments must not move eastward."[123] But even this order was not to stand, for two weeks later Chicherin telegraphed that all Czecho-Slovaks east of Omsk should return for embarkation at Archangel and Murmansk.[124] But these latter instructions were the product of negotiations Trotskii had been conducting with the Allies. It is time to turn to these developments.

11

British Efforts to
Co-opt the Czech Legion

By April 7, 1918, Wilson was more convinced than ever that the United States should neither condone nor participate in the Japanese intervention unless invited to do so by the Russians, because Japanese intervention without Russian approval would "throw Russians into the German arms."[1] However, Trotskii's negotiations with Lockhart had convinced the War Cabinet at least tentatively of Bolshevik willingness to cooperate. After Balfour made clear that the Allied position at Murmansk and Archangel differed from that at Vladivostok—since it involved the whole question of Allied intervention via Siberia—on April 17 the War Cabinet agreed to approve the policy adopted by the military leaders on the scene in order to prevent further encroachments in Russia by the Central Powers or Finland. The British now believed that Trotskii might be persuaded to authorize the use of the Czecho-Slovak forces in the vicinity of Archangel and Murmansk to protect both Russian and Allied interests.[2]

Lockhart had also interviewed the members of the Czecho-Slovak National Council, who were very concerned over Trotksii's order stopping the Czech movement after the Japanese landing at Vladivostok. Although that order had been rescinded and the Czechs were moving once again, the Czech leaders feared that the Allies might take further action in the Far East that would again detain the corps. In that event, the corps would make for Archangel. When Maxa, the Vice President of the Czecho-Slovak National Council in Russia, asked him if the British would send ships to remove them upon their arrival, Lockhart advised him to push toward Vladivostok. In the meantime, Lockhart promised to consult with the British Foreign Office regarding Archangel. Maxa, who had talked with the key Soviet leaders, thought that they were "honest enough" in their desire to fight Germany, but he doubted that they could do anything by themselves. Although he had never discussed the question of Allied intervention with the Bolsheviks, he thought that concluding an agreement with them would be difficult but not impossible. Lockhart's report of his discussion with the Czech leaders caused the British Foreign Office to ponder even more seriously the question of informing both Lockhart and the French regarding a firm Czech policy.[3] Therefore, it instructed Lockhart, in conjunction with local French representatives, to urge Trotskii to authorize the employment of the Czechs in opposing German aggression and intrigues at Archangel and Murmansk and along the railways leading to these ports. The British had already given instructions that Semenov was to cease his activities "for the time being" in eastern Siberia.[4]

Balfour was now much more optimistic over the possibility of cooperating with the Bolsheviks against Germany. Since the Bolshevik government was the de facto government of Russia, it seemed to him "impossible to go behind it." He informed Reading that "of late a very significant change" had come over Trotskii's attitude toward the Allies. He had "not only curbed anti-Allied tone of Bolshevist Press but he has approved of Allied cooperation at Murmansk and has suggested that the British naval officers should assist in restoring discipline in Black Sea fleet." If Trotskii was willing to accept the advance of Allied forces into Russia, Balfour believed that it would transform the whole situation in the east.[5] When he learned that Trotskii had proposed to use the Czech corps at Murmansk and that he was taking immediate steps to implement a plan with the French mission, Balfour was obviously pleased.[6] He informed House that the situation was "entirely altered by apparent willingness of Trotskii to invite Allied assistance against German aggression."[7] Wilson, in turn, agreed to reconsider the whole problem of intervention in "the new light" of Trotskii's willingness to cooperate.

Since Kikujiro Ishii, the new Japanese Ambassador, was scheduled to reach Washington on April 26, Wilson believed that a favorable opportunity had arrived to ascertain Japan's views of an intervention with the cooperation of American and Allied contingents. However, Wilson thought it would be better for Lansing to sound out Ishii on the new proposal without disclosing either the British proposal or Trotskii's invitation. Actually, he doubted Japan's willingness to intervene at all, particularly if accompanied by American and Allied contingents.[8]

Wilson's position can only be understood in the light of intelligence he had been receiving concerning Japan's operations in northern Manchuria and its efforts to seize control of the Chinese Eastern Railway. As early as April 4, the American legation at Harbin had transmitted to Washington translations of intercepted telegrams sent by General

Giichi Tanaka of the Japanese General Staff in Tokyo to General Masa-
take Nakajima at Harbin, which had been destined for delivery to
Horvath. These telegrams revealed Japan's efforts to control factions in
Siberia and northern Manchuria in order to receive special privileges
and advantages in those areas.[9] The Japanese were clearly backing
Horvath. The Japanese Minister in China had made clear to Horvath
their opposition to any acceptance of American assistance on the Chinese Eastern Railway in Manchuria. Moreover, the Russian Minister
had informed Reinsch personally that the Chinese Eastern Railway was
a Chinese enterprise in which Russia "had certain treaty rights and it
was supposed that the arrangements made for American assistance to
Russian railways did not refer to it."[10]

Reinsch had informed Wilson of the Russian reorganization of the
governing board of the Chinese Eastern Railway and of the Russians'
plans to engage in military action against the Bolsheviks, backed by
Japanese forces. The Japanese had agreed to finance the movement and
to provide military support if they could secure agreement to the
acceptance of certain conditions, which were described as "harsh."
Japanese plans were clearly designed to "suppress the Bolshevik uprising" and to cooperate with the Cossack troops to do it. Semenov was
being supplied with Japanese artillery. Reinsch strongly urged Wilson
to avoid any commitment to Semenov and to organize Allied action to
offset the Japanese.[11] At the same time, Morris had had interviews with
Shimpei Gotō, who had become Foreign Minister in April 1918, that
suggested that Germany might be in communication with prominent
Japanese officials. Morris was clearly concerned over the negotiation of
possible German-Japanese agreements as a result of the collapse of
Russia. Given Wilson's awareness of all of this information, it was not
surprising that he expressed considerable doubt to Reading about
Japan's willingness to intervene with Allied cooperation.[12]

In the meantime, by April 11, General Lavergne, the French Military Attaché in Moscow, had reported to Paris that conflicts had arisen
between the Czech Legion and the Bolshevik authorities. He was now
concerned whether the Czech Legion would actually be able to reach
Vladivostok, because Trotskii had given orders to stop its advance, and
there were continual differences of opinion about disarmament. Nevertheless, the Czechs were proceeding eastward, and he stressed that
their one desire was still to get to France. It was at this point that the
Paris government and the French General Staff approached their allies
for vessels to transport the Czechs from both Vladivostok and Archangel. According to Beneš, this was the first official suggestion by the

French government that a section of the Czech army might perhaps be transported by way of Archangel. Apparently, he was unaware of the decision regarding the Czechs in Joint Note No. 20.[13]

By April 30, the British through Lockhart had negotiated an agreement with Trotskii for the use of Czech troops to defend the northern Russian ports. Meanwhile, French military authorities informed the British that 45,000 of the Czech troops had been collected near Omsk, where they remained pending a decision by the Allies to send them to Murmansk or Vladivostok. When the advisability of retaining these troops in Siberia for an Allied intervention was discussed, the War Cabinet learned that the Czechs desired most of all to come to the Western Front. General George Macdonogh, the director of British military intelligence, reported that because they had been so badly treated in Russia the Czechs refused to fight there. However, a second Czech corps of almost 20,000 men was being organized near Omsk, and arrangements could probably be made for this corps to remain in Russia and be stationed, as was originally proposed, along the Murmansk and Archangel railways.[14]

On May 2, the Supreme War Council held its fifth session at Abbeville. It was attended by the military and political representatives of the Allied powers, including Clemenceau; Pichon; Foch; General Henri-Philippe Pétain; Lloyd George; Lord Milner, British Secretary of State for War; Sir Douglas Haig, chief of the British Expeditionary Force in France; General Charles John Sackville-West, British military representative on the Supreme War Council; Bliss; Orlando; and Sonnino. The Allied statesmen discussed the question of the transport of Czech troops from Russia and approved Joint Note No. 25 of the permanent military representatives. While Clemenceau raised no objections to routing a portion of the Czech corps through the northern ports, he wanted them transported to France "at the earliest possible date." Clemenceau's observations at Abbeville confirmed the views of Beneš about the "great importance that France attached to transfer of our troops to the Western front but not to their employment in Siberia."[15] The British were also successful in having incorporated into the note their long-desired scheme of sending to Archangel and Murmansk "all Czech troops which have not yet passed east of Omsk on the Trans-Siberian Railway." Moreover, Joint Note No. 25 instructed that until embarkation these troops could be employed profitably in defending Archangel and Murmansk and in guarding and protecting the Murmansk Railway. Similarly, Czech troops who had already proceeded east of Omsk could eventually be used, as had been recommended in Joint Note No. 20, to cooperate with the Allies in Siberia. However, at Clemenceau's urging, the Supreme War Council passed an additional resolution whereby the British agreed to arrange transportation from Russia for those Czech troops then in Vladivostok or on their way to that port. The French accepted responsibility for them until they embarked. Finally, the British agreed to approach Trotskii with the proposal to concentrate at Murmansk and Archangel those troops not belonging to the army corps that had left Omsk for Vladivostok.[16] Balfour gave Lockhart the task of approaching Trotskii, while the British War Office took the initiative in carrying out the decision of the Supreme War Council in cooperation with the Minister of Shipping.[17]

The Bolshevik government agreed and Paris was so informed. General O. G. Ogorodnikov, Bolshevik commander in northern Russia, reportedly had unofficially sanctioned the guarding of the northern Russian ports by the Czech troops. Moreover, with the help of Sadoul, Lavergne had secured Trotskii's permission to allot to the Czech troops a portion of the war matériel then collected at Archangel. All information concerning the Czechs and their movement was to be kept as secret as possible, and all Allied officers involved were warned accordingly. Trotskii had stipulated that if he did request Allied or Japanese assistance, his request must under no circumstances be published.[18] As a result of these negotiations, Chicherin issued an order designed to implement the Abbeville agreement to the local soviets along the Trans-Siberian Railway.

In the meantime, the confusion and difficulty surrounding the Czecho-Slovak movement to the east had been constantly increasing. On May 9, Maxa and two other members of the Czecho-Slovak National Council, learning of the new scheme to split the Czech corps, traveled from Omsk to Moscow in an effort to find a solution to their problems. On their arrival, they conferred with Lavergne, who verified Trotskii's agreement of the revised plan and his promise of all necessary aid to evacuate part of the legion via Archangel. They also discussed with Trotskii the work of the National Council among the prisoners of war and the continued Czecho-Slovak Communist agitation among the echelons. Trotskii appeared agreeable to all matters discussed but the last. That, he said, was the concern of the Commissar of Nationalities, Stalin. These discussions increased the mutual anticipation that the exit from Archangel would proceed without serious obstruction. The Czecho-Slovak envoys then decided to return to Omsk, agreeable to the new plan. Apparently they still believed it possible for the corps to be removed rapidly and safely.[19] Meanwhile, the Allied governments assumed that the Abbeville agreement was in the process of rapid implementation. Actually, within the next week the plans were obstructed and vitiated by a further series of events in Russia and Siberia, which will be noted later. These events, however, were not immediately known to the Allied governments.

Once Beneš learned that the Bolshevik authorities had agreed to the Abbeville resolution, he decided that the favorable moment had come to negotiate directly with London. To Beneš, these negotiations represented the "first decisive step" on England's part to promote Czecho-Slovak "national and political aims," and the decisive element was clearly the Czecho-Slovak army in Russia. Introduced to Balfour by Steed on May 10, Beneš outlined the situation in Austria-Hungary, particularly in Bohemia, and described the development of the Czech movement with special reference to the positive attitude of the French government and the growth and strength of the Czech armies in France, Italy, and Russia. He asked for recognition of the Czecho-Slovak National Council as the supreme organ of the Czecho-Slovak political movement and for recognition of the Czecho-Slovak national army as the French had done. At Balfour's request, he submitted two memoranda that explained the juridical situation of the Czecho-Slovak National Council in France and Italy and the significance of the military agreement signed by Clemenceau on February 7. Recognizing the ambivalent attitude of the British toward Austro-Hungarian affairs, Beneš urged them not to oppose the policy of the other Allies in Czech affairs.[20]

Balfour appeared sympathetic. He recognized the Czech endeavor to establish an army in France and Italy and was impressed by the fact that the Czechs had formed "the only element in Russia which had shown itself able to cope with the Bolshevik chaos and had held out longest on the eastern front against the Germans." He also expressed the desire to retain the Czecho-Slovak army in Russia. Balfour promised to let Beneš know within the next few days whether he could recognize the Czecho-Slovak National Council and publicly support Czech military aspirations.[21] Beneš also submitted the same requests to Cecil, who appeared very favorable.[22] Cecil suggested the possibility of issuing a manifesto addressing the use of "Czech troops within the scope of Allied military operations as a whole." However, he took the position that such a manifesto could not be regarded as a promise that the fighting would be continued until the Czechs were liberated, but merely that it would promise the eventual recognition of the sovereignty of the Czecho-Slovak National Council and of the Czech army as an Allied army. Beneš agreed to this interpretation.[23]

Given the desperate situation of the Allies on the Western Front and in Russia, the use of the Czechs in Russia had now become a matter of high governmental policy in Great Britain. On May 11, when the War Cabinet met, Lloyd George clearly favored building Allied intervention around the Czech Legion rather than opening up Russia to a large-scale Japanese invasion that might alienate the Russian people. He also suggested the possibility of diverting some Americans for duty at Vladivostok. By this time, he was strongly impressed with the telegrams from Lockhart indicating that it no longer suited Trotskii "to be under German domination." Lloyd George felt it "very desirable" that a nucleus of Allied troops be sent to Russia so that Trotskii would feel that he had some force behind him.[24] Lloyd George said that Trotskii could go no further than he had gone. Obviously, he could not make an open overture to the Allies, because the Germans would learn of it at once. Lloyd George proposed an immediate conference to consider the best methods of organizing assistance to Trotskii. The Allied governments had to be prepared to act immediately, since the Germans were now only three or four days from Petrograd.[25]

The War Cabinet discussions resulted in the decision to organize military resistance to the Germans in Russia while simultaneously negotiating with America and Japan about their intervention. The War Cabinet considered it anomalous that while great efforts were being made to secure the intervention of Japan and the United States, Czecho-Slovak troops should be removed from Russia to the Western Front. In any case, the shipping controller had reported that any transport would simply divert tonnage from the transport of equivalent numbers of American troops. Moreover, it seemed inadvisable to ask for Japanese tonnage for that purpose when the British were already putting pressure upon Japan for intervention in Russia, which clearly would absorb all of her tonnage. The War Cabinet agreed that the Czecho-Slovaks, either at or on their way to Vladivostok, should be placed under the command of the French, who would organize them into efficient fighting units. They proposed to inform Clemenceau of the difficulty involved in securing the Czechs' transport to France and ask whether, pending their eventual transport, the Czechs might be used to stiffen the Japanese as part of an Allied force of intervention in Russia. The War Cabinet believed that the collection and organization of large bodies of troops at the ports of Vladivostok, Archangel, and

Murmansk would in itself be a warning to Germany against the removal of further divisions to the Western Front.

The War Cabinet also agreed to send General Frederick C. Poole at once to Russia as British military representative to take charge of military affairs for the British government and to advise the War Office on all steps necessary to implement British intervention in Russia. Poole was to have the right of direct communication with the War Office. However, the War Cabinet stressed that Poole should be careful not to interfere in diplomatic affairs without previously consulting Lockhart. By this time, a French colonel had already arrived at Murmansk from Moscow with orders to go to Archangel to superintend the arrival there of the Czechs. Admiral Sir Rosslyn E. Wemyss, the First Sea Lord, agreed to send some 200 marines for the defense of Archangel, and the War Office promised to send such munitions and supplies as Poole might deem necessary for his mission. While holding and safeguarding the position at Murmansk and Archangel, Poole was to consider how far he could work up from Archangel toward Vologda with the forces at his disposal. The War Cabinet decided that it was inadvisable at that point to move either American or other Allied troops from the West to Russia. Convinced that it was virtually impossible for Trotskii to invite Allied intervention in Russia before an Allied force was on the front to protect him against the enemy—however much he might desire it—they agreed to press the American and Japanese governments to be satisfied "with the very strong expressions which had already fallen from Trotskii and the Bolshevik Foreign Minister without waiting for a formal invitation which the Bolshevik government could not be expected to make in their present situation."[26]

The decision to utilize the Czech troops both at Archangel and around Vladivostok to reinforce intervention was aimed initially at supporting Trotskii against the Germans. Lockhart's telegrams had indicated that such a move would be acceptable to Trotskii, at least insofar as northern Russia was concerned. Major E. Francis Riggs, American Assistant Military Attaché in Moscow, agreed that Trotskii at this time had a policy based on an entente with the Allies. Rejecting the view that Trotskii and Lenin were German agents, Riggs was convinced that Trotskii's idea was "to play the Allies off against the Germans and vice versa," and it was this plan that had led him to become a party, in connection with the French, to allowing a part of the Czecho-Slovaks to be directed to the northern ports. Riggs also reported that Trotskii had asked the Americans for instructors for his Red Guard and noted: "I know this for a fact because he asked *me*."[27]

On May 17, the day that General Poole left for Russia, the War Cabinet met once again to discuss Allied intervention in Siberia and in particular the use of Czecho-Slovak forces as a nucleus on which to base such intervention. Unable to obtain the assent of either the United States or Japan, Lloyd George was debating whether the British should now proceed without them. With the Germans withdrawing troops from the Russian front, the British army bearing the brunt of the attack on the Western Front, and no material American contribution arriving to assist them, Lloyd George opined that the British had every justification not to allow the Japanese and Americans to block any British attempts to stultify these German withdrawals. Although Balfour believed that the Japanese would be unwilling to agree to an intervention in Siberia without their taking a leading part, he felt sure that if the British proposed to act without them, the Japanese would immediately wish to join and that American cooperation would follow very soon thereafter.

Balfour was all for informing Wilson that "we had a large force of 20,000 Czecho-Slovaks who would fight well if properly officered, and asking if the United States Government saw any objection to these troops being used against the Germans, with the assistance of the Japanese." Milner, however, immediately pointed out the drawbacks to the proposed telegram. First, the French were still very insistent that Czecho-Slovak forces should be transported to France. Second, the Czecho-Slovaks themselves were still unwilling to be involved in the internal strife of Russia. Their desire was "to fight Germans and not Bolsheviks." Chancellor of the Exchequer Andrew Bonar Law quickly pointed out that the problems of Czech transportation and securing their cooperation in Russia might both be solved if the Czecho-Slovak forces were made a part of the Allied force, thus making it clear to them that they were not fighting Russians but Germans.[28]

Cecil was much impressed by these suggestions. He agreed with Balfour that once definite steps had actually been taken to implement intervention in Siberia, the rest of the Allies would soon conform, even the French. Cecil agreed to see Beneš and ascertain definitely whether the Czecho-Slovaks would cooperate if "the object of the expedition was to fight Germans." In the meantime, the General Staff would determine if anything effective could be done in Siberia without the cooperation of either the United States or Japan, using the Czecho-Slovak force as a nucleus, reinforced by Canadian railway elements, British troops from Hong Kong, and a French contingent. If after these actions had been taken there was any promise of a scheme being put into operation, the British Foreign Office then would take such diplomatic action as might be expedient with the United States, Japan, and France. The War Cabinet had devised a clever plan to "trigger both American and Japanese involvement in Asiatic Russia."[29]

On the following day, Cecil explained to Beneš the reasons for keeping the army in Russia. Beneš stated that the army would obey the orders of the National Council. However, if the army were asked to remain in Russia, Beneš requested that the Allied governments publicly recognize the Czecho-Slovak movement and the National Council and acknowledge them as a nationality with just claims to independence.[30] When Cecil submitted Beneš's request to the Foreign Office, he appended a significant note: "We are at this moment hoping for, and in a great measure counting upon the Czecho-Slovak forces in Russia to form the nucleus of intervention at Archangel and Vladivostok. It therefore seems to be important to give them all political encouragement possible—that is, to go as far as France and Italy and not wait for the United States."[31] The Foreign Office favored Beneš's proposals and wanted immediate action, because a solution to the problem of using the Czecho-Slovaks in Russia could not be postponed.[32] At the same time, Beneš reiterated that the Czecho-Slovak National Council desired to continue its arrangement with France for the transfer of a minimum of 30,000 troops from Russia.

On May 23, Cecil informed Beneš that the Czecho-Slovak movement had "every possible sympathy of His Majesty's Government" and that Britain would be glad to give the same recognition to the movement as had been given by France and Italy. The British were prepared to recognize the Czecho-Slovak National Council as the supreme organ of the Czecho-Slovak movement in the Allied countries, to recognize the "Czecho-Slovak army as an organized unit operating in the Allied cause," and to attach to it a British liaison officer. It was agreed to accord the National Council political rights concerning the civil affairs of the Czecho-Slovaks similar to those already accorded to the Polish National Committee. Although the War Cabinet was reluctant to take such a stand without first consulting the United States "and bringing her into line," nevertheless the urgency of getting the Czechs "to form an agreement of intervention at Archangel and Vladivostok" necessitated immediate action on the matter without waiting for the United States.[33] Thus the decisive element in the British decision to grant political recognition to the Czecho-Slovak National Council was Beneš's agreement to fight on the Eastern Front if it should be renewed.[34] Balfour now sought to make the necessary arrangements for intervention in Russia, presumably in support of the Bolshevik government and against the Germans.

At this crucial juncture, Lockhart reported that Lavergne was seeking to arrange the transfer of the Czechs to Archangel for future employment in France. Lockhart had informed the Czechs that the British could not supply the necessary ships to take them all via Vladivostok and that half would have to go via Archangel. The Czechs were willing to accept this, and Lenin had told Lavergne that he was agreeable if the Czechs would consent to the French request that half of their number be transported to France via Archangel. Lavergne was anxious that Lockhart support his request to Trotskii. When Lockhart sought approval from the Foreign Office, the request naturally threw Downing Street into a quandary. The British obviously objected to supplying the Czechs with provisions and ships at Archangel for transfer to France, since this would upset their plans for using the Czechs in Russia and their hopes for securing French agreement to those plans. In these circumstances, they thought it would be better to "get them all to Vladivostok, where they will swell the contingent which we hope will form part of the Allied expeditionary forces."[35]

On his return trip to Paris on May 20, Beneš had the opportunity to visit with General Charles Delmé-Radcliffe, chief of the British military mission in Italy, who was conveying to the French government reports from Cecil on the result of the Czech leader's negotiations in London. From that conversation, Beneš gathered that Cecil, on behalf of the British government, had reported the possibility of an agreement with France regarding the Czech army in Siberia and its utilization in accordance with the British point of view. Beneš later recorded the clear divergence of opinion that existed on this matter, as revealed by his discussions at the Quai d'Orsay with Pichon and General Henri Berthelot, chief of the French military mission in Rumania. The latter showed little confidence in the possibility of renewing the Eastern Front and apparently considered these attempts as simply a scheme to protect the interests of the British. Clemenceau agreed with Pichon and Berthelot.[36] Nevertheless, by May 23, Milner had received word from Clemenceau of his agreement "to the use of Czecho-Slovak troops at Murmansk and Archangel, except such as had already arrived at Vladivostok."[37] The British plans to utilize the Czecho-Slovaks as the spearhead for Allied intervention in Russia seemed on the verge of realization.

12

Outbreak of the
Czech-Bolshevik Conflict

May 1918 marked the most crucial period in the Czecho-Slovak liberation movement. The Czech Legion had fought its last official engage-
ment with the Germans in southwestern Russia and had begun its long
journey to Siberia with the official consent of the Soviet government.
The French government was eagerly awaiting the legion on the Western
Front. Masaryk had given explicit orders to the legion to maintain strict
neutrality, and the soldiers themselves were eager to get out of the
Russian turmoil as quickly as possible. Yet by May 25, the Soviet
government and the Czecho-Slovaks were engaged in a life and death
struggle that was to have profound international implications.

Considerable diversity of view surrounds the origin and development of the Czech-Bolshevik conflict. The Soviets charge that the conflict was planned, organized, and financed by the English and French
governments as a part of a much larger plan for a general offensive
against the Bolshevik government.[1] This version states that the Czech
Legion was ordered to seize the whole Trans-Siberian Railway as the
preliminary strategic move in an all-out attack upon the Soviet government. This was to be followed by the landing of large expeditionary
forces in European Russia and in the Far East. (Variations on this theme
have been further developed by several Western historians as well.)
Conversely, the Czecho-Slovak official version places the major responsibility upon the Soviet leaders, particularly Stalin and Trotskii. It
insists that the attack upon the legion was premeditated by the Bolsheviks with an intent to disband and incorporate it into the Red Army
and into labor battalions.[2] The obvious bias of these two official versions necessitates a careful analysis of the outbreak of the conflict.

In late April, all towns and cities along the Trans-Siberian Railway
were in the hands of the Bolsheviks. The Czech Legion was stretched
out from Penza, west of the Volga, to Vladivostok. Although the initial
movement of the Czechs had been slow because of the disorganization
of railway traffic, by April 30 some 6,000 to 8,000 Czechs had arrived at

Vladivostok, where the Soviets were furnishing barracks for them. By May 7, the Allies, in cooperation with Trotskii, had agreed that all Czecho-Slovaks who had not passed Omsk should be evacuated via Archangel. A telegram from Moscow on May 8 categorically forbade any further movement of Czecho-Slovak trains in the direction of Vladivostok and established Archangel as their destination.[3]

Accordingly, three Czech envoys—Maxa, Dr. Ivan Markovič, and František Janík—departed from Omsk for Vologda and Moscow to confer with Soviet and French authorities regarding the change in plan. Arriving on May 13, they consulted the following day with General Lavergne, who verified that Trotskii had promised to cooperate in the revised plan to evacuate part of the legion via Archangel. On May 15, the three Czechs left for Archangel, where they learned that transports could begin to arrive. Returning to Moscow, the Czech delegates continued their conversations with Trotskii, who urged them to put pressure on the Allies for a speedy removal to France.[4] In discussing the change of plans with the Czech leaders, Trotskii did not refer to the arrangements for additional collaboration with the Allies. Rather, he rationalized the change of direction by implying that "the Japanese landing in Vladivostok and the advance of the Semenov band made the further movement of the echelons to the east impossible." This no doubt pleased Maxa, Markovič, and Janík, who had already informed Lavergne of their desire to have the Czech army corps transported to France as rapidly as possible and freed from any service in Murmansk.[5] They now decided to return to Omsk to implement the plans for transferring part of the troops to the north. Apparently, they still believed it possible to remove the troops rapidly and safely.

The Allied plan for the change in the transport of the Czechs was not made known to the Czech leaders in Russia either in sufficient detail or in time for effective implementation. Negotiations had been carried out directly between the Allied representatives in Russia and the Soviet authorities, and it was probably as a result of the agreement between them that the central Soviet government issued its order stopping further transport of the Czechs by way of Irkutsk. Although Lavergne had notified the French government of Bolshevik acceptance of the new transport plan as early as April 27, it was not until May 10 that the official Czecho-Slovak organ published news of the approval of the plan. And even then, the Czech leaders in Siberia were not informed that the plan had received Allied agreement. This information did not arrive until May 17.[6] The order had given rise to the most varied conjectures among the Czech troops, especially because the

General Stanislav Čeček (National Archives)

Soviet government simultaneously had issued another order to trans-port German prisoners from eastern to western Siberia. The Czechs believed that the change in plan was the result of German pressure on Moscow. This widely prevalent view, strongly supported by anti-Bol-shevik leaders, assumed that "Moscow was ruled by the Kaiser's ambassador, Count Mirbach, who ruled all the Bolshevist provinces and whose obedient servants were Lenine and Trotskii." Thus, behind the Bolshevik policy to disarm any force fighting against the Germans in Russia stood Count von Mirbach or General Ludendorff.[7] The offi-cial Czech account of the Czech-Bolshevik conflict also rested on the opinion, "very widely spread through Russia," that the Soviet leaders were the paid agents of Germany. This conviction grew stronger as repeated attempts were made to disarm the soldiers.[8] Both Lieutenants Jan Syrový and Stanislav Čeček (later generals and commanders in Siberia) opposed the proposal, affirming that their opposition was shared by the vast majority. On May 12, Syrový categorically an-nounced that no Czecho-Slovaks would turn back toward Archangel.[9]

General Jan Syrový (National Archives)

On May 14, while Maxa and Čermák were gone, a catalytic incident erupted at Cheliabinsk, the first station in Siberia on the eastern side of the Urals. A train carrying German and Austro-Hungarian prisoners of war to the west stopped by the Cheliabinsk station just a few yards from a train carrying Czecho-Slovak soldiers moving eastwards. Although the Czech official version of the Cheliabinsk incident reported that the relations between the prisoners and the Czechs were "good," nevertheless, as the train was leaving, a prisoner threw a piece of iron out of the train, mortally wounding one of the Czecho-Slovak soldiers. The train was instantly stopped, a fight ensued, and the

Hungarian culprit was lynched. The local soviet immediately investigated the affair and arrested some Czecho-Slovaks. Furious at what they regarded as the illegal imprisonment of their fellows, the Czechs, led by their commanders, marched to the city, released their comrades, and disarmed the Red Guards.

According to Miller's vivid account of the events, only half of the 5,000 Czechs in Cheliabinsk were armed, but they were all called out. Within ten minutes, they had taken the station and the munitions warehouses and provided all with arms. Apparently the Bolsheviks offered little resistance to the capture of the city. Miller believed that this incident aroused the suspicions of the Bolsheviks and "made it impossible for the Czechs to go back through the Bolshevik strongholds . . . to Archangel, or at least so they thought."[10] For Lockhart, the result of this seemingly insignificant skirmish in a small Trans-Siberian Railway junction between two groups from a dying multinational empire was quite clear: "The first plank in the platform of the interventionists had been laid." The events at Cheliabinsk became the catalyst for war throughout Siberia.[11]

Notwithstanding this event, the circumstances were relatively favorable for the Czecho-Slovak legion's withdrawal from Russia. About 14,000 to 15,000 of the Czechs had already reached Vladivostok, and over 25,000 were already east of Omsk.[12] Others were scattered in echelons from Samara to Omsk. The Soviets had comparatively little to gain and a great deal to lose by a foolish policy of useless obstruction. On the other hand, the Czechs in their isolated situation saw the various delays, rerouting, and disarming attempts as a Bolshevik plot to hand them over to the Germans.[13] This fear had already resulted in plans by certain officers to make ready for "every and any contingency." While senior officers agreed with Generals Shokorov and Dietrichs that peaceful passage to Vladivostok was imperative, no matter what conditions the Bolsheviks might impose, still others thought that the right moment for shooting their way to Vladivostok had not come yet. A few, led by Captain (later General) Rudolf Gajda, commanding officer of the Seventh Regiment, were serious about taking immediate action against the Bolsheviks if they tried to block their way. Contemptuous of the Bolsheviks, the young, headstrong Gajda ordered Captain Eduard Kadlec, the only Czech officer with staff experience, to prepare plans for such a contingency. In the ensuing days, Gajda's idea of shooting his way to the east became more popular.[14]

On May 18, following the Cheliabinsk incident, a congress of Czech

General Rudolf Gajda (National Archives)

delegates chose a military executive committee of twelve (composed of six soldiers and six officers) to be in charge of the evacuation of the legionnaires from Siberia to France. The legion was divided into two with Čeček and Gajda commanders of the first and second divisions. Syrový was chief of the entire force. Commissars were elected to deal with local and regional soviets.[15]

The Cheliabinsk incident on May 14; the congress's decision that in view of the tense situation existing between the Soviet government and the Czecho-Slovaks, "vigorous measures must be taken immediately in order to secure the rapid passage of the trains toward Vladivostok"; and the May 20 order of the Council of People's Commissars to completely disarm all Czecho-Slovak echelons marked a turning point in

Cheliabinsk convention of the Czecho-Slovak army (*Bohemian Review*)

relations with the Bolsheviks.[16] When the order arrived from the Moscow Soviet that all arms were to be given up and that in the interim the Czech commissar of the army would be held as a hostage, the Czechs decided they would not give up their arms nor would they go by way of Archangel under the existing conditions. Instead, they decided to concentrate the entire first division around Cheliabinsk as soon as possible and then make for Vladivostok, seizing all the important towns along the way if any resistance was offered to their rapid transport. On May 24, Miller informed George Williams, his former YMCA colleague, now Consul at Samara: "So, if there are any reports in the press that the Tchéques are trying to capture Siberia, and oust the Soviet Government, we are to know that they are only making for Vladivostok, and are thru letting the Bolsheviks play with them longer."[17]

For the Bolshevik government, the Cheliabinsk incident was the last straw. The Czechs, even though "Allied" troops, seemed to be giving them nothing but trouble. Soviet permission for the Czechs to go to Vladivostok had been given against the wishes of the Siberian soviets, which were not only having to contend with Semenov but were also worried about the possibility of Japanese intervention. Moreover, the

Czechs who had already arrived in Vladivostok appeared to be stranded, for no Allied ships were in sight to remove them. In these circumstances, the Soviets decided that they would have an advantage in a showdown while the Czechs were still partially disarmed. On May 21, the day after instructions were sent to the local soviets to disarm the legion forcibly, Trotskii arrested Maxa and Čermák, another member of the presidium of the Russian branch of the Czecho-Slovak National Council, in Moscow and issued a decree abolishing the Russian branch of the Czecho-Slovak National Council.[18] Maxa and Čermák immediately signed an order to the legion to surrender all arms unconditionally to the representatives of local soviets. The order continued: "The safeguarding of the troops will rest altogether with the Soviet organ of the Russian Federated Republic. Whosoever should disobey this order shall be considered a traitor and declared an outlaw."[19]

On May 22, the "Congress of the Czecho-Slovak Revolutionary Army" at Cheliabinsk replied that it did not believe that the Soviet government had sufficient strength to guarantee free and safe transit of its troops to Vladivostok, and it unanimously refused to give up its arms until it could obtain a guarantee of free departure and of personal safety.[20] Believing that the orders issued by the Czecho-Slovak National Council members to the legion to surrender its arms had been either forged or secured under duress, the congress declared the orders invalid and delegated exclusive charge of the transportation of the Czecho-Slovak troops to a provisional executive committee chosen by the congress. It declared that any attempt to disarm them would be considered an "act of violence."[21] Despite the outraged protests of the French military representatives, the congress agreed unanimously to disregard the orders from Paris that half the corps should proceed to Archangel. On May 23, the members voted to defy the Bolsheviks and move the entire corps to Vladivostok, by force if necessary. Trotskii immediately ordered all Siberian Bolsheviks to shoot every armed Czecho-Slovak found on the railway. On May 25, Captain Gajda instructed all the commanders of the Czech echelons east of Novo Nikolaevsk "to proceed militarily to Vladivostok" and to take all the stations en route to Irkutsk.[22] The breach between the Czechs and the Bolsheviks was complete.

Evidently as a result of the telegram from Aralov and Trotskii, the Soviets first attempted to disarm a military transport at Maryanovka, near Omsk. On May 25, as the Czechs were approaching Omsk, they learned that an ambush was prepared for them, whereupon they retired to Station Maryanovka. In the meantime, the regimental band was playing on the station platform when two trains approached from Omsk. Without any warning whatsoever, heavy fire from machine guns and rifles was opened on the unsuspecting Czechs. After a brief but bloody battle, the Czechs retired to Station Issilkul, and negotiations started between the Czechs and the local soviet about the manner in which the Czechs could proceed.

Lacey G. Gray, American Vice Consul at Omsk, observed that the Czechs had received reports of Soviet efforts to disarm all the Czech echelons along the Siberian Railway simultaneously with the Maryanovka affair. The Czechs had concluded that "the Germans were forcing the Soviets to disarm them and keep them here as prisoners."[23] Gray also reported that after the battle at Maryanovka, the Czechs had captured a great deal of arms from the Red Guard and then received assistance from a Cossack division, led by Boris Vladimirovich Annenkov, which joined them later at Issilkul. On the same day, May 25, Kadlec and Gajda, in accordance with the resolution of the Cheliabinsk congress of May 23, proceeded eastward at their own discretion to occupy Mariinsk and Novo Nikolaevsk. According to the Soviet version of the fighting at Mariinsk and Maryanovka, the trouble started when some drunken Bolshevik sailors attacked the Czechs. According to the Czech version, the local soviet was working under instructions received from Moscow and was preparing to disarm the Czechs.[24] Ernest F. Campbell, YMCA man with the Czechs at Mariinsk, reported a different version of events. On the afternoon of May 25, after receiving "a signal telegram" from their commanding officers "that movement at all points was blocked and that the stations were to be seized," the Czechs proceeded to take the city and the Bolshevik train at the station within half an hour. They lost only two men, who were mistaken for Bolsheviks and shot by their own soldiers.[25]

The Cheliabinsk congress in mid-May was clearly a turning point for Czech actions in Siberia. When the delegates from the congress returned to Penza and informed their colleagues of the decision to force a passage through to Vladivostok, arms collected to be given to the Bolsheviks in accordance with the Moscow order were redistributed among the men. On May 27, at dawn, the Czech officers also received secret orders that their "action would begin at half hour after midnight," and patrols went into the town to secure intelligence for a troop advance. In the meantime, Vasilii Vladimirovich Kurajov, the chairman of the provincial soviet, called a meeting of the Czechs and personally requested their disarmament. The Czechs unanimously and emphatically refused. Shortly thereafter, while negotiations continued be-

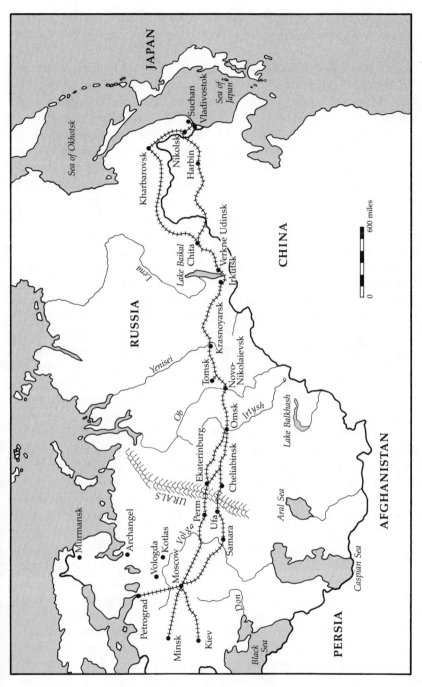

Map 2. Strategic Points on the Trans-Siberian and Chinese Eastern Railroads

tween the provincial soviet and the Czech military leaders, Čeček arrived and helped to organize preparations for the attack. The Czechs seized Penza on May 29 after heavy fighting. Overjoyed with their victory, especially with the capture of a vast quantity of rifles, ammunition, machine guns, and other military equipment, the Czechs had "no idea, what was going on on the railway line from Chelyabinsk to Vladivostok, [but] were ready to force [their] way alone, even to the very end of the world."[26] The Czechs were winning similar military successes at other points along the Trans-Siberian Railway: Novo Nikolaevsk and Cheliabinsk, on May 26; Syzran, May 28; and Tomsk, May 31. Until the time of battle, they were spread out from the Volga to Vladivostok. Now the legion was strategically well situated to seize the railway at its most vital points. Indeed, some Siberian Bolsheviks had already warned Trotskii that they were too weak to carry out his disarmament orders "in its full sense as you demand."[27]

In addition to the regular American consular officers, military attachés, and YMCA secretaries, close to the scene of the Czech-Bolshevik conflict was Colonel George H. Emerson, commander of the Russian Railway Service Corps, then stationed in Manchuria. In late March, Trotskii had requested that a group of American railway experts help the Soviet government to restore the operating efficiency of the Russian railways. However, Stevens, in Harbin, was reluctant to release Emerson, because he had finally succeeded in arranging the employment of Emerson's engineers on the Chinese Eastern Railway, which was then under Horvath's control. Stevens feared that any attempt to engage in Soviet service would so infuriate Horvath that he would become suspicious of the entire railway corps and that its employment in his area would be jeopardized. It was only after the State Department explained that the desire to improve the Soviet-controlled railway system was primarily connected with the military effort against Germany that Stevens finally agreed to dispatch Emerson to European Russia.[28]

Accompanied by six engineers, Emerson arrived in Vladivostok on May 5. Two days later, he received a message from Francis at Vologda that arrangements would be made for a special movement of the Emerson party. Chicherin instructed all railroad regional and local soviet deputies to give the Emerson mission "all assistance."[29] In Vladivostok, Major Slaughter, Assistant Military Attaché in the American embassy, joined the Emerson party to accompany some provisions being shipped to Vologda. As they continued their journey, they met several echelons of Czecho-Slovaks and, on May 24, met Robins, who

Front, left to right: Vice Consul Lacey G. Gray, Bohdan Pavlů, and Major Homer H. Slaughter, Ekaterinburg, Siberia (National Archives)

informed them that conditions were improving and that he had had a very successful trip from Moscow. On May 26, Emerson and his party arrived at Irkutsk, where they were greeted by Consul General Ernest L. Harris, who had been there only two weeks, and his associate, Consul David B. Macgowan. I. M. Geitzman, deputy agent in Irkutsk of the Moscow Commissariat for Foreign Affairs, who had established cordial relations with the Americans, welcomed the party on behalf of the local Soviet authorities.[30]

   In Irkutsk that afternoon, after the Emerson party had departed, while strolling in the public park directly across from the railway station, Harris witnessed the outbreak of one of the initial encounters between the Czechs and the Bolsheviks. He observed that when the Soviets attempted to carry out Aralov's order to disarm the Czecho-Slovak trains, fighting ensued. After a brief battle, the Czechs on this first train "gave up their arms voluntarily and further bloodshed was avoided, and this particular train shortly proceeded on its way." About ten o'clock that evening, two more Czech trains arrived at Innoken-tievskaya, which was about five miles west of Irkutsk and directly opposite an Austro-German prison camp, located about one and one-

Lacey G. Gray, *left,* and Ernest L. Harris, Omsk, Siberia (National Archives)

half miles across an open field. According to Harris and the French Consul General, Gaston Bourgeois, who personally investigated the incident, these trains were attacked about midnight by armed Austrian and German prisoners. However, the 1,000 Czechs engaged evidently made short work of the Austrians and Germans. While the conflict was in progress, Geitzman and Y. D. Yansen, the chairman of the Irkutsk Soviet, appeared at Harris's home and urged him to intervene to stop the bloodshed.

Knowing that the Czechs were under French command, Harris immediately called upon Bourgeois, and they proceeded at daybreak under a flag of truce to the scene of the action. By that time, the Czechs had captured twenty-two Austrians, four Germans, and nine Russians who were members of the Red Guard, all in the "uniforms of their respective nationalities."[31] Many Austrian and German wounded had been returned to the camp. Harris immediately visited the Russian commandant of the prison camp to get all the facts from both sides. An Austrian officer who accompanied him back to the Czech trains established the nationality of the prisoners; there had been five casualties (four Austrian and one German). Because all the prisoners except for two or three were in the uniforms of their respective nationalities, Harris concluded that many of the prisoners in Irkutsk were armed. According to the best intelligence available, there were then 600 armed prisoners in the city, who composed a large part of the Red Guard. Harris noted that he had seen a few Austrian prisoners in Austrian uniforms bearing arms. He and Bourgeois succeeded in disarming these two trains of Czechs as well as a third train that had arrived at another station a few miles west. The disarmament compact was agreed upon and signed by the Czech commanders, two Soviet commissars, Bourgeois, Harris, and Vergé, the French officer accompanying the Czechs. Although feeling was running high, Harris reported that the disarmament of these three trains was carried out without a hitch. A commissar of the Soviet was placed in each train, and Harris instructed Macgowan to accompany the whole lot to Vladivostok.[32]

Harris and Bourgeois knew nothing of the new orders that had been sent to either the Czechs from their commanders at Cheliabinsk, or to the local Soviet authorities from Trotskii and Aralov. They thought that the incident was the result of a misunderstanding and believed that it was their duty to expedite the passage of the Czechs to Vladivostok for transport to the Western Front. As a result of Harris's action, these trains had no further trouble.[33] Barely twenty-four hours after the signing of the disarmament agreement, a Czech courier arrived bringing the order from the Czech commander that all Czech troop trains should refuse to disarm and, if necessary, seize the railroad and fight their way to Vladivostok.[34]

A retrospective analysis of Harris's report reveals certain important facts. Clearly, in the fight at Irkutsk between the Czechs and the Soviets on May 26, both German and Austrian officers were killed while fighting in the ranks with the Red Guards.[35] Harris's telegram to Lansing gave a very definite impression that war prisoners led the Red Guard at Irkutsk and dominated the city. The most important fact was that Harris and Bourgeois persuaded, cajoled, or ordered the French officer in charge and the Czech echelon commander to give up Irkutsk, which they had captured, and to move on to Vladivostok. According to Gajda, by giving up Irkutsk they had endangered the entire Czech army. Had the Czechs held Irkutsk, there could hardly have been any real reason later for claiming that the Czechs were in danger, because within a few days, and practically without combat, the way to Manchuria would have been open, since the nearest Red troops were then at Chita, nearly 800 miles to the east, and the Lake Baikal tunnel section had fallen to the Czechs with Irkutsk.

As events turned out, the Czechs fought from June 1 to July 12 to recapture Irkutsk and, until the end of August, to recapture the tunnel region of Lake Baikal to reach Verkhneudinsk. While it cannot be proved that the one report of Harris and the action at Irkutsk determined the issue of intervention, the fact is that had the Czechs held Irkutsk, there could have been no excuse for intervention to save the Czechs; and, just as certainly, the report of war prisoners fighting Czechs at Irkutsk was the first authentic report from a United States source to support Allied claims of prisoners of war fighting with the Red army.[36] Moreover, as soon as the conflict began at Irkutsk, numerous reports of prisoner activity in the Amur region, at Chita, and at Irkutsk indicated that the war prisoners appeared to be the backbone of the attack on the Czechs. It is not too much to say, therefore, that Harris's action ultimately had some bearing on President Wilson's final decision to intervene in order to rescue the Czechs. At the same time, it is not surprising that Gajda, commander of the central Siberian group of Czechs, was furious when he learned what had occurred at Irkutsk and later told Emerson that if he ever caught up with the officers of these first trains, he would have them court-martialed for accepting the mediation and consenting to proceed.[37]

In the early morning of May 26, while Harris and Bourgeois were negotiating with the Czechs and Bolsheviks in Irkutsk, Czech troops attacked and overthrew the Bolshevik authorities at Novo Nikolaevsk. Immediately afterward, bands of armed Russians wearing white and green cockades and badges appeared in the town. These Russians assisted the Czechs in their military operations against the Bolsheviks and organized a new civil administration headed by a person styling himself the Commissar of the Siberian Provisional Government. In other places seized by the Czechs in the next few days, other commissars appeared who organized the local administration in the name of the new government. Apparently these local commissars worked quite independently of each other, and no explanation was given the public about the location of this Siberian Provisional Government or the persons who composed it until June 1. According to John A. Ray, Vice Consul in Novo Nikolaevsk, the Czechs maintained order while the local self-governing bodies were expected to organize affairs within their respective districts. The new Siberian government appeared to consist largely of members of the Social Revolutionary party and showed great reluctance to take any firm measures. They did, however, issue an order mobilizing all the officers in Siberia for active service and calling for volunteers for the army. Ray reported that the volunteers were not numerous and that the ranks of the new units had been filled up by officers serving as private soldiers.[38]

By the end of May, then, it was clear that the Czechs were seizing the towns and cities along the Trans-Siberian Railway in response to the orders of their own commanders. This state of affairs was not, however, generally known either in Siberia itself or abroad. Thus, while Harris and Bourgeois had restored the Bolsheviks to power and persuaded the Czechs to discontinue the fight at Irkutsk and continue the journey peacefully across Siberia, Gajda and his troops had ousted the Bolsheviks from control at Novo Nikolaevsk, Cheliabinsk, and Mariinsk and were cooperating in the establishment of a new Siberian government. But the Czech position in Vladivostok was quite different. Admiral Knight telegraphed Secretary of the Navy Daniels that 10,000 Czechs had arrived at Vladivostok and "were positively opposed" to conducting military operations in Siberia and Russia. They were unwilling to fight any Slavic race or faction but "enthusiastically eager" to fight against Germany. However, they were restless over the delays in transportation from Vladivostok of which no news had yet been received.[39]

While this patchwork of conflicting policies and confused events was unfolding in Siberia, a Franco-British conference in London had agreed on May 27 to stick to the Abbeville agreement to transfer the Czechs to the Western Front, but if necessary to retain a portion of the Czech army in Russia to hold Archangel. On the same day, Reading informed the State Department that British and French troops had landed at Murmansk on the Arctic coast and were "assisting the Bolshevists and the Russian Red Guards in protecting the Coast and Kola Railway from attacks by the White Guards."[40] At the same time, Lockhart informed the War Cabinet that Trotskii had no objection to Czech forces being sent to Archangel en route to France, but that they must be disarmed in transit through Russia and that Maxa was being held as a hostage for such disarmament.[41] Trotskii also requested a formal Allied demand for the transfer of the Czechs from Archangel and assurances that ships would be provided to "take them off." The British, who had been making every effort to persuade the French to retain the Czechs in Russia, were not about to comply with Trotskii's request. If the French insisted on their departure, then it was "surely for them to fight out the conditions with Trotskii."[42] To confuse matters further, the War Cabinet also received word that the Czechs were unwilling to intervene in Russian affairs and wished only to fight on the Western Front.[43] Lockhart reported that both the "Czech leaders and the Bolsheviks seem anxious to avoid further fighting so it is just possible that the conflict may end nominally." The French were doing their best to protect Czech interests, while Chicherin had asked Lockhart to use his "influence to obtain a peaceful settlement of the dispute."[44]

Emerson, too, now found himself involved in the role of mediator. Upon reaching Krasnoyarsk on May 27, he realized that the fighting that had occurred at Mariinsk would prevent his continuing to Vologda. Endeavoring to locate American Vice Consul Edward Thomas, he had come across Gregorii Weinbaum, President of the Soviet Committee of the province, who had informed him that the incident at Mariinsk was purely local. Thereupon, Emerson offered both his and Major Slaughter's services as mediators, making clear that their efforts were entirely unofficial. Slaughter immediately sent a wire to the commanding officer of the Czech troops at Mariinsk, asking him to defer all action until Emerson could confer with him and emphasizing the importance of the railway mission. At Soviet army headquarters not far from Mariinsk, Emerson conferred with Soviet officers, who claimed that the Czechs were responsible for the trouble. They refused to permit them to proceed unless they would disarm and also agree not to interfere directly or indirectly with internal affairs in Russia. If the Czechs complied, the Soviet authorities agreed to expedite their movement and to put a Red Guard on each Czech train to guarantee the safety of the Czech soldiers en route to Vladivostok.[45]

Through the cooperation of Weinbaum and the Russian and Czech commanders at the front, Emerson and Slaughter on May 29 negotiated with the Russian commander and then met with the Czech commander, Captain Kadlec, who insisted that the Czechs could not possibly disarm. Although Kadlec admitted that the Czechs had not been molested since leaving southern Russian territory, he now had very reliable information that "the Germans were actuating the Russian Soviet Government at Moscow to disarm them" and thus to keep them in Russia or central Siberia. They had no alternative but "to take up arms openly and fight their way to Vladivostok." Kadlec made it clear that the soldiers had disagreed with their civil officers and had elected Gajda, commanding officer at Novo Nikolaevsk, to be in charge.[46] Gajda alone had the authority to mediate the seizure of Siberian towns along the railway; the "concerted movement" was the result of this change in recognition of authority. Moreover, since they had taken over Novo Nikolaevsk, a new government had been instituted under Czech protection. Kadlec reiterated that the movement was a concerted one supported by the entire Czech army. He was convinced that the Czechs could exist in Siberia indefinitely and that they could control Siberia with little trouble.[47]

After further discussion, Kadlec, who preferred "open action with the Red Guard Army," reluctantly agreed to allow Emerson and his party, which included representatives of the Soviet government, to proceed westward and to meet Gajda at Novo Nikolaevsk.[48] However, when Weinbaum learned that a Soviet representative could not be taken along because of the unknown conditions on the railway, he opposed Emerson's decision to negotiate with Gajda and referred the entire matter to the Central Soviet Committee at Krasnoyarsk. Moreover, he declared that, regardless of Emerson's recommendations, the Soviet Committee had decided to start immediate action against the Czechs. "Very much excited," Weinbaum exclaimed, "France has, through concerted action with the Czech troops enroute, taken Siberia in 24 hours."[49]

On May 30, Emerson returned to Krasnoyarsk at noon and met a committee representing the Central Siberian Soviet at Irkutsk and two Czech officers. The committee informed him of the settlement that had been made by Harris and Bourgeois at Irkutsk, showed him a copy of the agreement, and also told him of their peaceable settlement with the Czech echelons at Nizhneudinsk and Kansk. They wished to continue westward in order to make a peaceful settlement with the other Czech echelons and asked the Emerson group to accompany them. Although glad to assist as mediators, Emerson's group wanted to have official support for their efforts. When Emerson wired Harris at Irkutsk through the good offices of Weinbaum, Harris informed him of the successful mediation at Irkutsk and authorized him to proceed to Mariinsk and endeavor to negotiate a similar agreement. Although Bourgeois was unable to leave Irkutsk at that time, he approved Emerson's efforts and offered to meet any delegates who would come to Irkutsk for negotiations. Harris then instructed Edward Thomas, Vice Consul in Irkutsk, to accompany Emerson on his mediation mission and emphasized that the Americans "must impress upon Czechs and upon soviet that we are all fighting the common enemy and in unity lies success."[50]

Now empowered with official authority from both Harris and Bourgeois, Emerson informed all the soviets and all the commanders of both the Soviet army and the Czech army from Irkutsk to Cheliabinsk of his appointment and requested that they cease all military action immediately until the arrival of his mission.[51] By June 1, the Czechs at Mariinsk and the Bolsheviks at Suslova had approved the armistice, and Emerson, with Soviet representatives from Irkutsk and Krasnoyarsk and two Czech officers, crossed the lines to Mariinsk on June 2, where they had separate conferences with Gajda and the Soviet representative.[52]

But events were taking a different turn at Vologda. On May 28, the Allied Ambassadors there held a conference, which was also attended by Lockhart and the French Military Attachés, and decided to urge intervention regardless of Bolshevik consent.[53] On June 1, Lavergne sent a memorandum describing the Czecho-Slovak break with the Soviets to the French Ministry of War. He reported that a new committee had been appointed to direct the Czechs on their journey, and that Trotskii was irreconcilable on the question of disarming the Czecho-Slovaks. He concluded that the presence of Czech forces at strategic points along the Trans-Siberian Railway could well be utilized for purposes of intervention.[54] By this time Francis also had received word of the hostilities in the Omsk area. Deeply concerned over the Czech disarmament, he expressed his regret to Lansing.[55] Chicherin, however, insisted that it was absolutely essential that the Czechs give up their weapons, cease their struggle against the Bolsheviks, and leave the country. In desperation he turned to Lockhart for help. He charged the Czechs with counterrevolutionary activity and said that telegrams had been seized also implicating British representatives. Nevertheless, he asked Lockhart to use his moral influence to induce the Czechs to stop fighting and to break the opposition of the "Czech mutineers."[56]

From the standpoint of British strategy in Russia at that moment, Lockhart and the British government were the last intermediaries whom the Soviets should have approached. By the end of May, the British War Cabinet was in a quandary. The strategy it had accepted on May 17 was now in trouble. The imponderables of Japanese and American policy continued to frustrate all its efforts to divert Germany's attention from the Western Front. Moreover, the French had adamantly refused to use the Czech Legion as the nucleus of an expeditionary force in Russia.[57]

In the wake of widespread Soviet preparations for fighting the

Dr. Václav Girsa at Czech headquarters, Vladivostok, Siberia (National Archives)

Czecho-Slovaks and in response to the various Soviet proposals to end the conflict, the representatives of the Czecho-Slovak National Council in Vladivostok, which had a far more favorable view of Bolshevik efforts to expedite the movements of the Czech Legion and which was still following Masaryk's original instructions, now transmitted a telegram to all legionnaires signed by Dr. Václav Girsa, Captain Vladimír Hurban, and Václav Houska. It blamed delayed departure from

Vladivostok on the absence of ships, and ordered all clashes along the railway to cease. The council added that the arms question was unimportant, since the quantity left by the Siberian Soviet was sufficient to insure the personal safety of the legion to Vladivostok. It affirmed that the road was absolutely safe from Karimskaya to Vladivostok; that the plan of sending the First Division to Archangel was proposed by the Allies because of transportation considerations; and that if the Czechs would be patient and not forget their ultimate aim, they would be able to achieve their mission.[58] The executive committee of the Vladivostok Soviet also cautioned all the Soviets along the vast mileage of the Trans-Siberian Railway: "Avoid everything which might create trouble with the Czecho-Slovak echelons. Do everything which may expedite them to Vladivostok."[59] Two weeks later, the Czecho-Slovak National Council at Vladivostok and Dietrichs sent a peace delegation to Omsk "to assure all our echelons on the way and especially Captain Gajda at Omsk, that the road is clear and that no danger is threatening our echelons on their way to Vladivostok."[60]

As Emerson prepared to mediate between the Soviets and the Czechs at Mariinsk, Consul Alfred R. Thomson at Omsk faced a similar situation. Here, too, the Soviets had appealed to the American officials for support. On the evening of May 31, the Soviet asked Thomson to attend a conference between the Soviet and the French-Czech delegates from Issilkul. At the conference the President of the Soviet read an intercepted telegram from the commander of the Czech troops at Cheliabinsk that had instructed other Czech echelons to disregard French control for the time. The single result of this meeting was a telegram sent by Major Alphonse Guinet, French military representative attached to the Czech Legion, which read: "To the Czechs at Isilkoul: Your action forces the French Mission to wash its hands of this affair. It will be a disgrace for the Czechs to become involved in Russian difficulties. If the Czechs persist in their activities everything must end between them and the French Government. The Czechs must take no action whatever until the French Mission [which was leaving Omsk immediately] arrives in Isilkoul." When the President of the Soviet asked Thomson whether he concurred in the telegram, he replied that he was not authorized to act in the matter, since he had been unable to wire Ambassador Francis for instructions. However, insofar as the matter lay within his competence in a personal capacity, he supported the attitude taken by the French delegates.[61] While the French military authorities sought to restrain the Czech military leaders, the local

Bolsheviks appealed for support in the struggle they now realized could not long be postponed.

On the evening of June 1, a second conference took place between the same parties, and again Thomson was invited. Since all the negotiations were carried on in Russian, Gray, the American Vice Consul at Omsk, attended the conference. To Gray, it seemed that the French were wavering on the disarmament of the Czechs, so, during an intermission in the meeting, Gray presented the facts to the French lieutenant who accompanied Major Guinet. When the meeting resumed, one Czech delegate insisted that the Czechs must never submit to Trotskii's order instructing them to be disarmed and confined in prison camps: "We will never consent! Sooner will we die!" The Soviet, however, insisted upon total disarmament. Guinet replied:

The Czechs are courageous troops. Armed, they know that they can attain their end and complete their journey. While en route, they have no desire to shed blood. Their aim is France. Concessions from both sides are imperative. You possess some strength and they possess some strength. Safety is necessary to them and must be guaranteed. At present it is only a question of time. It is premature to talk of the surrender of arms. This question must be referred to the coming conference at Cheliabinsk otherwise the Czechs will take Omsk, and, arms in hand will secure their onward progress.[62]

The Soviets thereupon adjourned to discuss the matter and determine their action. Meanwhile a telegram arrived from Issilkul recalling the French and Czech delegates immediately. When the Soviets reentered the room, they were informed of the new development. Before the meeting was adjourned, both sides agreed to keep the truce until further notification.

The Omsk Soviet immediately became active and pressed all workingmen into the army; recruited prisoners; terrorized the population by arresting the leading men and executing them; and also hunted White Guards, who had become very active. Gray reported that the Cossacks had openly joined with the Czechs. Shortly thereafter, on June 5, a second decisive battle between the Czechs and the Red Army occurred at Station Maryanovka outside of Omsk, where the Red Army had entrenched itself. On June 7, the Soviets and their families left Omsk on steamboats and White Guards appeared from their houses and took control.

On June 8, Thomson, Gray, and British Vice Consul Jordan called on the new government. They were told that the White Guard had been working for some time to overthrow the Bolsheviks and had a government "planned out," but that most of the members were still in places occupied by the Bolsheviks. They emphasized that their platform was renewal of war with Germany, nonrecognition of the Treaty of Brest-Litovsk, continuance of the alliance with the Allies, and treatment of foreign property and persons in accordance with existing international customs. They requested immediate assistance from the Allies. The American and Allied representatives responded that although they "had no instructions" from "their respective Governments," they personally felt that their platform would meet with the approval of the Allies. They promised to lend the new government "all the moral assistance possible" until they had received definite instructions.[63]

With the Czech defeat of the Red Army near Omsk, Thomson, Gray, and the Allied representatives called on Syrový and told him they were extremely pleased by their actions, that their respective governments would surely approve, and that they would receive support from the Allies. They also stated that the Czechs had achieved "one of the most important victories over the Germans the Allies had had, because if they had been one week later, the Germans would have had the whole of Siberia in their hands." The Russians immediately formed volunteer divisions, and all officers were called to the colors. The Czechs and Russians began to extend their field of operations and send forces in all directions. Thus it was that the Czechs at Omsk led by Syrový believed that they had been assured of the personal support of the American and Allied representatives in that area and that it was only a question of time before official support would be forthcoming.[64]

Back in Mariinsk, on June 2, Emerson and Slaughter were continuing their efforts to mediate the conflict, this time with Gajda himself.[65] Emerson explained that the Soviet representatives would arrange a cease-fire and assign a commissar to accompany each Czech echelon in safety to Vladivostok. He added that the American and Allied Consuls had arranged such a mediation at Irkutsk with success. Gajda responded that his people who had left Irkutsk would be punished, since they had no authority to leave. He informed Emerson that from Novo Nikolaevsk to Tomsk the government and the railway were in the hands of a new government, the Constitutional Assembly Government, apparently the same government that a few days later assumed power in Omsk. Emerson responded that the Soviet government was in full control of the railway from Mariinsk to Vladivostok. To this

Gajda replied that within ten days "there might be in Irkutsk another power."[66] He refused to consider disarmament of Czech troops and was pledged to support any organization in opposition to the Soviet government.[67]

During the conference with the Soviet representatives, Emerson persuaded them to allow the Czechs to proceed with full arms and equipment, provided they would agree not to cause disturbances en route or attempt to depose Soviet authorities. The Soviet authorities were deeply suspicious because wherever the Czechs had become established, it seemed that "the old regime got in power right away and have arrested all the Soviets which would make it appear that they are supporting the old regime." The Czechs, however, insisted that they would protect the representatives of the new government, which had supported them when they took control. Major Vergé, the French officer who had participated in the settlement of the dispute at Irkutsk on May 27, wired his strong support of Emerson's interpretation of conditions.[68]

Finally, in the early hours of June 4, the conferees signed a temporary armistice, which applied only to the Mariinsk front until June 10. The main obstacle to a settlement was clearly some kind of a Czech agreement with the White Guards in the area. The Czechs claimed that they could not honorably leave Mariinsk or any of the other captured towns, now occupied by the White Guards, "as they had found them." The conferees at Mariinsk agreed that a delegation of Czechs and Soviets would travel west of Mariinsk and there attempt to negotiate with all Czech troops tied up en route. The Emerson party was to accompany the mission. On June 4, the final morning of the conference, a message was received from Vergé at Chita, once again indicating his deep concern over the negotiations in progress, assuring Soviet cooperation in the Czech troop movement, and advising Gajda that "he must not do anything without first securing instructions from the French and American Consuls and that he must not forget the important and explicit instructions of professor Maserik."[69]

On June 5, the Emerson party and Vice Consul Ray arrived at Novo Nikolaevsk, which had been taken by the Czechs under Gajda on May 26 with the assistance of White Guards. They conferred once again with Gajda and two assistants, but the mediators had little success. Indeed, Ray reported a movement on foot in the town to lynch the representatives of the Soviet with the Emerson party. On June 6, Emerson was told that "any further peace conference had better be held at some other place" and that his train would proceed westward sometime during the day.[70] Shortly after the Emerson train left Novo Nikolaevsk, Harris at Mariinsk wired that he wished to be with them at the final conference at Omsk. The party waited at Kargat until June 8, when Harris and his group arrived, but no further mediation conferences were held.

Harris's trip west had revealed that new anti-Bolshevik governments had been established at every station controlled by the Czechs. Actually, prior to his departure from Novo Nikolaevsk, Emerson had met with Ivan A. Mikhailov, the representative of the new anti-Bolshevik government, who seemed particularly surprised to learn of the official nature of the Emerson party. Mikhailov claimed that when he had called on Francis two weeks earlier at Vologda, Francis had informed him that the Allies had recognized the new Central Siberian Government at Harbin under L. A. Ustrugov (later Minister of Ways of Communications in the Kolchak government at Omsk), which he represented.[71] Harris learned that these new governments sought first to establish order, second to repudiate the Brest-Litovsk Treaty, and finally to continue the war against Germany. They desired renewed support from the Allies. Harris assured them "that the moment the Allies were convinced that organization in Russia was being accomplished and that the Russian people were again Allies, from that moment they would find every imaginable help forthcoming."[72] The local Bolshevik authorities realized how critical the situation was and warned that they would "arm every prisoner-of-war against the Czechs if it became necessary."[73] The anti-Bolsheviks, in turn, realized "that in some places" the prisoners of war "would be and had been armed" against them, and they requested Allied help "by allowing the Czecho-Slovak trains to stay on in certain localities until the rule of the majority was established and prisoners of war returned to guarded camps." Harris replied that this question would have to be decided in Washington and in the other Allied capitals, but that for the present it seemed obvious that Czecho-Slovak troops were on the spot and were aiding the anti-Bolshevik forces.[74]

When the Harris party arrived at Mariinsk on June 6, Kadlec was not inclined to be friendly, since he was clearly dissatisfied with Harris's interference in the Irkutsk Czech-Bolshevik conflict. Moreover, according to Langdon Warner, Vice Consul at Harbin, Emerson's efforts had left a most unfriendly feeling. Warner was told: "We need proceed no further in the hope of patching up a peace, as the Czechs would fight their way to Vladivostok, or if necessary remain long enough to insure the safety of their comrades in the West and to establish the new

Temporary Government in power." Kadlec insisted that to leave them now would be to hand them over to the Bolsheviks, who would not hesitate to hang the members of the government who might fall into their hands and the peasants who had brought in food and supplies. He, too, considered that two weeks would be sufficient to see the new government established and organized against the Bolsheviks. The situation had become a military rather than a political one, and he proposed to "shape his course in such a way as to reach Vladivostok and the Western Front with his forces as little depleted as possible."[75] To Kadlec, the fate of Russia and Siberia was to become "a colony or a series of colonies of Germany or Japan or both." In fact, when Emerson had asked him what he would do if the Baikal tunnels were blown up, he answered, "We stay and we stay as masters of Siberia."[76]

After observing the Czechs and talking with members of the new Russian government established in their wake, Warner recommended that the United States act decisively to aid the new government when it became established and in the meantime render all possible assistance to its allies, the Czechs, in their attempt to reach the coast.[77] Drysdale agreed. He had traveled along the railway just prior to the Czech-Bolshevik outbreak and had noted much more discontent with the Soviet government in Siberia than had been visible during his trip the previous March. It seemed only a question of time before the Soviets would be replaced by some more moderate party even without the aid of the Czechs. To Drysdale, the situation offered "a wonderful opportunity to keep Czech Army inside Siberia and thus immediately to insure the retention in Siberian camps of at least one hundred and eighty thousand German, Austrian and Turkish prisoners of war and of bringing Siberia, at least, back into the war against the Central Powers." Drysdale was clearly not alone in this view.[78]

As the Czechs continued to seize railway towns throughout Siberia, Trotskii announced the concentration of Bolshevik troops against the Czecho-Slovaks on the fronts of the Volga, the Urals, and Siberia. He denounced the Czecho-Slovaks as direct allies of counterrevolution and agents of capitalism.[79] At the same time, I. M. Geitzman, Foreign Commissar of the Central Siberian Soviet, cabled an explanation of the origin and development of the Czech-Bolshevik conflict to Washington. He explained that Moscow's plan to pass a Czecho-Slovak army through Vladivostok as rapidly as possible had failed due to the catastrophic conditions of transport and supplies in late March and Semenov's threat to Siberian railroad communication in early May. According to Geitzman, these delays were misinterpreted by the

Czecho-Slovaks and used by reactionary elements against the Soviet government. The Czechs thought and were told that the Soviet authorities purposely kept them back. When, on May 25, the Central Siberian Soviet learned that armed Czecho-Slovaks had captured two or three railroad stations between Novo Nikolaevsk and Nizhneudinsk, it was baffled but took steps to safeguard the railroad from further capture.

The central Siberian authorities also commended Harris's mediation efforts at Irkutsk and believed that at that time both sides were convinced there were no reasons for a quarrel between the Soviet Republic and the Czecho-Slovak army. However, they were deeply disturbed because the Czech echelons at Nizhneudinsk, Mariinsk, and Novo Nikolaevsk had not settled matters peaceably with the Bolsheviks. The Soviet approved the efforts of the American consulate to settle the matter without bloodshed and confirmed the dissatisfaction of the leaders of the Czecho-Slovak National Council and chief Czech commanders at Vladivostok, who had categorically ordered their fellow countrymen located in the west to submit to the Soviets and instantly proceed eastward. The Soviet also approved of the armistice negotiated through the good offices of Emerson and declared that "the Russian Soviet Republic [was] respecting the ideas of Czecho-Slovaks as an oppressed nation" and had "neither reason to detain nor cause to conflict." It pledged to do all in its power to reach an amicable mutual understanding.[80]

Kadlec was not the only one who viewed the efforts of the peace mission as pro-Bolshevik. A few days after Harris's departure for western Siberia, the official organ of the Soviet government published an article reporting Harris's efforts to assist in the settlement of the Czech-Bolshevik conflict. It seemed to be a deliberate attempt to create the impression that Harris was siding with the Bolsheviks and had departed from a position of strict neutrality. This report was also spread verbally. On the day following the appearance of the article, Consul J. Paul Jameson, acting in Harris's absence, demanded an apology from the Commissar of Foreign Affairs. This was given verbally by Commissar Jakov D. Janson, but at Jameson's insistence a correction of the report appeared in the Irkutsk newspapers on June 8.[81]

On June 7, when Harris and his party reached Taiga, they learned from the Russian commander that Omsk had been taken by the Czechs. Once again Harris explained to the White Russian commanders of the new Siberian government the American policy of noninterference in Russian internal affairs. When the White Russian Commander emphasized the anti-Bolsheviks' desire to establish a firm foundation at home and then renew the war against the Germans (he added that "the presence of the Czechs" for at least two weeks was vital to obtaining this objective), Harris, in turn, assured him that he believed that railroad conditions alone would surely give him that fortnight. Harris's discussion with the White Russian Commander at Irkutsk revealed that the Czechs held the railway from Penza to the Pacific except for the area of Irkutsk and Krasnoyarsk. When Harris inquired whether they had "the unity of purpose to fight our common enemy" in the event of their success, the Russian commander responded: "That can be guaranteed. The larger part of our forces are officers who represent no political party, and will obey the instructions of the Temporary government which repudiates the Brest Treaty of peace. That should speak for itself."[82]

By the time that Harris had arrived at Kargat and realized the extent of the Czecho-Slovak success, he was convinced that he could no longer participate in any mediation efforts between the Czechs and the Soviet authorities. He immediately relieved Emerson of all responsibility for such activities and informed both the Soviet representatives and the Czech officers separately that the counter-Bolshevik movement had introduced a new factor into his mediation efforts with which "America can have nothing to do." He reaffirmed the instructions received from President Wilson that all consular and diplomatic officials of the United States in Russia and Siberia were to refrain from "mixing into any partisan or factional politics whatsoever."[83] Thus ended both Emerson's and Harris's efforts at mediation.

On June 10, when Harris returned to Irkutsk, he and Bourgeois sent a joint note to the Soviets protesting various actions hindering the Czechs' passage through Irkutsk and the anti-Czech campaign in the local newspapers.[84] Harris reported his mediation attempts to the State Department and added his view that the Bolsheviks would never agree to permit the Czechs to proceed fully armed and that the Czechs would refuse to be disarmed and would not permit the Bolsheviks to resume authority in the places where they, the Czechs, had helped White Guards to seize control.[85] Emerson, however, believed that he had secured Soviet agreement to permit the Czech troops to proceed to Vladivostok with a Soviet guard. Moreover, his mediation efforts revealed that the Czech military initiative had not had the official support of either the Czecho-Slovak National Council or the French military officers accompanying the legion.[86]

Vergé and Bourgeois continued their efforts to mediate the Czech-

Bolshevik dispute. Vergé again instructed the Czecho-Slovak forces that "the French Consul General wishes no interference" on their part "with the internal affairs of Russia." He had conferred with Geitzman and the Central Siberian Committee. It "sincerely wish[ed] to expedite Czech progress to the East." Two Czech representatives who had arrived in Irkutsk agreed with the Central Siberian Committee and were staying on for further information. The Soviet commanders en route also appeared eager to bring about peace. The Soviet commander of the station one hundred miles east of Nizhneudinsk had telephoned the Czech commander in that area seeking a possible arrangement to stop the fighting. Other Soviet representatives also called seeking a way to arrange peace. When Harris learned of the continued mediation efforts of Vergé and Bourgeois, he explained to the Czech commander why he decided to discontinue his own mediation.[87]

The final break between the Czecho-Slovaks and the Soviet government, on June 11, was precipitated by an order, signed by Lenin and others, that the Russian branch of the Czecho-Slovak National Council be abolished and its holdings surrendered to the Czecho-Slovak Bolsheviks connected to the Commissariat of Nationalities.[88] Drysdale, who had accompanied Harris in his efforts at mediation, now decided to take action. Recognizing that the armistice on the Mariinsk-Irkutsk front was to end on June 16, he feared that an agreement between the Czechs and the Bolsheviks was no longer probable. He now advised that, in that event, the Czech troops then in Vladivostok should be urged to return immediately to Karimskaya and Irkutsk to insure the safe passage of the Czechs then in western Siberia. In transmitting this message to Admiral Knight and to the legation at Peking, Drysdale emphasized the concurrence of the American and French Consuls General at Irkutsk.[89] Harris himself reported his conviction that an anti-Bolshevik movement was in progress throughout the whole of central Siberia. Moreover, he was certain that, under the current conditions, the Czechs would refuse to deliver up their arms and were prepared to fight.[90]

In the meantime, Emerson continued his efforts to reach Vologda. When he arrived at the Omsk station, he was joined by Thomson, who had been instructed to get to Vologda as soon as possible. Later they met Ray, who had been sent to Omsk by Francis to get supplies and who was accompanied by S. P. Labonov, who had been assigned by the Council of People's Commissars with Francis's approval to escort Emerson and his party to Vologda. Labonov spoke English and was accompanied by six armed men as a guard. Francis vouched for their fidelity and courage. "I am glad you are at last coming into Russia and hope to see you at Vologda in the near future. We shall confer here before you go to Moscow if you should go there at all or perhaps we shall go to Moscow together."[91] The meeting never took place. On June 13, Emerson arrived at Cheliabinsk, where he found many Czech echelons and met Guinet. Because of train difficulties west of Cheliabinsk, the Emerson party did not arrive at Miass until June 16. By that time the Czech forces had taken Labonov off their train and returned him to Omsk. It now appeared impractical to proceed any further west, as the lines were not clear to Vologda and the safe passage of the party could not be guaranteed. On June 21, the Provisional Executive Committee of the Czecho-Slovak army and the Russian Branch of the Czecho-Slovak National Council at Omsk telegraphed for instructions to the Czecho-Slovak National Council in Paris. They asked that negotiations be conducted directly with the representatives of the Allied governments, since the Allied representatives in Siberia had received no new directives in view of the "new situation created by us." On June 23, Guinet who had gone to Omsk, telegraphed the Emerson party that the Allies had "decided to intervene at the last of June and the Army Czecho-Slovac and the French Mission forms the Advance Guard of the Allied Army." The French Ambassador had instructed Guinet to thank the Czecho-Slovaks for their actions in "the name of all the Allies."[92] Yet it was not until June 29 that Colonel Paris telegraphed the French Minister of War via Tokyo that the Czechs were attacking in Central Siberia and requesting assistance in order to establish a new Eastern Front in the Ural Mountains against the Germans. They estimated that 100,000 troops were needed and that Japan might possibly provide these troops.[93]

This review of events reveals that the new "provisional" leadership elected at the Cheliabinsk congress was largely responsible for the Czech-Bolshevik revolt. Emerson's negotiations with these newly elected young Czech military leaders fully confirm this view. The Czech leadership in the Russian branch of the Czecho-Slovak National Council originally appointed by Masaryk made every effort to carry out Allied instructions to reroute part of the Czech Legion to the northern ports, while the Czech leadership in Vladivostok conscientiously sought to persuade the Czech troops having difficulties in central Siberia to stay neutral in all internal squabbles and to continue their efforts to reach Vladivostok. Moreover, the French officers with the Czechs also sought diligently to persuade, indeed order, them to adhere to Masaryk's instructions and concentrate on moving to

Vladivostok for repatriation. Americans on the scene verified that it was the Czech leaders on the spot who precipitated the revolt—a revolt of resolute young men against their timid local leaders, a sudden and seemingly spontaneous affair that surprised everybody, foe and friend alike.

The revolt can be better understood by considering the inexperience of the Czech leaders, both political and military; the muddle into which the leaders and the Allies got themselves by negotiating clumsily with the Bolsheviks; the morbid fear of the Germans, which was felt by both leaders and the rank and file; the unprincipled and purposeless adventurism of the young Czech officers; the lack of political foresight by the Czechs generally, when the revolt was sparked off; and, later, the misleading optimism of the junior Allied personnel when tolerating and supporting the revolt. It also seems clear that both Emerson and Harris made every effort to settle the dispute along their sections of the railway peacefully and in no way became involved with the internal political problems that arose. In fact they only ceased their activities after White Russian governments had been established and were operating in various other towns along the Trans-Siberian Railway, and they realized that further involvement would be contrary to Wilson's instructions to remain completely neutral. American records indicate that the Bolsheviks also sought to end the Czech revolt peaceably, but neither they nor the Czech leaders at Vladivostok were able to persuade Gajda and his men that Bolshevik offers for a peaceful resolution of the difficulties were sincere. Animated by a blind hatred of the Germans and hardened by years of war, which was heightened by the chaotic conditions in Siberia, Gajda sensed instinctively that his men felt as he did and insisted on action on his own. Yet, however much Gajda and some other officers might have talked tough, the revolt would have been impossible without their men's wholehearted consent. But that consent was based on a genuine belief of being betrayed by the Bolsheviks; a sense of mortal danger threatening them from (real or imagined) German-Bolshevik cooperation; a sincere conviction that there was a *need* to defend themselves; and a wish to overcome all obstructions and go to the Western Front to participate in the fight against the Central Powers. It must also be noted that once American and French efforts at negotiation had failed, Harris, Thomson, Gray, Warner, and Drysdale, without instruction, clearly indicated strong support for Czech efforts and displayed a sympathetic attitude toward the White Russian groups that had assumed power in collaboration with or in the wake of Czech successes.

13

Hope Grows for a
New Eastern Front

While Harris, Emerson, Thomson, Gray, Slaughter, Drysdale, and the YMCA secretaries were observing and participating in Czech activities in Siberia, American representatives in European Russia were becoming equally concerned about the Czechs. In March, when Russell M. Story, the YMCA secretary stationed in eastern Siberia, met with various officials in Moscow, he reported "a feeling that important events were impending in Siberia" associated with the Czech decision to proceed to Vladivostok for embarkation to France. The French Consul General in Moscow, Joseph Fernand Grenard, had intimated that a plan was being implemented to create a new Eastern Front by supporting an anti-Bolshevik government in Siberia, in cooperation with the "action of the French government in assuming the financial responsibility for the Czechs." This had persuaded Story "that a conflict with the Bolsheviks was inevitable."[1] Yet it must be noted that, as late as May 22, Clemenceau was vehemently opposed to allowing "even a fraction" of the Czecho-Slovak force to be used for "intervention in Russia."[2]

Whether Poole in Moscow had any knowledge of the plan to which Story referred is difficult to ascertain. Poole later recalled that meetings were held in his office throughout May and that among those who attended were Grenard; General Lavergne, chief of the French military mission; Eric Lebun, the French Consul in Moscow; Lockhart; and Major Allen Wardwell, of the Red Cross mission to Russia.[3] Once intervention had actually begun, Grenard wrote: "The intervention that we have tried to bring about and that is partly a result of our efforts has begun. Now it remains for us to see that it is victorious."[4]

By late May 1918, Francis had informed Washington of Trotskii's order to disarm the Czecho-Slovaks. He was deeply concerned because he believed that Germany would "probably" arm the prisoners of war loyal to the Central Empires still in Russia in order to oppose Allied intervention, and that armed Czech troops should be available "for resisting prisoners." He later reported that a body of Czech soldiers had declined to be disarmed and had taken the station near Ekaterinburg on the Trans-Siberian Railway. Slaughter informed Francis that the Czecho-Slovaks had joined Colonel Alexei Ilich Dutov, the Ataman of the Orenburg Cossacks, and had surrounded Ekaterinburg.[5]

On May 31, Poole informed Lansing that the difficulties between the local soviet and the Czecho-Slovaks in Samara had grown into serious conflict and that Soviet troops were being rushed to the scene. Similar reports arrived from Ekaterinburg, Omsk, and Cheliabinsk. Communications had broken down because of the fighting. The Foreign Commissariat expressed grave concern over Dutov's activities and the reactionary movement in the Don led by General Peter Nikolaevich Krasnov. Chicherin feared that the Czechs would join these anti-Bolshevik movements, particularly since they were allied to the French, who had actively encouraged and supported anti-Bolshevik and anti-German groups in the Don since the Bolsheviks seized power.[6] The Bolsheviks were exceedingly anxious to reach some agreement. They were prepared to guarantee in writing to forward the Czechs to Archangel as soon as possible on condition that their arms be handed over and that tonnage for their transport be guaranteed by the French and British governments. Both Noulens and Lavergne were opposed to disarming the Czechs and had urged that they be treated properly as an international force departing from Russia after the conclusion of peace between Germany and Russia. Francis agreed. Lockhart was even more specific: he was "afraid that the Czechs will not be of any advantage to us if they are once disarmed."[7] Fortunately for Francis, on May 29 the State Department had circulated its declaration that the aspirations of the Czecho-Slovaks had the "earnest sympathy" of the United States—precisely the kind of support that he needed. Francis immediately sent the telegram to Poole and instructed him to advise Chicherin of its contents informally. Poole not only complied but also informed Chicherin that if any controversy arose, the United States would be disposed to favor the Czechs.[8] Both Francis and Poole took these steps without authority from the State Department, but they felt it necessary to use their discretion to promote the interests of the Allies as they interpreted them, particularly in the absence of satisfactory cable communication and the emergency conditions. Throughout May, Francis had grown in the conviction that Allied intervention was advisable from every viewpoint, and that it was hopeless to wait for a Bolshevik invitation to intervene. Moreover, his Allied colleagues affirmed that Japan was likely to intervene without Allied consent.[9]

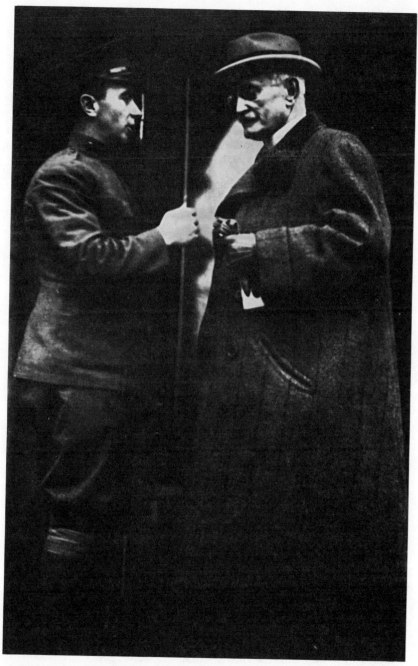

Ambassador David R. Francis, *right* (National Archives)

On June 1, Lavergne, in a telegraphic report from Moscow, made his first reference to the possibility of intervention in Russia as a result of the Czech-Bolshevik conflict. He also described Trotskii's hostile attitude toward the Czech army, which in turn distrusted the Soviets. On the other hand, Lavergne drew attention to the conciliatory attitude of Chicherin, who was anxious to avoid any conflict with the Czech troops or with the Allies.[10] Although Trotskii had sent Soviet troops to assist in the disarmament of the Czechs, he had released Maxa and Čermák so that they could return to their troops to dissuade them from making further trouble. Trotskii had no objections to the plan to send the Czechs to France; in fact, he wanted to get them out of Russia as soon as possible. To Lockhart, both the Czech leaders of the National Council and the Bolsheviks seemed anxious to avoid further fighting. Unaware of the actions of the Cheliabinsk congress, he was personally convinced that the Czechs had not been engaged in any counterrevolutionary plots, since their one aim was to get out of Russia. Yet the British Foreign Office was clearly making no great effort to bring the Czechs to France immediately.[11]

By June 2, Lockhart learned that the Czechs themselves had rejected the policies of both Masaryk and the Czech National Council at Cheliabinsk as being too moderate and too conciliatory toward the Bolsheviks. The troops were apparently ready to fight their way through to the Far East, and it would be difficult to persuade them now to move toward Archangel. Clearly, if intervention could take place within the next ten days, the Allies would have the great advantage of the presence of the Czechs in Siberia. Lavergne agreed. If delay continued, there was grave danger that the Czechs would be broken up and that they might be forced in self-defense to destroy large portions of the Trans-Siberian Railway. Lockhart saw the "German wall . . . closing in on every side." If the Allies did not act immediately, he feared that it would be difficult to insure a successful intervention.[12]

As the days passed and the Czech crisis became even more complicated, the Allied representatives in Moscow sought to create conditions that would persuade the Czechs to stay in Siberia or Russia as the spearhead of Allied intervention. On the other hand, although Clemenceau had agreed earlier to retain the Czechs in northern Russia temporarily, it was only as part of a plan that envisaged their rapid transportation to the Western Front as soon as tonnage could be made available.[13] Clemenceau was not only desperate for seasoned veterans who could be put into the line at once, but Beneš had convinced him that "when fifty thousand Czech troops were fighting in France a revolution would break out in Bohemia."[14] In the meantime, Masaryk in Washington was seeking to persuade Lansing of the advantages of removing the Czech army from Siberia and getting them to the Western Front.[15] The State Department, however, was receiving very different advice from Francis and Poole. Poole's views were similar to Lockhart's. He reported that the Czechs "are thoroughly exasperated with their treatment by the Bolsheviks, that they evince a very warlike spirit and talk of forcing their way to Vladivostok." He stressed that the Czechs were a "splendid, disciplined force, violently against the Germans."[16] Their presence in Russia provided a strong motivation for intervention and the reestablishment of an Eastern Front. Moreover, even if they got to Vladivostok, there were no ships to transport them. In these circumstances, it seemed to Poole to be the height of foolishness to consider their continued movement across Siberia.[17] He was convinced that the Germans were responsible for nagging the Bolsheviks to harass the Czecho-Slovaks. Obviously, he and a great many others believed that "it would be just as well if the Czecho-Slovaks did not get out in such a hurry because they would help to pin down a certain number of German troops in the east, troops which otherwise might be transferred to the Western Front."[18]

It was these considerations that motivated both Francis and Poole to present their protest to the Soviet Foreign Ministry on June 3 against the disarmament of the Czechs. Although Francis had no authority from Washington for his action, he wrote his son, "I have taken chances before, however, and another little chance will do me no harm."[19] When Lansing learned of Poole's actions, he was exceedingly displeased and rebuked Francis, admonishing him that any communications with the Soviet government "should so far as practicable, be limited to matters affecting American interests."[20] Francis and Poole, however, were not alone in their concern over the fate of the Czechs. The other chiefs of missions at Vologda, inspired by Francis's initiative, sent similar instructions to their representatives in Moscow. Although Poole had made his initial protest alone, to emphasize Allied solidarity he also accompanied the Allied representatives on a joint visit to Chicherin.[21]

Chicherin's reply to both Poole and the Allied representatives blamed the Czechs for the initial confrontations and insisted that the Soviet government had been forced to adopt a course of severe armed repression of the Czechs because of their direct counterrevolutionary armed rebellion. He expressed the hope that the Allies would announce their disapproval of what was clearly a patent intervention in

DeWitt C. Poole, Jr. (National Archives)

Russian domestic affairs. He insisted that "he had no objection to the departure of the Czechs if disarmed." Poole, however, strongly disagreed and urged Francis to make clear to Washington that the Czech outbreak had been the direct result of Soviet acquiescence in German demands, that the Czechs had not knowingly conspired with revolutionaries, that their only desire was to quit Russia with their arms in order to fight the Germans in France, and that the Soviets' final interference with them was "culminating proof of the subserviency of the Soviet government to German influence."[22] In response to Poole's plea, Francis informed Lansing that the Soviet order to disarm the Czechs was dictated by the Germans, that many German and Austrian prisoners of war were fighting with the Red Guard against "the Slovaks," and that the Soviet government was spreading Communist doctrine among the legionnaires and endeavoring in every way to interfere with their departure by claiming they were a counterrevolutionary movement.[23]

It was not until early June that certain German representatives in Moscow recognized the possibility of the Czecho-Slovak troops being used as a vehicle for the restoration of a bourgeois order in Russia with the aid of the Allies. Shortly thereafter, Kühlmann instructed Mirbach in Moscow to prevent the Czechs from traveling on to Vladivostok and to stop the transport of the Poles and the Czechs via the Murmansk Railway to the Western Front.[24] Mirbach lodged an official protest with the Bolsheviks and demanded that the transport of the Czecho-Slovaks across Siberia be forbidden as a violation of the Treaty of Brest-Litovsk.[25] On June 9, Ludendorff himself complained against the failure of the Soviet government to disarm the Czechs and against the cooperation of the Soviet authorities with the Entente in permitting the Czechs to occupy the Murmansk and the eastern Siberian railways.[26]

On June 3, the Supreme War Council approved Joint Note No. 31.[27] While Francis thoroughly agreed with this decision, he was astounded to learn that Rear Admiral Thomas W. Kemp, commander of the British squadron in the White Sea, the American and French naval officers at Murmansk, and General Poole were reported to have stated that recognition of the Soviet government was the only solution to the current Russian situation. Francis considered that such a step would be a tragic mistake, because the Soviet government was "a corpse which no one had the courage to bury." Convinced that the naval officers at Murmansk were totally oblivious of the real situation, he voiced his strong opposition to Lansing.[28] Lockhart was also urging action upon the British Foreign Office: "The French and Italians are trying their hardest to use this incident [the Czech-Bolshevik conflict] so as to force intervention as soon as possible. . . . If the Allies are ready to intervene, then by all means let us act with the greatest possible speed. We could never have a more favorable opportunity. Moment is ripe almost over-ripe."[29]

One reason for the disturbances along the Siberian railroad was the fact that the Allies had no transports in Vladivostok to expedite the departure of the Czecho-Slovaks. It was only natural that the Central Soviet Government at Irkutsk regarded the concentration of 10,000 Czecho-Slovaks at Vladivostok as highly undesirable. Harris in Irkutsk also expressed his concern.[30] Yet it was not until the beginning of June that the Supreme War Council had agreed to a resolution regarding the transport of the Czecho-Slovak troops. It was Clemenceau who had pushed the British to fulfill their agreement to transport the Czechs from Vladivostok to France. Clemenceau believed that while they were waiting for Wilson's decision about intervention, they would have time to transport the Czecho-Slovaks to France and thus overcome the immediate crisis. Faced with this pressure, Lloyd George had agreed to take action. By June 11 the British Ministry of War assured the French that they were taking the necessary measures to make two ships available to transport the Czechs at Vladivostok to Vancouver, Canada.[31]

On June 7, Omsk, the most populous city in western Siberia, surrendered to the Czechs, followed by Samara on the next day. George Williams, who provided a detailed report of the Czech-Bolshevik encounter, revealed that the Bolsheviks were both unprepared and untrained for the sharp fighting.[32] After the Czech victory, General Čeček had requested an interview with Williams to explain fully the origin and development of the Czech-Bolshevik conflict and to turn over certain documents for transmission to the American Ambassador and the other Allied representatives. To Williams, the documents clearly showed "the duplicity of the National Soviet in dealing" with the Czechs. Since Williams had no direct communication with Francis, he sent the documents to Poole with the message that it was indifferent to the Czechs where they were to fight and that, if the Allies so directed, they would gladly remain in their present position and establish a new anti-German front along the Volga. Williams added: "However, in the absence of other instructions, they will resume movement east as soon as railroad repaired which should be in a few days."[33] Just a few days earlier, Campbell, too, had reported that "the Czechs here feel that they are fighting with the Germans."[34] On June 12, he wrote from Mariinsk that Kadlec had returned from Omsk accompanied by 150 Russian soldiers who seemed anxious to assist in the wrenching of Siberia from the Bolsheviks. He went on: "The Czecho-Slovaks . . . think they are doing a good service by detaining the more than a million Germans in Russia and helping the Russians to work out for themselves some kind of a decent government. They are no longer in a rush to reach Vladivostok. They are confident that the Allies will come to their assistance in Russia when the real conditions are known."[35]

In the meantime, the Soviet government and the Siberian soviets continued to protest against the counterrevolutionary actions of the Czecho-Slovaks. Indeed, Weinbaum told Slaughter that he would arm every German and Austrian prisoner in the Krasnoyarsk district to defeat the Czechs.[36] There was good reason for Soviet concern.

Stretched from Samara on the Volga to Vladivostok on the Pacific, the Czechs had captured railway stations, towns, cities, and machinery. Although French agents reported large numbers of German and Austrian prisoners among the troops of the Red Army, no effective resistance had been offered thus far. According to French reports, when the Czechs entered a city, they occupied only the station and the railroad yards; they then issued a proclamation to the inhabitants that they would not interfere in their affairs but would only preserve order. Thus far this had resulted in the immediate overthrow of the Bolsheviks and the facilitation of a new government by a coalition of anti-Bolshevik parties.[37]

In mid-June, Drysdale, Harris, and Bourgeois at Irkutsk awaited the end of the armistice on the Omsk-Irkutsk front with some trepidation. Assuming that an agreement between the Czechs and Bolsheviks was improbable, Drysdale, it will be recalled, with the concurrence of his two colleagues, had already acted to secure support for the Czech troops in western Siberia.[38] Francis believed, on the basis of reports from Noulens, that the Supreme War Council had decided to permit the Czecho-Slovaks to remain in Russia for the present with the approval of the Czecho-Slovak National Council. Moreover, it had been "decided on" to land British, French, Italian, and American forces in the North. In these circumstances, Francis considered an Allied advance into Siberia very important, if not absolutely necessary. He informed Poole and Lansing that "armed Czechs" were "rapidly expanding domination westward, which Soviet government [was] powerless to prevent except by arming German prisoners of war which reported doing."[39]

By this time, the messages Poole had received from Francis and Williams seemed to indicate that the Allies had finally decided to intervene and therefore desired that the Czechs in the Urals and Siberia should remain roughly in the positions they then occupied. The Czechs had reported their willingness to remain in their present position in order to establish a new anti-German front along the Volga. However, Williams's message made Poole fear that, in the absence of any instructions, the Czechs would resume their movement to the east as soon as the railway was repaired. At this critical juncture, Poole learned that as a reaction to the Czech uprising, the Germans were planning to seize Moscow on June 21. This information galvanized Poole to action.[40]

At this point, Poole and many others doubted that the war could be won against Germany. And what Poole now determined to do needs to be interpreted in the light of that fear. He was thoroughly sympathetic with the Czechs' wish to extricate themselves from Siberia and get to the Western Front to fight; he was also aware of the failure of the plans to transport part of the Czech troops to Archangel. Moreover, even if they did get through to the seaboard, there was no tonnage available to move them across the sea. On the other hand, if they remained in Siberia, they would be an enemy with whom the Germans would have to reckon. Poole naturally saw the possibility of utilizing the Czecho-Slovak and anti-Bolshevik Russian elements as the vanguard to establish a new Eastern Front. At this crucial stage, when Moscow itself might be occupied by the Germans, there was no time for consultation with Francis, much less Washington. Poole believed that the Czechs in Siberia would perhaps have no way of knowing the position of the Allied governments from any other source but himself. Therefore, unless Poole took action, they might never learn of the Allied decision before they had abandoned the Urals and western Siberia, leaving these areas open to the reprisals of the Bolsheviks and to the military occupation of the Germans.[41]

Poole, after pondering deeply and consulting with Grenard, sent a telegram to Williams at Samara on June 18, telling him that if he had an opportunity to speak with the Czecho-Slovak commander there, he could say that

> pending further notice, the Allies will be glad from a political point of view to have them hold their present position. On the other hand, they should not be hampered in meeting military exigencies of the situation. It is desirable first of all that they should obtain control of the Trans-Siberian Railway and secondly, if this is assumed at the same time, if possible, to retain control over the territory they now dominate. Inform French representatives that the French Consul General joins in these instructions.[42]

Poole realized that he had no authority to send such a message; yet it was "hard to stand on protocol in a situation of that kind." Poole had sent the message in the name of the Allies. Yet the United States was not an Ally, strictly speaking; it was an associated power. Moreover, even if the United States had been an Ally, Poole had no authority to speak on its behalf. In later years, Poole excused himself, stating that his action was "one of those things a man does in a stressful situation. I don't apologize for it. Indeed, I think it was quite right. But I explain that it was completely *ultra vires*."[43]

As it turned out, Poole's message was not forwarded from Samara until July 22 and thus had no real effect upon the immediate decisions that were taken by the Czechs. Actually, a message from the French Ambassador provided the news for which both Gray and the Czechs had been waiting. On June 22, Guinet at Cheliabinsk received a coded message brought by courier and dated Perm, May 18: "The French Ambassador informs Major Guinet he can thank the Czecho-Slovaks for their action, this in the name of all the Allies, who have decided to intervene the end of June, and the Czech Army and French Mission form the advance guard of the Allied army. Recommendations will follow concerning political and military points with respect to occupation and organization."[44]

All of the internal evidence in this note suggests that the dates were wrong in the report that was forwarded to the State Department by Consul Alfred Thomson. The French Ambassador was not at Perm on May 18; the first conflict between the Czecho-Slovaks and the Soviets had occurred on May 14, and the Allied and associated ambassadors assembled at Vologda knew nothing or very little about it on May 18. Certainly they had taken no joint action to warrant such a message. It was not until June 3 that the Supreme War Council decided to send troops to the northern ports. However, from the first, Noulens had been an ardent advocate of Allied intervention, and, in a note sent to his government on May 14 and delivered by the French embassy in Washington, he had been quoted as urging the utilization of the Czecho-Slovak army as an "advance guard" of a joint intervention.[45]

Regardless of the date, the mysterious message received by Guinet was accepted as authentic by the French military and consular officers in Siberia and the American representatives. Until that date, Guinet in the Omsk district and Bourgeois and Vergé at Irkutsk had been doing their utmost to compose the quarrel between the Soviets and the Czecho-Slovaks and to facilitate the evacuation of the latter. Several days after receiving this message, Guinet addressed the Czecho-Slovak troops in their daily newspaper, lauding them for their energetic action, which he said was "a great honor to the whole Czecho-Slovak army." He also praised both the commanders in chief who had carried out their orders and the members of the military congress who had decided upon these actions. Although Guinet had not shared the views of those whom he was now lauding, he pointed out that the members of the French embassy had been "forced to find ways of keeping up connections with the Russian Soviet authorities." This was no longer necessary, and, Guinet wrote: "Now you will witness how we will with body and soul support the liberation movement of the Czecho-Slovak army. Thanks to you a new Russian front is established, but to our regrets, yet with small support from the flower of the Russian nation. This front is established against the true enemies of right and righteousness, that is against the Germans."[46]

The Czecho-Slovaks were hopeful and enthusiastic when these messages arrived. Despite their initial plans to go to France, they were quite willing to remain in Russia to fight the Germans and Bolsheviks, not only because they believed that the Red Army had attacked their echelons and because they could fight the Germans and Austro-Hungarians, but also because they believed the Allies would now be indebted to them and support the establishment of an independent Czecho-Slovak republic.

Thomson at Omsk was delighted with the message from Vologda.[47] One month later, Gray received Poole's cipher message emphasizing the desirability of Czech control of both the Trans-Siberian Railway and the territory that they then dominated. By that time, Gray and Harris had already accepted as authentic the message received by Guinet, and they had begun to support French efforts to implement it.[48] Both Poole and Harris had received their instructions from Francis, who sent them by courier from Vologda to Moscow during the early summer of 1918, although Francis had not been authorized by Washington to do so.[49] Through this diplomatic confusion, the Czecho-Slovaks were promised assistance that the United States Government never intended and was never ready to give. On July 24, Slaughter reported that the "French Consul Samara stated to new government French alone responsible action Czechs against Bolsheviks and Siberian Provisional Government therefore owes existence to the French."[50]

On June 20, Paris sent its first official instructions to Lavergne regarding the use of the Czecho-Slovaks in Russia. Since the Czech Legion had come to a standstill, the French government ordered retention of the positions occupied with a view to developing centers of resistance in cooperation with those Siberian and Cossack elements favorable to the reestablishment of order, completing the possession of the Trans-Siberian railroad, and preparing for eventual Allied intervention from the east. General Alby, who sent the instructions, also demanded that the Czecho-Slovaks refuse to be disarmed and that those Czechs who reached Vladivostok disarmed should be supplied with rifles and ammunition. The British and Japanese Foreign Offices were asked to cooperate. Janin and Beneš approved these arrangements. Lavergne, acting on these instructions from Paris, ordered the Czecho-Slovaks to halt, participate in no intervention in Russian affairs, and refrain from making the possibility of intervention hazardous.[51]

Events in the Russian Far East were changing rapidly. Harris reported that Irkutsk had been seized by German prisoners of war, supposedly with Soviet connivance, and that this had completely modified the attitude of the Czechs in Vladivostok toward the military situation. Admiral Knight believed that the Czechs were now ready to cooperate with the Allies against German activities in Siberia and in the reestablishment of an Eastern Front. Knight saw the Czech situation as the dominating factor in Siberia and perhaps in Russia. He cabled: "Should movement be contemplated for establishment of Eastern Front it will be enormously facilitated by present condition with a notable advantage that the Czech influence would greatly overcome that of Japanese removing chief antagonism of Russians to movement against German power and influence."[52]

The Bolshevik decision to arm German prisoners of war was clearly without the official sanction of the German government. When, on June 23, the Bolsheviks secretly submitted a proposal to the German government to arm the prisoners of war for use against the Czecho-Slovaks, the German response was negative. Not only was the German government absolutely opposed to supporting the Bolsheviks, it was also averse to having thousands of its soldiers exposed to attacks by the Czecho-Slovaks.[53] Yet Francis reported to Lansing on June 19 that intelligence received from Noulens and other sources revealed that Trotskii and Chicherin had had several conferences on the previous day with some unknown person, presumably Mirbach, and that the Soviet government had accepted German aid against the Czechs, which up to this time had been refused. Two German army corps were to occupy Moscow immediately.[54]

A turning point was also approaching in Vladivostok. On June 25, the Allied Consuls at Vladivostok met two of the principal members of the Czech National Council, who had now concluded that even if they were willing, the Soviets were powerless to prevent armed prisoners from interfering with the movement of the Czech troops eastward. Therefore, in response to orders from Gajda, who had wired that the Czech passage through Siberia was "only possible by force of arms," the leaders of the council had determined that the 15,000 Czech troops at Vladivostok should return to the west to assist their compatriots. Both Harris and Bourgeois at Irkutsk believed that such action was justified and had cooperated with Gajda in the transmission of these orders to the Czech commanders at Vladivostok. The Czechs requested arms and ammunition as well as a supporting armed Allied force. All of the Allied Consuls agreed to recommend immediate favorable action to their respective governments on both requests, for the double purpose of assisting "a splendid body of Allied troops in their just fight against armed war prisoners, and of checking German activity in Siberia."[55] The Czecho-Slovaks explained their departure from Masaryk's dictum of neutrality on the grounds that "the Central Government of Siberia is without doubt, under a strong or dominant influence of Germans and Magyars."[56]

On June 26, members of the Czecho-Slovak National Council visited Admiral Knight and reported that the Czechs controlled the Siberian railroad from Penza to Nizhneudinsk with a force of approximately 40,000, and that the Soviets had been overthrown in the region controlled by the Czechs and had been replaced by a new government wholly Russian but anti-Bolshevik. The Czech forces at Vladivostok had received orders from Gajda, their commanding officer at Novo Nikolaevsk, to proceed westward to open and hold the railway and join forces from the west to attack an Austro-German force at Irkutsk. The Czech representatives asked Admiral Knight what kind of help could be expected from the United States and the Allied powers. If they succeeded in obtaining control of the Siberian railroad from Vladivostok to the Volga, would the associated powers want them to hold the road in the expectation that they would join them in the establishment of a new Eastern Front? If they remained in Siberia to fight on a new Eastern Front, would this action be accepted by the associated powers as the equivalent of fighting on the Western Front and as entitling them to the same consideration when peace terms were finally agreed upon as if they had proceeded to the Western Front in accordance with their original agreement with the French government? These questions had been submitted to Knight "in the finest spirit of loyalty and with no intimation or intent to abate in any degree their determination to fight on any one front or another, whatever the reply to their question might be."[57]

Without waiting to receive a reply, on June 29 the Czechs occupied Vladivostok and disarmed the Red Guard. Although the Japanese and British landed large armed parties in the morning, they did not participate in the fighting. Knight landed a small detachment of marines in the evening to guard the American consulate.[58]

With the capture of Vladivostok by the Czechs, the Washington government now faced the decision of responding to the Czechs' request for aid in their efforts to help their brethren in the interior as well as to initiate the establishment of a new Eastern Front. By this time Francis, virtually all of the American Consuls and Military Attachés who had made contact with the Czechs en route, and all of the YMCA men attached to the Czech trains enthusiastically favored supporting the Czechs and had demonstrated that support even before they had received official instructions from the American government.

14

Wilson's Fateful Decision
of July 6, 1918

The Czech advance in Russia and Siberia aroused tremendous enthusiasm in the United States. Both Masaryk and Beneš later emphasized that in 1918, the actions of the Czech Legion in Siberia became the most effective propaganda tool for eliciting American support of Czech liberation. Beneš avowed that it "contributed towards our recognition . . . mainly by its mere existence."[1] As the news of Czech successes arrived, Masaryk found "the effect in America was astonishing and almost incredible—all at once the Czechs and Czechoslovaks were known to everybody."[2] And so we must ask to what extent did the activities of the Czechs in Siberia ultimately contribute to their recognition by both the Allies and the United States?[3]

Throughout May, the Allies had brought increasing pressure to bear upon Wilson to secure his consent to an Allied intervention in northern Russia and in Siberia. By May 31, virtually all the American representatives in Russia, Siberia, and China supported the call of the British, French, and Japanese for immediate intervention.[4] Numerous plans envisaged the Czechs playing a major role in such an intervention force. Deeply opposed to lone Japanese intervention, Long had already suggested on May 21 that if a decision were made to support Semenov, the Czecho-Slovak troops "would be most useful," particularly if "taken over by this Government and assisted by American officers." Long discussed the matter with Basil Miles, then in charge of Russian affairs, and Lansing, to whom he expressed his wish that Wilson would consult with Masaryk.[5] By the end of May, the department had begun to consider proposals for action in Siberia. Fearing the dangers of Allied military intervention in Russia and knowing Wilson's opposition to lone Japanese intervention, Lansing conferred with Francis and Stevens about using the Russian Railway Service Corps as the "preeminent" factor in a policy of Allied economic assistance to Russia. Its activities would be protected by an American and Allied military force. Although it would be difficult to attain numerically equal participation in such a military policy, Lansing believed that Japanese participation could be equalized by American and Chinese forces and the "valuable Bohemian troops now gathering at Vladivostok." Increments from the Allies could be added to such a force, but "American preeminence in all matters pertaining to the Railroad and in connection with propaganda and other economic assistance would be insisted upon and maintained." Since Trotskii had already requested American railway help and Emerson and a group of railway engineers had been sent to Vologda to confer with Trotskii and Francis, Lansing instructed Francis:

> If, however, as a result of your conference and cooperation with Emerson it might be arranged that any reasonable and proper suggestions or requests by the Soviet authorities be favorably considered by the Embassy and the Railway Corps with the distinct proviso and 'quid pro quo' that the railway assistance in European Russia should be accompanied by permission for the corps to extend its activities in Siberia, this program might immediately be commenced with the advantage of the tacit acquiescence of such authorities.[6]

Support for utilizing the Czechs came from other quarters. Reinsch, the American Minister to China, strongly opposed lone intervention by the Japanese because he feared their imperialistic motivations in both Russia and Manchuria. He saw the Czecho-Slovaks as an ideal vehicle for intervention.[7] He discussed the matter at length with the Allied ministers in Peking and asked why the Japanese should be invited into Siberia when the Czech force, already in Siberia, was admirably adapted to whatever purposes the Americans and Allies desired. Moreover, the Czechs would pose none of the problems presented by a possible Japanese penetration of eastern Siberia and Manchuria.[8] He had made his views known to the State Department, where they were held in high regard. However, when Lansing asked Masaryk on June 3 what the United States could do to help the Czecho-Slovaks, Masaryk immediately responded that the "greatest help" would be the transportation of the Czecho-Slovak troops from Russia to France. Lansing promised to give the matter his attention.[9] On June 7, the British Foreign Office informed the State Department of its readiness to recognize the Czecho-Slovak National Council in the same manner as had the French and Italian governments. Its decision had been strongly influenced by the hope of utilizing the Czechs as the nucleus for an Allied intervention in Russia. It was prepared to attach a liaison officer to the Czech army as soon as seemed advisable.[10]

As Wilson struggled to make a decision about intervention in both northern Russia and Siberia, the State Department wrestled with the related problems regarding recognition of the Czecho-Slovak National Council and approval of tentative plans for transporting at least some of the Czechs from Vladivostok to the Western Front. Those considerations were complicated by still another matter. At a recent conference at Versailles, the premiers of France, Great Britain, and Italy had advocated "the creation of a united, independent Polish state, with free access to the sea." Critical observers interpreted this as an implementation of Wilsonian principles and regarded such action as "sure to stimulate the revolutionary efforts of the Bohemian and other Slavs against the Habsburg autocracy."[11]

Following the Polish example, the Czecho-Slovak National Council sought to define and strengthen the position of the Czech "nation" with the associated governments and submitted to France a political program essentially involving recognition of "the *de facto* existence of a Czech nation with a national entity" and permission for the Czecho-Slovak National Council to represent "the political and administrative interests of that nation until it is able to adopt a final constitution." The French government favored granting these special prerogatives to the Czecho-Slovak National Council, as it already had for the Polish National Council. However, before implementing that policy, France wanted assurance that such a procedure would harmonize with Wilson's views. The French assumed that, given Wilson's statement of principles regarding self-determination and the rights of small nations, their action would thoroughly comport "with the ideas for which the American people under the energetic impulsion of their President are fighting by the side of the French people."[12] Since Lansing already knew that the British were prepared to follow the French and Italian modes of recognizing the Czecho-Slovak National Council, he immediately sought full information concerning the entire matter from Paris.[13]

Meanwhile, the British proceeded with their plans for intervention in northern Russia. The British hopes that the initial force would be strengthened considerably by Czecho-Slovak troops once they had reached the northern ports came closer to reality when by mid-June the Supreme War Council and Beneš had approved the utilization of some 20,000 Czechs to defend the Russian Arctic ports in the northwest prior to their transport to France. Bliss had agreed to the proposal only insofar as the forces required would be drawn from Czech units then in Russia and would therefore require the transport of no more than two American battalions. The Czech forces were to be strengthened by the addition of British, French, Italian, and American troops. Joint Note No. 31 had been approved, then, on the assumption that Czech troops would arrive at Archangel and Murmansk to be stiffened by not more than a total of six Allied battalions. Wilson had made it clear that he would not participate in the enterprise unless it was approved by Foch.[14] Foch, in answer to the queries of Bliss and Wilson, had confirmed his approval.[15]

By this time, Wilson was objecting less strenuously to intervention at the northern ports, where there was no question of Japanese participation. However, he saw no advantage to be gained by intervention in Siberia. Yet in his last speech Wilson had made clear that the United States would "stand by" Russia. The question of how he proposed to help Russia now became the subject of much discussion in the newspapers and by the public.[16] The whole issue was complicated by the State Department's knowledge that Great Britain, France, and Italy were inviting Japan to a lone intervention, a course of action it regarded as hazardous, not only for the course of intervention itself, but for the future of eastern Siberia and Manchuria.[17]

As Lansing struggled with the whole question of intervention, he was forced to conclude that in many respects it rested primarily upon the ability to transport troops.[18] At this point the British informed Washington that the Allied governments were reconsidering the question of transportation to France of the Czecho-Slovak troops in Russia. They had requested that the Japanese divert tonnage for this purpose until it was needed for Allied intervention in Siberia. This new British information presented the State Department with a dilemma, particularly since many members, including Lansing, had been thinking seriously of using the Czech troops as the nucleus of an intervening force if Wilson should decide on intervention. The State Department decided temporarily to withhold acknowledgment of the note and wait a few days pending further developments. In any case, since all available American ships were transporting troops to the Western Front, none could be spared for transporting troops across the Pacific.[19]

As Lansing pondered the question of transport, his mind naturally turned to the larger issue of Allied intervention in Russia. While he favored doing as Foch desired at the northern ports, he felt it would be "a grave error" for Japan alone to send an expedition to Siberia. Thus, the only other method of opposing German penetration in Siberia, "unless the Czecho-Slovaks are willing to resist Russians who ally themselves with the Germans," was peaceful assistance through a commission of agricultural, labor, and financial advisers. While he recognized that an international police force might be necessary to protect the commission, it need not be large. Lansing had instructed Auchincloss to write such a proposal, which he planned to deliver to Wilson over his own signature. House had endorsed the plan enthusiastically and written Wilson accordingly. He also had discussed the plan confidentially with Wiseman, who was so enthusiastic that he immediately informed Reading in order to "get him to cooperate with us in putting it through."[20] On June 14, Wiseman found Wilson still firmly opposed to lone intervention by the Japanese, and even to Allied intervention, on the ground that the latter would be the same thing, since the Japanese would supply the major part of the military force. Moreover, Wilson still desired an invitation to enter Russia from the Bolsheviks or somebody really representing Russian opinion. Nevertheless, Wiseman thought that Wilson might be ready to consider sending a civil commission in the nature of a relief organization, possibly with Herbert Hoover as its head. Actually, only the day before, Wilson had told Secretary of Commerce William Cox Redfield of his intention to confer with him and Mott about the organization of an "original kind of relief expedition for Russia." While this certainly was not the kind of intervention desired by the British, Wiseman hoped that the commission might be an entering wedge for military intervention and advised the Foreign Office to encourage the scheme.[21]

By mid-June the dual problems of transporting the Czechs from Russia and arriving at a decision about intervention in Russia appeared to be closely related and filled with contradictions. Although Wilson was still absolutely opposed to a Siberian intervention, he recognized that if Allied military operations were contemplated from Murmansk and Archangel, the Czech contingents might be "especially valuable" for such an expedition because of their familiarity with the Russian language and their previous employment on the Russian front.[22] The Far Eastern Division of the State Department had also come to see in the Czechs a vehicle for an intervention that would both solve the immediate problems in Russo-American relations and prevent the use of extensive numbers of Japanese troops. Reinsch had also enthusiastically presented this view to the State Department. Francis, strongly supported by Poole, had already indicated his strong sympathy and support for the Czechs, indeed without departmental approval. They, too, believed that immediate intervention was necessary with the use of the Czech forces. Poole had already taken personal steps to egg the Czechs to fight.[23] To complicate matters further, the Japanese had made independent agreements with the Chinese to send Japanese troops

into Siberia and Manchuria, ostensibly to oppose the Bolsheviks whenever the moment seemed propitious. Reinsch had sent the text of the
agreements of May 16 on June 5. Emile V. Cutrer, the Military Attaché at
Peking, reported that Japan was negotiating an additional secret treaty
with the Chinese to secure monopolies over certain trades and "taking
every advantage" of the weakness, disorganization, and rampant
internal dissensions within China.[24] Wilson also knew that the Allies
were in the process of seeking Japan's agreement to a lone Japanese
intervention. At the same time, both Britain and France had been
urging Wilson to support recognition of the Czecho-Slovak National
Council and to agree to a joint intervention in Russia in cooperation
with both the Czechs and the Japanese.

As pleas for intervention continued to pour into Washington,
Wilson pondered the various proposals and memoranda that had been
sent to him, especially two documents submitted by Reinsch and
Poole. He had "the greatest confidence" in Reinsch's "discretion and
judgment."[25] As he considered Reinsch's proposal to use the Czecho-
Slovaks in Siberia in a larger plan for intervention, there seemed to
Wilson "to emerge . . . the shadow of a plan that might be worked,
with Japanese and other assistance." After all, these people were the
"cousins of the Russians."[26]

The second document from Poole presented the views toward intervention of the All-Russian Union of Cooperative Societies, an organization that had refrained from all political activity and was regarded as
nonpolitical. The cooperative societies were primarily concerned with
the economic calamity facing the people of Russia and felt it their duty
to save the Russian people from starvation. While the cooperatives
were able to work with the Bolsheviks and even the Germans, their
political sympathies were really with the Allies. Moreover, their members were pro-American and very anti-Japanese. It appeared that the
cooperatives would support Allied intervention, particularly one
which included Americans, but would oppose lone Japanese intervention.[27] "Very much" interested in Poole's dispatch, Wilson informed
Lansing: "These associations may be of very great service as instru-
ments for what we are now planning to do in Siberia."[28]

As the State Department waited uneasily for Wilson to formulate
his decision about Russia, Charles R. Crane continued his efforts to
secure an audience for Masaryk with leaders of the administration.
Although Masaryk had seen Lansing, he described his discussions
with him as "not quite adequate, although satisfactory in a preliminary
way."[29] Crane also appealed to Wilson to see Masaryk—"one of the

wisest and best of Christians."[30] Wilson received Crane's note when he was deeply involved in working out a scheme for the relief of Russia that did not involve military intervention. Thus Masaryk's earlier memorandum on the subject must surely have met with his approval. In any case, Wilson responded immediately that he would try to see Masaryk, that he had been planning to have a joint conference with him and with others to work out his plan.[31] On June 18, Wilson saw Mott, Jusserand, and Regnault, the new French Ambassador to Japan. To all of them he indicated that he had not made a final decision regarding Russia and that he would not do so until after he had seen various persons, most notably Masaryk. After a Cabinet meeting that afternoon, he also conferred with Lansing on the Russian situation.[32]

Wilson was now well informed of the views of Baker and the War Department about intervention in Russia. Baker himself would have liked "to take everybody out of Russia" and "let the Russians . . . settle their own affairs." Realizing that this was impossible, he thought the best that could be done to help the Russian people was to expose "the falsity and treachery of German propaganda in that country" by providing "such military assistance as may be . . . accomplished by men who not only represent our feeling and point of view but are themselves interested in Russia and the Russian people" and would be "subtle in their comprehension, and generous and tolerant in their sympathies."[33] Obviously, these were not the Japanese. Both Baker and Bliss shared Wilson's concerns about lone Japanese intervention, and Baker sent Wilson a number of reports from Bliss, who had voiced his opposition to the continued efforts of Lloyd George and Clemenceau to secure a large Japanese military intervention in Siberia. Wilson was grateful for Baker's comments and for the enclosures from Bliss, whom he regarded as a "remarkable man, a real thinking man, who takes the pains to think straight."[34]

When Wilson finally received Masaryk, he was of course meeting a man whose views on intervention were similar to his own. While Masaryk's memoranda and speeches had emphasized that 50,000 Slavic prisoners of war were organized in Russia ready to fight against their oppressors, he had also urged the importance of transferring them to France. He, like Wilson, was opposed to any interference in Russian affairs and had pledged Czech troops to neutrality in Russia. Also like Wilson, Masaryk strongly supported help for Russia to rebuild the administrative and economic life of the country. However, he had made clear that whoever would aid Russia had to be on good terms with the Bolsheviks. Masaryk explained: "I do not mean necessarily that this

Government should be formally recognized; that is not so important. But the recovery of Russia is essential, and the work done to that end must not be frustrated. You can't work against the Government." Masaryk doubted the value of military intervention and had publicly announced his conviction that the Bolsheviks were growing more and more anti-German. He had criticized the weakness of the other parties in Russia and had emphasized his refusal to permit his legion to join them. However, if the Russians were to be helped, the Russian railways must be supported and rehabilitated, and the Allies must buy Russian grain and sell it where it was needed, thereby preventing the Germans and Austrians from acquiring it, and provide basic manufactured goods to the people. Transactions should be carried out through a barter system.[35]

Masaryk spoke with the President from 5:00 to 5:45 on June 19. He later recorded that the "main subject of the discussion" had been the "question of intervention in Russia, and whether the Japanese could intervene in Siberia and organize Siberia, and whether our Bohemian troops could be used to that end." Masaryk explained that he was "not in favor of a so-called intervention," because he did "not see what it would bring about." He felt that an army of one million Japanese troops would be required to fight Germany in Russia, and he agreed with Wilson that Japan would demand territory in Russia as compensation. "The eyes must be clear about that," said Masaryk. However, Masaryk did approve of the President's plan for the creation of a "Commission for the Relief of Russia," which Lansing had proposed as the means of at least "for the time being, dispos[ing] of the proposal of armed intervention." Wilson told Masaryk of the plan for propaganda work, of sending "business men with goods, conducting a barter, because the Russians would not accept money for their grain and the goods," and sending representatives from the YMCA and the Red Cross. The proposal was strikingly similar to the one that Masaryk himself had suggested to the President in April. Wilson was pleased that Masaryk "seemed to think well of the plan." Masaryk then asked the President "to help our men from Russia to be brought to France." He spoke of the great political effect of Bohemian troops fighting in France, describing it as "the most effective anti-Austrian propaganda among all non-German and non-Magyar nations in Austria." Masaryk also "emphasized the necessity of dismembering Austria if the war should be won." He recorded that the "President accepted this view and consented." Masaryk found the President "very friendly indeed." Obviously, given Masaryk's views on the neutrality of Czech troops in Russia and his earnest pleas for shipping to transfer the Czech Legion to France, he had not agreed to Lansing's plan to allow his troops to form the nucleus of a military occupation of the Trans-Siberian Railway and, in fact, had so informed the President. Yet, by this time both Beneš and Štefánik, the two other members of the Czech triumvirate, had agreed to Allied plans independently.[36]

Several days later, news arrived in Washington that completely changed the attitude of both the leaders in the State Department and Masaryk himself. It was an urgent cable from Balfour based on reports received from Lockhart. Balfour said that inter-Allied intervention must take place immediately, because the Bolshevik loss of power during the last month might well induce the Germans to checkmate the Allies by supporting a counterrevolution with pro-German tendencies. Balfour urged simultaneous intervention at Murmansk, Archangel, and especially in Siberia, since the force which controlled Siberia would be the economic master of central Russia. He believed that Bolshevik consent would not be given and indeed was no longer of vital importance. The memorandum said that inter-Allied intervention would cement such Russian elements as remained favorable to the Allies, revive the energies of Allied friends, and perhaps revive the national spirit in Russia, all of which would have a decisive effect on the issue of the war. Spurred to action, Lansing sent Wilson a copy of Balfour's memorandum and advised him that the Czecho-Slovak forces in western Siberia had created "a new condition which should receive careful consideration."[37]

Following Balfour's cable came one from Knight to Daniels reporting that the attitude of the Czechs toward the military situation was "completely modified" as a result of the seizure of Irkutsk by German prisoners of war, supposedly with Soviet connivance, and the German-Bolshevik obstruction of the withdrawal of the Czech forces now west of Irkutsk. The Czechs were now ready to cooperate with the Allied movements against German activities in Siberia and to reestablish an Eastern Front. The Czech situation and "its future movement," said Knight, "have become dominating factors in Siberia and perhaps Russian situation." He reported that the only Czech forces now east of Irkutsk were the 16,000 men at Vladivostok. West of Irkutsk, approximately 45,000 very adequately armed Czechs were prepared to hold the railroad and dominate the situation. Knight added:

Should movement be contemplated for establishment of Eastern front it will be enormously facilitated by present condition with the notable advantage the Czech influence would greatly overcome that of Japanese removing chief antagonism of Russians to movement against German power and influence. Belief is widespread that great number of former Russian soldiers would join Czechs who are of Allied race and recognized as former comrades in arms. Armed prisoners of war under German officers still control Irkutsk, conditions very bad, and apparently Consul is not allowed to communicate by code.[38]

As soon as Knight's cable arrived, J. Butler Wright passed it on to Miles with a handwritten note: "This is a 'Godsend,' it is just the news we want. Masaryk is in town! Let's concentrate on this with all our power at once."[39]

These events all unfolded as the State Department pondered a response to the question raised by the British about the transport of Czech troops from Siberia. In light of the new intelligence, the department "obviously" recognized "the advisability of retaining the Czecho-Slovak forces in the Far East for the present, pending the development of the situation on the eastern front where they might be needed to reinforce possible Russian opposition to the further encroachments by Germany."[40] Lansing, however, doubted the wisdom of going on record to retain the Czechs in Siberia, not only because of Masaryk's clear opposition, but also because of the State Department's strong opposition to Japanese intervention for the past six months. Therefore, he requested the views of his Assistant Secretary, William Phillips, as well as Miles and Grew, now head of the Division of Western European Affairs.[41] On June 24 Phillips reported to Long that "Professor Masaryk has changed his views."[42] Clearly Masaryk's change of mind was the product not only of the persuasion of the Russian Division of the State Department, but also of the fact that conditions in Siberia themselves had now changed, and that the Czechs appeared to have been prevented from continuing their eastward march to Vladivostok by the German prisoners of war presumably aided and abetted by the Bolsheviks. These events now placed the State Department in a quandary, and it was not until August 21 that Lansing finally responded to the British memorandum on transport of the Czechs. He then simply pointed out that the delay had been unavoidable because of the uncertainty of the Siberian situation and that the State Department would reserve judgment until the situation clarified.[43]

Leaders in London were by this time almost frantic with worry. The strong anti-Bolshevik wing of the government was determined to resume aid to Semenov. Moreover, the British war leaders were in a panic about the prospect of German penetration farther into Russia, not just in Europe but in Asia as well. Lord Curzon was convinced that the best method to save Asia from "the German clutch" was through Japanese intervention. The question was how to win Wilson's approval of such a plan. The Foreign Office had exhausted virtually all of its arguments by this time. As John D. Gregory, a member of the Russian section of the Foreign Office, admitted, "There remains only the Czechoslovak complication to use as a lever." Strong encouragement now came from the French, who were enthusiastically behind Japanese intervention, especially Clemenceau, who was even willing to leave the Czech Legion in Siberia. Unable to persuade Wilson to accept Japanese intervention and aware that the Germans had recalled from Russia a number of divisions destined for the Western Front, the French now felt that it was absolutely urgent to arm the Czechs in Siberia.[44]

To Lansing, the plight of the Czecho-Slovak forces in western Siberia seemed "to create a new condition which should receive careful consideration." As he wrote to Wilson, the efforts of the Czechs to reach Vladivostok were being opposed "by the Bolsheviks" and the Czechs were fighting the Red Guards along the Siberian line with more or less success. "As these troops are most loyal to our cause and have been most unjustly treated by the various Soviets," Lansing asked, "ought we not to consider whether something can not be done to support them?" Describing the number and position of the Czech troops in Siberia, Lansing added: "Is it not possible that in this body of capable and loyal troops may be found a nucleus for military occupation of the Siberian Railway?"[45]

As Wilson studied Lansing's memorandum, he received additional strong representations from his military advisers who opposed military intervention through Siberia for the purpose of reestablishing an Eastern Front. Wilson had specifically sought General March's advice on a long, unsigned memorandum of June 17, which proposed a scheme for intervention in Siberia and Russia with a large Japanese force. March responded that the plan was "neither practical nor practicable." He believed that the whole matter came down to a decision as to whether the Japanese should be given a "free hand in Siberia," and he regarded as "wholly inadmissible" solving the Russian problem by "giving Japan a portion of Siberia." Bliss and Baker also opposed such proposals for strategic reasons but were especially emphatic concerning their opposition to lone Japanese intervention. Wilson agreed totally with March.[46] And yet the pressures on Wilson for intervention in Siberia were almost overwhelming and, as one dedicated advocate of Wilson's position pointed out, "scarcely resistible."[47]

On the evening of June 24, Reading and Wilson had a long discussion about Russia. Reading soon discovered that the only proposal Wilson was considering seriously was that of a relief commission to Siberia supported by a protective armed guard and headed by a special commissioner. Reading learned that the War Department and others were studying the problem and that Wilson wanted a definite plan. Although gratified that Wilson now recognized the necessity for a military force to accompany the civil commission, Reading had urged the use of Allied troops as a cooperating force along with the Japanese, if only to offset any unfavorable response by the Russians to a force consisting mainly of Japanese. Wilson would go no further than to approve a relief commission with an armed guard, and he still adamantly opposed the purely military policy of intervention by a large Japanese army supplemented by contingents of American and Allied forces. Reading reported the bad news to Balfour at once.[48]

Wilson was deeply aware of the terrific strain that a German offensive in the West would place on the moral and military resources of France and Great Britain. Yet intervention would be incompatible with a just and enduring peace and with any trustworthy international organization strong enough to guarantee the future security and liberties of all nations. However, it looked as if the time had come when Wilson had to abandon the diplomatic isolation he had hitherto preserved and seek a better understanding with the Allies. He had to negotiate an agreement with them for a joint economic, military, and political policy in Russia. Neither he nor they could afford to let the existing differences of purpose persist. The news media had been arguing for political unity ever since the United States entered the war, but now it was becoming indispensable. The question was, on what basis could it be best achieved? Wilson believed that his own program, if honestly and intelligently carried out, was much better calculated to unify the Allies and to frustrate the German attack on the liberties of the world. But the appearance of the Czecho-Slovak Legion in Siberia had introduced a new and "sentimental" element into the whole issue of intervention in Russia, and the Allies were determined to use it to the greatest possible advantage in securing Wilson's agreement and participation in the military plans that they were formulating for the re-creation of a Russian front.[49]

In the meantime, in response to Lansing's request for more information on which to base a decision regarding recognition of the

Czecho-Slovak National Council, Sharp conferred at length with Beneš in Paris. Thereupon he wrote Lansing enthusiastically about Beneš, noting two points especially: first, that Balfour had already promised British recognition, and, second, that the chief objective of the Czecho-Slovak National Council at that time was "to formulate plans for the placing of Czecho-Slovak troops . . . in Russia at the disposition of the Allies."[50] On June 25, Phillips passed all of this information on to Lansing. He also reported that the French had submitted a political program embodying recognition of the Czecho-Slovak state and the de facto recognition of the National Council as the lawful government of that state. Phillips emphasized the importance of Masaryk's role as President of the National Council and Sharp's information about Allied use of the Czecho-Slovak troops in Russia. He recommended that the United States "recognize the *de facto* existence of the Council and so advise the British, French and Italian Governments."[51] On June 25, Lansing's agenda was full with matters relating to Russia, Siberia, and the Czechs. He discussed the Siberian question and recognition of the Czechs with Jusserand, the Czech crisis in Siberia with Miles, and, in the midst of these discussions, received a call from the White House asking him to a conference on Siberia with Wilson and other Cabinet officers that evening.

In the morning, Masaryk himself saw Lansing, who questioned him on the possibility of using the Czechs as a police force for the American mission in Siberia.[52] Masaryk said yes. He assured Lansing that the Czechs' only wish was to fight the common enemy and to help the Russians. However, he was clearly opposed to having his Czechs fight the Bolsheviks and sought Lansing's help to "order our relationship to the Bolsheviks peacefully." He secured Lansing's permission to address a note to Chicherin in order to refute Soviet claims that the Czecho-Slovaks had engaged in counterrevolutionary activity. Masaryk was still willing to agree to disarmament if the Soviets would provide free and unmolested passage to France. Masaryk also sought to get Lansing to "recognize us: not only the Council but as a government." He had already raised the question earlier that day with Phillips, who had "objected that we do not have any territory."[53]

Masaryk's discussions with Lansing also encompassed "the question of cancelling Mr. Wilson's declarations" concerning self-determination, which Masaryk felt were contradictory. Masaryk offered many "good arguments" for enunciating "a new, clear, and unequivocal declaration." He criticized the apparent inconsistency in Wilson's speeches: the principle that no people should be forced to live under any sovereignty repugnant to them conflicted directly with Wilson's assertion that "we do not wish in any way to impair or to rearrange the Austro-Hungarian Empire." He also noted Wilson's failure to recognize Austro-Hungarian responsibility for provoking the war. Moreover, said Masaryk, Wilson had to recognize that Austria was a medieval state, the leader of the Counter-Reformation, an artificial conglomeration of various nations, antinational, antidemocratic, and a dynasty recklessly using the church and religion for materialistic aims. Masaryk insisted that the Allies had to make the dismemberment of Austria-Hungary their primary objective in the East—that Germany could only be really defeated if the Czecho-Slovaks, Poles, South Slavs, and Rumanians were liberated from Austro-Hungarian despotism. Moreover, Italy's national aims could not be satisfied if Austria-Hungary's integrity was maintained. Thus, the Italian and the Eastern fronts must be used and Russia must be helped. On the day following his conference with Lansing, Masaryk sent him a copy of his earlier notes on the President's program, as well as a paper containing "a better explanation" of the Austrian problem.[54]

By this time, Miles, Grew, Lansing, and Phillips, as well as the Russian and Far Eastern divisions of the State Department, all agreed that it would be highly desirable to have the Czecho-Slovak troops remain in Siberia. Nevertheless, they were averse to recommending this to London because of their previous attitude toward Japanese intervention and their knowledge of Masaryk's avowed unwillingness to retain the Czech troops in Siberia. On June 25, after Masaryk's conference with Lansing, it became clear that the latter reason was no longer valid, since Masaryk "had changed his mind."[55] It was now obvious that if the United States cooperated with the Czechs in Siberia as allies, a further official declaration of American support for the freedom and independence of the Czecho-Slovaks was required immediately. Not surprisingly then, Lansing spent a good part of the day preparing a memorandum for Wilson on dismembering Austria-Hungary. After the Cabinet meeting that afternoon, Lansing conferred with Wilson for half an hour on the "nationalities in Austria and on Siberia" and also presented his memorandum on "Policy in Relation to the Nationalities now within the Austro-Hungarian Empire."[56] Wilson read and returned it to him on the same day.

Lansing's memorandum reiterated his view that a separate peace with Austria was now impossible in view of the Sixtus letter. He advocated a definite policy of dismemberment toward the Austrian Empire with specific reference to independence for the Czechs. His arguments clearly bore the imprint of Masaryk's ideas. Despite Lansing's earlier and later criticism of the principle of "self-determination," he used it extensively to convince Wilson of the importance of freeing the Czechs from Austro-Hungarian rule. He argued that the United States had already gone part of the way by declaring for an independent Poland and by expressing "sympathy with the nationalistic aspirations" of the Czecho-Slovaks and Yugoslavs. The United States need have no qualms over dismemberment, since the Habsburg monarchy was organized on the "principle of conquest and not on the principle of 'self-determination.'" Moreover, the announcement of this policy, "which is founded on the just principle that the nationalities possess the inherent right of self-government," would exert a decided influence in eliminating Austria-Hungary as a factor in the war. Shortly after his conference with Wilson, Lansing dispatched an urgent request to Caldwell for a full report on the number, character, and morale of the Czecho-Slovaks and their officers at Vladivostok; an outline of their military organization; and the character, quality, and quantity of their arms and ammunition.[57] On the evening of June 25, Wilson held a conference on Siberia at the White House, attended by Secretaries Baker, Houston, Redfield, Lansing, and William B. Wilson.[58] The evening was spent matching ideas about Russia.[59]

After an interview with Lansing on June 26, Reading concluded that opinion in Washington was crystallizing in favor of an economic commission to Russia with "an idea of using the Czechoslovaks at Vladivostok . . . for the purpose of protecting the commission." Since the Czecho-Slovaks were insufficiently armed, Lansing had even asked about the possibility of reserving the rumored 800,000 Russian rifles and many millions of cartridges in England, which had not yet been converted for British use. Reading did not assume that Lansing's comments revealed a definite policy devised by Wilson but simply that his mind was turning to the "equipment and arming of the Czechoslovaks" both at Vladivostok and elsewhere and of such Russians as might join these forces, but it did "not at all follow that the President intends to adopt it."[60]

Later that day, Reading saw Jusserand, who had also received news of the rumored desire to rearm the Czechs at Vladivostok. Jusserand's information was that Russian rifles in sufficient numbers were already in the town under English control. Jusserand had also received a cablegram to the effect that Foch had reported the recent withdrawal of several German divisions from Russia and had said that it had become necessary to create a diversion. Jusserand had immediately conveyed this information to Wilson.[61] The Imperial War Cabinet now directed the British delegates to the Supreme War Council to propose a reasoned resolution urging Wilson to accept the policy of economic assistance to Russia. Reading advised Wilson that it would be a serious blow to the associated cause if he committed himself publicly against such a policy at the present time.[62]

On June 26, despite his reluctance to decide on the proposed commission to Russia, Wilson indicated his full agreement with Lansing's memorandum on the nationalities of Austria-Hungary. He wrote, "We can no longer respect or regard the integrity of the artificial Austrian Empire."[63] On the following day, Lansing issued a formal statement to the press announcing "the position of the United States Government to [be] that all branches of the Slav race should be completely freed of German and Austrian rule." Masaryk's conversation with Lansing had made an impression.[64] Was it also only a coincidence that on the same day Masaryk had agreed to the retention of his Czechs in Siberia?

By late June and early July, the Czecho-Slovak response to the plea for help from their compatriots in western Siberia had created a totally new situation, which in turn initiated the implementation of new or modified American and Allied policies, not only toward Russia and Siberia, but also toward the Czecho-Slovak liberation movement itself. As Knight awaited a response to his questions from Washington, Ambassador Ishii informed Lansing of Japan's reluctance to agree to the Allied proposal for intervention in Siberia without Washington's concurrence.[65] Wilson had read Japan's response with "genuine pleasure" because it seemed that, at least temporarily, he had been able to forestall plans for massive Japanese military intervention in Siberia. However, it now appeared that the Allies might soon be able to substitute the Czechs in place of the Japanese.[66]

The British War Cabinet had also received information that Japan was ready to intervene in Siberia if Wilson agreed and if the commander in chief was a Japanese. But the Japanese were unwilling to go beyond central Siberia. Because the real British objective was to induce the anti-German elements in Russia to unite against Germany, they were somewhat disturbed by Japan's position. Yet if Japanese intervention would enable the Czecho-Slovaks to succeed in reestablishing a Russian front, then clearly it should be encouraged.[67] By the end of June, the French had issued instructions to the Czecho-Slovaks to rally all anti-Bolsheviks around them.[68] Foch had also telegraphed Wilson personally, urging an expedition to Siberia composed mainly of Japanese elements, but with the cooperation of one or two American regiments. When Jusserand gave Wilson Foch's telegram, he summarized the principal French reasons for intervention and insisted that even if the intervention forces never met the Germans, the news of it would greatly disturb them. He emphasized the Allied good fortune in the success of the Czechs and argued that it would be an "enormous error" not "to profit" from this and "immoral" to abandon them.[69] Wilson was apparently unmoved. When Secretary Daniels approached him with the report from Knight seeking a response to the questions raised by the Czechs at Vladivostok, Wilson informed him that it was not advisable "to reply to questions of Czechs."[70] The Chief of Naval Operations, Admiral William S. Benson, was advised that America's Russian policy was to protect Allied property and munitions of war at Vladivostok and Murmansk and to accept the assistance of the Czecho-Slovak forces in that endeavor. However, American forces were to conduct no active operations on Russian soil against any power or party except on the invitation of a recognized authority within Russia. They were to make no promises to the Czecho-Slovak troops, but were to transport them to France if they desired to go.[71]

Drysdale, whose views were strongly supported by Knight and Warner, was now cabling that the establishment of an anti-Bolshevik Siberian government was probable, that it was eager to resume hostilities against Germany, and that the 50,000 Czechs provided a "splendidly adequate nucleus for a new Siberian Army." He believed that this army, with Allied support, could be augmented by the following spring to operate against the Germans in European Russia, which might well bring Russia back into the war. Drysdale urged strong consideration of his plan as conceivably offering quick and effective aid to the Allied cause.[72] By this time, the Czechs controlled Vladivostok and were ready to move westward.

On June 29, Jusserand again urged Lansing to join the French the following day in a public and solemn declaration "to recognize the National Council as the supreme organization of the Czech-Slovak movement in the Entente countries." The French were prepared to support in "all earnestness the aspirations to independence" for which Czecho-Slovak soldiers were fighting in the ranks of the Allies.[73] Lansing sent the French requests to Wilson along with various other related memoranda from both the French and British embassies.[74] Since he had already issued his own statement to the press just a few days earlier, which embodied a similar declaration to the Serbs, he wrote Wilson: "The Allies are constantly seeking to have us act jointly with them in political matters, and this is another effort in that direction." Lansing felt that it was best "to act independently."[75] Wilson agreed.[76]

The French government recognized the Czecho-Slovak National Council on June 30.[77] Balfour sent a telegram to Pichon associating London with the sentiments expressed by France. Despite Wilson's refusal to participate, Pichon declared that in recognizing the Czecho-Slovak National Council, France had been "inspired by the sentiments and high ideals expressed by President Wilson."[78] The French action was the first instance in which a member of the Entente had recognized the belligerency of one of the subject peoples in the Dual Monarchy through its organized committee abroad. On June 30, Clemenceau also cabled the French Military Mission with the Czechs to confirm the orders for Allied intervention sent to General Lavergne on June 20.

As these momentous events were happening in Paris, the Russian branch of the Czecho-Slovak National Council and Dietrichs in Vladivostok issued a proclamation to the citizens of both Vladivostok and the Maritime Province. They explained that the initiating force for their military takeover was a Soviet order to forward the arms, ammunition, locomotives, and trucks then at Vladivostok to Nikolsk and Habarovsk to be used to arm Soviet troops (German and Hungarian war prisoners) to be sent to Irkutsk to fight against "our brothers." They declared that it was necessary to go back to aid their compatriots, and that their departure from the neutrality ordered by Masaryk had been necessitated by the change in conditions. They had no choice but to defend themselves. They professed to be disinterested in the political coloration of any new government elected by the Russian people. They insisted that until they had "executed" their military aims—to assist their "brothers before Irkutsk" and, eventually, to assemble all Czechs in Vladivostok for shipment to France—it was "all the same" to them whatever "kind of authority" the Russians accepted. They wanted only one thing—noninterference with their echelons on their way to Vladivostok and France.[79]

The Czechs under Dietrichs now began to fight the Bolsheviks with considerable success along the railroad between Vladivostok and Habarovsk.[80] Francis at Vologda wrote his many friends in the United States that, in his judgment, the "Soviet G. is about finished."[81] In official circles in Washington, the achievements of the Czechs and the Russian situation were the main topics of conversation. Charles R. Crane took advantage of the occasion to invite Lansing to dinner, no doubt to present Masaryk's views. Miles plied Lansing with reports from Vladivostok and informed him of General March's possible approval of arms for the Czechs. Phillips seized the opportunity to press for further consideration of the recognition of the Czecho-Slovak National Council in Paris.[82] The Belgian government transmitted information from its Consul in Moscow that the Soviet government was "powerless" against the Czechs, and that 12,000 German war prisoners, wearing Russian uniforms and acting in agreement with the Russian government, had left Petrograd to take the field against the Czecho-Slovak troops.[83]

On July 2, the Peking legation sent Harris at Irkutsk the instructions sent to Lavergne from Paris on June 20. He was asked to transmit the information to Bourgeois, who was to send it to Guinet at Omsk, who in turn would make it known to all French officers on mission with the Czechs. The instructions provided for the temporary retention of the Czech divisions in their present zone with a view to developing centers of resistance and grouping around them the Siberian and Cossack groups favorable to the reestablishment of order; second, completing the possession of the Trans-Siberian Railway; and third, preparing for and covering eventual Allied intervention from the east. French officers were instructed to oppose "energetically" the possible disarming of the Czechs and to keep them in organized units so as to insure their continued cohesion.[84] Clemenceau himself had signed the necessary order.[85] French officers were already implementing these plans as a result of the message they had received earlier from Ambassador Noulens. French military objectives clearly envisaged seizure and control of the Trans-Siberian Railway by the Czechs. Colonel Marie Constantin Robert Paris, chief of the French military mission to the Czech Legion, was ordered not only to connect the scattered Czech units along the Trans-Siberian Railway and to provide for effective occupation and defense of the lines of the railway as a means of supply, but also to lend technical and financial assistance to all groups capable of giving effective cooperation. The third article of the instructions was a secret addition that noted: "The French Military Attaché advised from Paris War Office of a project for eventual organization of a line of communication with the Czechs in the Omsk region from Araucaria by the Strait and Sea of Kara and the Obi [sic] River, communication from Archangel to Obdorak being assured by an ice breaker and thence by existing Obi River steamers; advise as to the possibility of project, . . . commandants' opinion requested as to its necessity and the most important required Czech forces."[86]

Thus when the Supreme War Council met on July 2, a complete change had occurred in the situation in Russia and Siberia, which convinced the council that Allied intervention was an urgent and imperative necessity. Not only had the Czecho-Slovak action "materially altered the situation," but to Wiseman it appeared that it would be "the determining factor."[87] The Supreme War Council viewed the Czechs as being totally disinterested in the internal politics of Russia, yet determined to fight Germany for the liberation of their own country. If intervention was to take place in time, there would have to be a Slavic army in western Siberia to which the Russian patriots could rally and which would eliminate the opposition of the Russian public to intervention by forces almost entirely Japanese. General Alby warned that the measures already taken to rally the Czechs would be of "no value" unless followed by a full-fledged intervention prepared by the Allies. He urged an immediate effort to bring about intervention by the Japanese army and the "most active negotiations" with the United States and Japan to support the Czechs. The deliberations of the Supreme War Council stressed the waning power of the Bolsheviks and the importance of supporting the Czecho-Slovak troops in western Siberia. The Allies were never so unanimous as they now appeared to be on the necessity for intervention.[88]

The Supreme War Council now presented a final appeal to Wilson. It stressed the changed situation in Siberia and predicted that if action were taken immediately, the Allies might well gain control of the railway through the whole of Siberia as far as the Urals in a very few weeks. The appeal presented it as the unanimous opinion of Foch and the Allied military advisers of the Council that the immediate dispatch of a considerable Allied force to Siberia was essential for the victory of the Allied armies.[89] When Reading went to discuss the Council's appeal with Wilson on July 3, he laid "great stress on the condition of the Czecho-Slovaks and the grave injury that would result to our cause if we were unable to afford fully adequate protection to them against German or Austro-Hungarian prisoners of war and on the necessity for immediate action taking advantage of present favorable conditions."[90] Wilson made relatively little response, and Reading came out of the meeting convinced that he would never agree to a new Eastern Front. In this judgment, Reading was absolutely correct.[91] Later, "speaking of War Council's advice on Russia" at the Cabinet meeting, Wilson said, "they propose such impractical things to be done immediately that he often wondered whether he was crazy or whether they were."[92]

Wiseman now sought to convey to the British Foreign Office Wilson's true feelings in regard to intervention. "The President," he said, was not only "unconvinced by all the political arguments in favor of Allied intervention," but was even less "impressed by the military arguments in favor of re-creating an Eastern front." He continued to think that "it would be a great blunder for the Allies to intervene without an unmistakable invitation from the Soviet Government. Anyone who has studied his Mexican policy will understand the remarkable parallel which the Russian situation presents, and realise that this is to him more than a passing political question, but a matter of principle." The British, Wiseman emphasized, had to realize that they were "up against a new conception of foreign policy which no amount of argument" would "reconcile with . . . traditional British policy." Nevertheless, Wiseman thought that ultimately the Czecho-Slovak position would be the determining factor.[93]

Back in Paris, Clemenceau had urged the Allies to consider what they would do if Wilson would not agree to their proposal for intervention. An immediate decision was vital so as to implement plans before winter arrived. While awaiting a reply from Wilson, the Supreme War Council approved a British proposal to send immediately to Vladivostok the 14,000 rifles and the necessary ammunition required for the armament of the Czecho-Slovak forces. Reading also talked at length with Lansing and impressed upon him the serious importance of the British and Supreme War Council appeals, which he noted, "Lansing fully recognizes."[94]

Lansing's position was quite different from that of the President. On July 4, he addressed a memorandum to Wilson, explaining that the Czechs' capture of Vladivostok and their success in western Siberia had materially altered the situation by "introducing a sentimental element into the question of our duty." He declared that if the United States failed to aid the Czechs and if they were destroyed, "we would be held culpable or at least generally blamed, especially by their compatriots in this country and western Europe." Whereas his earlier memorandum had stressed the Bolshevik attack on Czech troops, he now emphasized that American responsibility was made almost imperative because the Czechs were being attacked by released Germans and Austrians. Sensitive to Wilson's strong opposition to intervention in Russian affairs, Lansing wrote that "furnishing protection and assistance to the Czecho-Slovaks, who are so loyal to our cause," was a very different thing from sending an army into Siberia to restore order or to save the Russians from themselves. There was, he added, "a moral obligation to save these men from our common enemies, if we are able to do so." While the United States would have to rely chiefly upon Japan to supply the troops for any considerable expeditionary force, he thought that it would be wise for the United States and the Allies also to send troops. He advised that the Czecho-Slovaks be notified immediately of the intended assistance, that this notification should be accompanied by a declaration that there was no intention to interfere in the "internal affairs of Russia," and that, once the danger from German and Austrian aggression was over, the military forces would be withdrawn unless Russia desired further aid in resisting the Central Powers. The Russians should be informed that the territory and sovereignty of Russia would be unimpaired after the expeditionary forces had accomplished their purposes. He recommended the attachment to the force of a peaceful commission of representatives, "moral, industrial, commercial, financial and agricultural with a political High Commissioner at its head." "They should seek to restore normal conditions of trade, industry and social order. This commission should proceed westward from Vladivostok following as closely as possible with due regard to safety, the Czecho-Slovaks."[95]

Of all the reasons for intervention presented by the Supreme War Council, Lansing had seized upon the rescue of the Czechs as the most important. The Supreme War Council appeal had itself stressed that Czecho-Slovak success had transformed the Siberian situation and had demonstrated that the bulk of the Siberian population was no longer sympathetic to the Bolsheviks and must therefore be friendly to the Allied cause. The Czecho-Slovak force was in "grave danger of being cut off by the organization of German and Austro-Hungarian prisoners of war at Irkutsk," and therefore the Czech National Council had appealed to the Allied council at Vladivostok for "immediate military assistance."[96] Nevertheless, the Supreme War Council pointed out that to push a force through to Irkutsk to overwhelm the German prisoner organization and join hands with the Czecho-Slovaks "would probably be a simple and rapid matter if it were taken in hand immediately." In actuality, the Czechs did not feel in any danger. The Bolsheviks were powerless. Yet on July 3, the Supreme War Council in Paris stated: "The Czechs in danger of being cut off. The Bolsheviki are down and out. We must intervene to save the Czechs and to gain easy possession of Siberia." It was a contradictory series of statements, which contained only one untruth: "We must intervene to save the Czechs." Yet Lansing employed this one untruth to justify Allied intervention. Did he believe that it was true—proved true by trusted American agents and their reports of events? Or did he know about the contemplated Allied-Czech action in Siberia and feel compelled to adopt intervention in conjunction with Japan in order to restrain and control Allied action in

Siberia and Russia? It is true that by July 5 Clemenceau's orders to General Lavergne and the French Military Mission in Russia and Siberia to instruct the Czechs to seize the entire length of the Trans-Siberian Railroad, to rally anti-Bolshevik forces around them, and to prepare for eventual Allied intervention had been received in the State Department and "tallied" to Basil Miles. There is no evidence to indicate that Wilson ever saw them.[97]

As Wilson pondered Lansing's memorandum of July 4, Lansing continued to study the Siberian situation, while Miles kept him fully informed with reports from Harris, Caldwell, and Knight.[98] Harris had sent a long and impassioned cable denouncing the Bolsheviks and urging Allied intervention with Japanese assistance to fight the common enemy. Once again he advocated the utilization of the Czechs as the nucleus of an army to overthrow the Bolsheviks and added that many anti-Bolsheviks were "now rallying the Czechs for the purpose of overthrowing Bolsheviks." He concluded: "If Allies do not intervene and Czechs are removed or left unsupported there is grave danger of Germany gaining Siberian Railroad line through armed war prisoners. If Czechs are not supported the danger [is] that they may be overthrown by Bolsheviks and war prisoners."[99] Caldwell in Vladivostok agreed.[100] Knight also described the dangers confronting the Czechs from the advance of several thousand Red Guards and war prisoners. He reported "Bolshevic power entirely overthrown" in Vladivostok and that the "threatened danger" was from war prisoners and spies. Daniels sent Knight's urgent cable for instructions to Wilson with the request that it be answered that day.[101]

On July 5, Lansing instructed Caldwell: "Inform Czech leaders verbally that . . . your Government regards Czech forces in Russia as inspiring element of the military forces now engaged against the Central Powers. Also that you consider conduct of leaders at Vladivostok and in Western Siberia beyond criticism and deserving of the support and approval of all Governments engaged in war against Germany and Austria." A similar telegram was sent to Poole at Moscow to be communicated to the Czech leaders at Samara and Cheliabinsk, who had evinced a willingness to try to establish a front on the Volga or to proceed through Siberia according to the wishes of the Allied governments.[102] Surely such comments by the Secretary of State could only lead the Czechs to believe, in view of the proposals already made to them by the British and French, that the American government supported their actions.

On July 6, the Czechs were engaged in a serious battle near Nikolsk, fifty miles from Vladivostok, reportedly with three to four thousand Austrians and Germans accompanied by one thousand Red Guards commanded by German officers. Knight reported that although the situation was critical, he had every hope that the Czechs would win. "Reliable information" indicated that 30,000 war prisoners were already armed and that the Soviet government had announced they would arm every prisoner in Siberia. To Knight, the evidence pointed to a "prolonged and desperate fight against Germans both in this vicinity and throughout the length of Siberian Railroad."[103] By this time, Semenov had been defeated, and he had retreated to the vicinity of the Chinese border. Admiral Aleksandr Vasilevich Kolchak, former Russian commander of the Black Sea fleet, sent by the British to head an anti-Bolshevik movement in Siberia, had begun a movement toward Pogranichnaya and Vladivostok but without any tangible success, and reportedly he had resigned.[104]

Throughout the morning of July 6, Lansing was deluged with matters relating to the Czechs and to Siberia. When Auchincloss approached him about aid to the Czechs, he read him the memorandum he had prepared for Wilson. Lansing also discussed at length with Miles the recent telegrams from Russia and particularly Knight's reports.[105] At two o'clock that afternoon, July 6, Lansing, Baker, and Daniels, along with General March and Admiral Benson, arrived at the White House for a conference on the Russian situation. After Wilson offered his views on the matter, the group discussed the changed conditions in Siberia created by the Czecho-Slovak seizure of Vladivostok; the landing of American, British, French, and Japanese forces in that port; and the occupation of the railway through western Siberia by other Czecho-Slovaks and their reported capture of Irkutsk. After reviewing the Supreme War Council's appeal favoring the restoration of an Eastern Front against the Central Powers, as well as the memorandum presented by Lansing, Wilson announced his decisions. First, he rejected the establishment of an Eastern Front through a military expedition, even if it was wise to employ a large Japanese force. Second, he rejected any advance west of Irkutsk as unworthy of further consideration. He determined: "The present situation of the Czecho-Slovaks requires this Government and other Governments to make an effort to aid those at Vladivostok in forming a junction with their compatriots in western Siberia; and that this Government on sentimental grounds and because of the effect upon the friendly Slavs everywhere would be subject to criticism if it did not make this effort and would doubtless be held responsible if they were defeated by lack of such effort." Given the American inability to furnish any considerable force within a short time to assist the Czecho-Slovaks, Wilson agreed that the Japanese government should be asked to cooperate with the United States in furnishing arms and ammunition to the Czecho-Slovaks and in assembling a military force at Vladivostok composed of approximately 7,000 Americans and 7,000 Japanese "to guard the line of communication of the Czecho-Slovaks proceeding towards Irkutsk." The Japanese were to be asked to send troops at once. Wilson advised the immediate landing of available forces from American and Allied naval vessels to hold Vladivostok and cooperate with the Czecho-Slovaks. The entire endeavor was to be announced in a public declaration by the United States and Japanese governments that the purpose of landing the troops was to aid the Czecho-Slovaks against the German and Austrian prisoners, that there was no purpose to interfere with the internal affairs of Russia, and that they guaranteed not to impair the political or territorial sovereignty of Russia. Any further steps would have to await future developments.[106]

Although March voiced his strong opposition to Wilson's proposals, Lansing, Daniels, and Baker assented to them. Fully aware of the "tremendous drive" that had been "made upon the President to get the U. S. committed to sending troops to Siberia," March, from a military standpoint, still regarded the plan as "a very undesirable diversion of U. S. forces."[107] When Wilson, who understood March's opposition, said: "You are opposed to this because you do not think Japan will limit herself to seven thousand men, and that this decision will further her schemes for territorial aggrandizement," March immediately agreed. Wilson then replied, "Well we will have to take that chance."[108]

Immediately after the White House conference, instructions were sent to Knight, Morris, and Caldwell that Vladivostok was to be kept available as a base for the safety of the Czechs and as a means of "egress for them should the necessity arise." Knight was authorized to utilize his own force to aid the Czechs. However, American forces were to avoid any action tending to offend Russian sentiment or to involve them in any political questions.[109] On the same day the Allied powers issued a proclamation taking Vladivostok and its vicinity under their temporary protection.[110] By this time the Czechs had already committed themselves to act as the vanguard of an intervening force to take control of the Trans-Siberian Railway and to cooperate with the Allies in the reestablishment of an Eastern Front. Yet, when Wilson agreed to act to save the Czechs, he made unequivocally clear his complete and absolute opposition to the reestablishment of an Eastern Front.

On July 7, the executive committee of the Czech army in Siberia made the decision to set up an anti-Bolshevik front in the Volga area, to begin an advance against the Soviets, and to proceed farther into central Russia. It took this action on instructions from Guinet and an elusive figure, named Jeaneau, the French Consul at Samara, but without the approval of either Masaryk or Beneš. Jeaneau's instructions specifically indicated that the aim of the Czech echelons must no longer be to leave for France via Vladivostok, but to act as the avant-garde of the Allies to reestablish an Eastern Front on the Volga. The reward for such an action was an "independent Czecho-Slovak nation."[111]

As the Czechs set out, the State Department was deluged with telegrams from Knight and Caldwell describing the conditions of battle and the numerous armed German and Austro-Hungarian prisoners of war taking the field against the Czechs. In accordance with naval instructions, an Allied naval force was cooperating in the defense of Vladivostok. The naval commanders urged immediate military aid to the Czechs.[112] Moreover, even before the Japanese had received the appeal from the United States Government for arms to support the Czechs, they had responded affirmatively to a similar French request. The Japanese General Staff noted that although the Czechs initially had been reluctant to fight the Russians, since they had received word of the "abuse and the holding of their comrades West of Irkutsk," they were "very anxious to rescue them."[113]

As soon as Horvath, in Harbin, learned that the Czechs had started hostilities against the Bolsheviks at Vladivostok, he ordered his detachments to move to their assistance. Ivan Kalmikov, Ataman of the Ussuri Cossacks, captured Grodekovo, Horvatovo, and Golenki, but the Czechs had occupied Nikolsk before the arrival of Horvath's main force. Immediately the commander of Horvath's troops entered into negotiations with the Czechs to offer further combined action. To his astonishment, the Czechs not only refused his cooperation, but even showed ill will, "being apparently in favor of a Socialistic Siberian Government." To Horvath, the situation seemed absurd, since both the Czechs and Horvath's troops were being supplied with arms and money by Japan and France. Moreover, it was Japan who had urged him to organize an anti-Bolshevik government in the Far East in March 1918. Although his efforts had been largely confined to Harbin and the zone of the Chinese Eastern Railway, on July 9 at Grodekovo he declared his intention to organize a nonpartisan government for all of Siberia.[114] A constitutional monarchist by choice, he now announced his willingness to work as a conservative democrat.

When the consular representatives at Vladivostok learned of Horvath's proclamation, they feared civil strife that would prevent the Czechs from passing through Manchuria. They immediately advised British, French, and Japanese representatives at Peking to suggest that Horvath withdraw his proclamation and return to Harbin to facilitate the use of the Chinese Eastern Railway for the Czechs in their passage. They urged an early answer.[115] Horvath was not alone in his desire to cooperate with the Czecho-Slovaks. Semenov also announced that notwithstanding his lack of strength, he felt compelled to undertake an offensive in order to relieve the Czechs from Bolshevik attack and to support the White Guards in Trans-Baikalia. He, too, stressed the great importance of immediate intervention by the Allies.[116] At the same time, local representatives of the Provisional Government of Autonomous Siberia presented notes to the local Allied Consuls requesting Allied military intervention in Siberia and Russia with the object of interning Austrian and German war prisoners and establishing a new front against Germany.[117] Tereshchenko, too, saw the Czecho-Slovak movement as a "desperate effort to gain foothold," which should receive open support from the Allies and "assistance from America in particular." Strongly opposed to any intervention in which the Japanese might take a "dominating part," he obviously welcomed the Czecho-Slovak action.[118]

While these events were occurring in Siberia, the Allies proceeded with their own plans for intervention. Macdonogh, the director of British military intelligence, went to Paris to negotiate details for financing the Czecho-Slovaks in Siberia. The French agreed to pay for the Czechs so long as they remained in Siberia, while the British agreed to be responsible for their expenses from the time of their embarkation at a Russian port.[119] On July 9, the British Ambassador in Japan asked the Vice Minister for Foreign Affairs, Kijuro Shidehara, to support the appeal of the Allied Consuls at Peking to facilitate the movement of the Czechs through Manchuria. Shidehara agreed to consult the Chinese government about the matter, but he thought that, as far as the Chinese Eastern Railway was concerned, the request should be made to Horvath.[120] Also, on July 9 the British at Vladivostok announced what amounted to a proclamation of intervention and on July 10 issued orders to the British battalion at Hong Kong to proceed to Vladivostok.[121] The French, of course, had already issued their orders for intervention on June 20. On July 13, Japan proposed to China that Japan take over the Chinese Eastern Railway at once.[122] Obviously the plans of the Allies in Russia and Siberia differed sharply from those of the United States.

15

American and Allied Conflict
of Objectives in Siberia

After Wilson's decision of July 6, the State Department concentrated on securing Japanese approval of his proposal for a joint Japanese-American expedition to rescue the Czechs, while Masaryk sought to use the changed position of the Czechs in Russia as a lever to secure further support for the recognition of the Czecho-Slovak National Council as the trustee for an independent, sovereign Czecho-Slovak state. On July 8, Ishii approved the American plan and told Lansing that he believed that his government would find it acceptable. Lansing then discussed with Ishii "the possible consequence" of the Czecho-Slovaks "forming a nucleus" about which friendly Russians "might rally even to the extent of becoming again a military factor in the war." The two men agreed to keep these possibilities in mind, but to make no plans to implement them.[1]

Lansing now became deeply concerned about the secrecy of the negotiations with Japan, because the Washington government would be very embarrassed in its relations with Britain and the other Allies if Japan consulted the British government about the American proposal. On the other hand, both Lansing and Wilson believed that the Chinese should be asked to cooperate in the proposed Siberian expedition, since they already held the Manchurian railway east and west of Harbin and could aid the Czechs by continuing to guard it.[2] Wilson, however, was unwilling to inform any of the Allies of his plans until the Japanese had responded. He refused also to be hurried to reply to the Supreme War Council's demands despite pressure from Reading and Jusserand.[3]

When Wilson saw Reading on July 8, he told him about the White House conference on the Siberian expedition and indicated that both his military and naval advisers had produced reports that he had returned for further elucidation. Although aware of the "urgency of the matter," Wilson would not answer the questions from the Allied governments until he had received the complete reports from his advisers and the results of the current discussions between Lansing and Ishii.

Reading was not optimistic about his response. Jusserand, however, believed that the news about Czech successes would be a valuable argument in securing Wilson's cooperation. Moreover, he was heartened by the continued campaign for intervention in the American press.[4]

While Lansing negotiated with Ishii, events were moving rapidly in Siberia. The French, British, and Japanese Ministers in Peking, responding to the Allied consular appeal from Vladivostok to aid in the transfer of Czech forces from Vladivostok to western Siberia, were asking the Russian legation to arrange with the Russian railway authorities at Harbin for their transportation by the Chinese Eastern Railway. Once they received a favorable reply, they intended simply to inform the Chinese government of the passage of these forces through Manchuria. In view of Horvath's projected effort to establish a provisional Siberian government outside of the railway zone and the Chinese desire to take over the railway zone, such a proposal was likely to arouse considerable complications among the contenders for control of the railway. American Chargé at Peking John Van A. MacMurray felt it unwise to associate with these proposals, which might entail conflict with the Bolshevik forces near Chita and thus initiate intervention. Faced with this dilemma, he requested instructions about all the movements of the Czech forces in Siberia.[5]

To Wilson and Lansing, these requests offered an excellent opportunity "to bring the Chinese Government into participation in aiding the Czecho-Slovaks."[6] No sooner had Lansing consulted with Wilson than he learned through Langdon Warner, who telegraphed from Horvath's train at Grodekovo, that Japanese officers who had arrived in that area as mediators had indicated their intention to disarm the Czechs if they did not recognize Horvath. Warner found that Horvath himself was "deeply mixed with Japan."[7] Fearful of the effect of Horvath's projected action upon the transfer of Czecho-Slovak troops, the Allied Ministers in Peking finally persuaded the Russian Minister to join them in urging Horvath to refrain from any action that might impede the Czecho-Slovaks and to return to Harbin so as to facilitate the passage of the Czechs over the Chinese Eastern Railway.[8]

When the Allied Ambassadors in Washington learned of the American proposal to Japan for a joint expedition to Siberia, they were very much disturbed and feared that Washington wanted to confine the entire Siberian enterprise to Japanese and American troops. Reading, accompanied by the French and Italian Ambassadors, took the lead in an interview with Lansing on July 9. Lansing assured them that it was useless to consider details about Allied involvement until the Japanese had approved the general plan. Reading was "manifestly disturbed." When he asked "why the British had been omitted," Lansing "told him straight that in Russia the British were regarded as imperialists and unsympathetic to the Revolution." He told Jusserand that the French were not invited because they had identified with reactionary factions within Russia, especially the Semenov revolutionary forces. Nevertheless, Jusserand appeared "happy and delighted" that the United States was to take a hand. Although he believed that American reluctance to accept intervention was largely due to "repugnance" at accepting Japanese action, he also recognized Wilson's displeasure with the intensive Allied pressure. Thus he approved of Washington's approaching Tokyo alone, since this would solve the latter problem. In any case, a recent conversation with House had "confirmed" his impression that events were taking "the direction we desire."[9]

Immediately after the interview with Lansing, Reading advised both Balfour and Lloyd George that the American position regarding intervention had changed because of the changed situation of the Czecho-Slovaks in Siberia. Because of the Czechs' urgent need for assistance, Wilson did not plan to wait for the formation of an economic commission but would send troops first, thus reversing the order of the original proposal. Although the proposal discussed with the Japanese "did not apparently include the participation of either French, Italian or British troops," the fact that Wilson should take a "leading" part in a "military movement in Siberia was so important a change in the policy hitherto prevailing" that, despite its limitations, the "Ambassadors regarded the step as a distinct advance in the direction" of Allied policy.[10]

On the following day, Wilson reassured Reading that the only reason for consulting Ishii immediately was to save time and to avoid preliminary discussions with five governments. After Japan's answer was received, there would be immediate consultation with the Allies. Although Reading knew that Wilson was still not willing to cooperate in the re-creation of an Eastern Front, he was reassured by his conversation with Lansing who had "said this expedition may well be the means eventually of creating a Russian Front." Obviously Wilson and Lansing had different views about the ultimate objectives of the expedition. Reading believed that the Supreme War Council's resolutions and Foch's appeal were largely responsible for Wilson's step, "partial, as it is."[11]

The British Foreign Office cordially welcomed Wilson's decision as a

far-reaching change of policy, although it realized that Wilson's proposals offered little support for their own objectives. Clearly, 14,000
men added to the Czecho-Slovak army were not going to "deny Siberia
to the Germans or reconstitute the Russian Front."[12] Lloyd George
thought that it was surely possible to do "something more effective in a
military sense" that was "not inconsistent with Russia's distrust of a
purely Japanese intervention," particularly in view of the "large
Czecho-Slovak forces already on the spot." Regardless, the movement
had to be initiated without delay before the onset of the Siberian winter.
The French agreed.[13]

To expedite matters, the British decided to send General Knox to
Siberia to head British operations at Vladivostok. Reading was appalled, especially since the Foreign Office had indicated that Knox
might visit Washington en route to Vladivostok. He immediately
advised Lloyd George confidentially that there was a strong impression
in Washington that Knox had always been against the revolution and
that American leaders naturally feared that he would be likely to
assemble in Russia the ex-imperial officers and supporters and thus
give the British part of the expedition a reactionary appearance. It was
obvious to Reading that Wilson was clearly apprehensive lest any
intervention "should be converted into an anti-Soviet movement and
an interference with the right of Russians to choose their own form of
government." For this reason, Reading urged Lloyd George to give a
"liberal turn to our assistance to Russia" and take care "to reassure
opinion here in order to carry the President with us in any further
movement that may become necessary."[14] Lloyd George rejected Reading's fears about Knox's possible reactionary tendencies. He regarded
Knox as the best man for the job and believed that no man in the British
army "knows Russia as Knox does." He emphasized that Knox would
not be concerned with politics.[15]

As the State Department initiated its negotiations with Ishii regarding the proposed joint expedition to Siberia, dangers along the borders
of Manchuria, arising from the defeat of Semenov and Horvath's effort
to move into Siberia, had prompted the Japanese to implement the
provisions of the Sino-Japanese Military Pact of May 16. Japan appeared
to be preparing to move a considerable portion of its Kwantung gar-
rison to northern Manchuria. Morris indicated that the implementation
of the pact included "taking over the control of the Chinese Eastern
Railway."[16] Lansing immediately informed Stevens, then at Harbin, of
the success of the Czecho-Slovak troops in occupying Vladivostok and
urged him to summon his men from Nagasaki to Vladivostok at once.

Stevens was delighted and assured Lansing that with a fortnight's notice he would "put railways on the map quickly."[17]

When the Japanese Cabinet met to consider implementation of the Sino-Japanese pact, it also considered the American proposal concerning Siberia. On July 13, after strenuous debate and an all-day session, a compromise was finally reached whereby Japan reserved the right to dispatch additional troops to Siberia if needed to protect the Czecho-Slovak soldiers. Thus, while abandoning the original idea of a large-scale expedition, Japan reserved freedom of action for the future.[18] Wilson opposed both the proposal for an independent Japanese expedition to Siberia and Japanese support of Horvath. He insisted that "a military occupation of Manchuria would arouse deep resentment in Russia which would be greatly increased by any apparent support by the Allies of plans to restore monarchy." He also informed Tokyo that the United States was not prepared to support "any of the factions claiming to govern Siberia."[19] In the meantime, Ishii informed the State Department that a decision would be facilitated if the Americans would give the Japanese the command of the proposed joint expedition.[20] When Polk explained to Wilson that approval of Ishii's request would result "very shortly" in Japanese willingness to cooperate, he agreed to let the Japanese have the supreme command when they landed in Vladivostok.[21]

The Japanese newspapers were now filled with long inspired articles alleging that the United States had sent definite proposals concerning Siberia. Knight and Warner, now Acting Vice Consul at Harbin, who had recently arrived in Tokyo after a two-month trip through central Siberia, were reporting that German and Magyar prisoners organized by German agents had finally obtained mastery in the Central Soviet Government of Siberia and had thus forced the issue with the Czecho-Slovak army. They urged the Allies to give prompt support to enable the Czechs to hold their strategic position.[22]

In central Siberia, Harris and Emerson had been isolated from the outside world for some time. Harris had had no communication with Vladivostok since May 26 or with Peking since July 2. He was aware, however, that the Czechs had thrown the Bolsheviks out of Vladivostok, and he had received the message from the legation in Peking confirming French official support for intervention and consolidation of the Czech forces in central Siberia. He urged Emerson to go to Vladivostok as soon as railway conditions would permit.[23] In response, Emerson wired Guinet and Gajda and offered to cooperate with Czech forces to repair the railroad damaged during military operations.

Gajda, now a colonel, immediately accepted Emerson's services and arranged for American engineers to assist Czech engineers at once in repairing the Irkutsk bridge. Thus, even before an official public announcement regarding the joint expedition had been issued, Emerson and his railway engineers had begun to support Gajda and the French in their efforts in central Siberia.[24]

On July 17, Wilson sent his statement, or aide-mémoire, on intervention in Russia to the Allied Ambassadors. After clearly indicating his complete opposition to any kind of military intervention in Russia (it would be "merely a method of making use of Russia, not a method of serving her"), he added that military action was admissible in Russia only to help the Czecho-Slovaks "consolidate their forces and get into successful cooperation with their Slavic kinsmen and to steady any efforts at self-government or self-defense in which the Russians themselves may be willing to accept assistance." Despite the "immediate necessity and sufficient justification" for helping the Czecho-Slovaks, Wilson emphasized that he had no intention of taking part in organized intervention from either Vladivostok or Murmansk and Archangel. Moreover, American troops could be used only for the purposes he had clearly stated. He would "feel obliged to withdraw those forces if the plans in whose execution it was then intended that they should cooperate, should develop into others inconsistent with the policy to which the Government of the United States felt constrained to restrict itself." At Lansing's insistence, Wilson had added that in stipulating American purposes, he did not wish to restrict or to set limits to the actions of his associates or to define their policies. He indicated his hope of carrying out the plans to safeguard the rear of the Czecho-Slovaks operating from Vladivostok in cooperation with a small military force from Japan and, if necessary, from the Allies. He announced his intention of pledging and asking his associates to pledge to the Russian people in the most public and solemn manner that none of the governments uniting in action either in Siberia or in northern Russia contemplated "any interference of any kind with the political sovereignty of Russia, any intervention in her internal affairs, or any impairment of her territorial integrity either now or hereafter."

Wilson also indicated his intention to send to Siberia, at the earliest opportunity, a commission of merchants, agricultural experts, labor advisers, Red Cross representatives, and agents of the YMCA accustomed to organizing the best methods of spreading useful information and rendering educational help of a modest sort, in order to relieve the immediate economic necessities of the people in a systematic way.[25]

A comparison of Wilson's statement with an earlier draft prepared in Lansing's office on July 11 reveals the obvious differences between Wilson and Lansing regarding the character and objectives of the joint expedition. Lansing's draft did not spell out opposition to military intervention in Russia and also indicated the possibility of operating not only against the Germans and Austrian prisoners of war, but also against the Red Guards engaged in giving aid or support to the armed prisoners.[26]

Although Wilson's proposal did not receive the wholehearted support of the State Department, it was far more in accord with Masaryk's position than were the Allied proposals to use the Czechs. Indeed, one close observer gave Masaryk the "entire" credit for "persuading the President to act."[27] British reaction to the statement was mixed. Lloyd George found it difficult "not to take exception to the tone of the President's *aide-mémoire.*" He had serious misgivings concerning the adequacy of the proposed force. Since the British government regarded a force of 20,000 men insufficient to rescue the Czecho-Slovaks from Samara to Irkutsk, it deplored the decision to confine the military aid of the Japanese to 7,000 men. Lloyd George urged Wilson to make the primary object of his policy the establishment of effective Russian and Allied control over the whole of the Siberian railway to the Urals before the winter set in. He regarded the Czechs as the key to the situation. Recognizing Wilson's concern over a predominant Japanese force, Lloyd George pointed out that, together, the Czech, American, British, and French troops outnumbered the Japanese and "ought to . . . insure political control of the intervention while military operations for giving effect to Allied policy could be entrusted to the Japanese."[28] Obviously, Wilson and Lloyd George had two completely different views of the objectives of the Siberian expedition. Balfour shared many of Lloyd George's misgivings. Yet, sensitive to Wilson's fears that through French or British action Americans would be dragged into interfering with Russian domestic affairs, Balfour urged that Wilson be informed in "most emphatic terms that such interference would be quite contrary to our wishes and to our firm intention."[29] To Jusserand, Wilson seemed to be protecting himself in advance against the possibility that the Allies might present him with a fait accompli of a large intervention versus the Bolsheviks. Yet the French expressed satisfaction with the American proposal to Japan.[30]

In the meantime, Japan had informed Peking of both the Allied project to send the Czecho-Slovaks from Vladivostok to western Siberia by either the Amur or the Chinese Eastern railways, or by both, and of Japan's proposal to the United States that Allied forces cover the rear of the Czechs and establish patrols on the railway. The Japanese Foreign Office told Peking that, in any event, Japanese forces would establish such railway patrols in Manchuria and would expect Peking's approval as a part of the existing Sino-Japanese military convention, "although forces of other nations would, of course, have to obtain the specific consent of China for that purpose."[31] To Wilson this information seemed "to throw some exceedingly interesting sidelights on the action and policy of Japan." He immediately advised that China's part in the proposed enterprise "should be the guarding of the Railway connections within Manchuria, and that there she should act alone." He was particularly disturbed by Japan's statement that it would "in any event" establish military patrols back of the Czecho-Slovaks. To him, this meant that Japan would proceed on her own, regardless of whether she made an agreement with the United States or not.[32]

American concerns over a large Japanese intervention were supported by a recent telegram from Voska to the Military Intelligence Branch of the War Department. He strongly advised against Japanese intervention in Russia, which would only throw Russia into the hands of Germany because of Russian hatred of the Japanese. Voska urged that the United States send in an American command consisting of an American force of 5,000 men and another force consisting of the Czecho-Slovak army and Polish and Russian units led by American officers. Such forces would be heartily welcomed by the Russian people. Voska advised the United States "to issue proclamation showing clearly purpose of intervention, announcing to Russian people that it was solely for the purpose of policing their country until such time as Russian people could establish some form of government."[33]

Both Polk and Baker sent Voska's telegram to Wilson, and each praised the ability of the sender and the good sense of the communication.[34] Wilson fully agreed with Voska's admonitions against sending a large Japanese force to Russia. He feared that it would be difficult to induce the Japanese to leave Siberia, because their ultimate goal was control of eastern Siberia and northern Manchuria. Wilson now sought in every way to limit the size of the Japanese army, to lay down conditions for its withdrawal, and to provide for lone Chinese patrol of the Chinese Eastern Railway, despite the Sino-Japanese military pact signed earlier in the spring.[35]

While Wilson struggled to confine Japanese objectives in Siberia to the "rescue of the Czechs," the Czech revolt in Siberia was having an "astonishing and almost incredible" effect upon American public opinion. Political circles were also affected by it. Czech control of the railway and occupation of Vladivostok had "the glamour of a fairy tale," which glowed even more brightly against the dark background of German successes in France.[36] Taking advantage of this popular response, Masaryk and Beneš renewed their efforts to obtain full recognition of Czecho-Slovak national sovereignty. In mid-July, Masaryk wired Beneš of the difficulties facing the Czech army, largely because the Czecho-Slovak National Council had only semisovereignty over its movement. Recognition of the Czecho-Slovak National Council as a provisional government had now become more urgent than ever, not only because of the Czech position in Siberia but also because of the hasty decision of "so-called intervention in Siberia."[37]

In the days immediately following the issuance of the aide-mémoire, Masaryk besieged key personnel in the executive branch of the government with letters, memoranda, and personal visits.[38] On July 20, he sent a request to Polk for aid to the Czecho-Slovak army in Siberia. In an enclosed memorandum, he raised the issue of recognition and urged that the United States join France in recognizing the Czecho-Slovak National Council in Paris as the representative of the future government of a free Czecho-Slovak state. In support of that request, he drew heavily upon the Czech position in Siberia. He noted: "I think that this recognition has become practically necessary: I dispose of three armies (in Russia, France and Italy). I am, as a wit said, the master of Siberia and half of Russia, and yet I am in the United States formally a private man." He emphasized that, according to international custom, the Czechs in their army had the most essential attribute of sovereignty. Despite their lack of territory, France had overlooked customary criteria for sovereignty and extended recognition. He urged the United States to follow the French example.[39]

Masaryk's confidential memorandum to Polk traced the history and international position of the Czech army, emphasized the perfidy of the Bolsheviks in breaking their agreement, and made it clear that the Czechs had defended themselves only after having been attacked "in a very treacherous manner." He reported that Austria and Germany were daily increasing their occupation of Russia and were using her in an "absolutely mean and egotistical manner." Finally, Masaryk dwelt upon the objectives of the Czech army in Russia. He noted: "I shall not touch upon the various political questions nor do I intend to discuss the more distant future."[40] He only wished to make the best possible use of the army for the benefit of Russia and the Allies.

Masaryk also wrote a note to Wilson to explain the reasons for the changed situation of the Czechs—the disloyalty of the Bolsheviks and the local Soviets—and the need for American and Allied help for the Czech army in Russia. He enclosed a message from Špaček and Girsa of the Vladivostok National Council that detailed the Bolshevik treachery in preventing the Czechs from making their journey across Siberia peacefully. They expressed their support for the reconstitution of a Russian-German front in the east, and observed that an "army cannot be raised by Russia." Then they had posed the same question Knight had already relayed to Washington: "If new German-Russian front is established by Allies we ask for instructions as to whether we should stay here to fight in Russia by the side of the Allies and of Russia."[41]

Wilson, adamantly opposed to the reestablishment of an Eastern Front and deeply involved in negotiating a limited agreement with Japan for purposes of "rescuing the Czechs," was obviously not prepared to answer this final question in the affirmative. Nevertheless, he thanked Masaryk for his letter with its enclosure and assured him that nothing was giving him "more concern at present than the position of the Czecho-Slovak forces in Siberia." He also added that he, Lansing, and Baker were "trying to work out a policy which would be of real service." In the meantime, Masaryk wired the Czech army in Russia to "stay in Russia for the present, and assisted by the Allies, work against the 'common enemy.' "[42]

As Wilson sought to prevent or at least limit Japanese activity in Manchuria and Russia, Ishii arrived at the State Department to deliver orally his government's response to the American proposal. Japan agreed to accept the plan, but with certain reservations. For one thing, the Japanese government believed that a larger force of men should be sent, and it reserved the right to send in more than 7,000 troops. Second, Japan was also unwilling to give a joint guarantee to respect the political and territorial integrity of Russia and to refrain from interference in Russian internal affairs, but would give a separate one.[43]

Wilson was "very much put out" by the Japanese response. He was particularly concerned over the impression given by Japan's draft announcement "that large military units were to be sent" in view of Japan's "special position in Siberia." Both Wilson and Polk agreed that Japan, in fact, had sent a "new proposal," and that if they did not protest, they would be approving Japan's procedure in Siberia and thus would become a party to what might be "the most serious developments."[44] While Wilson did not wish to cause Japan any embarrassment, "nevertheless, their plan was so different from ours that he thought it best not to act at all."[45] Polk then sent for Ishii, explained Wilson's views, and told him that "it would be wise to leave out all mention of Japan's special position, etc."[46] Wilson and Polk felt that by sending troops not only without any numerical limitation, but even indicating that more troops would be sent if the occasion demanded, the Russians might naturally think that the expedition had more in view than "merely assisting the Czechs."[47] Polk now informed Morris of Wilson's opposition to Japan's reference to "special interests," particularly in view of the declaration in the Lansing-Ishii Agreement[48] and the fact that the Japanese were to have the supreme command and a larger number of troops than all the other powers put together.[49]

At the same time that they had sent their official response, the Japanese had insisted that a patrol of troops along the Chinese Eastern Railway was a military necessity. Wilson replied that the Chinese request to participate in the Siberian expedition should be granted, that Chinese troops should control that part of the Chinese Eastern Railway within Manchuria "without interference from any of the governments participating in the Siberian enterprise," and also that "a small contingent of Chinese troops be . . . added to the international force at Vladivostok."[50]

The Japanese agreed to permit the Chinese to cooperate at least to the extent of about 2,000 men.[51] However, the Chinese government, unable to withstand the pressure from Japan, now formally acknowledged the existence of a condition that would necessitate bringing the Sino-Japanese Military Pact of May 16 into force. Shortly thereafter, Japanese troops began to move from southern to northern Manchuria and to take up positions in the neighborhood of Manchouli on the Manchurian-Siberian border. The American government thus had failed in its efforts, first to prevent the Japanese expedition into northern Manchuria and, second, to have the Chinese Eastern Railway patrolled by Chinese troops alone.[52] Wilson's fears about Japanese motives in Siberia and in Manchuria intensified when, on July 30, the Secretary of the Japanese embassy informed Long that because the Bolsheviks were making trouble at certain points on the Siberian coast and the Amur River, "his Government had decided to send at once to certain points in Siberia Japanese destroyers." Phillips found the proposal absolutely "astounding." Knight confirmed that a Japanese fleet, consisting of warships, destroyers, and torpedo boats, was proceeding northward to protect Japanese interests along the Amur River against the Bolsheviks.[53] Knight later discovered that the Japanese naval force had been sent at the request of the Czech commander.[54]

While Masaryk sought to use the exploits of the Czech army in Siberia to secure recognition for the Czecho-Slovak National Council and acquire additional support in Washington for that army, Beneš sought to use the Czech Legion to lobby for full recognition of the Czecho-Slovak National Council in London. In pressing for such recognition, Beneš played on a point of particular importance to the British at that time: "the preparations made in Siberia and the role which we could play there." He now fully realized that Czech troops might render considerable service to Great Britain and her allies by facilitating an intervention in Russia. He, therefore, promised the British and French to leave these troops *provisionally* in Russia to carry out military operations, to hold the Trans-Siberian Railway for the Allies, to enlist the Russian population, and to prepare for Japanese and American intervention. To achieve these purposes, the Czecho-Slovak National Council had agreed with the French Foreign Ministry that Janin and Štefánik should be sent to Siberia to consolidate the Czecho-Slovak forces, give them a definite plan, and provide the necessary unity to prepare for decisive Allied intervention. These officers, then, would become the center around which all those working for the reconstitution of the Eastern Front could gather. Beneš assured Masaryk that the Czechs would remain in Siberia only "temporarily," or as long as there was no possibility of transporting them to France. After achieving their task, Janin would direct their transport to Europe. Although this plan had been conceived in France and supported by the Czecho-Slovak National Council, Beneš insisted that a necessary condition for its implementation was British agreement that the Czecho-Slovak National Council would be given "Real Sovereignty As A Government."[55]

On July 25, Beneš sent a memorandum incorporating these terms to the appropriate authorities in Britain and elaborated his views in a personal interview with Sir Lewis B. Namier, a special friend of the Czechs employed in the East European department of the Foreign Office. Namier, in turn, conveyed them to Sir William Tyrrell of the British Foreign Office.[56] On the following day, when Beneš spoke with Lord Robert Cecil, Beneš requested a clear concession that the Czecho-Slovak National Council have sovereign power over its "three National Armies." Cecil reported this conversation to Balfour and combined Beneš's request with the arguments in the memorandum received earlier from Masaryk, which made absolutely clear that Allied use of Czech soldiers for intervention in Siberia had to be accompanied by a precise declaration by the British government of the full sovereignty of the National Czecho-Slovak Council over its armies and that the council constituted the provisional government of Czecho-Slovakia.[57] Balfour recognized the validity of Beneš's arguments and told him that he agreed in principle with the idea of issuing a British declaration on behalf of the Czechs; but as in the previous discussions in May, he advised Beneš to have further and more detailed discussions on the matter with Cecil.[58]

By July 27, the Allies had accepted the Czech army as one of the Allied armies. On that day, in response to the telegram of the Czech National Council in Vladivostok of July 14, Masaryk sent instructions from Washington, in the name of the Czecho-Slovak National Council, ordering the Czech troops to remain in Siberia for the time being. Masaryk added that the Czecho-Slovaks occupied "unparalleled" strategic positions and that the question of whether they were to leave Russia was not a strictly Czech decision. He concluded: "It must be decided by the Allies, as the Czecho-Slovak Army is one of the Allied Armies and is under command of the Versailles War Council. It is beyond question that the Czecho-Slovaks wish to avoid participation in the Civil War in Russia, although they understand that by remaining there they might be able to render vastly greater service than if they were transported to France. They *are placing themselves at the disposal of the Supreme Allied Council.*"[59]

As Wilson struggled to hammer out a Siberian policy that would limit American-Japanese and, if possible, Allied intervention to the rescue of the Czechs, prevent the Japanese from seizing either Manchuria or eastern Siberia, and oppose any form of military intervention in the affairs of the Russian people, American officials in Siberia, out of contact with their superiors, had arrived at quite a different position and were supporting a totally different policy. American Consuls wrestled not only with the problem of what to do about the Czech military successes in Siberia, but also with what policy to follow toward the new Siberian governments that had arisen as a result of Czech successes. Consul John A. Ray, who had been detailed from Odessa to Tomsk, questioned Harris about the attitude of the United States toward recognition of the Siberian Provisional Government, if the control of the railway was offered to the United States. Apparently the new government believed that Japanese intervention would be less perilous if the railroad were controlled by Americans, preferably in some disguised form. Ray reported that French agents were in Omsk seeking to organize an all-Russian government through a coalition of the Siberian government and certain members of the Constituent Assembly. Ray himself opposed such a coalition.[60]

At the same time, Howard D. Hadley, Vice Consul at Samara, reported the hearty cooperation of the Cossacks with the Czecho-Slovaks and leaders of the Constituent Assembly in military operations in the Orenburg area. He urged the importance of maintaining the present front along the Volga as well as getting word to Washington about Czech successes. He had dined with Čeček, whom he described as the commander in chief of all of the Czecho-Slovak troops in Russia, who had said: "America better send troops here rather than to Western Front . . . even one-hundred fifty or two-hundred thousand troops do wonders. . . . Russian people would welcome American troops as heartily as they have welcomed Czecho-Slovaks." Hadley also suggested that it would be well if "Japan and America worked together in aiding Russia."[61] Knight warned of the danger of delay in announcing and carrying out the proposed aid to the Czechs.[62] Williams at Samara reported glowingly on the new anti-Bolshevik government composed of former delegates to the Constituent Assembly who had agreed, when they met in Petrograd during the winter, to arrange a meeting, which had finally occurred in Samara. Some fifteen of the thirty originally comprising the committee were at Samara trying to solve their many problems. Although eager to fight the Germans, the Czechs were delayed by continued Bolshevik hostility and anxiously awaited a statement of the Allied plan. Williams advocated their full support and noted that "Samara is center of movement and Volga logical front."[63]

In the meantime, the ciphered dispatch from Poole at Moscow dated June 22, 1918, the message originally sent on June 18, 1918, had arrived at Omsk, advising the Czecho-Slovaks leaders confidentially that the Allies would be glad "from a political point of view to have them hold their present positions," secure the control of the Trans-Siberian Railroad, and then, if possible, "retain control over the territory where they now dominate." Harris immediately telegraphed the Omsk consulate: "I consider this wise in view of the fact that the Allies wish the Czechs to be the main backbone and support of Allied action in Siberia and Russia against Germany." As Gray explained: "We all therefore felt certain that the Allies would immediately come to the support of the Czechs . . . as soon as the railway was open to Vladivostok, and did not hesitate to confer with the Czechs on this basis and make plans accordingly. Therefore the Czechs and Russians were absolutely sure Allied troops would be rushed to their assistance immediately."[64]

The Czechs began to act on this assumption. On July 23, they held a conference at Omsk with representatives from all the regiments attending. Their objective was to elect a national council to act in their affairs in Siberia and Russia and devise the many needed rules regarding their fighting forces. At the outset of the conference, Siberian governmental ministers, leading people of Omsk, and foreign consuls made many speeches of welcome. Gray also said a few words welcoming the Czechs as Allies. According to one Czech authority, Harris also attended the last day of the conference at Omsk on August 4, greeted them in the name of the United States government, and thanked them for the work they had done. Pavlů, who answered for the Czechs, expressed his appreciation for American support and his anticipation of fighting "side by side" with the American army in Russia to the "final and joyful victory of the Allies." Gajda and Syrový were made generals in place of Russian officers, who had been in command from the time the Czech troops left the Russian-German front.[65] The Czechs by this time had initiated a bold plan of military operations. Three groups of Czecho-Slovak troops were formed: one, under Čeček, was to establish itself on the lower Volga; another, under Syrový, was to take Ekaterinburg and press forward toward Vologda; and a third, under Gajda, was to proceed eastward along the Trans-Siberian Railway, establishing permanent and secure communications with Vladivostok.[66]

The Czechs had to provide political and police security throughout the regions in which they were operating because they could not depend upon the "Temporary Siberian Government." As a result, the Czecho-Slovak National Council exercised actual oversight and coordination of the political power in Siberia until well into the autumn of 1918. Colonel Edwin C. Landon, American Military Attaché on detail in Siberia, described the attitude of this body as that of a "mild Tsar, not anxious or zealous to interfere as long as things go right, but unhesitating and vigorous and prompt to quell any disturbance regardless of who the disturber is."[67]

On July 26, Harris reported that the Czechs, who had complete control of the railway from Penza to Lake Baikal, had also taken Ekaterinburg and were cooperating effectively with the Cossacks in that area. Moreover, the Siberian Provisional Government was forming at Omsk and asking for Allied support. While Harris recommended caution about recognition, he urgently advised immediate intervention from the east with various Allied armies to consolidate the whole situation in the Allies' favor and to "impress on Russian people that political and factional strife which still prevail in new government must be shelved until war with Germany is over." He believed that a military dictatorship was necessary to hammer Russia into shape as an active "ally." This, he said, was also the opinion of the Czechs and Cossacks.

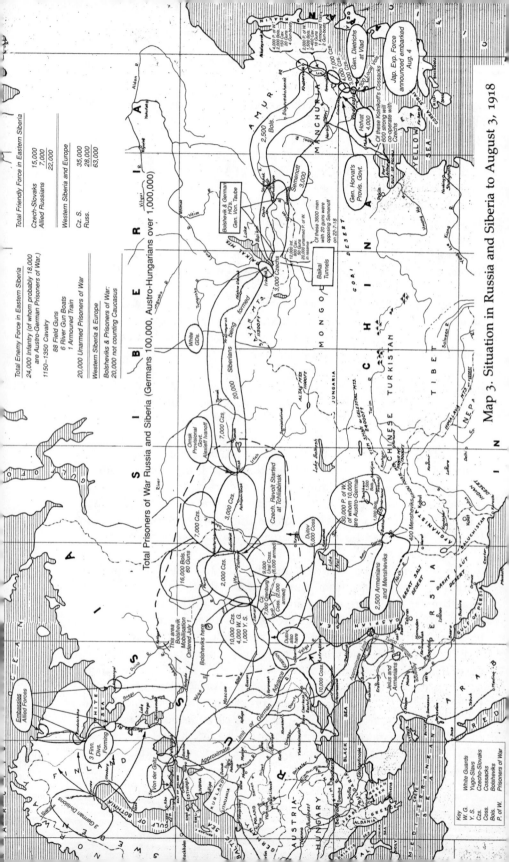

Map 3. Situation in Russia and Siberia to August 3, 1918

He reported that Gajda hoped to clear the railway in eastern Siberia of all Bolsheviks within three weeks.[68] Harris then argued that it was absolutely necessary that the Czecho-Slovak troops remain in Russia: "No one knows the frame of mind, customs, and habits of the Russian people better than the Czechs. They all speak Russian, and if their units are left unimpaired they will form the backbone of Allied intervention and in once more reestablishing a front against Germany in Russia." The "psychological moment" had "unquestionably arrived in the history of Russia." "A handful of Czecho-Slovak soldiers, men of unparalleled courage," had against tremendous odds "performed a deed which will live in history as long as the deeds of mankind shall be worthy of chronicling."[69] Harris urged the Allies to come immediately to the assistance of the Czechs to clinch and hold "immense advantage already gained."[70]

In the meantime, the Soviet government was protesting against "invasion of Soviet territory by Anglo-French troops" and against "political support which Allied powers are giving Czecho-Slovaks." Yet even under these conditions, Chicherin did not desire to break diplomatic relations with the Allies and hoped that the departure of the Allied Ambassadors from Vologda to Archangel would not be so interpreted.[71] Expressing his deep regret over their refusal to come to Moscow, he nevertheless saw no reason why diplomatic relations could not be maintained with the Entente through their representatives who remained in Moscow.[72]

In Vladivostok, Caldwell found his position very difficult. Members of the Horvath government had collected there and had announced publicly their desire to help the Czechs travel westward via Harbin. Every day the Czechs and Allied Consuls were asking him "to take action or give advice" or "approval of steps taken by them." In deep frustration he sought an intimation of the State Department's attitude toward not only the Czechs, but also the Siberian and Horvath governments.[73] The situation became even more complicated when the Bolsheviks once again won control of Vladivostok in the city elections.[74]

In Washington, Wilson agonized over a very different policy for public announcement. In a press release, which he drafted in late July, he again avowed his complete disapproval of military intervention and spelled out specifically why the United States could not approve it. In so doing, however, it appeared that he was trying once again to limit the actions of the Allies, a condition he had been persuaded to eliminate from his aide-mémoire. When Polk and Baker read Wilson's draft, they both gasped, "Impossible," and agreed that it ought to be modified to remove any statements that might provide information or be of propaganda value to the Germans. This meant that nothing could be stated to even imply a division of opinion among the Allies. Moreover, Polk feared that the statement "would seriously embarrass our associates in case they attempted intervention on their own hook." Therefore, both Polk and Baker advised a press release that made it clear that the expression of American views was not meant to "restrict" the activities of the Allies "or set limits on their actions and policies."[75]

The Russian problem was obviously giving Wilson "much anxiety." Clearly Wilson was moving into an area involving decisions of a military character in which he had not been previously involved personally. Indeed, only twice did he interfere with the military operations of the War Department during the war, and these concerned the northern Russian and the Siberian expeditions. Wilson later told Baker that he was perfectly satisfied with the soundness of the War Department's view, "but that, for other than military reasons, he felt obliged to cooperate in a limited way in both proposed expeditions." Wilson's reasons were diplomatic, and Baker believed him to be justified in his decision. Deeply concerned over the tremendous pressure being exerted upon him by his Allies, Wilson told Baker: "I wholly agree with all you say from a military point of view, but we are fighting this war with Allies and I have felt obliged to fall in with their wishes here. I have, however, stipulated that the American contingent in both cases be small."[76] Moreover, Wilson intended to give the commander of the expedition very explicit instructions.[77] On July 23, Washington informed Bliss about the President's decision to permit limited participation of American troops in the Murmansk expedition. However, these troops, along with those for the northern Russian expedition at Archangel, were for "purely and specifically defensive purposes, namely the retention of these ports." From this point on, Bliss emphasized to the Allies that the United States had definitely declined to take part in organized intervention in the interior of Russia in adequate force from either Murmansk or Archangel.[78]

Meanwhile, the Czech position in Siberia was becoming critical. Telegrams from Knight predicted that the coming six weeks would probably decide the issue of their safety. Dietrichs feared that if he sent the bulk of his forces at Vladivostok westward to support the Czechs east of Lake Baikal, it would leave the total force covering Vladivostok seriously inadequate. Moreover, the Bolshevik victory in the recent elections at Vladivostok added an additional unfavorable element to the situation. Polk believed that the situation was urgent.[79] British military intelligence reported that conditions were also bad on the Ussuri front, where the Czechs were greatly outnumbered and were withdrawing southward.[80] Jusserand urged immediate action in Vladivostok and questioned Polk about the advisability of placing the Czechs immediately under the high command of the Japanese general. Polk quickly opposed the suggestion; once again he emphasized that the Japanese general was there to command a force whose sole purpose was to relieve the situation around Vladivostok.[81]

Wilson, genuinely concerned about the plight of the Czechs, discussed the entire matter on August 1 with Baker, who advised that the State Department summon Ishii and "call his attention to the serious situation in Siberia." Wilson once again made clear that he was concerned to limit the number of Japanese troops, confine their presence to Vladivostok, and determine a limitation on additional troops. Polk urged Ishii to "hurry up their answer" in view of the crisis confronting the Czechs.[82]

On August 3, before any formal Japanese statement arrived, Premier Terauchi announced Japan's declaration of intervention. While it did attempt to meet some of Washington's earlier objections and made no reference to either Japan's "special position" in Siberia or to the dispatch of additional Japanese troops at a later date, significantly, the declaration did not mention the number of troops participating in the venture. The avowed purpose of the expedition was to assist the "Czecho-Slovak troops, aspiring to secure a free and independent existence for their race and loyally espousing the common cause of the Allies." Japan agreed to respect the territorial integrity of Russia and to abstain from all interference in her internal politics. Moreover, once the realization of the defined objectives had been achieved, Japan would withdraw immediately from Russian territory, leaving unimpaired the political and military sovereignty of Russia. The Japanese declaration made no mention either of the British plan to reconstitute the Eastern Front or of the American proposal to send economic aid to Siberia. At the same time, Terauchi expressed no doubts about military intervention per se, as Wilson had done.[83]

On August 3, Ishii assured Polk that while the Japanese accepted the American limitations, they reserved "the question as to the sending of additional troops to Vladivostok or elsewhere until circumstances should arise which might make it necessary." In the event that Japanese forces needed to move out of Vladivostok or send reinforcements "to prevent the slaughter of the Czechs" if a real emergency arose, Japan "wished to say frankly that they would be compelled . . . to move without consultation." On August 5, Gotō Shimpei, Minister of Foreign Affairs, assured Morris that the number of troops would not exceed 12,000, although he doubted whether this force would be sufficient to meet the increasingly serious conditions developing in northern Manchuria and eastern Siberia.[84]

While the Japanese answer was not complete, it was sufficiently satisfactory to proceed. Nevertheless, Wilson was "mad" and Phillips shared his anger.[85] "The Japanese have moved in circles all around us," Phillips wrote. "They have beaten us out everywhere. Not only have they secured our consent to a Japanese command, but their troops have entered Siberia before ours even began to move." This is "just the opposite of the way the President intended." Although Wilson was indignant with the Japanese and thought that they had got the better of him, Polk prevailed upon him to let the matter stand, since Japan's response and her public announcement had just reached the United States through press channels. At that point Wilson's aide-mémoire was once again discussed and altered in various particulars in accordance with the suggestions made earlier by both Polk and Baker. The selection of General William S. Graves as commander of the Siberian expedition was confirmed. Wilson then directed Polk to make public the American announcement "that we were prepared to go into Siberia for the purpose of assisting the Czechs."[86]

Wilson's public announcement, which he typed on his own typewriter and released to the press on the afternoon of August 3, declared once more his strong opposition to military intervention. It would add to "the present sad confusion in Russia rather than cure it, injure her rather than help her, and . . . would be of no advantage in the prosecution or main design to win the war against Germany." The United States would take no part in such intervention or sanction it in principle. Military action was admissible in Russia only to help the Czechs, to "steady any efforts at self-governing or self-defense in which the Russians themselves may be willing to accept assistance," and to guard military stores that Russian forces might subsequently need. Wilson also announced his approval of the use of American troops at Murmansk and Archangel for these same objectives.[87]

The official Bolshevik response to the American declaration, enunciated by Trotskii, labeled the whole document an American lie. He charged that in April the Japanese General Staff had used the threatened attack of German and Austro-Hungarian war prisoners on the Siberian railroad as its justification for landing troops in Vladivostok.

When Trotskii had sent American and British officers to the Siberian line from Moscow, they had confirmed officially that all such rumors were "nothing but silly inventions." This fact, he said, was well known to both Francis and Robins, the former chief of the American Red Cross in Russia. Now that intervention by the Allies had become an established fact, the American government had picked up the Japanese lie and attempted to hand it to the world in "a warmed up condition."[88] The Czech uprising was a counterrevolutionary act and the product of an Anglo-French plot. In response, the Soviet government began a systematic internment of English and French citizens. However, Chicherin explained that the Soviet attitude was "entirely different toward American citizens to whom this measure did not extend, because, although the United States government was forced by its allies to agree to participate in intervention, so far only formally, but it seems to us this decision is not irrevocable." Nevertheless, the Bolsheviks admitted that the battle against the Czechs was a question of the life or death of the Soviet government.[89]

Masaryk was deeply grateful for the United States's decision to render military help to the Czecho-Slovak army in Russia.[90] He interpreted the decision as a guarantee that the "American principle of 'consent of the governed' will be realized." Emphasizing his belief that Czecho-Slovak efforts in Russia would constitute a strong argument for the recognition of an independent Czecho-Slovakia, Masaryk wrote the President: "It is for these principles that our nation has been contending not only in this war, but already long ago; it is for these principles that our boys are shedding their blood on the endless plains of Russia and Siberia." He added: "Your name, Mr. President, as you no doubt know, is cheered in the streets of Prague. Our nation will be forever grateful to you and the people of the United States, and we know how to be grateful!"[91]

Obviously, Wilson accepted intervention only with the greatest reluctance. In finally surrendering to the insistent demands of the Supreme War Council and the pleas of the Czechs, Wilson emphasized that his major objectives were to rescue the Czechs while adhering to the principle of noninterference in Russia's internal affairs. The Americans were in a very difficult situation. Although they formally opposed Japanese intervention, they were unable to state their real reasons for doing so, since Japan was their associate. Throughout the war, Wilson had regarded Japan's activities in Asia with deep suspicion. He saw the military clique taking advantage of every possible opening while the Western powers were too involved in the war to counter Japanese moves. The Japanese had revealed their purposes in their Twenty-One Demands in 1915, in their occupation of Shantung, and in their political and economic penetration of Manchuria and northern China. Wilson hoped to limit and direct their activities in a way that would prevent their encroachment in both northern Manchuria and eastern Siberia. He had joined the expedition not because he believed in it, but because he thought he could "impose greater restraint on Japan within rather than outside it."[92] Wilson's conversation on July 25 with Henri Bergson, the well-known French philosopher, reveals most clearly his deep distrust of the Japanese. As Bergson noted, Wilson believed the Allies wished to "force his hand" to make the declaration of July 17, and that the British were behind the "extraordinary" articles in the *New York Times* favoring intervention. Clearly, the President was "loath to set the Japanese in motion." He had always "hoped to avoid intervention, even the appearance of intervening in Russian affairs." He was thoroughly exasperated with the ambiguous declaration of the Japanese on the subject and suspected that Japanese demands for enormous supplies, especially of steel, to conduct the expeditions were greater than necessary. Bergson believed the President might well suspect Japanese preparations for a future war, possibly "against the Americans."[93]

The public declarations of Japan, Great Britain, and the United States clearly revealed the differences of opinion among the three nations concerning the scope, character, and purposes of the Siberian expedition. Indeed, the British declaration of August 8, issued after British troops had already landed in Vladivostok, did not mention the Czech need of assistance. It stated that the Allies were coming as friends to stop German penetration of Russia and to bring economic relief.[94] Wilson agreed with Polk that the British proclamation envisaged "a very different plan" from his own and could not "possibly meet the situation." It "went too far and promised too much" and would "mislead the Russian people."[95]

The opportunity that now presented itself to the Allies was not the limited intervention that Wilson envisaged, but the possible establishment of an effective Eastern Front against Germany. Their own operations in northern Russia, the availability of the Czecho-Slovaks as the nucleus of a new army, the rise of anti-Bolshevik forces in Siberia, and large-scale intervention at Vladivostok became linked in the minds of the Allied high command as parts of an ambitious program to overthrow the Soviet state and launch a new attack on Germany. Clemenceau himself, on August 8, sent telegrams to the French military attachés in Tokyo, Peking, Archangel, and especially for Commander

Guinet, with specific instructions to utilize the Czechs in the realization of this objective.[96] Yet Wilson continued to adhere to his stated purpose for sending troops to Russia, a purpose which he refused to regard as intervention. In the following week, in accordance with his instructions, Polk emphasized to the Allied representatives that the United States had no intention of intervening and that American help would be limited to the precise reasons publicly stated.[97]

16

Masaryk and Anglo-French
Plans in Russia

Each section of the Czech army now operated in accordance with its own assessment of the situation and its own interpretation of the policies of the various Allies. Thus, while the Czechs at Vladivostok were proceeding westward, presumably to rescue their brethren in central Siberia, the Czechs in western Siberia moved northward and westward and seized Kazan, Simbirsk, Penza, and Ekaterinburg. All this was done while Gajda was proceeding to the east from Novo Nikolaevsk. As soon as the Czechs seized control of the railway, anti-Bolshevik Russian leaders began to organize provisional governments in the captured areas.[1]

On July 31, Captain Digby Jones, a British officer, arrived in Samara with instructions from General Poole. They ordered the Czechs to advance northward to take Perm and Viatka in order to effect a junction with the Allies at Vologda at the earliest possible moment. Captain Jones informed the Czecho-Slovaks that 25,000 Anglo-French soldiers were already at Vologda and that many more were expected shortly. As they sought to achieve this objective, the Czechs met unexpected and strong resistance and soon realized that it would be virtually impossible for them to succeed without reinforcements from the Allies. They placed no hope in Russian mobilization, guns were not available, and they were tiring fast. They immediately sent a courier to the east to seek urgent aid and reinforcements.[2] Henry Palmer, recently appointed American Vice Consul at Ekaterinburg, emphasized that reinforcements were "urgently and immediately indispensable" as "recent battles" had "been exclusively with German-Austro prisoners commanded by German and Austrian officers." He also asked the Allies in the east to "inform General Poole at Murmansk that Czechs here hard-pressed and unless reinforcements are forthcoming immediately will be unable to carry out General Poole's instructions as above stated regarding junction at Vologda."[3]

In the meantime, Harris in Cheliabinsk acted in accordance with the instructions presumably from Consul Poole in Moscow and from the French mission under Guinet. He told Slaughter, who was en route to Samara on a mission of investigation, that the Czechs were American allies as well as allies of France and England. He noted: "Anything they do under the exigencies or immediate necessities of the military situation we will approve and back them up. . . . Let that be known to such Czechs as you see fit." Harris sincerely believed that he knew the objectives of both Wilson and the Allies; indeed, he regarded the United States as "now dictating the policy of the Allies in Russia and in Europe—politically all."[4] Harris was appalled when he learned that enemy resistance had forced the Czechs to put off indefinitely their plans to capture Perm. After the Czechs reported that the "enemy" was planning attacks on Ekaterinburg, Harris sought desperately to communicate with Allied forces in eastern Siberia to hasten reinforcements for the Czechs fighting in western Siberia. Like Palmer, Harris added urgency to his plea by reaffirming the Czech intelligence that the opponents had been "entirely German and Austrian prisoners under their own officers," thus making it unnecessary "for the Allies to fear fighting against the Russian Bolsheviks." He, too, informed the Allies that General Poole's instructions to have the Czechs effect a juncture with the Allies at Vologda were doomed to fail unless reinforcements were forthcoming.[5]

By this time, the situation in northern Russia had altered considerably. On August 2, a Supreme Directorate of the northern region had been temporarily established in power in Archangel, supported by Russian White Guards and Allied forces. The Bolsheviks had been thrown into a state of complete demoralization.[6] On August 9, General Poole met with the Allied representatives, who agreed unanimously to urge the Allied governments to expedite the departure of troops already earmarked for Russia and to add a division to these troops. Poole believed that with 5,000 men actually on the spot, he could occupy Vologda and Viatka immediately and join not only the Czechs, but probably General Alexeev also.[7]

In central Siberia, the Czechs faced a critical situation south of Lake Baikal, where the enemy had recently blown up the tunnel between them and Irkutsk. At a conference of the American and Allied naval and military representatives held on board USS *Brooklyn* on July 31, Dietrichs had proposed that he proceed with his forces, then numbering only 4,000 men, via Harbin to rescue their comrades. He estimated that 6,000 Allied troops would be necessary to strengthen forces for the defense of the Nikolsk front, an additional 20,000 men were needed to

Czecho-Slovak armored train (National Archives)

relieve the Czechs at Baikal, and another 20,000 had to be sent to the Ussuri front. The Allied representatives unanimously agreed that two divisions of Allied troops should be sent to support the Czechs immediately. All but the American representatives, who believed that the Czechs required no help, recommended the immediate dispatch of Japanese troops.[8] As soon as Lloyd George received word from Dietrichs about the critical situation of the Czecho-Slovaks, he wired both Washington and Tokyo and urged immediate action to save the Czechs. The British War Cabinet also telephoned Clemenceau and urged him to press both Wilson and the Japanese for instant action.[9]

In the meantime, a memorandum from Girsa and two other members of the Czecho-Slovak National Council in Russia presented Masaryk with the Czech dilemma in somewhat different terms. The memorandum explained that the advance guard of the western Czech group was in a critical position and required help immediately. The Czechs in Vladivostok could not help unless the Allies immediately landed troops to protect their rear, freed them from Vladivostok, and also supported them by sending one additional division with the Czech force. Given this help, they could move immediately toward Chita on the Manchurian railway and thus connect in five weeks with their force advancing from Irkutsk. It would then be possible to proceed either to Dairen or to Vladivostok if the winter was to be spent in that area. Observing that the men were in excellent spirits and health, the memorandum continued: "In undertaking this, we maintain the principle of keeping ourselves free from Russian domestic affairs, unless our interference is absolutely essential for the protection of our force and for carrying on military operations." Noting that Bolshevism seemed to be disappearing, they asked Masaryk whether, "in view of the new situation thus presented," they should "stay in Russia, supposing this to be possible, and if so, under what conditions."[10] Masaryk immediately forwarded copies of the memorandum to the State Department and to Reading.[11]

Upon receipt of the Czech memorandum the British War Cabinet was thrown into a quandary. The message presented two questions: Should the Czecho-Slovaks concentrate at Vladivostok, or should they "clear out of Russia"? If the War Cabinet agreed to the latter proposition, General Sir Henry Wilson, chief of the Imperial General Staff, said the Allies would have to abandon all hopes for a new Eastern Front. This would place the Allied contingents at Murmansk and Archangel in an untenable position. To the British War Cabinet, the value of the Czechs to the Allied cause lay in their *dispersion* along some 2,300 miles of railway from Penza to Irkutsk; therefore, Masaryk's recommendation to concentrate the Czech army in Vladivostok or elsewhere was directly opposed to British objectives. General Wilson thought that it was crucial to prevent any hasty or premature action by President Wilson, "whose one idea in consenting to Allied action in the Far East had been to save the Czecho-Slovaks."[12] At the same time, it was important to persuade the Czech leaders not to aim at the withdrawal of the Czech forces at Vladivostok.[13]

As the War Cabinet engaged in its deliberations over the Czech crisis, Beneš increased his efforts to secure a British declaration recognizing, among other things, the right of the Czecho-Slovak National Council to exercise "supreme authority" over its army in Russia. It was no coincidence that negotiations on this subject proceeded quite rapidly within the next few days. Cecil and Balfour now accepted all of Beneš's earlier objections to the British initial proposal in principle and sent the revised official declaration to Beneš on August 9. It recognized the Czecho-Slovaks as an Allied nation and the three Czecho-Slovak armies as an Allied and belligerent army waging regular warfare against Austria-Hungary and Germany. Although the British government declined to recognize the Czecho-Slovak National Council unreservedly as an interim government, Balfour recognized it as the "Supreme Organ of the Czecho-Slovak National Interest and the present trustee of the future Czecho-Slovak Government," with supreme authority over its Allied and belligerent army.[14] Beneš had finally secured recognition from the British, and the Czecho-Slovak army in Russia and Siberia had played the decisive role in that final decision. Beneš now requested that Cecil notify the other Allies officially of the British declaration in the hope that it would prompt similar recognition by the others.

Although Balfour had now secured the agreement of the Czechs to use their troops in Siberia according to the British plan, he was keenly aware of Wilson's strong opposition to that plan and that he had agreed to send troops to Vladivostok only to save the Czechs. Moreover, he had no illusions that the Americans had ever accepted the expeditions to Archangel and Murmansk as being linked with the British policy in the Far East. In the face of Wilson's possible agreement to remove the Czechs from Russia, Balfour now suggested Anglo-French cooperation in explaining the case to Beneš and to Wilson in order to insure "that the president of the United States should not commit himself definitely and prematurely on the subject."[15]

As a result of these discussions, the British government sent a series of desperate appeals to the State Department alleging the critical position of the Czechs and urging expansion of the expedition to Siberia. Polk responded that plans were being implemented to help the Czechs, that the Japanese-American agreement had been reached "precisely in order to save the Czechs," and, since Japanese and other troops were actually on the way, there was nothing more that could be done for the present "without departing from the agreement." When Reading suggested that Polk ask Japan to take immediate measures to relieve the situation, he met a strong negative response. Polk expressed his amazement that the question of "emergency" had been raised by the British government at so early a date.[16] When di Cellere brought a message from Great Britain regarding expediting the troops to Vladivostok, Polk reiterated: "We had no intention of intervening, as we had stated to the British time and time again," and the President was "very much opposed to any expansion of the expedition."[17]

The undaunted British now devised a new approach: they affirmed that the safety of the Czech forces was "an obligation of honour resting on all the Allies." Because the Japanese alone appeared able to save the situation by immediate action, Balfour "earnestly" sought Wilson's aid in asking Japan formally "to send as quickly as possible whatever military help the Japanese and Czech military experts may think necessary or desirable." The current situation clearly "justified an emergency and demanded" extraordinary measures. Balfour added that if Wilson was unwilling to make such a request, in view "of the fact that any disaster to these brave people [the Czechs] would be deeply resented by public opinion here, we feel bound to make such a request unless the President sees grave objection."[18] The French Foreign Ministry made a similar request and suggested that approximately 80,000 men would suffice.[19]

Wilson was "irritated beyond words" by the continued British pressure to "invite the Japanese to send additional troops into Siberia," particularly after spending a month seeking to limit the size of the Japanese expedition. He drafted a "stiff reply" that rejected the British scheme in clear and unmistakable terms.[20] The British were not alone in urging the expansion of Japanese troop operations in Siberia. The Japanese were also exerting similar pressures, albeit for different reasons. On August 5, Gotō had informed Morris about the "increasingly serious conditions developing in northern Manchuria and eastern Siberia." Semenov's defeat and "the invasion of Chinese territory by Bolsheviks and organized German war prisoners [were] giving them more concern than the Czech situation."[21] On August 13, Tokyo informed Washington of its decision to send an independent Japanese force to protect the Manchurian border from invasion by the Bolsheviks. This the Japanese would do under the terms of the Sino-Japanese Military Agreement of May 16, 1918. Japan stated that China had consented to the operation and that troops would be withdrawn as soon as the temporary emergency was over. Tokyo added that its expedition into the zone of the Chinese Eastern Railway was "entirely different in nature from the present joint intervention in Vladivostok, or from military action in Russian territory, and the only nations that have interests involved are Japan and China."[22]

The Chinese version of the affair differed from the Japanese. Koo told Lansing that when, on August 8, the Japanese Minister at Peking had requested China's consent to the implementation of measures for joint defense against the enemy under the terms of the Sino-Japanese Military Agreement, Chinese Premier Tuan Ch'i-jui had replied that China would give her consent when the necessity arose. Japan had then proceeded to move troops into northern Manchuria. Koo pointed out that apparently Japan had interpreted the casual reply of the Premier as China's consent to an immediate occupation. China denied absolutely that Bolshevik or enemy forces had either bombarded Manchouli or otherwise made military encroachments on Chinese territory.[23]

Lansing and Long agreed that the Czech and the entire Siberian situations were getting out of hand. Lansing advised an enlargement of the military policy in Siberia. He directed Long to draft a memorandum outlining the salient points of the problem as the basis for a letter to Wilson.[24] Long's memorandum, written on August 17, emphasized the difference in direction that the situation in Siberia was developing from the policy outlined by Wilson. Not only was Japan planning to send a larger military force than anticipated, but the military exigencies of the situation seemed to require a larger military force, particularly on the railway line between "Manchouli and Chita, where it was expected that the enemy would launch a marauding expedition." Both Dietrichs and the Russian branch of the Czecho-Slovak National Council had urged more extensive Allied military assistance "to save their troops in Western Siberia." They reported that war prisoners were being armed faster than Allied assistance could arrive under current plans.[25] Long argued that "whether we will or not, circumstances will develop which we cannot control and which will jeopardize our position in Far Eastern affairs if we do not now change our policy." Therefore, he advocated an enlargement of the program as an immediate necessity. Even if the United States itself was not willing to send additional forces, it should fully support the efforts of other governments to do so and to send all necessary supplies as fast as possible to the Czecho-Slovak forces.[26]

On the following day, August 18, Lansing directed a letter to Wilson based upon Long's memorandum and accompanied by a series of documents from Jusserand, Knight, and Dietrichs. These documents had convinced Lansing that a reconsideration of Wilson's policy was required. Lansing explained Japan's intention to send a larger number of troops to Vladivostok and Manchouli. Moreover, although the Czecho-Slovaks had captured Irkutsk on July 7, some 25,000 Austro-German prisoners controlled the railway between that city and Lake Baikal and the Chinese border. The 2,000 to 6,000 Czech troops who had traveled from Vladivostok to Harbin were apparently utterly inadequate to push westward to Irkutsk against the superior numbers near Manchouli. No further troops could be sent from Vladivostok because a strong force of Austro-Germans and Red Guards, estimated at 80,000, was alleged to have gathered north of Vladivostok along the Amur

River. All the Czechs remaining in the city were required, together with the Allied forces already there, to resist an attack on that port. The question, therefore, was how to relieve the Czecho-Slovaks in western Siberia. Lansing anticipated that Japan, with the undoubted approval of the Allies, would assert that military conditions required her to send a much larger force both to Vladivostok and to the western border of Manchuria, "whether we liked it or not." Lansing concluded: "If we reach the conclusion that Japan will follow this course in any event, would we or would we not be in a better position to control the situation in the future by asserting that present conditions require Japan to send sufficient troops to open the railroad to Irkutsk and to keep it open so that we can send supplies to the Czechs?"[27]

Wilson's response, given on August 20, was clear and unequivocal. Unmoved by Lansing's appeal, he authorized a memorandum stating bluntly that the United States could not aid in equipping, transporting, or maintaining any troops beyond the numbers agreed upon between the United States and Japan. Moreover, he was not in favor of proceeding west of Irkutsk to relieve the Czecho-Slovaks in western Siberia. Rather, he favored their retirement eastward from western Siberia as rapidly as safety would permit, and the concentration of all troops in eastern Siberia. He preferred to defer a consideration of the future movement of the Czecho-Slovaks, whether eastward to France or westward to Russia, until after eastern Siberia had been cleared of enemies.[28] To Knight's plea that "assistance to Czechs by American and other forces be extended to the Manchuria front and Baikhar region instead of being confined to the Ussuri front," Secretary Daniels responded that American forces were "not intended for intervention in Russia but solely for the purposes specifically set forth in the President's *aide-mémoire*."[29]

The response of the British War Cabinet to both the "desperate situation" of the Czecho-Slovak forces and Japan's desire to increase its force was quite different from Wilson's. Although Curzon declared "*that the refusal of President Wilson to allow the Japanese to increase their force threw upon him a very great moral responsibility if the C-S were exterminated,*" there was some disagreement over how to handle the matter. Some members suggested that Foch be telegraphed to urge Wilson that unless the Czecho-Slovak forces were relieved, his campaign in the west would be ruined. Cecil disagreed. After all, Wilson was well aware of British views on the matter; but he simply did not believe in the possibility of reconstituting the Eastern Front. Also, it was Wilson's principle, said Cecil, "not to intervene in the internal affairs of any country unless requested to do so by the inhabitants." Nevertheless, Cecil agreed to telegraph the Japanese and the Czecho-Slovaks immediately. He believed that a direct appeal from the Czecho-Slovaks might have a greater effect on Wilson. The War Cabinet also instructed Cecil to consult with Reading, then visiting London.[30]

When Reading advised that the most effective pressure would be a communication from Foch to Wilson, Cecil initiated the necessary action.[31] In the meantime, Reading had hit upon a new approach—an appeal to Wilson through House. Reading urged Wiseman to lay the facts before House, who might then offer suggestions that would be acceptable to Wilson.[32] Although uninformed about the latest developments in Siberia, House suggested that since the Japanese had the military direction of the expedition, they were the "right people to press U.S.G. to increase the expedition to whatever size they consider necessary in order to enable the Czecho-Slovaks to retire in safety." Actually, in an earlier interview with Knox in Washington, House had told him "to tell the Japs that the main thing was that they should go in and go in quickly."[33] House could not have offered advice less likely to please Wilson.

Neither Wiseman nor Reading had any illusions about Wilson's real attitude toward Britain's request to enlarge the size of the expedition in Siberia. As Wiseman explained to Reading he had

> always thought that time and circumstances would modify the President's original policy regarding Russia, and I see indications even now that this is so. The danger now is—to be quite frank—that he is beginning to feel that the Allies are trying to rush, even trick, him into a policy which he has refused to accept. He is well aware that he is committed to the task of rescuing the Czechs, but thinks the Allies are already trying to change the character of the expedition into a full-fledged military intervention with the object of reconstituting the Eastern Front.[34]

In the meantime, in Vladivostok, the Japanese had already taken the necessary action. After Dietrichs had described the desperate situation of the Czechs at an Allied military conference, General Kikuzo Otani, commander of the Japanese troops, requested that the military representatives inform their governments that 70,000 troops were needed immediately if the Czechs were to be saved from defeat before winter.[35] By August 21, Japan had stationed 12,000 troops along the Chinese Eastern Railway. Koo had personally informed Lansing that these troops had been sent "without agreement."[36] Moreover, the American consular staff in Mukden believed that Japan would "never" withdraw this force from Chinese territory until it suited its own convenience to do so.[37] A few days later, Tokyo announced its intention to send 10,000 additional soldiers to the Maritime Province. Allied policy in Siberia seemed to have triumphed.[38]

Both the British and French wanted a unified political control in Siberia, because the Russians were so divided among themselves. The Czech force could be used for policing purposes. Caldwell also considered that some measure of martial law was necessary. Wilson, however, rejected these suggestions as an unwise interference in Russian local affairs. American opposition, however, did not stifle Anglo-French efforts. The British appointed Charles Eliot as High Commissioner in Siberia to represent Great Britain in all political matters. London hoped that Washington would follow its example in order to facilitate cooperative action by the Allies. Paris suggested that an inter-Allied civilian board also be established to settle any political, economic, or technical questions that might arise in Siberia. The French government appointed Regnault as representative on the board and as French High Commissioner at Vladivostok. They offered the chairmanship of the board to the United States.[39]

Wilson refused. He interpreted these Anglo-French requests as simply "another move to impress our action in Siberia with the character of intervention rather than relief of the Czechs." Furthermore, he regarded the suggestion that an American high commissioner be the head of the civilian board as "bait to draw us into a policy which has been so insistently urged by Great Britain for the past six months."[40] To Lansing, he wrote: "Please make it plain to the French ambassador that we do not think cooperation in *political* action necessary or desirable in Eastern Siberia because we contemplate no political action of any kind there, but only the action of friends who stand at hand and wait to see how they can help. The more plain and emphatic that is made, the less danger will there be of subsequent misunderstanding and irritations."[41]

On the other hand, the Washington government was exceedingly prompt in seeking to implement efforts to assist in the reorganization and operation of the Siberian and the Chinese Eastern Railways. Stevens was encouraged to have his men cooperate with the Russians running the railways and use his "best efforts to forward movement of Czecho-Slovaks and Allied resistance to German and Austrian prisoners of war." At the same time, he, as well as Caldwell, was warned "to avoid alliance with or support to any political group or faction in Russia." These instructions were far easier to send than to implement, as Stevens discovered, because he had "no shadow of authority." He urged the State Department to advise the Czechs directly that "we are ready to aid every possible way." He reported that he was involved with no political faction and was simply trying to work with the railway authorities, which he found very difficult since every faction appeared to be claiming jurisdiction.[42]

The matter of the efficient management and operation of the Trans-Siberian Railway became vital after Allied troops reached Siberia.[43] As Japanese troops began to pour into Siberia and northern Manchuria, Stevens warned the State Department that the Japanese were seeking to control the operation of the railways and would succeed unless Washington took a firm stand. He described the Russian operation as "merely a joke," while giving advice to the Russians was a farce, especially with Japanese influence predominating. If Japanese operation was to be permitted, he advised that all American railway men should be sent home.[44] He recommended that the railways be taken under military control at once and that he and the Russian Railway Service Corps be authorized to operate them.[45] In the meantime, Emerson had received a wire to proceed on the first train to Verkh-neudinsk. There, about August 21, he met Harris and Gajda. Harris informed him that the new Siberian government and the Czechs were very anxious to have Emerson take over the operation of the railroad. Both Gajda and Guinet had already urged such action earlier. Emerson was reluctant, however, to make such an agreement, because at that time he did not know what policy his home government had adopted.[46]

By the end of August, it had become obvious to Graves, Morris, and Stevens that Japan's policy was "as clear as the sun which gave birth to her imperial family." The superficial and temporary concessions won by the liberal faction within the Japanese government in July and early August actually represented a "bargain in words rather than a meeting of minds." In fact, the interventionists had won. It now appeared that the prointerventionist forces were implementing their plans for a large expedition to the Amur basin to bolster a pro-Japanese government in the Russian territories, gain control of the Chinese Eastern Railway and the Siberian railways east of Irkutsk, and harness the entire region to the Japanese economy.[47] General Graves, commander of the American expedition to Siberia, declared that no one could have been associated with the Japanese military representatives as he was in Siberia and escape the conviction that "they always hoped to occupy Eastern Sibe-

General William S. Graves (National Archives)

ria."[48] Morris was convinced that the Japanese General Staff had a "definite policy in Siberia and that it proposes to pursue this policy leaving to the Foreign Office and Viscount Ishii the task of explaining after the event." Stevens shared these views.[49] By this time Washington was aware of Japanese intentions to propose a change in the gauge of the Chinese Eastern Railway to conform to that of the South Manchuria Railroad, which would virtually disrupt this system and its connections with the Trans-Siberian Railway. Moreover, reports indicated that the Japanese were seeking to take over military control of the railways themselves.[50]

Despite his strong opposition to Japanese actions, Wilson instructed Lansing to make no formal statement of disapproval over the expansion of the Japanese expedition to Siberia.[51] On the advice of E. T. Williams, Lansing had advised allowing General Otani to carry out his plans in the hope that in return Japan would agree to cooperate in the operation of the railways by Stevens and the Russian Railway Service Corps.[52] Williams had argued that Otani was "not likely to accept American management of the railways unless we show willingness to cooperate heartily, but if we will waive the matter of number of troops and let Otani have a free hand in aid of the Czechs we may in return expect the Japanese not to object to management by American engineers of the railways."[53]

Wilson in conference with Lansing agreed to propose to Tokyo that the Stevens mission and the Russian Railway Service Corps be given the general direction of the Trans-Siberian and the Chinese Eastern Railways and their several branches, on the ground that these units were the agents of the Russian people and were being paid and supported by their Ambassador in the United States from funds belonging to them. Lansing felt that "further complications would not arise and best results would be had" if Stevens were to act on behalf of the Russian people for this purpose. It was "a delicate matter but would prevent the road being taken over entirely by the Japanese." Actually, the details given to Morris regarding the proposal were inaccurate. While it is true that the members of the Russian Railway Service Corps were paid from Russian funds, they took their orders from Stevens, who was paid out of American funds. Moreover, while in the Far East, Stevens was answerable only to Wilson and Lansing.[54]

Meanwhile, Balfour was becoming increasingly distressed because Wilson appeared to be "unwilling" to admit the precarious position of the Czech troops in Siberia. British information, which came largely from the Japanese, was not given to Washington by the Japanese themselves nor confirmed by Masaryk; therefore Balfour believed that the British efforts to impress the real state of affairs on Washington were "regarded as merely an attempt to involve the U. S. more completely in the Siberian adventure." To remedy this, Balfour, at Wiseman's suggestion, asked the Japanese to take the appropriate action and Beneš to impress upon Masaryk the "real seriousness of the position." In the meantime, Dietrichs had addressed a memorandum to the Czecho-Slovak National Council exposing the gravity of the Czech position.[55]

Beneš immediately cabled Masaryk and enclosed a copy of the telegram just received from Dietrichs. Beneš noted the continuous increase in the number of Austro-German prisoners, estimating their numbers from 25,000 to 30,000 armed men. Dietrichs insisted that if new forces were not sent immediately to the Trans-Baikal region, the 4,000 to 5,000 Czechs at Irkutsk, who were short of ammunition, would be overwhelmed. Unless Dietrichs's urgent appeal was answered immediately, Beneš said, the Allies would be unable to carry out any further military operations in Siberia. If Irkutsk should fall, there would be no more hope of saving the Czechs. Actually, Caldwell had already forwarded a summary of Dietrichs's report on August 15. Beneš reaffirmed that Otani, who had taken command of the Allied troops in the eastern Ussuri area on August 21, had also warned that if Japanese assistance did not arrive promptly, Irkutsk would be retaken by the Bolsheviks, "that Siberia will be lost to us, and that 50,000 Czechs will die this winter."[56]

Masaryk moved into action when he received the Japanese report. He forwarded Beneš's cablegram to both Baker and Lansing, conferred with Lansing personally, and submitted one of the memoranda he had promised earlier. Lansing had informed him that while Wilson had accepted the economic plan for Russia they had discussed earlier and wanted to help the Czecho-Slovaks, he did not want to restore the Eastern Front. Lansing had then comforted Masaryk by saying that after the connection between the Czech forces in the east and west had been made, a definite plan would then be decided: whether to go to France or stay in Siberia. Masaryk had remonstrated with Lansing, saying that a definite plan must be made immediately because 50,000 men could not be transported to the east only to be returned.[57] Masaryk's memorandum presented a series of additions and explanations to the request for help to the Czecho-Slovak army in Russia that Masaryk had made on July 20 and obviously reflected the pressures from London and Paris. He made it clear that he regarded the declaration of August 3 as binding the Allies and the United States to swift aid to Russia as well as to the Czech army. Before Wilson's declaration of August 3, some form of negotiation with the Moscow government might have been possible. Now, Masaryk said, it was impossible, particularly because the Bolsheviks, "led by the Austrians and Germans, declared a holy war against the Allies and especially against the Czecho-Slovak army." Masaryk now proposed an Allied military and political plan. It included a union of the Czech forces in the eastern part of Russia with the Allied forces in Siberia and the Urals; these two forces would join together all the way to Archangel. Here was General Poole's plan, emanating from the pen of Masaryk! Although he emphasized the need to restore order throughout Russia, Masaryk warned that the Russians were incapable of doing the job.

Masaryk had no illusions about the size of the army required to accomplish his objectives. It had to include a much larger Japanese contingent than had been planned, since he expected no effective help for a considerable period from any newly formed Russian army. Speed and immediate action were required because of the onset of winter. He urged the necessity of a unified command in Siberia and suggested a Japanese commander in chief, since Japan had the strongest contingent of troops. The Allied units would be represented in a common military council of which Dietrichs would also be a member.

Masaryk noted that the military situation at Vladivostok was no longer dangerous, because of the arrival of Allied contingents. It was western Siberia that was in danger; the army there was scattered over a great, expansive country with inadequate arms, clothing, and equipment. The enemy would seek to defeat and, if possible, to annihilate the Czech units on the Volga and the Urals first, and after that, those in Siberia. Thus, it must be the special task of the Czech army at Vladivostok to effect a contact with the western area. Allied reinforcements had to be sent at the earliest moment to aid the Czechs in the west. Masaryk saw the Trans-Siberian Railway as playing the chief role in the whole relief action. It was therefore necessary that it be maintained "at its best."

Masaryk emphasized that the military and political objective of the Czecho-Slovak army in Russia was to make war against the Central Powers. That had been the reason for its formation. That was why the Austrians and Germans had endeavored to prevent the Czech army from going to France; that was why "they forced the Bolsheviks to break their agreements and pledges"; and that was why they were organizing their war prisoners against the Czechs and the Allies.[58]

Masaryk proposed that once Siberia had been stabilized—which he believed could be accomplished before winter—half of the Czech army be transported to France while the other half remained in Russia. He reminded the State Department that the Czech army had passed under the military and financial administration of the Allies and had been declared a part of the Czech army in France. France, Italy, and Great Britain had recognized the Czech army as an Allied force and "recognized the justice of the efforts of the Czechs and Slovaks for complete independence." Thus, the aid extended to the Czech army was extended to a part of the Allied forces. He requested that American aid to the Czech army be advanced in the same way and noted that formal recognition of the Czecho-Slovak National Council and the belligerency of the Czech army would clear up the situation. He promised to submit a separate memorandum on this subject.[59]

Wilson was sympathetic to the Czech appeals for supplies, particularly nonmilitary ones. And yet efforts to aid the Czechs even in this regard presented serious difficulties, because of the amorphous state of the Czech army as a belligerent from the American standpoint. When Masaryk had expressed his gratitude to Wilson for his declaration of August 3, he had also appended a list of supplies and asked that arrangements be made for their transmission to the Czechs in Siberia. Wilson had referred the matter to the War and State Departments.[60] After a long conversation with Baker, in which he reaffirmed the importance of assisting the Czecho-Slovak forces, Lansing urged that "we should immediately provide them with arms, ammunition, uniforms, and warm clothing," since they were "menaced by armed German and Austrian prisoners of war and by the near approach of the Siberian winter." Lansing argued that the position of the Czecho-Slovak forces in Siberia, which prevented Siberian supplies from going to Germany and prevented repatriation of German and Austrian prisoners of war, had a direct bearing upon the campaign on the Western Front. They were, in effect, saving the lives of American soldiers in France, and thus "the honor as well as the interest of America" was involved "in their immediate relief and support against German and Austrian prisoners-of-war."[61]

By the end of August, Wilson had taken no steps to implement his plans for an economic commission for Siberia because he had simply not found the right man to head the mission. The British and French in the meantime were proceeding with their own arrangements for economic commissions.[62] Despite the continued efforts of Long, Auchincloss, Miles, and Lansing, the effort to send supplies to the Czechs continued to lag. There was some concern that General March himself was obstructing the efforts. Lansing continued to urge Wilson to action.[63] Although Wilson had directed Bernard Baruch to handle the matter, he had understood that Japan would supply the necessary military supplies for the Czechs at once. By this time, he had become deeply concerned because the Japanese appeared to be "doing the fighting on their own plan and letting the Czecho-Slovaks tag along, instead of acting themselves as a supporting force." Moreover, the whole problem of supplying military aid to the Czechs, to say nothing of financial aid, was a legal "rat hole," since the Czechs had not yet been officially recognized on even a de facto basis.[64]

It was now clear that Masaryk had completely reversed his attitude toward the Bolsheviks and the Czech mission in Russia. He had accepted the views of the Czech commanders in Russia regarding Bolshevik collusion with the Austro-German prisoners of war as well as Anglo-French plans for participation in the establishment of an Eastern Front in Russia, which necessitated the overthrow of German-Bolshevik power. Wilson, whose aide-mémoire of July 17 and press release of August 3 had strongly opposed both these policies, now faced a dreadful dilemma.

17

American Recognition of
Czecho-Slovak Belligerency

Throughout August, pressures mounted in the United States to recognize Czecho-Slovak independence. By mid-August, public support, Masaryk's influence, the British declaration of de facto recognition, antagonism to the German domination of Austria-Hungary, the need to secure greater leverage to control Czech actions in Russia, and the legal problems of aiding the Czechs financially and militarily led Wilson and Lansing to consider making a further declaration "giving more complete definition to our attitude in order to encourage the Czecho-Slovaks in their struggle against the Central Powers."[1]

This need to clarify American policy toward the Czecho-Slovaks now fighting alongside the Allies abroad was made even more urgent by the hardships the Czecho-Slovaks in the United States were suffering because of their technical status as enemy aliens. Czecho-Slovak volunteers in military services had been denied naturalization and thrown into "casual camps," along with Germans and Hungarians. Others found it difficult to secure employment in war industries because of their nationality. Yet Phillips believed nothing could be done until the United States decided to recognize the Czecho-Slovak National Council, at which time the Czecho-Slovaks could be reclassified as friendly aliens. Both Phillips and Miles strongly favored recognition of the Czecho-Slovak National Council.[2]

By the end of August, intelligence from Europe indicated that the Austro-Hungarian political situation was "very serious." Everything seemed to point to a general uprising of Czechs, Poles, and Yugoslavs all over the Empire. Austrian parliamentary discussions and governmental crises were described as "totally irrelevant."[3] "The Austro-Hungarian Government was thrown into a state of consternation" by British recognition of the Czecho-Slovaks, as it was "at that moment prepared to launch a peace offensive based upon previous utterances by Messrs. Lloyd George and Balfour."[4] Vienna had emphatically repudiated the Declaration of Recognition by the British government.

The Austrians claimed that the Czecho-Slovak National Council was a committee of private persons who had no mandate from the Czecho-Slovak people and still less from the Czecho-Slovak "nation," which existed, they claimed, only in the imagination of the Entente. They regarded as equally absurd the committee's claim to represent a future government. Moreover, notwithstanding the Entente's recognition of the Czecho-Slovak "army" as a part of the Entente army, these "disloyal elements" when caught would be treated as traitors.[5]

The American press was enthusiastic about the British declaration. The action was anticipated as a forerunner of American recognition and the death knell of the Austro-Hungarian Empire.[6] Press support of Czech recognition clearly removed one obstacle to American recognition of Czech independence, because Wilson had been quoted as saying, "No action could be taken, or at least usefully taken, unless it received the support of the great majority of the American people."[7] Lansing thought that the time was now ripe for some form of recognition of the Czecho-Slovak National Council. No single factor in this consideration was more important than his admiration of Czech bravery and belligerency in Siberia. In a letter to Wilson,[8] he emphasized that strong popular pressure to recognize the Czecho-Slovaks as an independent nationality was the natural consequence of the "heroic and romantic withdrawal of Czecho-Slovak troops from the Ukrainian Front and their remarkable migration across Siberia. No tale of military achievement in this war is more astounding."[9] Lansing suggested two possible courses. First, the Allies could recognize the belligerency of the "Czecho-Slovak revolutionists" in view of their military organization operating in Siberia and eastern Russia against Austrian loyalists and their German allies. This would make possible the recognition of the Czecho-Slovak National Council, with Masaryk at its head, as a de facto revolutionary government and the provision of such aid as seemed expedient. Since this action was based on the Czech state of belligerency, the Yugoslavs thus would have no similar ground to claim recognition. Secondly, Lansing thought that to avoid any future charge of deception or secretiveness, it might be wise to issue a frank declaration that, because of its utter subservience to Germany, Austria-Hungary had forfeited whatever right it once enjoyed to be treated as an independent state and that the nationalities aspiring to be free from Austro-Hungarian rule should receive not only the sympathy, but also the material aid of all nations that realized the evil ambitions of Germany's rulers. With this rationale, the American government would be prepared to advance the cause of national freedom by assuming relations with any council or body of men truly representative of revolutionists against the Austro-Hungarian government who sought national independence by force of arms. The second approach would avoid the questions of defined territory and of naming any particular nationality, though the latter would have to be done later when a military organization was in actual operation.

Wilson agreed that the time had come to take definitive action in regard to "this important matter." Although his inclination was to follow the second course described by Lansing, there were considerations that restrained him from it. He promised to explain these to Lansing orally at their next interview, since they were too complex for a brief memorandum.[10] Wilson was not yet ready to agree to the dismemberment of Austria-Hungary. Polk, Long, and Phillips clearly disagreed with the President, although not openly.[11] For whatever reasons, Wilson agreed with Lansing that the first alternative suggested seemed to be the best one to accept. It seemed to Wilson to be "as far as we need go at this time." He instructed Lansing to prepare a public announcement for his consideration.[12]

On August 30, after conferring with Wilson about both the Siberian situation and the Czecho-Slovaks, Lansing drafted a public statement recognizing the Czecho-Slovak National Council as a de facto belligerent government.[13] On August 31, he sent this draft to Wilson and reminded him that there was "a disposition among newspaper men to discuss—possibly to criticize—our silence in regard to this matter." Public pressure was now "getting out of hand," and he hoped that something could be done "very shortly."

Wilson made a partial modification of Lansing's draft and then typed out on his own portable typewriter—the unmistakable machine with the purple ribbon and small widely spaced type—the final draft of September 2, 1918.[14] The declaration was a straightforward statement:

> The Czecho-Slovak peoples having taken up arms against the German and Austro-Hungarian Empires, and having placed organized armies in the field which are waging war against those empires under officers of their own nationality and in accordance with the rules and practices of civilized nations; and The Czecho-Slovaks having, in prosecution of their independent purposes in the present war, confided supreme political authority to the Czecho-Slovak National Council.
>
> The Government of the United States recognizes that a state of belligerency exists between the Czecho-Slovaks thus organized and the German and Austro-Hungarian Empires.

It also recognizes the Czecho-Slovak National Council as a *de facto* belligerent government, clothed with proper authority to direct the military and political affairs of the Czecho-Slovaks.

The Government of the United States further declares that it is prepared to enter formally into relations with the *de facto* government thus recognized for the purpose of prosecuting the war against the common enemy, the Empires of Germany and Austria-Hungary.[15]

On September 3, at noon, Lansing formally presented Masaryk with a copy of the declaration. Masaryk, "much pleased," thanked Lansing heartily.[16] In a public announcement, Masaryk noted that the American recognition differed from the French and British in that these nations had recognized the right to Czech independence directly, whereas the American wording recognized "in the first place our army and the National Council." While the British text recognized the Czecho-Slovak National Council as the present trustee of the future government, the United States recognized the council directly as the de facto government. The American declaration stressed the belligerency and emphasized the organization of the nation as demonstrated, first, in mobilizing armies, and second, in confiding all political affairs to the authority of the National Council. He added: "In accordance with the humanitarian principles of the American Constitution the military practice of our armies (this applies especially to our army in Russia) is acknowledged."[17]

Masaryk immediately sought and received the help of Long in arranging an audience with Wilson to express his appreciation personally "on behalf of his countrymen."[18] Masaryk telegraphed his good friend, Crane, thanking him not only for his good wishes but "also for the help you have given me in my political endeavors."[19] To Wilson, Masaryk wrote of his appreciation that "the United States had recognized the justice of our struggle for independence and national unity" and thanked him "in the name of the whole nation, for the act of political generosity, justice and political wisdom." America's recognition would strengthen the Czech armies and the whole nation in their unshakable decision to sacrifice everything for the liberation of Europe and of mankind.[20] Masaryk's letter gave Wilson "a great deal of gratification" because it reassured him that Masaryk approved the method by which he was supporting the Czecho-Slovak movement. At the same time, Wilson expressed to Masaryk how much he and Lansing had "valued the counsel and guidance" that Masaryk had given them, and that it would "always be a matter of profound gratitude to me if it should turn out that we have been able to render service which will redound to the permanent advantage and happiness of the great group of peoples whom you represent."[21]

On September 11, Masaryk met briefly with Wilson at the White House. After Masaryk offered his personal thanks to Wilson for recognition, Wilson apologized for the delay in getting aid to the Czechs in Russia. Wilson also expressed his concerns over British, French, and Japanese policies in Russia. He was disturbed over the British assumption of control of intervention in Russia to implement their own interests. He feared Japanese assumption of the high command of the Allied troops in Siberia and hoped that since the Czechs might well have the largest number of troops there, the command would be given to the Czech leadership. He expressed his concern over the failure of the French to be properly sensitive to the "feelings" of the Russian people. Both men agreed on the importance of negotiating peacefully the differences that existed among the Russians and the futility of attempting to solve these problems through "shooting."[22]

The United States's de facto recognition of the Czecho-Slovak nation recognized for the first time a nation whose boundary lines had not yet been determined and whose sovereign name and power had not been clearly indicated.[23] Following the United States's declaration on September 3, the National Council changed, according to its decision of September 28, into a provisional government.

At this very time, the Bolshevik government, having completed its military preparations, was initiating an advance against the Czech legionnaires in Russia and Siberia.[24] Yet from the vantage point of Graves, who had arrived in Vladivostok on September 3, the Czech question in Siberia had already been settled, since by mid-September the Czechs controlled virtually the whole Siberian Railway line with the aid of Japan. Now the problem was how to keep Japan from taking over the complete control and operation of the railways in Siberia and Manchuria.[25] Even as the American government moved swiftly to forestall such an event, Graves reported that, despite the gravity of the situation on the Volga front, the Czechs from the west had joined with the Czechs from the east along the Chinese Eastern Railroad at Chita. The only resistance appeared to be at Habarovsk. It was slight and would disappear as soon as the destroyed bridges on the Siberian railway were repaired. The railroads were open from Vladivostok through Manchuria to Samara.[26] MacMurray affirmed that the Czechs held Chita and Karimskaya and that telegraphic communications with

Irkutsk via Penza had been reopened.[27] It now seemed possible that through railway service could be established to Manchouli, thus releasing all the Czech forces in Siberia. Morris reported that the Japanese General Staff still feared the activities of the Austrians and Germans in the Amur region and had fully mobilized the third Japanese division for departure to Manchouli, but that in central Siberia close cooperation existed between the Czechs and the Central Siberian army.[28]

Thus, in the very week in September in which the United States announced its de facto recognition of the Czecho-Slovak National Council, railway connections between eastern and western Siberia were reestablished, and the Czechs were in a position to withdraw to Vladivostok and from there return to France. Wilson's position seemed to have been vindicated.[29] Moreover, it was clear that, just as it had for Britain and France, the Czech Legion in Siberia had played the crucial role for the United States in its decision to recognize Czecho-Slovak belligerency. Wilson now faced the task not only of competing with the British, French, Japanese, and newly created Siberian governments for Czecho-Slovak acceptance of his policies in Russia and Siberia, but also of getting his own representatives to follow American rather than Allied policies.

On September 4, 1918, David R. Francis was delighted to see the arrival of about 4,800 American troops at Archangel. Interpreting Wilson's aide-mémoire very broadly, he planned to encourage them to join General Poole's forces in the British plan to form a junction with the Czechs moving northward from the Volga area.[30] DeWitt Poole reported that "disaffection from the Bolsheviks" continued to be marked and was "almost complete among the peasants," while the rapprochement between the Germans and the Bolsheviks became more clearly defined every day. He urged that the Czechs must "not only be promptly supported in the rear, but a junction effected in the north without further delay."[31] Harris greatly feared that unless reinforcements were sent immediately, the Czechs would be unable to carry out General Poole's instructions regarding a junction at Vologda. He was now also aware of the Czech destruction of the Bolshevik army east of Lake Baikal and the establishment of communications with Harbin and Vladivostok. Moreover, the Cossacks were cooperating with the Czechs, and a provisional Siberian government formed at Omsk was asking for Allied intervention, having declared war against Germany and assumed responsibility for foreign loans. At the same time, telegrams from Vladivostok reported that the Czech forces at Irkutsk had forced their way eastward, taken Chita and Karimskaya, and made connection with the Czech and Japanese forces moving westward from Manchouli.[32] Given all of these new developments, Lansing decided to review Wilson's policy and determine whether it was "now advisable to change and allow Czechs to move westward and with the Russians to fight west of the Urals."[33]

Bliss, at Supreme War Council headquarters, did not believe that such a review was necessary. He reported his views to March:

It is one thing to help the Czecho-Slovaks to keep from being wiped out by the Bolsheviks and then march them to Vladivostok and help them get out of the country. . . . I certainly do not suppose that we are going to help the Czecho-Slovaks if they want to set up a government of their own; nor do I suppose that we want to face the possibility of having a force of 7,000 Americans wiped out in an attempt to reach Germany's Eastern Front against the will of the Russians. . . . As I have said before, if our Allies have any axes to grind in Russia, let them go and do it. I think that the war has got to be ended on this Western Front. . . .

Bliss also strongly opposed sending reinforcements to northern Russia and was indignant because London's instructions to General Poole had been sent without the knowledge of the military representatives at Paris.[34]

Wilson fully agreed with Bliss. For several days, he had been mulling over Harris's message of August 30, which described Poole's plan for a junction with the Czechs. It was now clear to Wilson that both the northern expedition under the aggressive Poole and the Siberian expedition were being expedited and implemented in the "most striking" and "utter disregard of the policy to which we expressly confined ourselves in our statement about our action in Siberia." Wilson wrote Lansing in exasperation: "It is out of the question to send reinforcements from eastern Siberia . . . to Perm; and we have expressly notified those in charge of those forces that the Czecho-Slovaks must (so far as our aid was to be used) be brought out eastward, not got out westward. Is there no way,—no form of expression,—by which we can get this comprehended?"[35] But even as Wilson expressed his anger over the changed objectives of both the Czechs and his associates in Russia, news came pouring into the State Department of Czech successes in Siberia, along with ominous warnings that unless aid was sent immediately and "unless Allies make strenuous efforts half the results of Czech victories will be lost."[36]

Actually, as Graves reported, the Czechs had easily overcome Bolshevik opposition. By the time that he had arrived in Vladivostok on
September 3, 1918, it was "perfectly clear" that "the military resistance
to the Czecho-Slovaks had practically disappeared." Graves himself
believed that most of the German-Austrian war prisoners would return
to their prison camps and that there would be no more "trouble in
Siberia."[37] Emerson agreed and added that the physical condition of the
railway, then open to Samara, was first class except for a few bridges
that were then being repaired. He found law and order prevailing in the
cities and towns along the railroad and thought that conditions on the
whole seemed very hopeful.[38] Harris, however, was convinced that the
Czechs were not strong enough to hold their grip on such a large
territory and would be destroyed unless the Allies hurried to their
assistance.[39]

The news of Czech successes in Siberia that most impressed Lansing was Knight's report that "extraordinary favorable military situation is indicated by a reliable report from the West." Knight had
received his information from Gajda, now Commander in Chief of all
the Czech forces succeeding Dietrichs. Gajda had reported that 90,000
Czechs, along with a large force of Russians, were under his command
in central Siberia, totaling approximately 160,000 men, while large
numbers of Russians were mobilizing by authority of the Provisional
Government. He pleaded urgently for arms, ammunition, and clothing
for a much larger force than had heretofore been believed possible. He
reported that 400,000 German-Austrian prisoners were under control
and that all prisoner and Bolshevik opposition had broken down. The
railroad was clear to a point beyond the Volga where "a formidable
front already exists."[40]

To Lansing, the complexities of the Russian situation involving the
changed situation of the Czechs, the urgent problem of getting supplies to them, the activities of the Japanese, and the possibility of
changed objectives for the entire expedition to Siberia necessitated a
full reconsideration of the matter. He instructed Auchincloss to review
the recent Russian telegrams and sketch out a letter to Wilson covering
the entire Russian problem.[41] After discussing his draft with Long,
Miles, and Vance McCormick and receiving their approval, Auchincloss completed the final draft and then read it to House, who also
approved it. Although Auchincloss was fearful that the "president
would balk at it," Lansing approved the letter virtually without change
and sent it on to Wilson.[42]

Lansing's letter noted that "our confidence in the Czech forces has been justified," that there was "strong evidence to prove that the Russians are entirely satisfied to cooperate with the Czechs in Russia and that assistance to the Czechs amounts to assistance to the Russians." There were, however, certain problems that Lansing feared might "seriously impair" American prestige, not only with the Russians and the Czechs, but also with the Allies and Japanese. Recalling to Wilson his reason for sending military forces to Russia, he reminded him of his eventual hope and purpose to send economic and other relief to the Russian people, following, but in no way embarrassing, the military assistance rendered to the Czecho-Slovaks. Moreover, Wilson had indicated that his purpose was not to desert the Czecho-Slovak army engaged in conflict with nationals of the Central Powers in Siberia and had demonstrated his sympathy with the Czecho-Slovaks by recognizing the National Council as a de facto government at war with the Central Powers.[43] Lansing saw the major problems presented by the recent telegrams as aid to the Czecho-Slovaks operating both in Siberia and the eastern part of Europe and Russia, and aid to the civilian populations in Siberia, along the Murmansk coast, and in the Archangel district. He suggested that one of the war boards handle the financial questions involved in these operations and recommended Vance McCormick as particularly fitted to direct such a project.[44] Lansing had earlier advised that since the Czecho-Slovak National Council had been recognized as a de facto government, it "might be possible to make them a loan sufficient to purchase supplies in this country. The entire responsibility and work of purchasing and arranging for transportation of the supplies would then fall upon Professor Masaryk and his colleagues."[45]

Wilson now discussed the Auchincloss plan with various advisers and designated Baruch, McCormick, and Edward N. Hurley of the Shipping Board to handle war supplies, economic help, and shipping, and to make sure that supplies got through; however, he was reluctant to create a separate organization to arrange the problem of supplies and relief. After McCormick explained the matter fully to Wilson, he agreed to help expedite the aid in as administratively efficient a way as possible.[46]

Now that the Czecho-Slovaks were in control of the whole Trans-Siberian Railway, General Wilson insisted that a definite decision be made concerning their strategic employment east and west of the Urals. With their line of communications secured and their rear protected by the Japanese forces east of Lake Baikal, the refitting and equipping of the Czecho-Slovaks were insured, and they would be at liberty to concentrate on action in whatever direction seemed most desirable. To General Wilson, it now seemed imperative for the Czechs to join Poole's forces to secure Allied control of the railways from Ekaterinburg through Perm and Viatka to Vologda in order to establish through communication with Archangel and to enable supplies from western Siberia to be sent to the people of northern Russia, who otherwise would starve. The time seemed propitious to General Wilson for such an advance, since four American battalions had just arrived in northern Russia and were advancing "successfully" to Vologda. To carry out these operations, it was essential that the Japanese move westward along the Siberian railway, take over the guarding of the railway, and release all Czecho-Slovak troops for concentration west of the Urals.[47]

In mid-September, Girsa reported that the Red Army and units from the German army were advancing against the Czechs on the Volga front and that the Czech forces that had fought their way through Siberia would have to return to that front. The return movement had begun on September 9 under Gajda. Dietrichs had assumed the command and organization of the Russian forces that had been cooperating with the Czechs, including the forces from central to western Siberia under the command of Semenov and Kalmikov, all of whom had agreed to the change.[48]

Gajda had sent Captain Husarek, his aide de camp, to Vladivostok with an urgent message for Knight and Graves. Gajda's statement emphasized the dangers presented by the war prisoners armed by the Bolsheviks even though they had been defeated in a series of battles. He reported that the Bolsheviks had been scattered and the prisoners returned to their camps, where 4,000 of them were being guarded by the Czechs assisted by loyal Russian soldiers. The Czechs had been welcomed by the "mass of Russian people," who "took advantage of the opportunity to overthrow the Soviet Government." Now, Gajda reported, the whole of Siberia from Chita to the Urals was quiet; a Russian army of several thousand men had been organized and armed and was acting loyally and efficiently under the command of the Czechs. However, conditions were serious on the Volga front not only for the Czechs, but also for Allied forces who were seeking to effect a junction with the Czechs from both Archangel and the Caspian region. It was urgent to strengthen the line eastward. Bolshevism was apparently dead in Siberia, and all classes, including former Bolsheviks, were now awaiting the arrival of the Allied forces and promised cooperation. Gajda appealed for help from Allied forces at the earliest possible moment and especially from American forces, which, he insisted, would be received with enthusiasm and would stimulate recruiting among the Russians as nothing else could.[49] Gajda was now publicly announcing the opening of a new front against the Germans in Russia. The Czecho-Slovak army would not go to the French Front.[50]

Both Knight and Graves were persuaded that the Czechs did need moral and material aid, including clothing, blankets, arms, ammunition, and especially field artillery. Graves agreed that the American flag was best for moral support, but that Japan was the only nation in a position to give much material assistance. He saw no need for more than 1,000 troops at Vladivostok and believed that the farther American troops went west, the better the effect would be. Since the matter involved more than military questions, Graves requested instructions from the War Department. Both of these cables were sent on to Wilson.[51]

By September 12, the situation on the Volga had become critical. Kazan had fallen, Simbirsk was being evacuated, and Samara and the Volga front were thus endangered. General Syrový cabled in desperation: "It is impossible to continue to operate without immediate assistance of strong allied force. . . . Failure to render immediate assistance will prevent us from clearing further than Urals. There is small hope of aid from Russian Army in near future. There is no time for consideration and conference. Telegraph immediately answer of Allies."[52]

On September 13, Harris confirmed that the Czechs were in full retreat from Kazan and that the Czech staff at Samara had asked him to telegraph the Allies for urgent help. Harris noted that there were between 30,000 and 40,000 Bolsheviks and Austro-German war prisoners around Ekaterinburg commanded by an Austrian general and that everywhere the Bolsheviks were showing better organization and were "very active under German direction." He doubted that the town could be held since there were only 12,000 Czechs and Cossacks opposing them.[53]

In the meantime, at Chita, from which the Czechs had been withdrawn to aid in the critical situation on the Volga, and which the Japanese had entered, conditions were described as extremely unsettled. Consul J. Paul Jameson reported the prevalence of factionalism with various groups favoring Horvath, the Omsk government, the Semenov faction, and the Japanese. Jameson noted: "The people I spoke with were very anxious for the Allies to come in, and specially for the American and Czech troops to come at the earliest possible moment."[54] On September 14, Pavlů and the Czech and White Russian staffs at Samara wired both the State Department and Graves for immediate Allied help. They wanted to know "immediately and very definitely just what policy Allies will pursue in Russia and to what extent Czechs can positively rely upon their help."[55]

In the midst of these desperate pleas, the Austrian government on September 14 appealed to all the belligerents to send representatives to a neutral state for "confidential non-binding conversations over the fundamental principles of the Peace Treaty."[56] The Austrian proposal, delivered on the afternoon of September 16, was "the sensation of the day."[57] When the Associated Press asked Lansing about its significance, he replied that it "showed Austria breaking and we should strike all the harder."[58] Wilson had immediately telephoned Lansing about answering the Austrians with a flat refusal. Lansing agreed. Wilson then typed a sixty-eight word reply, which Lansing gave to the newspapermen at 6:50 that evening.[59] The note stated simply that the United States could "entertain no proposal for a conference upon a matter concerning which it had made its position and purpose so plain."[60]

Masaryk was enthusiastic about Wilson's response. He now believed that the solution to the future peace of the world was possible.[61] The British press in general also universally approved Wilson's answer to the Austrian note.[62] Stovall in Switzerland agreed that the Austrian offer was unworthy of serious consideration. After conferring with leaders of the Polish, Czech, and Yugoslav movements, he wrote: "I am informed by persons in positions to know conditions, that if responsibility for continuing the war can be clearly laid on Germany, revolts will spring up before the end of the year in both Austria-Hungary and Bulgaria."[63]

Coincidentally, at the very time of the Austrian peace appeal, a great mass meeting of historic interest to the peoples of the oppressed nationalities of Austria-Hungary was held in Carnegie Hall in New York on September 15. The Committee on Public Information had encouraged the meeting to focus public attention on the objectives of the war, particularly in the light of the recent de facto recognition of the Czecho-Slovak National Council. Several American organizations assisted, including the YMCA and the YWCA. The meeting was called "The Will Of The Peoples of Austria-Hungary. Victory Meeting For The Oppressed Nationalities of Central Europe."[64] Senator Gilbert M. Hitchcock of Nebraska presided, and the leading speakers were Masaryk and Paderewski. Masaryk explained that the meeting was called to express to Wilson and the American people the gratitude of the Czechs for their recognition. It was the "first occasion on which representatives of the seven oppressed nations of Austria had sunk their differences and met on the common ground of war to the death against their common oppressor." A resolution was formally adopted calling for the dissolution of the Austro-Hungarian Empire.[65]

On September 20, Masaryk presented the resolutions to Wilson in a brief speech. Wilson then replied that Austria had been viewed as an old building whose sides had been held together by props and that it was now clear that the props must be removed. It was not a long interview—about a half hour—but when it was concluded, "Doctor Masaryk's weary old face shone." According to Creel, who had escorted them, Masaryk exclaimed, "And they told me that he was cold! Why, your President is the most intensely human man I have ever met. He's actually incandescent with feeling."[66]

By this time Wilson had finally determined that the most effective way to handle the Czech financial problem was to authorize Baruch to draw on the President's war fund in the sum of $1,500,000 to send the Czecho-Slovaks the supplies that Baruch had carefully listed in a letter to him on September 16. Wilson had insisted that the English should be asked to make their contribution to Czech relief exactly "as we are making ours," and he was "happy to learn that they are in a position to do so." He had also secured General March's approval for the transfer of winter overcoats and shoes so desperately needed by the Czechs, which could be supplied from current stocks in Vladivostok itself. He was ready to supply Masaryk with "the means" for "getting together an organization of engineers to inspect supplies here."[67] It now appeared that supplies for the Czechs were "sure to be started."[68]

By mid-September, after the fall of Kazan to superior Bolshevik forces, the Czechs were once again losing the possibility of forming a junction with Archangel. Pavlů had telegraphed Irkutsk that neither the Samara army nor the Siberian army was in a position to render any effective aid. Moreover, there were no arms. Pavlů had addressed a special appeal to the Allies for early help and evinced hope for an early agreement for the formation of an all-Russian government in Siberia.[69] Consul Poole reported that the "whole situation on the Eastern Front" was "critical, requiring promptest action taken on our part to extend to the Czechs and the few remaining anti-German Russian fighting units the support promised in our recent official declaration."[70]

Clemenceau now sent an urgent and extremely confidential message to Wilson urging the transfer of five additional American battalions to Murmansk. The French had secured Foch's endorsement of

Clemenceau's request. Bliss, however, reported that Foch had consented only out of deference to Clemenceau and would not misunderstand Wilson's declining. Both Bliss and Baker agreed that "yielding to this request would only open the door to further diversion of American forces as French and British will not send theirs and will join in requests upon us."[71] The request for additional battalions for northern Russia may well have been in part at least the result of pressure from American representatives there. Francis had sent an urgent telegram to Foch's headquarters demanding that reinforcements be sent "without telling . . . how many or what kind." He asked Bliss and Colonel T. Bentley Mott, Military Attaché at Paris, to bring the matter to Pershing's attention. An angry Bliss explained to Mott that General Poole was engaging in a campaign that "we have never contemplated nor recommended and that it was up to him to obey his instructions and confine himself to the defense of the Arctic ports."[72]

Major E. Francis Riggs, assistant to Colonel Ruggles at Archangel, had also appeared in Versailles at the headquarters of the Supreme War Council. Riggs presented a letter to Bliss from Francis urging the sending of reinforcements. He seemed to think that with this additional help, General Poole could "force himself to parts of Russia where he will secure volunteers and where he can then get into contact with the Czechs and as a result of it they will practically conquer Western Russia and re-establish a front against the Germans." To Bliss, Riggs's conversation sounded "wild." Apparently Francis, in his letter to Consul Poole, made the amazing statement that General Poole had told him that he had been promised at least 10,000 American troops. Bliss told Riggs "that if anyone made such a statement to General Poole it was difficult to characterize it as other than a deliberate falsification of facts."[73] When March received news of these developments from Bliss, he immediately sent a copy of Bliss's letter to Wilson and expressed his strong opposition to what he thought was being effected and included a copy of the instructions issued by the British War Office to General Poole. Wilson was fully sympathetic. To March, he wrote, "I think you know already that the judgments expressed are my own also."[74]

Masaryk in the meantime was making every effort to implement Wilson's plan to aid the Czechs. He spoke to Long at length "about the Czechs, their distress in the Volga and Ekaterinburg Districts, the preponderance there of German and Austrian prisoners, the state of physical exhaustion of the Czechs and their need for moral and physical support." All that Masaryk said was being borne out by the cablegrams coming into the State and War departments.[75]

At this crucial point, Janin and Štefánik arrived in America en route to Siberia under orders to assume command of the Czechs there.[76] When Janin, accompanied by Jusserand, visited the White House, he sought to impress upon Wilson the need for sending additional troops to Murmansk and Archangel—the five battalions that Clemenceau had requested. Wilson responded to his remarks very negatively and labeled the entire operation "foolish." Although Wilson's attitude toward the Czecho-Slovaks was most sympathetic, he insisted upon their retreat to eastern Siberia if they wished to be assured of support from the rear. The entire conversation struck Janin as revealing an absolutely negative attitude on Wilson's part toward the entire Russian enterprise.[77]

As Wilson sought to persuade the Czechs to retire to the east of the Urals, he continued to seek Japan's approval for placing the Trans-Siberian and Chinese Eastern Railways under the direction of Stevens and the Russian Railway Service Corps. He also requested Lansing to consider ways of indicating American disapproval of the large numbers of troops that Japan had sent to Siberia and Manchuria under the guise of rescuing the Czechs.[78] By the end of August, the State Department had presented Stevens's proposal for railway control to Japan and China. Lansing had informed the Chinese government that the suggested policy seemed to be the "only solution of a problem which is very complicated and which may otherwise become most embarrassing."[79] Although it favored the American plan, China hesitated to give its formal consent in the fear of antagonizing Japan. On the other hand, Japan formally rejected the plan as "constituting intervention in Russia's domestic administration which it has always been the avowed policy of Associated Governments to denounce."[80]

Washington was unimpressed by Gotō's objections, and with good reason. During the first week in September, Graves, Stevens, and Harris had cabled reports that Otani had issued an order placing all of the Trans-Siberian Railroad under military control. Graves immediately questioned him concerning the matter, while Stevens urged "quick action . . . or American Railroad men are out of business completely." Wilson was "very much disturbed by this report" and could not believe that it represented Japan's desires or intentions.[81] He immediately telephoned Lansing to consider ways to oppose such a scheme.[82] Lansing thereupon instructed Morris to protest that the rumored Japanese actions were quite at variance with Washington's purpose to aid Russia, in which purpose the United States was confident Japan concurred.[83] When Morris conveyed Lansing's protest,

General Pierre T. Janin (National Archives)

Gotō seemed completely at a loss to explain the matter.[84] When Graves asked Otani about the military takeover, Otani responded that he had "never busied himself concerning the railroad in general or their stock" and that apparently the rumor concerning the takeover was "the result of a misunderstanding perhaps in translation."[85] Ishii was equally at a loss to account for these reports. Morris concluded reluctantly that the Japanese General Staff had its own policy in Siberia, which it was carrying out regardless of the wishes of the Foreign Office and of Ishii. The latter was left with the task of explaining.[86]

Lansing's efforts increased with the news that the Japanese had been strongly urging Horvath to turn over control of the Chinese Eastern Railway to them. Naturally this greatly concerned the Chinese, who inquired anxiously about the progress of the American-Japanese railway negotiations. Although the Chinese Minister in Washington made it clear that the Japanese dispatch of troops to Manchouli had been without Peking's formal assent, MacMurray reported that so complete was Japanese domination over the Chinese government, he thought that Peking would not dare to act upon the American proposal unless assured that the project had the support of all the other Allies.[87] Thereupon the State Department opened negotiations with the British, French, and Italian governments, and also with Masaryk. Stevens and the Russian Railway Service Corps were "agents of the Russian people," Lansing said, and the United States had no desire to control the Russian railways. It was merely doing what it thought best for the Russian people in a spirit of unselfishness and disinterestedness.[88] The French and Italian governments promised to support the American proposal, as did Masaryk.[89] However, Great Britain appeared unwilling to follow suit. Nevertheless, Balfour had advised Japan of the desirability of cooperating with the United States in railway measures, "if only with a view to engaging the U. S. as deeply as possible in Siberian adventure and to securing their material help in supplying the needs of the railroads upon recommendations of their own engineers."[90]

Wilson had now become deeply concerned about the disposition of both Czech and Japanese troops in Siberia and in Manchuria. He was considering the wisdom of asking Japan courteously but plainly what she proposed to do with her large army in Siberia, since the Trans-Siberian Railway was open and controlled by friends from Vladivostok to Samara. Moreover, impeccable intelligence seemed to indicate that the hostile forces that were said to be in the intervening regions had been dispersed or brought under control. Wilson feared that there was some "influence at work to pull absolutely away from the plan which we proposed and to which the other governments assented, and proceed to do what we said we would not do, namely form a new Eastern Front." While Wilson agreed that it might be necessary to leave some portion of the Czecho-Slovak troops in western Siberia near the Urals to prevent the Germans from taking agricultural and other supplies, nevertheless, by the time winter had closed the country, it was his "clear judgment" that the United States should insist that the Czecho-Slovaks be brought out eastward to Vladivostok and conveyed to the Western Front in Europe. Now, fully aware of what his associates were seeking to do at Archangel, Wilson wrote to Lansing on September 17: "I am clear that we should insist upon taking no part in attempting to form a new Eastern Front and that any attempt to use the Czecho-Slovaks in conjunction with what is being attempted at Archangel would also be walking into the same trap."[91] The Allies, said Wilson, should be informed that the United States would "not be a party to any attempt to form an Eastern Front, deeming it absolutely impractical from a military point of view and unwise as a matter of political action." Moreover, they should be kindly but definitely made to understand that the most the United States was ready to do was to assist in the holding of Archangel or Murmansk until the spring, as the exigencies of the winter dictated, and that in Siberia the United States would cooperate with the Czecho-Slovak troops only if they withdrew to eastern Siberia there to await the determination of the best military disposition of their forces. As Wilson put it, "we cannot act too soon or speak too plainly."[92]

On September 20, Lansing handed Phillips the two letters from Wilson regarding the Czecho-Slovak situation. By mid-September, it was clear that Wilson was clashing head-on not only with the Japanese, but with the British as well. The differences between the British and Americans regarding the continued use of the Czechs had simply exacerbated "the predictable clash between British 'traditional' policy and Wilson's 'new conception of foreign policy.' "[93] Balfour was deeply worried about British relations with the United States concerning Siberia.[94] Neither House nor Wiseman could think of a way out of the impasse. House, indeed, disagreed "almost entirely" with the manner in which Wilson had handled the Russian situation, although he agreed heartily with his objectives.[95] American distrust of British motives was so strong by mid-September that Masaryk went to the British embassy and asked that reassurances be given to Wilson. He reported that he had heard suspicions of the British expressed frequently, not only in the

State Department, but even by Wilson himself.[96] Lansing now had a long talk with Wiseman. "The Czech forces," he remarked, "are moving West when they ought to be going East." Lansing said that American policy was clear, unaltered, and in entire accord with Japan's policy to rescue the Czechs and not to assist them in recreating an Eastern Front. The Japanese should go to Irkutsk with the understanding that the Czechs would withdraw to a certain point, from which the Japanese would retire eastward with them, and both forces would evacuate Russian territory.[97]

Masaryk himself was caught between the divergent policies of the British and the Americans. While Janin had been in Washington, he and Masaryk had discussed the Russian situation thoroughly, on September 21. They had agreed that the front against the Germans in Russia could not be restored without the entire Japanese army. Moreover, they doubted the ability of the anti-Bolshevik Russians, if left to themselves, to raise a large enough army to control Russia. Yet Masaryk feared that if the Bolsheviks had a military agreement with the Germans, the Germans would send an army against the Czechs. This army would try to organize prisoners of war, of whom it was estimated there might be a considerable number in Russia, even some 100,000. In these circumstances, both Janin and Masaryk thought that it might be advisable for the Czechs in northern Russia to retire over the Urals. But if the Czechs retreated, "what would be the fate of the Allied contingents at Archangel and Murmansk or of the numerous Americans, English, French, Bohemians, etc. in Moscow and elsewhere in Russia?" The question of how far to retreat over the Urals would depend on the strength of the enemy in Siberia. On the other hand, if Siberia could be held, the whole of Siberia would be under one government and the Russians there could organize an army. Masaryk's conversations with Janin were incorporated in a memorandum.[98]

On the same day that Masaryk signed this memorandum with Janin, he also had a similar discussion with Lansing, as Wilson had requested. Lansing asked Masaryk what the definite plans and intentions of the Czechs were. Masaryk replied that he emphatically agreed with Wilson that the restoration of an Eastern Front was absolutely out of the question. It would require the entire Japanese army to do it.[99] He also agreed that the wisest course for the Czecho-Slovaks on the Volga and in eastern Russia was to retire through Siberia as soon as that could be done with safety. Lansing reported that "in every way" Masaryk was "most thoroughly in accord with our policy."[100] He was convinced of Masaryk's desire to have the Czechs moved eastward.[101]

Obviously this was a plan that was bound to meet steadfast opposition from the British. In negotiations with Beneš, the British had agreed to recognize the Czecho-Slovak National Council as the trustee of a future Czecho-Slovak sovereign state, but largely on the understanding that Czech troops in Siberia would be used to support the British plan, which was also supported strongly by the French. Indeed, when Masaryk had expressed his gratitude to Lloyd George for the War Office's generous appreciation of the Czech army in Russia, he made it clear that the primary reason for joining the Allies and sticking with them was "to insure that in the final victory Austria-Hungary was not preserved in any form."[102]

On the same day that he spoke with Masaryk—that is, September 21—Lansing also responded to Wilson's note regarding the withdrawal of the Czecho-Slovaks. While concurring with Wilson's views, he again called Wilson's attention to the aide-mémoire of July 17. Lansing suggested that while "we should make our position clear that we will not send forces into the interior to support the Czecho-Slovaks and that in our opinion they should proceed to a zone of safety," nevertheless, he was "a little embarrassed by the suggestion that we 'insist' that they shall be brought out eastward to Vladivostok and conveyed to the Western Front in Europe if necessary." He suggested merely restating American policy on the matter and emphasizing the impracticality of the restoration of an Eastern Front.[103] Reluctantly Wilson agreed that Lansing was "quite right" and that they should merely urge the advisability of what was, in their judgment, "a wise and necessary course."[104]

Wilson was now determined to confront the Japanese. He sent Morris to Vladivostok in mid-September to investigate the entire Siberian situation and to confer with Stevens. Morris saw no practical difficulty in authorizing Otani, as senior officer of the Allied forces, to assume the military protection of the railways and to designate Stevens, the representative of the Russian people, as director general with full powers to operate the entire system.[105] Gotō had intimated to Morris that Japan was willing to agree that Stevens's engineers should take over operation of the Chinese Eastern and Trans-Siberian railways under Japanese military protection.[106] However, Wilson and the State Department officials were reluctant to turn over military control of the railways to Japan, even under Stevens's direction.[107]

It was Masaryk and the Czech Legion that now provided a way out of the apparent impasse. On September 23, a day devoted almost exclusively to efforts to implement the plan for direction and control of the Trans-Siberian Railway, Long invited Masaryk to come to the State Department. There, he discussed with him the subject of the Trans-Siberian Railway system and its operation by Stevens and the Russian Railway Service Corps under the military protection of such military authorities as might be in control of the different sections through which the railroad passed. Long told Masaryk that the French had unconditionally approved the American proposal, that the Japanese had now agreed, that the Chinese Cabinet was considering the matter favorably and would probably agree, and that the English had not yet responded. Long asked Masaryk whether he would approve if the Russian Railway Corps operated the road under the control of the Czecho-Slovaks. Masaryk responded positively and said that he would urge the French and the Czech commanders in Siberia to cooperate. Masaryk also offered the services of the Czecho-Slovak railway regiment to serve under Stevens's direction as part of the operating personnel for the railroad.[108]

Thus by the last week in September, the prospects in Washington for limiting American support of the Czechs in Siberia to the objectives defined in Wilson's aide-mémoire seemed promising. Wilson had made clear his opposition to the use of the Czechs in the reestablishment of an Eastern Front, expressed his disapproval of Japanese troop expansion in Siberia and Manchuria, and co-opted Masaryk's troops into his plan for administering and controlling the Trans-Siberian and Chinese-Eastern railways under the leadership of the Stevens mission. At the same time, he had rejected Austro-Hungarian proposals for preliminary peace talks and strengthened his support for Czecho-Slovak independence. The news on the Western Front was also improving. The Allied armies had now regained nearly all the territory they had lost in the March offensive and were everywhere approaching the Hindenburg Line.[109]

18

Masaryk's Dilemma and the End of Austria-Hungary

In Siberia itself, there seemed little likelihood of implementing the American plans to use the Czechs to police the railways under the control and direction of Stevens. Morris reported that the Czechs were actively engaged in the civil war in western Siberia and were making no real effort to proceed to Vladivostok.[1] Harris warned that "if Czechs were removed from any city in Siberia, Urals or Samara districts, Bolsheviks would immediately get control again."[2] From Archangel, where American troops had already landed and General Poole was attempting to implement his plans for making a juncture with the Czechs in the Volga area, Ambassador Francis telegraphed: "Can Department advise me whether a state of war exists between the United States and the Bolshevik Government?"[3]

The leaders of the Czech forces in the Volga region were pleading for immediate assistance. Morris recommended that American troops be sent to the vicinity of Omsk to cooperate with British and French troops in aiding the Czechs and their Russian friends to maintain their position in European Russia. Morris found that the British and French representatives, particularly Generals Knox and Paris, were influencing the Czech leaders with impractical plans to create by force a new Russian army and a new Eastern Front. General Gajda, he said, "who is very young, had been impressed by these schemes and misled by unauthorized suggestions of ultimate unlimited American support." Morris believed that "General Graves's presence in western Siberia would steady the Czechs' leaders and make clear to them and to the Russian people our policy and purpose." He urged that whatever action was decided upon be announced to the Czech commanders immediately, since Gajda's plans for the winter depended upon the character and extent of the assistance from the Americans and the Allies. Both Graves and Knight supported these views.[4]

Lansing was thoroughly perplexed and distressed by Morris's report. He sympathized with "the spirit of the Czecho-Slovaks" when

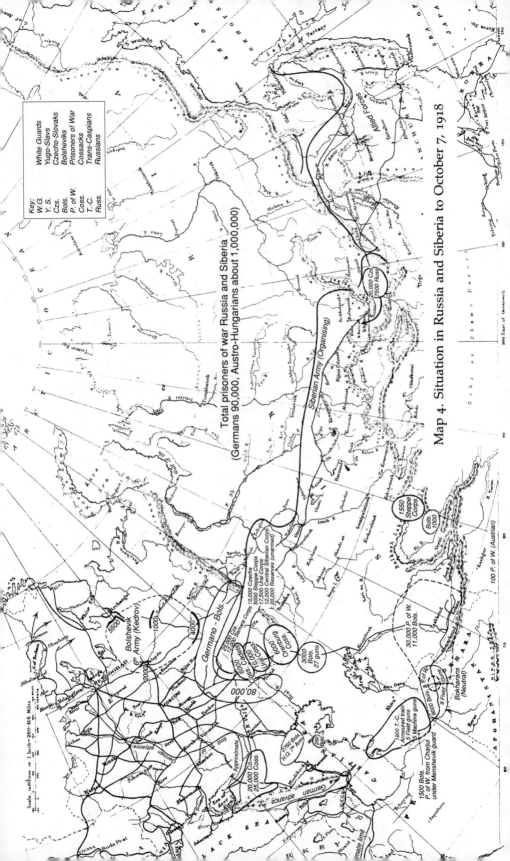

Map 4. Situation in Russia and Siberia to October 7, 1918

Key:
W.G.   White Guards
Y.S.   Yugo-Slavs
Czs.   Czecho-Slovaks
Bols. Bolsheviks
P. of W. Prisoners of War
Coss. Cossacks
T.-C. Trans-Caspians
Russ. Russians

Total prisoners of war Russia and Siberia
(Germans 90,000, Austro-Hungarians about 1,000,000)

Scale 1:8,650,000 or 1 Inch=250–416 Miles

Siberian Army (Organising)

Allied Forces

Bolshevik 6th Army (Kedrov)

Germano – Bols.

German advance

German advance

Approximate

they said that they could not "abandon their helpless friends to certain massacre and pillage."[5] Lansing now had information from reliable sources that the peaceable Russian citizens of Moscow, Petrograd, and other cities were suffering from an openly avowed campaign of mass terrorism—the Red Terror—and were subject to wholesale executions. Lansing believed that all civilized nations should register their abhorrence of such barbarism in order to check the further increase of the indiscriminate slaughter of Russian citizens.[6] Moreover, Lansing feared that the United States would be generally criticized if it told the Czechs that it was their duty, regardless of their Russian allies, to join their compatriots in Siberia. Revealing his perplexity to Wilson, Lansing wrote: "We cannot abandon the Czecho-Slovaks on the ground that they will not abandon their Russian friends. Of course that would never do. And yet, what is the alternative, or is there any?"[7]

The situation was complicated by a complete turnabout in Masaryk's views. Whereas a few days earlier he had assured Lansing that he agreed thoroughly with the American position against the reestablishment of the Eastern Front and that he did not believe that the United States could count upon the Russians reorganizing as a military force, he was now presenting a totally different view. Masaryk now asked support for a larger army to assist the Czechs and indicated that it was the only way to hold that part of Russia leading up to Archangel and to save Siberia from the Germans. Masaryk insisted that the plan he proposed did not "in any way imply the restoration of the Russian Front."[8]

Wilson found himself in a quandary. On September 24, he discussed Russia at some length with House, and together they "looked at the map and tried to find what was best for the Czech Army . . . to do in the circumstances."[9] As he pondered over a response to Morris's proposals and to Masaryk's plea for further aid, the British requested the views of the United States concerning the immediate training of those Russian officers and volunteers who were willing to support the Allies.[10] Wilson instructed Lansing to urge that action be withheld pending Janin's arrival in Siberia.[11] At this crucial point the French government presented the formal request by Clemenceau and supported by Foch, but not sanctioned by the military representatives of the Supreme War Council, that the American government send five additional battalions to Archangel to be put at General Poole's disposal.[12]

Wilson's response was an immediate, firm refusal. Then after considering the entire Russian and Siberian situation with great care and discussing it with House and General March, Wilson, on September 26, typed a series of memoranda to Lansing defining American policy. He disapproved definitively of Graves's suggestion that he establish himself at Omsk or at some other point in the far interior. However, he did authorize Graves to establish his headquarters at some place such as Harbin, where he could be in touch with an open port during the winter and from whence he could make the best use of his force to safeguard the railways and keep the eastward routes open for the Czechs. Moreover, although all available supplies that could be spared from the Western Front were to be moved forward as fast as possible for the use of the Czech forces, they would not be sent west of the Urals, despite Masaryk's plea. Wilson emphasized that American assistance could not be given to carry out any other program, and he concluded: "All that the British Commander at Archangel expected to happen upon the sending of Allied and American troops to the northern ports has failed of realization and this Government cannot cooperate in an effort to establish lines of operation and defense through from Siberia to Archangel."[13]

Wilson instructed Lansing to convey his views to Francis and Morris. Specifically, Francis was to be informed that he should act "on the certain assumption that no more American troops will be sent to the northern ports." He should be told that, "it being in our view plain that no gathering of any effective force by the Russians is to be hoped for, we shall insist with the other Governments, so far as our cooperation is concerned, that all military effort in that part of Russia be given up except the guarding of the ports themselves and as much of the country round about them as may develop threatening conditions." This information was also to be sent to London, Paris, Rome, and to Allied representatives at Vladivostok and Archangel. Finally, Wilson noted: "Please make it clear to Morris that the ideas and purposes of the Allies with respect to what should be done in Siberia and 'on the Volga Front' are ideas and purposes with which we have no sympathy and that the representatives of the Allies at Vladivostok are trying their best to 'work' General Graves and every other American in sight and [the Allies] should be made to understand that there is absolutely 'nothing doing.'"[14] Lansing sent a forceful though modified reply to Morris's proposal in which he concluded: "You will please impress upon the military, naval, and civil authorities of the United States Government at Vladivostok that, notwithstanding any pressure to the contrary, they are expected to be governed wholly and absolutely by the policy of this Government as expressed herein."[15] On the following day, Lansing informed Francis that the United States did "not consider that its efforts to safeguard supplies at Archangel or to help the Czechs in Siberia have created a state of war with the Bolsheviki."[16]

The Allied response to Wilson's virtual ultimatum was scarcely conciliatory. Masaryk immediately registered his protests and explained his unwillingness to acquiesce in the American policy. He declared that the statement of September 27 was a radical change from Wilson's statement of August 3. Why, he asked, had the earlier statement been canceled at a time "when the whole situation, political and military, is changing so favorably?" He was reluctant to decide such important strategic questions so far from the scene of action and in the light of continually changing military events. He considered it absolutely vital to hear the opinions of Janin, then on his way to Vladivostok, as well as of the Allied commanders in Siberia, before he could agree to abandon the territory west of the Ural Mountains.

Masaryk suggested that the recent reverses of the Germans in the west and the promising developments on the Eastern Front might very well lower the "Germano- and Austro-Philism" of the Bolsheviks: "I would use this change and try to get paid for the retirement, to put it bluntly." He recognized that this was not an easy diplomatic job but said that he would try anything to "help our common cause." He added, "I explained clearly enough my views of the Bolsheviks; I do not agree with them and their tactics, but, if I may use one of President Wilson's utterances about Mexico, I would speak even with the Devil. It is my conviction that the attitude of the Allies toward the Bolsheviks has been a wrong one from the beginning; it was and is not right to withdraw from Russia and leave her and the Bolsheviks entirely to the Germans and Austrians."[17] Masaryk was clearly in a very difficult position. Obviously, if Allied policy regarding the Czechs differed from Wilson's, he was faced with the dilemma of whose policy he must direct his Czechs to follow. He consulted with both Wiseman and House, but there appeared to be no way out of the impasse.[18]

The British War Cabinet was thrown into something of a quandary upon receipt of Lansing's memorandum. Balfour immediately asked the British military authorities whether they would be able to do anything in Europe and Russia if America actually refused to help beyond the point she had indicated. Cecil was eager to know whether the Japanese and the French alone could supply the Czechs with everything necessary to achieve their objectives. Balfour had serious doubts. Although the War Cabinet considered the possibility of simply continuing its current policy without giving any information to Wilson, it finally decided to send a dispatch to Washington.[19]

Accordingly, the British Foreign Office informed the State Department that the American decision to hold its troops in eastern Siberia would not affect Britain's determination to aid the Czechs in holding their position west of the Urals and assisting those Russians who had been loyal to the Allies throughout the war. If the Czechs withdrew to the east of the Urals, the "loyal" Russians would be left to the mercy of their enemies. Therefore, the British government intended to continue its efforts in their behalf and to ask the French and Japanese to do the same. The Foreign Office added, somewhat plaintively, that it hoped that the United States would not discourage the other Allies from helping the British.[20]

The French were less conciliatory. Jusserand expressed his resentment to Lansing on September 28.[21] While accepting the President's right to have his own "less optimistic opinion" on the question, Jusserand asked: "But how can one justify decisions by which not only the hoped-for-aid is refused but by which the realization of our hopes by our own methods is rendered more difficult. It is no longer a question of advancing or staying where we are but of abandoning what we now hold and have great interest in protecting." Moreover, a retreat without a fight would run the risk of a massacre. In that event, said Jusserand: "This blood will be on your head, not on ours, and it will be a grave responsibility to have caused these deaths." Such an attitude caused the "sharpest pain" to the Allies, and Jusserand hoped that the President would not oppose the efforts of the Allies to avoid the misfortunes predicted by the President and to take advantage of whatever circumstances might develop to achieve Allied objectives.[22] The Allies now began to pursue their own plans to rehabilitate the Volga front. A small detachment of British and French troops proceeded westward to cooperate with the Czechs on the Volga,[23] presumably to expedite the movement of Czecho-Slovaks from eastern Siberia to the west, which had begun from Vladivostok on September 9.[24] Francis, deeply sympathetic to Allied efforts, proposed to organize an American-Slavic Legion at the request of many Russians who professed preference for such service over that in similar legions being organized by the French and British.[25] Wilson had "very serious doubts about the American Slavic Legion" and suggested that Francis be "asked to consider the consequences which may follow."[26]

Although Wilson had disapproved of any plan to lend American military assistance to the Czechs on the Volga front or in north Russia, he had given McCormick full authority to implement the plans for economic aid to the Czechs.[27] He had also approved the department's plan for a loan to the Czechs. There seemed to be no legal drawback to a loan now that the Czecho-Slovak government had been recognized as a de facto belligerent government at war with Germany and since it urgently needed funds to make purchases in the United States in order to prosecute the war.[28] On October 5, Wilson authorized a $5,000,000 credit for the Czecho-Slovak government, to be used by McCormick to finance supplies to the Czecho-Slovaks in Russia, pending the establishment of formal de jure relations with the Czecho-Slovak government.[29]

Meanwhile, the military situation throughout Siberia continued to deteriorate. Samara faced a military crisis. According to Consul Alfred R. Thomson, the Czechs and the Russians were tired from "weeks of constant fighting [an enemy] five times superior numerically," with no new forces to relieve them and at a time when the "German officers were making a new army out of the enemy." He pleaded desperately for additional help, not only to prevent the Volga front from falling into the hands of the Germans, but also to prevent German domination of the whole country.[30] Girsa informed Graves that daily reports from the commanders on the Volga front were showing more and more clearly the tragic situation of the Czech troops. They had been living for nine months in filthy boxcars and suffered from overwork, a lack of food that had reduced them to extreme weakness, and a total lack of sanitary provisions. They had been fighting continuously for the last four months because they had no replacements. Nevertheless, they had informed Girsa that they would do their duty to the end, despite their total exhaustion. They requested that their "Father," Masaryk, be informed that all "to the last man preferred death rather than to tarnish the honor and glory of the Czecho-Slovak Army." To Girsa, it seemed clear beyond any doubt that the die was cast for the Czech troops, and that their loss was to be expected.[31]

Syrový had decided to retreat from the Volga front toward Ufa and to direct all Czech forces coming from the east toward the region of Ekaterinburg in an offensive aimed at occupying Perm and fortifying themselves there. He described the situation as very critical and the arrival of Allied reinforcements as an absolute necessity.[32] At this grave juncture, General Poole informed Francis that he was going to England himself for thirty days to explain the seriousness of the Russian situation but that he would surely return. Francis doubted this, since it was

Czech troops outside city limits of Ekaterinburg, Russia (National Archives)

rumored that Trotskii had asserted that after dispersing the Czecho-Slovaks on the Volga front and throughout Siberia, he would next turn his attention to Archangel.[33]

The situation had become so critical, especially at Samara, that the city was being evacuated with the probable loss of the entire district. The Czechs, however, continued to wait and hope for Allied and American assistance. In desperation, Jameson urged immediate confirmation of "American failure to advance so that large bodies of Czechs may not wait for expected assistance and be annihilated."[34] Frantic appeals were coming from all Siberian, Czech, and Slovak associations to send at least one hundred American soldiers by special train to Ekaterinburg and Cheliabinsk to encourage the Czechs, who were losing their morale because the expected aid was not arriving.[35] Syrový transmitted an urgent message to the American government describing the crisis facing the Czechs on the Volga, the political and military importance of Samara, and the fact that loss of the city would mean the loss of all southern Russia. He concluded: "We cannot believe that all our work is going to be frustrated and I count on your aid."[36]

The British had been deeply distressed over the failure to augment Allied efforts in Siberia. The War Cabinet was convinced that it was "absolutely necessary" to change Allied policy in Siberia, even if the objective were "restricted to the rescue of the Czecho-Slovak troops and their transfer to Vladivostok and to France." To that end, the British embassy once again approached the State Department with a plan for the reorganization of the Allied machinery for the administration of aid in Siberia.[37] However, Wilson's position remained firm. Realizing this, the British, and the French, also, now pinned their hopes on Japan, and in mid-September both Knox and Clemenceau made separate urgent appeals to the Japanese government for a massive intervention. The British note delivered to Japan on October 16 reiterated the British position, namely that the Japanese push on at least to Omsk. Japan's response completely killed any further idea of decisive intervention. On October 23, the Japanese government replied that it was not interested in restoring Russia as a great power, that it had its own interests to pursue in Siberia, and that it would not act in accordance with Allied wishes.[38]

As Allied efforts on the Eastern Front deteriorated, their situation on the Western Front improved dramatically. On September 29, Bulgaria collapsed. The Austro-Hungarian monarchy was now exposed and vulnerable from the south because the main burden of defending the southeastern flank against the rapidly advancing Allied armies rested on the ragged, demoralized Austrian army. It was the beginning of the end. The Crown Council met in Vienna on September 27 and decided to send a second note to Washington.[39] That note, sent on October 7, asked for an armistice on the basis of the Fourteen Points, the four principles of Wilson's address of February 12, and his speech at the Metropolitan Opera on September 27. The Kaiser's government had appealed to Wilson for an armistice on October 6.[40]

Lansing immediately advised Wilson to refuse to conclude an armistice or to enter into negotiations with the Austro-Hungarian government until after it had met certain conditions: an unconditional acceptance of the principles that Wilson had laid down, withdrawal from all occupied territory, denouncement of the treaties of Brest-Litovsk and Bucharest, and a declaration that these acts would be performed regardless of the course pursued by Germany—that is on the basis of a separate peace.[41] Rather than rejecting the German overture in a peremptory fashion, Lansing initially favored holding out at least a ray of hope that the war could be ended if the German war lords would comply with reasonable military demands and if Germany would accept democracy. In other words, Lansing advocated playing upon the hopes of the German people and on the despair of the Austro-Hungarians, clearly giving "the impression that we intend to end forever the Austro-Hungarian Empire."[42]

The Vatican was deeply concerned over the possible dissolution of the Austro-Hungarian Empire, and it began frenzied activity to prevent the worst. Appeals and interventions were made in several directions, either to American representatives in Rome or through Cardinal Gibbons in America.[43] Not only the Pope, but also Austro-Hungarian statesmen and Masaryk believed that the destiny of the Habsburgs was in Wilson's hands. Fully aware of Point Ten, they awaited Wilson's reply to the Austrian note with great anticipation. At the same time, to forestall Wilson's intervention in Austria's internal affairs, projects for federalization were discussed endlessly. Julius Andrássy, the last Austro-Hungarian Foreign Minister, wrote: "Wilson was to be convinced by means of a *fait accompli* that there was determination to adapt the situation to his principles."[44]

On October 11, Andrássy went to Switzerland to get into contact with the Allied diplomats, but the British and French Ministers in Bern refused to see him unless he brought a message of capitulation.[45] Andrássy was followed by Tarnowski, who failed to get in touch with Stovall.[46] Lammasch was asked to see Herron to relay to Washington Austria's willingness to comply with Wilson's program. Although Herron dutifully forwarded Lammasch's telegrams, his comments on them were not calculated to incline Washington favorably toward Vienna.[47] Wilson had clearly become the arbiter, not only of peace, but also of the internal affairs of the Habsburg monarchy. His influence abroad was reaching its climax.

Herron wrote a special note to Wilson on October 14 reporting the arrival of a second telegram from Lammasch to be communicated to him personally and immediately. The note indicated that Vienna was dealing seriously with Point Ten and that it would be met in the near future. Herron advised Wilson that for the United States to treat with Austria-Hungary, or to preserve the Habsburg Empire after the pledges it had made to the nationalities, would justly be regarded by them "as a betrayal of our cause."[48] Stovall reported that not only would the Emperor issue a manifesto immediately granting autonomy and a new system of government to the people of the Dual Monarchy, but his manifesto would probably also be supported by the Kaiser himself.[49]

The Czecho-Slovak National Council knew that it faced a crucial period. A separate or premature peace would nullify all its efforts and blast all hopes for Czecho-Slovak independence. Masaryk, who had been deeply involved with seeking ways to save the Czech situation on the Volga, informed Lansing on October 14 that the Czech army at the Volga front had decided to evacuate the territory and to retire over the Urals to Ekaterinburg. This, in effect, was an affirmative response to Wilson's request of September 27. Although Masaryk had no knowledge of the strategic and political consequences of his decision, the interchange of notes with Germany and Austria had now taken precedence over all other events and was unquestionably "the great event of the war." To that end, he took the liberty of submitting to Lansing a few remarks reiterating that the principles and commitments that Wilson had already enumerated could justify only a negative response to the peace proposals of both Germany and the Austro-Hungarian Empire.[50]

On October 14, the Czecho-Slovak National Council constituted itself a provisional government with its seat in Paris and began accrediting Czecho-Slovak representatives to the Allied governments.[51] In taking such action, Beneš made it clear that he had the support and mandate of Czech representatives in Prague. The French accorded this provisional government de jure recognition on October 15.[52] On October 16, Emperor Charles, to save the dynasty, issued a manifesto proclaiming that Austria would become a federal state in which each "race" would be free to establish its own body politic within its own territory.[53]

Wilson, however, had already made up his mind. Before the Swedish Minister had transmitted the second Austro-Hungarian note, Wilson stressed to Sir Eric Geddes, First Lord of the Admiralty, on October 7 and 13, and to Wiseman the "absolute necessity" for the breakup of the monarchy because of American commitments to the oppressed nationalities, specifically the Czecho-Slovaks.[54] When Geddes suggested that the Austrian government might bring representatives of the various nationalities to the peace conference, Wilson replied: "We have already recognized Masaryk. . . . We cannot listen to anybody else."[55]

In the meantime, Masaryk had been hard at work preparing a Czecho-Slovak declaration of independence with the help of Professor Miller and devoted American friends. Wilson had told Masaryk that no

Declaration of Independence (*Bohemian Review*)

decisions would be made concerning Austria-Hungary until he had been consulted.[56] Masaryk sent the first draft of the declaration to Lansing on October 16, noting that his decision to publish it had been made some weeks earlier because of the "insincere promises of the Austro-Hungarian Government to reorganize the Empire" but that if Wilson had any objections, he could delay publication until after Wilson had sent his answer to Charles.[57] When Lansing did not respond immediately, on October 18, Masaryk cabled the declaration to Beneš in Paris. Numerous copies were then multigraphed, and a special type-written copy was made for Wilson.[58]

The Czecho-Slovak declaration of independence was designed to nullify Emperor Charles's manifesto promising federalization and autonomy to the dissatisfied nationalities and was therefore partly polemical; nevertheless, those sections dealing with the ideals and hopes that animated the Czecho-Slovak leaders were eloquent and inspiring and paid tribute to the "American principles as laid down by President Wilson: the principles of liberated mankind—of the actual equality of nations—and of governments deriving all their just powers from the consent of the governed." Affirming that "no people should be forced to live under sovereignty they do not recognize," the declaration ringingly affirmed that freedom was the first prerequisite for federalization. While rejecting federalization within the Habsburg Empire, Masaryk expressed the hope that the free nations of Central and Eastern Europe might easily federate, "should they find it necessary," after they had achieved their freedom.[59]

Even as Masaryk released his declaration to the world, Wilson was hard at work composing his reply to Austria. He typed the final draft of the note to Austria-Hungary on his own typewriter. His note emphasized that he could no longer entertain the suggestion concerning federalization presented by the Austro-Hungarian government "because of certain events of the utmost importance" that had occurred since the delivery of his Fourteen Points Address and his enunciation of Point Ten. Wilson continued: "Since that sentence was written and uttered to the Congress of the United States the Government of the United States has recognized the belligerency of the Czecho-Slovak forces operating in Siberia and has consented to deal with the Czecho-Slovak Council as with an independent national authority and has also recognized in the fullest manner the justice of the national aspirations of the Jugo-Slavic peoples."[60]

Wilson was therefore no longer at liberty to accept mere "autonomy of these peoples as the basis of peace." Wilson asked Lansing to revise his statement in a "more official and definite manner." Significantly, in doing so, Lansing removed Wilson's direct reference to the "belligerency of the Czecho-Slovak forces operating in Siberia" as the major factor in bringing about the revision of Point Ten and substituted for it the following general statement:

> The United States has recognized that a state of belligerency exists between the Czecho-Slovaks and the German and Austro-Hungarian Empires and that the Czecho-Slovak National Council is a *de facto* belligerent Government. . . . The President is therefore, no longer at liberty to accept the mere 'autonomy' of these peoples as a basis of peace, but is obliged to insist that they, and not he, shall be the judges of what action on the part of the Austro-Hungarian Government will satisfy their aspirations and their conceptions of their rights.[61]

Wilson's reply "struck Vienna like lightning." "It caused a panic at court and in the Ministry of Foreign Affairs. It was . . . the death sentence of the Habsburg Dynasty" and completed "the demoralization of the country."[62] Local administrative parliaments were being organized as quickly as possible by the Czechs, Germans, Ruthenians, Poles, and Yugoslavs despite vain appeals to the people from Vienna to retain the current governmental administration until new ones could be created to take their places. Moreover, shortly after Wilson's reply had been received in Austria-Hungary, Stránskí, a Czech leader, announced that all negotiations with the government of the Czecho-Slovaks must be addressed to the National Council in Paris, inasmuch as the 150 delegates of the Czech people in the Parliament of Austria no longer regarded themselves as authorized to negotiate on behalf of the Czecho-Slovak nation. In addition, the Czech leaders and the Czech delegates in the Parliament under the presidency of Kramář had recently held a conference at Prague and had adopted resolutions proclaiming that the new state was to be democratic in principle and treat all peoples of the state with justice, without distinction of "race."[63]

In the meantime, the military situation was disintegrating. On October 24, the Italians struck at the Austrian lines all the way from Trentino to the Adriatic. Within a week, the resistance of the Austrian army collapsed completely, the army disintegrated, and the soldiers headed home in a disorderly rout. On October 21, the German members of the Reichsrat, basing themselves on the Emperor's manifesto, declared the German Austrian territories an independent state and themselves the Provisional National Assembly. Two days later, the Hungarian National Council was formed in Budapest under Count Michael Károlyi. Because the Emperor was unable to save the situation, the government headed by Baron Max von Hussarek was replaced on October 26 with one under Lammasch. It became known as the Ministry of Liquidation.[64]

Andrássy had been apppointed Foreign Minister with the task of saving what he could. Seeing only "one way out of the difficulty" and "with a heavy heart," he began negotiations for a rapid and immediate peace. This meant betraying the forty-year-old Austro-German alliance which his father had helped to create.[65] On October 27, Charles telegraphed the Kaiser of his irrevocable determination to propose within twenty-four hours a *separate peace* and an immediate armistice.[66]

On October 28, Andrássy asked the Swedish government to send Washington a note accepting Wilson's conditions as a basis for peace.[67] The Czecho-Slovaks and Yugoslavs assumed Andrássy's note released them from allegiance to the Empire and proceeded to set up their own governments. On October 28, a bloodless revolution occurred in Prague, thanks largely to the perfection of the Maffia's organization. That evening, the Czech National Committee in Prague issued its first "law," which began: "The independent Czech-Slovak state has come into being." An accompanying manifesto exhorted the Czech people to preserve law and order and make themselves worthy of their "liberators, Masaryk and Wilson."[68] On October 30, unaware of the Prague declaration, the Slovak National Council declared independence and union with the Czechs.[69] The Croatians, Rumanians, and Ukrainians within the Empire quickly followed the Czech and Slovak examples.

While the Habsburg Empire was falling apart under the influence of his principle, Wilson, hardly conscious of it, was grappling uneasily with the Andrássy note. The formal notes from the Swedish legation had arrived on October 29.[70] Meanwhile, leading political figures in Bohemia and in the United States were urging the unconditional surrender of both Germany and Austria-Hungary and the immediate freeing of the subject races.[71] In a blistering note to Lansing, Masaryk denounced Vienna's response.[72] After scanning it hastily, Lansing sent Masaryk's comments to Wilson and asked him to return them after reading them.[73] Wilson, however, was already engaged in drafting a reply to the Austro-Hungarian note. It stated quite simply that he understood the Austrian note to mean that Vienna had consented to deal with the Czecho-Slovaks and the Yugoslavs, and that he would submit its request for an armistice to the Allied governments for their consideration.[74] On October 30, Lansing submitted a counterdraft, and the question was still in the process of discussion in the Cabinet when another note arrived from Andrássy, addressed personally to Lansing and begging him desperately to intercede with Wilson to grant Austria an immediate armistice to end the futile slaughter.[75] Lansing immediately sent Andrássy's note to Wilson, whom he asked what course of action he deemed advisable.[76] After an hour-long conference with Baker and Lansing on October 31, Wilson decided to send no reply to Vienna but to reply orally through the Swedish Minister that the Austrian request would be referred to the Allied governments.[77]

In the meantime, the Austrian commander in chief had already initiated armistice negotiations directly with the Italians. Grew, who had accompanied House, Wilson's special representative in Paris, had the satisfaction of translating the text of the Austro-Hungarian note of surrender when it arrived. On November 3, in the Villa Giusti near Padua, an armistice was signed. It went into effect twenty-four hours later. The proud House of Habsburg-Lorraine, which had ruled Austria for six centuries and Bohemia and Hungary for four, had formally come to an end.[78]

The entire National Council had every reason to feel proud of its achievements when, alone of the succession states, Czechoslovakia was represented by Beneš in the plenary session of the Supreme War Council at Versailles on November 4, when armistice terms were drawn up. Beneš himself was in a state of high excitement on that afternoon when he took his seat in a motor car decorated with the Czech flag and drove through Paris to Versailles. It was hard for him to believe that three years before he had escaped across the frontiers of Bohemia, crawling through the thickets to avoid being seen by the Austrian-Bavarian police and staking his whole future on what destiny might bring. Now he sat in conference with the representatives of France, Great Britain, the United States, Italy, Japan, Serbia, Greece, Belgium, and Portugal to decide with them the fate of the empires of William and Charles, and to sign the terms of their capitulation.[79]

Before his departure for Europe, Masaryk bade farewell to all those persons who had supported his efforts in Washington. In his farewell address, Masaryk emphasized the importance of the United States in the regeneration of Eastern Europe and also the need for a strong and independent Russia. By this time, the National Assembly at Prague had proclaimed Masaryk President. In addition, Wilson had authorized a loan of $7,000,000 to the Czecho-Slovak National Council.[80] Masaryk sailed for England on November 20. Upon his arrival in Paris, he was received officially by President Raymond Poincaré and accorded full military honors. In various interviews, both in London and Paris, he emphasized that without a strongly organized Russia, no stable peace would be possible and that the Russia of the future must be a counterweight to Germany. He expressed his hope that the United States and the Allies would soon reach a decision regarding their policy toward Russia so that the Czecho-Slovak troops in Siberia might be released for the occupation of Slovakia.[81] Although clearly less patient with Allied vacillation in formulating a definite policy, Masaryk indicated that the Czechs would be willing to remain in Russia if the Allies would make up their minds and support them properly.[82]

In his first presidential address, delivered from the ancient royal castle in Prague on December 25, 1918, Masaryk again conveyed his deep appreciation for the support of Wilson and the American people in winning Czecho-Slovak independence. Acknowledging the Czech debt to America, he noted that the Czech liberation movement was especially grateful to the American people for money. Again, he emphasized that it was the Czech army fighting on three fronts and especially in Siberia that had "won our liberty for us."[83] Masaryk also cabled his heartfelt thanks to Wilson: "Our nation shall never forget that it was you, Mr. President, who by his kind sense of freedom and justice has brought about the disruption of the immoral state combination called Austria-Hungary and it was you by his knowledge of our right in the most critical moment has made possible the revolution which brought us our national independence."[84]

The State Department now increased its efforts to gather the necessary information to grant formal de jure recognition to the Czecho-slovak nation. Although the United States had recognized the state of belligerency between the Czecho-Slovaks and the German and Austro-Hungarian Empires and had also recognized the Czecho-Slovak National Council as a de facto belligerent government as of September 3, 1918, it had not granted formal diplomatic recognition to the Czecho-slovak government.[85] Polk thought that the Washington government should accord the republic some degree of recognition to hold it responsible for the financial advances from the Treasury Department, signed by Charles Pergler, whom Masaryk had appointed as commissioner in the United States on November 5, 1918, but Lansing disapproved.[86] He did not consider further recognition desirable, since the frontiers of the Czech state had not been definitely determined, but he did approve sending a diplomatic representative to Prague. Richard Crane, who had been so deeply supportive of Masaryk's efforts to secure recognition in Washington, was so appointed.[87] The dilemma surrounding Czechoslovakia's de jure legal status continued until the summer of 1923, when the Solicitor General of the Department of State finally decided that Lansing's letter of November 14, 1918, actually had determined the issue. At that time, Lansing had informed the Secretary of the Treasury:

> The United States Government on 3 September 1918 accorded recognition to the Czecho-Slovak National Council as a *de facto* belligerent government clothed with proper authority to direct the military and political affairs of the Czecho-Slovaks. The Czecho-Slovak National Council is, in the opinion of this Department, a foreign government engaged in war with the enemies of the United States. I am of the opinion that obligations executed at this time by President Mazaryk in the name and on behalf of the Czecho-Slovak National Council, purchased at par by the Secretary of the Treasury under the authority of the Liberty Bond Acts, will be valid and binding internationally, and such obligations will have the sanction of this Department.[88]

The office of the Solicitor General ruled that the de facto recognition of the Czecho-Slovak National Council on September 3 constituted a specific recognition of the existence of the Czechoslovak state.[89] That statement, which had been extended on the basis of Czecho-Slovak belligerency against the common enemies of the United States, became the only official recognition of the Czechoslovak republic. Yet, in the mind of Wilson, recognition was granted because of the Czecho-Slovak struggle against German and Austro-Hungarian prisoners of war in Siberia who presumably tried to prevent the Czechs from leaving Russia to join the Allies to fight for their liberation on the Western Front. Thus for both the Allies and the United States, the action of the Czecho-Slovak Legion in Russia and Siberia was the determining factor in the decision to recognize Czechoslovakia, each of course interpreting that action in the light of its own specific and conflicting aims and objectives in Russia. President Wilson refused to be drawn into the Allied schemes for reestablishing an Eastern Front or overthrowing the Bolshevik government. Indeed, within the limits of coalition diplomacy, he tried to act as a brake on his own allies. After failing to "rescue the Czechs," he sought to co-opt the Czech Legion into serving as a police force to implement the American plan to operate the Trans-Siberian and Chinese Eastern Railways and thus prevent Japan from securing control, not only of the railways, but also of northern Manchuria and eastern Siberia. So it was that American policy toward the Czechs was ultimately directed toward the American objectives of preserving the territorial integrity not only of the Soviet Union, but also of the Republic of China, as well as preserving the Open Door in northern Manchuria and eastern Siberia. Meanwhile, the response of the United States and the Allies to the belligerency of the Czecho-Slovak Legion in Russia had played the crucial role in the dissolution of the Austro-Hungarian Empire and the recognition of an independent Czechoslovak state.

19

Epilogue

Although the Armistice on the Western Front brought no change in Allied plans for the Czech Legion, Admiral Kolchak's takeover of the Omsk government on November 18 removed Czech troops from military cooperation with the White Russians. The legion gradually withdrew from the Volga front, handing it over to the Russians and retaining only the railway for its own purposes.[1] Before the Czecho-Slovak National Council could formulate its policy toward the Kolchak government, General Gajda complicated matters by announcing that he favored Kolchak to bring order and expel Bolshevism. Many of the soldiers disagreed. They refused to fight for a dictator supported by reactionaries. They looked to the Czech National Council in Russia, mostly Social Revolutionary in composition, for their orders, rather than to Gajda. However, early in 1919, Kolchak placed Gajda, although a foreigner and under thirty, in command of the Siberian army, a position he held until the tide turned against the Whites.[2]

While the State Department wrestled with the triple problem of Czech demoralization, the Kolchak coup, and the effort to secure the cooperation of the Japanese in the railway plan, Secretary Baker revealed to President Wilson his grave doubts and misgivings about the entire enterprise. Baker believed that the Czechs no longer needed military aid from the Americans. "Undoubtedly" they could be expedited to their own country, "where, of course, they ought to be." He was deeply concerned over the activities of the Japanese in Siberia. They had "seized the Chinese Eastern Railroad" and were busy building up a pro-Japanese faction among the Russians themselves. Thus the presence of the American troops in Siberia was being used by the Japanese as a cloak for their own operations there, and, said Baker: "The Czecho-Slovak people are quite lost sight of in any of the operations now taking place." Insofar as Baker understood Bolshevism, he did not like it, but if the Russians liked it, he believed that they were

Admiral Aleksandr V. Kolchak (National Archives)

entitled to have it and that it did not "lie with us to say that only ten percent of the Russian people are Bolsheviks and therefore we will assist the other ninety percent in resisting it." Moreover, Baker dreaded "to think how we should all feel if we are rudely awakened someday to a realization that Japan had gone in under our wing and so completely mastered the country that she cannot be either induced out or forced out by any action either of the Russians or the Allies."[3]

Japan now had 72,400 men in Siberia and northern Manchuria, all of them under the direct control of the General Staff in Tokyo.[4] The United States continued to protest vigorously against Japanese actions; at the same time, it sought to place the railways under international military control and to operate them through the Russian Railway Service Corps. After months of patient negotiation and an internal struggle within the Japanese government, an Inter-Allied Railway Agreement was finally reached.[5] Wilson regarded the railway plan as of "inestimable value to the people of Russia and the United States, as well as the world in general."[6] This agreement changed completely the character of intervention in Siberia. The primary concern of American military forces became the restoration and protection of the railways instead of the rescue of the Czechs, who were now participating in the execution of the railway plan. In effect, the improvement of the transportation system served to aid the anti-Bolshevik cause and, despite its denials, the United States became an active participant in the Russian Civil War.[7]

The situation in Siberia was complicated for Wilson by the action of the other Allied leaders, who had supported the establishment of Kolchak's government. As the peace conference neared its end, reports arrived in Paris that Kolchak was doing well in his struggle against the Bolsheviks, and both the British and Wilson's own subordinates brought heavy pressure to bear on him to give support and recognition to Kolchak. Kolchak, however, was supported by independent Cossack leaders, who used the chaotic conditions in Siberia as a means of increasing their own wealth and power. The Cossacks also destroyed railway transportation, interrupted telegraphic communications, and terrorized the eastern regions. Furthermore, Japan directly encouraged and supported the Cossacks.[8] At the same time, the Kolchak authorities were provoked by what they regarded as the "unneutral" policy of American troops. Kolchak's government at Omsk stated flatly that American troops were accomplishing no useful purpose in Siberia and even accused them of pro-Bolshevik activities. The British and French governments sustained the objections of the Omsk government.[9]

Wilson was obviously deeply troubled about the entire Siberian situation. He presented his problem to the Council of Four in Paris. Wilson's dilemma was quite evident. Although he favored a neutral policy in both northern Russia and Siberia, at the same time he did not wish to withdraw American soldiers from Siberia and leave Japan in control. Under heavy pressure, Wilson finally agreed to offer support to Kolchak, although he insisted that democratic pledges be secured from him. Wilson's discussions in the Council of Four, however, clearly indicated that he had no confidence in the entire enterprise, nor in Allied or Japanese motivations for promoting it. [10]

General Janin supported Wilson's views. On February 1, 1919, Janin reported to Paris that the Russians were sabotaging absolutely everything he did, even Czech evacuation. [11] Deeply distressed with the incompetence and incapacity, to say nothing of the factional quarrels of the Kolchak regime, Janin became completely disillusioned with its capacity to launch an offensive against the Bolsheviks, and he so informed his superiors in Paris. [12] Initially, the Czechs found the guarding of the railway an easy enough assignment. However, with the increased claims on the peasants by the Kolchak regime and the decrease in the popularity of the Czech guardians, the Siberians began to form partisan detachments and attack the railway. Thus the Czechs were soon involved in fighting again, and they detested engaging in antipartisan operations on behalf of the Kolchak regime. Consequently, they were bone tired, eager to return home, and on the verge of mutiny. On April 19, Štefánik, on his return journey to Czechoslovakia, telegraphed Janin to withdraw the legion from guard duty and concentrate it around Irkutsk to be ready for the final evacuation. At the same time, the French government sent orders that in effect instructed the Czechs to take part in the final military action against the Bolsheviks. Janin decided to obey the orders of his home government and to ignore those from Štefánik. From this point on, the Czechs and the Allies were engaged in a kind of see-saw action: Should the legion be evacuated or not? [13]

The Czechs at home and Beneš, who was in Paris representing the new republic at the peace conference, were quite content with the position of the legion in Siberia. As long as it did practically no fighting, it was a useful reminder to the victorious Allies that the Czechs were still operating in their behalf and that they deserved benevolent treatment. However, there was no clear Czech-Allied agreement on the legion, and while the Czechs wished it to remain passive, the Allies had other plans. On May 9, 1919, Clemenceau asked Janin point blank whether Czech morale had been restored and whether the legion could be sent to the front. Janin made another round of inspections, held consultations with Czech officers, and responded in the negative. Clearly this report did not impress the Allies in Paris.

Then suddenly the Czechs themselves manifested their hostility to any further fighting. On June 13, 1919, Janin reported large-scale mutinies among the Czechs. He telegraphed Beneš of the absolute necessity of evacuating the legion.[14] Toward the close of June 1919, the Allies recognized that the situation at the front was serious. They agreed that the legion should make a last effort to save the hard-pressed Whites. Since Janin had reported that the Czechs would not fight directly, the Allies discussed "indirect plans." As early as June 11, Winston S. Churchill, the new British War Minister, had suggested a plan by which 30,000 of the Czechs might fight their way to Archangel and be repatriated there by British shipping, while the remainder worked their way to Vladivostok.[15] Actually, Churchill believed that a plan of evacuation by southern Russia was preferable. The legion would fight its way through the Bolshevik front and join General Anton I. Denikin, around whom British military hopes were now centered. From thence evacuation would be easy. The plan was ingenious on paper; the Czechs would get their evacuation, the Allies much needed troops, and the Whites a morale booster—for this evacuation implied that the Bolshevik front would be broken. By this time, Stevens found the Czech predicament dangerous. He feared that the legion's dissatisfaction would lead them to defy their officers and make a deal with the Bolsheviks to go home.[16] Morris agreed. The American mission in Paris was also deeply concerned about Czech demoralization. Both McCormick and Lansing agreed that the Czech troops had to be repatriated immediately.[17] However, Kramář, Prime Minister and now head of the Czechoslovak peace delegation, had indicated his support of a plan similar to Churchill's. He believed that the overland plan offered the quickest and earliest way of getting the Czechs home. Kramář, a longtime Russophile, was particularly eager to have the Czechs render this last service to Russia.[18] Apparently Churchill was able to persuade Beneš of the efficacy of his plan, and so it was that, on July 9, Janin received orders for evacuation via Archangel or southern Russia.[19]

Janin immediately refused his consent. Churchill's plan made no sense to him. The Archangel alternative was out of the question, if only for psychological reasons. The southern Russian alternative presumed a first-class fighting force to pierce the front and march some 500 miles to the territories under General Denikin's control.[20] On July 10, General

Syrový informed Janin that the Czechs would not fight. Janin sent the message to Paris.[21] Foreign Minister Pichon agreed to the evacuation of the Czecho-Slovak troops, but only if the Americans would send a few troops to reinforce the Japanese. General Bliss said no, because the American troops had been sent to Siberia to help the Czechs to leave it. Once the Czechs were evacuated, he said, there would be no pretext to justify the retention of American troops in the country. Pichon responded that if the United States would not take on the task, it remained for the Japanese to do so; otherwise the whole country "would become a prey to Bolshevism." Keishiro Matsui, one of the Japanese representatives at the Paris Peace Conference, agreed to ask Japan to assume responsibility for guarding the Siberian railroad.[22] Given Morris's view that, despite the railway plan, the Japanese were continuing "in their organized attempt to take possession of the Chinese Eastern and Trans-Siberian railways as far as Chita and thus dominate eastern Siberia and northern Manchuria," there was little likelihood that the President would be sympathetic to the proposal.[23] Indeed, Wilson personally felt that the Japanese presence would "stiffen the Bolshevik resistance to a greater degree than they would help Kolchak."[24]

On July 17, some one thousand wounded, sick, and disabled Czecho-Slovak troops from Siberia, who had been evacuated early by American ships across the Pacific, arrived in Washington, where the President had agreed to review and address them. The President extended a cordial welcome to this "brilliant detachment," noting: "From afar we have watched your deeds and have been moved to admiration of your actions under the most adverse of circumstances." He went on:

> In the history of the modern world, and perhaps in all history, there is no more wonderful or brilliant record than the withdrawal of your forces in opposition to the armies of Germany and Austria through a population which developed an hostility, and the march of your armies for thousands of miles across the great regions of Siberia, keeping steadfastly in mind the necessity for order and organization.
> You are returning now to your native land, today a free and independent country. May you take back with you that stamina which you so well manifested all through your trying experiences in Russia and Siberia.[25]

In Siberia, the remainder of the Czechs, some 50,000 strong, dominated the Siberian railway from Irkutsk to Omsk. They were living in boxcars at various points along the railway and efficiently guarding their part of the railway. They were determined not to spend another winter in Siberia.[26] By this time it was clear that no one, not even Beneš, was willing to urge the Czech soldiers to fight. Indeed, there was no certainty that a peaceful evacuation could be secured. The Czechs sent several delegations to Prague to request their evacuation, and the Czech government now made clear that it would not consent to the Czecho-Slovak Legion fighting its way out eastwards unless the British government would guarantee that the Allied expedition operating from Archangel would remain in northern Russia until the legion's arrival. Prague was now under strong political pressure, and evacuation would have to be carried out. To complicate matters, one of the local leaders in Siberia, Pavlů, suddenly changed his mind on the urgency of evacuation and postponed the final decision once more.[27] Since Janin's orders from Paris bade him to keep the Czech corps in Siberia, he proceeded to seize on the Pavlů plan as a last hope. The plan was little more than a slightly modified version of the Churchill-Beneš proposals.[28] Encouraged by Denikin's successes, Pavlů dreamed of joining him in the joy ride to Moscow. Kramář had also come out in support of the plan. Thus it appeared to have the Czechoslovak government's backing. To create a suitable atmosphere for the march to Moscow, Pavlů sent an officer to Omsk to negotiate with the Kolchak government for incentives for the Czech soldiers. Pavlů himself started a newspaper campaign to convince the soldiers that they should march home via Russia. He urged the soldiers to help the Russian Whites in their hour of need. He also offered them danger money, for in the meantime, Kolchak, menaced by the Bolsheviks in his capital at Omsk, was willing to hand the Czechs the Russian gold reserve provided they came and got it. The scheme finally collapsed when Masaryk suddenly and unexpectedly dismissed Kramář as Prime Minister and repudiated Pavlů's plan. On July 28, 1919, after so many orders and counterorders, Janin finally agreed to begin evacuating the sick and wounded.[29]

Secretary Baker now recommended that Wilson discontinue American military cooperation in Siberia, on the grounds that the Czecho-Slovak forces had been rescued and that the subsequent restoration of order in Siberia was the business of the Siberian people.[30] Long and Lansing insisted that the withdrawal note to Japan must clearly spell out the strong differences between the United States and Japan on the implementation of policy in Siberia.[31] Wilson approved the note in principle.[32] As finally sent on August 30, 1919, the American note to Japan carefully reviewed the events that had led to intervention and the later developments that had contributed to the making of the Inter-Allied Railway Agreement. Citing the major differences existing between the United States and Japan in regard to Siberian policy, the note frankly placed the blame for the failure of the railway plan upon Japanese lack of cooperation.[33] In the meantime, the Czechs remained in Siberia with their French Commander in Chief, torn between following the orders of the Czechs and the French. By this time repatriation had become a burning political question in Czechoslovakia—one which might possibly result in an overthrow of the government. On August 26, 1919, Janin received still another telegram from Beneš urging him to start general evacuation.[34]

The American mission in Paris agreed on the importance of providing transportation and financial assistance to insure the return of the Czech troops. Phillips now devised a plan to advance additional credits to the Czechoslovak government up to twelve million dollars, which was the estimated cost of repatriating 50,000 men. With the President's approval, Phillips intended to advise Polk to request that Great Britain and France each bear one-fourth of such a loan. He urged the President to authorize the Shipping Board to set aside the necessary tonnage for the movement. He insisted that the political and moral considerations in this particular instance were paramount even to the urgent demand on commercial routes for the vessels that had been engaged in returning American troops from France.[35] Phillips also pressed the matter with Carter Glass, Secretary of the Treasury, requesting his help.[36] Wilson immediately approved Phillips's proposal.[37]

Although the military situation at Omsk appeared unchanged, the Czechs were increasingly restless and more openly antagonistic to the Kolchak government, which had formally recognized both Kalmikov and Semenov in eastern Siberia. It was impossible for American agencies to cooperate with these atamans. Thus the Americans found themselves in disagreement not only with Japanese policy, but also with the official representatives of the Kolchak government in eastern Siberia. Morris noted: "We thus have the doubly anomalous situation that the Czechs, by their presence are responsible for the continued existence of a Government against which they are now intriguing while we are endeavoring to find means of cooperation with a government many of whose representatives are openly hostile."[38]

On September 25, probably after another contradictory order, Janin tried again to bargain with Beneš over the evacuation of the Czechs. But Beneš was no longer in a position to bargain. The problem of the "forgotten Czech legion in Siberia" had become a burning domestic

issue in Prague. Wives and relatives of the soldiers lobbied their deputies in Parliament, and street rioting broke out. Frightened by the riots,
the Czech government issued firm orders to Beneš, who passed them
on to Janin. On September 26, Janin was told to evacuate the legion
even against Allied wishes. Beneš was now apparently convinced that
"the legion was ready to shoot its way out to Vladivostok or negotiate
its passage west with the Bolsheviks." This threat of mutiny finally
decided the issue. On September 29, detailed orders of evacuation
went out to all Czech units in Siberia.[39]

The impending withdrawal of the Czecho-Slovak troops posed
grave problems both to the Kolchak government and to the American
inspectors assigned to insure the effective operation of the Trans-
Siberian Railway in those areas guarded by the Czech troops. The
failure of the Allied governments to come to any decision concerning
the protection of the Trans-Siberian after the departure of the Czech
troops greatly affected the entire strategical situation in Siberia.
Kolchak was forced to withdraw two of his divisions from the front for
the purpose of protecting the railway.[40] At the same time, practically all
of the original members of the Russian Railway Service Corps, including Colonel Emerson, agreed that their efforts were useless under the
existing arrangements, particularly in those areas controlled by the
Kolchak government and Kolchak's troops. There, the railway inspectors found that their instructions and orders were "in every way
ignored by officials of railways." In view of this "hopeless situation"
they requested to be relieved of their duties as soon as possible.[41]

By this time the President had become seriously ill and the State
Department had to assume full responsibility for America's Siberian
policy. To that end, despite the fact that the United States had indicated
its plans to withdraw from Siberia and to evacuate the Czechs as
rapidly as possible, Acting Secretary of State Phillips informed the
Commission to Negotiate Peace in confidence that, "as soon as President Wilson is able to attend to business the Secretary is seriously
considering recommending to him that formal recognition be granted
to the Omsk Government."[42]

In early October, Lansing sent a note to Japan requesting a reply to
the American withdrawal note of August 30. He also instructed Morris
to bring to the attention of the Japanese government the grave conditions existing in Siberia due to the activities of Japanese subordinate
military officers and Cossack leaders.[43] Yet throughout this period,
Harris continued to urge both greater assistance to and formal recognition of Kolchak. Moreover, Lansing found that it was also the "unan-

imous judgment" of his advisers to recognize the Kolchak government.[44] Lansing himself confided to his diary his reasons for opposing such recognition. He believed that the Kolchak government was not sufficiently stable, and that Kolchak's officials were corrupt, incompetent, reactionary, and without the support of the people. The only effective military power in Siberia seemed to center around the Czecho-Slovak troops, who were "desirous of returning home." If they declined to fight, Lansing believed that Kolchak would "have to retire to Irkutsk."[45] Lansing had scarcely made these observations when incoming intelligence revealed that the anti-Bolshevik forces in European Russia had recently had decisive military successes. Now more than ever before, Lansing believed that the Bolshevik government would fall. Thus it was more important than ever that Kolchak be supported. Lansing informed the mission at Paris, Stevens, and the American embassy in Tokyo: "Everything possible is being done to this end in Washington." In these circumstances, a withdrawal of the Allied railway inspectors would bring about a "most difficult situation for Admiral Kolchak at the very moment when everything else is more favorable to the success of his movement than at any time in the past." Incoming reports revealed so radical an improvement in the general situation in Siberia that Lansing felt justified in asking "that the inspectors be retained under Russian guard at least until the culmination of the critical events then taking place in European Russia."[46] Stevens's response to Lansing's plea was hesitant at first. Nevertheless, in view of Lansing's personal plea, Stevens reported on October 25: "Have no anxiety, there will [be] no abandonment [of] the work of Service Corps unless the Bolsheviks run some of them out."[47]

When Polk conferred with the other Allied leaders in Paris concerning the recognition of Kolchak, he found Pichon in full agreement. Polk suggested that the United States take the lead, since Great Britain and France were merely waiting for an opportunity to follow. Moreover, in view of all the help given Denikin by Great Britain, Polk believed that such an action would help American prestige. He added: "As Petrograd may be taken soon it would be better to grant recognition now, if you intend ultimately to grant recognition, rather than to wait."[48]

In the meantime, the Omsk government was carrying on unofficial negotiations with the Czechs to return to the front and "save the situation." Harris urged the department to use its influence, possibly with the government at Prague, in order to bring this about. He added: "With the assistance of a few thousand Czechs on this front the Bolsheviki can be definitely defeated."[49] While Poole, now head of the Russian

Division in the State Department, believed that although it would be "very desirable . . . to have Czechs remain," their return had now become a crucial political issue in Czechoslovakia. However, he agreed that Harris's appeal should be transmitted to Paris and Prague. Poole wanted the legation in Prague to make clear to the government of Czechoslovakia that negotiations were under way for the return of the Czech troops by water and that the suggestions from Siberia would not affect those negotiations; nevertheless, the department believed that if these Czech forces should loyally assist Kolchak, it might very probably mean that they would get home sooner across Russia than if they were brought by sea.[50] Apparently Allied pressure on the Czech government caused Beneš to hesitate once again. Throughout October 1919, he had sent several inquiries to Janin as to whether a limited or even large-scale action by the Czechs against the Bolsheviks could be contemplated. On October 31, Janin replied rather categorically that the Czechs would not go to the front to fight and therefore had to be evacuated as soon as possible.[51]

Even as the Allies sought to provide further support to Kolchak, his situation had begun to deteriorate. With the success of the Bolsheviks near Petrograd and the checkmating of General Denikin, it appeared the Bolsheviks had scored on all fronts and had gained a new lease on life. Although Harris assured the department that there was nothing immediately alarming, he believed it might shortly become so. Reiterating that if Kolchak fell, Bolshevism would extend at least to Lake Baikal, he pressed the department to take the initiative to urge the Prague government to issue an order for 25,000 Czechs to advance to the Siberian front and save the situation. He also urged that the Allies recognize Kolchak. Harris added, "Why do the allies delay longer? I am now satisfied that Kolchak cannot last much longer unaided. . . . The Siberian Army is fighting well, yet if the Bolsheviki continue to advance as rapidly as at present Omsk will fall in four weeks' time. It is believed that at least fifty percent of the Czech soldiers are willing to fight Bolshevism again, and thus secure their return home across European Russia."[52]

The State Department immediately sent Harris's desperate appeal to Polk in Paris. Phillips especially emphasized Harris's belief that the situation would be saved if 25,000 Czechs would join at once with Kolchak in an anti-Bolshevik offensive. Convinced that it was no longer possible to wait upon the British and French governments respecting the movement of the Czechs, he urged a proposal to the government at Prague that the United States would begin immediately the movement of a portion of the Czechs from Vladivostok by sea upon the clear understanding that "not less than 25,000 of them would at once cooperate with Kolchak in a counteroffensive against the Bolsheviks" in order to obtain a way home. Phillips added: "From our point of view this is practical." Since the President had "approved of the extension of credits and the allocation of shipping for the repatriation of the Czechs" chiefly to prevent interior political difficulties in Czechoslovakia, this aspect of the situation would be met by the repatriation of a portion of the Czecho-Slovaks. Phillips continued: "If you concur I am sure that the necessary specific authorization of the President can be obtained so that the first American ships will be at Vladivostok within sixty days ready to load Czech troops."[53] But Phillips's proposal was based upon unreliable reports from Harris in Siberia. Up until November 1, Harris was insisting that everything was all right, and he continued so to report in the face of the most positive evidence to the contrary. Major Slaughter informed Colonel Emerson of the story and indicated that the attitude of the State Department was "entirely based on the glowing reports which they were getting from Mr. Harris, when the situation on the ground was diametrically opposite to the information which he was giving them."[54]

Kolchak announced that "no matter what happened he was determined to fight on to the last."[55] In desperation, he sent a proposal to General Gajda offering to make him commander in chief of the Siberian army in return for his support. Gajda refused, stating that within a few weeks the Kolchak government would fall.[56] General Dietrichs had already resigned due to a difference of opinion about future military plans. Thus Kolchak was forced personally to assume duties as Commander in Chief.[57] The Omsk telegraph office had now been evacuated, and all ministers and governmental heads except Kolchak had left for Irkutsk.[58]

From Vladivostok, Gajda now began to plot the downfall of Kolchak. He had decided to use the Social Revolutionary party for this attempt, and, as early as September 1919, he had organized Social Revolutionary Bureaus at Krasnoyarsk, Irkutsk, and Vladivostok. The French government had apparently got wind of the projected plans and sought to abort them. Pichon telegraphed Gajda that if he consented to leave Siberia, the French representatives of all countries would have orders to receive him with all the honors due his rank. Gajda refused the invitation. He believed that it was simply another effort to get rid of him and was the result of repeated telegrams from General Janin, General Knox, and Admiral Kolchak. He professed a desire to remain with the Czecho-Slovaks until they were evacuated.[59] Although Gajda had announced that his job was to establish democratic government in Siberia, General Čeček had issued an order to Czech friends declaring that any Czech who joined Gajda would be treated as a deserter.[60]

On November 10, the Bolsheviks unexpectedly appeared in Omsk and took it with its immense stores of arms and ammunition intact. The Kolchak regime simply faded away. On November 17, Gajda led the first uprising at Vladivostok.[61] Although his attempt failed, the Social Revolutionary rebels were victorious at Krasnoyarsk and Irkutsk. The latter victories had incalculable consequences for Kolchak and even for the Czechs. Krasnoyarsk was an important railway junction, and disorders there meant delays in evacuation. On November 16, General Syrový had refused to suppress the Social Revolutionary coup but instead ordered the Czechs to take over the Trans-Siberian Railway west of the city. This meant that Kolchak and his army commanders could not move reinforcements into the contested areas.

By mid-November, the Czech Legion found its position virtually intolerable. It could no longer protect a government whose actions it had come to regard as contrary to all Czech aspirations and also to the elementary demands of humanity and justice. Under the protection of Czech bayonets, the local military were engaging in actions which the Czechs claimed would "stupefy the whole civilized world." These included the burning of villages, murders by the hundreds of "peaceable Russian inhabitants, [arrests] without trial of democratic men merely suspected of disaffection," and other injustices the Czechs found they could no longer condone. They believed that these activities were the direct result of Czech neutrality and nonintervention in Russian domestic affairs, but that this very neutrality, while conducted in good faith, had forced them to become "accomplices in crime." In these critical circumstances, Pavlů and Girsa drafted an appeal to the Allied powers describing their "intolerable situation" and once again requesting the Allies to expedite their return home. The Czech Legion affirmed that it would always be a "faithful ally," but it considered it "necessary to take all measures to inform nations of the world in what tragic moral position Czech army is being placed and the causes of this situation."[62]

At the same time, the Czechs refused to expedite Kolchak's journey eastward. Delay followed delay, for since the legion completely controlled the operation of the railway, Kolchak could only proceed eastward at its pleasure. At last something appears to have snapped in Kolchak's troubled mind, and he struck out in impotent rage at his tormenters. From Krasnoyarsk, Kolchak wired his subordinate, General Semenov, to oppose the passage of the Czechs at all costs and, if necessary, to blow up the bridges and tunnels that lay between the Czech trains and Vladivostok.[63] The Czechs, of course, intercepted this telegram, and henceforth what had been simple obstructionism became undeclared war. For the remainder of the journey to Irkutsk, Kolchak was a prisoner, his coach guarded by four Czechs by day and twelve by night.[64]

During the next few weeks, the Czechs fought first against Semenov's troops and then, together with the remnants of Kolchak's forces, against the Red Army. With one hundred Czech trains stalled west of Irkutsk, and the Fifth Red Army in hot pursuit, the problem was to get to Vladivostok with all possible speed. The Czechs turned to the systematic destruction of the very route they had so wearily guarded over the previous year and a half, blowing up tracks and leveling bridges. At this point, both the Czechs and the Bolsheviks, frustrated by this needless loss of men and the destruction of the railway, decided on a conference to establish a neutral zone between the two armies and negotiate conditions for a peace. The decision seemed a sensible and pragmatic one to the Czechs, desperate to leave Russia. Harris, however, regarded the action as treachery, particularly after the surrender of Kolchak to the "political authorities" at Irkutsk on January 15.[65] The last Czech personnel left Irkutsk on February 25, 1920. Stevens tried manfully to evacuate at least three trains a day, but even this modest number was difficult to attain in the face of Japanese opposition.[66] Lieutenant Colonel B. O. Johnson of the Railway Service Corps was now convinced that if Japanese harassment continued, the Czechs would fight anyone to get out of the "white hell" of Siberia.[67] But evacuation was at hand.

The American proposal that Britain and the United States together evacuate the entire force had been accepted by the British government on December 22.[68] General Frank T. Hines proposed to begin the American part of the operation on February 1, 1920, and to evacuate 10,000 men a month. To Lansing, the continued presence of the American forces during the operation was an obvious corollary to the plan. He believed that the United States mission would not be accomplished until the safe evacuation of the Czechs was assured "and a substantial portion of them actually afloat." Meanwhile, American troops had been withdrawn from northern Russia in June 1919. They were followed by British and other Allied contingents in October 1919.

The last American ship to evacuate the Czech Legion was the

Czecho-Slovak soldiers preparing to return home via the United States
(National Archives)

Heffron. It departed Vladivostok September 2, 1920, with 1,175 pas-
sengers, including 178 Hungarian prisoners. With its departure, the
American contribution came to an end. Under the auspices of the
United States, 34,123 Czechs were removed in the general evacuation,
3,000 invalids had crossed the United States, and 1,880 other nationals
had come out with the legion.[69] The American expedition itself
departed on April 1, 1920, while the Japanese band stood on the dock
and played, "Hard Times, Come Again No More." Japan refused to
withdraw its troops from Siberia until November 1922, and it did not
evacuate northern Sakhalin, seized as indemnity for losses at the hands
of Soviet troops, until 1925. Japan had overrun northern Manchuria and
extended its privileges and influence there. It had fought pitched

battles against the Bolsheviks. But it had detached no Russian territory. So it was that almost two years after the war ended, Woodrow Wilson was able to rescue the Czechs and to set the stage for Japanese withdrawal from Siberia without the seizure of either Russian or Chinese territory.[70]

Notes

Abbreviations Used in the Notes

CAB War Cabinet Papers, Public Record Office, London.
CPI Records of the Committee on Public Information, RG 63, National Archives, Washington, D.C.
DF Decimal File
DSNA General Records of the Department of State, National Archives, Washington, D.C.
FFM-Ar France, Foreign Ministry Archives, Paris.
FMD-Ar France, Ministry of Defense Archives, Paris.
FRUS U.S. Department of State. *Foreign Relations of the United States*. Cited by year and subtitle.
Lansing Papers U.S. Department of State. *Foreign Relations of the United States: The Lansing Papers, 1914–1920*. 2 vols. Washington, D.C., 1939–40.
LC Library of Congress, Washington, D.C.
NA National Archives, Washington, D.C.
NRCNA Naval Records Collection of the Office of Naval Records and Library, RG 45, National Archives, Washington, D.C.
Official German Documents Carnegie Endowment for International Peace. *Official German Documents Relating to the World War.* 2 vols. New York, 1923.
PRO Public Record Office, London.
PWW Link, Arthur S.; David W. Hirst; John E. Little; et al., eds. *The Papers of Woodrow Wilson*. 59 vols. to date. Princeton, N.J., 1966–.
RG Record Group
RWWC Russian War Work Collection, YMCA Archives, University of Minnesota, St. Paul, Minn.
WRCNA War Records Collection, National Archives, Washington, D.C.

Chapter 1

1. Abrash, "War Aims toward Austria-Hungary," 78–79.
2. Mamatey, *The United States and East Central Europe*, 20; Robert J. Kerner, "Digest of Memorandum on Racial Participation in the Government of

Austria-Hungary," A.E.F. General Headquarters G-2, RG 256, Records of the American Commission to Negotiate Peace, State Department Records, National Archives, Washington, D.C. (hereafter cited as RG 256, DSNA).

3. Hantsch, *Die Geschichte Österreichs,* 2:191; Korbel, *Twentieth Century Czechoslovakia,* 26.

4. Zeman, *Break-Up of the Habsburg Empire,* 13–17, 53; Kerner, "White Mountain to World War," 46–47. For a discussion of the evolution of Kramář's Russophile views and the popularity of the pan-Slavic movement among the Czechs prior to the war, see Bradley, *La Légion tchécoslovaque,* 14–22; Kramář, "L'Avenir de l'Autriche," 577–600, and "Europe and the Bohemian Question," 183–205; Jiří Kořalka, "The Czech Question in International Relations at the Beginning of the 20th Century," 254–57.

5. Masaryk, *Making of a State,* 13–22; Kerner, "White Mountain to World War," 46–48; Davenport, *Too Strong for Fantasy,* 317–18; Miliukov, "Masaryk," 399–400; Seton-Watson, *Masaryk in England,* 26–27; Korbel, *Twentieth Century Czechoslovakia,* 12–18.

6. Seton-Watson, *Masaryk in England,* 20; Zeman, *Break-Up of Habsburg Empire,* 77–78.

7. Legras, "La Russie tsariste et la question tchécoslovaque," 125–30; Bradley, *La Légion tchécoslovaque,* 24–25.

8. Kenneth D. Miller, "The Czecho-Slovak Revolutionary Movement," in the Harris Papers.

9. Steed, *Through Thirty Years,* 2:42–45; Seton-Watson, *Masaryk in England,* 33–34.

10. Masaryk, *Making of a State,* 28; Seton-Watson, *Masaryk in England,* 20–23, 36–38, 40–47; Hanak, *Great Britain and Austria-Hungary,* 100–103.

11. Masaryk, *Making of a State,* 28–29.

12. Seton-Watson, *Masaryk in England,* 40–47; K. Čapek, *Masaryk Tells His Story,* 231–32.

13. Zeman, *Break-Up of Habsburg Empire,* 82.

14. Einstein, *A Diplomat Looks Back,* 199–200; "Address of Dr. Eduard Beneš before the National Assembly in Prague," September 30, 1919, DF 860f.00/49, DSNA; Korbel, *Twentieth Century Czechoslovakia,* 27–28.

15. Masaryk, "The Czecho-Slovak Nation," 4–5; Kerner, "Winning of Czechoslovak Independence," 310–11.

16. P. Janin, *Milan Rastislav Štefánik,* 13, 33, 35, 65; "General Štefánik," 148–51; E. Beneš, *My War Memoirs,* 84.

17. Thomson, *Czechoslovakia in European History,* 240.

18. E. Beneš, *My War Memoirs,* 115.

19. Willert, *Road to Safety,* 23–24.

20. Seton-Watson, *Masaryk in England,* 22; Hanak, *Great Britain and Austria-Hungary,* 6–10, 103.

21. Seton-Watson, *Masaryk in England,* 67–72; E. Beneš, *My War Memoirs,* 87.

22. K. Čapek, *Masaryk Tells His Story,* 251; Seton-Watson, *Masaryk in England,* 23.

23. Masaryk to Seton-Watson, November 30, 1915, in Seton-Watson, *Masaryk in England,* 76.

24. Steed, *Through Thirty Years*, 2:125.

25. Masaryk, *Making of a State*, 40–41; Hanak, *Great Britain and Austria-Hungary*, 117–18; E. Beneš, *My War Memoirs*, 123; Calder, *Britain and Origins of New Europe*, 59.

26. Asquith, *Memories and Reflections*, 2:8; Papoušek, *Czechoslovak Nation's Struggle*, 5–6; Abrash, "War Aims towards Austria-Hungary," 110–12.

27. Churchill, *The World Crisis*, 1:487.

28. May, "R. W. Seton-Watson and British Anti-Habsburg Sentiment," 40.

29. August 7, 1916, CAB (INET Papers) 42/17, PRO. See also Lloyd George, *Peace Treaties*, 1:31, 43–44; Lloyd George states that this was the "first official pronouncement in which what came to be known as self-determination constituted the principle of a readjustment of national boundaries" (p. 31).

30. Papoušek, *Czechoslovak Nation's Struggle*, 5; Clemenceau, *Grandeur and Misery of Victory*, 180; E. Beneš, *Souvenirs de guerre*, 1:261.

31. "Dissolution of Austria-Hungary," [1918], No. 38, Inquiry Archives, RG 256, DSNA.

32. Seton-Watson, *Masaryk in England*, 51, 82–83; E. Beneš, *My War Memoirs*, 87; Claudel, *Accompagnements*, 182–83.

33. E. Beneš, *My War Memoirs*, 82; Kerner, "White Mountain to the World War," 53–54.

34. E. Beneš, *My War Memoirs*, 82.

35. "Lois Fondamentales (Statuts) de Conseil National tchécoslovaque," (cont.) and "Decisions du conseil National tchécoslovaque du 10 fevrier 1916," in dispatch no. 6731, William G. Sharp (Ambassador to France) to Secretary of State, October 28, 1918, Paris, DF 860f.01/7, DSNA. Dürich renounced his position in the spring of 1918.

36. E. Beneš, *My War Memoirs*, 77, 85–87; Masaryk, *Making of a State*, 102; Kerner, "Winning of Czechoslovak Independence," 314; Glaise-Horstenau, *Collapse of the Austro-Hungarian Empire*, 46–47.

37. "Central Europe Liberation as Final Aim in War: Professor Masaryk Says Czech Demand Will Tally with Highest Interests of Allies," *Christian Science Monitor*, 3 March 1916, 2.

38. T. G. Masaryk to Charles R. Crane, April 10, 1918, DF 861.00/2721, DSNA.

39. E. Beneš, *My War Memoirs*, 115, 123.

40. Bradley, *La Légion tchécoslovaque*, 30.

41. Lieutenant Colonel B. Vuchterle, "The Beginning of the Czecho-Slovak Army in Russia," Czecho-Slovak History, File 314.7, RG 395, Records of the U.S. Army Overseas Operations and Commands, 1898–1942, WRCNA (hereafter cited as RG 395, WRCNA); Laurance B. Packard, "The Czecho Slovaks in Russia," April 15, 1919, DF 861.00/6052, DSNA (hereafter cited as Packard Report, DF 861.00/6052, DSNA).

42. For conflicting evidence regarding the attitude of the Tsar and Sazonov toward Czech independence, see Abrash, "War Aims toward Austria-Hungary," 86–91, 96–100; E. Beneš, *Souvenirs de guerre*, 1:314; Kramář, "M. Kramář et la politique slave," 294; Malone, "War Aims toward Germany," 142–43; Paléologue, *La Russie des tsars*, 1:93–94, 246–47; Sazonov, *Fateful Years, 1909–1916*,

273-74; Papoušek, *Czechoslovak Nation's Struggle*, 18-19, 23-28; Renzi, "Who Composed 'Sazonov's Thirteen Points'?" 349-50.

43. Papoušek, *Czechoslovak Nation's Struggle*, 19; Masaryk, *Making of a State*, 149.

44. Packard Report, DF 861.00/6052, DSNA.

45. Ján Papánek, *La Tchécoslovaquie*, 33.

46. Packard Report, DF 861.00/6052, DSNA.

47. Papoušek, *Czechoslovak Nation's Struggle*, 24.

48. Elsa Brändström, *Among Prisoners of War in Russia and Siberia*, 56-57.

49. Vuchterle, "Beginning of Czecho-Slovak Army in Russia," File 314.7, RG 395, WRCNA.

50. The Austrians denied the desertions but at the same time issued orders promising dishonor and disgrace for all Czechs who followed in the footsteps of their brethren. *Christian Science Monitor*, December 31, 1915.

51. Vuchterle, "Beginning of Czecho-Slovak Army in Russia," File 314.7, RG 395, WRCNA. "How, When, and Where were the First Fighting Units Formed in Russia Entirely of Czechs," File 314.7, RG 395, WRCNA; E. Beneš, *My War Memoirs*, 86-87; Papoušek, *Czechoslovak Nation's Struggle*, 24-29; Henry and De Means, *L'Armée tchécoslovaque*, 42-44; and Bradley, *La Légion tchécoslovaque*, 25-59.

52. Papoušek, *Czechoslovak Nation's Struggle*, 24, 27, 30.

53. E. Beneš, *My War Memoirs*, 95; Masaryk, *Making of a State*, 86, 88-89.

54. Bradley, *La Légion tchécoslovaque*, 35-36; Abrash, "War Aims toward Austria-Hungary," 101-18.

55. E. Beneš, *My War Memoirs*, 123-26; Masaryk, *Making of a State*, 152-62; Henry and De Means, *L'Armée tchécoslovaque*, 74. See also Holotík, *Štefánikovská*, 421, 426-27, 437.

56. Mamatey, *United States and East Central Europe*, 32-33.

57. E. Beneš, *My War Memoirs*, 96-98, 131-32; Masaryk, *Making of a State*, 86-89; Papoušek, *Czechoslovak Nation's Struggle*, 28-30; Bradley, *La Légion tchécoslovaque*, 33, 39-41.

58. E. Beneš, *My War Memoirs*, 159, 162-63; Seton-Watson, *Masaryk in England*, 59; Valiani, *End of Austria-Hungary*, 97, 151.

59. Holotík, *Štefánikovská*, 427; Valiani, *End of Austria-Hungary*, 172-73.

Chapter 2

1. *PWW*, 1:307-14.

2. W. Wilson, "The Dual Monarchies." See also Pergler, *Struggle for Czechoslovak Independence*, 36-40; *Bohemian Review* 1 (February 1917).

3. *The Voice of Freedom*, October 1916, 5, 154, copy in the Wilson Papers.

4. For example, see Mayer, *Political Origins of New Diplomacy*, 75, 341-44, 352-53; Pomerance, "The United States and Self-Determination," 2.

5. "An Address on Preparedness to the Manhattan Club," November 4, 1915, *PWW*, 35:168. For Wilson's thought on self-government, see generally Link, *Wilson: Revolution, War, and Peace*, 10-11; Notter, *Origins of Foreign Policy*,

651–52; Unterberger, "National Self-Determination," 2:638–41; Pomerance, "The United States and Self-Determination," 1–27.

6. *PWW*, 37:115.

7. *New York Times*, July 8, 9, 19, 1914, pictorial section, 1; Joseph C. Grew to Ulysses Grant-Smith, April 7, 1917, Grew Papers; Allen W. Dulles to Lansing, April 29, 1917, Lansing Papers, LC; Dulles to John W. Foster, May 21, 1917, Dulles Papers.

8. Gwynn, *The Letters of Sir Cecil Spring Rice*, 2:193; House to Wilson, September 6, 1914, *PWW*, 31:5.

9. Wilson to Francis Joseph I, June 28, 1914, *PWW*, 30:222; *FRUS, 1914*, 26; *New York Times*, June 29, 1914.

10. Willian Jennings Bryan to Penfield, August 4, 1914, *FRUS, 1914, Supp., World War*, 42; *New York Times*, July 28, 1914.

11. Penfield to Bryan, August 7, 1914, *FRUS, 1914, Supp., World War*, 48–50, 60–61, 78–79.

12. Neutrality Proclamation, August 19, 1914, ibid., 551.

13. Crane to Wilson, August 4, 1914, C. R. Crane Papers; *New York Times*, August 2, 1914; Notter, *Origins of Foreign Policy*, 315.

14. Wilson to Crane, August 4, 1914, C. R. Crane Papers and *PWW*, 30:343; Crane to Wilson, August 4, 1914, Wilson Papers.

15. Herbert Bruce Brougham, "Memorandum of Interview with the President," December 14, 1914, *PWW*, 31:458–60.

16. Dumba, *Memoirs*, 192.

17. Wilson to Lansing, June 16, 1915, and William Phillips to Lansing, June 16, 1915, DF 763.72114/550, DSNA; Wilson to House, April 1, 1915, and Tsar Nicholas to President Wilson, April 15, 1915, *PWW*, 32:462, 525–26; Dumba, *Memoirs*, 195–97; Brändström, *Among Prisoners of War in Russia and Siberia*, 27–28; Bryan to Wilson, April 27, 1915, Wilson Papers. Shortly thereafter, the Russian government agreed to permit the American Red Cross to operate in Siberia and throughout Russia. The Austro-Hungarian Ambassador was so informed. DF 763.7214/684, DSNA.

18. Wilson to Lansing, September 8, 15, 1915, *Lansing Papers*, 1:82, 83; *PWW*, 34:425–26, 432–33, 446, n. 5, 471; Link, *Struggle for Neutrality*, 648; House Diary, June 23, 1916.

19. What the American government did not know was that a German submarine flying the Austrian flag had done the deed and that the Austro-Hungarian government had agreed to assume full responsiblity. Link, *Wilson: Confusion and Crises*, 67; Wilson to Edith Bolling Galt, November 17, 1915, with enclosures, *PWW*, 35:208–9.

20. Lansing to Wilson, December 3, 1915, *Lansing Papers*, 1:497–98; *PWW*, 35:282, 286–89; Lansing to Penfield, December 6, 1915, *FRUS, 1915, Supp., World War*, 623–25.

21. Wilson to Lansing, December 5, 1915, *Lansing Papers*, 1:498. See also Wilson to Lansing, December 5, 1915, with enclosure, *PWW*, 35:286–89.

22. Lansing to Wilson, December 17, 1915, and Lansing, "Draft Telegram," all in *Lansing Papers*, 1:499–500; Lansing to Penfield, December 19, 1915, *FRUS, 1915, Supp., World War*, 647–48. Lansing to Wilson, December 17, 1915, with

enclosure, and Wilson to Lansing, December 18, 1915, with enclosures, *PWW*, 35:364–66, 368–70.

23. *Lansing Papers*, 1:501–5. Memorandum of Conversation with Baron Zwiedinek, December 18, 1915, and Penfield to Lansing, December 24, 1915, DF 865.857 AN2/93 1/2 and AN2/88, DSNA; Wilson to Lansing, December 27, 1915, *PWW*, 35:394.

24. Lansing to Wilson, December 28, 1915, *PWW*, 35:403–4; *Lansing Papers*, 1:506–8.

25. Wilson to Lansing, December 29, 1915, *PWW*, 35:406–7; *Lansing Papers*, 1:508–9.

26. Penfield to Lansing, December 29, 1915, *FRUS, 1915, Supp., World War*, 655–58. Even Lansing admitted that the note had made a "splendid impression." Lansing to House, January 7, 1916, *PWW*, 35:446.

27. Penfield to Lansing, December 29, 1915, *Lansing Papers*, 1:507–8; *PWW*, 35:403–4, 420; Penfield to Lansing, December 29, 1915, *FRUS, 1915, Supp., World War*, 655. Penfield to Lansing, December 31, 1915; Wilson to Lansing, January 2, 1916; and Lansing to Wilson, December 28, 1915, all in *Lansing Papers*, 1:507, 512. *Christian Science Monitor*, January 1, 1916.

28. Wilson to Lansing, December 31, 1915, *PWW*, 35:411.

29. Müller, *The Kaiser and His Court*, 120.

30. Penfield to Lansing, April 15, 1916, and Wilson to Lansing, May 12, 1916, DF 763.72/2664 1/2 and 2665 1/2, DSNA; Lansing to Wilson, May 9, 1916, with enclosures, *PWW*, 37:4–5, 24.

31. Lloyd George, *War Memoirs*, 2:277–78; Lloyd George to Robert Donald, January 8, 1916, quoted in D. R. Woodward, "David Lloyd George, A Negotiated Peace with Germany, and the Kühlmann Peace Kites of September 1917," 75–76.

32. *Christian Science Monitor*, March 24, 1916.

33. Link, *Wilson: Confusion and Crises*, 141.

34. Penfield to House, June 5, 1916, House Papers; House Diary, June 23, 1916. Penfield sent a similar letter marked "personal and private" to Lansing who sent it to Wilson. Penfield to Lansing, June 3, 1916, and Lansing to Wilson, June 21, 1916, DF 763.72/2803 1/2, DSNA; *PWW*, 37:273–75. However, it was Wilson's hope that recent Russian successes had altered the Austrian attitude, which had been cockier because of German successes in the North Sea. Wilson to Lansing, June 21, 1916, DF 763.72/2804 1/2, DSNA, and *PWW*, 37:275. See also Joseph Edward Willard to Wilson, May 11, 1916, *PWW*, 37:19–20.

35. *Official German Documents*, 2:1060; see also 1:223–423. The final conference at Pless was on November 4, 1916.

36. *FRUS, 1916, Supp., World War*, 65.

37. Hindenburg, *Out of My Life*, 253–54. See also *Official German Documents*, 2:869–71.

38. House Diary, November 14, 1916; *PWW*, 38:645–47. The State Department had already been secretly informed both of Germany's interest in considering peace proposals as well as the possibility of "ruthless and indiscriminate submarine warfare" at any time. Report, May 1916/April 1917, Grew Papers.

39. *Christian Science Monitor,* March 27, 1916.
40. Pribram, *Austrian Foreign Policy,* 102–3; Valiani, *End of Austria-Hungary,* 183–84, 253.
41. *New York Times,* November 22, 23, 26, 1916; *Christian Science Monitor,* November 23, 1916; Müller, *The Kaiser and His Court,* 219–20.
42. *Christian Science Monitor,* November 25, 1916; *New York Times,* January 7, 21, 1917.
43. Lloyd George, *War Memoirs,* 4:1934–35.
44. Penfield to Lansing, December 26, 1916, *FRUS, 1916, Supp., World War,* 110.

Chapter 3

1. U.S. Department of Commerce, *Statistical Abstract of the United States,* 1916, 106–7; Ferrell, "The United States and East Central Europe before 1941," 21; Miller, "The Rebirth of a Nation: The Czechoslovaks," 117–20; Thomson, *Czechoslovakia in European History,* 240, 247–48; Monroe, *Bohemia and the Czechs,* 13–15. For an early account of the Bohemians in the U.S. prior to 1914, see T. Čapek, *Památky českých emigrantů v Americe.*
2. Not until the spring of 1918 did the term "Czech" begin to appear in American newspapers and periodicals. Prior to that time, the Czechs were known only as "Bohemians." The Czech national organization was called the Bohemian National Alliance, and the national journal, *Bohemian Review.* As a noted authority on Czech history points out, "The use of these names creates problems for the student of the Czechs and their influence on Wilson, since the Czechs in America continued to call themselves Bohemians even after the start of the war, while the political exiles in Europe used the term 'Czech.' " Odložilík, "The Czechs," 207, 209.
3. Francis Sindelár, *Z Boja Za Svobodu Otciny,* as quoted in Pergler, *Struggle for Czechoslovak Independence,* 20–22.
4. E. Beneš, *My War Memoirs,* 98; *Sokol Ameriky,* November 1916, as quoted in Pergler, *Struggle for Czechoslovak Independence,* 21–23; *New York Times,* November 28, 1914.
5. E. Beneš, *My War Memoirs,* 99.
6. Pergler, *Struggle for Czechoslovak Independence,* 23–24; E. Beneš, *My War Memoirs,* 117; *New York Times,* April 4, 22, 1915.
7. E. Beneš, *My War Memoirs,* 100–101.
8. Voska and Irwin, *Spy and Counterspy,* 16, 200; E. Beneš, *My War Memoirs,* 100, 117; *New York Times,* April 22, August 31, November 9, 1915.
9. C. R. Crane Memoirs, 53, 53A; Masaryk, *Making of a State,* 212; Davenport, *Too Strong for Fantasy,* 319; Paul Selver, *Masaryk,* 195–96.
10. C. R. Crane Memoirs, 152–55, 168; Crane to Josephine Crane Bradley, January [n.d.], 1914, C. R. Crane Papers; David F. Houston to Charles W. Eliot, December 1, 1916, Houston Papers; E. B. Wilson, *My Memoir,* 100, 345; Masaryk, *Making of a State,* 221.

11. C. R. Crane Memoirs, 153–54; Houston to Eliot, December 1, 1916, Houston Papers; *PWW*, 24:554.

12. Wilson to Mark Sullivan, January 7, 1915, *PWW*, 30:31, 46, 58, 32:25; Wilson to Crane, May 15, 1914, Wilson Papers; Crane to Wilson, May 18, 1914, and Wilson to Crane, May 21, 1914, C. R. Crane Papers; *New York Times*, January 30, February 3, 1914.

13. *New York Times*, February 23, 1915; Houston to House, July 24, 1915, Houston Papers; Crane to House, Summer 1915, C. R. Crane Papers; Phillips to House, July 31, 1915, House Papers.

14. C. R. Crane Memoirs, 65; Harper, *The Russia I Believe In*, vii, 9, 107.

15. Miller, "Nationalism in Bohemia and Poland," 879–86, and "What Wilson Meant to Czechoslovakia," 71–72, 74; Miller to Lansing, September 2, 1914, DF 763.72/684, DSNA.

16. Pergler, *Struggle for Czechoslovak Independence*, 58–59; Voska and Irwin, *Spy and Counterspy*, 200; E. Beneš, *My War Memoirs*, 118.

17. Voska and Irwin, *Spy and Counterspy*, x–xii. Voska is in error about the dates.

18. Ibid., 20, 29; Dedijer, *Sarajevo, 1914*, 275.

19. Voska and Irwin, *Spy and Counterspy*, 36; Calder, *Britain and Origins of New Europe*, 51.

20. Gaunt, *The Yield of the Years*, 167–68; Voska and Irwin, *Spy and Counterspy*, 15–16, 38; Lansing to Wilson, December 1, 1915, Personal and Confidential Letters from Secretary of State Lansing to President Wilson, 1915–1918, State Department Records, RG 59 (hereafter cited as Confidential Letters, RG 59, DSNA). See also Tuchman, *The Zimmerman Telegram*, 72–75; Baerlein, *March of the Seventy Thousand*, 4–17; and Calder, *Britain and Origins of New Europe*, 52.

21. Wiseman to Masaryk, July 31, 1918, Wiseman Papers; Crane to Josephine Crane Bradley, February 14, 1917, C. R. Crane Papers; Willert, *Road to Safety*, 24, 63–64; Calder, *Britain and Origins of New Europe*, 53.

22. McDowell, "Tried in Her Father's Stead," 116; *New York Times*, April 28, 1916; Balch, *Our Slavic Fellow-Citizens to the Great Settlement*; Miller, "What Wilson Meant to Czechoslovakia," 71–74.

23. Masaryk to Crane, March 11, 1915, C. R. Crane Papers.

24. *New York Times*, March 10, 1915; Masaryk to Roger H. Williams, November 15, 1915, C. R. Crane Papers; Voska and Irwin, *Spy and Counterspy*, 16. Pergler later revealed that the "whole Czecho-Slovak movement originally was financed by subscriptions from America," which continued to be a main source of funds. Pergler to Lansing, March 6, 1918, CPI, RG 63, NA.

25. Masaryk, *Making of a State*, 92; for a full account of the Alice Masaryk affair, see Unterberger, "The Arrest of Alice Masaryk," 91–106.

26. Penfield to Lansing, April 6, 1916, Charles L. Hoover to Penfield, March 11, 1916, DF 364.64/63, DSNA; Richard C. Crane to Crane, April 24, 1916, C. R. Crane Papers.

27. Masaryk to Crane, November 15, 29, 1915, C. R. Crane Papers.

28. Crane to J. C. Bradley, April 20, 1916, ibid.; *New York Times*, April 9, 21, 28, 1916; *Denní Hlasatel*, April 19, 1916.

29. Crane to J. C. Bradley, April 20, 1916, and Frederick Dickson to Crane,

April 20, 1915, C. R. Crane Papers; *Christian Science Monitor,* December 1, 1915, March 3, 5, 1916.

30. *New York Times,* November 9, 1915. For Sabath's later efforts to influence Wilson on behalf of Bohemian independence, see Kisch, "Wilson and Independence of Small Nations," 235–38.

31. *Denní Hlasatel,* April 21, 1916.

32. *New York Times,* April 21, 1916; Frank L. Polk (Acting Secretary of State) to Sabath, June 3, 1916, DF 363.64/63, DSNA.

33. Secretary of State to Charles L. Hoover, Prague, March 2, 1916, DF 364.64/35a, DSNA.

34. Penfield to Lansing, April 6, 1916, and Hoover to Penfield, March 11, 1916, DF 364.64/63, DSNA; Polk to Julia Lathrop, April 21, 1916, DF 364.64/43, DSNA; *Denní Hlasatel,* April 28, 1916.

35. *Chicago Tribune,* April 27, 1916. See also *Denní Hlasatel,* April 27, 1916.

36. *Christian Science Monitor,* April 27, 1916.

37. *Chicago Tribune,* May 15, 1916; *Denní Hlasatel,* May 10, 1916.

38. *New York Times,* May 9, 1916.

39. *New York Times,* August 20, 1916. *Christian Science Monitor,* August 21, 1916, reported that she was freed on July 3.

40. *Denní Hlasatel,* August 21, 1916.

41. Steed, *Through Thirty Years,* 2:98.

Chapter 4

1. Link, *Wilson: Progressivism and Peace,* 187–88; Grew to Lansing, November 17, 21, 25, 28, 1916, *FRUS, 1916, Supp. 1, World War,* 64–65, 67, 69–70, 71–74; House Diary, November 14, 1916; *PWW,* 38:645–47; Report, May 1916–April 1917, Grew to W. H. Buckler, April 3, 1917, Grew Papers.

2. Foerster, *Failures of Peace,* chap. 6; Valiani, *End of Austria-Hungary,* 257–58.

3. Grew to the Secretary of State, December 12, 1916, *FRUS, 1916, Supp. 1, World War,* 85–90; *PWW,* 40:230–31; Brunauer, "Peace Proposals of December 1916/January 1917," 560–61.

4. Lansing to Diplomatic Representatives to Great Britain, France, Russia, Italy, Japan, Roumania, and Serbia, and to the Consul at Havre for transmission to the Belgian Government, December 16, 1916, *FRUS, 1916, Supp. 1, World War,* 94–95.

5. Ibid., 97–99; Wilson to Lansing, December 18, 1916, with enclosure, "An Appeal for a Statement of War Aims"; and Wilson to House, December 19, 1918, *PWW,* 40:272–76.

6. Scott, *Official Statements,* 22–24; Gerard to Lansing, December 26, 1916, and Penfield to Lansing, December 26, 1916, *FRUS, 1916, Supp. 1, World War,* 117–19; see also *PWW,* 40:331.

7. Link, *Wilson: Revolution, War, and Peace,* 57–58. See also Doerries, "Imperial Germany and Washington," 43–44.

8. Penfield to Lansing, December 22, November 21, December 26, 1916, *FRUS, 1916, Supp. 1, World War,* 109–10, 114–15, 118–19.

9. Suarez, *Briand*, 4:101; W. H. Page to Lansing, December 15, 1916, *PWW*, 40:247–48. Sharp to Lansing, December 16, 1916; W. H. Page to Lansing, December 18, 1916; Bliss (Counselor of the Embassy in Paris, acting in the temporary absence of Ambassador Sharp) to Lansing, December 18, 1916; T. N. Page to Lansing, December 19, 1916; and Sharp to Lansing, December 19, 1916; all in *FRUS, 1916, Supp. 1, World War*, 95, 96, 99, 100, 102.

10. Great Britain, *Parliamentary Debates* (Commons), 5th ser., 88 (December 19, 1916): 1333–34.

11. Robert Cecil to Sir Cecil Spring Rice (British Ambassador to the United States), December 18, 1916, FO 371/2805, No. 255553, 337–38, PRO; Eric Drummond to Cecil, December 21, 1916, Balfour Papers; Suarez, *Briand*, 4:90–92; *London Chronicle*, December 22, 1916; *New York Times*, December 23, 1916; *London Times*, December 22, 23, 1916.

12. Wilson to Lansing, December 21, 1916, *PWW*, 40:307–8, n. 1.

13. Scott, *Official Statements*, 26–28; Lloyd George, *War Memoirs*, 3:60–63; Link, *Wilson: Progressivism and Peace*, 231–32.

14. "On Wilson's Note to the Belligerent Governments," in Seton-Watson, *Masaryk in England*, 92–93.

15. Lloyd George, *Peace Treaties*, 1:41.

16. Ibid., 2:870; "The Peace Settlement in Europe: A Memorandum of the Right Hon. A. J. Balfour, November 1916," in Dugdale, *Balfour*, 2:328–34; Valiani, *End of Austria-Hungary*, 169–70; Young, *Arthur James Balfour*, 377.

17. Wiseman telegram, December 13, 1916, Wiseman Papers.

18. Calder, *Britain and Origins of New Europe*, 107; Valiani, *End of Austria-Hungary*, 169.

19. E. Beneš, *My War Memoirs*, 154–56; *New York Times*, January 6, 1917; Valiani, *End of Austria-Hungary*, 171.

20. E. Beneš, *My War Memoirs*, 157; Cecil, *A Great Experiment*, 46; Suarez, *Briand*, 4:102; Valiani, *End of Austria-Hungary*, 169–70.

21. E. Beneš, *My War Memoirs*, 157–58; Seton-Watson, *History of Czechs and Slovaks*, 291; Masaryk, *Making of a State*, 124; Abrash, "War Aims toward Austria-Hungary," 118.

22. Masaryk to Crane, April 10, 1918, DF 861.00/2721, DSNA. Thomas Čapek suggests that the French decision was the result of Štefánik's acquaintance with Philippe Berthelot of the French Foreign Ministry and the friendly attitude of Premier Briand. See T. Čapek, *Origins of the Czechoslovak State*, 57–58. Briand's sympathy is confirmed in Suarez, *Briand*, 4:114–15; Berthelot's in Valiani, *End of Austria-Hungary*, 169–70. Cecil and Berthelot were charged with the task of drafting definite war aims. Lloyd George, *Peace Treaties*, 1:38; *History of The Times: 1912–1920*, 320.

23. Rosen, *Forty Years of Diplomacy*, 2:229.

24. Sharp to Lansing, January 10, 1917, *PWW*, 40:439–41; *FRUS, 1917, Supp. 1, World War*, 8. On the illogic of mentioning the Slavs in general and then adding the Czecho-Slovaks as if they were not Slavs, see Valiani, *End of Austria-Hungary*, 170–72.

25. E. Beneš, *My War Memoirs*, 154–58; Abrash, "War Aims toward Austria-Hungary," 117–18.

26. Suarez, *Briand*, 4:115. See T. Čapek, *Origins of Czechoslovak State*, 46. Masaryk, however, insisted emphatically that Briand was the first statesman "who publicly promised to our nation the help of France." Masaryk to C. R. Crane, April 10, 1918, DF 861.00/2721, DSNA.

27. Lloyd George, *War Memoirs*, 5:23; Calder, *Britain and Origins of New Europe*, 108.

28. Masaryk, "Embers of Revolt in Austria-Hungary."

29. "Brief Memorandum; The Czecho-Slovaks and the War, Especially in Relation to the Policy of the Western Allies and the United States" by R. J. Kerner, collaborator [1918], No. 308, Inquiry Archives, RG 256, DSNA; E. Beneš, *My War Memoirs*, 158; *New York Times*, January 6, 1917.

30. Zeman, *Break-Up of Habsburg Empire*, 114–18; Mamatey, *United States and East Central Europe*, 48–49.

31. Penfield to Lansing, January 12, 1917, *FRUS, 1917, Supp. 1, World War*, 11.

32. Penfield to Lansing, January 27, 1917, enclosing Tisza to Penfield, January 25, 1917, ibid., 34.

33. "What the Papers Say," *Bohemian Review* 1 (February 1917): 17–18; *Chicago Tribune*, January 28, 1917.

34. Hapgood to Wilson, January 29, 1917, and Masaryk to Hapgood, January 27, 1917, with enclosure marked "Strictly Confidential" and entitled *At the Eleventh Hour: A Memorandum on the Military Situation* (London, 1916), in Wilson Papers. See also *PWW*, 41:56–58.

35. Text in *PWW*, 40:533–39.

36. Kerner, "Brief Memorandum," No. 308, Inquiry Archives, RG 256, DSNA.

37. Jusserand to Briand, n.d., received March 7, 1917, Guerre 1914–1918, Etats-Unis, 505:280–81, FFM-Ar; *PWW*, 41:354–57.

38. Gerard to Lansing, January 31, 1917, and Count Johann von Bernstorff (German Ambassador to the United States) to House, January 31, 1917, *PWW*, 41:79–82; Link, *Wilson: Revolution, War, and Peace*, 64–65.

39. House Diary, February 1, 1917; *PWW*, 41:86–89; Link, *Wilson: Revolution, War, and Peace*, 66.

40. May, *Passing of the Habsburg Monarchy*, 1:476–82.

41. *New York Times*, February 4, 1917; *Bohemian Review* 1 (March 1917): 15.

42. Lansing to Wilson, October 26, 1916, Wilson Papers; *PWW*, 38:544–45. Wilson agreed. Wilson to Lansing, October 30, 1916, ibid., 560.

43. Phillips, *Ventures in Diplomacy*, 7, 14, 18, 32–34, 62, 73.

44. Phillips Diary, February 3, 1917; *Christian Science Monitor*, November 11, 1916.

45. House Diary, February 1, 1917; *PWW*, 41:86–89; Seymour, *Intimate Papers*, 2:449.

46. Lansing to Penfield, February 4, 1917, *FRUS, 1917, Supp. 1, World War*, 112–13.

47. Ibid.; Penfield to Lansing, February 1, 1917, ibid., 104–5; Phillips Diary, February 3, 1917.

48. Phillips Diary, February 4, 1917; Polk Diary, February 5, 1917.

49. Penfield to Lansing, February 4, 1917, *FRUS, 1917, Supp. 1, World War*, 113.

50. Polk Memorandum of Interview with Tarnowski, February 3, 1917, Polk Papers; Phillips Diary, February 5, 7, 1917.

51. Penfield to Lansing, February 5, 1917, *PWW*, 41:129–30.

52. Czernin to Tarnowski, February 6, 1917, Krieg 61a, Amerika I, as quoted in G. H. Davis, "The Diplomatic Relations between the United States and Austria-Hungary, 1913–1917," (Ph.D. diss., Vanderbilt University, 1958), 245.

53. Czernin, *In the World War*, 131; May, *Passing of the Habsburg Monarchy*, 1:476–78.

54. Phillips Diary, February 9, 10, 11, 14, 15, 1917.

55. Link, *Wilson: Progressivism and Peace*, 315–16.

56. Lansing to Page, February 8, 1917, *FRUS, 1917, Supp. 1, World War*, 40–41; shorthand draft in Wilson Papers.

57. Page to Lansing, February 11, 1917, *PWW*, 41:210–14.

58. Lloyd George, *Peace Treaties*, 1:41.

59. CAB 23/13, War Cabinet 37(a)/1, Minutes of Meeting on January 18, 1917, PRO. The War Cabinet was a small committee of the Cabinet established by Lloyd George in December 1916. The original committee of five, later expanded to seven, made all important decisions concerning the war.

60. Page to Lansing, February 20, 21, 1917, *FRUS, 1917, Supp. 1, World War*, 55–56; Lansing, *The Big Four*, 78; *PWW*, 41:211–14; R. S. Baker, *Wilson: Life and Letters*, 6:467–68; Hendrick, *Life and Letters of Walter Hines Page*, 3:366–72.

61. Handwritten note from Lansing to Wilson with draft instructions corrected by the President, February 21, 1917, Lansing Papers, Princeton; Lansing to Penfield, February 22, 1917, *PWW*, 41:267–68.

62. Penfield to Lansing, February 27, March 13, 1917, *PWW*, 41:297–98, 398–99.

63. White House Executive Appointment Diary, 1917, March 6, 1917, Wilson Papers. Jusserand to Briand, n.d., received March 7, 1917, Guerre 1914–1918, Etats-Unis, 505:280–81, FFM-Ar; *PWW*, 41:354–57.

64. Penfield to Wilson, March 13, 1917, *PWW*, 41:398–99.

65. Wilson to Lansing, March 3, 1917, with corrected enclosure, and Lansing to Penfield, March 3, 1917, DF 763.72119/8389, DSNA; *PWW*, 41:313.

66. Penfield to Wilson, March 13, 1917, *PWW*, 41:398–99.

67. Lansing to Wilson, March 17, 1917, *Lansing Papers*, 1:24–25; *PWW*, 41:421–22.

68. Penfield to Lansing, February 1, 1917; "Address of the President of the United States to Congress, February 3, 1917"; Lansing to Penfield, February 4, 1917; all in *FRUS, 1917, Supp. 1, World War*, 104–6, 109–12, 113.

69. House Diary, February 1, 1917; *PWW*, 41:86–89.

70. Lansing to Penfield, February 4, 1917, and Penfield to Lansing, February 4, 1917, *FRUS, 1917, Supp. 1, World War*, 112–13.

71. Polk Memorandum of Conversation with Swiss Minister, February 16, 1917, Polk Papers.

72. Phillips Diary, February 9, 10, 11, 14, 15, 1917; Lansing to Wilson, February 10, 1917, *PWW*, 41:185.

73. See Secretary of State to the Diplomatic Representatives in Neutral Countries, February 3, 1917, *PWW*, 41:116.

74. Czernin, *In the World War,* 127.

75. Phillips Diary, February 26, March 1, 1917.

76. Ibid., March 4, 6, 1917; Penfield to Lansing, March 2, 1917, *FRUS, 1917, Supp. 1, World War,* 161–68.

77. Grew to Abraham Elkus (Ambassador to Turkey), March 15, 1917, and Grew to Mrs. Edward Grew, March 16, 1917, Grew Papers.

78. Phillips Diary, March 16, 1917; Penfield to Lansing, March 6, 14, 1917, *FRUS, 1917, Supp. 1, World War,* 169, 177; Polk Diary, March 15, 1917; Grew, *Turbulent Era,* 1:318–21.

79. Phillips Diary, March 7, 1917; Lansing to Penfield, March 18, 1917, *FRUS, 1917, Supp. 1, World War,* 178–80.

80. Lansing to David R. Francis (Ambassador in Russia), March 20, 1917, *FRUS, 1918, Russia,* 1:12.

81. Palmer, *Newton D. Baker,* 1:89.

82. Wilson to Lansing, March 27, 1917, *PWW,* 41:477–78; Lansing to Penfield, March 28, 1917, *FRUS, 1917, Supp. 1, World War,* 188.

83. Memorandum of Interview with Count Tarnowski, March 29, 1917, Lansing Papers, LC; Phillips Diary, March 30, 1917.

84. *FRUS, 1917, Supp. 1, World War,* 195–203.

85. Bernstorff, *My Three Years in America,* 385.

86. Lansing to Elkus, March 31, 1917, and Lansing to Ambassadors, April 2, 1917, *FRUS, 1917, Supp. 1, World War,* 191, 194–203.

87. Lansing, *War Memoirs,* 245.

88. Phillips to Lansing, March 28, 1917, DF 701.6311/271, DSNA; Phillips Diary, April 9, 1917.

89. Balfour to Lloyd George, April 26, 1917, FO 115/2202, 3–7, PRO.

90. Jusserand to the Foreign Ministry, n.d., received April 24, 1917, Guerre 1914–1918, Etats-Unis, 506:281, FFM-Ar; *PWW,* 42:127–29.

91. "Enclosure," March 22, 1917, *PWW,* 42:328–42.

92. House Diary, April 22, 28, 1917; *PWW,* 42:155–58; Seymour, *Intimate Papers,* 3:43–44, 47–49. See also "Balfour's Statement on Foreign Policy to the Imperial War Council," enclosure in Balfour to Lansing, May 18, 1917, *PWW,* 42:327–42.

93. Wilson to Mamatey, March 7, 1917, Wilson Papers.

94. For example, see U.S. Congress, *Congressional Record,* 65th Cong., 2nd sess., 1917, 55, pt. 2:1873–74.

95. *Bohemian Review* 1 (May 1917): 14.

96. Mamatey to Wilson, June 23, 1917, Wilson Papers.

97. *Bohemian Review* 1 (February 1917): 17, and 1 (April 1917): 15.

98. Pergler to Lansing, March 6, 1917, CPI, RG 63, NA.

99. Pergler, *Struggle for Czechoslovak Independence,* 27–32, 62–64; *Bohemian Review* 1 (May 1917): 16.

100. U.S. Congress, *Congressional Record,* 65th Cong., 1st sess., 1917, 55, pt. 2:1819; pt. 3:2856; Kisch, "Wilson and Independence of Small Nations," 235.

101. Pergler, "The Bohemian Question," 155–60; Pergler to the Editor, *New Republic* (May 5, 1917): 21–22; Mika, "Rearranging Austro-Hungary," 314–15.

102. J. S. Williams, "War to Stop War," 178–85.

103. John S. Williams to Wilson, April 27, 1917, J. S. Williams Papers.

104. Wilson to Williams, April 4, 1917, J. S. Williams Papers.

105. Newton D. Baker (Secretary of War) to Wilson, May 5, 1917, Wilson Papers; *PWW*, 42:227; Wilson to Williams, May 8, 1917, and Williams to Wilson, May 11, 1917, J. S. Williams Papers.

106. Holotík, *Štefánikovská*, 421; Henry and De Means, *L'Armée tchéco-slovaque*, 77.

107. Mamatey, *United States and East Central Europe*, 132; Lansing to Wilson, June 21, 1917, *PWW*, 42:552–53; Phillips Diary, November 20, 1917. See also Baker to Wilson, May 31, 1917, Baker Papers; *PWW*, 42:431–32.

108. E. Beneš, *My War Memoirs*, 181–84.

109. *New York Times*, April 26, 1917.

110. *FRUS, 1917, Supp. 2, World War*, 1:97–100; Wilson to House, June 1, 1917, House Papers; *PWW*, 42:432–33.

111. *FRUS, 1917, Supp. 2, World War*, 1:98; Kerner, "Brief Memorandum," Inquiry Archives, RG 256/308, DSNA; Pergler, *Struggle for Czechoslovak Independence*, 42–44.

112. Voska to House, June 29, 1917, House Papers.

113. Pergler, *Struggle for Czechoslovak Independence*, 44. See *New York Times*, January 14, 1917, for a two-page review of Chéradame's *The Pan-German Plot Unmasked*.

114. Leonard, *War Addresses of Woodrow Wilson*, 68–69; Pergler, *Struggle for Czechoslovak Independence*, 44.

115. *Washington Post*, June 4, August 28, 1917.

Chapter 5

1. Lansing, *War Memoirs*, 245–47, 261.

2. House Diary, May 18, 1917; Phillips Diary, May 28, July 27, 1917; Grew to Thomas D. M. Cardeza, June 20, 1917, and Grew to Ellis Dresel and Hugh R. Wilson, July 5, 1917, Grew Papers; Phillips to House, June 30, 1917, House Papers.

3. Dulles to John W. Foster, May 21, 1917, Dulles Papers.

4. House Diary, August 3, 1917.

5. Memorandum of My Last Interview with Count Tarnowski before His Departure from Washington, May 1, 1917, Lansing Papers, LC, partially reproduced in Lansing, *War Memoirs*, 254–55.

6. Ibid.

7. Tarnowski to Lansing, May 3, 1917, Lansing Papers, Princeton; Lansing, *War Memoirs*, 255.

8. Tarnowski to Lansing, May 3, 1917, Lansing Papers, Princeton; Phillips Diary, May 4, 1917.

9. Müller, *The Kaiser and His Court*, 252, 259; Czernin, *In the World War*, 143.

10. Vivian, *Emperor Charles of Austria*, 119; Lloyd George, *War Memoirs*, 4:231–32; May, *Passing of the Habsburg Monarchy*, 1:486–91.

11. Page to Lansing, April 18, 1917, DF 763.72119/564, DSNA; Lloyd George, *Peace Treaties*, 2:773–74; Lloyd George, *War Memoirs*, 4:234–35.

12. CAB 23/16, War Cabinet 391A, Secret, April 15, 1918, PRO.

13. Lloyd George, *Peace Treaties*, 2:773–74; Lloyd George, *War Memoirs*, 4:239; Page to Wilson, June 22, 1917, Page Papers.

14. De Manteyer, *Austria's Peace Offer*, 154; Hankey, *The Supreme Command*, 2:735.

15. CAB 23/13, War Cabinet 135 (A)/19, Minutes of Meeting on May 9, 1917 at 12 P.M., PRO.

16. A. J. P. Taylor, *The Troublemakers*, 147–48.

17. CAB 23/16, War Cabinet 159(A), Minutes of Meeting on June 8, 1917; "The Present Military Situation in Russia and its Effect on Our Future Plans," Secret, July 29, 1917, CAB 24/GT 1549; CAB 23/12, War Cabinet Minutes, July 31, 1917, PRO.

18. Czernin, *In the World War*, 164.

19. Seton-Watson, *History of the Roumanians*, 500; May, *Passing of the Habsburg Monarchy*, 1:495.

20. Vivian, *Emperor Charles of Austria*, 127–29; Müller, *The Kaiser and His Court*, 252; Czernin, *In the World War*, 168.

21. Balfour to Wilson, May 18, 1917, Balfour Papers; *PWW*, 42:327; Phillips Diary, July 10, 1917. Not all of the agreements had been included. Link, *Wilson: Revolution, War, and Peace*, 78. It should be noted that the proceedings of the Imperial War Council were absolutely secret.

22. Balfour to Lansing, May 18, 1917, *Lansing Papers*, 2:19; see also *PWW*, 42:328–42. English translations of the text of the Allied secret treaties drawn from the Russian press had been sent to the State Department by the American Ambassador in Petrograd on December 5 and reached the State Department on December 27, 1917.

23. While there is no evidence that he ever actually read the copies that Balfour sent him, Wilson was obviously aware of Allied war aims.

24. Balfour to Lloyd George, April 26, 1917, FO 371 3119/86512, PRO; *PWW*, 42:140–41; Gardner, *Safe for Democracy*, 93.

25. Phillips Diary, July 10, 1917.

26. Ibid., July 27, 1917; Pribram, *Austrian Foreign Policy*, 110–11.

27. *Literary Digest* (September 1, 1917): 17–18.

28. Page to Lansing, August 15, 1917, FRUS, 1917, Supp. 2, World War, 1:161–64.

29. May, *Passing of the Habsburg Monarchy*, 2:522.

30. E. Beneš, *Souvenirs de guerre*, 1:523. Lansing was inclined to agree. Lansing to Wilson, August 13, 1917, Lansing Papers, Princeton; *PWW*, 43:438.

31. Wilson to House, August 16, 1917, House Papers; *PWW*, 43:488–89. For a detailed account of Wilson's views and response, see Zivojinović, "The Vatican, Woodrow Wilson and the Dissolution of the Habsburg Monarchy," 41.

32. House to Wilson, January 27, 1917, *PWW*, 41:39–40; House Diary, August 15, 1917; *PWW*, 43:486.

33. Lansing to Wilson, August 13, 1917, Lansing Papers, Princeton; Lansing to Wilson, August 20, 1917, *PWW*, 43:438–39, 523–25.

34. For the Allied response, see House to Wilson, August 22, 1917, with enclosures from Balfour and Wiseman, Wilson Collection, Princeton; *PWW,* 44:30–31; Dawson, *War Memoirs of William G. Sharp,* 202; *FRUS, 1917, Supp. 2, World War,* 1:165–76; Lansing to Wilson, August 21, 1917, Wilson Papers; *PWW,* 44:22.

35. Steffens, *Autobiography,* 765.

36. Wilson to House, August 23, 1917, with enclosure, House Papers; *PWW,* 44:33–36.

37. Lansing to Page, August 27, 1917, *PWW,* 44:57–59.

38. Sir Edward Grey, ennobled as Viscount Grey of Fallodon on July 27, 1916. *PWW,* 37:32.

39. Phillips Diary, August 28, 1917; House to Wilson, August 29, 1917; House to Wilson, August 31, 1917, with enclosure from David Hunter Miller to House, August 30, 1917; and House to Wilson, September 4, 1917, Wilson Papers; *PWW,* 44:83–84, 105–6, 149–50; FO 115/2264, 44, PRO.

40. Williams to Wilson, August 29, 1917, J. S. Williams Papers; John R. Mott to Wilson, August 30, 1917, Wilson Collection, Princeton; *PWW,* 44:94.

41. Kerner, "Brief Memorandum," Inquiry Archives, RG 256/308, DSNA; May, *Passing of the Habsburg Monarchy,* 2:523–24.

42. CAB 23/12, War Cabinet Minutes 200, July 31, 1917; CAB 23/13, War Cabinet Minutes 247 (B)/100, Minutes of Meeting on October 11, 1917, at 11:30 A.M., PRO.

43. Lloyd George to Wilson, September 3, 1917, handed by Reading to Wilson on September 20, 1917, *PWW,* 44:125–30.

44. Auchincloss Diary, May 29 to July 22, 1917; House Diary, September 16, 22, 1917; see also *PWW,* 44:200–203; Fowler, *British-American Relations,* 71–72.

45. House Diary, September 16, 1917; *PWW,* 44:200–203; Trask, *U.S. in Supreme War Council,* 14, 183–84, n. 33; Fowler, *British-American Relations,* 75–76.

46. Trask, *U.S. in Supreme War Council,* 15, 18–19.

47. Drummond to Balfour, September 23, 1917, Balfour Papers.

48. Wiseman to Drummond, October 4, 1917, Balfour Papers.

49. Wilson to House, September 2, 19, 1917, House Papers; *PWW,* 44:120–21, 216–19; Gelfand, *The Inquiry,* 26–27.

50. Mezes, "Preparations for Peace," 5.

51. House to Wilson, September 20, 1917, Wilson Papers; *PWW,* 44:226. Wilson, who had a high regard for Mezes and Lippmann, heartily approved of their selection. Wilson to House, September 24, 1917, House Papers; *PWW,* 44:244–45.

52. Lansing to Mezes, November 5, 1917, Mezes Papers. Mezes tried to keep Lansing fully informed of The Inquiry's efforts and progress. Mezes to Lansing, November 9, 1917, ibid.; Wilson to House, September 19, 1917, *PWW,* 44:216–19; Memorandum on Certain Essentials of a Stable Peace, October 24, 1917, Lansing Papers, LC.

53. Putney to Lansing, May 26, 1917, with memorandum, "Nationalistic Aspirations in the Near East," DF 763.72119/623a, DSNA. This is the "lost" or "misplaced" document Mamatey was unable to locate in the State Department files. Mamatey, *United States and East Central Europe,* 92.

54. "Supplement to Memorandum on Nationalistic Aspirations in the Near East, Containing Some Suggestions as to a Settlement of Peace Along the Lines of Nationality," enclosed in Putney to Lansing, June 5, 1917, DF 763.72119/9597, DSNA.

55. Memorandum on Certain Essentials of a Stable Peace, October 24, 1917, Lansing Papers, LC.

56. Ibid. According to Professor George Barany, this memorandum clearly shows Lansing as one of the spiritual fathers of an independent Central Europe. See his article, "Wilsonian Central Europe," 229.

57. Memorandum by Walter Lippmann, n.d., Confidential, Mezes Papers.

58. Mamatey, *United States and East Central Europe*, 129–31, 132.

59. Štefánik to Polk, October 17, 1917, Polk Papers.

60. Ibid.

61. Henry and De Means, *L'Armée tchécoslovaque*, 77.

62. Pergler to Lansing, March 6, 1918, Kerner Papers.

63. *New York Times*, September 17, 1917; *Bohemian Review* 1 (October 1917): 13.

64. New York *World*, October 28, 1917.

65. Mezes to E. S. Martin, November 7, 1917, Mezes Papers.

66. Mamatey, *United States and East Central Europe*, 133.

67. Balfour to Reading, October 31, 1917, MSS Europe, FO 118/114, India Office Library and Records, in Wilson Collection, Princeton.

68. *FRUS, 1918, Russia*, 1:253.

69. Unterberger, *America's Siberian Expedition, 1918–1920*, 19–20.

70. British Foreign Office to Reading, November 1, 1917, and Reading to Lloyd George and Balfour, November 2, 1917, both in India Office Library and Records, in Wilson Collection, Princeton; *PWW*, 44:294–95.

71. FO 115/2318, 174, PRO; House to Wiseman, December 18, 1917, Wiseman Papers; *PWW*, 45:322–23.

72. E. Beneš, *My War Memoirs*, 192–93.

73. Papoušek, *Czechoslovak Nation's Struggle*, 50–51; Thomson, *Czechoslovakia in European History*, 261; Ullman, *Intervention and the War*, 151; Nosek, *Independent Bohemia*, 92.

74. Thomson, *Czechoslovakia in European History*, 264; Valiani, *End of Austria-Hungary*, 244–45.

75. Packard Report, DF 861.00/6052, DSNA; House to Wilson, London, November 9, 1917; House to Wilson, November 9, 1917, with enclosure from William Hepburn Buckler to House; Wilson to House, December 1, 1917; all in Wilson Papers; see also *PWW*, 44:545–49; *PWW*, 45:176.

76. *FRUS, 1917, Supp. 2, World War*, 1:302.

77. Ibid., 282–88. See also T. N. Page to Wilson, October 2, November 4, 1917, Confidential, Wilson Papers; *PWW*, 44:295, 506–9. See editorial, "Austria and the United States," *New York Times*, October 21, 1917.

78. *FRUS, 1917, Supp. 2, World War*, 1:334.

79. *FRUS, 1917, Supp. 2, World War*, 1:308; Seymour, *Intimate Papers*, 3:220–21; R. S. Baker, *Wilson: Life and Letters*, 7:366. The Supreme War Council consisted of the Prime Minister and one permanent military representative from each government fighting on the Western Front. House represented Wilson. The

military representatives were General Maxime Weygand, France; General Sir Henry Wilson, Great Britain; General Luigi Cadorna, Italy; and General Tasker H. Bliss, United States.

80. Phillips Diary, November 28, 1917.

81. *FRUS, 1917, Supp. 2, World War,* 1:351; Phillips Diary, November 5, 9, 19, 1917.

82. Ibid., November 19, 1917.

83. Ibid.; British Embassy to State Department, November 5, 1917, *FRUS, 1917, Supp. 2, World War,* 1:289; Lansing to Wilson, November 5, 1917, with enclosure, Wilson Papers; *PWW,* 44:513–14.

84. House to Wilson and Lansing, November 28, 1917, House Papers; House Diary, November 29, 1917; CAB 23/16, War Cabinet 311(a), Minutes of Meeting on January 2, 1918, PRO.

85. CAB 23/13, War Cabinet Minutes 247(B)/100, Minutes of Meeting on October 11, 1917, at 11:30 A.M., PRO; Seymour, *Intimate Papers,* 3:376–77; Valiani, *End of Austria-Hungary,* 264.

86. May, *Passing of the Habsburg Monarchy,* 2:525–26; Valiani, *End of Austria-Hungary,* 202–3, 264.

87. Smuts to Lloyd George, December 27, 1917, CAB 1/25, PRO; Hancock, *Smuts: The Sanguine Years 1870–1919,* 466–67.

88. Sharp to Lansing, December 1, 1917, *FRUS, 1917, Supp. 2, World War,* 1:332–33. See also Lansing to Wilson, November 15, 1917, with enclosure from George Talbot Odell to Lansing, November 10, 1917, DF 763.72119/10473, DSNA; *PWW,* 45:55–58.

89. House to Wilson, November 28, 1917, House Papers; Wilson to House, December 3, 1917, Wilson Papers; *PWW,* 45:151–52, 187.

90. Lansing, *War Memoirs,* 258.

91. Lansing to Wilson, November 20, 1917, *Lansing Papers,* 2:61.

92. Woolsey to Mezes, December 7, 1917, Mezes Papers.

93. Lansing, *War Memoirs,* 248, 255, 258.

94. Seymour, *Intimate Papers,* 3:274–77; Wilson to House, December 3, 1917, Wilson Papers.

95. *FRUS, 1917,* ix, xvi. Only a few weeks earlier in a public address, Wilson had indicated his full awareness of German domination of Austria-Hungary, and of the latter's desire for peace because their peoples knew that at the war's end they would "in effect themselves be vassals of Germany, notwithstanding that their populations are compounded of all the peoples of that part of the world"; *An Address of President Wilson to the American Federation of Labor Convention.*

96. Lansing Diary, December 4, 1917; Phillips Diary, December 4, 5, 1917.

97. Ibid., December 5, 1917; Cronon, *Cabinet Diaries of Daniels,* 246.

98. Phillips Diary, December 4, 7, 1917.

99. Roosevelt, *Roosevelt and the Kansas City Star,* 65; *Literary Digest* (December 8, 1917): 17; *New York Times,* August 23, May 7, December 3, 1917; *Washington Post,* December 7, 1917.

100. R. S. Baker, *Wilson: Life and Letters,* 7:397–98; Scott, *Official Statements,* 205. In this respect Czernin regarded Wilson's views as "great and important

progress which we have a great interest in recognizing and grasping." Wilson to Lansing, December 8, 1917, DF 763.72/8021, DSNA.

101. May, *Passing of the Habsburg Monarchy,* 2:530–31.

102. Masaryk to Wilson, December 13, 1917, Wilson Papers; an enlarged version in DF 763.73/8108, DSNA, acknowledged by the State Department in Phillips to Slav Press Bureau, January 17, 1918, ibid.

103. Kerner, "Brief Memorandum," Inquiry Archives, RG 256/308, DSNA; *Bohemian Review* 1 (December 1917): 1; *Literary Digest* (January 22, 1918): 15. See also George H. Mika to the Editor, *New Republic* 13 (1918): 314–15.

104. Kerner, "Brief Memorandum," Inquiry Archives, RG 256/308, DSNA.

105. Pergler to Lansing, December 18, 1917, DF 763.72119/1241, DSNA; *Washington Post,* December 12, 1917. For Lansing's criticism of what he regarded as the ambiguity in Wilson's position, see his *War Memoirs,* 259–60.

106. *Bohemian Review* 1 (August 1917): 16; V. Beneš, "How Bohemians Organized," 5–8.

107. Wilson had explained his position earlier to Baron Ludovic Moncheur, former Belgian Minister to the United States (1901–1909), in an interview in August. He recognized that the "races forming the Austro-Hungarian agglomeration would wish to be emancipated" after the war. He argued that the "Dual Monarchy would continue to exist, but each people of the confederation would have liberal autonomy." This would be the greatest obstacle to the consolidation of the *Mittel Europa* bloc, for the "many non-German elements of the Austro-Hungarian Empire" would act as a check upon the "German policy of the country" and would "prevent Vienna from submitting docilely to Berlin's orders." Moreover, they would be hostile to the "whole idea of a new war." Moncheur to Baron Charles de Broqueville, August 14, 1917, *PWW,* 43:465–70.

Chapter 6

1. Bradley, *La Légion tchécoslovaque,* 48.

2. *Christian Science Monitor,* April 9, 1917; Price, *Reminiscences of Russian Revolution,* 18.

3. Selver, *Masaryk,* 271; Stewart, *White Armies of Russia,* 99; Papoušek, *Czechoslovak Nation's Struggle,* 45; Masaryk, *Making of a State,* 154–69.

4. Bradley, *La Légion tchécoslovaque,* 50–51; Papoušek, *Czechoslovak Nation's Struggle,* 46–47.

5. *New York Times,* June 26, July 7, 15, October 14, June 5, 1917.

6. *Bohemian Review* 1 (June 1917): 16.

7. E. Beneš, *My War Memoirs,* 186, 197–98, 352; Masaryk, *Making of a State,* 166.

8. Seton-Watson, *Masaryk in England,* 102–3; Fic, *Bolsheviks and the Czechoslovak Legion,* 2.

9. Masaryk, *Making of a State,* 164–65; Papoušek, *Czechoslovak Nation's Struggle,* 47–48; Fic, *Bolsheviks and the Czechoslovak Legion,* 32; E. Beneš, *My War Memoirs,* 352–53. For Shokorov's order and later similar appeals for strict

neutrality, see *Dokumenty a materiály k dějinám československo-sovětských vztahů,* Doc. 4 and 11, 23–24, 32–33 (hereafter cited as *Dokumenty a materiály*).

10. Beaumont, *Heroic Story,* 55–56; *Bohemian Review* 1 (December 1917): 18.

11. C. R. Crane Memoirs, 193; Crane to Mildred Nelson Page, June 27, 1918, C. R. Crane Papers; Unterberger, *America's Siberian Expedition,* 7–9; *FRUS, 1918, Russia,* 3:11–25.

12. Crane to Mildred Nelson Page, June 27, 1917, and Crane to Richard Crane, July 6, 1917, C. R. Crane Papers; Richard Crane to Wilson, July 27, 1917, with enclosure from Crane to Richard Crane, Petrograd, July 21, 1917, Wilson Papers; *PWW,* 43:298–99.

13. Wiseman to Drummond, June 16, 20, 1917, Wiseman Papers.

14. Wiseman to Drummond, June 16, 1917, and Wiseman, "Russia," May 15, 1918, Wiseman Papers; House Diary, May 15, 16, 21, 1917.

15. Lansing to Wilson, June 8, 1917, with enclosures entitled "Russia," June 8, 1917, DF 861.00/423 1/2A, DSNA; *PWW,* 42:463–66. Wilson approved the project orally on June 15, 1917. DF 861.00/423 1/2A, DSNA.

16. Wiseman to Drummond, June 16, 20, 1917, Wiseman Papers; see also *PWW,* 42:529–30.

17. Maugham later described his work for the secret service and the activity of Czech agents in a novel entitled *Ashenden, or the British Agent* (London, 1927). Czech agents also appeared in some of his other novels, where they were described as "the greatest secret agents in this war." Calder, *Britain and Origins of New Europe,* 239, n. 106.

18. W. Somerset Maugham Report, December 7, 1917, Polk Papers; Report and Suggestions on Propaganda Work in Russia. Submitted to His Excellency, Sir Edward Carson and Hon. E. M. House by Emanuel V. Voska, November 6, 1917, Wiseman Papers; Fowler, *British-American Relations,* 109–18; Voska and Irwin, *Spy and Counterspy,* 214. DeWitt C. Poole, Jr., newly appointed American Vice Consul to Moscow, later to become Consul General, met Maugham en route to his post and traveled with him across Siberia; Poole Memoirs, 82–84.

19. Sir Henry Wilson, "Possibilities of Guerrilla Warfare in Russia," March 7, 1918, CAB 24/44/GT 3842; Brigadier General H. W. Studd, "The Situation in the Eastern Theater," March 26, 1918, CAB 25/72; and Brigadier General Alfred Knox, "Subject: Bolshevik Revolt and Commencement of Negotiations for an Armistice," December 4, 1917, War Office, 106/1097, PRO. For a description of Knox, see Fleming, *Fate of Admiral Kolchak,* 94.

20. Memorandum by Macdonogh, November 20, 1917, FO 381/3018, PRO.

21. CAB/4, War Cabinet, Minutes of Meeting on November 21, 1917, at 11:30 A.M.; CAB 23/4, War Cabinet 280/66, Minutes of Meeting on November 22, 1917, at 11:30 A.M., PRO.

22. Pichon to Paul Cambon (French Ambassador to London), December 18, 1917, Guerre, 1914–1918, nos. 5258–59, 357:49, FFM-Ar; Foch, *Memoirs of Marshal Foch,* 225–26; W. Somerset Maugham Report, December 7, 1917, Polk Papers; Fowler, *British-American Relations,* 109–18.

23. K. Čapek, *Masaryk Tells His Story,* 274; E. Beneš, *My War Memoirs,* 353.

24. Khabas, "K istorii bor'by s chekhoslovatskim myatezhom," 57; Popov, *Chekho-Slovatskii miatezh i samarskaia uchredilka,* 19.

25. Gorky, *History of the Civil War*, 2:259; Polner, "Czech Legion and the Bolsheviks."

26. Bunyan and Fisher, *Bolshevik Revolution, Documents*, 425–26. For Alexeev's appeal to the French Military Mission at Kiev, see *Dokumenty a materiály*, Doc. 24, dated February 9, 1918, 48–51.

27. CAB 23/4, War Cabinet 289/55, Minutes of Meeting on December 3, 1917, at 11:30 A.M., PRO.

28. Most notably, one by Voska. See Report and Suggestions on Propaganda Work in Russia. Submitted to His Excellency Sir Edward Carson and Hon. Colonel E. M. House by Emanuel V. Voska, November 6, 1917, Wiseman Papers.

29. House to Wiseman, December 18, 1917, ibid.; Wilson to Lansing, December 12, 1917, with enclosures, and Wilson to Lansing, January 1, 1918, with enclosure, *PWW*, 45:274–75, 417–19.

30. Beaumont, *Heroic Story*, 55–57; Stewart, *White Armies of Russia*, 100–101.

31. *Československý deník*, No. 15, February 7, 1918, Doc. 22, *Dokumenty a materiály*, 47–48. Kennan, "Czechoslovak Legion," 6–7; Beaumont, *Heroic Story*, 55–58; Stewart, *White Armies of Russia*, 101; Masaryk, *Making of a State*, 176, 244.

32. Masaryk, *Making of a State*, 176–77; E. Beneš, *My War Memoirs*, 353–54; Fic, *Bolsheviks and the Czechoslovak Legion*, 4–5.

33. Bradley, *La Légion tchécoslovaque*, 72; Karel Zmrhal, "The Break between the Soviets and the Czecho-Slovaks," in Long Papers.

34. "The Czecho-Slovak Incident," Records of Adjutant General, RG 407, WRCNA. Statement of Captain Hurban in Masaryk to Frank L. Polk, August 7, 1918, DF 861.00/2465 1/2, DSNA.

35. Antonov Ovsjanko (Commander in Chief of the Soviet armies of the Republic of Southern Russia) to all Revolutionary Armies of Southern Russia, March 16, 1918, no. 92, in Zmrhal, "The Break between the Soviets and the Czecho-Slovaks," Long Papers; see also DF 861.00/3816, DSNA, and Packard Report, DF 861.00/6052, DSNA.

36. Kennan, "The Czechoslovak Legion," 6; Stewart, *White Armies of Russia*, 101–2.

37. Doc. 29, *Dokumenty a materiály*, 55–57; E. Beneš, *My War Memoirs*, 355; Kennan, *Decision to Intervene*, 139–40; White, *Siberian Intervention*, 244–45.

38. British War Office to Under Secretary of State for Foreign Affairs, April 3, 1918, FO 371.W38/59310/500420, PRO; Carley, "The Origin of the French Intervention," 420–21; Fic, *Bolsheviks and the Czechoslovak Legion*, 14.

39. Stalin, by order of the Soviet of National Commissaries, to the representatives of the Czechoslovak Army Corps, Moscow, March 26, 1918, in Zmrhal, "Break Between Soviets and Czecho-Slovaks," Long Papers, and Doc. 34, *Dokumenty a materiály*, 62–63; Bunyan, *Intervention, Civil War, and Communism*, 78–82.

40. Mott to Wilson, April 21, 1917, Wilson Collection, Princeton; Wilson to Mott, April 25 and November 9, 1917, Mott Papers; White House Memorandum for the President, November 20, 1917, and Mott to Wilson, November 20, 1917, Wilson Collection, Princeton; D. Davis and Trani, "The American Y.M.C.A. and the Russian Revolution," 464–91; Colton, *Forty Years with Russians*, 80–95.

41. Gardiner H. Miller to Samuel T. Hubbard, June 27, 1918, Polk Papers. Miller and others attached to the Czechs were eager to "be fighting side by side with the people who wish to fight."

42. The Association with the Czecho-Slovaks, April 14, 1918, RWWC; E. T. Heald to Jerome Miller, October 30 to November 12, 1917, Kenneth C. Miller to Wheeler, February 10/23, 1918, Russia-Kiev Correspondence and Reports, 1917–1918, YMCA Archives.

43. Miller to Heald, January 10/23, 1918, Russia-Kiev Correspondence and Reports, 1917–1918, YMCA Archives.

44. Cooperation with the United States Government Agencies in Russia, "Report on War Time Activities of the Y.M.C.A. in Russia, 1917–1919," World Service Materials, YMCA Archives; Poole Memoirs, 206–7. R. M. Story to Mott, in Russia, March 9, 1919, Colton Papers, YMCA Archives. Statement of E. F. Campbell, March 21, 1918, in "Statements made by men of the Russian staff regarding the past and future of the YMCA and their personal plans in present situation," Samara, March 21, 1918, World Service Materials, YMCA Archives. Ethan T. Colton, head of the YMCA in Russia, wanted the YMCA "to be kept wholly clear from performing any kind of propaganda services with either the Consulate or the Committee on Public Information." Colton to C. V. Hibbard, May 9, 1918, World Service Materials, YMCA Archives.

45. Colton Memoirs, Hoover Institution, 57–58.

46. Mott to Colton, April 9, 1919, RWWC. See also Mott to Colton, April 18, 1918, State Department Records, Archangel Consular Files, RG 84, DSNA.

47. Phillips Diary, March 30, 1917; Cronon, *Cabinet Diaries of Daniels*, 125–26; Baker to Lansing, March 31, 1917, and Page to Lansing, March 31, 1917, *FRUS, 1918, Russia*, 3:183–84.

48. Baker to Wilson, March 31, 1917, Baker Papers; *PWW*, 41:511; Stanley K. Hornbeck, "The American Expeditionary Force in Siberia," Division of Far Eastern Affairs, in Hornbeck Papers.

49. Franklin K. Lane to Wilson, April 14, 1917, Wilson Papers.

50. Wilson to Lansing, May 17, 1917, Wilson Papers.

51. Francis to Lansing, May 15, 1917, *FRUS, 1918, Russia*, 3:190.

52. Repington, *First World War*, 1:432, 437–40, 442–43, 469–71, 477, 491; Nabokov, *Ordeal of a Diplomat*, 244–45.

53. Wilson to J. S. Williams, August 13, 1917, J. S. Williams Papers; Sharp to Wilson, June 30, 1917, Wilson Papers; *PWW*, 43:57–59.

54. Noulens, *Mon ambassade*, 2:46.

55. CAB 23/4, War Cabinet 250/64, Minutes of Meeting on October 16, 1917, at 11:30 A.M., PRO; *Literary Digest* (September 15, 1917): 12, and (October 13, 1917): 25. Notes on Russian Situation as It Effects the Allied Cause, Office of Naval Intelligence, October 31, 1917, WA6, Russian Situation, 1917–1919, NRCNA; Reading to Lansing, November 1, 1917, *FRUS, 1918, Russia*, 2:1; Francis to Lansing, November 6, 1917, *FRUS, 1918, Russia*, 1:221.

56. Seymour, *Intimate Papers*, 3:386–88; Phillips Diary, December 24, 1917; House to Lansing, December 1, 1917, House Papers.

57. J. S. Williams to Wilson, August 10, 1917, J. S. Williams Papers and Baker Papers; Wilson to J. S. Williams, August 13, 1917, J. S. Williams Papers.

58. Spring Rice to the Foreign Office, December 22, 27, 1917, FO 115/2318, 266–67, 297–98, PRO.

59. FO 115/2318, 65, PRO.

60. Willard to Lansing, October 8, 1917, and Lansing to Wilson, February 14, 1918, DF 861.77/187 and 291, DSNA; *PWW*, 46:344–45; *FRUS, 1918, Russia*, 3: 213, 216; Hornbeck, "American Expeditionary Force in Siberia," Hornbeck Papers.

61. *FRUS, 1918, Russia*, 3:213, 216; Hornbeck, "American Expeditionary Force in Siberia," Hornbeck Papers.

62. Memorandum from Far Eastern Division, March 5, 1918, DF 761.94/137 1/2, DSNA (also in Hornbeck Papers).

63. Ibid., Memorandum, March 5, 1918, Long Papers; Reinsch to Lansing, May 16, 1918, *PWW*, 48:72; Isvolsky to Sazonov, June 26, 1916, *Un livre noir, diplomatie d'avant guerre et de guerre*, 3:82–83.

64. Polk Diary, January 9, 1918. See also Long Diary, December 31, 1917, January 15, 1918, Long Papers.

65. See also Lansing to Wilson, September 25, 1917, with memoranda of Lansing's conferences with Japanese Special Ambassador Ishii on September 6 and 22, 1917, *PWW*, 44:249–56. Ishii had informed Lansing "that through various channels the German Government had three times sought to persuade Japan to withdraw from the Allies and to remain neutral, but that in every case his Government had firmly rejected the suggestion." Enclosure of September 6, 1917, ibid. Wilson was obviously concerned about this information and spent half an hour with Ishii himself in which he apparently did "most of the talking" in order to give Ishii his "*full* thought" on some of the issues discussed. Wilson to Lansing, September 25, 1917, DF 793.94/583 1/2, DSNA; see also *PWW*, 44:264.

66. Tsao, *The Chinese Eastern Railway*, 29; LaFargue, *China and the World War*, 160.

67. Griswold, *Far Eastern Policy*, 227–28; Grondijs, *La Guerre en Russie et en Sibérie*, 513.

68. Hornbeck, "American Expeditionary Force in Siberia," Hornbeck Papers.

69. Roland S. Morris (Ambassador in Japan) to Lansing, December 24, 1917, *FRUS, 1918, Russia*, 2:11–13. For British efforts to secure American participation in a joint landing with the Japanese at Vladivostok to prevent lone Japanese action, and American opposition, see FO 115/2318, 248, 256, 258, 266–67, 294, 297, PRO.

Chapter 7

1. Notes on Interview with the President, January 23, 1918, Wiseman Papers; *PWW*, 45:323–27; Seymour, *Intimate Papers*, 3:278–86.

2. Balfour to Wilson, May 18, 1917, *PWW*, 42:327–42.

3. House to Wilson, November 30, 1917, *FRUS, 1917, Supp. 2, World War*, 1:328, 352–53.

4. Ibid., 1:328; Seymour, *Intimate Papers*, 3:285, 278-90; House to Wilson, December 1, 2, 1917, House Papers; *PWW*, 45-177, 184-85.

5. Francis to Lansing, November 29, 1917, *FRUS, 1918, Russia*, 1:253.

6. Golder, *Documents of Russian History*, 620.

7. Bunyan and Fisher, eds., *Bolshevik Revolution, Documents*, 282.

8. Francis to Lansing, December 6, 1917, *FRUS, 1918, Russia*, 1:258.

9. Ira N. Morris (Minister to Sweden) to Lansing, December 27, 1917, *FRUS, 1918, Russia*, 1:404. Actually these points, adopted by the Petrograd Soviet as a peace program as early as April 1917, had stimulated the first use of the term "self-determination" among the Czechs in Prague. E. Beneš, *My War Memoirs*, 339.

10. Wheeler-Bennett, *Brest-Litovsk*, 118-20; Price, *Reminiscences of Russian Revolution*, 191.

11. Czernin, *In the World War*, 223-24; Wheeler-Bennett, *Brest-Litovsk*, 121; Fenwick, "Notes on International Affairs," 706-7.

12. Mayer, *Political Origins of New Diplomacy*, 306; Wheeler-Bennett, *Brest-Litovsk*, 129.

13. Francis to Lansing, December 31, 1917, *PWW*, 45:411-14.

14. House Diary, November 29, 1917; Mamatey, *United States and East Central Europe*, 151.

15. Smuts to Lloyd George, December 26, 1917, CAB 1/25, PRO.

16. Mamatey, *United States and East Central Europe*, 150-52; CAB 23/13, War Cabinet 308 (a) 157, Draft Minutes of the Meeting on December 31, 1917, PRO.

17. CAB 23/5, War Cabinet 312/13, Minutes of Meeting on January 3, 1918, at 11:30 A.M., PRO; L. Woodward, *Great Britain and the War of 1914-1918*, 401; Mayer, *Political Origins of New Diplomacy*, 313-28. Czernin's response to the Bolsheviks was accepted by the War Cabinet as a reaffirmation of the British interpretation of the Smuts-Mensdorff conversation, thus providing a renewed opportunity for separating the Austro-Hungarians from the Germans. CAB 23/5, War Cabinet 315/13, Minutes of Meeting on January 5, 1918, PRO. See also Notes on an Interview with the President, January 23, 1918, Wiseman Papers, and *PWW*, 46:85-88; also D. Woodward, "The Origins and Intent of David Lloyd George's January 5 War Aims Speech," 22-39.

18. CAB 23/5, War Cabinet 313/13, Minutes of Meeting on January 3, 1918, at 5:00 P.M., PRO.

19. CAB 23/5, War Cabinet 314/13, Minutes of Meeting on January 4, 1918, PRO. Jusserand was "rather perturbed at the effect in the United States of the news that the Allies were planning an official answer to German-Russian peace terms." Spring Rice to Foreign Office, January 2, 1918, FO 115/2371, 274, PRO; *PWW*, 46:431-32.

20. CAB 23/5, War Cabinet 314/13, Minutes of Meeting on January 4, 1918, PRO. For full address, see *FRUS, 1918, Supp. 1, World War*, 1:4-12, and Lloyd George, *War Memoirs*, 5:63-73. See also *PWW*, 45:487-88, n. 2.

21. *FRUS, 1918, Russia*, 1:244, 253, 258, 405-8.

22. Wilson to Lansing, January 1, 1918, Wilson Papers.

23. Frank William Taussig to Wilson, January 3, 1918, Wilson Collection,

Princeton; *PWW,* 45:440–41; Wheeler-Bennett, *Brest-Litovsk,* 121; Fenwick, "Notes on International Affairs," 706–7.

24. Wheeler-Bennett, *Brest-Litovsk,* 127–36; Price, *Reminiscences of Russian Revolution,* 191; Phillips Diary, January 4, 1918.

25. Francis to Lansing, December 31, 1918, *FRUS, 1918, Russia,* 1:405–8.

26. Phillips Diary, January 2, 3, 1918; Polk Diary, January 3, 1918, Memorandum for the Secretary of State from Basil Miles, January 1, 1918, DF 861.00/935 1/2, DSNA. For Francis's initial opposition to a response and his later change of mind, see Francis to Lansing, December 29, 1917, and January 2, 1918, *FRUS, 1918, Russia,* 1:405, 419–21; Francis to Wilson, January 3, 1918, DF 763.72119/1072, DSNA; *PWW,* 45:433–35.

27. Wilson to Lansing, January 1, 1918, DF 861.00/936 1/2, DSNA; *PWW,* 45:417.

28. Lansing to Wilson, January 2, 1918, Wilson Papers; *PWW,* 45:427–30.

29. Ibid., 428. Interestingly enough, Lansing did not provide a definition of "nationalities." He surely must have perceived that his criticism of the Bolsheviks applied equally to Wilson's position.

30. House Diary, January 3, 1918; Wiseman, The Attitude of the United States and of Wilson towards the Peace Conference, ca. October 20, 1918, Wiseman Papers; reproduced in Fowler, *British-American Relations,* 290–96. Wilson to Lansing, January 29, 1918, DF 763.72119/1266 1/2, DSNA; *PWW,* 46:149.

31. Ronald Hugh Campbell to House, January 2, 1918, Wilson Collection, Princeton. The full report is printed in Lloyd George, *War Memoirs,* 5:21–36.

32. Gwynn, *Letters of Sir Cecil Spring Rice,* 2:422–25.

33. Spring Rice to Balfour, January 4, 1918, Balfour Papers; *PWW,* 45:454–58.

34. Ibid.; Spring Rice to Balfour, January 4, 1918, Balfour Papers. Wilson expressed many of these views to Spring Rice so that they might be conveyed to Balfour, although he preferred that they not be transmitted to Lloyd George. Balfour to Spring Rice, January 5, 1918, ibid.; Cronon, *Cabinet Diaries of Daniels,* 243; Phillips Diary, December 18, 1917; Memorandum for the Secretary of State by Basil Miles, Acting Chief of the Russian Division, January 1, 1918, Wilson to Lansing, January 1, 1918, DF 861.00/935 1/2 and 936 1/2, DSNA; *PWW,* 45:417.

35. Unterberger, "Woodrow Wilson and the Russian Revolution," 52–53.

36. Unterberger, *America's Siberian Expedition,* 22–25; Memorandum from Robert Cecil to the British Embassy, January 1, 1918, Wilson Papers; *PWW,* 45:420.

37. The Inquiry, Memorandum submitted December 22, 1917, "The Present Situation: The War Aims and Peace Terms It Suggests," in *FRUS: Paris Peace Conference, 1919,* 1:41–53.

38. House Diary, January 4, 9, 1918; *PWW,* 45:458–59, 550–59; Mezes, Miller, and Lippmann, "The Present Situation: The War Aims and Peace Terms it Suggests," *PWW,* 45:459–74. For the first drafts of the Fourteen Points, see ibid., 476–86. See also Mezes, Miller, and Lippmann, "Memorandum, January 2, 1917 [1918], A Suggested Statement of Peace Terms"; Wilson Papers, and *PWW,* 45:459, n. 1.

39. Wilson to Lansing, December 22, 28, 1917, *FRUS, 1917, Supp. 2, World War*, 1:483, 511–12.

40. H. R. Wilson to Lansing, December 28, 1917, DF 763.72119/10068, DSNA; *PWW*, 45:415–17; Mamatey, *United States and East Central Europe*, 174. On July 19, the *Reichstag* had passed a peace resolution supporting a peace of "mutual agreements and the enduring reconciliation of peoples." *FRUS, 1917, Supp. 2, World War*, 1:139–40.

41. Wilson to Lansing, January 1, 1918, DF 763.72119/10068, DSNA; *PWW*, 45:415–17. The well-known Austrian historian Heinrich Benedikt believes that insufficient attention has been paid to the Meinl talks, which in his opinion had the best chance of success. See the introduction to his book, *Die Friedens-aktion der Meinlgruppe*, and 308. See also Valiani, *End of Austria-Hungary*, 267–85.

42. Lansing to Grew, January 2, 1918, and Lansing to H. R. Wilson, January 2, 1918, DF 763.72119/10068, DSNA; Barany, "Origin of Wilson's Point 10," 220.

43. Grew to Lansing, January 3, 1918, DF 763.72119/1058, DSNA; H. R. Wilson to Lansing, January 7, 1918, Wilson Papers. For Barany's view, see "Origin of Wilson's Point 10," 220–21.

44. Italics inserted. Balfour to House, January 2, 1918, Wilson Collection, Princeton. The latter phrase was quoted verbatim to Mensdorff in the Smuts-Mensdorff conversation and again quoted specifically to Wilson when Balfour informed him of those conversations two weeks later. The phrase appeared without alteration in Wilson's Point 10.

45. R. S. Baker, *Woodrow Wilson and World Settlement*, 3:38; *PWW*, 45:481–82, 485, 514.

46. Wilson to Lansing, January 29, 1918, DF 763.72119/1266 1/2, DSNA; *PWW*, 46:149.

47. *FRUS, 1918, Supp. 1, World War*, 1:15; *PWW*, 45:514.

48. See Sisson, *One Hundred Red Days*, 209, 211, and *Literary Digest* (March 2, 1918): 17, for an account of how the Fourteen Points were used in Russia.

49. Italics inserted. *PWW*, 45:534–39; Unterberger, "Woodrow Wilson and the Bolsheviks," 71–72.

50. Balfour to House, January 2, 1918, Wilson Papers.

51. Mamatey, *United States and East Central Europe*, 179–80; Pomerance, "The United States and Self-Determination," 1–27.

52. "Critique on Kerner's Memoranda on Austria-Hungary," Inquiry Archives, RG 256/306, DSNA.

53. Baron Ludovic Moncheur to Baron Charles de Broqueville, August 14, 1917, *PWW*, 43:465–70; Cronon, *Cabinet Diaries of Daniels*, 265; Polk to Wilson, January 22, 1918, Wilson Papers; Wilson to Polk, January 23, 1918, DF 763.72119/1166, DSNA; *PWW*, 46:83; Link, *Wilson: Revolution, War, and Peace*, 76.

54. Lansing Diary, January 7, 1918; House Diary, January 9, 1918; *PWW*, 45:550–59.

55. Memorandum on Subject of the President's War Aims Address on January 8, 1918, Which are Open to Debate, January 10, 1918, Lansing Papers, Princeton; Lansing, *War Memoirs*, 261.

56. Lippmann to Mrs. Jess Lyon, January 31, 1967, Fullerton, Calif.; courtesy of Mrs. Lyon.

57. Spring Rice to Wilson, January 13, 1918, FO 115/2432, 53, PRO; Spring Rice to Balfour, January 17, 1918, FO 115/2432, 52, PRO.

58. *FRUS, 1918, Supp. 1, World War,* 1:17–21; T. N. Page to Lansing, January 29, 1918, DF 763.72/8706 1/2, DSNA; T. N. Page to Wilson, January 29, 1918, Wilson Papers; *PWW,* 46:155–60. Lansing's concern over the Italian response led him to advocate sending an American military commission to Italy as soon as possible as the "next best move that we can make" outside of sending a contingent of American troops. Lansing to Wilson, February 18, 1918, Wilson Papers; *PWW,* 46:375–78.

59. American Military Intelligence Report, American Embassy, Rome, January 11, 1918, DF 763.72/9021, DSNA; T. N. Page to Wilson, January 29, 1918, Wilson Papers.

60. Notes on Interview with the President, January 23, 1918, Wiseman Papers, and *PWW,* 46:85–88.

61. Herron to H. R. Wilson, January 25, 1918, Herron Papers; *New York Times,* May 26, 1918.

62. Voska and Irwin, *Spy and Counterspy,* 253; *Denní Hlasatel,* January 14, 1918.

63. House Diary, January 29, 1918; *PWW,* 46:167–68; A Memorandum by William C. Bullitt prepared for Colonel House, January 29, 1918, entitled "Hertling's Address," Wilson Papers; *PWW,* 46:162–67; Auchincloss to Wilson, January 31, 1918, with enclosure from House entitled "Political Developments in Germany since Hertling's Address," prepared by William C. Bullitt, Wilson Papers; *PWW,* 46:183–93.

64. *PWW,* 46:183–93; *New York Times,* January 22, 1918.

65. Villard, *Fighting Years,* 340–41. They were also known in the United States because on January 25, 26, 28, 29, 1918, they had been published in the *Evening Post.*

66. Wheeler-Bennett, *Brest-Litovsk,* 201–4.

67. *FRUS, 1918, Supp. 1, World War,* 54–59. Czernin claimed that he had sent a copy of his speech to Wilson before it was actually delivered. Lansing, however, denied this. Lansing to Page, January 29, 1918, ibid., 51–52. See also Scott, *Official Statements,* 255–60.

68. Czernin, *In the World War,* 188–89.

69. Herron to H. R. Wilson, January 29, 1918, Herron Papers; H. R. Wilson to Lansing, January 30, 1918, House Papers; *PWW,* 46:172–73.

70. CAB 23/16, War Cabinet 325 (a), Minutes of Meeting on January 18, 1918, PRO.

71. Ibid.

72. CAB 23/16, War Cabinet 331 (a), Minutes of Meeting on January 28, 1918, PRO.

73. House Diary, January 31, 1918; House to Wilson, January 31, 1918, Wilson Papers; *PWW,* 46:181–83. In answer to Czernin's speech replying to Wilson's address, House had advised Wilson to "do nothing for the present." Wilson concurred. They both agreed that the "situation was becoming more and more favorable for peace." House Diary, January 27, 1918.

Chapter 8

1. Lansing to Wilson, December 17, 1917, Confidential Letters, RG 59, DSNA; "Preparatory Remarks," Germany, I, Herron Papers; Phillips to Ellis Loring Dresel, May 19, 1917, Dresel Papers; H. R. Wilson, *Diplomat between Wars*, 6–7.

2. Phillips Diary, October 18, 1917; H. R. Wilson, *Diplomat between Wars*, 11–12; Dulles to John W. Foster, May 21, 1917, Dulles Papers; Lansing to Wilson, December 17, 1917, Confidential Letters, RG 59, DSNA.

3. Polk to American Legation (Bern), January 11, 1918, DF 863.00/68a, DSNA. Herron to Sharp, January 28, 1918, House Papers.

4. Grew to Wilson, February 12, 1918, Grew Papers; Allen C. Dulles was assigned to the races and politics of Austria-Hungary, the Balkans, and Turkey. H. R. Wilson, *Diplomat between Wars*, 11–12; Dulles to Foster, May 21, 1917, Dulles Papers.

5. H. R. Wilson, *Diplomat between Wars*, 23–24.

6. Auchincloss Diary, January 30, February 1, 1918. Richard Crane to Lansing, January [n.d.], 1918; W. H. Lamar to Burleson, January 15, 1918; Woodrow Wilson to Lansing, January [n.d.], 1918; all in DF 861.00/1011, DSNA. H. R. Wilson, *Diplomat between Wars*, 23.

7. H. R. Wilson to Mitchel Pirie Briggs, September 3, 1929, and Herron to Morris Hillquit, November 11, 1924, Herron Papers.

8. Briggs, *Herron and the European Settlement*, 9, 25.

9. Wilson to Mitchell Kennerly, October 1, 1917, Herron Papers; *PWW*, 44:287; Theodore K. Shipkoff to Crane, September 23, 1919, C. R. Crane Papers; Samuel Huston Thompson, Jr., to Wilson, December 9, 1917, Wilson Papers; *PWW*, 45:255–56.

10. Herron to Morris Hillquit, November 11, 1914, Herron Papers.

11. Wilson to Polk, August 10, 1918, Lansing Papers, Princeton; H. R. Wilson to Briggs, September 2, 1929, Herron Papers; Lansing to Sharp, January 15, 1918, *FRUS, 1918, Supp. 1, World War,* 1:31; Grew to H. R. Wilson, February 19, 1918, Grew Papers. See also Wilson to Lansing, February 4, 1918, DF 763.72119/1267 1/2, DSNA; *PWW*, 46:235; Shipkoff to Crane, September 23, 1919, C. R. Crane Papers; and Wilson to Lansing, February 16, 1918, DF 763.72119/1300 1/2, DSNA; *PWW*, 46:357.

12. "Preparatory Remarks," Germany, I, Herron Papers; H. R. Wilson, *Diplomat between Wars*, 20–22.

13. Briggs, *Herron and the European Settlement*, 116. It was a view shared by both Grew and Dulles, who had both served in Vienna. Dulles to Foster, May 2, 1917, Dulles Papers.

14. "Preparatory Remarks," Germany, I, also V, Document I, 5–7, Herron Papers; Osuský, "Secret Peace Negotiations," 657–58.

15. Herron to H. R. Wilson, January 29, 1918, Austria: Document II, Herron Papers; H. R. Wilson to Lansing, January 31, 1918, Lansing Papers, Princeton; *PWW*, 46:198–200; H. R. Wilson, *Diplomat between Wars*, 35–37; Herron, "A Golden Bridge Unbuilt," 378. For the efforts of Meinl and Lammasch to find a way of initiating peace feelers with President Wilson, see Polzer-Hoditz, *Kaiser*

Karl, 453; Valiani, *End of Austria-Hungary,* 185, 219, 267–69; and Benedikt, *Die Friedensaktion der Meinlgruppe,* 231.

16. H. R. Wilson to Lansing, January 31, 1918, DF 763.72119/8155, DSNA, and Lansing Papers, Princeton; *PWW,* 46:198–200.

17. H. R. Wilson to Lansing, January 31, 1918, ibid. For confirmation of Herron's view, see Memorandum of a Conversation by Professor George Herron, February 3, 1918, Austria: Document IV, 1–6, Herron Papers; *PWW,* 46:242–47.

18. H. R. Wilson to Lansing, January 31, 1918, *PWW,* 46:198–200.

19. Muehlon was described as a "man of unusual personality, clarity of mind, and with great belief in the future of a regenerated Germany." He had apparently given up his position as one of the directors of Krupp while still quite young, because of his conviction that Germany was both "profoundly wrong in the current struggle and a menace to civilization." H. R. Wilson to Lansing, February 8, 1918, *FRUS, 1918, Supp. 1, World War,* 1:82–105; H. R. Wilson, *Diplomat between Wars,* 36; H. R. Wilson to Lansing, February 5, 1918, Lansing Papers, Princeton; *PWW,* 46:253–54.

20. Memorandum of Conversation by Professor George Herron, February 3, 1918, Austria: Document IV, 1–6, Herron Papers; also in Wilson Papers; *PWW,* 46:242–47; H. R. Wilson to Lansing, January 31, 1918, *PWW,* 46:198–200.

21. Memorandum of Conversation, Prof. George D. Herron, February 3, 1918, enclosure in H. R. Wilson to Lansing, February 4, 1918, Wilson Papers; *PWW,* 46:241–47.

22. Memorandum of a Conversation with Professor Herron, Austria: Document V, 1–10, Herron Papers.

23. Wilson to House, January 31, 1918, House Papers, and *PWW,* 46:178.

24. *PWW,* 46:178; Wiseman to Drummond and Balfour, February 4, 1918, Wiseman Papers; *PWW,* 46:247–50.

25. Sharp to Lansing, February 2, 1918, *FRUS, 1918, Supp. 1, World War,* 1:70–71; Scott, *Official Statements,* 271–73.

26. Sharp to House, February 2, 1918, enclosing statement of Supreme War Council, House Papers; Scott, *Official Statements,* 263; Wiseman to Drummond and Balfour, February 4, 1918, Wiseman Papers; enclosure dated February 2, 1918, in Woodrow Wilson to Lansing, February 4, 1918, *PWW,* 46:233–35; see also *PWW,* 46:247–50.

27. House to Wilson, February 3, 1918, Wilson Papers; Wilson to Lansing, February 4, 1918, House Papers; both printed in *PWW,* 46:221, 233. Balfour supported the announcement and despite sharp Parliamentary criticism adhered to the position that diplomacy at that moment provided no means of ending the war. Scott, *Official Statements,* 273–77.

28. Wilson to Lansing, February 4, 1918, Wilson Papers, and *PWW,* 46:233; Polk to Sharp, February 5, 1918, *FRUS, 1918, Supp. 1, World War,* 1:81–82. The President demonstrated his anger in a blunt response to his allies, which he agreed to let Lansing temper, but not without making them aware of the gravity of his objections. Wilson to Lansing, February 16, 1918, DF 763.72 SU/32 1/2, DSNA, and also in *PWW,* 46:360–61. Notes were sent to the British, French, and Italian Ambassadors and telegrams to London, Rome, and Paris.

The original note was written on the President's typewriter. See Wilson Papers. See also *FRUS, 1918, Supp. 1, World War,* 1:81–82, for the President's instructions to Arthur Hugh Frazier (Counselor of Embassy in Paris) that hereafter any Allied statement which might be considered political should be first referred to the President for his approval or a disclaimer issued that it had not been submitted to the American government. For the printed note to the Ambassadors of Britain, France, and Italy, see ibid., 125.

29. House to Wilson, February 3, 1918, Wilson Papers; *PWW,* 46:221; Wiseman to Drummond and Balfour, February 4, 1918, and Reading to Foreign Office, February 19, 1918, Wiseman Papers. See also Reading to Balfour, February 26, 1918, Wiseman Papers, and *PWW,* 46:247–50, 465–67.

30. *PWW,* 46:241–47, 261–63; H. R. Wilson to Lansing, February 6, 1918, Lansing Papers, Princeton; Dulles to Lansing, February 11, 1918, Dulles Papers.

31. Lansing, "Memorandum on Dr. Heinrich Lammasch," February 10, 1918, Wilson Papers, and *PWW,* 46:315–16.

32. Wiseman to Drummond and Balfour, February 4, 1918, Wiseman Papers; *PWW,* 46:247–50; Balfour to House, February 8, 1918, House Papers, original in Balfour Papers; Briggs, *Herron and the European Settlement,* 83; see also Bullitt's support of this policy in his Memorandum for Colonel House, February 7, 1918, enclosure in Auchincloss to Wilson, February 7, 1918, Wilson Papers, and also *PWW,* 46:265–68.

33. Lansing Diary, February 11, 1918; *New York Times,* February 12, 1918.

34. *PWW,* 46:318–24; *FRUS, 1918, Supp. 1, World War,* 1:108–13; Scott, *Official Statements,* 265–71. To Wilson the "thing at stake now" was "the peace of the World." "An Outline of an Address to a Joint Session of Congress," ca. February 8, 1918, Wilson Papers, and *PWW,* 46:273–74. For the various drafts of his address, see ibid., 274–79, 291–97.

35. W. H. Page to House, February 8, 1918, House Papers.

36. Auchincloss Diary, February 18, 1918; Lansing Diary, February 12, 1918; Voska and Irwin, *Spy and Counterspy,* 253.

37. Voska and Irwin, *Spy and Counterspy,* 255–58; Phillip Patchin to Creel, April 1, 1918, CPI, RG 63, NA.

38. Lansing to H. R. Wilson, February 15, 1918, DF 763.72119/8184a, DSNA, and also in *PWW,* 46:353.

39. H. R. Wilson to Lansing, February 21, 1918, Lansing Papers, Princeton, and also in *PWW,* 46:412–13.

40. H. R. Wilson to Lansing, February 16, 1918, *PWW,* 46:365–66; Valiani, *End of Austria-Hungary,* 281.

41. H. R. Wilson to Lansing, February 19, 1918, Lansing Papers, Princeton, and *PWW,* 46:388; Osuský, "Secret Peace Negotiations," 667; Briggs, *Herron and the European Settlement,* 84.

42. W. H. Page to Lansing, February 20, 1918, *PWW,* 46:397–400; Seymour, *Intimate Papers,* 3:372–73.

43. W. H. Page to Lansing, February 21, 1918, DF 763.72119/7727, DSNA, and *PWW,* 46:397–400, 411–12; Page Diary, February 23, 1918.

44. *PWW,* 46:397–400.

45. Lansing to Wilson, February 23, 1918, Lansing Papers, Princeton, and *PWW*, 46:424.

46. House Diary, February 24, 1918; House to Balfour, February 24, 1918, Wiseman Papers, House Papers, and *PWW*, 46:432.

47. House Diary, February 26, 1918; *PWW*, 46:467–68.

48. Lansing Diary, February 26, 1918; Wiseman to Drummond, February 26, 1918, Wiseman Papers; *PWW*, 46:464.

49. Lansing Diary, February 25, 1918.

50. House Diary, February 26, 1918; *PWW*, 46:467–68; Alfonso XIII to the President, February 25, 1918, Wilson Papers, and also *PWW*, 46:440–42; W. H. Page to Lansing, March 6, 1918, *FRUS, 1918, Supp. 1, World War,* 1:149.

51. House Diary, February 28, 1918; Lansing Diary, February 28, 1918; Lansing to Wilson, February 23, 1918, Lansing Papers, Princeton; A Draft of a Telegram to Alfonso XIII, February 28, 1918, Wilson Papers, and also *PWW*, 46:486–87.

52. "Memorandum on the President's Proposed Reply to the Emperor Karl's Personal Communication," February 28, 1918, Lansing Papers, LC.

53. Ibid.

54. Balfour to House, February 27, 1918, FO 115/2388, 106–7, PRO; also in Wilson Papers, Wiseman Papers, and *PWW*, 46:483–84; original in Balfour Papers.

55. Page to Lansing and the President only, February 27, 1918, Lansing Papers, Princeton, and also *PWW*, 46:473–74. See also *Corriere della Sera* (Milan), February 14, 1918, for a forthright editorial comment on Wilson and Czernin. North Winship to Lansing, February 15, 1918, CPI, RG 63, NA.

56. Wiseman to Drummond, March 1, 1918, Wiseman Papers; *PWW*, 46:507–8.

57. *FRUS, 1918, Supp. 1, World War,* 1:183–84; *PWW*, 46:508.

58. Lansing Diary, March 1, 1918; Lansing to Reading, March 1, 1918, *Lansing Papers,* 2:109; Lansing to Reading, March 1, 1918, FO 115/2429, 228–29, PRO; Polk Diary, March 1, 1918.

59. Wilson to J. S. Williams, February 18, 1918, J. S. Williams Papers; *PWW*, 46:369–70.

60. Clemenceau, *Grandeur and Misery of Victory,* 190–92; Wheeler-Bennett, *Brest-Litovsk,* 363–66.

61. E. Beneš, *My War Memoirs,* 197; Papoušek, *Czechoslovak Nation's Struggle,* 61–62.

62. CAB 23/16, War Cabinet 357a, Very Secret Minutes of Meeting on March 1, 1918, PRO.

63. Ibid.

64. Mamatey, *United States and East Central Europe,* 230.

65. CAB 23/16, War Cabinet 359a, Minutes of Meeting on March 5, 1918, PRO.

66. Fürstenberg to Czernin, March 5, 1918, intercepted by British Intelligence, DF 763.72119/8735, DSNA; *PWW*, 46:551–53.

67. CAB 23/16, War Cabinet 360a, Minutes of Meeting on March 6, 1918, PRO.

68. Balfour to House, March 7, 1918, Wiseman Papers; House to Wilson, March 8, 1918, Wilson Papers; *PWW*, 46:574–75. House could not "quite understand why Austria would want to continue conversations with England while they are having them with us"; ibid.

69. Page to Lansing, March 12, 1918, DF 763.72/930 1/2, DSNA.

70. Balfour to House, March 13, 1918, Wiseman Papers, original in Balfour Papers; House to Wilson, March 13, 1918, Wilson Papers; *PWW*, 46:11–12.

71. Stovall to Lansing, March 18, 1918, DF 763.72/9523, DSNA. Lloyd George, *War Memoirs*, 5:50–53; Seymour, *Intimate Papers*, 3:379–81.

72. Stovall to Lansing, March 5, 1918, *FRUS, 1918, Supp. 1, World War*, 1:150–51.

73. Stovall to Lansing, March 23, 1918, *PWW*, 47:127–29; Polk to H. R. Wilson, March 23, 1918, DF 763.72119/8730, DSNA.

74. "Memorandum on Parliament and Government in Austria, March–July 1918," Political Intelligence Department, Foreign Office Austria, August 15, 1918, Records of War Department to General Staff, RG 165, WRCNA.

75. Herron, A Visit from Count Windisch-Graetz, Geneva, November 22, 1918, Austria: Document XLIII, Herron Papers.

76. Wilson to Polk, March 10, 1918, Lansing Papers, Princeton, commenting on H. R. Wilson to Lansing, February 8, 1918. See the Herron-Lammasch conversations, February 3, 4, 1918, *FRUS, 1918, Supp. 1, World War*, 1:82–105.

77. Mamatey, *United States and East Central Europe*, 232.

78. Emperor Charles to Wilson, March 23, 1918, *FRUS, 1918, Supp. 1, World War*, 1:184–86. The intercepted message bears no date of receipt in Washington.

79. Mamatey, *United States and East Central Europe*, 232; R. S. Baker, *Wilson: Life and Letters*, 8:39–40.

80. Stovall to Lansing, March 25, 1918, DF 763.72/9534, DSNA.

81. Balfour to House, April 3, 1918, Wiseman Papers.

82. Herron to H. R. Wilson, April 11, 1918, Austria: Document XIX, 4–7, Herron Papers; Shipkoff to Crane, September 23, 1919, C. R. Crane Papers.

83. Herron to H. R. Wilson, April 11, 1918, Austria: Document XIX, 10–12, Herron Papers.

84. Garrett to Lansing, April 3, 1918, *FRUS, 1918, Supp. 1, World War*, 1:189–95; Valiani, *End of Austria-Hungary*, 219–20.

85. Garrett to Lansing, April 3, 1918, *FRUS, 1918, Supp. 1, World War*, 1:189–95. Except for his mention of France, Czernin's address was similar to the Emperor's letter.

86. Thomson, *Czechoslovakia in European History*, 278.

87. E. Taylor, *The Fall of the Dynasties*, 342–43; Valiani, *End of Austria-Hungary*, 221.

88. De Manteyer, *Austria's Peace Offer*, 36–38, 83–84; Vivian, *Emperor Charles of Austria*, 130.

89. Lansing, *War Memoirs*, 263–64; R. S. Baker, *Wilson: Life and Letters*, 8:68–69, 81.

90. Mamatey, *United States and East Central Europe*, 235–36.

91. Herron to H. R. Wilson, April 19, 1918, DF 763.72119/1662, DSNA.

92. Sharp to Lansing, April 14, 1918, *FRUS, 1918, Supp. 1, World War*, 1:213–14; Egan (Copenhagen) to Lansing, April 13, 1918, DF 763.72/9553, DSNA.

93. E. Beneš, *My War Memoirs*, 326.

94. CAB 23/16, War Cabinet 391A, *Secret*. Personal Note by the Secretary of a Discussion with regard to the letter from the Austrian Emperor, published by authority of the French Government, April 1918, PRO. Discussion took place on April 15, 1918, as part of War Cabinet 391. (The Secretary was instructed to make no official minutes of the meeting, but for purposes of the record it was felt advisable to prepare a personal note.)

95. Address of President Wilson Delivered at Baltimore, April 6, 1918, *PWW*, 47:267–70.

96. "Memorandum on the Making Public, by M. Clemenceau, of the Austrian Emperor's Letter to Prince Sixtus de Bourbon, April 12, 1918," Lansing Papers, LC.

97. Herron to Sharp, April 13, 1918, DF 763.72119/1602, DSNA. Polk sent the note to the President and Lansing.

98. Herron to H. R. Wilson, April 16, 1918, DF 763.72119/1661, DSNA.

99. Herron to President Wilson, April 19, 1918, Austria: Document XIV, Herron Papers.

Chapter 9

1. Briggs, *Herron and the European Settlement*, 73–75. See also *Denní Hlasatel*, May 23, 1918.

2. Hanak, *Great Britain and Austria-Hungary*, 276–79; Steed, *Through Thirty Years*, 2:185–220; Calder, *Britain and Origins of New Europe*, 176–77.

3. E. Beneš, *My War Memoirs*, 328. The State Department received the details of this meeting on May 3, through Colonel Mervyn C. Buckey, the American Military Attaché in Rome. Page to Lansing, May 3, 1918, *FRUS, 1918, Supp. 1, World War*, 1:799–802. See also John F. Bass, "Report on the International Committee for Propaganda in Enemy Countries" (April 28, 1918), which strongly recommended American cooperation with the Committee's efforts, particularly on the Italian front. CPI, 20-B3, RG 63, NA.

4. CAB 23/5, War Cabinet 359, March 5, 1918, PRO; E. Beneš, *My War Memoirs*, 329.

5. Calder, *Britain and Origins of New Europe*, 180.

6. Ibid.; Zeman, *Break-Up of Habsburg Empire*, 192.

7. CAB 23/5, War Cabinet 359, March 6, 1918, PRO; E. Beneš, *My War Memoirs*, 329.

8. Sharp to Lansing, March 24, 1918, DF 763.72119/8784, DSNA.

9. Page to Lansing, April 9, 1918, *FRUS, 1918, Supp. 1, World War*, 1:795–96.

10. Page to Lansing, April 12, 1918, *FRUS, 1918, Supp. 1, World War*, 1:796–97; Bass, "Report on Committee for Propaganda," CPI, 20-B3, RG 63, NA.

11. Bass, "Report on Committee for Propaganda," CPI, 20-B3, RG 63, NA; Page to Lansing, May 3, 1918, *FRUS, 1918, Supp. 1, World War*, 1:799–802.

12. *FRUS, 1918, Supp. 1, World War,* 1:801–2.

13. When Phillip Patchin of the Committee on Public Information was asked to take advantage of the situation by "means of appropriate publicity," he was "personally . . . at a loss to know" just what could be done and sought counsel from others on the committee. Patchin to Will Irwin, May 2, 1918, CPI, 17 A6, RG 63, NA.

14. See Inquiry Archives, RG 256/283 and 256/997, DSNA; H. W. Steed, "A Program for Peace," 18, Inquiry Archives, RG 256/38, DSNA.

15. Edward Vaczy to Creel, February 11, 1918, CPI, RG 63, NA.

16. "Memorandum of Suggestions for Stimulating Revolutions in Austria-Hungary among Her Subject Peoples through Immigrants from These Peoples in the United States" (May 2, 1918), in CPI, 17 A6, RG 63, NA; Louis J. Piro to Herbert Miller, May 5, 1918, ibid.

17. Auchincloss Diary, January 30, February 18, 1918; Lansing Diary, March 20, 1918; Voska and Irwin, *Spy and Counterspy,* vii–viii, 259.

18. Masaryk to Crane, April 10, 1918, DF 861.00/2721, DSNA; *PWW,* 47:548–52; Masaryk, *Making of a State,* 201–2; *Japan Advertiser,* April 11, 1918. For an edited version of the memorandum with additional comments, see Seton-Watson, *Masaryk in England,* 103–7.

19. Morris to Lansing, April 13, 1918, *FRUS, 1918, Russia,* 2:122.

20. E. Beneš, *My War Memoirs,* 359–60; Seton-Watson, *Masaryk in England,* 112.

21. Long to Secretary of Treasury, April 17, 1918, DF 861.00/1579, DSNA.

22. "Preparatory Remarks," January 1, 1918, Germany, I, Herron Papers; Herron to Wilson, April 19, 1918, Austria: Document XXV, ibid. Briggs, *Herron and the European Settlement,* 116–17.

23. Stovall to Lansing, April 24, 1918, DF 763.72119/8793, DSNA.

24. Sharp to Lansing, April 23, 1918, ibid.

25. Reading to Lansing, May 4, 1918, DF 763.72/9812, DSNA.

26. Page to Lansing, May 7, 1918, DF 763.72/9893 1/2, DSNA; Valiani, *End of Austria-Hungary,* 244.

27. Masaryk, *Making of A State,* 207; *Denní Hlasatel,* May 6, 1918.

28. *Washington Post,* May 5, 1918; *New York Times,* May 6, 1918.

29. J. S. Williams to Wilson, May 6, 1918, and MSS of speech, May 14, 1918, J. S. Williams Papers.

30. Wilson to J. S. Williams, May 8, 1918, Wilson Papers; *PWW,* 47:561.

31. Lansing Diary, May 16, 18, 1918.

32. Masaryk, *Making of a State,* 224. Herbert Hoover claimed an intimacy with Masaryk and felt that he was responsible for securing through Secretary Houston his original introduction to Wilson. Hoover had a high regard for Masaryk and saw a good deal of him prior to the armistice; Hoover, *Memoirs,* 1:379. Professor Guido Kisch gives Sabath a primary role in preparing the way for and cooperating with Masaryk in the promotion of the Czech liberation movement. See "Wilson and Independence of Small Nations," 235–38. The decisive role in getting Masaryk's appointment with Wilson on June 19 has also been assigned to Mott. See Long and Hopkins, "T. G. Masaryk and Czechoslovak Independence," 96.

33. Lansing Diary, May 6, 1918. This is the first time that Masaryk's name appears in Lansing's diary.

34. Crane to Wilson, May 8, 1918, Wilson Papers; PWW, 47:561.

35. Tumulty to Wilson, May 9, 1918; Wilson to Tumulty, May 10, 1918; Richard Crane to Wilson, May 7, 1918, enclosing Masaryk's memorandum; all in Wilson Papers and PWW, 47:548–52.

36. Putney, Memorandum on the Slavs of Austria, May 8, 1918, and Summary of the important sections of Mr. Putney's memorandum on the Slavs of Austria, both in Long Papers.

37. Lansing to Wilson, May 10, 1918, PWW, 47:589–91.

38. Wilson to Madam Paderewski, May 9, 1918, Wilson Papers; PWW, 47:576–77.

39. Lansing Diary, May 10, 1918. Wilson returned to Lansing at this time his letter of May 10. See handwritten notation on Lansing to Wilson, May 10, 1918, Lansing Papers, Princeton; PWW, 47:589–91.

40. Mamatey, "Dissolution of Austria-Hungary," 269.

41. Richard Crane to Wilson, May 11, 1918, Wilson Papers; PWW, 47:610–11. Wilson explained in a handwritten note that he was "so pressed just now that I *must* postpone it."

42. Lansing Diary, May 15, 1918.

43. Lansing to Wilson, May 13, 1918, enclosing Lansing to Page, May 11, 1918, Lansing Papers, Princeton. Page was also asked for his personal view.

44. Lansing to Wilson, May 13, 1918, ibid.

45. Lansing to Wilson, May 13, 1918, Lansing Papers, 2:128; Page to Lansing, May 18, 1918, DF 763.71/10101, DSNA.

46. Lansing to Wilson, May 21, 1918, DF 763.72/10103, DSNA; PWW, 48:96–97.

47. Stovall to Lansing, May 13, 16, 1918, DF 763.72119/1668 and 1669, DSNA; Stovall to Lansing, May 13, 1918, and Page to Lansing, May 18, 1918, DF 763.72/10229 and 10103, DSNA.

48. Lansing to Wilson, May 13, 1918, Lansing Papers, 2:128.

49. Memorandum of a Conversation with Professor Masaryk, May 16, 1918, Long Papers; Lansing Diary, May 15, 1918.

50. Phillips to Lansing, May 25, 1918, DF 763.72/10294 1/2, DSNA. The Serbian Minister suggested using the phrase "aspirations for liberty and independence had the earnest sympathy," etc.

51. Substance of the Note Exchanged Between the Japanese and Chinese Governments on the 25th of March 1918, DF 861.00/1865 1/2, DSNA, also in Wilson Papers; Memorandum for the Secretary of State, May 21, 1918, Long Papers; Long Diary, April 8, 9, May 18, 1918; see also PWW, 48:104–7. For the text of the Sino-Japanese Military Agreements, MacMurray, *Treaties*, 2:1406–7.

52. Long Diary, May 24, 1918.

53. Crane to Phillips, May 24, 1918, DF 861.00/1940, DSNA.

54. *New York Times*, May 23, 26, 1918. Regrettably, other than newspaper accounts, no record of these speeches exists. Since Masaryk spoke extemporaneously, advance copies of his speeches were not normally available to the press. Dr. Ruza L. Stuerm, Masaryk Institute, Inc., to William Shepard, November 4, 1965, courtesy of Professor Shepard.

55. Phillips to Lansing, May 25, 1918, DF 763.72/10294 1/2, DSNA; Francis to Lansing, May 31, 1918, citing Circular Telegram, May 29, 1918, *FRUS, 1918, Russia,* 2:183. One Czech spokesman identified Putney as the author of the memorandum. See Pergler, *Struggle for Czechoslovak Independence,* 91. A comparison of the announcement with Putney's memorandum clearly shows a strong similarity if not virtual identity of terminology.

56. Dr. L. J. Fisher to Lansing, May 30, 1918, DF 763.72/10185, DSNA.

57. *FRUS, 1918, Supp. 1, World War,* 1:808–9; *Denní Hlasatel,* May 30, 1918.

58. L. Michailovitch (Serbian Minister) to Lansing, June 14, 1918, DF 763.72119/1747, DSNA. For Masaryk's comment, see note by Masaryk written on his own typewriter, entitled "Confidential and Private Audience with Mr. Lansing, June 3, 1918," Masaryk Archives, in Křížek, "T. G. Masaryk," 656–57.

59. Mamatey, "Dissolution of Austria-Hungary," 269.

60. Wiseman to Drummond, May 30, 1918, Wiseman Papers; *PWW,* 48:203–6.

Chapter 10

1. Zmrhal, "Break Between Soviets and Czecho-Slovaks," Long Papers; "Czecho-Slovak Incident," RG 407, WRCNA.

2. Masaryk to Crane, April 10, 1918, DF 861.00/2721, DSNA; Beaumont, *Heroic Story,* 68.

3. "Czecho-Slovak Incident," RG 407, WRCNA.

4. Bunyan, *Intervention, Civil War, and Communism,* 80–81.

5. Mints and Gorodetsky, *Dokumenty po istorii grazhdanskoi voiny v SSSR,* 1:199.

6. MacAdam, "Anabasis of the Czecho-Slovaks," 627; Packard Report, DF 861.00/6052, DSNA; Fic, *Bolsheviks and the Czechoslovak Legion,* 7, 12–13.

7. Story to Mott, March 9, 1919, RWWC; CAB 23/6, War Cabinet 401/68, Minutes of Meeting on April 30, 1918, PRO.

8. Poole to Lansing, August 12, 1919, DF 861.00/5181 1/2, DSNA.

9. Fic, *Bolsheviks and the Czechoslovak Legion,* 16.

10. "Czecho-Slovak Incident," RG 407, WRCNA; MacAdam, "Anabasis of the Czecho-Slovaks," 628; Zmrhal, "Break Between Soviets and Czecho-Slovaks," Long Papers. For Stalin's order, see Doc. 34, *Dokumenty a materiály,* 62–63.

11. Bunyan, *Intervention, Civil War, and Communism,* 79.

12. Daily News Resumé, April 5, 1918, Francis Papers.

13. Rainey, "History of the Czecho-Slovak Movement"; Edwin Landon, "Report on a Trip to Western Siberia and Eastern Russia"; Major H. H. Slaughter, "Report on Trip into Siberia and Russia, May 19 to September 15, 1918"; all in RG 120, WRCNA (hereafter cited as Rainey Report, Landon Report, or Slaughter Report, RG 120, WRCNA). See also "Report of Movements of Czecho-Slovak Trains at Present in Mariinsk to Date, June 8, 1918," by Ernest T. Campbell, DF 861.00/2984, DSNA; Bunyan, *Intervention, Civil War, and Communism,* 78–80; White, *Siberian Intervention,* 245; E. Beneš, *My War*

Memoirs, 365; Beaumont, *Heroic Story,* 68–69. Masaryk himself wrote that since the Corps was "going to France, they need not have their rifles as they will be armed in France." Masaryk to Crane, April 10, 1918, DF 861.00/2721, DSNA.

14. Zmrhal, "Break Between Soviets and Czecho-Slovaks," Long Papers; Doc. 39, *Dokumenty a materiály,* 70–71; Bunyan, *Intervention, Civil War, and Communism,* 81–82.

15. Sadoul, *Notes sur la révolution bolchévique,* 367; Doc. 32 and 42, *Dokumenty a materiály,* 59–61, 71–72; Fic, *Bolsheviks and the Czechoslovak Legion,* 32–35.

16. Story to Mott, March 9, 1919, RWWC, YMCA Archives; Zmrhal, "Break Between Soviets and Czecho-Slovaks," Long Papers.

17. Trotskii, *Sochineniia,* pt. 1:278; Polner, "Czech Legion and the Bolsheviks," 23–24. For a differing view of the role of the Russian commanders in the Czech corps, see Fic, *Bolsheviks and the Czechoslovak Legion,* 35.

18. Polner, "Czech Legion and the Bolsheviks," 23–24.

19. Packard Report, DF 861.00/6052, DSNA.

20. Ibid.; "Czecho-Slovak Incident," RG 120, WRCNA; Bunyan, *Intervention, Civil War, and Communism,* 83–85.

21. Bunyan, *Intervention, Civil War, and Communism,* 68–95.

22. "Czecho-Slovak Incident," RG 120, WRCNA; Beaumont, *Heroic Story,* 68–69.

23. "Czecho-Slovak Incident," RG 120, WRCNA; Packard Report, DF 861.00/6052, DSNA; Bunyan, *Intervention, Civil War, and Communism,* 83–85.

24. Orsen M. Nielsen to Francis, April 1, 1918, Francis Papers; Diary of William V. Duncan, February 28, March 31, 1918, in Duncan Papers (hereafter cited as Duncan Diary).

25. David B. Macgowan to Maddin Summers (Consul General in Moscow), April 3, 1918, Francis Papers.

26. Nielsen to Summers, April 2, 1918, and Nielsen Report, April 8, 1918, ibid.; Duncan Diary, March 10, 1918.

27. Polner, "Czech Legion and the Bolsheviks," 40; Fic, *Bolsheviks and the Czechoslovak Legion,* 30–31.

28. Willing Spencer (Chargé d'Affaires at Peking) to Lansing, March 6, 1918, and Reinsch to Lansing, April 10, 1918, *FRUS, 1918, Russia,* 2:69–70, 117.

29. March 18, 1918, Polk Papers.

30. Unterberger, *America's Siberian Expedition,* 46.

31. Graves, *America's Siberian Adventure,* 26.

32. Reinsch to Lansing, April 10, 1918, *FRUS, 1918, Russia,* 2:117.

33. Masaryk to Crane, April 10, 1918, DF 861.00/2721, DSNA; *PWW,* 47:548–52.

34. Story to Mott, March 9, 1919, RWWC, YMCA Archives.

35. Lansing to Wilson, March 24, 1918, *PWW,* 47:131–32.

36. Drummond to Wiseman, January 30, 1918, and Wiseman to Drummond, February 1, 1918, Wiseman Papers; *PWW,* 46:213; House to Wilson, February 2, 1918, Wilson Papers; *PWW,* 46:214–15; Lansing to Bliss, February 2, 1918, Bliss Papers; *PWW,* 46:219–20; Wilson to Lansing, February 4, 1918, DF 861.00/1097, DSNA.

37. A Memorandum by Colville A. de Rune Barclay, British Chargé,

February 6, 1918, handed to Polk, February 7, 1918, DF 861.00/1098, DSNA; *PWW,* 46:270–71.

38. Bliss to Peyton C. March, February 20, 1918, Bliss Papers; see also Baker to Wilson, February 26, 1918, with enclosure from Bliss, *PWW,* 46:452–54.

39. March, *Nation at War,* 115.

40. Morris to Lansing, February 8, 1918, *FRUS, 1918, Russia,* 2:42–43; *PWW,* 46:345, n. 1.

41. Lansing to Wilson, enclosing Department Memorandum, February 9, 1918, signed by E. T. Williams and B. Long with Wilson's response noted on the document. DF 861.00/1097, DSNA, and *PWW,* 46:301–3.

42. Lansing to W. H. Page, February 13, 1918, DF 861.00/1066, DSNA; *PWW,* 46:339–41. Over a year earlier, Wilson had instructed Reinsch to tell the Chinese government of his "sincere" desire "to help China" and that "we are constantly trying to shield her against the selfishness of her neighbor." Wilson to Lansing, February 10, 1917, DF 763.72/3275, DSNA; *PWW,* 41:186.

43. Reinsch to Lansing, February 21, 1918, *FRUS, 1918, Russia,* 2:53.

44. "Memoirs of General Dmitri L. Horvath," chap. 5, in Horvath Papers.

45. "Memorandum of Conversation had with the Chinese Minister Today" by Breckinridge Long, February 26, 1918, DF 861.00/1249, DSNA; Long Diary, February 26, 1918.

46. Long Diary, February 22, 17, 1918.

47. Ibid., February 24, 1918.

48. Wiseman to Reading, February 12, 1918, and Wiseman to Drummond, February 19, 1918, Wiseman Papers, and also *PWW,* 46:333–34, 389; Wilson to Lansing, February 13, 1918, Lansing Papers, Princeton; Fowler, *British-American Relations,* 170.

49. Reinsch to Lansing, February 24, 1918, *FRUS, 1918, Russia,* 2:55–56; E. T. Williams to Lansing, February 25, 1918, DF 861.00/1165 1/2, DSNA.

50. Millard to Crane, March 12, 1918, C. R. Crane Papers; Long Diary, January 31, 1918; Lansing Diary, January 31, 1918; House Diary, February 13, 1918; Lansing Diary, February 27, 1918.

51. Wilson to Lansing, February 4, 1918; Lansing to Wilson, February 9, 1918; and Memoranda by Long and E. T. Williams, February 8, 9, 1918; all in DF 861.00/1097, DSNA, and in Wilson Papers; *PWW,* 46:236, 301–4; Cronon, *Cabinet Diaries of Daniels,* 269–70; Wilson to Polk, with enclosures, January 19, 1918, *PWW,* 46:34–35; Polk to American Embassies (London, Paris, Peking), January 21, 1918, DF 861.00/945, DSNA.

52. Lansing to W. H. Page, February 27, 1918, *FRUS, 1918, Russia,* 2:57–58; Long Diary, February 26, 1918.

53. Unterberger, *America's Siberian Expedition,* 28–29; Kennan, *Russia Leaves the War,* 465–74.

54. CAB 23/5, War Cabinet 350, February 20, 1918, PRO.

55. CAB 23/5, War Cabinet 353/14, Minutes of Meeting on February 25, 1918, PRO.

56. Reading to Wilson, February 27, 1918, with two enclosures from Balfour to Reading, dated February 26, 1918, Wilson Papers, also in Wiseman Papers; *PWW,* 46:470–72.

57. Reading to Balfour, February 27, 1918, FO 115/2445, 91, PRO; *PWW*, 46:472.

58. Reading to Balfour, February 27, 1918, Wiseman Papers; FO 115/2445, 93–94, PRO; *PWW*, 46:482.

59. For the French distortion of the Japanese pledge of disinterest and its willingness to go beyond Irkutsk "so far as the Urals" to fight the Germans, see Pichon to Jusserand, no. 510, February 26, 1918 (draft by Berthelot), Guerre, 750:63, FFM-Ar; Kennan, *Russia Leaves the War*, 475; Lansing to Wilson, with enclosure, February 27, 1918, *PWW*, 46:474–76. See also Jusserand to the French Foreign Ministry, received February 28, 1918, État-major de l'armée de terre, 16N3012, FMD-Ar.

60. Reading to British Foreign Office, February 15, 1918, FO 371/3486, PRO; *PWW*, 46:353–57.

61. Reading to Balfour, February 27, 1918, Wiseman Papers, and *PWW*, 46:482; Lansing to Wilson, February 27, 1918, *PWW*, 46:474–76.

62. Morris to Lansing, February 27, 1918, *FRUS, 1918, Russia*, 2:57. Jusserand confirmed Japan's willingness "to act so far as the Ural Mountains" and to promise publicly her disinterest. Summary of a telegram from Eugène L. G. Regnault, French Ambassador at Tokyo, February 27, 1918, Wilson Papers; *PWW*, 46:476.

63. Final Report of Tasker H. Bliss, Joint Note No. 16, February 18, 1918, DF 763.72SU/99, DSNA. Bliss to Henry Pinckney McCain for Lansing, Baker, and March, February 19, 1918, Wilson Papers; *PWW*, 46:391–92.

64. Benedict Crowell, Acting Secretary of War, to Wilson, March 2, 1918, Wilson Papers.

65. Wiseman to Drummond and Balfour, February 4, 1918, Wiseman Papers; *PWW*, 46:247–50.

66. Reading to Balfour, March 2, 1918, FO 115/2445, 100, PRO.

67. A Draft of an Aide-Mémoire, handed to Lansing, March 1, 1918, DF 861.00/1246, DSNA; *PWW*, 46:498; Wiseman to Drummond, March 2, 1918, Wiseman Papers.

68. A Draft of an Aide-Mémoire handed to Lansing, March 1, 1918, DF 861.00/1246, DSNA; *PWW*, 46:498.

69. Lansing to Wilson, March 1, 1918, Long Papers; *PWW*, 46:499.

70. To: The Secretary. Subject: An International Commission to China. Resumé: A plan outlined at the request of the President. Sent as enclosure with Lansing to Wilson, March 1, 1918, Long Papers.

71. E. T. Williams to Lansing, February 21, 1918, enclosure with Lansing to Wilson, March 1, 1918, Long Papers; *PWW*, 46:500–501.

72. A Draft of an Aide-Mémoire handed to Lansing, March 1, 1918, DF 861.00/1246, DSNA; *PWW*, 46:498.

73. Polk to Lansing, March 15, 1918, *FRUS, 1918, Russia*, 2:68–69; Kennan, *Russia Leaves the War*, 479.

74. House Diary, February 25, 1918; Wiseman to Balfour, March 4, 1918, *PWW*, 46:530–31.

75. House to Wilson, March 3, 1918, Wilson Papers, and *PWW*, 46:518–19; House to Balfour, March 4, 1918, Wiseman Papers; House Diary, March 3, 1918. See also Seymour, *Intimate Papers*, 3:392–93; and DF 861.00/1290 1/2, DSNA.

76. Auchincloss Diary, March 3, 1918; House to Wilson, March 3, 1918, and Bullitt to Polk, March 2, 1918, DF 861.00/1290 1/2, DSNA, Wilson Papers, and *PWW,* 46:510–13, 518–19.

77. *PWW,* 46:513; see also *Manchester Guardian,* March 1, 1918.

78. *PWW,* 46:510–13; Cronon, *Cabinet Diaries of Daniels,* 285; Lane and Wall, *Letters of Franklin K. Lane,* 266–67.

79. Benedict Crowell to Wilson, March 5, 1918, with two enclosures from Judson to Acting Chief of Staff entitled "Action in Russia," February 26, March 4, 1918; and memorandum for General Judson, March 4, 1918, entitled "Japanese Intervention in Siberia," by Lieutenant Colonel Sherman Miles, former Military Attaché in Russia; Wilson to Crowell, March 6, 1918, Wilson Papers, and *PWW,* 46:532–44.

80. Auchincloss Diary, March 3, 1918; House to Wilson, March 3, 1918, House Papers and Wilson Papers. See also House Diary, March 3, 4, 5, 1918; and *PWW,* 46:518–19, 532, 553.

81. CAB 23/5, War Cabinet 358/14, Minutes of Meeting on March 4, 1918, PRO; Reading to Foreign Office, March 4, 1918, *PWW,* 46:506–7; Seymour, *Intimate Papers,* 3:397; Unterberger, *America's Siberian Expedition,* 67; Kennan, *Russia Leaves the War,* 480–81.

82. Polk to Morris, March 5, 1918, *FRUS, 1918, Russia,* 2:67–68, and *PWW,* 46:545–46; Kennan, *Russia Leaves the War,* 482.

83. Reading to British Foreign Office, March 5, 1918, FO 115/2445, 107, PRO, and in Wiseman Papers; Polk Diary, March 6, 1918.

84. Notes for a Cable from the Ambassador to the Foreign Office, March 9, 1918, Wiseman Papers, and *PWW,* 46:590–91.

85. Balfour to House, March 6, 1918, Wiseman Papers, and *PWW,* 46:576–77. Reading had tried to argue the question with House but to no avail. FO 115/2445, 110, PRO.

86. Balfour to House, March 6, 1918, *PWW,* 46:576–77; Drummond to Wiseman, March 26, 1918, Wiseman Papers. See also *PWW,* 47:156–57.

87. House to Balfour, March 4, 1918; paraphrase of telegram from the Foreign Office to the British Embassy at Tokyo, March 4, 1918, both in Wiseman Papers. See also Polk to Wilson, March 5, 1918, with enclosure, *PWW,* 46:547–48.

88. CAB 23/5, War Cabinet 358/14, Minutes of Meeting on March 4, 1918, PRO; Ullman, *Intervention and the War,* 115–17; Kennan, *Russia Leaves the War,* 490–91.

89. CAB 23/5, War Cabinet 359/14, Minutes of Meeting on March 5, 1918, PRO; Balfour to House, March 6, 1918, Wiseman Papers; *PWW,* 46:576–77.

90. Reading to Balfour, March 10, 1918, FO 115/2445, 111, PRO; House to Wilson, March 10, 1918, Wilson Papers, and *PWW,* 46:597.

91. To the Fourth All-Russian Congress of Soviets, March 11, 1918, *PWW,* 46:598; Polk Diary, March 11, 1918; *PWW,* 46:597; Polk to M. Summers, March 11, 1918, *FRUS, 1918, Russia,* 1:395–96. Both Crane and Mott heartily approved the message. Mott to Wilson, March 11, 1918, and Crane to Tumulty, March 12, 1918, Wilson Papers; *PWW,* 46:604–5, 619.

92. Reading to Balfour, March 10, 1918, FO 115/2445, 111, PRO; Balfour to Reading, March 11, 1918, Wiseman Papers, and *PWW*, 46:605–6.

93. Morris to Lansing, March 19, 1918, *PWW*, 47:77–78; Wiseman to Reading, March 22, 1918, Balfour Papers.

94. Balfour to Reading, March 11, 1918, Wiseman Papers, and *PWW*, 46:605–6.

95. Doc. 37, *Dokumenty a materiály*, 66–68; E. Beneš, *My War Memoirs*, 357–58, 365–66.

96. Spiers to W.O., March 31, 1918, FO 371.3323/57780, PRO. Foreign Office to Lockhart, April 20, 1918, FO 371.3323/68874, PRO; E. Beneš, *My War Memoirs*, 362.

97. Paraphrase of a telegram from Lockhart, March 28, 1918, handed by Reading to State Department, April 2, 1918, DF 861.00/1438 1/2, DSNA; *PWW*, 47:245–46; Francis to Lansing, April 4, 1918, *FRUS*, *1918*, *Russia*, 1:493; James A. Ruggles (Military Attaché at Vologda) to Milstaff, April 15, 1918, enclosure in E. H. Van Deman to Chief of Staff, Military Intelligence Branch, Executive Division, April 26, 1918, RG 165, file 2266-D-22, WRCNA.

98. Bunyan, *Intervention, Civil War, and Communism*, 62; Ullman, *Intervention and the War*, 121; E. Beneš, *My War Memoirs*, 357–58, 365–66.

99. Summers to Francis, March 27, 1918, Francis Papers; Robins to Francis, March 31, 1918, Robins Papers; Report of Major Thomas D. Thacher, American Red Cross, April 6, 1918, WA6, RG 45, NRCNA; Ullman, *Intervention and the War*, 118–19.

100. Italics inserted. Joint Note No. 20, April 8, 1918, Supreme War Council, RG 407, Records of Adjutant General, WRCNA. At this point, they believed they could secure Trotskii's agreement to this.

101. Lansing to Wilson, February 19, 1918, DF 861.77/309, DSNA, and *PWW*, 46:387.

102. *FRUS*, *1918*, *Russia*, 3:221, 224.

103. Balfour to Reading, February 26, 1918, in Reading to Wilson, February 27, 1918, Wilson Papers; *PWW*, 46:470–72.

104. To the Fourth All-Russian Congress of Soviets, March 11, 1918, *PWW*, 46:598. Polk to Summers, March 11, 1918, *FRUS*, *1918*, *Russia*, 1:395–96; Polk to Wilson, March 9, 1918, Lansing Papers, Princeton; *PWW*, 46:585–88; Polk Diary, March 11, 1918. Jusserand was critical of the message. Polk Diary, March 12, 1918.

105. Wilson to Polk, March 10, 1918, and Polk to Wilson, March 9, 1918, enclosing Memorandum of Imperial Japanese Embassy, handed to Long, March 7, 1918, all in Lansing Papers, Princeton; Polk Diary, March 11, 12, 1918. The Japanese had requested this statement so as to determine their policy toward Russia in the future. See also Polk to Page (Great Britain), March 12, 1918, *FRUS*, *1918*, *Russia*, 1:397, and paraphrase of a cable from Sir William Conyngham Greene (British Ambassador in Tokyo) to the Foreign Office, March 7, 1918, with handwritten note from House to Wilson. Wilson Papers; *PWW*, 46:571–72.

106. Lansing to Wilson, March 24, 1918, DF 861.00/1433 1/2, DSNA; *PWW*, 47:131–32.

107. Wilson to Lansing, March 22, 1918, handwritten note to Lansing in Lansing to Wilson, March 24, 1918, DF 861.00/1433 1/2, DSNA; *PWW*, 47:106, 131–32.

108. Reading to Balfour, March 27, 1918, Wiseman Papers.

109. Unterberger, *America's Siberian Expedition*, 38.

110. No. 291 from Tokyo, March 27, 1918, to Balfour, FO 115/2445, 219–20, PRO; Reading to Balfour, March 27, 1918, Wiseman Papers; Balfour to House, April 3, 1918, Wiseman Papers (original in Balfour Papers); also FO 115/2445, 243, PRO.

111. Balfour to House, April 3, 1918, Wiseman Papers; paraphrase of telegram from Lockhart, March 28, 1918, DF 861.00/1438 1/2, DSNA; *PWW*, 47:245–46.

112. Lansing to Francis, April 5, 1918, *FRUS, 1918, Russia*, 2:100–101. The Japanese admiral furnished a copy of his statement to the commanders of both the British and American vessels. Noulens, *Mon ambassade*, 2:65.

113. Caldwell to Lansing, April 6, 1918, *FRUS, 1918, Russia*, 2:105.

114. Noulens, *Mon ambassade*, 2:66–67; Bunyan, *Intervention, Civil War, and Communism*, 68–95; Cumming and Pettit, *Russian-American Relations*, 194–95.

115. Reading to Balfour, April 7, 1918, FO 115/2445, 261, PRO; *PWW*, 47:281–82.

116. Reading to Balfour, April 10, 1918, FO 115/2445, 295, PRO.

117. Reading to Balfour, March 19, 1918, FO 115/2445, 172–78, PRO; *PWW*, 47:78–82.

118. Nielsen Report, April 8, 1918, Francis Papers; Ackerman, *Trailing the Bolsheviki*, 123; Irkutsk to Comrade Trotskii, April 5, 1918; Lenin to Irkutsk-Siberian Central Executive Committee, April 5–8, 1918; Jakovlev, Chairman of the Siberian Central Executive Committee to Moscow, April 5, 1918, in Meijer, *Trostky Papers*, 1:33, 35, 37, 39.

119. Bunyan, *Intervention, Civil War, and Communism*, 82.

120. Poole to Lansing, April 6, 1918, *FRUS, 1918, Russia*, 2:104–5. For selected documents on the Bolshevik reaction to the Anglo-Japanese landing, see Degras, *Soviet Documents on Foreign Policy*, 1:67–69.

121. Lockhart, *British Agent*, 268–69; British Foreign Office to Lockhart, April 7, 1918, and Morris to Lansing, April 13, 1918, *FRUS, 1918, Russia*, 2:109, 121.

122. Great Britain, *House of Commons Debates*, 5th ser., 104:1611–12; London *Times*, April 12, 1918.

123. Chicherin to Soviet of Krasnoyarsk, April 21, 1918, in Zmrhal, "Break Between the Soviets and the Czecho-Slovaks," Long Papers; Papoušek, *Chekhoslovaki i Sovety*, 23; Polner, "Czech Legion and the Bolsheviks," 41.

124. It was at this point that Macgowan telegraphed to Summers his concern over the fighting between the Bolsheviks and the Czecho-Slovaks. He added "a collison is evident, although details are lacking as the Czecho-Slovaks are unwilling to surrender their arms." He added, however, that nothing of a serious nature had been observed during the middle of that week by Story and his YMCA party as they passed through the area. Macgowan to Summers, April 17, 1918, Francis Papers.

Chapter 11

1. Reading to Balfour, April 7, 1918, FO 115/2445, 261, PRO; *PWW*, 47:281–82.
2. CAB 23/6, War Cabinet 393/69, April 17, 1918, 11:30 A.M., Minute 17, PRO.
3. Lockhart to Foreign Office, April 15, 1918, FO 371.W38/50420/69996, PRO.
4. CAB 23/6, War Cabinet 393/69, April 17, 1918, 11:30 A.M., Minute 17, PRO. See also FO 371.W38/60520/688740, PRO; Foreign Office to Lockhart, April 20, 1918, FO 371.W38/50420/68874, PRO.
5. Balfour to Reading, April 18, 1918, Reading Papers; *PWW*, 47:366–69. For American confirmation, see Ruggles to Milstaff, April 15, 1918, and E. H. Van Deman to Chief of Staff, April 26, 1918, RG 165, file 2266-22, WRCNA.
6. Lockhart to Foreign Office, April 21, 1918, FO 371.W38/73544/50420, PRO.
7. Balfour to Reading, April 23, 1918, Reading Papers; original handwritten note in Balfour Papers; *PWW*, 47:412; House to Wilson, April 24, 1918, Wilson Papers; *PWW*, 47:417–18; House Diary, April 24, 1918. See also Ullman, *Intervention and the War*, 160–61.
8. Reading to Balfour, April 25, 1918, FO 115/2446, 8–11, PRO; *PWW*, 47:440–41.
9. Moser to Lansing, with enclosures, April 4, 1918, Wilson Papers; Hosoya, "Japanese Documents on the Siberian Intervention," 30–37.
10. Reinsch to Lansing, April 8, 1918, "For the President," Wilson Papers.
11. Reinsch to Lansing, April 25, 1918, ibid.
12. Lansing to Wilson, April 25, 1918, with enclosures, and Morris to Lansing, January 10, 22, 1918, ibid.; *PWW*, 47:426–30, 440–41; Reading to Balfour, April 25, 1918, FO 115/2446, 8–11, PRO; Morley, *Japanese Thrust into Siberia*, 136–56.
13. E. Beneš, *My War Memoirs*, 357–58, 362, 365–66.
14. CAB 23/6, War Cabinet 401/68, Minutes of Meeting of April 30, 1918, and 402/66, Minutes of Meeting of May 1, 1918, at 11:30 A.M., PRO; British Embassy to Department of State, n.d., *FRUS, 1918, Russia*, 2:140. See also Macdonogh to Balfour, March 30, 1918, FO W38/57780, No. 0149/5067.
15. E. Beneš, *My War Memoirs*, 368; Resolution in Regard to the Transportation of Czech Troops from Russia, Passed by the Supreme War Council at its Fifth Session, May 2, 1918, Joint Note No. 25, Records of the Adjutant General, RG 407, WRCNA.
16. Resolution of May 2, 1918, Joint Note No. 25, RG 407, WRCNA. General Bliss conveyed this information to the War Department on May 4, while the French Foreign Office informed Washington of the possibility of transporting certain of these Czechs via Murmansk and Archangel. See ibid. and Sharp to Lansing, May 1, 1918, DF 861.00/1703, DSNA. Kennan observes that the wording of this note, combined with the failure of the Allies to seek seriously to provide shipping either at Vladivostok or at the northern ports, seems to indicate that the idea of dividing the corps was, in the minds of its authors, a disingenuous scheme designed "to give perfunctory recognition to the principle of the eventual removal of the Czech units to France but actually to assure their availability for service in Russia in the event of Allied intervention." Kennan, *Decision to Intervene*, 136–65.

17. CAB 23/6, War Cabinet 405/69, Minutes of Meeting on May 6, 1918, at 12:00 noon, PRO. "Transportation of Czech Troops from Russia," Joint Note No. 25, April 27, 1918, Records of the American Section of the Supreme War Council, RG 407, WRCNA; see also Memorandum for Colonel H. S. Hawkins, Liaison Officer for the War Department with the Department of State, May [n.d.], 1918, RG 165, file 2266-D-29, WRCNA. Trask, *U.S. in Supreme War Council,* 115–16.

18. Lockhart to British Foreign Office, May 6, 1918, Very Secret. FO 371.W38.81744/50420, PRO; Reading to Balfour, May 2, 1918, FO 115/2445, 416; *PWW,* 47:486; E. Beneš, *My War Memoirs,* 363–64.

19. Polner, "Czech Legion and the Bolsheviks," 45–57; Bunyan, *Intervention, Civil War, and Communism,* 86; Lockhart to Foreign Office, May 18, 1918, FO 371.W38.93398/50420, PRO.

20. Beneš to Balfour, with enclosures, May 10, 1918, FO 371.W38/82727/64427, PRO; Beneš to Balfour, May 11, 1918, FO 371.3135/85869, PRO; also in Inquiry Archives, RG 256, DSNA; E. Beneš, *My War Memoirs,* 373–76.

21. E. Beneš, *My War Memoirs,* 373.

22. Cecil Memo, May 18, 1918, FO 371.W3.89425/64427, PRO.

23. E. Beneš, *My War Memoirs,* 373.

24. CAB 23/14, War Cabinet 409A, Draft Minutes of Meeting held in Secretary of State for War's room, War Office, Whitehall, S W on May 11, 1918, PRO. See also D. Woodward, "The British Government and Japanese Intervention," 676.

25. CAB 23/14, War Cabinet 409A, May 11, 1918, PRO; Reading to Balfour, May 2, 1918, FO 115/2445, 416, PRO.

26. CAB 23/6, War Cabinet 410/69, Minutes of Meeting May 13, 1918 at 12:00 noon, PRO; J. C. Smuts to Whitehall, May 11, 1918, Appendix G. T. 4519; Ministry of Shipping to British Foreign Office, May 11, 1918; British Foreign Office to Hodgson (Vladivostok), May 16, 1918; R. Graham to British War Office, May 17, 1918, copy to Ministry of Shipping, all in FO W38.84358/50420, PRO.

27. Statement of Major E. F. Riggs on the Situation in Russia, "Selected Documents Concerning the Czecho-Slovak Forces in Russia during 1918," RG 120, WRCNA; Chicherin to all Siberian, Lake Baikal and Railroad Soviet Deputies, May 11, 1918, *Česká Družina* Collection; Ruggles to Warcolstaf, March 12, 1918, enclosed in Lansing to Wilson, March 25, 1918, Lansing Papers, Princeton.

28. CAB 23/6, War Cabinet 413/66, Minutes of Meeting on May 17, 1918 at 12:00 noon, PRO.

29. Ibid.; D. Woodward, "The British Government and Japanese Intervention," 677; Kennan, *Decision to Intervene,* 136–65.

30. Cecil Memo, May 18, 1918, FO 371.3443/89880, PRO.

31. Cecil Memo, May 18, 1918, FO 371.W3.89425/64427, PRO.

32. Nicolson, Oliphant, and Clerk Minutes, May 20, 1918, FO 371.3135/89425, PRO.

33. FO 371.W3.89425/64427, PRO. It was agreed to inform the United States of the proposed action.

34. It should be stressed, however, that Beneš's commitment to the use of Czech troops in western Russia was as part of a massive Allied intervention against the Germans and provided there was no interference in Russian internal affairs. L. S. Amery, Note on a Conversation with Dr. Beneš, May 14, 1918, in J. Bradley, *Allied Intervention in Russia*, 81. See also Ullman, *Intervention and the War*, 1:170.

35. Lockhart to Foreign Office, May 18, 1918; Copy to D.M.I., FO 371.W38.93398/50420, PRO; Noulens, *Mon ambassade*, 2:86; E. Beneš, *Souvenirs de guerre*, 2:258–59.

36. E. Beneš, *My War Memoirs*, 376–77; Ullman, *Intervention and the War*, 1:171.

37. CAB 23/6, War Cabinet 415/64, Minutes of Meeting of May 23, 1918, at 12:00 noon, PRO.

Chapter 12

1. For some recent examples, see Berezkin, *Oktiabr'skaia revoliutsiia i SShA, 1917–1922 gg.* [The October Revolution and the USA, 1917–1922]; Gvishiani, *Sovetskaia Rossiia i SShA, 1917–1920* [Soviet Russia and the USA, 1917–1920]. See also Ganelin, *Sovetsko-amerikanskie otnoshenii v kontse 1917–nachale 1918 g.* [Soviet-American Relations from late 1917 to early 1918]. For the evolution of Soviet historiography on intervention, see Thompson, "Allied and American Intervention in Russia 1918–1921," 319–80; J. Bradley, *Allied Intervention in Russia*, xi–xix; and Kennan, "Soviet Historiography and America's Role in the Intervention," 302–22. For the evolution of American historiography on the American role in the Russian civil war, see Unterberger, ed., *American Intervention in the Russian Civil War*.

2. E. Beneš, *Souvenirs de guerre*, 2:198; E. Beneš, *Světová válka a naše revoluce*, 3:Doc. 284; Packard Report, DF 861.00/6052, DSNA; Horvath Memoirs, chap. 10; Caldwell to Lansing, April 30, 1918, *FRUS, 1918, Russia*, 2:148; George H. Emerson and H. H. Slaughter, "Report of the American Engineers who were in Siberia at the time of the Czecho-Slovak Movement Which Resulted in the Overthrow of the Bolshevik and Central Powers War Prisoners Associated with Them, May 5 to September 9, 1918," 2, DF 861.77/541, DSNA (hereafter cited as Emerson Report, DF 861.77/541, DSNA).

3. Lieutenant Colonel David P. Barrows, American Military Attaché at Peking, estimated their number at 10,000. "Memoirs of David P. Barrows," 142–48, Barrows Papers (hereafter cited as Barrows Memoirs). Report of Captain Yanick of the Czecho-Slovak Staff Submitted to General William S. Graves, Graves Papers (hereafter cited as Yanick Report, Graves Papers); Lavergne to Minister of War, May 5, 1918, E. Beneš, *Souvenirs de guerre*, 2:256.

4. George W. Williams to Poole, June 1, 1918, DF 861.00/2718, DSNA; also in Harris Papers; Papoušek, *Czechoslovak Nation's Struggle*, 39; Fic, *Bolsheviks and the Czechoslovak Legion*, 202–5.

5. *Izvestiia*, May 30, 1918; Papoušek, *Czechoslovak Nation's Struggle*, 65–66; E. Beneš, *Světová válke a naše revoluce*, 3:Doc. 283. See also Polner, "Czech Legion and the Bolsheviks," 45–47.

6. E. Beneš, *Světová válke a naše revoluce*, 3:Doc. 280; Schwanda, *The Czechoslovak Troops in Russia and Siberia*, 11; Polner, "Czech Legion and the Bolsheviks," 43–45.

7. E. Beneš, *Světová válke a naše revoluce*, 3:Doc. 277; Catherine E. Breshkovsky to Polk, March 10, 1919, DF 861.00/4320, DSNA; George Lazarov to Mrs. C. W. Dietrich, February 2, 1928, Breshkovsky Papers. See also Yanick Report, Graves Papers. This view was not shared by the American Military Attaché in Moscow. See statement of Major E. F. Riggs, September 27, 1918, RG 120, WRCNA.

8. "Czecho-Slovak Incident," 5, RG 407, WRCNA; Bulletin: Russian Situation, May 22–28, Allied and Associated Powers (1914–1920), Supreme War Council, American Section, Fuller Papers.

9. White, *Siberian Intervention*, 246; E. Beneš, *Souvenirs de guerre*, 1:363; Polner, "Czech Legion and the Bolsheviks," 42–43.

10. Williams to Poole, June 1, 1918, enclosures in Sheldon Whitehouse (Chargé d'Affaires ad interim, Vologda) to Lansing, August 23, 1918, DF 861.00/2718, DSNA; Poole Memoirs, 237–49; "Czecho-Slovak Incident," 2–3, RG 407, WRCNA.

11. Lockhart, *British Agent*, 282. For varying accounts of this incident, see Zmrhal, "Break Between Soviets and Czecho-Slovaks," Long Papers, 3–4; C. R. Crane Memoirs, 215–17; Papoušek, *Czechoslovak Nation's Struggle*, 66–68; Beaumont, *Heroic Story*, 70–73; Thomson to Lansing, July 14, 1918, FRUS, *1918*, *Russia*, 2:248–49; Nosek, *Independent Bohemia*, 98.

12. Rainey Report, RG 120, WRCNA, i; Major Walter S. Drysdale (Military Attaché to China), Report to the American Ambassador to China on the Situation in Russia, Vladivostok, June 25, 1918, 7, RG 120, WRCNA (hereafter cited as Drysdale Report, RG 120, WRCNA).

13. Rainey Report, RG 120, WRCNA, i; see also note 7 above.

14. J. Bradley, *Allied Intervention in Russia*, 88–89; Kennan, *Decision to Intervene*, 163. For a somewhat different version, see Fic, *Bolsheviks and the Czechoslovak Legion*, 229, 260–62.

15. Viest reports that nine members were selected to implement the decisions taken at the Military Congress: Captain Gajda (C.O., 7th Regt.) as president; four members of the Russian section of the Czecho-Slovak National Council; and four representatives of the troops (two from each division). Translation of report of Sub-Lieutenant Viest on the Events in Western Siberia, Czecho-Slovak History, Vladivostok, June 26, 1918, File 314.7, Records of the Adjutant General, RG 407, WRCNA; Fic, *Bolsheviks and the Czechoslovak Legion*, xviii, 220–21. See also Zmrhal, "Break Between Soviets and Czecho-Slovaks," 5, Long Papers; "Czecho-Slovak Incident," 5, RG 407, WRCNA; Yanick Report, Graves Papers; Breshkovsky to Polk, March 10, 1919, DF 861.00/4320, DSNA.

16. On May 20, Aralov, Trotskii's assistant, wired all soviets along the Penza-Omsk railroad: "Detrain the Czechoslovaks, and organize them into labor cartels or draft them into the Soviet Red Army. Do everything to assist the Czechoslovak Communists." E. Beneš, *Světová válke a naše revoluce*, 3:Docs. 284 and 286; Bunyan, *Intervention, Civil War, and Communism*, 88. These

instructions to V. V. Kuraev, chairman of the Penza Soviet, are dated May 23 in Doc. 50, *Dokumenty a materiály,* 81–82; "Czecho-Slovak Incident," 3, RG 407, WRCNA; Packard Report, 8, DF 861.00/6052, DSNA; Fic, *Bolsheviks and the Czechoslovak Legion,* xviii.

17. Williams to Lansing, June 5, 1918, DF 861.00/2718, DSNA, and Harris Papers; "Czecho-Slovak Incident," 5, RG 407, WRCNA; Packard Report, 9, DF 861.00/6052, DSNA.

18. Trotskii, *Sochineniia,* pt. 3:482; Bunyan, *Intervention, Civil War, and Communism,* 88.

19. Zmrhal, "Break Between Soviets and Czecho-Slovaks," Long Papers, 5; Doc. 49, *Dokumenty a materiály,* 81; Bunyan, *Intervention, Civil War, and Communism,* 89. Maxa continued his efforts to arrange a truce between the Czechs and the Bolsheviks. He was apparently absolutely opposed to the action taken by the Cheliabinsk congress, which, in effect, defied both Masaryk's orders and those of the French military mission. When both he and the legion returned to Czechoslovakia, he publicly accused the leaders of the congress of treason. Van S. Merle-Smith to Richard Crane, July 9, 1920, DF 861.00/2983, DSNA. As late as 1920 the State Department was still trying to unravel the mystery of the actual origin of the Czech-Bolshevik conflict; ibid.

20. Zmrhal, "Break Between Soviets and Czecho-Slovaks," Long Papers, 7; Bunyan, *Intervention, Civil War, and Communism,* 89.

21. Bunyan, *Intervention, Civil War, and Communism,* 90; Doc. 60, *Dokumenty a materiály,* 93–94; Lockhart to Foreign Office, June 2, 1918, FO 371.W38.106181/50420, PRO.

22. For the text of these resolutions, see Bunyan, *Intervention, Civil War, and Communism,* 89–91; E. Beneš, *My War Memoirs,* 366–67. For Gajda's instructions, see Doc. 53, *Dokumenty a materiály,* 85–86. Gajda cautioned the Czechs against engaging in "robberies, thefts or disorders en route." They were not to disturb passenger traffic.

23. E. Beneš, *Světová válke a naše revoluce,* 3:Docs. 287 and 288; E. Beneš, *My War Memoirs,* 366–67; Packard Report, DF 861.00/6052, DSNA; Ernest F. Campbell to E. L. Harris (American Consul General for Siberia), June 8, 1918, Harris Papers; Emerson Report, 6, DF 861.77/541, DSNA.

24. Campbell to Harris, June 8, 1918, Harris Papers; L. S. Gray (Vice Consul at Omsk) to Harris, "Political Situation in the Omsk District Covering Period from May 10, 1918 to Date," November 10, 1918, 1–2, Harris Papers (hereafter cited as Gray Report, Harris Papers); Yanick Report, Graves Papers; Stewart, *White Armies of Russia,* 107.

25. Ernest F. Campbell, "Report of Movements of Czecho-Slovak Trains at Present in Mariinsk to Date," June 8, 1918, DF 861.00/2984, DSNA (hereafter cited as Campbell Report, DF 861.00/2984, DSNA).

26. Extract of Diary of Dr. Pitra, Volunteer of Company No. 7, First Czechoslovak Regiment, in Some Remarks on History of Czechoslovaks in Russia, Records of Adjutant General, RG 407, WRCNA; J. Bradley, *Allied Intervention in Russia,* 96.

27. Bunyan, *Intervention, Civil War, and Communism,* 92, 99–100.

28. Statement of Major E. F. Riggs, September 7, 1918, RG 120, WRCNA;

Lockhart (Moscow) to Foreign Office, March 21, 1918, received March 26, 1918, No. 42, Very Secret, FO 371/3290, Russia, 55299, PRO; Lansing to Stevens, April 23, 1918, Emerson Report, 1, DF 861.77/541, DSNA; Kennan, *Decision to Intervene*, 280–81. See also Hard, *Raymond Robins's Own Story*, 101, and Ross, *The Russian Soviet Republic*, 34–36.

 29. Copy of telegram from Moscow, May 11, 1918, No. 109, Box No. B/N, Česká Družina Collection.

 30. Emerson Report, DSNA, 1–5, DF 861.77/541.

 31. Harris to Lansing, June 2, 1918, *FRUS, 1918, Russia*, 2:184–86.

 32. Agreement between the Representatives of the Central Siberian Soviet and the Czecho-Slovak Forces, May 27, 1918, ibid., 186–87.

 33. Ibid.; Hornbeck, "American Expeditionary Force in Siberia," 17, Hornbeck Papers.

 34. Report of Langdon B. Warner (Vice Consul at Harbin), June 6, 1918, DF 861.00/2376, DSNA. According to Warner, this order had been issued when the Czechs at Kansk and Nizhneudinsk had intercepted a message from the Central Siberian Soviet at Irkutsk, which was thought to have been inspired by the Germans in Moscow. The message in translation read: "All Czechs to be disarmed. If their resistance becomes effective, trains to be delayed either by refusal of rolling stock or as a last resort, by the destruction of railways ahead. Keep us informed of your actions." See also Bunyan, *Intervention, Civil War, and Communism*, 91.

 35. Commander Jean Pichon to the French Minister of War, May 23, 1918, DF 861.00/2440, DSNA.

 36. Hornbeck, "American Expeditionary Force in Siberia," 17–18, Hornbeck Papers.

 37. Ibid., 18–19; Emerson Report, 21, DF 861.77/541, DSNA. Kennan draws his account of this entire episode largely from the Swedish Red Cross records as reported by Klante, *Von der Wolga zum Amur*. Kennan, *Decision to Intervene*, 283–84. According to that account, it was the Czechs who started the trouble this time and the Communists who reacted in self-defense.

 38. John A. Ray to Lansing, September 4, 1918, DF 861.00/3180, DSNA.

 39. Admiral Austin M. Knight to Daniels, May 27, 1918, *FRUS, 1918, Russia*, 2:174.

 40. Reading to Phillips, May 27, 1918, DF 861.00/1941, DSNA; E. Beneš, *Souvenirs de guerre*, 2:219–20.

 41. CAB 23/14, War Cabinet 418 A/10, Draft Minutes of Meeting on May 27, 1918, PRO.

 42. Lockhart to Foreign Office, May 24, 1918, FO 371.W38.93425/50420, PRO; E. Beneš, *Souvenirs de guerre*, 2:250–51.

 43. CAB 23/6, War Cabinet 418/54, Minutes of Meeting on May 27, 1918, at 12:00 noon, PRO. Interestingly enough, the minutes note that "great efforts are being made by enemy agents to turn them away from their purpose."

 44. Lockhart to Foreign Office, June 1, 1918, FO 371.W38/50420/104125, PRO.

 45. Emerson Report, 7–8, DF 861.77/541, DSNA. For the full account of Emerson's negotiation efforts, see Unterberger, "The United States and the Czech-Bolshevik Conflict, 1918," 145–53.

46. Emerson Report, 8, DF 861.77/541, DSNA; Emerson to Harris, June 4, 1918, DF 861.00/2984, DSNA.

47. Emerson Report, 9, DF 861.77/541, DSNA.

48. Ibid., 11.

49. Ibid., 12; Stewart, *White Armies of Russia*, 107.

50. Emerson to Harris, May 30, 1918; Emerson and Slaughter to Stevens and Harris, May 30, 1918; Harris to Emerson, May 31, 1918; Telegraph Conversation between Colonel Emerson and Consul General Harris, Krasnoyarsk and Irkutsk, May 31, 1918; all in Emerson Report, 15–19, DF 861.77/541, DSNA.

51. Ibid., 20; Emerson to Harris, June 4, 1918, DF 861.00/2984, DSNA; Edward Thomas to Samuel N. Harper, October 10, 1918, Harper Papers. Thomas indicated that he was "opposed to the plan" of mediation but had cooperated at the Consul General's instructions.

52. Emerson Report, 15, DF 861.77/541, DSNA.

53. Lockhart, *British Agent*, 280–81.

54. E. Beneš, *Souvenirs de guerre*, 2:250–51.

55. Francis to Lansing, May 28, 1918, DF 861.00/1962, DSNA.

56. Chicherin to Lockhart, May 28, 1918, *Correspondance diplomatique entre la République Russe et les puissances de l'Entente*, 7; Lockhart to Foreign Office, Moscow, June 1, 1918, FO 371.W38/50420/104125, PRO.

57. CAB 23/16, War Cabinet 420, May 29, 1918, PRO.

58. Geitzman to Lansing, June 9, 1918, DF 861.00/1986, DSNA; Coates and Coates, *Armed Intervention in Russia*, 107–8.

59. Geitzman to Lansing, June 9, DF 861.00/1986, DSNA; see also Yakovlev to Sukhanov, June 1, 1918, Telegram No. 3106, Records of Adjutant General, RG 407, WRCNA.

60. Geitzman to Lansing, Irkutsk, June 9, 1918, DF 861.00/1986, DSNA. Baerlein, *March of the Seventy Thousand*, 123, contains a discussion of the last-minute peace overtures. See also *Pravda*, No. 123, June 1918; Maksakov and Turunov, *Khronika grazhdanskoi voiny v Sibiri*, 165–67; and Polner, "Czech Legion and the Bolsheviks," 79–80.

61. Gray Report, 3–4, Harris Papers.

62. Ibid., 4. For the Protocols of the three sessions of the Executive Committee of the Czech army, supporting the account of Guinet's views, see Holotík, *Štefánikovská*, 462–66.

63. Gray Report, 5–6, Harris Papers.

64. Ibid., 5–7. These announcements by United States and Allied representatives were taken extremely seriously by the Czechs, and no one "questioned their feasibility." Ackerman to Colonel House and Long, January 2, 1919, Long Papers; Caldwell to Lansing, November 9, 1918, DF 861.00/3195, DSNA.

65. Emerson Report, 20, DF 861.77/541, DSNA; Emerson to Harris, June 4, 1918, DF 861.00/2984, DSNA.

66. Emerson Report, 21, 24–26, DF 861.77/541, DSNA; Gray Report, 6, Harris Papers.

67. Emerson Report, 25–33, DF 861.77/541, DSNA; Emerson to Harris, June 4, 1918, DF 861.00/2984, DSNA.

68. Vergé to Gajda, June 1 (or 2) 1918, Emerson Report, 37, DF 861.77/541, DSNA; Bradley, *Allied Intervention in Russia*, 97.

69. Emerson Report, 44–45, DF 861.77/541, DSNA; Holotík, *Štefánikovská*, 462. Gajda never forgave Vergé for disrupting his operations.

70. Emerson Report, 46, DF 861.77/541, DSNA.

71. Harris Conference Notes: Nizhneudinsk, June 4, 1918; Kansk, June 5, 1918; Mariinsk, June 6, 1918, all in DF 861.00/2984, DSNA; and Warner Report, June 6, 1918, DF 861.00/2376, DSNA.

72. Warner Report, June 4, 1918, DF 861.00/2376, DSNA.

73. Conference between Consul General Harris and three representatives of the newly established "Menshevik Government at Nizhneudinsk," June 4, 1918, DF 861.00/2984, DSNA.

74. Summary of Intelligence, No. 10, Relative to Affairs in Siberia for the Period ending June 4, 1918, General Staff (M.I.D.), War Office, RG 165, WRCNA.

75. Warner Report, Mariinsk, June 6, 1918, and Harris Conference with Captain Kadlec of the Czechoslovak Echelons at Mariinsk, June 6, 1918, DF 861.00/2376 and 2984, DSNA.

76. Conference with Captain Kadlec at Mariinsk, June 6, 1918, DF 861.00/2984, DSNA.

77. Warner Report, June 6, 1918, DF 861.00/2376. See also Bowie, *Langdon Warner through His Letters*, 90–98.

78. Drysdale to Reinsch, Report on the Situation in Russia, June 25, 1918, in Drysdale Report, 8, RG 120, WRCNA.

79. Sharp to Lansing, June 7, 1918, *FRUS, 1918, Russia*, 2:194.

80. Geitzman to Lansing, Irkutsk, June 9, 1918, DF 861.00/1986, DSNA. This position is confirmed in Yakovlev (Irkutsk) to Sukhanov (Vladivostok Soviet), Telegram No. 3106, Records of Adjutant General, RG 407, WRCNA. See also Caldwell to Lansing, June 5, 1918, DF 861.00/1957, DSNA.

81. Harris to Lansing, June 30, 1918, DF 861.00/2977, DSNA; *Vlast Truda*, June 6, 8, 1918.

82. Conversation of Consul General Harris with staff commanders of the New Siberian Government, Taiga, June 7, 1918, DF 861.00/2984, DSNA; Warner Report, Taiga, June 7, 1918, ibid.

83. Emerson Report, 47–52, DF 861.77/541, DSNA; Emerson and Harris Conference at Kargat, Siberia, June 8, 1918, DF 861.00/2984, DSNA.

84. Caldwell to State Department, June 12, 1918, DF 861.00/2040, DSNA.

85. Harris Conversation Notes, Nizhneudinsk, June 11, 1918, DF 861.00/2984, DSNA; Caldwell to State Department, June 10, 1918, DF 861.00/1989, DSNA.

86. Ernest F. Campbell, Report of "Movements of Czecho-Slovak Trains at Present in Mariinsk to Date," June 15, 1918, DF 861.00/2984, DSNA.

87. Notes on Conversation with Czech commander at Nizhneudinsk, June 11, 1918, DF 861.00/2984, DSNA.

88. Bunyan, *Intervention, Civil War, and Communism*, 98–100; *Izvestiia*, June 21, 1918.

89. Paraphrase of cyphered message sent to American Consul at Vla-

divostok on behalf of Major Drysdale, U.S.A., for transmission to Knight and to Legation at Peking, June 14, 1918, Harris Papers.

90. Harris to State Department, June 14, 1918, DF 861.00/2021, DSNA.

91. Francis to Emerson, Vologda, May 17, 1918, Emerson Report, 53, DF 861.77/541, DSNA.

92. Emerson Report, 53–56, DF 861.77/541, DSNA; Doc. 106, signed by Pavlů, chairman, and others in *Dokumenty a materiály,* 137–38; Holotík, *Štefánikovská,* 465–66; Graves, *America's Siberian Adventure,* 49. Guinet's telegram was published in the *Československý Deník,* June 14, 1918.

93. Colonel Paris to French Ministry of War, June 29, 1918, E. Beneš, *Světová válke a naše revoluce,* 3:Doc. 299.

Chapter 13

1. Story to Mott, March 9, 1919, Report of Story, 10, RWWC.

2. Clemenceau to Cecil, May 22, 1918, FO 371.W38.93904/50420, PRO. For Clemenceau's insistence on bringing the Czech troops to the Western Front, see E. Beneš, *Souvenirs de guerre,* 2:191–92, and E. Beneš, *Světová válke a naše revoluce,* 3:Doc. 278.

3. Poole Memoirs, 320.

4. Marty, *La révolte de la mer Noire,* 61.

5. Francis to Lansing, May 28, 1918, DF 861.00/1962, DSNA; Francis to Lansing, May [31], 1918, and Poole to Lansing, May 31, 1918, *FRUS, 1918, Russia,* 2:183–84; Thomson to Lansing, August 16, 1919, DF 861.00/5305, DSNA.

6. Poole to Lansing, May 31, 1918, *FRUS, 1918, Russia,* 2:183–84; Carley, "The Origins of French Intervention," 426–27.

7. Paraphrase of telegram from Lockhart (Moscow) to Foreign Office, June 2, 1918, DF 861.00/2082 1/2, DSNA; Lockhart to Foreign Office, June 2, 1918, No. 250, FO 371.W38.106181/50420, PRO.

8. Francis to Lansing, June 3, 1918, *FRUS, 1918, Russia,* 2:188; Francis to Lansing, August 27, 1918, DF 861.00/2944, DSNA; Kennan, *Decision to Intervene,* 305.

9. Francis to Lansing, May 29, 1918, *FRUS, 1918, Russia,* 2:179, 207–8; Francis to Lansing, August 27, 1918, DF 861.00/2944, DSNA.

10. Lavergne to Ministry of War, June 1, 1918, E. Beneš, *Souvenirs de guerre,* 2:250–51; Lockhart to Foreign Office, June 1, 1918, FO 371.W38/50420/104125, PRO. See also DF 861.00/2082 1/2, DSNA.

11. Lockhart (Moscow) to British Foreign Office, June 1, 1918, FO 371.W38/50420/104125, PRO; paraphrase of telegram from Lockhart (Moscow) to Foreign Office, June 2, 1918, DF 861.00/2082 1/2, DSNA.

12. Lockhart to British Foreign Office, June 2, 1918, Urgent, FO 371.W38/106181/50420, PRO; E. Beneš, *Souvenirs de guerre,* 2:251.

13. See Joint Note No. 31, June 3, 1918, Records of Supreme War Council, DF 861.00/6731, DSNA.

14. Sharp to Lansing, June 4, 1918, DF 763.72 SU/44, DSNA; Clemenceau to Cecil, May 22, 1918, FO 371.W38/93904/50420, PRO; Jusserand to French Foreign

Ministry, May 29, 1918, Nos. 658 and 659, Etat-major de l'armée de terre, 4N46, FMD-Ar; *PWW*, 48:202–3.

15. Lansing Diary, June 3, 1918.

16. Poole to Lansing, June 2, 1918, *FRUS, 1918, Russia*, 2:187.

17. Poole Memoirs, 267.

18. Ibid., 236; Francis to Lansing, June 3, 1918, *FRUS, 1918, Russia*, 2:188.

19. Francis to Perry Francis, June 3, 1918, Francis Papers.

20. Polk to Francis, June 10, 1918, *FRUS, 1918, Russia*, 2:201.

21. Poole to Francis, June 5, 1918, Francis Papers. For Lavergne's report of the Allied visit to Chicherin, see E. Beneš, *Světová válke a naše revoluce*, 3:Doc. 292.

22. Poole to Francis, June 5, 1918, Francis Papers; Francis to Lansing, June 7, 1918, DF 861.00/1977, DSNA. Poole claimed that "Chicherin admitted to me personally that the Germans had brought pressure to bear concerning the Czecho-Slovaks." Poole to Lansing, August 12, 1918, DF 861.00/518 1/2, DSNA.

23. Francis to Lansing, June 7, 1918, DF 861.00/1977, DSNA; E. Beneš, *Souvenirs de guerre*, 2:202; E. Beneš, *Světová válke a naše revoluce*, 3:Docs. 294 and 295.

24. Zeman, *Germany and the Revolution in Russia*, 129–33; Chicherin to Ioffe (Soviet representative to German Government), June 11, 1918, Doc. 95, *Dokumenty a materiály*, 125–27.

25. Ibid.; E. Beneš, *Souvenirs de guerre*, 2:203; E. Beneš, *Světová válke a naše revoluce*, 3:Doc. 295; Polner, "Czech Legion and the Bolsheviks," 72.

26. Zeman, *Germany and the Revolution in Russia*, 134.

27. Joint Note No. 31, Joint Note to the Supreme War Council by its Military Representatives, June 3, 1918, RG 120, WRCNA.

28. Francis to Lansing, June 6, 1918, *FRUS, 1918, Russia*, 1:552–53.

29. Lockhart to British Foreign Office, June 6, 1918, FO 371.W38/107587/50420, PRO. Lockhart's cable was not received at the Foreign Office until June 17.

30. Caldwell to Lansing, June 5, 1918, DF 861.00/1057, DSNA.

31. CAB 23/6, War Cabinet 426/59, Minutes of Meeting on June 5, 1918, at 12:00 noon, PRO; E. Beneš, *Světová válke a naše revoluce*, 3:Docs. 296 and 297; Sharp to Lansing, June 3 and June 4, 1918, DF 763.72 SU/44 and SU/53, DSNA.

32. Williams to Poole, June 5, 1918, Poole Memoirs, 240–41. For conflicting reports of the military clashes, see *FRUS, 1918, Russia*, 2:177–88; George Lazarev to Mrs. C. W. Dietrich, February 7, 1928, Breshkovsky Papers; Stewart, *White Armies of Russia*, chap. 5; Dupuy, *Perish by the Sword*; and White, *Siberian Intervention*, 92–93.

33. Williams to Poole, June 12, 1918, DF 861.00/2718, DSNA; also in Harris Papers; Poole to Lansing, June 17, 1918, *FRUS, 1918, Russia*, 2:214–15. See also Poole Memoirs, 241–49.

34. Campbell Report, June 8, 1918, DF 861.00/2984, DSNA.

35. Campbell with the Czechoslovaks from Mariinsk to Nizhneudinsk, June 12, 1918, Harris Papers.

36. *Izvestiia*, June 13, 1918; Cumming and Pettit, *Russian-American Relations*, 224–26; Paraphrase of a Telegram from Lockhart to British Foreign Office, June

13, 1918, and Ira A. Morris (Stockholm) to Lansing, June 13, 1918, DF 861.00/2217 1/2 and 2016, DSNA; Poole to Francis, June 13, 1918, Francis Papers; Memorandum received from Captain Slaughter, U.S.A., while at the station Kargat on June 9, 1918, DF 861.00/2984, DSNA.

37. Poole to Lansing, June 9, 1918, DF 861.00/2063, DSNA. See also Ruggles to Milstaff, Vologda, June 13, 1918, No. 45, MID 2266-D-51, RG 165, WRCNA.

38. Drysdale to Knight, June 14, 1918, Harris Papers; see also Caldwell to Lansing, June 15, 1918, DF 861.00/2029, DSNA. Caldwell's message reached Washington on June 15.

39. Francis to Poole, June 13, 1918, Francis Papers; Francis to Lansing, June 15, 1918, *FRUS, 1918, Russia*, 2:213–14.

40. Poole to Francis, June 15, 1918, Francis Papers; Kennan, *Decision to Intervene*, 314–15. See also Ludendorff to Kühlmann, June 9, 1918, in Zeman, *Germany and the Revolution in Russia*, 135.

41. Poole Memoirs, 253–54.

42. Cyphered Dispatch from American Consul General Poole (Moscow) to American Consul Williams (Samara), June 18, 1918, RG 407, WRCNA; Poole Memoirs, 253–54, 307. The copy of this telegram in the Harris Papers does not contain the last sentence and was sent by Gray from Omsk to Harris. It is undated.

43. Poole Memoirs, 307. For Graves's evaluation of this action, see Graves, *America's Siberian Adventure*, 70–73.

44. It should be noted that the original message in French, which is in the Records of the Adjutant General's Office, is dated June 18, Perm, and June 22, Cheliabinsk. See "Message Delivered to Czechs by Major (now Lieutenant Colonel) Guinet of the French Military Mission," Records of Adjutant General, RG 407, WRCNA. For the original note in English dated May 18, 1918, see Thomson to Harris, July 22, 1918, DF 861.00/2983, DSNA. Emerson received a copy of the telegram from Major Guinet at Omsk on June 23. Emerson Report, 56, DF 861.77/541, DSNA. Graves, *America's Siberian Adventure*, 49. See also Doc. 114, *Dokumenty a materiály*, 148.

45. Merle-Smith to Hugh C. Wallace (Ambassador at Paris), July 9, 1920, DF 861.00/2983, DSNA; Sharp to Lansing, May 26, 1918, *FRUS, 1918, Russia*, 2:172–74; Carley, "The Origins of French Intervention," 426–27.

46. "The Allies and the Czecho-Slovaks," in Documents Concerning Operations of the Czech Army, Hoover Institution on War, Revolution and Peace. See also Bunyan, *Intervention, Civil War, and Communism*, 106, and Dragomiretskii, *Chekhoslovaki v Rossii 1914–1920*, 69. The latter was a Russian apologist for the Czechs who refers to Guinet's support of the Czech endeavor at this point.

47. Thomson to Lansing, July 4, 1918, DF 861.00/2983, DSNA.

48. Gray Report, 10, Harris Papers. Ackerman, *Trailing the Bolsheviki*, 135.

49. Ackerman, *Trailing the Bolsheviki*, 136.

50. Slaughter Report, 11, RG 120, WRCNA; Packard Report, chap. 10, DF 861.00/6052, DSNA.

51. Alby to Lavergne, June 30, 1918, E. Beneš, *Souvenirs de guerre*, 2:252–53; MacMurray (Peking) to Harris, July 2, 1918, Fuller Papers; Chamberlin, *Russian*

Revolution, 2:10. Compare also Medek, *Czech Anabasis across Russia and Siberia*, 21.

52. Knight to Daniels, June 29, 1918, DF 861.00/2165 1/2, DSNA.

53. Bothmer, *Mit Graf Mirbach in Moskau*, 63–64.

54. Francis to Lansing, June 19, 1918, *FRUS, 1918, Russia*, 1:564.

55. Caldwell to Lansing, June 25, 1918, ibid., 2:226. For Gajda's orders see undated handwritten note from Harris to Caldwell at Vladivostok: "Communiqued following to Tscheck commanders in Vladivostok quote Gaida, commander of all Tschek forces, orders all Tschecks back from Vladivostok direction Irkutsk stop Seize railway stop Passage through Siberia of Tschecks only possible by force of arms stop Act quickly stop Tschecks into action stop unquote. In view of situation railway French Consul General and I after conference feel [that we cannot interfere with Tscheck movements] that such action is justified" (Harris Papers). The part in brackets was crossed out in the original.

56. Representatives of the Czecho-Slovak National Council to the Consuls of the Allied Powers, June 25, 1918, *FRUS, 1918, Russia*, 2:265–67.

57. Knight to Daniels, June 26, 1918, *PWW*, 48:458–60.

58. Caldwell to Lansing, July 29, 1918, ibid., 2:235. For differing evaluations of the Czech action, see Stewart, *White Armies of Russia*, 112, and Norton, *The Far Eastern Republic of Siberia*, 63. For a detailed and laudatory account of the Vladivostok takeover, see George Gleason, Siberian Report Letter No. 10, November 4, 1918, RWWC. On June 28, Dietrichs informed Caldwell that an ultimatum would be delivered to the Soviet on the following day, demanding the latter's disarmament by June 30 at 6:00 P.M. Caldwell to Lansing, June 28, 1918, *FRUS, 1918, Russia*, 2:234.

Chapter 14

1. E. Beneš, *My War Memoirs*, 119, 367–68.

2. Masaryk, *Making of a State*, 255.

3. Griswold, *Far Eastern Policy*, 233; Vondracek, *Foreign Policy of Czechoslovakia*, 125–26; Valiani, *End of Austria-Hungary*, 243; Kennan, *Decision to Intervene*, 165.

4. Long Diary, May 31, 1918; Unterberger, *America's Siberian Expedition*, 48–49, 60.

5. Memorandum for the Secretary of State, May 21, 1918, Long Papers; Long Diary, May 21, 1918; Lansing Diary, May 21, 1918. In late April, Richard Crane had suggested a scheme of economic penetration in Siberia using the Japanese, and Lansing had asked him to prepare a memorandum. Ibid., April 27, 1918.

6. Lansing to Francis, May 29, 1918, and Lansing to Stevens through Moser, May 29, 1918, DF 861.00/2079 1/2, DSNA.

7. Reinsch to Lansing, June 5, 1918, *FRUS, 1918, Russia*, 2:189. The Japanese threat was largely responsible for converting Reinsch to military intervention. See Pugach, *Paul S. Reinsch*, 241–42.

8. Sir James Jordan to British Foreign Office, June 13, 1918, Very Confidential, FO 371.W38.106087/50420, PRO; Reinsch to State Department, June 13, 1918, DF 861.00/2014, DSNA; Lansing Diary, June 14, 1918. This concern over Japanese intervention in Siberia was most forcefully presented to the State Department by an American Red Cross official returning from that area who regarded the Japanese as pro-German and feared an ultimate German-Japanese alliance. Memorandum of Conversation with Mr. Anderson by E. T. Williams, June 13, 1918, DF 861.00/2082, DSNA.

9. Memorandum of Breckinridge Long, June 7, 1918, Long Papers; also in DF 861.00/2008, DSNA; Masaryk's notes in Křížek, "T. G. Masaryk," 657.

10. Vance McCormick to State Department, June 7, 1918, DF 763.72/10279, DSNA. The State Department acknowledged receipt of the British memorandum on June 13, 1918. See ibid.

11. Sosnowski to Lansing, June 15, 1918, Lansing Papers, Princeton.

12. Embassy of French Republic to Secretary of State, June 15, 1918, DF 763.72/10415, DSNA.

13. Lansing to Baker, June 17, 1918, Records of War Department to General Staff, RG 165, WRCNA; Lansing to Sharp, June 18, 1918, DF 763.72/10279, DSNA.

14. Milner to Reading, June 11, 1918, Baker Papers; Long, "American Intervention in Russia," 53. In the meantime, Milner had initiated a new plan for a much larger Allied expedition, which at that point was approved by neither Bliss nor Foch. Milner had directed his proposal to Wilson. Foch, who had not been consulted on the plan by Milner, felt that it constituted a new proposal that required action by the Supreme War Council. Joint Note No. 31, Supreme War Council Military Representatives, June 3, 1918, DF 861.00/6731, DSNA; Bliss to Baker, June 19, 1918, Baker Papers; Bliss to Baker, June 22, 1918, Bliss Final Report, 126–27, DF 763.72SU/99, DSNA; Baker to Wilson, June 20, 1918, Baker Papers; Barclay to Lloyd George and Milner, June 22, 1918, FO 800/223, H M 06770, PRO. See also *PWW*, 48:395–97.

15. Balfour to Reading, June 11, 1918, Wiseman Papers; *PWW*, 48:285–88.

16. Reading to Foreign Office, May 23, 1918, FO 115/2446, 338–40, PRO; *PWW*, 48:133–34.

17. Lansing Diary, June 11, 1918; R. S. Morris to Lansing, June 13, 1918, DF 861.00/1992, DSNA.

18. Lansing Diary, June 12, 1918.

19. Memorandum from His Majesty's Government, June 10, 1918, and Draft Note of Secretary of State to Ambassador of Great Britain, June 17, 1918, both in DF 763.72/10309, DSNA; Lansing Diary, June 12, 1918.

20. Auchincloss Diary, June 13, 1918; Lansing Diary, June 13, 1918; Lansing to Wilson, June 13, 1918, Wilson Papers; House Diary, June 13, 14, 1918; see also *PWW*, 48:305–6, 310.

21. Wilson to William Cox Redfield, June 13, 1918, Wilson Papers; Wiseman to Drummond, Cable, June 14, 1918, *Most Secret*, Wiseman Papers; *PWW*, 48:303, 315–16.

22. Lansing to Wilson, May 21, 1918, enclosing Russian Division memorandum, "The Military Advance of Semeneff," Wilson Papers; *PWW*, 48:104–7;

Baker to Bliss, May 31, 1918, Records of the American Section of the Supreme War Council, No. 316, RG 120, WRCNA; *PWW*, 48:218–19; Unterberger, *America's Siberian Expedition*, 54–57.

23. Poole to Francis, June 21, 1918, Francis Papers.

24. Cutrer to Milstaff, Peking, June 8, 1918, No. 9, MID 2266-1-8, RG 165, WRCNA.

25. Wilson to Reinsch, December 27, 1916, Reinsch Papers; Crane to Wilson, January 20, 1917, and Wilson to Crane, January 23, 1917, Wilson Papers; *PWW*, 40:335. Reinsch, a former professor of political science at the University of Wisconsin, was well aware of the importance of railway concessions and the strategic and commercial importance of the Siberian railway system in particular. See his *World Politics at the End of the Nineteenth Century as Influenced by the Oriental Situation*, 133–55. For a broader exposition of his views, see Reinsch, *Intellectual and Political Currents in the Far East*, and *Secret Diplomacy: How Far Can It Be Eliminated?*

26. Wilson to Lansing, June 17, 1918, DF 861.00/2145 1/2, DSNA; *PWW*, 48:335.

27. Poole to Lansing, June 12, 17, 1918, *FRUS, 1918, Russia*, 2:205, 214–15; see also *PWW*, 48:359–60.

28. Lansing to Wilson, June 19, 1918, and Wilson to Lansing, June 19, 1918, *Lansing Papers*, 2:363–64; see also *PWW*, 48:358–60.

29. Crane to House, June 18, 1918, C. R. Crane Papers.

30. Crane to Wilson, June 9, 1918, ibid.; *PWW*, 48:273.

31. Wilson to Crane, June 11, 1918, Wilson Papers; *PWW*, 48:283. Crane continued to keep Wilson informed of Masaryk's whereabouts and his scheduled arrival in Washington. Crane to R. Forster, White House, June 14, 1918, Wilson Papers. Masaryk was expected to remain in Washington for a week or two. Pergler to Lillian D. Wald, June 14, 1918, Wald Papers.

32. Auchincloss Diary, June 18, 1918; Lansing Diary, June 18, 1918; Jusserand to French Foreign Ministry, received June 18, 1918, Série E Japon, Intervention en Sibérie, E6212/18-20, FMD-Ar; *PWW*, 48:355–56. See also Long and Hopkins, "T. G. Masaryk and the Strategy of Czechoslovak Independence," 96. Long and Hopkins err in overriding Masaryk's view that Crane played the decisive role in bringing Masaryk and Wilson together. See Masaryk, *Making of a State*, 221, and Masaryk, *Světová revoluce*, 366–75. The view of Long and Hopkins, that Mott arranged the interview, rests upon a document written by Mott many years later. See "Experiences Dealing with Rulers," University Club, Winter Park, Fla., 1945, Mott Papers.

33. Baker to Wilson, June 19, 1918, Baker Papers.

34. Wilson to Baker, June 19, 1918, ibid.; Bliss to Baker, June 18, 1918, Wilson Papers; *PWW*, 48:367–70; Palmer, *Newton D. Baker*, 321.

35. *New York Times*, May 27, 1918; Masaryk to Crane, April 10, 1918, DF 861.00/2721, DSNA; Richard Crane to Wilson, May 7, 1918, with Masaryk enclosure, Wilson Papers; *PWW*, 47:548–52; Jusserand to Pichon, June 9, 1918, Papiers Jusserand, Lettres Politiques, 1918, 17:166–68, FFM-Ar; *PWW*, 48:273–74.

36. Masaryk's typewritten notes in English on his meeting with the President are in the Richard T. Crane Papers. His handwritten notes in Czech

are in *Dokumenty o protilidové*, 21. See also Lansing to Wilson, June 13, 1918, *PWW*, 48:305–7; Lansing Diary, June 12, 1918; Wilson to Lansing, June 19, 1918, DF 861.00/2148 1/2, DSNA; *PWW*, 48:358; Mamatey, *United States and East Central Europe*, 285–86.

37. Balfour to Reading, June 20, 1918 (received June 21), Wiseman Papers; Paraphrase of a telegram from Lockhart to the Foreign Office, June 20, 1918, Lansing to Wilson, June 23, 1918, both in DF 861.00/2164 1/2, DSNA; *PWW*, 48:380–81, 398–99.

38. Knight to Daniels, June 21, 1918, DF 861.00/2165 1/2, DSNA. On June 17, the War Department had received word from Ruggles, Military Attaché at Vologda, that railroad and wire communication with Siberia had been cut and the Bolsheviks in Siberia more or less overthrown, that Siberia had "declared itself independent republic based on universal suffrage and constituent assembly." Ruggles to Milstaff, Vologda, June 13, 1918, No. 45, MID 2266-D-51, and also Ruggles to Milstaff, May 10, 1918, No. 24, MID 2266-D-29, RG 165, WRCNA.

39. Handwritten note on DF 861.00/2615 1/2, DSNA.

40. DF 763.72/10209, DSNA.

41. Phillips to Lansing, June 21, 1918, and Lansing to Phillips, June 21, 1918, DF 763.72/10308, DSNA.

42. Phillips to Long, June 24, 1918, DF 763.72/10308, DSNA; Long Diary, June 24, 1918.

43. Draft Note, June 20, 1918, DF 763.72/10309, DSNA. See also Grew to Phillips, and Phillips to Grew, June 25, 1918, DF 763.72/10308, DSNA.

44. Balfour to Reading, June 21, 1918, FO 371/3324, No. 110145, 16, PRO, and DF 861.00/2164 1/2, DSNA; CAB 23/41, Imperial War Cabinet 19, Notes of meeting on June 20, 1918, PRO; CAB 23/41, Imperial War Cabinet 20, Notes of meeting on June 25, 1918, PRO; Memorandum by Gregory, June 17, 1918, FO 371/3319, PRO. Clemenceau to Jusserand, June 23, 1918, Camille Barrière to the French Foreign Ministry, June 27, 1918, Jusserand to the French Foreign Ministry, June 27, 1918, all in Etat-major de l'armée de terre, 4N46, FMD-Ar. See also *PWW*, 48:446–47; Woodward, "The British Government and Japanese Intervention," 680–81. Francis had written for instructions in view of an expected collapse of the Bolshevik government. Polk to Wilson, June 6, 1918, with enclosure, DF 861.00/1945, DSNA.

45. Lansing to Wilson, June 23, 1918, Paraphrase of Telegram from Lockhart to Foreign Office, June 20, 1918, DF 861.00/2164 1/2, DSNA; *PWW*, 48:398–99. Wilson read and returned the memo on June 25.

46. Wilson to Baker, June 19, 1918, and March to Baker, June 24, 1918, Wilson Papers; Bliss to March, June 24, 1918, Bliss Papers; March to Wilson, June 24, 1918, in March, *Nation at War*, 116–20. See also *PWW*, 48:357, 418–21.

47. Bullitt to House, June 24, 1918, House Papers. Many preached the need for intervention, urging that Bolshevism was a greater threat than was the menace of Japan. They insisted that the only means of helping Russia was by overthrowing Bolshevism. See "Intervention in Russia," *New Republic*, June 1, 1918, 130–33; Mason, "Japan and Bolshevism," 259–61; London *Times*, June 15, 19, July 4, 1918; *New York Times*, June 3, 4, 1918. By June 1918 even members of

Congress had begun to urge that the U.S. adopt the policy of Siberian intervention. *Congressional Record,* 56, pt. 8:7557, 7997–8001, 8065–67, 8580.

48. Reading to Balfour, June 25, 1918, FO 115/2447, 146–51, PRO; *PWW,* 48:429–31.

49. "The Approaching Crisis," *New Republic,* June 22, 1918, 217–20; "Russia and Recognition," *Nation,* June 22, 1918, 727–28.

50. Sharp to Lansing, June 22, 1918, DF 763.72/10463, DSNA.

51. Phillips to Lansing, June 25, 1918, Subject: Recognition of Czecho-Slovak National Council, DF 860f.01/17. Jusserand continued to pressure Lansing in person on both the recognition of the Czechs and intervention in Siberia. Lansing Diary, June 25, 1918.

52. Lansing Diary, June 25, 1918; Long Diary, June 24, 1918. Jusserand had discussed the matter with Lansing on June 20 as well. Lansing Diary, June 20, 1918. On the same day, Lansing also agreed to see Raymond Robins while Long discussed the Siberian issue with Dr. Harper; Long Diary, June 25, 1918. Robins discussed the Russian situation with Lansing and favored the proposal of sending an economic commission; Lansing Diary, June 26, 1918.

53. Masaryk's handwritten, unpublished note of his June 25 meeting with Lansing in Křížek, "T. G. Masaryk," 662; Masaryk to Chicherin, June 25, 1918, DF 861.00/2180a, DSNA.

54. Masaryk to Lansing, June 26, 1918, DF 763.72119/673 1/2, DSNA; also in Czechoslovak Republic, Ministerstvo zahranicnich veci, *Archiv diplomatických dokumentů československých,* dated June 26, 1918. The State Department acknowledged with sincere thanks Masaryk's personal note and the "valuable information" it contained; Phillips to Masaryk, July 1, 1918, DF 763.72119/673 1/2, DSNA.

55. Phillips to Long, June 24, 1918, DF 763.72/10309, DSNA.

56. Memorandum handed by Lansing to Wilson, June 25, 1918; Lansing to Wilson, June 27, 1918, Lansing Papers, LC; *PWW,* 48:435–37, 447–48. Lansing Diary, June 25, 1918.

57. Lansing to Caldwell, June 25, 1918, 5 P.M., *FRUS, 1918, Russia,* 2:224.

58. Lansing Diary, June 25, 1918.

59. Tumulty to Wilson, June 27, 1918, and Wilson to Tumulty, June 27, 1918, Wilson Papers; *PWW,* 48:444.

60. British Embassy (Washington) to British Foreign Office, June 26, 1918, FO 371/3324, No. 114697, PRO. See also FO 115/2447, 157–58, PRO, dated June 27, 1918.

61. FO 115/2447, 157–58, PRO.

62. Balfour to Reading, June 28, 1918, Wiseman Papers; Reading to Wilson, June 28, 1918, FO 115/2447, 301A, PRO; *PWW,* 48:463. Jusserand had already informed Reading that the economic policy would be a "very distinct step in advance of the position held thus far." British Embassy (Washington) to Foreign Office, June 26, 1918, FO 115/2447, 159, PRO.

63. Lansing Diary, June 27, 1918; Wilson to Lansing, June 26, 1918, in "Policy in Relation to the Nationalities Now Included within the Austro-Hungarian Empire," June 27, 1918, Lansing Papers, LC; see also *PWW,* 48:435–37, 447–48.

64. *PWW,* 48:435–37; Lansing Diary, June 28, 1918. See also Lansing to T. N.

Page, June 27, 1918, DF 763.72/10291, DSNA. Pergler, Masaryk's secretary, later claimed that the supplementary declaration issued on June 28 was from the pen of Putney. See Pergler, *Struggle for Czechoslovak Independence*, 91. This authorship does not appear to be confirmed in the Lansing Diary. The British regarded the American announcement as an important step; FO 371.W38/117101/64427, PRO.

65. *PWW*, 48:458–60, and Caldwell to Lansing, June 25, 1918, ibid., 428–29.

66. Ishii to Lansing, June 26, 1918, and Wilson to Lansing, June 28, 1918, DF 861.00/2215 1/2 and 2216 1/2, DSNA; also enclosed in Lansing to Wilson, June 27, 1918; Wilson to Lansing, June 28, 1918, Wilson Papers; *PWW*, 48:448–49, 457.

67. CAB 23/44, Imperial War Cabinet 20A, Notes of Meeting on June 26, 1918, A Meeting of the Prime Ministers, PRO.

68. American Legation (Peking) to Harris, July 2, 1918, and Morris to American Legation (Peking), July 1, 1918, DF 861.00/2194 and 2195, DSNA; Chamberlin, *Russian Revolution*, 2:10; Medek, *Czech Anabasis across Russia and Siberia*, 21.

69. Foch to Wilson, June 27, 1918, Baker Papers; Jusserand to the French Foreign Ministry, received June 29, 1918, Etat-major de l'armée de terre, 4N46, FMD-Ar. Henri Bergson, the noted French philosopher, also had a long conversation with Wilson, beseeching him for an energetic intervention, emphasizing its importance for success on the Western Front, and warning him of the "grave responsibility" he assumed if he failed to act. He sought to allay Wilson's concerns about Japanese seizure of territory by assuring him that the Allies would oppose territorial concessions in China and only agree to trade commissions. Bergson was hopeful that Wilson's consideration of a limited economic mission might result in the development of a policy "close to ours." Bergson to the French Foreign Ministry, through Jusserand, June 28, 1918, ibid. See also *PWW*, 48:441–44, 445–46.

70. Daniels to Wilson, June 27, 1918, Baker Papers.

71. Memorandum for Chief of Naval Operations, June 27, 1918, RG 45, WA6, NRCNA.

72. Caldwell to Lansing, June 28, 1918, DF 861.00/2239, DSNA. For Warner's view of the Czech peril, see Bowie, *Langdon Warner through His Letters*, 81–102.

73. Jusserand to Lansing, June 29, 1918, DF 763.72/10592, DSNA. For Beneš's efforts to secure an Allied commitment of solidarity toward the Czecho-Slovak National Council and to secure French agreement to pressure the Allies to that end, see E. Beneš, *My War Memoirs*, 384–85.

74. Lansing to Wilson, June 29, 1918, DF 860f.01/17, DSNA.

75. Lansing to Wilson, June 29, 1918, *PWW*, 48:464.

76. Lansing Diary, June 30, 1918. A year later, on August 19, 1919, at a conference at the White House with a group of senators, Wilson was questioned concerning his familiarity with the agreements made by the Allied governments with the Czecho-Slovak National Council. He responded that he was aware of "arrangements similar to those that we had ourselves made recognizing those national committees as provisional representatives of the people" and indicated that the recognition by the U.S. was "purely informal." It was not an international recognition, but merely an agreement to deal with

them as representatives. See appendix 4 in Lodge, *The Senate and the League of Nations*, 338.

77. For Foreign Minister Stéphen Pichon's speech proclaiming the right of the Czecho-Slovak nation to independence, see Pichon's text, June 30, 1918, Records of War Department General Staff, RG 165, WRCNA; Thomson, *Czechoslovakia in European History*, 268.

78. *New York Times*, July 2, 1918. Like the *New York Times*, the *Washington Post* reported and praised French action and expressed the wish that Wilson would follow their example; *Washington Post*, July 3, 1918.

79. "By the Czecho-Slovak National Council to the Citizens of Vladivostok and of the Maritime Province" in "An authorized and verified translation of the official version of the incident given by the temporary Executive Committee of the Czecho-Slovak Army," Major David P. Barrows to Chief of Military Intelligence Division, October 20, 1918, 314.7, Czecho-Slovak History, Records of Adjutant General, RG 407, WRCNA.

80. "Statement of General Dietrichs Concerning the Operations in Taking Nikolsk," Records of Adjutant General, RG 407, WRCNA.

81. See Francis correspondence, July 1–8, 1918, Francis Papers.

82. Auchincloss Diary, July 1, 1918.

83. Belgian Government to Lansing, July 2, 1918, DF 763.72/10594, DSNA.

84. American Legation (Peking) to American Consul General (Irkutsk), July 2, 1918, DF 861.00/2194, DSNA. A copy of this telegram appears in the Irkutsk Consular Files, RG 84, DSNA; see Harris Papers and also Fuller Papers. See also E. Beneš, *Světová válke a naše revoluce*, 3:Doc. 300. The telegram was repeated in toto to the department in the legation's telegram of July 2, 1918; see DF 861.00/2194, DSNA. For a careful inquiry into the events surrounding the French initial plans for intervention via the instructions of General Lavergne and the knowledge of these instructions by Harris and Emerson, see "Reported Plan for Allied Intervention in Russia in 1918," *Strictly Confidential*, Peking, February 16, 1933, DF 861.00/11522, DSNA.

85. See documents mentioned in note 84. DF 861.00/2194 and 861.00/11512A, DSNA.

86. MacMurray to Lansing, July 12, 1918, DF 861.00/2263, DSNA.

87. Wiseman to Arthur Murray, July 4, 1918, Wiseman Papers; *PWW*, 48:523–25.

88. Memorandum by General Alby, July 2, 1918, Doc. 117, *Dokumenty a materiály*, 152–64; Balfour to Reading, July 2, 1918, Wiseman Papers; *PWW*, 48:496–501.

89. Reading to Wilson, July 3, 1918, enclosing Supreme War Council Resolution in Balfour to Reading, July 2, 1918, Wilson Papers; *PWW*, 48:493–501; Diplomatic Liaison Officer, Supreme War Council (Frazier) to Lansing, July 2, 1918, *FRUS, 1918, Russia*, 2:241–46. See also Murray to Wiseman, July 3, 1918, Wiseman Papers.

90. March to Wilson, July 3, 1918, enclosing Bliss to Lansing, Baker, and March, July 2, 1918, Wilson Papers; *PWW*, 48:503–6; Reading to Balfour, July 3, 1918, Wiseman Papers; Ullman, *Intervention and the War*, 211–12.

91. Reading to Balfour, July 3, 1918, Wiseman Papers; FO 115/2447, 297–301, PRO; Auchincloss Diary, July 3, 1918; *PWW*, 48:511–14.

92. Cronon, *Cabinet Diaries of Daniels*, 318.

93. Wiseman to House, July 4, 1918, and Wiseman to Murray, July 4, 1918, Wiseman Papers; *PWW*, 48:523–29.

94. Frazier through Ambassador Sharp (Paris) to State Department, July 4, 1918, DF 763.73 SU/89, DSNA; Lansing Diary, July 4, 1918; Reading to Foreign Office, July 4, 1918, Wiseman Papers.

95. "Memorandum on the Siberian Situation," Office of the Secretary, July 4, 1918, DF 861.00/2292 1/2, DSNA. See also Memorandum for Secretary of State from Basil Miles, and penciled addendum, July 5, 1918, DF 861.00/2908, DSNA.

96. Balfour to Reading, July 3, 1918, Wiseman Papers; *PWW*, 48:496–501.

97. MacMurray to Harris, July 2, 1918, DF 861.00/2194, DSNA; Hornbeck, "American Expeditionary Force in Siberia," Hornbeck Papers, 18–19. When General Graves later pointed out that both Poole and Harris knew that the Czechs were not in need of help at least one month before his own arrival, he was speaking from solid evidence. See Graves, *America's Siberian Adventure*, 343–46. When he indicated that Harris had the full support of the Russian section of the State Department and perhaps even one step higher in the hierarchy of the State Department, his view also seems to be borne out by the evidence available; ibid., 217–18.

98. Lansing Diary, July 5, 1918.

99. Harris to State Department, July 5, 1918, DF 861.00/2205, DSNA.

100. Caldwell to Lansing, July 5, 1918, *FRUS, 1918, Russia*, 2:261.

101. Knight to Daniels, July 5, 1918, RG 45, WA6, NRCNA; Daniels to Wilson, July 5, 1918, with enclosure from Knight requesting instructions, Wilson Papers; *PWW*, 48:527–28.

102. Lansing to Caldwell, July 5, 1918, DF 861.00/2181, DSNA.

103. Knight to Daniels, July 6, 1918, RG 45, WA6, NRCNA. Lansing immediately reported this information to Francis at Vologda. Lansing to Francis, July 6, 1918, DF 861.00/2335e, DSNA.

104. Lansing to Francis, July 6, 1918, *FRUS, 1918, Russia*, 1:571.

105. Lansing Diary, July 6, 1918.

106. Memorandum of the Secretary of State of a Conference at the White House in Reference to the Siberian Situation, July 6, 1918, *PWW*, 48:542–43; Lansing Diary, July 6, 1918.

107. March to General John J. Pershing, July 5, 1918, March Papers.

108. March, *Nation at War*, 126.

109. Daniels to Knight, July 6, 1918, RG 45, WA6, NRCNA; Lansing to Morris, July 6, 1918, *FRUS, 1918, Russia*, 2:263–64.

110. Unterberger, *America's Siberian Expedition*, 70. Balfour immediately informed the State Department that the British action had been adopted without any intention of starting intervention but solely for insuring order in Vladivostok, securing the communications of the Czech forces, and safeguarding the Allied stores in the city. Balfour to Reading, July 10, 1918, *FRUS, 1918, Russia*, 2:275.

111. Doc. 85, *Dokumenty a materiály,* 114–51; Doc. 55, Holotík, *Štefánikovská,* 467; Šteidler, *Československé hnutí na Rusi,* 68–69; Medek, *Za svobodu,* 3, pt. 4:187; Bordes Report, Archives de l'armée de terre; J. Bradley, *Allied Intervention in Russia,* 98–99.

112. Caldwell to Lansing, July 7, 1918, *FRUS, 1918, Russia,* 2:264; Knight to Daniels, July 7, 1918, I.N. 2309, Special Dispatches, RG 45, NRCNA.

113. Morris to Lansing, July 7, 1918, DF 861.00/2212, DSNA; Report of a Conference of Japanese General Staff on June 27, July 4, 1918, dated July 9, 1918, RG 165, WRCNA.

114. Horvath at Grodekovo to Ambassador Krupensky at Tokyo, Horvath Memoirs, 14–16; Unterberger, *America's Siberian Expedition,* 14–15.

115. Paraphrase of telegram from British Minister (Peking) to British Foreign Office, July 2, 1918, DF 861.00/3493, DSNA.

116. Paraphrase of telegram from British Minister (Peking) to British Foreign Office, July 8, 1918, DF 861.00/2333, DSNA.

117. Caldwell to Lansing, July 8, 1918, DF 861.00/2289, DSNA.

118. Sims to Opnav, July 9, 1918, RG 45, WA6, NRCNA.

119. CAB 23/7, War Cabinet 442/30, Minutes of Meeting on July 8, 1918, at 12:00 noon, PRO.

120. Paraphrase of telegram from British Ambassador (Tokyo) to Foreign Office, July 9, 1918, DF 861.00/2334, DSNA. This information was conveyed to the State Department on July 13, and received in the department on July 17; ibid.

121. CAB 23/7, War Cabinet 444/30, Minutes of Meeting on July 11, 1918, at 11:30 A.M., PRO.

122. Hornbeck, "American Expeditionary Force in Siberia," Hornbeck Papers; Morris to Lansing, July 15, 1918, *FRUS, 1918, Russia,* 2:283.

Chapter 15

1. Memorandum of the Secretary of State, July 8, 1918, *PWW,* 48:559–60. Wilson was informed of Lansing's conference with Ishii. Lansing Diary, July 8, 1918.

2. Lansing to Wilson, July 8, 1918, DF 861.00/2292 1/2, DSNA; *PWW,* 48:560–61. For popular knowledge of American negotiations regarding Siberia, see *New York Times,* July 9, 1918.

3. Jusserand to French Foreign Ministry, received July 4 and 5, 1918, Nos. 852 and 855, Etat-major de l'armée de terre, 4N46, FMD-Ar; Wiseman to British Foreign Office, July 8, 1918, Wiseman Papers. Cecil sought to exert personal pressure through Colonel House. Cecil to House, July 8, 1918, ibid. *PWW,* 48:566–67.

4. Reading to Foreign Office, July 8, 1918, FO 115/2448, 135–38, PRO; *PWW,* 48:565–66; Jusserand to French Foreign Ministry, July 10, 1918, Etat-major de l'armée de terre, 4N46, FMD-Ar; Reading conveyed the substance of his observations to the French and Italian Ambassadors.

5. MacMurray to Lansing, Peking, July 9, 1918, *FRUS, 1918, Russia,* 2:271–72.

6. Lansing to Wilson, July 11, 1918, DF 861.00/2241, DSNA.

7. MacMurray to Lansing, July 13, 1918, *FRUS, 1918, Russia,* 2:280; Gajda, *Moje paměti,* 159.

8. MacMurray to Lansing, July 16, 1918, DF 861.00/2467, DSNA.

9. Phillips Diary, July 9, 1918; Jusserand to French Foreign Ministry, received July 12, 1918, Etat-major de l'armée de terre, 4N46, FMD-Ar. See also Auchincloss Diary, July 9, 1918; Lansing to Wilson, July 9, 1918, *PWW,* 48:574–75.

10. Reading to Lloyd George and Balfour, July 9, 1918, Wiseman Papers.

11. Reading to Lloyd George and Balfour, July 10, 1918, *PWW,* 48:586–87.

12. Lloyd George to Reading, July 10, 1918, Wiseman Papers; *PWW,* 48:587–89.

13. Jusserand to French Foreign Ministry, July 10, 1918, Etat-major de l'armée de terre, 4N46, FMD-Ar.

14. Reading to Lloyd George, July 12, 1918, Wiseman Papers; *PWW,* 48:602–3.

15. Lloyd George to Reading, July 18, 1918, Balfour Papers.

16. Morris to Lansing, July 13, 1918, *FRUS, 1918, Russia,* 1:281; LaFargue, *China and the World War,* 169; Takeuchi, *War and Diplomacy,* 205–7.

17. Lansing to Morris, July 10, 1918, and Stevens to Lansing, July 18, 1918, *FRUS, 1918, Russia,* 3:237.

18. Takeuchi, *War and Diplomacy,* 207; Morley, *Japanese Thrust into Siberia,* 264–66.

19. Polk to Morris, July 19, 1918, *FRUS, 1918, Russia,* 2:297; LaFargue, *China and the World War,* 169.

20. Polk Diary, July 13, 1918. The Imperial War Cabinet had already indicated that they would have no objection to the Japanese command. CAB 23/44, Imperial War Cabinet 20A, Notes of Meeting of Prime Ministers on June 26, 1918, PRO.

21. Polk to Wilson, July 15, 1918, *PWW,* 48:621–22; Polk Diary, July 16, 1918. Polk suggested that no formal statement be given out, but that the Japanese should simply send an officer of sufficient rank with their forces, and it would be "understood that our forces would be under his command."

22. Morris to Lansing, July 15, 1918, *FRUS, 1918, Russia,* 2:283.

23. Harris to Ray, Irkutsk, July 15, 1918, DF 861.77/541, DSNA; Emerson Report, 58, DF 861.77/541, DSNA.

24. Emerson Report, 59, DF 861.77/541, DSNA. See also W. R. Castle (Acting Secretary of State) to Nelson T. Johnson (American Minister in China), January 11, 1933, DF 861.00/11512A, DSNA.

25. Secretary of State to Allied Ambassadors, July 17, 1918, *FRUS, 1918, Russia,* 2:287–90.

26. Office of the Secretary, July 11, 1918, DF 861.00/2293 1/2, DSNA; see also Draft of an Aide-Mémoire, July 16, 1918, Polk Papers; *PWW,* 48:624–27.

27. Anderson Diary, July 19, 1918, Anderson Papers. Anderson corroborates, at least in part, the view set forth by Masaryk in the Czech and German versions of his war memoirs. See Masaryk, *Světová revoluce,* 367, and Masaryk, *Die Welt-Revolution,* 310. Masaryk claims that although it was not through his

personal influence alone, nevertheless he "was able, step by step, to persuade" both Wilson and Lansing to accept his program. See also Kalvoda, "Masaryk in America," 85–86.

28. Lloyd George to Reading, Very Secret, July 17, 1918, Wiseman Papers; CAB 23/7, War Cabinet 450, July 22, 1918, Minute 8, PRO; Balfour to Reading, July 22, 1918, handed by Barclay to State Department, July 30, 1918, DF 861.00/2957, DSNA; also in Wiseman Papers.

29. Balfour to Reading, July 22, 1918, Balfour Papers.

30. Reading to Balfour, July 23, 1918, FO 115/2448, 257–60, PRO; Jusserand to French Foreign Ministry, received July 19, 1918, Etat-major de l'armée de terre, 16N3012, FMD-Ar; Reading to Balfour, July 19, 1918, *PWW*, 49:36.

31. MacMurray to Lansing, July 24, 1918, Long Papers.

32. Wilson to Long, July 26, 1918, ibid.

33. Polk to Wilson, July 20, 1918, with enclosure, Warburton to Military Intelligence Branch, Executive Division, General Staff, War Department, Paris, July 17, 1918, Wilson Papers; *PWW*, 49:41–42; Czecho-Slovak Organization Who's Who, Confidential, July 1, 1918, in RG 165, WRCNA.

34. Polk to Wilson, July 20, 1918, Wilson Papers; also in DF 861.00/3920f, DSNA; Baker to Wilson, July 20, 1918, Wilson Papers and Baker Papers; *PWW*, 49:41–42.

35. Seymour, *Intimate Papers*, 3:415; Long to Koo, July 26, 1918, *FRUS, 1918, Russia*, 2:304. Wilson was quite adamant about the latter matter. Polk to MacMurray, July 26, 1918, ibid., 2:305.

36. Masaryk, *Making of a State*, 276; "Recognition of the Provisional Government," *Bohemian Review* 2 (July 1918): 97; Selver, *Masaryk*, 287.

37. Copy of telegram from Masaryk to Beneš, received in Paris, July 15, 1918, FO 371/3135; Recognition of Czecho-Slovak National Sovereignty, July 27, 1918, FO 371.W3/135132/F64427, PRO; Masaryk to Polk, July 20, 1918, DF 763.72/11171 1/2, DSNA; Hugh Gibson, Report of an Interview with Mr. Edward Beneš of the Czecho-Slovak National Council, Gibson Papers.

38. Polk Diary, July 19, 1918; Jusserand to French Foreign Ministry, received July 19, 1918, Etat-major de l'armée de terre, 16N3012, FMD-Ar.

39. Memorandum on the Czecho-Slovak Army in Russia, enclosure in Masaryk to Polk, July 20, 1918, DF 861.00/2346, DSNA; *PWW*, 49:44–46.

40. Masaryk, "Help of the Allies to the Czecho-Slovak Army in Russia Necessary," July 20, 1918, Confidential, DF 861.00/2346, DSNA; *PWW*, 49:44–46.

41. Masaryk to Wilson, July 20, 1918, with enclosure from members of the Czecho-Slovak National Council (Girsa, Špaček) to the President of the Czecho-Slovak National Council (Masaryk), sent by British Consul at Vladivostok, July 14, 1918, Wilson Papers; *PWW*, 49:44–46.

42. Wilson to Masaryk, ca. July 22, 1918, Wilson Collection, Princeton; *PWW*, 49:53. Wilson had already conveyed this same information to Reading, who in turn informed Jusserand that he would make no decision without first consulting fully with Lansing and Baker. Jusserand to French Foreign Ministry, received July 5, 1918, Etat-major de l'armée de terre, 4N46, FMD-Ar. For

Masaryk's telegram to the Czech army, see Doc. 128, July 21, 1918, in *Dokumenty a materiály,* 164.

43. Polk to Wilson, July 24, 1918, *PWW,* 49:75–76; Auchincloss Diary, July 24, 25, 1918.

44. Polk Diary, July 25, 1918; Phillips Diary, July 25, 1918; Polk to Morris, July 27, 1918; *FRUS, 1918, Russia,* 2:307.

45. Auchincloss Diary, July 25, 1918.

46. Phillips Diary, July 25, 1918; *PWW,* 49:97.

47. *PWW,* 49:110–11; Wilson regarded the Japanese answer as a "counter-proposal." Reading to Balfour and Lloyd George, July 26, 1918, Reading Papers.

48. The Lansing-Ishii Agreement of November 2, 1917, had acknowledged Japan's "special interest" in China, and reaffirmed the adherence of both powers to the Open Door policy. Despite its ambiguity, the agreement was hailed as a great triumph, since it was vital to the war effort that relations between the two nations assume a friendlier tone. MacMurray, *Treaties,* 2:1394–96. For diplomatic exchanges relating to the agreement, see *FRUS, 1917,* 258–75.

49. Polk to Morris, July 27, 1918, *FRUS, 1918, Russia,* 2:306–7.

50. Morris to Lansing, July 23, 1918, and Polk to Morris, July 29, 1918, *FRUS, 1918, Russia,* 2:300–301, 314.

51. Polk to Lansing, July 29, 1918, DF 861.00/2403 1/2, DSNA.

52. LaFargue, *China and the World War,* 169–70.

53. Phillips Diary, July 30, 31, 1918; Polk to Morris, July 30, 1918, Long Papers.

54. Knight to Daniels, August 3, 1918, RG 45, WA6, NRCNA.

55. Beneš to Masaryk, July 28, 1918, in Holotík, *Štefánikovská,* Doc. 53, 459–61; FO 371.W3/130680/64427, PRO; see also Recognition of Czecho-Slovak National Sovereignty, July 27, 1918, FO 371.W3/135132/F64427, PRO, and Pichon to Beneš, June 29, 1918, Gibson Papers.

56. Interview between Namier and Beneš, July 26, 1918; report transmitted to Sir William Tyrrell, FO 371, PID 266, vol. 4366, PRO.

57. Recognition of Czecho-Slovak National Sovereignty, July 27, 1918, FO 371.W3/135132/F64427, PRO.

58. Beneš to Cecil, August 3, 1918, FO 371.W3/135903/64427, PRO. See also Memorandum from Beneš, July 29, 1918, FO 371.W3/132422/64427, PRO; notes and conversations between Beneš and Cecil, August 2, 1918, FO 371.W3/135135/64427, PRO; E. Beneš, *My War Memoirs,* 403–4; Steed, *Through Thirty Years,* 2:231–33.

59. Statement of the Czecho-Slovak National Council at Washington on the aims of the Czecho-Slovaks in Russia, July 27, 1918, in Scott, *Official Statements,* 357. A draft of Masaryk's original telegram of July 21 to the Czech Legion is in the Masaryk Papers. A note to the draft telegram, not sent, instructs the legion to fight "in the first place" the Austrians and Germans, but "Russian troops & parties united with Austrians" and Germans "must be fought too." An illuminating discussion of this statement appears in typescript MSS, Volia Rossii, chaps. 8–9, Golovine Papers.

60. Ray to Harris, July 21, 1918, Harris Papers.

61. Hadley to Harris, July 21, 1918, ibid.

62. Miles to Polk, July 22, 1918, DF 861.00/2298 1/2, DSNA.

63. Williams to Harris, July 22, 1918, Harris Papers.

64. Gray Report, 9–10, Harris Papers. See also Medek, *Za svobodu*, 3, pt. 4:805.

65. Medek, *Za svobodu*, 3, pt. 4:804–5; Gray Report, 9–10, Harris Papers; Thünig-Nittner, *Die Tschechoslowakische Legion in Russland*, 67–69.

66. Packard Report, 65, DF 861.00/6052, DSNA.

67. Landon Report, 8, RG 120, WRCNA; Packard Report, DF 861.00/6052, DSNA.

68. Harris to Legation at Peking, No. 10, July 26, 1918, Harris Papers.

69. Harris to Lansing, July 29, 1918, *FRUS, 1918, Russia*, 2:309–14.

70. Harris to Legation at Peking, No. 10, July 26, 1918, Harris Papers.

71. Francis and the Allied Ambassadors had left Petrograd for Vologda at the height of the Brest-Litovsk crisis. After the assassination of Mirbach on July 4, 1918, the Soviet leaders, fearing for the safety of the Vologda diplomats, invited them to come to Moscow. However, by mid-July the diplomats had received a secret communication from General Poole, commander of the North Russian expedition, which definitely confirmed the British intentions to intervene in Archangel at the end of the month. They were, therefore, urged to get out of Soviet-held territory before the expedition arrived. They departed for Archangel on July 23. Kennan, *Russia and the West under Lenin and Stalin*, 80–83.

72. Poole to Lansing, July 25, 1918, *FRUS, 1918, Russia*, 1:623. The YMCA reported that despite the Czech successes against the Bolsheviks in Siberia, the Bolsheviks were not hampering the YMCA efforts in many areas. They considered it "remarkable and unexpected" that in "a number of localities the Bolsheviki are sympathetic and even helpful," particularly in Vladivostok. Memorandum on Association work in Russia, April 25, 1918, World Service Materials, YMCA Archives.

73. Caldwell to Lansing, July 31, 1918, DF 861.00/2391, DSNA.

74. Polk to Caldwell, July 31, 1918, DF 861.00/2390, DSNA.

75. Phillips Diary, July 20, 1918; Polk to Wilson, July 20, 1918, Polk Papers and Wilson Papers; *PWW*, 49:37–40, 51.

76. Baker, "Foreword," in Graves, *America's Siberian Adventure*, viii–ix.

77. Baker to Mrs. John B. Casserly, November 15, 1924, Wilson Papers.

78. Baker to Wilson, July 20, 1918, Wilson Papers; Final Bliss Report, 130, DF 763.72SU/99, DSNA; *PWW*, 49:43–44. Wilson agreed to divert three battalions of infantry, provided Foch could spare them, and three companies of engineers, if General Pershing could spare them. March to Bliss, July 22, 1918, RG 407, WRCNA; *PWW*, 49:57.

79. Polk to Morris, August 1, 1918, *FRUS, 1918, Russia*, 2:322; Knight to Daniels, July 30, 31, 1918, RG 45, WA6, NRCNA; *PWW*, 49:150–53.

80. Knight to Daniels, August 2, 1918, RG 45, WA6, NRCNA.

81. Polk Diary, August 1, 1918.

82. Ibid., August 2, 3, 1918.

83. *FRUS, 1918, Russia*, 2:324–25; Stewart, *White Armies of Russia*, 134–35.

84. Polk Diary, August 3, 1918; Unterberger, *America's Siberian Expedition*, 85.

85. Long Diary, August 3, 1918; Polk Diary, August 3, 1918.

86. Phillips Diary, August 3, 1918; Polk Diary, August 3, 1918; *PWW*, 49:178–79.

87. Polk to Morris, August 3, 1918, *FRUS, 1918, Russia*, 2:328–29.

88. *Izvestiia*, August 23, 1918; *Berliner Tageblatt*, August 8, 1918; Cumming and Pettit, *Russian-American Relations*, 249–50.

89. Extract from Chicherin's Report made before the Meeting of the Central Executive Committee on September 2, 1918, DF 861.00/2980, DSNA; *Berliner Tageblatt*, August 9, 1918.

90. Masaryk to Polk, August 5, 1918, Polk to Masaryk, August 6, 1918, Polk Papers; Masaryk to Wilson, August 5, 1918, *PWW*, 49:185; Miller, "What Wilson Meant to Czechoslovakia," 79.

91. Masaryk to Wilson, August 5, 1918, Wilson Papers; *PWW*, 49:185; *Denní Hlasatel*, August 7, 1918. Copies of Masaryk's letter were sent to the British, French, Italian, and Japanese Ambassadors. *New York Times*, August 7, 1918.

92. Peffer, "Japan's Absorption of Siberia," 367–68; Dennis, *The Foreign Policies of Soviet Russia*, 280–81; Griswold, *Far Eastern Policy*, 234–39; Baker, "Foreword," in Graves, *America's Siberian Adventure*, viii–ix. John F. Stevens, in reminiscing over his activities in Russia and Siberia as head of the Russian Railway Service Corps, noted that after four years he was convinced that while the U.S. had never proclaimed its policy as that of keeping the "open door" or "so-called John Hay policy intact, but the truth of the matter is it was for just that purpose. And as against our own ally—Japan." He added, "And I am very free to say—however egotistical it may sound, that after matching wits for four long years—secretly of course—I prevented the Japanese from taking the Chinese Eastern Railway." "Stevens Account of His Activities in Russia and Siberia," Railway Service Corps Papers.

93. "Notes réunies ainsi par H. B. lui-même," Papiers d'Agents, Bergson, vol. 3, FFM-Ar.

94. Barclay to Lansing, August 8, 1918, *FRUS, 1918, Russia*, 2:333–34.

95. Polk to Wilson, July 27, 1918; paraphrase of telegram from Balfour to Reading, July 25, 1918; draft proclamation, note by the President, July 29, 1918; all in DF 861.00/7412, DSNA; Barclay to Foreign Office, July 30, 1918, FO 115/2448, 321, PRO.

96. CAB 23/7, War Cabinet 455/30, Minutes of Meeting on August 7, 1918, PRO; Doc. 56 and 57, Holotík, *Štefánikovská*, 469–74.

97. Polk Diary, August 8, 1918.

Chapter 16

1. Rainey Report, 1–2, RG 120, WRCNA; Harris to Lansing, September 10, 1918, enclosing Extract of Letter from Vice Consul Williams to Vice Consul Hadley (Samara), August 2, 1918, DF 861.00/3164, DSNA. Czech Official Record, August 10, 1918, RG 120, WRCNA; Bordes Report, Archives de

l'armée de terre; Becvar, *The Lost Legion: A Czechoslovak Epic*, 175; J. F. N. Bradley, *La Légion tchécoslovaque*, 96.

2. Henry Palmer (Vice Consul at Ekaterinburg) to American Consul at Omsk, August 1918, Harris Papers; Williams to Hadley (Samara), August 2, 1918, DF 861.00/3164, DSNA; Merle-Smith to John W. Davis (American Ambassador at London), July 9, 1920, DF 861.00/2983, DSNA. Bordes Report, Archives de l'armée de terre; see also "Instructions Issued by War Office to General Poole," in H. W. Studd, Brigadier General, Acting British Military Representative, Supreme War Council to Permanent Military Representative, American Section, Supreme War Council, August 16, 1918, RG 120, WRCNA, and Docs. 56 and 57, Holotík, *Štefánikovská*, 469–74.

3. Palmer to Harris, August 1918, Harris Papers.

4. Statement of the American Consul General at Cheliabinsk, August 6, 1918. Recorded by H. H. Slaughter, Graves Papers; statement also affirmed as a true copy by R. L. Eichelberger, Lieutenant Colonel, General Staff, U.S. Army, ibid.

5. Paraphrase of cipher received from Consul General Harris at Novo Nikolaevsk to forward to Peking, August 13, 1918, Harris Papers.

6. Paraphrase of telegram from Archangel, August 6, 1918, DF 861.00/2450, DSNA.

7. Paraphrase of telegram from Lindley to the Foreign Office, August 9, 1918, DF 861.00/3487, DSNA. The French supported this plan. Bordes Report, Archives de l'armée de terre.

8. Balfour to Reading, August 7, 1918, *FRUS, 1918, Russia*, 2:337.

9. CAB 23/7, War Cabinet 454/30, Minutes of Meeting on August 4, 1918, at 1:15 P.M., PRO.

10. Members of the Czecho-Slovak National Council to Masaryk, July 31, 1918, *FRUS, 1918, Russia*, 2:319.

11. Masaryk to Polk, August 5, 1918, Polk Papers; Polk to Tumulty, August 8, 1918, DF 861.00/2530, DSNA; CAB 23/7, War Cabinet 455/4, August 7, 1918, PRO.

12. CAB 23/7, War Cabinet 455/30, Draft extract from the Minutes of Meeting on August 7, 1918, PRO.

13. Notes on War Cabinet Minutes No. 455, FO 371.W57/170344/6, vol. 3365, PRO.

14. E. Beneš, *My War Memoirs*, 407. The official agreement was prepared in duplicate on September 3 and sent to the American Ambassador on September 9. See Page to Lansing, September 9, 1918, DF 763.72/11350, DSNA; Thomson, *Czechoslovakia in European History*, 269; Miller, "What Wilson Meant to Czechoslovakia," 79; Steed, *Through Thirty Years*, 2:231–33. Balfour to Beneš, August 9, 1918, in Ješina, *The Birth of Czechoslovakia*, 63.

15. CAB 23/7, War Cabinet 455/30, Minutes of Meeting on August 7, 1918, PRO.

16. Reading to British Foreign Office, August 9, 1918, Wiseman Papers; British Embassy to Department of State, August 12, 1918, *FRUS, 1918, Russia*, 2:341–42.

17. Polk Diary, August 8, 1918.

18. Balfour to Barclay, August 10, 1918, Wiseman Papers; British Embassy to State Department, August 12, 1918, *FRUS, 1918, Russia,* 2:341–42. See also British Foreign Office to Reading, August 10, 1918, Wiseman Papers.

19. Jusserand to Lansing, August 17, 1918, *Lansing Papers,* 2:376–77.

20. Phillips Diary, August 13, 14, 1918. Lansing Diary, August 14, 1918; *PWW,* 49:261–62; Wilson to Lansing, August 14, 1918, DF 861.00/2501.

21. Morris to Lansing, August 5, 1918, *FRUS, 1918, Russia,* 2:330.

22. Morris to Lansing, August 13, 1918, *FRUS, 1918, Russia,* 2:343–46. See also *New York Times,* August 18, 1918.

23. Koo to Lansing, September 13, 1918, MacMurray to Lansing, August 15, 1918, *FRUS, 1918, Russia,* 2:378, 348–49. For the Japanese version of the Bolshevik and prisoner-of-war danger, see Ishii to Lansing, August 17, 1918, DF 861.00/2602 1/2, DSNA; *PWW,* 49:282–84.

24. Lansing Diary, August 15, 1918; Long Diary, August 17, 1918.

25. Beneš to Masaryk, August 11, 1918, in Czechoslovak Republic, Ministerstvo zahranicnich veci, *Archiv diplomatických dokumentů československých;* Russian Branch of Czechoslovak National Council to Masaryk, August 10, 1918, *Dokumenty a materiály,* 170–77; Long to Lansing, August 17, 1918, DF 861.00/2601 1/2, DSNA; Caldwell to Lansing, August 15, 1918, *FRUS, 1918, Russia,* 2:346–48.

26. Long to Lansing, August 17, 1918, DF 861.00/2601 1/2, DSNA.

27. Lansing to Wilson, August 18, 1918, *PWW,* 49:282–84.

28. Lansing Diary, August 20, 1918, *FRUS, 1918, Russia,* 2:351.

29. Knight to Daniels, August 15, 1918, *PWW,* 49:262–63; Opnav to Commander in Chief, Asiatic Fleet, August 17, 1918, RG 45, WA6, NRCNA.

30. CAB 23/7, War Cabinet 462/30, Minutes of Meeting on August 21, 1918, PRO.

31. CAB 23/7, War Cabinet 463/30, Minutes of Meeting on August 22, 1918 at 11:30 A.M., PRO.

32. Reading to Wiseman, August 20, 1918, Wiseman Papers; *PWW,* 49:302–3.

33. Wiseman to Reading, August 22, 1918, ibid.; Knox to Macdonogh, July 28, 1918, Macdonogh to Clerk, September 4, 1918, FO 371.154818/3365, PRO.

34. Wiseman to Reading, August 23, 1918, Wiseman Papers; *PWW,* 49:345. Balfour acted upon Wiseman's advice. See Balfour to Barclay, August 28, 1918, ibid.

35. Substance of Report from Col. Robertson at Vladivostok, received August 22, 1918, DF 861.00/3486, DSNA.

36. Koo to Lansing, September 13, 1918, *FRUS, 1918, Russia,* 2:378; Lansing Diary, August 21, 1918. For a report of Koo's conversation with Long, see *FRUS, 1918, Russia,* 2:353.

37. E. Carleton Baker to Lansing, August 21, 1918, DF 861.00/2909, DSNA.

38. Morris to Lansing, August 26, 1918, and Ishii to Lansing, August 27, 1918, *FRUS, 1918, Russia,* 2:356–58.

39. Ibid., 339–41, 349–50, 354–55, 361.

40. Wilson to Lansing, September 2, 1918, Long Papers; Lansing to Wilson, August 22, 1918, *Lansing Papers,* 2:378.

41. Wilson to Lansing, August 23, 1918, *PWW,* 49:332. Lansing to Jusserand,

August 31, 1918, *FRUS, 1918, Russia*, 2:362. Barclay reported that Lansing was rather sharp in delivering Wilson's message. Barclay to Foreign Office, September 4, 1918, FO 115/2449, 260, PRO.

42. Stevens to Lansing, August 13, 1918; Lansing to Caldwell, August 15, 1918; and Polk to Moser, August 10, 1918; all in *FRUS, 1918, Russia*, 3:237–38.

43. Newton D. Baker to Lansing, August 19, 1918, DF 861.00/2535, DSNA. Lansing was informed of the seriousness of the situation.

44. Stevens to Lansing, August 26, 1918, *FRUS, 1918, Russia*, 3:239.

45. Morris to Lansing, August 23, 1918, ibid., 139–40.

46. Emerson Report, 65–66, DF 861.77/541, DSNA.

47. Lengyel, *Siberia*, 233–34; Morley, *Japanese Thrust into Siberia*, 307–9; Millard, *Democracy and the Eastern Question*, 300.

48. Graves, *America's Siberian Adventure*, 62.

49. Morris to Lansing, September 8, 1918, *FRUS, 1918, Russia*, 3:245–46.

50. Lansing to Morris, August 30, 1918, ibid., 239–40.

51. Lansing to Morris, August 30, 1918, ibid., 240; Morris to Lansing, September 8, 1918, ibid., 371.

52. Long to Morris, August 30, 1918, ibid., 240.

53. E. T. Williams to Long, August 29, 1918, DF 861.00/2583, DSNA.

54. Lansing to Morris, August 30, 1918, *FRUS, 1918, Russia*, 3:239–40; Lansing to Wilson, August 30, 1918, DF 861.77/471, DSNA; *PWW*, 49:396–97; Lansing Diary, August 30, 1918.

55. Balfour to Barclay, August 28, 1918, Wiseman Papers.

56. Masaryk to Baker, August 28, 1918, RG 165, WRCNA; Masaryk to Lansing, August 28, 1918, DF 763.72/11171 1/2, DSNA. For a summary of the reports of Girsa and Dietrichs, already received in the State Department, see Caldwell to Lansing, August 15, 1918, *PWW*, 49:263. David P. Barrows, head of a small American "intelligence detachment" of fifty men who could speak Russian, Czech, and Swedish, also reported that Bolshevik strength had been "greatly exaggerated" by the Japanese staff. Although assured by the Japanese that there were "15,000 Red Guard and enemy prisoners" on the Ussuri front, he observed they "could not have exceeded half that number"; chap. 7, "Ussuri Campaign," 2–3, Barrows Memoirs.

57. From Masaryk's notes, Masaryk Archives, XV, Amerika, pt. 24, as discussed in Vávra, "K historiografické interpretaci," 40–41; British Embassy to Foreign Office, August 28, 1918, FO 115/2449, 183–84, PRO; White House Appointment Book, August 27, 1918; Barclay to Balfour, August 30, 1918, FO 115/2449, 235–36, PRO; *PWW*, 49:373.

58. Masaryk to Lansing, August 28, 1918, DF 763.72/11171 1/2, DSNA; Masaryk, "The Situation in Russia and the Military Help of the Allies and the United States," RG 120, WRCNA.

59. Masaryk to Lansing, August 28, 1918, DF 763.72/11171 1/2, DSNA. See also Barclay to Balfour, August 30, 1918, FO 115/2449, 235–36, PRO; *PWW*, 49:373.

60. Baker to Lansing, August 16, 1918, DF 861.00/2513, DSNA.

61. Lansing to Baker, August 15, 1918, DF 860.24/6B, DSNA; "Memorandum Concerning Supplies Being Furnished by the Red Cross for the Czecho-Slovaks," Long Papers.

62. Lansing Diary, September 4, 1918; Long Diary, September 8, 1918; Wiseman to Reading, August 27, 1918, Wiseman Papers; *PWW*, 49:366.

63. Lansing Diary, August 29, September 4, 1918; Lansing to Wilson, August 29, 1918, DF 860F.24/9A, DSNA; *PWW*, 49:383.

64. Wilson to Lansing, September 2, 1918, DF 860F.24/9 1/2, DSNA; *PWW*, 49:383.

Chapter 17

1. American Consul General in London to Lansing, August 14, 1918, DF 763.72/11116, DSNA; Federation Franco-Tchèque des Etats-Unis Tchèques to Lansing, August 18, 1918, DF 763.72/11425, DSNA; Lansing to Wilson, August 19, 1918, *Lansing Papers*, 2:139–41; *New York Times*, September 8, 1918.

2. Albert Hlavac, Jr., Lt., USNA, to Leland Harrison, Esq., Office of the Secretary of State, July 27, 1918; J. R. Grew to Lester H. Woolsey, Office of the Solicitor, August 12, 1918, and additional notes from State Department personnel on the matter, all in DF 860f.01/36, DSNA.

3. Memorandum from Cecil, August 27, 1918, FO 371.W3.2002/148060, PRO; Political Intelligence Department, Foreign Office, Austria, August 15, 1918, RG 165, WRCNA.

4. Sharp to Lansing, September 23, 1918, DF 763.72119/8824, DSNA. Sharp immediately sent this information on to both Lansing and House.

5. Scott, *Official Statements*, 373; *New York Times*, August 18, 1918.

6. *New York Times*, August 14, 15, 18, 1918; *Literary Digest*, August 31, 1918, 21.

7. Spring Rice to Balfour, January 4, 1918, Balfour Papers; Gwynn, *Letters of Spring Rice*, 2:423; Mamatey, *United States and East Central Europe*, 78.

8. Lansing Diary, August 15, 1918; Lansing to Wilson, August 19, 1918, *Lansing Papers*, 2:139–41.

9. Woolsey to Lansing, "Recognition of Czecho-Slovak Belligerency," August 23, 1918, Office of the Secretary, DF 763.72/11133 1/2, DSNA; Lansing Diary, August 23, 1918; "Memorandum on the Recognition of the Czechoslovaks as a National Entity," August 23, 1918, Lansing Papers, LC.

10. Wilson to Lansing, August 22, 1918, *PWW*, 49:313.

11. Phillips Diary, August 12, 1918.

12. Wilson to Lansing, August 22, 1918, *Lansing Papers*, 2:141.

13. Lansing Diary, August 30, 1918; Office of the Secretary, Draft of Public Declaration, August 30, 1918, DF 763.72/11135 1/2, DSNA.

14. Lansing to Wilson, August 31, 1918, *Lansing Papers*, 2:143; Wilson to Lansing, September 2, 1918, DF 763.72/11136 1/2, DSNA; Ferrell, "The United States and East Central Europe Before 1941," 35–38; Mamatey, "Dissolution of Austria-Hungary," 269–70. See also DF 763.72119/2540, DSNA.

15. *FRUS, 1918, Supp. 1, World War*, 1:824–25; E. Beneš, *My War Memoirs*, 416–17; Wilson to Lansing, September 2, 1918, *Lansing Papers*, 2:144.

16. Lansing Diary, September 3, 1918; E. Beneš, *My War Memoirs*, 416–17.

17. Long Diary, September 3, 1918; "Czechs Recognized by U.S.," *Current History Magazine of New York Times* 9 (October 1918): 85.

18. Long to Tumulty, September 6, 1918, Wilson Papers; also in Long Papers; Tumulty to Long, September 7, 1918, DF 763.72/12024, DSNA.

19. Masaryk to Crane, September 6, 1918, C. R. Crane Papers.

20. Masaryk to Wilson, September 7, 1918, Wilson Papers.

21. Wilson to Masaryk, September 10, 1918, ibid.

22. Notes of a meeting with Wilson by Masaryk on September 11, 1918, *Dokumenty o protilidové,* 22; also in Kovtun, *Masaryk and America,* 61-62.

23. Acting Secretary of Labor to Lansing, September 10, 1918, DF 763.72/11423, DSNA; Fenwick, "Notes on International Affairs," 715-16.

24. E. Beneš, *My War Memoirs,* 370-71.

25. Caldwell to Graves, September 9, 1918; Graves to Caldwell, September 12, 1918; Otani to Graves, September 14, 1918; all in Graves Papers. Graves, *America's Siberian Adventure,* 79-80.

26. Graves to the Adjutant General, September 3, 1918, DF 861.00/3465, DSNA.

27. MacMurray to Lansing, September 4, 1918, DF 861.00/2619 3/4, DSNA.

28. "The Situation on the Volga Front from August 31, 1918, and Schematic Outline of the Union of Two Groups of Czecho-Slovak Forces in the Station of Olovjannaja on August 31, 1918," Czech Offical Record, RG 120, WRCNA; Memorandum, August 31, 1918, Graves Papers; Morris to Lansing, September 5, 1918, *FRUS, 1918, Russia,* 2:368.

29. Long Diary, September 4, 1918; Morris to Lansing, September 5, 1918, *FRUS, 1918, Russia,* 2:368; Varneck and Fisher, *Testimony of Kolchak,* 371-72; Baerlein, *March of the Seventy Thousand,* 186.

30. Francis to Lansing, September 4, 1918, *FRUS, 1918, Russia,* 2:519.

31. Hopper to Lansing, September 8, 1918, DF 861.00/2650, DSNA.

32. All of this information was immediately relayed to Francis. Lansing to Francis at Archangel, September 6, 1918, DF 861.00/2725A, DSNA.

33. Long Diary, September 5, 1918; Lansing Diary, September 5, 1918.

34. Bliss to March, September 3, 1918, RG 120, WRCNA.

35. Wilson to Lansing, September 5, 1918, DF 861.00/7381, DSNA.

36. MacMurray to Lansing, September 6, 1918, and Caldwell to Lansing, September 5, 1918, DF 861.00/2639 and 2629, DSNA.

37. Graves to the Adjutant General of the Army, September 6, 1918, Graves Papers.

38. Graves to the Adjutant General, September 9, 1918, RG 45, WA6, NRCNA; also in DF 861.00/3454, DSNA.

39. MacMurray to Lansing, September 5, 1918, DF 861.00/2628, DSNA.

40. Knight to Daniels, September 6, 1918, telegram, enclosed in Lansing to Wilson, September 9, 1918, Wilson Papers; Lansing Diary, September 7, 1918.

41. Auchincloss Diary, September 7, 1918.

42. Ibid., September 8, 9, 1918; Long Diary, September 8, 1918.

43. Lansing to Wilson, September 9, 1918, Wilson Papers; also in DF 861.00/2783F, DSNA.

44. Auchincloss Diary, September 8, 9, 1918; Long Diary, September 8, 1918; Lansing to Wilson, September 9, 1918, Wilson Papers; also in DF 861.00/2783F, DSNA.

45. Lansing to Wilson, September 4, 1918, DF 860F.24/9 1/2A, DSNA.
46. Auchincloss Diary, September 13, 1918; Lansing Diary, September 14, 16, 1918.
47. CAB, 24/63, G. T. 5648, Notes on the Situation in Russia and Siberia, September 9, 1918, by Henry Wilson, Chief of the Imperial General Staff, PRO.
48. Caldwell to Lansing, September 12, 1918, *FRUS, 1918, Russia*, 2:377.
49. Graves to Adjutant General, September 12, 1918, DF 861.00/3464, DSNA; Knight to Daniels, September 12, 1918, DF 861.00/2760 1/2, DSNA; Lansing to Wilson, September 13, 1918, DF 861.00/2760 1/2A, DSNA.
50. Graves to Adjutant General, September 12, 1918, DF 861.00/3464, DSNA; newspaper report of a press conference with Gajda, September 17, 1918, *Golos Premoria* (Vladivostok), Doc. 145, *Dokumenty a materiály*, 181–83.
51. Doc. 145, *Dokumenty a materiály*, 181–83; Knight to Daniels, September 12, 1918, DF 861.00/2760 1/2, DSNA; Lansing to Wilson, September 13, 1918, DF 861.00/2760 1/2A, DSNA.
52. Caldwell to Lansing, September 16, 1918, DF 861.00/2714, DSNA; *PWW*, 51:51, n. 2. Syrový's appeal arrived in the State Department on September 17.
53. MacMurray to Lansing, September 13, 1918, DF 861.00/2692, DSNA; Duncan Diary, September 12, 1918; Caldwell to Lansing, September 15, 1918, DF 861.00/2695, DSNA.
54. J. P. Jameson to Lansing, September 14, 1918, DF 861.00/3321, DSNA.
55. MacMurray to Lansing, September 14, 1918, DF 861.00/2702, DSNA.
56. Swedish Minister (Ekengren) to Lansing, September 16, 1918, *FRUS, 1918, Supp. 1*, 1:306–9; *PWW*, 51:11, n. 1; Rudin, *Armistice, 1918*, 32–41.
57. House Diary, September 16, 1918; *PWW*, 51:23; "Peace Proposals," September 16, 1918, CPI, RG 63, NA.
58. Lansing Diary, September 15, 1918.
59. Ibid., September 16, 1918; House Diary, September 16, 1918; Auchincloss Diary, September 16, 1918; Wilson to Lansing, September 16, 1918, Lansing Papers, Princeton; *PWW*, 51:10–11, 23–24.
60. Lansing to Ekengren, September 17, 1918, *FRUS, 1918, Supp. 1*, 1:309–310; Rudin, *Armistice, 1918*, 32–41.
61. "Memorandum of Conversation Had with Professor Masaryk This Evening," September 17, 1918, Long Papers. Many others were very enthusiastic about Wilson's way of handling the matter, and he was deeply appreciative of their support. For example, see Wilson to Williams, September 21, 1918, J. S. Williams Papers; Lansing to Chandler P. Anderson, September 23, 1918, Lansing Papers, LC.
62. Page to Lansing, September 19, 1918, DF 763.72119/1926, DSNA.
63. Stovall to Lansing, September 19, 1918, DF 763.72119/1937, DSNA.
64. *New York Times*, September 15, 1918; Masaryk to Lansing, September 15, 1918, DF 763.72119/1894 1/2, DSNA.
65. *New York Times*, September 16, 1918; New York *World*, September 16, 1918.
66. Creel, "Woodrow Wilson, the Man Behind the Legend," 42.
67. Wilson to Bernard Baruch, chairman of the War Industries Board, September 17, 1918, Wilson Papers; *PWW*, 51:26.

68. Lansing to Caldwell, September 18, 1918, *FRUS, 1918, Russia,* 2:385; Long Diary, September 17, 1918.

69. MacMurray to Lansing, September 16, 1918, DF 861.00/2716, DSNA.

70. Letcher to Lansing, October 8, 1918, DF 861.00/2924, DSNA.

71. Baker to Wilson, September 15, 1918, Baker Papers; *PWW,* 51:17. Interestingly enough, the military advisers at Versailles had considered the subject and unanimously but informally agreed that no further forces of any kind should be sent to Murmansk that year. The English and French representatives had concurred.

72. Bliss to March, September 7, 1918, RG 120, WRCNA; *PWW,* 51:52–55.

73. *PWW,* 51:52–55; "Report of Lecture Given by Major Riggs to General Lochridge and the Other Officers of the American Section, Supreme War Council, at Versailles, September 16, 1918," in Selected Documents Concerning the Czecho-Slovak Forces in Russia during 1918, RG 120, WRCNA. The lecture had been given on September 7.

74. Bliss to March, September 7, 1918, and Wilson to March, September 18, 1918, RG 120, WRCNA; *PWW,* 51:51–55.

75. "Memorandum of Conversation with Masaryk," September 17, 1918, Long Papers.

76. Long to Tumulty, September 13, 1918, Long Papers; Lansing Diary, September 17, 1918. Wilson agreed to receive General Janin on September 18. Long to Jusserand, September 17, 1918, Long Papers; *PWW,* 51:85.

77. British Embassy to Foreign Office, September 20, 1918, FO 371/3324, No. 160450, 572A, PRO; *PWW,* 51:85; British Embassy to Foreign Office, September 20, 1918, FO 115/2450, 58, PRO. P. Janin, "Fragments de mon journal Sibérien," 2–5.

78. Lansing to Wilson, September 13, 1918, and Wilson to Lansing, September 20, 1918, DF 861.00/3645, DSNA; *PWW,* 51:78–80.

79. Lansing to Morris, August 30, 1918, and Lansing to MacMurray, August 31, 1918, *FRUS, 1918, Russia,* 3:239–41.

80. Ibid., 243–44, 248, 255–56, 257–58.

81. MacMurray to Lansing, September 7, 1918, ibid., 243–45; Graves to Otani, September 5, 1918, Graves Papers. See also Long Diary, September 4, 1918; Lansing to Morris, September 6, 1918, *FRUS, 1918, Russia,* 3:242.

82. Lansing Diary, September 5, 1918.

83. Lansing to Morris, September 6, 1918, *FRUS, 1918, Russia,* 3:242; Long Diary, September 5, 1918; Lansing Diary, September 5, 1918.

84. Morris to Lansing, September 8, 1918, *FRUS, 1918, Russia,* 3:245–46.

85. Caldwell to Graves, September 10, 1918; Graves to Caldwell, September 13, 1918; Otani to Graves, September 14, 1918; all in Graves Papers.

86. Morris to Lansing, September 8, 1918, *FRUS, 1918, Russia,* 3:245–46. For an analysis of the differences in Japanese opinion regarding intervention, see "What Japan Thinks," *New Republic,* August 31, 1918, 124–25.

87. Koo to Lansing, September 13, 1918, and MacMurray to Lansing, September 12, 1918, *FRUS, 1918, Russia,* 2:378, 3:248; Lansing Diary, September 12, 1918.

88. Lansing to Page, September 13, 1918, *FRUS, 1918, Russia,* 3:249–52.

89. Sharp to Lansing, September 18, 1918, and Macchi di Cellere to Lansing, September 20, 1918, ibid., 259, 261–62.

90. Balfour to Barclay, September 19, 1918, FO 115/2450, 35–36, PRO.

91. Wilson to Lansing, September 17, 1918, DF 861.00/3009, DSNA; *PWW*, 51:25–26.

92. Wilson to Lansing, September 18, 1918, DF 861.00/3010, DSNA, and *PWW*, 51:50–51.

93. Fowler, *British-American Relations*, 195.

94. CAB 23/7, War Cabinet 475/32, Meeting on September 23, 1918, at 12:00 noon, PRO.

95. House Diary, September 19, 1918.

96. Fowler, *British-American Relations*, 193–94.

97. Wiseman to Reading and Drummond, September 21, 1918, Reading Papers.

98. Masaryk, "Agreement with General Janin on the Situation in Siberia," Confidential, Long Papers. Also in DF 861.00/2920, DSNA; *PWW*, 51:95–96, n. 2.

99. Wiseman to Reading and Drummond, September 21, 1918, Reading Papers; Vávra, "K historiografické interpretaci," 43.

100. Lansing to Wilson, September 21, 1918, DF 861.00/2783D, DSNA; *PWW*, 51:86–87. See also Lansing Diary, September 21, 1918.

101. *PWW*, 51:86–87; Lansing Diary, September 21, 1918; Long Diary, September 21, 1918.

102. Masaryk to Lloyd George, September 21, 1918, FO 371.W3/159999/64227, PRO.

103. Lansing to Wilson, September 21, 1918, DF 861.00/3010, DSNA; *PWW*, 51:87.

104. Wilson to Lansing, September 23, 1918, DF 861.00/3013, DSNA; *PWW*, 51:91.

105. Morris to Lansing, September 18, 1918, *FRUS, 1918, Russia*, 3:258–59. See also *PWW*, 51:86.

106. MacMurray to Lansing, September 19, 1918, and Morris to Lansing, September 20, 1918, *FRUS, 1918, Russia*, 3:259–60, 262.

107. Long Diary, September 19, 1918.

108. Memorandum, Re: Conversation with Dr. Masaryk, September 23, 1918, Long Papers; Long Diary, September 23, 1918; Long to American Legation at Peking, September 23, 1918, Long Papers.

109. Phillips Diary, September 20, 1918; Lansing Diary, September 20, 1918; Lansing to Francis, September 14, 1918, DF 861.00/2722a, DSNA.

Chapter 18

1. Lansing to Francis, September 14, 1918, DF 861.00/2722a, DSNA; Morris to Lansing, September 23, 1918, *FRUS, 1918, Russia*, 2:387–90; *PWW*, 51:98–101.

2. Harris to Lansing, September 23, 1918, *FRUS, 1918, Russia*, 2:385–86; *PWW*, 51:101–2.

3. Francis to Lansing, September 23, 1918, *FRUS, 1918, Russia,* 2:543–44.
4. Morris to Lansing, September 23, 1918, ibid., 387–90; *PWW,* 51:98–101.
5. Lansing to Wilson, September 24, 1918, *PWW,* 51:97–98.
6. Lansing to Francis, September 24, 1918, DF 861.00/2783b, DSNA.
7. Lansing to Wilson, September 24, 1918, *PWW,* 51:97–98.
8. Masaryk to Lansing, September 23, 1918, and Lansing to Wilson, September 24, 1918, Wilson Papers. The latter note also contained in DF 861.00/2783C, DSNA; *PWW,* 51:95–97.
9. House Diary, September 24, 1918; *PWW,* 51:102–110.
10. Barclay to Lansing, September 23, 1918, *FRUS, 1918, Russia,* 2:386.
11. Barclay to British Foreign Office, September 24, 1918, "Memorandum," Lansing to British Embassy, October 1, 1918, FO 115/2450, 93, 236–37, PRO.
12. Jusserand to Lansing, September 25, 1918, DF 861.00/2858, DSNA.
13. Wilson to Lansing, September 26, 1918, Long Papers; *PWW,* 51:121–22; March, *Nation at War,* 303.
14. Wilson to Lansing, September 26, 1918, Long Papers; Lansing Diary, September 25, 26, 1918; March to Bliss, September 26, 1918, March Papers; *PWW,* 51:121–22, 139.
15. Lansing to Morris, September 26, 1918, *FRUS, 1918, Russia,* 2:392–94; see also *PWW,* 51:97–101. Lansing to Barclay, September 27, 1918 (enclosing memorandum), FO 115/2450, 141, 143–47, PRO; *FRUS, 1918, Russia,* 2:392–94, 543–44, 548. Actually, the State Department found it difficult to draft a memorandum, since its chief officers did not agree with Wilson's position and, as they pointed out, his statement in the aide-mémoire of July 17 had been modified by the department to indicate that the American position was not intended as a criticism "of any independent action which the other governments might care to take." Long Diary, September 20, 1918; Phillips Diary, September 20, 1918; Lansing Diary, September 20, 1918. For the exchanges and negotiations surrounding the drafting of this memorandum, see Lansing to Wilson, September 20, 1918, DF 861.00/2783, DSNA; Lansing Diary, September 21, 1918; Long Diary, September 21, 1918; Lansing to Wilson, September 21, 1918, DF 861.00/3010, DSNA; Wilson to Lansing, September 23, 1918, DF 861.00/3013, DSNA; *PWW,* 51:91.
16. *FRUS, 1918, Russia,* 2:543–44, 548.
17. Masaryk to Lansing, September 30, 1918, *Lansing Papers,* 2:388–91.
18. House Diary, October 1, 1918; Masaryk to Wiseman, October 1, 1918, Wiseman Papers. A copy of Masaryk's notes (September 30) on Lansing's September 27 memorandum are in the Wiseman Papers. Fowler, *British-American Relations,* 195.
19. CAB 23/8, War Cabinet 481, October 2, 1918, PRO.
20. Barclay to Lansing, October 3, 1918, *FRUS, 1918, Russia,* 2:403–4.
21. Lansing Diary, September 28, 1918; Bliss to March, October 5, 1918, RG 165, WRCNA.
22. A Translation of a Telegram from Jean Jules Jusserand to the Foreign Ministry, n.d. [September 28, 1918], Wilson Collection, Princeton; *PWW,* 51:152–54.
23. Lansing to MacMurray, October 9, 1918, DF 861.00/2841, DSNA.

24. Undated Memorandum in Graves Papers.

25. Basil Miles, "American Slavic Legion at Archangel," Memorandum for the Secretary of State, September 30, 1918, DF 861.00/2912, DSNA.

26. Wilson to Lansing, October 2, 1918, and Lansing to Miles, October 3, 1918, DF 861.00/2910, DSNA; *PWW*, 51:178.

27. Wilson to Lansing, September 12, 1918, DF 861.48/651, DSNA; *PWW*, 49:529; Baruch to Wilson, September 16, 1918, and Wilson to Baruch, September 17, 1918, Baruch Papers; Long Diary, October 3, 1918; *PWW*, 51:26.

28. McAdoo to Wilson, October 4, 1918, and Wilson to McAdoo, October 5, 1918, Bureau of Accounts (Treasury), Country File, Czecho-Slovakia Treasury Reports, RG 39, NA; Lansing Diary, October 5, 1918.

29. McAdoo to Secretary of State, October 4, 1918, and Polk to Wilson, October 10, 1918, DF 850F.51/2 1/2, DSNA.

30. Thomson to American Legation in Peking, September 29, 1918, Harris Papers.

31. Girsa to Graves, September 29, 1918, Czecho-Slovak National Council, No. 1086, RG 120, WRCNA. These appeals from Thomson and Girsa were immediately transmitted to the State Department. DF 861.00/2841 and 2867, DSNA. General Paris to General Janin, September 27, 1918, Barrows Papers. For a detailed account of Czech difficulties, see David P. Barrows, "An American Officer in Siberia," Barrows Papers, and "Reorganization and Difficulties," October–November 1918, chap. 12, Packard Report, 95–103, DF 861.00/6052, DSNA.

32. Girsa to Graves, October 3, 1918, Czecho-Slovak National Council, No. 125, RG 120, WRCNA; Medek, *Za svobodu*, 3, pt. 4:804.

33. Paraphrase of telegram from Ambassador Francis, Archangel, October 4, 1918, RG 45, WA6, NRCNA.

34. MacMurray to Lansing, received October 7, 1918, DF 861.00/2898, DSNA.

35. Caldwell to Lansing, October 7, 1918, DF 861.00/2899, DSNA. For Lansing's summary of the situation, see Lansing to Francis, October 8, 1918, DF 861.00/3037a, DSNA. See also Caldwell to Lansing, October 7, 1918, DF 861.00/2914, DSNA; MacMurray to Lansing, October 9, 1918, DF 861.00/2919, DSNA.

36. Caldwell to Lansing, October 8, 1918, DF 861.00/2916, DSNA.

37. Barclay to Lansing, October 1, 1918, *FRUS, 1918, Russia*, 2:399–401.

38. Bradley, *Allied Intervention in Russia*, 108–10.

39. Zivojinović, "The Vatican, Woodrow Wilson, and the Dissolution of the Habsburg Monarchy," 53.

40. Swedish Minister (Ekengren) to Lansing, October 7, 1918, *PWW*, 51:258–59; Swiss Chargé to Wilson, October 6, 1918, *PWW*, 51:252–54; Seymour, *Letters from the Paris Peace Conference*, 3.

41. Lansing to Wilson, October 7, 1918, *PWW*, 51:258–59; Long Diary, October 7, 1918.

42. Memorandum on Policy as to Overtures of Peace by Germany and Austria-Hungary, October 7, 1918, Lansing Papers, LC.

43. Zivojinović, "The Vatican, Woodrow Wilson, and the Dissolution of the

Habsburg Monarchy," 53; Ellis, *Life of Cardinal Gibbons*, 2:256–57; Mamatey, *United States and East Central Europe*, 327; Perman, *Shaping of the Czecho-Slovak State*, 49.

44. Andrássy, *Diplomacy and the War*, 255.

45. Ibid., 253.

46. Stovall to Lansing, October 18, 1918, *FRUS, 1918, Supp. 1, World War*, 1:369.

47. Mamatey, *United States and East Central Europe*, 326.

48. Herron to the President, Geneva, October 14, 1918, Herron Papers.

49. Stovall to Lansing, October 15, 1918, DF 763.72/11775, DSNA; Stovall to Lansing, October 17, 1918, and Godson (Bern) to Washington, October 17, 1918, RG 165, WRCNA, enclosing a clipping from the *Frankfurter Zeitung* reporting that a general strike was spreading throughout Bohemia. See also *New York Times*, October 16, 1918, for German press response to Czech "treason" and its effect on the outcome of the war.

50. Masaryk to Lansing, October 14, 1918, with enclosure entitled, "Germany's Answer of October 13," DF 861.00/3118, DSNA.

51. Sharp to Lansing, October 16, 1918, DF 861.00/2968; Masaryk, *Making of a State*, 508–9; Thomson, *Czechoslovakia in European History*, 273. It was at this point that Pergler was appointed "chargé d'affaires" of the Czecho-Slovak legation in Washington. Sharp to Lansing, October 16, 1918, *FRUS, 1918, Supp. 1, World War*, 1:846.

52. Sharp to Lansing, October 16, 1918, *FRUS, 1918, Supp. 1, World War*, 1:846–47. Copy of a note addressed to Beneš from Pichon, October 15, 1918, in No. 6752, Sharp to Lansing, November 5, 1918, DF 860f.01/9, DSNA. See also Kovtun, *Czechoslovak Declaration of Independence*, 12–13, 20. At Masaryk's request, the text of the French official note of recognition was transmitted to Lansing on October 26. See DF 861.00/3052, DSNA.

53. Stovall to Lansing, October 18, 1918, *FRUS, 1918, Supp. 1, World War*, 1:367; Long Diary, October 18, 1918; Pribram, *Austrian Foreign Policy*, 123; *New York Times*, October 16, 1918.

54. Sir Eric Geddes to Lloyd George, October 13, 1918, and House to Balfour, October 13, 1918, Eric Geddes Papers, ADM 116/1809, PRO; *PWW*, 51:325–27. See also Lloyd George, *War Memoirs*, 5:260–61; Walworth, *Woodrow Wilson, American Prophet*, 189; Wiseman to Reading and Drummond, October 16, 1918, Wiseman Papers.

55. Notes of an Interview with the President at the White House, October 16, 1918, Geddes Papers; *PWW*, 51:347–52.

56. Miller, "What Wilson Meant to Czechoslovakia," 83.

57. Masaryk to Lansing, October 16, 1918, *FRUS, 1918, Supp. 1, World War*, 1:846, and enclosure (not printed), DF 861.00/2970, DSNA.

58. Masaryk to Lansing, October 18, 1918, DF 861.00/3124, DSNA; Miller, "What Wilson Meant to Czechoslovakia," 83–84; Mamatey, *United States and East Central Europe*, 331–32.

59. Declaration of Independence of the Czecho-Slovak Nation by its Provisional Government, enclosure in Masaryk to Lansing, October 18, 1918, *FRUS, 1918, Supp. 1, World War*, 1:847–51; R. S. Baker, *Wilson: Life and Letters*,

8:497–99. The "draft" declaration sent to Lansing on October 16 had been a summary of Masaryk's memorandum to Lansing of August 31 properly adapted to the occasion. DF 861.00/2970, DSNA. See also *PWW*, 51:395.

60. Memorandum by President Wilson entitled "For Reply to the Austro-Hungarian Government," [ca. October 19, 1918], DF 763.72119/2540, DSNA, and *PWW*, 51:383.

61. *FRUS, 1918, Supp. 1, World War*, 1:368.

62. Masaryk, *Making of a State*, 394; *FRUS, 1918, Supp. 1, World War*, 1:392.

63. Stovall to Lansing, October 25, 1918, No. 5395, RG 165, WRCNA.

64. Mamatey, *United States and East Central Europe*, 337.

65. Andrássy, *Diplomacy and the War*, 271.

66. Mamatey, *United States and East Central Europe*, 338.

67. Associated Press Dispatch from Paris, October 27, 1918, DF 763.72119/2367 1/2, DSNA, substantiated in note from Stovall to Lansing, October 28, 1918, in DF 763.72119/2380, DSNA. See also the formal note in Ekengren to Lansing, October 29, 1918, *PWW*, 51:505–6.

68. Thomson, *Czechoslovakia in European History*, 282.

69. Mamatey, *United States and East Central Europe*, 339.

70. Lansing to Wilson, October 29, 1918, DF 763.72119/2464 and 2465, DSNA, and *PWW*, 51:506–8.

71. Lansing Diary, October 29, 1918.

72. Masaryk to Lansing, October 29, 1918, *PWW*, 51:506–8, with enclosure, DF 763.72119/2464, DSNA; also in Czechoslovak Republic, Ministerstvo zahranicnich veci, *Archiv diplomatických dokumentů československých*.

73. Lansing to Wilson, October 29, 1918, DF 763.72119/2464, DSNA; *PWW*, 51:506–8.

74. Draft reply, undated, Wilson Papers.

75. Ekengren to Lansing, October 30, 1918, *PWW*, 51:526–27; Scott, *Official Statements*, 441–42; Houston, *Eight Years with Wilson's Cabinet*, 1:319–20.

76. Lansing to Wilson, October 31, 1918, DF 763.72119/2600, DSNA; *PWW*, 51:526–27.

77. Lansing Diary, October 31, 1918; Lansing Memorandum, October 31, 1918, *PWW*, 51:527.

78. House to Wilson, October 31, 1918; *PWW*, 51:531–34; House to Lansing, November 1, 1918, *FRUS, 1918, Supp. 1. World War*, 1:433–35; Scott, *Official Statements*, 472; Grew, *Turbulent Era*, 1:344; Long Diary, November 2, 1918; Lansing Diary, November 3, 1918; Pribram, *Austrian Foreign Policy*, 127.

79. House to Wilson, November 4, 1918, Wilson Collection, Princeton; *PWW*, 51:580–82; E. Beneš, *My War Memoirs*, 460–61; Masaryk, *Making of a State*, 508–9; Thomson, *Czechoslovakia in European History*, 270.

80. Memorandum for Secretary of the Treasury from Albert Rathbone, November 19, 1918, Bureau of Accounts (Treasury) International Fiscal Relationships: Country File, Czecho-Slovakia, Treasury Department, RG 39, NA; *New York Times*, November 17, 1918; Phillips to National City Bank, May 31, 1922, DF 86of.01/140, DSNA.

81. *New York Times*, December 2, 9, 1918.

82. Ibid., December 11, 12, 1918.

83. "Masaryk's First Presidential Message," sent to Albert H. Putney, Department of State, by Director, Czecho-Slovak Information Bureau, January 28, 1919, DF 86of.01/27, DSNA.

84. President Masaryk to President Woodrow Wilson, Rome, Italy, January 2, 1919, Wilson Papers; *PWW*, 53:590.

85. Polk to American Embassy at Paris, January 2, 1919, DF 763.72119/3149, DSNA.

86. Polk to American Mission at Paris, February 7, 1919, for Secretary Lansing, DF 86of.01/28A, DSNA.

87. Lansing (Paris) to Washington, February 14, 1919, DF 86of.01/29, DSNA.

88. Lansing to Carter Glass, November 14, 1918, DF 861.00/2898, DSNA; R. Harrison to C. C. Hyde, June 2, 1923, DF 86oF.01/148 1/2, DSNA; see also DF 86oF.01/149 1/2 and 800.51 W89, Czechoslovakia/52 1/2, DSNA.

89. Harrison to Hyde, June 2, 1923, DF 86oF.01/148 1/2, DSNA; see also DF 86oF.01/146 1/2, DSNA.

Chapter 19

1. Harris to Lansing, November 19, 1918, *FRUS, 1918, Russia*, 2:435.

2. Harris to American Legation at Peking, November 21, 1918, and Palmer to Harris, November 21, 1918, Harris Papers; Harris to Lansing, November 28, 1918, DF 861.00/3343, DSNA.

3. Baker to Wilson, November 27, 1918, Wilson Papers; Palmer, *Newton D. Baker*, 2:394–95.

4. Intelligence summary No. 32, November 22, 1918. Prepared by Lieutenant Colonel Barrows, Cavalry, U.S.A., RG 165, Records of the War Department General and Special Staffs, Military Intelligence Division, 1917–1941; Morris to Lansing, November 20, 1918, DF 861.00/3252, DSNA; Aide-mémoire, November 20, 1918, RG 84, Records of Foreign Service Posts of Department of State, Diplomatic Correspondence, Vol. 12 (1918), file 800R. Ingersoll to F. Leonard, November 17, 1918, DF 861A.01/131, DSNA; Memorandum on the Japanese role in the Intervention in Siberia, October 15, 1918, Wiseman Papers.

5. Polk Diary, December 23, 1918; *FRUS, 1919, Russia*, 239.

6. *FRUS, 1919, Russia*, 146–48.

7. Ibid., 244, 250–51, 494; Memorandum of John F. Stevens, Railway Service Corps Papers; Notes of a Meeting held at President Wilson's House in the Place des Etats-Unis, Paris, May 9, 1919, *FRUS, 1919, Russia*, 345–47.

8. Reinsch to Polk, December 9, 1918; Polk to Lansing, January 2, 1919; Morris to Lansing, January 10, 1919, DF 861.00/3368, 3617b, and 3622, DSNA; Graves, *America's Siberian Adventure*, 86, 90, 108, 215, 246.

9. Omsk Government to Boris A. Bakhmetev (Ambassasdor to Washington of the Provisional Government), April 24, 1919, *FRUS, 1919, Russia*, 494–96. The British regarded General Graves as "sympathizing with the Bolsheviks rather than with the Omsk authorities." Polk Diary, May 10, 1919; Polk to Lansing, May 9, 1919, *FRUS, 1919, Russia*, 493–94.

10. Grayson Diary, May 27, 1919; *FRUS, 1919, Russia,* 345–47, 351–53, 367–70; Bliss to Wilson, May 9, 1919, Wilson Papers.

11. J. Bradley, *Allied Intervention in Russia,* 118.

12. Masaryk, *The Making of a State,* 102.

13. Caldwell to Lansing, March 14, 1919, Girsa to Pergler, April 3, 1919, DF 861.00/4080 and 4223 1/2, DSNA.

14. J. Bradley, *Allied Intervention in Russia,* 121–22.

15. Bliss, Paris Peace Conference Diary, June 11, 1919, Bliss Papers.

16. Stevens to Department of State, June 16, 1919, Reinsch to Acting Secretary of State, June 21, 1919, *FRUS, 1919, Russia,* 281, 283.

17. Stevens to Lansing and McCormick, June 16, 1919, American Mission to Secretary of State, June 24, 1919, Polk to Lansing and McCormick, June 20, 1919, DF 861.00/4694, 4748, and 4717, DSNA.

18. American Mission to Secretary of State, June 24, 1919, DF 861.00/4748, DSNA; Translation of message received from Washington, June 28, 1919, Harris Papers.

19. J. Bradley, *Allied Intervention in Russia,* 122.

20. Harris to Department of State, July 5, 1919, and Polk to Lansing, July 10, 1919, DF 861.00/4748 and 4802, DSNA.

21. J. Bradley, *Allied Intervention in Russia,* 123; see also DF 861.00/4877, DSNA.

22. Notes of a Meeting in M. Pichon's Room, July 9, 1919, *FRUS, Paris Peace Conference, 1919,* 7:64–65.

23. Morris (temporarily at Irkutsk) to Secretary of State, July 17, 1919, DF 861.77/945, DSNA.

24. Polk to Wilson, July 16, 1919, Wilson Papers.

25. Remarks by the President of the United States on reviewing a detachment of the Czecho-Slovak army, Washington, July 18, 1919, DF 861.00/4873a, DSNA. See also Long to Tumulty, July 17, 1919, enclosing memoranda for the President of July 15 and 17, 1919, Wilson Collection, Princeton.

26. Morris to Department of State, July 22, 1918, DF 861.00/4905, DSNA.

27. Lansing to Morris, July 24, 1919, DF 861.00/4877, DSNA; J. Bradley, *Allied Intervention in Russia,* 123.

28. Ray Atherton (Secretary of Embassy at Tokyo) to Lansing, August 7, 1919, DF 861.00/4989, DSNA.

29. J. Bradley, *Allied Intervention in Russia,* 123–34.

30. Baker to Lansing, August 29, 1919, Baker Papers. Baker had been engaged in personal efforts to secure American assistance to bring the Czechs home. R. J. Caldwell to George Peabody, June 18, 1919, and Peabody to Baker, June 18, 1919, ibid.

31. Long to Lansing, August 29, 1919, Long Papers; Lansing to Baker, August 30, 1919, Baker Papers.

32. Lansing to Wilson, August 30, 1919, Wilson Papers; Long Memorandum on Withdrawal of American Troops, August 29, 1919, Long Papers.

33. Lansing to Atherton, August 30, 1919, *FRUS, 1919, Russia,* 573–78.

34. J. Bradley, *Allied Intervention in Russia,* 124.

35. American Mission in Paris to Lansing, September 17, 1919, DF 861.00/5229, DSNA; Phillips to Wilson, September 19, 1919, Wilson Papers.

36. Phillips to Glass, September 19, 1919, DF 861.00/5229, DSNA.

37. Wilson to Phillips, September 20, 1919, Wilson Papers; also in DF 861.00/5245, DSNA. When Glass requested the President's approval for the loan, he indicated that he intended to discuss with the Treasuries of Britain and France the proportions to be borne by them of the necessary advances. Wilson approved entirely of Glass's proposal. Phillips to Lansing, September 25, 1919, *FRUS, 1919, Russia*, 299–300; Glass to Wilson, September 25, 1919, and Wilson to Glass, September 25, 1919, Wilson Papers.

38. Morris to Lansing, September 23, 1919, DF 861.00/5264, DSNA.

39. J. Bradley, *Allied Intervention in Russia*, 124–25.

40. Grew to Lansing, October 20, 1919, and Polk to Lansing, October 20, 1919, DF 861.00/5578 and 5428, DSNA.

41. Emerson to Johnson, Blunt, Cantrell (Harbin), October 20, 1919, Russian Railway Service Corps Papers; Stevens to Lansing, October 20, 1919, *FRUS, 1919, Russia*, 534.

42. Phillips to Commission to Negotiate Peace, October 1, 1919, *FRUS, 1919, Russia*, 436; Cronon, *Cabinet Diaries of Daniels*, 444.

43. Lansing to Morris, October 10, 1919, *FRUS, 1919, Russia*, 586–87.

44. Polk to Lansing, October 24, 1919, *FRUS, 1919, Russia*, 444–45; Lansing Diary, October 9, 1919.

45. Lansing Diary, October 9, 1919.

46. Lansing to Jenkins, October 21, 1919, *FRUS, 1919, Russia*, 536; Lansing to American Mission, October 22, 1919, DF 861.00/5428, DSNA. Caldwell reported that Kolchak's failure might result in "break up [of] Russia into military states under foreign domination and permanent occupation of Eastern Siberia by Japan which may be nearer fait accompli than is supposed and which the United States alone can prevent by prompt action commensurate with magnitude of the task." This information had been repeated to Paris for Polk. Lansing to the American Mission, October 22, 1919, DF 861.00/5513a, DSNA.

47. Stevens to Lansing, October 24, 25, 1919, *FRUS, 1919, Russia*, 537–38; Stevens to Lansing, October 25, 1919, DF 861.00/5484, DSNA.

48. Commission to Negotiate Peace to Lansing, October 24, 1919, *FRUS, 1919, Russia*, 444.

49. Charles Tenney (Secretary of Legation at Peking) to Lansing, October 28, 1919, DF 861.00/5507, DSNA.

50. D. C. Poole to Western European Division, November 1, 1919, with memorandum, November 1, 1919, DF 861.00/5507, DSNA.

51. Janin to Beneš, October 31, 1919, in J. Bradley, *Allied Intervention in Russia*, 125.

52. Tenney to Lansing, October 31, 1919, *FRUS, 1919, Russia*, 445–46.

53. Phillips to Polk, November 1, 1919, DF 861.00/5543, DSNA.

54. Johnson, en route, Tomsk railroad (Taiga) to Emerson (Irkutsk), November 25, 1919, Emerson Papers; also in Railway Service Corps Papers.

55. Harris to Lansing, November 2, 1919, DF 861.00/5558, DSNA; Lansing to Commission to Negotiate Peace, November 3, 1919, *FRUS, 1919, Russia*, 222.

56. Commanding Officer, U.S.S. *New Orleans,* to Commander in Chief, U.S. Asiatic Fleet, November 3, 1919, WA-6, NRCNA.

57. Johnson (Omsk) to Emerson (Irkutsk), November 4, 1919, Railway Service Corps Papers.

58. Johnson to Emerson, November 11, 1919, ibid.

59. Gajda to Gaston Bourgeois, November 5, 1919, and General Graves to the Adjutant General of the Army, Washington, D.C., November 11, 1919, RG 165, WRCNA; Commanding Officer, U.S.S. *New Orleans,* to Commander in Chief, U.S. Asiatic Fleet, November 8, 11, 1919, WA-6, NRCNA. See also J. Bradley, *Allied Intervention in Russia,* 126–27.

60. Macgowan to Lansing, November 17, 1919, *FRUS, 1919, Russia,* 313–14. This information was conveyed to Morris, Harris, Stevens, and General March, and a copy was sent to the War Department. "Declaration to the Allied Representatives," *Czechoslovak Daily News,* November 14, 1919, in Railway Service Corps Papers. See also *London Daily Herald,* January 7, 1920.

61. Tenney to Lansing, November 17, 1919, and McGowan to Lansing, November 17, 18, 1919, DF 861.00/5681, 5682, and 5699, DSNA; Lampson to Curzon, November 17 and 18, 1919, in J. Bradley, *Allied Intervention in Russia,* 126–27.

62. Macgowan to Lansing, November 16, 1919, DF 861.00/5678, DSNA.

63. Tenney to Secretary of State, December 28, 1919, DF 861.00/6027, DSNA. Semenov and his bloodthirsty troops emerge as the archvillains of the civil war in Siberia. He commanded a gaggle of desperate adventurers totally devoted to their own excesses. General Graves characterized him as "a murderer, robber and most dissolute scoundrel." Tupper, *To the Great Ocean,* 380. His headquarters presented to another observer "an atmosphere of laziness, rodomontade, alcohol, lucrative requisitions, dirty money, and the killing of the innocent." Fleming, *Fate of Admiral Kolchak,* 52.

64. Fleming, *Fate of Admiral Kolchak,* 196.

65. Harris to Department of State, February 22, 1920, DF 861.00/6482, DSNA. When the Czechs had surrendered Kolchak, Harris had cabled the department, "Under these circumstances in my judgement the Czechs have forfeited any claim they might have to American protection in the matter [of] being evacuated from Siberia." February 21, 1920, DF 861.00/6484, DSNA. For the Czech-Bolshevik conditions of peace, signed February 7, 1920, see Doc. 263, *Dokumenty a materiály,* 339–41.

66. Stevens to Secretary of State, February 28, 1920, DF 861.00/6474, DSNA.

67. Harris reported on February 4 that in Siberia, north of a line running from Irkutsk to Leipzig, the usual temperature was 55 degrees below zero. General Kappel, Kolchak's commander in chief, froze to death. R. A. Williams, "The Odyssey of the Czechs," 37, n. 92.

68. Ibid., 30–31.

69. Ibid., 31, 33–34.

70. Unterberger, *Did the United States Try to Overthrow the Soviet Government, 1918–1920?,* 22.

Bibliography

Primary Works

Archival Sources

Government Documents

France, Foreign Ministry Archives, Paris.
    Guerre 1914–18 Etats-Unis.
    Papiers d'Agents, Bergson, 1918.
    Papiers Jusserand, Lettres Politiques, 1918.
France, Ministry of Defense Archives, Paris.
    Etat-major de l'armée de terre.
Great Britain, Public Record Office, London.
    Foreign Office Papers, 1916–18.
    War Cabinet Papers, 1917–18.
United States, National Archives, Washington, D.C.
    RG 39: Bureau of Accounts (Treasury), Country File, Czecho-Slovakia
        Treasury Reports.
    RG 45: Naval Records Collection of the Office of Naval Records and Library.
    RG 59: General Records of the Department of State.
    RG 63: Records of the Committee on Public Information.
    RG 84: Records of the Foreign Service Posts of the Department of State.
    RG 120: Records of the American Expeditionary Forces (World War I),
        1917–23.
    RG 165: Records of the War Department General and Special Staffs.
    RG 182: Records of the War Trade Board.
    RG 256: Records of the American Commission to Negotiate Peace.
    RG 395: Records of the United States Overseas Operations and Commands,
        1898–1942.
    RG 407: Records of the Adjutant General's Office, 1917–.

Private Papers

Anderson, Chandler P. Diary and Papers. Library of Congress. Washington,
    D.C.
Auchincloss, Gordon. Diary. Yale University Library. New Haven, Conn.
Baker, Newton D. Papers. Library of Congress. Washington, D.C.
Balfour, Arthur James. Papers. Public Record Office, London.
Barrows, David P. Memoirs and Papers. Library of University of California at
    Berkeley. Berkeley, Calif.

Baruch, Bernard M. Papers. Princeton University Library. Princeton, N.J.
Bliss, Tasker H. Papers. Library of Congress. Washington, D.C.
Bordes Report. Archives de l'armée de terre. Château de Vincennes. Vincennes, France.
Breshkovsky, Catherine E. Papers. New York Public Library. New York, N.Y.
Bullard, Arthur. Papers. Princeton University Library. Princeton, N.J.
Česká Družina Collection. Hoover Institution on War, Revolution and Peace. Stanford, Calif.
Colton, Ethan T. Memoirs and Papers. Hoover Institution on War, Revolution and Peace. Stanford, Calif.
———. Papers. YMCA Archives. University of Minnesota. St. Paul, Minn.
Crane, Charles R. Memoirs and Papers. Columbia University Library. New York, N.Y.
Crane, Richard T. Papers. Georgetown University Library. Washington, D.C.
Dresel, Ellis Loring. Papers. Harvard University Library. Cambridge, Mass.
Dulles, Allen W. Papers. Princeton University Library. Princeton, N.J.
Duncan, William V. Diary and Papers. Hoover Institution on War, Revolution and Peace. Stanford, Calif.
Emerson, George B. Papers. Hoover Institution on War, Revolution and Peace. Stanford, Calif.
Francis, David R. Papers. Missouri Historical Society. St. Louis, Mo.
Fuller, B. A. G. Papers. Hoover Institution on War, Revolution and Peace. Stanford, Calif.
Geddes, Sir Eric. Papers. Public Record Office. London.
Gibson, Hugh. Papers. Hoover Institution on War, Revolution and Peace. Stanford, Calif.
Golovine, N. N. Papers. Hoover Institution on War, Revolution and Peace. Stanford, Calif.
Graves, William S. Papers. Hoover Institution on War, Revolution and Peace. Stanford, Calif.
———. Papers. U.S. Military Academy Library. West Point, N.Y.
Grayson, Cary T. Diary. In possession of Cary T. Grayson, Jr.
Grew, Joseph C. Papers. Harvard University Library. Cambridge, Mass.
Harper, Samuel N. Papers. University of Chicago Library. Chicago, Ill.
Harris, Ernest L. Papers. Hoover Institution on War, Revolution and Peace. Stanford, Calif.
Herron, George D. Papers. Hoover Institution on War, Revolution and Peace. Stanford, Calif.
Hornbeck, Stanley K. Papers. Hoover Institution on War, Revolution and Peace. Stanford, Calif.
Horvath, Dmitri L. "Memoirs of General Dmitri L. Horvath." In Horvath Papers. Hoover Institution on War, Revolution and Peace. Stanford, Calif.
House, Edward M. Diary and Papers. Yale University Library. New Haven, Conn.
Houston, David Franklin. Papers. Harvard University Library. Cambridge, Mass.

Kerner, Robert J. Papers. Library of University of California at Berkeley. Berkeley, Calif.

Lansing, Robert. Papers. Library of Congress. Washington, D.C.

———. Selected Papers. Princeton University Library. Princeton, N.J.

Long, Breckinridge. Papers. Library of Congress. Washington, D.C.

Masaryk, Thomas G. Papers. University of Pittsburgh Library. Pittsburgh, Pa.

Mezes, Sidney E. Papers. Columbia University Library. New York, N.Y.

Mott, John R. Papers. Yale University Library. New Haven, Conn.

Page, Walter Hines. Papers. Harvard University Library. Cambridge, Mass.

Phillips, William. Journal and Notes of A Diplomatic Courier. Harvard University Library. Cambridge, Mass.

Polk, Frank L. Diary and Papers. Yale University Library. New Haven, Conn.

Poole, DeWitt C. Oral Memoirs. Oral History Research Office, Columbia University Library. New York, N.Y.

Railway Service Corps Papers. Hoover Institution on War, Revolution and Peace. Stanford, Calif.

Reinsch, Paul S. Papers. Wisconsin Historical Society. Madison, Wis.

Robins, Raymond. Papers. Wisconsin Historical Society. Madison, Wis.

Russia-Kiev Correspondence, 1917–1918. YMCA Archives. University of Minnesota. St. Paul, Minn.

Russian War Work Collection. YMCA Archives. University of Minnesota. St. Paul, Minn.

Wald, Lillian. Papers. Columbia University Library. New York, N.Y.

Williams, John Sharp. Papers. Library of Congress. Washington, D.C.

Wilson, Woodrow. Collection. Princeton University Library. Princeton, N.J.

———. Papers. Library of Congress. Washington, D.C.

Wiseman, William. Papers. Yale University Library. New Haven, Conn.

World Service Materials. YMCA Archives. University of Minnesota. St. Paul, Minn.

Published Sources

Public Documents

An Address of President Wilson to the American Federation of Labor Convention. Washington, D.C., 1917.

Bunyan, James. *Intervention, Civil War, and Communism.* Baltimore, 1936.

Bunyan, James, and H. H. Fisher. *The Bolshevik Revolution, 1917–1918: Documents and Materials.* Stanford, Calif., 1934.

Carnegie Endowment for International Peace. *Official German Documents Relating to the World War.* 2 vols. New York, 1923.

Correspondance diplomatique se rapportant aux relations entre la République Russe et les puissances de l'Entente, 1918. Moscow, 1919.

Cumming, C. K., and Walter W. Pettit. *Russian-American Relations, March 1917–March 1920.* New York, 1920.

Czechoslovak Republic. Ministerstvo zahranicnich veci. *Archiv diplomatických dokumentů československých.* Prague, 1927.

Degras, Jane, ed. *Soviet Documents on Foreign Policy.* 2 vols. London, 1951.

Dokumenty a materiály k dějinám československo-sovětských vztahů. Part 1. November 1917–August 1922. Prague, 1975.

Dokumenty o protilidové a protinárodní politice T. G. Masaryka. Prague, 1953.

Golder, Frank A., ed. *Documents of Russian History, 1914–1917.* New York, 1927.

Great Britain. *Parliamentary Debates.* 5th ser. 1916–1919.

Hosoya, Chihiro. "Japanese Documents on the Siberian Intervention, 1917–1922: Part 1. November 1917–January 1919." *Hitotsubashi Journal of Law and Politics* 1 (April 1960): 30–37.

Janin, Pierre T. "Fragments de mon journal Sibérien." *Le Monde slave* (December 1924): 2–5.

Un livre noir, diplomatie d'avant guerre et de guerre d'après les documents des archives russes, 1910–1917. Paris, 1934.

MacMurray, John Van A. *Treaties and Agreements with and Concerning China 1894–1919.* 2 vols. New York, 1973.

Medek, Rudolf, ed. *Za svobodu: Obrázková kronika československého revolučního hnutí na Rusi, 1914–1920.* 4 vols. Prague, 1922–29.

Meijer, Jan, ed. *Trotsky Papers.* 2 vols. London, 1964.

Mints, I., and E. Gorodetsky, eds. *Dokumenty po istorii grazhdanskoi voiny v SSSR.* Vol. 1. Moscow, 1940.

Scott, James Brown, ed. *Official Statements of War Aims and Peace Proposals, December 1916 to November 1918.* Washington, D.C., 1921.

U.S. Congress. *Congressional Record.* 64th Cong., 1st sess. Washington, D.C., 1916.

———. 65th Cong., 1st and 2d sess. Washington, D.C., 1917–18.

U.S. Department of Commerce. *Statistical Abstract of the United States, 1916.* Washington, D.C., 1917.

U.S. Department of State. *Foreign Relations of the United States: The Lansing Papers, 1914–1920.* 2 vols. Washington, D.C., 1939–40.

———. *Foreign Relations of the United States, 1914.* Washington, D.C., 1922.

———. *Foreign Relations of the United States, 1914, Supplement, The World War.* Washington, D.C., 1928.

———. *Foreign Relations of the United States, 1915, Supplement, The World War.* Washington, D.C., 1928.

———. *Foreign Relations of the United States, 1916, Supplement, The World War.* Washington, D.C., 1929.

———. *Foreign Relations of the United States, 1917.* Washington, D.C., 1926.

———. *Foreign Relations of the United States, 1917, Supplement 1, The World War.* Washington, D.C., 1931.

———. *Foreign Relations of the United States, 1917, Supplement 2, The World War.* 2 vols. Washington, D.C., 1932.

———. *Foreign Relations of the United States, 1918, Russia.* 3 vols. Washington, D.C., 1931–33.

———. *Foreign Relations of the United States, 1918, Supplement 1, The World War.* 2 vols. Washington, D.C., 1933.

———. *Foreign Relations of the United States: The Paris Peace Conference, 1919.* 13 vols. Washington, D.C., 1942–47.

————. *Foreign Relations of the United States, 1919, Russia.* Washington, D.C., 1937.

Varneck, Elena, and H. H. Fisher. *The Testimony of Kolchak and Other Siberian Materials.* Stanford, Calif., 1935.

Zeman, Z. A. B., ed. *Germany and the Revolution in Russia, 1915–1918.* London, 1958.

Letters, Diaries, and Memoirs

Andrássy, Julius. *Diplomacy and the War.* London, 1921.

Asquith, Herbert H. *Memories and Reflections, 1852–1927.* 2 vols. Boston, 1928.

Baker, Ray Stannard, ed. *Woodrow Wilson and World Settlement.* 3 vols. New York, 1927.

————. *Woodrow Wilson: Life and Letters.* 8 vols. New York, 1939.

Baker, Ray S., and William E. Dodd, eds. *The New Democracy: Presidential Messages, Addresses and Other Papers.* 2 vols. New York, 1926.

————. *The Public Papers of Woodrow Wilson.* 6 vols. New York, 1925–27.

Beneš, Edvard. *My War Memoirs.* London, 1928.

————. *Souvenirs de guerre et de révolution, 1914–1918.* 2 vols. Paris, 1929.

————. *Světová válke a naše revoluce.* 3 vols. Prague, 1935.

Bernstorff, Johann von. *My Three Years in America.* New York, 1920.

Bothmer, Freiherr Karl von. *Mit Graf Mirbach in Moskau.* Tübingen, 1929.

Bowie, Theodore, ed. *Langdon Warner through His Letters.* London, 1966.

Čapek, Karel. *President Masaryk Tells His Story.* New York, 1935.

Cecil, Robert. *A Great Experiment: An Autobiography.* New York, 1941.

Československá obec legionářská Prague. *Sborník vzpomínek na T. G. Masaryka.* Prague, 1930.

Colton, Ethan T. *Forty Years with Russians.* New York, 1940.

Cronon, E. David, ed. *The Cabinet Diaries of Josephus Daniels, 1913–1921.* Lincoln, Nebr., 1963.

Czernin, Ottokar. *In the World War.* London, 1919.

Dawson, Warrington, ed. *War Memoirs of William G. Sharp.* London, 1931.

Dumba, Constantin T. *Memoirs of a Diplomat.* Translated by Ian F. D. Morrow. London, 1933.

Einstein, Lewis. *A Diplomat Looks Back.* Edited by Lawrence E. Gelfand. New Haven, Conn., 1968.

Foch, Ferdinand. *The Memoirs of Marshal Foch.* Translated by Col. T. Bentley Mott. New York, 1931.

Gajda, Rudolf. *Moje paměti; Československá anabase; Zpět na Ural proti bolševikům; Admirál Kolčak.* Prague, 1920.

Graves, William S. *America's Siberian Adventure.* New York, 1931.

Grew, Joseph C. *Turbulent Era.* Edited by Walter Johnson. 2 vols. Boston, 1952.

Gwynn, Stephen L., ed. *The Letters and Friendships of Sir Cecil Spring Rice.* 2 vols. Boston, 1929.

Hard, William. *Raymond Robins' Own Story.* New York, 1920.

Harper, Samuel N. *The Russia I Believe In: The Memoirs of Samuel N. Harper, 1902–1941.* Edited by Paul V. Harper. Chicago, 1945.

Hendrick, Burton J., ed. *The Life and Letters of Walter Hines Page.* 3 vols. New York, 1922–25.
Hindenburg, Paul von. *Out of My Life.* Translated by F. A. Holt. London, 1920.
Hoover, Herbert. *The Memoirs of Herbert Hoover: Years of Adventure, 1874–1920.* New York, 1951.
House, Edward M., and Charles Seymour, eds. *What Really Happened at Paris.* New York, 1921.
Houston, David F. *Eight Years with Wilson's Cabinet, 1913–1920.* New York, 1926.
Janin, Maurice. *Ma mission en Sibérie, 1918–1920.* Paris, 1933.
———. *Moje účast na československém boji za svobodu.* Prague, [1920].
Lane, Anne W., and Louise H. Wall, eds. *The Letters of Franklin K. Lane, Personal and Political.* Boston, 1922.
Lansing, Robert. *The Big Four—And Others of the Peace Conference.* London, 1922.
———. *War Memoirs of Robert Lansing, Secretary of State.* Indianapolis, Ind., 1935.
Leonard, Arthur Roy, ed. *War Addresses of Woodrow Wilson.* Boston, 1918.
Link, Arthur S.; David W. Hirst; John E. Little; et al., eds. *The Papers of Woodrow Wilson.* 59 vols. to date. Princeton, N.J., 1966–.
Lloyd George, David. *War Memoirs of David Lloyd George.* 6 vols. London, 1933–37.
Lockhart, R. H. Bruce. *British Agent.* New York, 1933.
March, Peyton C. *Nation at War.* Garden City, N.Y., 1932.
Masaryk, T. G. *The Making of a State: Memories and Observations, 1914–1918.* New York, 1969.
———. *Světová revoluce. Za války a ve válce 1914–1918.* Prague, 1925.
———. *Die Welt-Revolution: Erinnerungen und Betrachtungen 1914–1918.* Berlin, 1927.
Müller, Georg Alexander von. *The Kaiser and His Court.* Edited by Walter Görlitz and translated by Mervyn Savil. New York, 1964.
Nabokov, Constantin. *The Ordeal of a Diplomat.* London, 1921.
Noulens, Joseph. *Mon ambassade en Russie soviétique, 1917–1919.* 2 vols. Paris, 1933.
Phillips, William. *Ventures in Diplomacy.* Boston, 1952.
Price, Morgan Phillips. *My Reminiscences of the Russian Revolution.* London, 1921.
Repington, Charles à Court. *The First World War, 1914–1918: Personal Experiences.* 2 vols. Boston, 1920.
Riddell, George A. *Lord Riddell's War Diary, 1914–1918.* London, 1933.
Rosen, Roman Romanovich. *Forty Years of Diplomacy.* 2 vols. London, 1922.
Sazonov, Sergei D. *Fateful Years, 1909–1916.* London, 1928.
Seymour, Charles. *Letters from the Paris Peace Conference.* Edited by Harold B. Whiteman, Jr. New Haven, Conn., 1965.
Seymour, Charles, ed. *The Intimate Papers of Colonel House.* 4 vols. Boston, 1926–28.
Sisson, Edgar. *One Hundred Red Days.* New Haven, Conn., 1931.
Steed, Henry Wickham. *Through Thirty Years, 1892–1922.* 2 vols. New York, 1925.

Steffens, Lincoln. *The Autobiography of Lincoln Steffens*. New York, 1931.
Suarez, George. *Briand: Sa vie, 1916–1918*. 6 vols. Paris, 1938–52.
Villard, Oswald. *Fighting Years: Memoirs of a Liberal Editor*. New York, 1939.
Voska, Emanuel V., and Will Irwin. *Spy and Counterspy*. New York, 1940.
Wilson, Edith B. *My Memoir*. Indianapolis, Ind., 1938.
Wilson, Hugh R. *Diplomat between Wars*. New York, 1941.

Newspapers and Contemporary Periodicals

Berliner Tageblatt, 1918
Corriere della Sera (Milan), 1918
Chicago Tribune, 1915–1919
Christian Science Monitor, 1914–1919
Československý Deník, 1918–1919
Denní Hlasatel, 1915–1918
Evening Post (New York), 1918
Frankfurter Zeitung, 1918
Izvestiia, 1918
Japan Advertiser, 1918
Literary Digest, 1914–1918
London Chronicle, 1916–1918
London Daily Herald, 1919
London *Times*, 1916–1918
Manchester Guardian, 1918
Le Matin, 1917
New York Times, 1914–1919
New York *World*, 1917–1918
Pravda, 1918
Le Temps, 1916
Vlast Truda, 1918
Washington Post, 1917–1918

Secondary Works

Books

Ackerman, Carl W. *Trailing the Bolsheviki*. New York, 1919.
Baerlein, Henry. *March of the Seventy Thousand*. London, 1926.
Balch, Emily Greene. *Our Slavic Fellow-Citizens to the Great Settlement*. New York, 1910.
Beaumont, A. *Heroic Story of the Czecho-Slovak Legion*. Prague, 1919.
Becvar, Gustav. *The Lost Legion: A Czechoslovak Epic*. London, 1939.
Benedikt, Heinrich. *Die Friedensaktion der Meinlgruppe 1917–18: Die Bemühungen um einen Verständigungsfrieden nach Dokumenten, Aktenstücken und Brieffen*. Graz and Cologne, 1962.
Berezkin, A. V. *Oktiabr'skaia revoliutsiia i SShA, 1917–1922 gg*. Moscow, 1967.
Bonsal, Stephen. *Suitors and Suppliants*. New York, 1939.
Bradley, J. F. N. *La Légion tchécoslovaque en Russie, 1914–1920*. Paris, 1965.

Bradley, John. *Allied Intervention in Russia*. Landham, Md., 1984.

Brändström, Elsa. *Among Prisoners of War in Russia and Siberia*. London, 1929.

Briggs, Mitchell Pirie. *George D. Herron and the European Settlement*. Stanford, Calif., 1932.

Calder, Kenneth J. *Britain and the Origins of the New Europe, 1914–1918*. London, 1976.

Čapek, Thomas. *Origins of the Czechoslovak State*. New York, 1926.

———. *Pámatky českých emigrantů v Americe*. Omaha, Nebr., 1907.

Carley, Michael J. *Revolution and Intervention: The French Government and the Russian Civil War, 1917–1919*. Kingston, Canada, 1983.

Chamberlin, William H. *The Russian Revolution, 1917–1921*. 2 vols. New York, 1935.

Churchill, Winston. *The World Crisis*. 4 vols. London, 1923–28.

Claudel, Paul. *Accompagnements*. Paris, 1949.

Clemenceau, Georges. *Grandeur and Misery of Victory*. Translated by F. M. Atkinson. New York, 1930.

Coates, W. P., and Zelda Coates. *Armed Intervention in Russia, 1918–1922*. London, 1935.

Davenport, Marcia. *Too Strong for Fantasy*. New York, 1967.

Dedijer, Vladimir. *Sarajevo, 1914*. Belgrade, 1966.

De Manteyer, G., ed. *Austria's Peace Offer, 1916–1917*. London, 1921.

Dennis, Alfred L. P. *The Foreign Policies of Soviet Russia*. New York, 1924.

Dragomiretskii, V. S. *Chekhoslovaki v Rossii 1914–1920*. Paris and Prague, 1928.

Dugdale, Blanche E. C. *Arthur James Balfour, First Earl of Balfour*. 2 vols. London, 1936.

Dupuy, R. E. *Perish by the Sword*. Harrisburg, Pa., 1938.

Ellis, John T. *The Life of Cardinal Gibbons, Archbishop of Baltimore, 1834–1921*. 2 vols. Milwaukee, Wis., 1952.

Fic, Victor M. *Bolsheviks and the Czechoslovak Legion: Origin of Their Armed Conflict*. New Delhi, 1978.

———. *Revolutionary War for Independence and the Russian Question: Czechoslovak Army in Russia, 1914–1918*. New Delhi, 1977.

Fleming, Peter. *The Fate of Admiral Kolchak*. London, 1963.

Foerster, Kent. *The Failures of Peace: The Search for a Negotiated Peace during the First World War*. Washington, D.C., 1941.

Fowler, W. B. *British-American Relations, 1917–1918: The Role of Sir William Wiseman*. Princeton, N.J., 1969.

Ganelin, R. Sh. *Sovetsko-amerikanskie otnosheniia v kontse 1917–nachale 1918 g.* Leningrad, 1975.

Gardner, Lloyd C. *Safe for Democracy: The Anglo-American Response to Revolution, 1913–1923*. New York, 1984.

Gaunt, Guy. *The Yield of the Years*. London, 1940.

Gelfand, Lawrence O. *The Inquiry: American Preparations for Peace, 1917–1919*. New Haven, Conn., 1963.

Getting, Milan. *Americkí Slováci a vývin československej myšlienky v rokoch 1914–1918*. Masaryktown, Fla., 1933.

Glaise-Horstenau, Edmund von. *The Collapse of the Austro-Hungarian Empire*. London, 1930.

Gorky, M., ed. *The History of the Civil War in the USSR*. 2 vols. New York, 1937.

Griswold, A. Whitney. *Far Eastern Policy of the United States*. New York, 1939.

Grondijs, Ludovic H. *La Guerre en Russie et en Sibérie*. Paris, 1922.

Gvishiani, L. A. *Sovetskaia Rossiia i SShA, 1917–1920*. Moscow, 1970.

Hanak, Harry. *Great Britain and Austria-Hungary during the First World War*. London, 1962.

Hancock, W. K. *Smuts: The Sanguine Years 1870–1919*. Cambridge, 1962.

Hankey, Maurice. *The Supreme Command, 1914–1918*. 2 vols. London, 1961.

Hantsch, Hugo. *Die Geschichte Österreichs*. 2 vols. Graz, 1953.

Henry, Charles, and F. De Means. *L'Armée tchécoslovaque*. Paris, 1928.

Herben, Jan. *T. G. Masaryk*. 3 vols. Prague, 1927–28.

The History of The Times: *The 150th Anniversary and Beyond, 1912–1948*. Part 1. *1912–1920*. London, 1952.

Holotík, Ludovít. *Štefánikovská legenda a vznik ČSR*. Bratislava, 1960.

Janin, Pierre T. *Milan Rastislav Štefánik*. Prague, 1932.

Ješina, Čestmír, ed. *The Birth of Czechoslovakia*. Washington, D.C., 1968.

Kennan, George. *The Decision to Intervene*. Princeton, N.J., 1958.

———. *Russia and the West under Lenin and Stalin*. New York, 1960.

———. *Russia Leaves the War*. Princeton, N.J., 1956.

Klante, Margarete. *Von der Wolga zum Amur*. Berlin, 1931.

Kohn, Hans. *The Habsburg Empire, 1804–1918*. Princeton, N.J., 1961.

Korbel, Josef. *Twentieth Century Czechoslovakia*. New York, 1977.

Kovtun, George J. *The Czechoslovak Declaration of Independence: A History of the Document*. Washington, D.C., 1985.

———. *Masaryk and America: Testimony of a Relationship*. Washington, D.C., 1988.

LaFargue, Thomas E. *China and the World War*. Stanford, Calif., 1937.

Lengyel, Emil. *Siberia*. New York, 1943.

Link, Arthur S. *The Struggle for Neutrality, 1914–1915*. Princeton, N.J., 1960.

———. *Wilson: Campaigns for Progressivism and Peace, 1916–1917*. Princeton, N.J., 1965.

———. *Wilson: Confusion and Crises*. Princeton, N.J., 1964.

———. *Woodrow Wilson: Revolution, War, and Peace*. Arlington Heights, Ill., 1979.

Lloyd George, David. *The Truth about the Peace Treaties*. 2 vols. London, 1938.

Lodge, Henry Cabot. *The Senate and the League of Nations*. New York, 1925.

Macartney, C. A. *The Habsburg Empire, 1790–1918*. London, 1969.

Maksakov, V., and A. Turunov. *Khronika grazhdanskoi voiny v Sibiri 1917–1918*. Moscow, 1926.

Mamatey, Victor S. *The United States and East Central Europe, 1914–1918: A Study in Wilsonian Diplomacy and Propaganda*. Princeton, N.J., 1957.

Marty, André. *La révolte de la mer Noire*. Paris, 1949.

May, Arthur J. *The Passing of the Habsburg Monarchy, 1914–1918*. 2 vols. Philadelphia, 1968.

Mayer, Arno J. *Political Origins of the New Diplomacy, 1917–1918*. New Haven, Conn., 1959.

Medek, Rudolph. *Czech Anabasis across Russia and Siberia*. London, 1929.

Millard, Thomas F. *Democracy and the Eastern Question*. New York, 1919.

Monroe, Will S. *Bohemia and the Czechs.* Boston, 1910.

Morley, James. *The Japanese Thrust into Siberia, 1918.* New York, 1957.

Norton, Henry Kittridge. *The Far Eastern Republic of Siberia.* London, 1923.

Nosek, Vladimir. *Independent Bohemia.* London, 1918.

Notter, Harley. *The Origins of the Foreign Policy of Woodrow Wilson.* Baltimore, Md., 1937.

Paléologue, Maurice. *La Russie des tsars pendant la grande guerre.* 2 vols. Paris, 1921–22.

Palmer, Frederick. *Newton D. Baker: America at War.* 2 vols. New York, 1931.

Papánek, Ján. *La Tchécoslovaquie, histoire politique et juridique de sa création.* Prague, 1923.

Papoušek, Jaroslav. *Chekhoslovaki i Sovety.* Prague, 1928.

———. *The Czechoslovak Nation's Struggle for Independence.* Prague, 1928.

Pergler, Charles. *America in the Struggle for Czechoslovak Independence.* Philadelphia, 1926.

Perman, Dagmar. *The Shaping of the Czecho-Slovak State: Diplomatic History of the Boundaries of Czechoslovakia, 1914–1920.* Leiden, 1962.

Polzer-Hoditz, Arthur. *Kaiser Karl.* Vienna, 1929.

Popov, F. G. *Chekho-Slovatskii miatezh i samarskaia uchredilka.* Moscow, 1933.

Pribram, Alfred Francis. *Austrian Foreign Policy, 1908–1918.* London, 1923.

Pugach, Noel H. *Paul S. Reinsch: Open Door Diplomat in Action.* Millwood, N.Y., 1979.

Reinsch, Paul S. *Intellectual and Political Currents in the Far East.* Boston, 1911.

———. *Secret Diplomacy: How Far Can It Be Eliminated?* New York, 1922.

———. *World Politics at the End of the Nineteenth Century as Influenced by the Oriental Situation.* London, 1919.

Roosevelt, Theodore. *Roosevelt and the Kansas City Star.* Boston, 1921.

Ross, Edward A. *The Russian Soviet Republic.* New York, 1923.

Rudin, Harry R. *Armistice, 1918.* New Haven, Conn., 1944.

Sadoul, Jacques. *Notes sur la révolution bolchévique.* Paris, 1926.

Schuman, Frederick L. *American Policy toward Russia since 1917: A Study of Diplomatic History, International Law and Public Opinion.* New York, 1928.

Schwanda, Charles B. *The Czechoslovak Troops in Russia and Siberia.* New York, 1924.

Selver, Paul. *Masaryk.* London, 1940.

Seton-Watson, Robert W. *A History of the Czechs and Slovaks.* Hamden, Conn., 1943.

———. *History of the Roumanians.* Cambridge, 1934.

———. *Masaryk in England.* New York, 1943.

Šteidler, František. *Československé hnutí na Rusi.* Prague, 1922.

Stewart, George. *The White Armies of Russia.* New York, 1939.

Takeuchi, Tatsuji. *War and Diplomacy in the Japanese Empire.* New York, 1935.

Taylor, A. J. P. *The Habsburg Monarchy, 1809–1918.* London, 1964.

Taylor, Edmond. *The Fall of the Dynasties.* New York, 1963.

Thomson, S. Harrison. *Czechoslovakia in European History.* Princeton, N.J., 1943.

Thünig-Nittner, Gerburg. *Die Tschechoslowakische Legion in Russland.* Wiesbaden, 1970.

Trask, David F. *The United States in the Supreme War Council: American War Aims and Inter-Allied Strategy, 1917–1918.* Middletown, Conn., 1961.

Trotskii, Leon. *Sochineniia.* Moscow, 1926.

Tsao, Lien-en. *The Chinese Eastern Railway: An Analytic Study.* Shanghai, 1930.

Tuchman, Barbara. *The Zimmermann Telegram.* New York, 1958.

Tupper, Harmon. *To the Great Ocean.* Boston, 1965.

Ullman, Richard H. *Intervention and the War.* Princeton, N.J., 1961.

Unterberger, Betty M. *America's Siberian Expedition, 1918–1920: A Study of National Policy.* 1956. Reprint. New York, 1969.

————. *Intervention against Communism: Did the United States Try to Overthrow the Soviet Government, 1918–1920?* College Station, Tex., 1987.

Unterberger, Betty M., ed. *American Intervention in the Russian Civil War.* Lexington, Mass., 1969.

Valiani, Leo. *The End of Austria-Hungary.* New York, 1973.

Vivian, Herbert. *The Life of Emperor Charles of Austria.* London, 1932.

Vondracek, Felix John. *The Foreign Policy of Czechoslovakia.* New York, 1937.

Walworth, Arthur. *Woodrow Wilson, American Prophet.* New York, 1958.

Wheeler-Bennett, John. *Brest-Litovsk: The Forgotten Peace, March 1918.* 2d ed. New York, 1956.

White, John Albert. *The Siberian Intervention.* Princeton, N.J., 1950.

Willert, Arthur. *The Road to Safety: A Study in Anglo-American Relations.* London, 1952.

Woodward, Llewellyn. *Great Britain and the War of 1914–1918.* London, 1967.

Young, Kenneth. *Arthur James Balfour.* London, 1963.

Zeman, Z. A. B. *The Break-Up of the Habsburg Empire, 1914–1918.* London, 1961.

Articles and Dissertations

Abrash, Merritt. "War Aims toward Austria-Hungary, the Czechoslovak Pivot." In *Russian Diplomacy in Eastern Europe, 1914–1917,* edited by Alexander Dallin, 78–118. New York, 1963.

"The Approaching Crisis." *New Republic,* 22 June 1918, 217–20.

"The Austro-Serbian Conflict." *Outlook,* 29 August 1914, 1028–30.

Barany, George. "A Note on the Origin of Wilson's Point 10: The Meinl Mission and the Department of State, 1917–1918." *Journal of Central European Affairs* 23 (July 1963): 219–22.

————. "Wilsonian Central Europe: Lansing's Contribution." *Historian* 28 (February 1966): 244–51.

Beneš, Vojta. "How Bohemians Organized." *Bohemian Review* 1 (September 1917): 5–8.

"Bohemian Cause in Magazines." *Bohemian Review* 1 (October 1917): 16.

Bonsal, Stephen. "Bohemia, the Submerged Front." *North American Review* 206 (September 1917): 426–35.

Brunauer, E. C. "Peace Proposals of December 1916/January 1917." *Journal of Modern History* 4 (December 1932): 544–71.

Bruno, Guido. "The Czechs and Their Bohemia." *Pearson's Magazine* 38 (September 1917): 110–11.

Carley, Michael Jabara. "The Origins of the French Intervention in the Russian

Civil War, January–May 1918: A Reappraisal." *Journal of Modern History* 48 (September 1976): 413–39.

"Central Europe Liberation as Final Aim in War: Professor Masaryk Says Czech Demand Will Tally with Highest Interests of Allies." *Christian Science Monitor,* 3 March 1916, 2.

Creel, George. "Woodrow Wilson, the Man Behind the Legend." *Saturday Evening Post* 103 (March 28, 1931): 37–44.

Davis, Donald E., and Eugene P. Trani. "The American Y.M.C.A. and the Russian Revolution." *Slavic Review* 33 (September 1974): 464–91.

Davis, Gerald H. "The Diplomatic Relations between the United States and Austria-Hungary, 1913–1917." Ph.D. diss., Vanderbilt University, 1958.

Doerries, Reinhard R. "Imperial Germany and Washington: New Light on Germany's Foreign Policy and America's Entry into World War I." *Central European History* 11 (March 1978): 43–44.

Fenwick, Charles G. "Notes on International Affairs." *American Political Science Review* 12 (November 1918): 706–21.

Ferrell, Robert H. "The United States and East Central Europe before 1941." In *The Fate of East Central Europe,* edited by Stephen D. Kertesz, 21–51. Notre Dame, Ind., 1956.

"General Štefánik." *Czechoslovak Review* 3 (June 1919): 148–51.

Hard, William. "The Case of Austria-Hungary." *Metropolitan* 46 (October 1917): 23–24.

Herron, George D. "A Golden Bridge Unbuilt." *World Tomorrow,* December 1921, 378.

"Intervention in Russia." *New Republic,* 1 June 1918, 130–33.

Kalvoda, Josef. "Masaryk in America in 1918." *Jahrbücher für Geschichte Osteuropas* 27 (1979): H.1.

Kennan, George. "The Czechoslovak Legion." *Russian Review* 16 (October 1957): 3–16.

———. "Soviet Historiography and America's Role in the Intervention." *American Historical Review* 65 (January 1960): 302–22.

Kerner, Robert J. "American Interests and the Bohemian Question." *Bohemian Review* 1 (December 1917): 7–11.

———. "The Czechoslovaks from the Battle of White Mountain to the World War." In *Czechoslovakia,* edited by Robert J. Kerner, 29–50. Berkeley, 1940.

———. "The Winning of Czechoslovak Independence." *Foreign Affairs* 7 (January 1929): 308–16.

Khabas, R. "K istorii bor'by s chekhoslovatskim myatezhom." *Proletarskaia Revoliutsiia* No. 5 (1928): 57.

Kisch, Guido. "Woodrow Wilson and the Independence of Small Nations in Central Europe." *Journal of Modern History* 19 (1947): 235–38.

Kořalka, Jiří. "The Czech Question in International Relations at the Beginning of the 20th Century." *Slavonic and East European Review* 48 (April 1970): 248–68.

Kramář, Karel. "Europe and the Bohemian Question." *National Review* 40 (October 1902): 183–205.

———. "L'Avenir de l'Autriche." *Revue de Paris* 1 (February 1899): 577–600.

————. "M. Kramář et la politique slave." *Le Monde slave,* November 1926, 294.

Křížek, Jaroslav. "T. G. Masaryk a vystoupení čs legií na jaře 1918." *Československý časopis historický* 14 (1966): 637–666.

Legras, Jules. "La Russie tsariste et la question tchécoslovaque." *Le Monde slave,* November 1924, 123–38.

Lippmann, Walter. "The World Conflict in Its Relation to American Democracy." *Annals of The American Academy of Political and Social Sciences* 72 (July 1917): 1–10.

Long, John W. "American Intervention in Russia: The North Russian Expedition, 1918–1919." *Diplomatic History* 6 (Winter 1982): 45–67.

Long, John W., and C. Howard Hopkins. "T. G. Masaryk and the Strategy of Czechoslovak Independence: An Interview in Russia on 27 June 1917." *Slavonic and East European Review* 56 (January 1978): 88–96.

MacAdam, George. "The Anabasis of the Czecho-Slovaks." *World's Work* 36 (October 1918): 625–28.

McDowell, Mary. "Tried in Her Father's Stead." *Survey,* 29 April 1916, 116.

Malone, Gifford D. "War Aims toward Germany." In *Russian Diplomacy in Eastern Europe, 1914–1917,* edited by Alexander Dallin, 124–62. New York, 1963.

Mamatey, Victor. "The United States and the Dissolution of Austria-Hungary." *Journal of Central European Affairs* 10 (October 1950): 256–70.

Masaryk, Thomas G. "The Czecho-Slovak Nation." *Nation,* 5 October 1918, 4–5.

————. "Embers of Revolt in Austria-Hungary." *New York Times,* 26 May 1918.

Mason, Gregory. "Japan and Bolshevism." *Outlook,* 12 June 1918, 259–61.

May, Arthur J. "R. W. Seton-Watson and British Anti-Habsburg Sentiment." *American Slavic and East European Review* 20 (February 1961): 40–54.

————. "Woodrow Wilson and Austria-Hungry to the End of 1917." In *Festschrift für Heinrich Benedikt,* edited by Hugo Hantsch and Alexander Novotny, 213–42. Vienna, 1957.

Mezes, Sidney Edward. "Preparations for Peace." In *What Really Happened at Paris,* edited by Edward M. House and Charles Seymour, 1–14. New York, 1921.

Mika, G. H. "Rearranging Austro-Hungary." *New Republic,* 12 January 1918, 314–15.

Miliukov, Paul. "Masaryk." *Foreign Affairs* 8 (April 1930): 399–400.

Miller, Herbert A. "The Bulwark of Freedom." *Survey,* 5 October 1918, 5–10.

————. "Nationalism in Bohemia and Poland." *North American Review* 200 (December 1914): 879–86.

————. "The Rebirth of a Nation: The Czechoslovaks." *Survey,* 2 November 1918, 117–20.

————. "What Woodrow Wilson and America Meant to Czechoslovakia." In *Czechoslovakia,* edited by Robert J. Kerner, 71–87. Berkeley, Calif., 1940.

Odložilík, Otakar. "The Czechs." In *The Immigrants' Influence on Wilson's Peace Policies,* edited by Joseph P. O'Grady, 204–23. Lexington, Ky., 1967.

Osuský, Stefan. "The Secret Peace Negotiations between Vienna and Washington." *Slavonic and East European Review* 4 (March 1926): 657–68.

————. "Why Czechoslovakia?" *Foreign Affairs* 15 (April 1957): 455–71.

"Our New Ally, Siberia." *Outlook*, 24 July 1918, 478.

Patton, Albert J. "The Eager Bohemians." *Chamberlain's* 15 (September 1917): 7–8.

Peffer, Nathaniel. "Japan's Absorption of Siberia." *Nation*, 5 October 1921, 367–69.

Pergler, Charles. "The Bohemian Question." *Annals of the American Academy of Political and Social Science* 72 (July 1917): 155–60.

Polner, Murray. "The Czech Legion and the Bolsheviks." Ph.D. diss., Columbia University, 1955.

Pomerance, Michla. "The United States and Self-Determination: Perspectives on the Wilsonian Conception." *American Journal of International Law* 70 (1976): 1–27.

Renzi, William A. "Who Composed 'Sazonov's Thirteen Points'? A Re-Examination of Russia's War Aims of 1914." *American Historical Review* 88 (April 1983): 347–57.

Scott, James Brown. "Foreign Enlistments in the United States." *American Journal of International Law* 12 (January 1918): 172–74.

Thompson, John M. "Allied and American Intervention in Russia, 1918–1921." In *Rewriting Russian History: Soviet Interpretations of Russia's Past*, edited by Cyril E. Black, 319–80. 2d rev. ed. New York, 1962.

Unterberger, Betty M. "The Arrest of Alice Masaryk." *Slavic Review: An American Quarterly of Soviet and East European Studies* 33 (March 1974): 91–106.

———. "National Self-Determination." In *Encyclopedia of American Foreign Policy*, edited by Alexander DeConde. 3 vols. New York, 1978.

———. "The Russian Revolution and Wilson's Far Eastern Policy." *Russian Review* 16 (April 1957): 35–46.

———. "The United States and the Czech-Bolshevik Conflict, 1918." In *Proceedings of the Conference on War and Diplomacy*, edited by David B. White, 145–53. The Citadel, S.C., 1976.

———. "Woodrow Wilson and the Bolsheviks: The 'Acid Test' of Soviet-American Relations." *Diplomatic History* 11 (Spring 1987): 71–91.

———. "Woodrow Wilson and the Russian Revolution." In *Woodrow Wilson and a Revolutionary World, 1913–1921*, edited by Arthur S. Link, 49–104. Chapel Hill, N.C., 1982.

Vávra, Vlastimil, "K historiografické interpretaci poměru T. G. Masaryka vůči Sovětskému Rusku v roce 1918." *Československý časopis historický* 21 (1973): 13–44.

"What the Papers Say." *Bohemian Review* 1 (February 1917): 17–18.

Williams, John S. "War to Stop War." *Annals of the American Academy of Political and Social Science* 72 (July 1917): 178–85.

Williams, Rowan A. "The Odyssey of the Czechs." *East European Quarterly* 9 (Spring 1975): 15–38.

Wilson, Woodrow. "The Dual Monarchies." In *The State: Elements of Historical and Practical Politics*, chap. 9. Rev. ed. Boston, 1904.

Woodward, David R. "The British Government and Japanese Intervention in Russia During World War I." *Journal of Modern History* 46 (December 1974): 663–85.

———. "David Lloyd George: A Negotiated Peace with Germany and the Kühlmann Peace Kites of September 1917." *Canadian Journal of History* 6 (March 1917): 75–93.

———. "The Origins and Intent of David Lloyd George's January 5 War Aims Speech." *Historian* 34 (November 1971): 22–39.

Zivojinović, Dragan R. "The Vatican, Woodrow Wilson and the Dissolution of the Habsburg Monarchy, 1914–1918." *East European Quarterly* 3 (1969): 31–70.

Index

Publication of Supplementary Volumes to *The Papers of Woodrow Wilson* is assisted from time to time by the Woodrow Wilson Foundation in order to encourage scholarly work about Woodrow Wilson and his time. All volumes have passed the review procedures of the publishers and the Editor and the Editorial Advisory Committee of *The Papers of Woodrow Wilson*. Inquiries about the Series should be addressed to The Editor, Papers of Woodrow Wilson, Firestone Library, Princeton University, Princeton, N.J. 08540.

Inga Floto, *Colonel House in Paris: A Study of American Policy at the Paris Peace Conference 1919* (Princeton University Press, 1981)

Raymond B. Fosdick, *Letters on the League of Nations. From the Files of Raymond B. Fosdick* (Princeton University Press, 1966)

Wilton B. Fowler, *British-American Relations, 1917–1918: The Role of Sir William Wiseman* (Princeton University Press, 1969)

John M. Mulder, *Woodrow Wilson: The Years of Preparation* (Princeton University Press, 1978)

George Egerton, *Great Britain and the Creation of the League of Nations* (University of North Carolina Press, 1978)

Stephen L. Vaughn, *Holding Fast the Inner Lines: Democracy, Nationalism, and the Committee on Public Information* (University of North Carolina Press, 1980)

Robert C. Hilderbrand, *Power and the People: Executive Management of Public Opinion in Foreign Affairs, 1897–1921* (University of North Carolina Press, 1980)

Edwin A. Weinstein, *Woodrow Wilson: A Medical and Psychological Biography* (Princeton University Press, 1981)

Arthur S. Link (ed.), *Woodrow Wilson and a Revolutionary World, 1913–1921* (University of North Carolina Press, 1982)

Valerie Jean Conner, *The National War Labor Board: Stability, Social Justice, and the Voluntary State in World War I* (University of North Carolina Press, 1983)

Klaus Schwabe, *Woodrow Wilson, Revolutionary Germany, and Peacemaking 1918–1919: Missionary Diplomacy and the Realities of Power* (University of North Carolina Press, 1985)

Frances Saunders, *Ellen Axson Wilson: Between Two Worlds* (University of North Carolina Press, 1985)

Reinhard R. Doerries, *Imperial Challenge: Ambassador Count Bernstorff and German-American Relations, 1908–1917* (University of North Carolina Press, 1989)

Betty Miller Unterberger, *The United States, Revolutionary Russia, and the Rise of Czechoslovakia* (University of North Carolina Press, 1989)